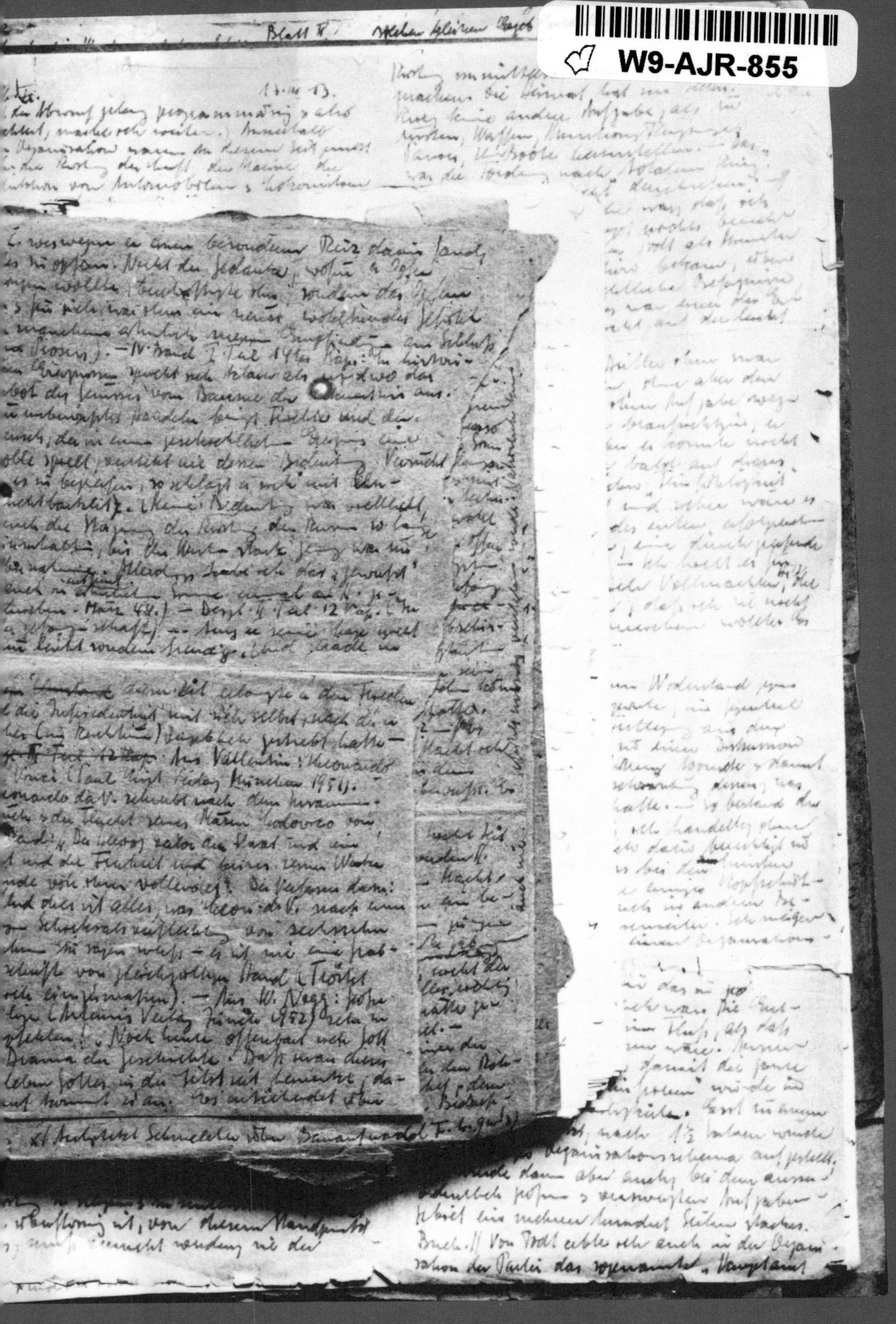

INSIDE THE THIRD REICH

INSIDE THE THIRD REICH

MEMOIRS

BY

ALBERT SPEER

Translated from the German by

RICHARD and CLARA WINSTON

Introduction by Eugene Davidson

THE MACMILLAN COMPANY

The Macmillan Company
866 Third Avenue, New York, N.Y. 10022
Collier-Macmillan Canada Ltd., Toronto, Canada

Library of Congress Catalog Card Number: 70-119132

The original edition of this book was published in Germany in 1969 under the title *Erinnerungen* © 1969 by Verlag Ullstein GmbH.

First Printing

Printed in the United States of America

Contents

PART

ONE

(v)

PART

THREE

32 Annihilation   *471*

Hitler's condition—Fear and pity—Last birthday—Goering goes to
Berchtesgaden—My flight—In the Hamburg radio bunker—Last visit
to Hitler—Situation conference—Farewell to Magda Goebbels and
Eva Braun—Last words with Hitler—Himmler and his notions—
Doenitz—Tears—Responsibility

EPILOGUE

PHOTOGRAPHS FOLLOW PAGES 166, 286 AND 406

Introduction

THE UNRESOLVED QUESTIONS OF THE PERIOD OF NATIONAL SOCIALISM REMAIN with us. The enormity of the crimes committed, the huge scale of victory and defeat are subjects of continuous exploration and analysis. How could one of the chief centers of the civilized world have become a torture chamber for millions of people, a country ruled by criminals so effectively that it conquered most of Europe, moving out toward other continents, planting its swastika standards from Norway to the Caucasus and Africa before it was brought down at the cost of some thirty million lives? What had happened to the nation of thinkers and poets, the "good" Germans that the nineteenth century knew? And how did intelligent, well-intentioned, educated, principled people like Albert Speer become so caught up in the movement, so captivated by Hitler's magnetism that they could accept everything—the secret police, the concentration camps, the nonsensical rhetoric of Aryan heroism and anti-Semitism, the slaughter of the Fuehrer's wars—and devote all their resources to keeping this regime in power? In these memoirs of the man who was very likely the most gifted member of the government hierarchy we have some of the answers to these riddles and as complete a view as we are ever likely to get of the inside of the Nazi state.

When he joined the Party in 1931, Speer had never given much thought to politics. He came from an upper-middle-class family, one of the most prominent in Mannheim, supported in high style by the father's flourishing architectural practice and involved mainly in the cultural and social life of the city. Speer's father did read the liberal *Frankfurter Zeitung,* an unusual paper for a conservative architect to have in his home, but he utterly rejected the Nazis because he believed them to be more socialist than nationalist. The family suffered financial reverses during the inflation in 1923 but always lived well in a *bürgerlicher* comfort enjoyed by very few people in post-World War I Germany.

Albert Speer was not one of the disoriented, rejected millions who were out of a job and a place in society; he joined the National Socialist Party because his faint interest in politics was roused more than it had ever been before when he heard Hitler give a speech in 1931. Most young men brought up like Speer did not care much for Hitler and his street fighters in 1931; Hitler's strength went up and down with the numbers of unemployed. Left-wing Berlin, where Speer heard Hitler speak, gave Hitler only 22.5 percent of the vote in the last free election held in November 1932, and even after the *Reichstag* fire, when almost 44.0 percent of the rest of Germany voted for Hitler, the National Socialists got only 31.3 percent of the Berlin vote. So Speer made his own decisions in his own way. Like a good many other people he was looking for a new, powerful doctrine to clear up his own thinking. He had dabbled in philosophical ideas; had read Spengler and become depressed by him; had heard the prophecies of doom from the post-World War I intellectuals and seen them borne out in the confusion and hopelessness of the cities; and now he was rejecting much of what he had been brought up to believe in because none of it seemed to have any relevance to the chaos around him.

The speech Speer heard was made for university and technical students and faculties. Like every skillful politician, Hitler pitched his style to his audience. He wore a sober blue suit instead of his street fighter's brown shirt and spoke earnestly, in a relatively low key, of a revitalized Germany. To Speer, his conviction seemed to be an antidote to Spengler's pessimism and at the same time fulfillment of his prophecy of the *Imperator* to come. These were the good tidings, it seemed, the complete answer to the threat of Communism and the political futility of the Weimar governments. In a time when nothing in the democratic process seemed to work, Hitler's words sounded a loud call to many young men who by 1931 were convinced of the necessity for bold, new remedies for Germany's deep troubles. The succession of patched-up coalition governments that governed neither long nor well and could find no answers at all to Germany's economic depression, social unrest, and military powerlessness had to be replaced by a man and a party with new solutions, by a leader who knew the meaning of strength and law and order. The anti-Semitism of the Nazis could be condoned or ignored as merely a passing "children's disease" if one liked the rest of their program. As Machiavelli once wrote, political misjudgments and wrong turns are like tuberculosis, hard to detect and easy to cure in the beginning and easy to diagnose and very hard to cure at the end.

But it was not the Party as a political instrument that appealed to Speer. What drew him was the personality of the Fuehrer, the scale of the blueprints for recovery, and later the wonderful opportunity to design buildings. It was through Hitler and the Party that Speer could realize his youthful architectural ambitions and acquire new ones beyond anything he had imagined. He tried not to see any of the barbarities committed by the National Socialist Party or the state although, as he tells us, the broken panes of the Jewish shops vandalized during the *Kristallnacht* lay shattered in front of him. But what he was able to accomplish in his profession and later in his key government posts so dazzled his vision that he could shut his eyes to almost everything, no matter how repulsive, that might disturb his purposes. What he wanted to do was to design and build and to work for a new order. Here the means were abundantly at hand if he did not look too closely at the price being paid for them.

Speer has had a long time to ask himself questions about his role in the Third Reich. At Nuremberg he was sentenced to twenty years for crimes against humanity and for war crimes; he served this sentence to the last hour. Some of these years he used to write these memoirs. They were intended for his children, but perhaps even more for himself. They had to be written clandestinely, often on scraps of paper or sheets torn from rolls used by the prison painters, and hidden behind a book Speer pretended to be reading as he lay on his cot. They were smuggled out of Spandau by one of the prison staff, a Dutchman who had himself been a slave laborer.

Speer, as the reader will discover, is not given to facile self-exculpation. When in defeat he finally came face to face with himself, with the bitter knowledge of what manner of man and what kind of state he had helped survive, he was as unrelenting toward himself as toward his collaborators. He told the court at Nuremberg, knowing that he risked his life when he said it, that as a member of Hitler's government he took full responsibility for the crimes committed, for the slave labor in the factories under his authority, for his collaboration with the SS when it provided concentration camp prisoners for his production lines, and his conspicuous role in a regime that killed—although with no direct help from him—six million Jews. He had been accused on all four counts of the Nuremberg indictment: of having plotted to wage aggressive war, of participating in it, and of committing war crimes and crimes against humanity. He fully accepted what lay behind the charges—the accusation that was mainly an echo of his own conscience—that he had served all too well as Minister of Armaments and War Production in a criminal state.

The court found him not guilty on the first two counts. With regard to the other charges, a majority (the Russians voted for death) took note of extenuating circumstances, on the evidence that Speer had tried to provide his workers with adequate food and housing, to make their lot as endurable and their work as efficient as possible. The court also noted that he had openly opposed Hitler (and indeed had planned to kill him when he saw that the Fuehrer was ready to destroy Germany only to gain a little more time for himself); and, too, Speer had had the uncommon courage to protest Hitler's mistaken identification of his own fate with that of the country to a Fuehrer who had many a man executed for uttering merely defeatist sentiments.

The court, especially the Russians on it, knew from experience as well as from the evidence before them how much Speer had accomplished for the Reich. He had kept Germany armed against a world of enemies both inside and outside its boundaries. Far more than Goering, he had become the second man in the Reich; one English newspaper had even written, toward the end of the war, that he was more important to the German war effort than Hitler himself. There is truth in this statement. By the time of Stalingrad, Hitler's mystique was fading and his decisions becoming more and more bizarre; it was Speer who kept the war machine running in high gear and increasingly productive until 1945. Only when the cities lay in ruins and at Hitler's orders the last factories were to be blown up did Speer come to suspect what many of his compatriots like Goerdeler, Witzleben, and Rudolf Pechel had long known: that a Hitlerian victory would have worse consequences for Germany than any defeat.

In prison Speer set himself the task of finding out why it had taken him so long to see the error in the way he had chosen. He put himself through a long and careful self-analysis, a process that prison was ideally suited to further. He could read almost any nonpolitical books he chose; so he turned to psychology, philosophy, and metaphysics, the kind of books, he says, he never in the world would have read or thought he had had the time to read when he was in civil life. And he could look inward, ask himself questions as he went over the days of his life, questions that a man sometimes asks during or after major crises but that seldom can be thoroughly investigated amid the intense preoccupations of making a career in the contemporary world. Speer was unhampered by the demands of such a life; he had gnawing problems, to be sure—the well-being of his family and the appalling state of the country he had helped to keep at war and thus had helped destroy—but his main preoccupation was to try to explain himself to himself. He could do this best by writing it all down. In what he said he had nothing to lose. He was condemned and sentenced; he had acknowledged his guilt; now it was his job to understand what he had done and why. So the reader of these memoirs is fortunate: he will be told, as far as the author is capable of telling him, precisely why Speer acted as he did. Thus this chronicle of National Socialist Germany seen from within also becomes a self-revealing account of one of the most able men who served it.

Inwardness is especially unusual in a technician. A man like Speer, working with blueprints, ordering vast projects, is likely to exhaust himself in manipulation, in transforming the outer world, in carrying out production goals with all the means at hand. His was not introspective work, but in Spandau Speer had to turn not to others to carry out his planning, but only, day after day and night after night, to himself. It was a rare opportunity and he took full advantage of it. He could do it the more readily because he was convinced the court had acted justly in his case; he had much the same interest as the prosecution in finding out what had happened.

This objectivity has stayed with him. One of the suggestions made to him in connection with the publication of this book in England was that he meet the former chief British prosecutor, Lord Shawcross (at the time of the trial, Sir Hartley Shawcross), on the BBC to discuss the Nuremberg case. Speer said he would be pleased to meet with the British or American or any other prosecutor; he bears no rancor against the people who helped put him in prison for twenty years, and he has no objection to meeting anyone who has a serious interest in the history in which he played such a conspicuous role.

When he returned to Heidelberg after his twenty-one-year absence he did the simple, ordinary things a man might do who must start all over again. He went back to the summer house above the Neckar where he had lived as a child; and because when he was a boy he had had a St. Bernard dog, he got himself another one, to help him return to the beginnings again, to bridge the long exile. He planned to resume his architectural practice, although on a very small scale this time. Men take disaster in very different ways. Admiral Doenitz, for example, will not discuss Spandau. He says he has put it away in a trunk and doesn't want to talk about it. Speer on the other hand talks easily about his imprisonment—more than easily: with serenity.

Of course, motives may remain unrevealed, whatever Speer's earnest attempts to seek them out. It is unlikely that any man, despite his good intentions, can rid himself entirely of the need to see himself in a better light than his critics see him. Hans Frank, a co-defendant of Speer's, wrote his memoirs while awaiting execution; it was he who made the often quoted remark, "A thousand years shall pass and this guilt of Germany will not have been erased." Although disgusted with himself, Frank could not avoid telling in his recollections how he had respected the law and had tried to get the Fuehrer to respect it too. In this and other ways he salvaged what he could from a career he now deplored. Albert Speer may not be entirely immune from this human failing, but he has no intention of covering up or decorating anything. He put his life on the line in the Nuremberg courtroom and he now meets his German and foreign critics with calm assurance, with sorrow for the irretrievable mistakes he made but the conviction that he has paid for them as far as he could and as far as his judges thought he should.

Some of his self-discoveries leave him still with ambivalent judgments. When he first met the Fuehrer, Speer writes, it was at a time in his career when, like Faust, he would have gladly sold his soul to the devil in exchange for a patron who would make use of his architectural services. And something resembling the Faustian pact was made. All his energies and abilities Speer eagerly placed at Hitler's disposal, although he fought off everyone, including Hitler, who obstructed his single-minded drive to do his job. Speer's early admiration for the Fuehrer slowly diminished as Hitler became increasingly capricious and unapproachable; when Hitler ordered everything blown up, Speer refused to obey him and was ready to kill him to prevent the orders from being carried out. Nevertheless, he made a flight to the bunker in Berlin under the guns of the Russian planes and troops a few days before Hitler's suicide in order to say good-bye.

Speer has given us two versions of this flight. In an interview published in *Der Spiegel* just after he was released from Spandau he said he went to Berlin to attempt to persuade one of his close collaborators, Friedrich Lüschen, to leave the city. In these memoirs, however, the story is told somewhat differently. Speer writes that he did have Lüschen's rescue in mind and also wanted to save Dr. Brandt, an old friend and Hitler's personal physician, who had fallen into the hands of Himmler's SS. In the last stages of his trip to Berlin Speer learned that Brandt was no longer in the city and he could not reach Lüschen, but he nevertheless decided to continue his journey. He knows now that he had to go to Berlin to say farewell to the man whom he owed so much and for whom he felt such deeply mixed emotions.

Speer always intends to be as ruthlessly honest in his self-portrait as he is in those he draws of others. He has written that even today he is glad that he said farewell to the wreck of a man who, when Speer departed, absent-mindedly gave him a limp hand to shake, without a word that spoke of their long association. What made him change his mind about the reasons for the flight? I suggest that the change is evidence of the continuing reevaluation of his reasons for acting as he did. It seems likely that during the interview in *Der Spiegel* he told reporters what readily came to mind and that only later, as he reexamined his present feelings in the context of these memoirs, did he see clearly why he had gone to Berlin and how even today he is not rid of the spell of the Fuehrer he served for so many crowded years. Speer has no prettified self-image to protect. His fellow prisoner, von Schirach, who was released from Spandau at the same time as Speer, may defend what he takes to be his own services to Germany, but Speer bears the full burden of his past and attempts to carry out his self-imposed obligation to come to grips with whatever he has done no matter what the cost to his self-esteem. So the true story emerges, as I think it has, as far as the author is able to re-member and comprehend it, throughout these pages.

This careful self-scrutiny occurs too in connection with his part in the treatment of the Jews. Actually Speer played no role whatever in the Jew-baiting or in the exterminations. The exterminations were known to comparatively few people. Even those most concerned, the Jews in con-centration camps, and incredibly, many of those within sight of the gas chambers, refused to believe the stories they heard.* The mass killings were beyond imagination—they sounded like clumsy propaganda; Speer, however, was in a position to find out about them. He tells us that one of his friends, Gauleiter Hanke, had visited Auschwitz and warned him in the summer of 1944 against making a similar visit. But the Minister of Armaments and War Production had no business that required him to be concerned with rumors of any death mills; his business was with the prisoners who could man his factories, so he never pursued the matter, never looked behind the terrible curtain Hanke had pointed out to him. He preferred not to know, to turn his face away, to concentrate on his own huge task. He believes this was a grievous failure, a sin of omission more inexcusable than any crime he may have committed.

It is for this reason that Speer did not resist his long prison term as did, for example, Admiral Doenitz. Doenitz always felt himself unjustly convicted; he has a large volume of letters from British and American naval officers sharing his view who wrote to him, on their own initiative, to protest the Nuremberg court's verdict and his sentence of ten years. In Speer's case too, non-Germans, including the three Western governors of the prison, had taken the view that he had been given an excessive sentence and had recommended a commutation, but the Russians who had voted to hang Speer held him to his full term. Speer has no complaint to make against the Russians or anyone else. He came to know the Russian guards well at Spandau; they exchanged stories about their children and families and no one ever mentioned the past. Speer was grateful for that; he knew his jailers had undoubtedly lost friends and relatives because he had kept the German war machine rolling and that they had good reason to be hostile. But they were not hostile; nor was the

---

* Two recent publications have dealt with this astonishing incomprehension. One, *The Destruction of the Dutch Jews,* was witten by Jacob Presser, who was him-self a concentration camp prisoner. The other is an article by Louis de Jong, director of the Dutch Institute of War Documentation; it is entitled "Die Niederländer und Auschwitz" and appeared in the January 1969 issue of the *Vierteljahrshefte,* pub-lished by the Institut für Zeitgeschichte in Munich.

former slave laborer who befriended Speer in prison, because he thought Speer had seen to it, in the days of his forced labor, that he be tolerably treated.

It is Speer's spirit of contrition, this complete acknowledgment of so much that went wrong, of so much that he feels was lacking in him in his days of power, as well as the perceptiveness of his observations, that makes this book such an unusual document. It tells us much of how history was made, and something too of the moral dilemma of a civilized man who had been given an enormous administrative assignment, that at first had seemed to him more a technological than a human problem. Much of what Speer tells us is related to an old story of *hubris*, of temptations of pride and position, and of the opportunity to create on a heroic scale. In the euphoria of history-making activity, unpleasant facts were ignored; they were no more than obstacles to the achievement of the grand design. But with the collapse of everything he had lived for and lived by, Speer came to judge himself more strictly than the Nuremberg court could judge him. It is in this long, painful struggle for self-enlightenment that we may see that whatever he lost when he made his pact with Adolf Hitler, it was not his soul.

EUGENE DAVIDSON

May 1970

Every autobiography is a dubious enterprise. For the underlying assumption is that a chair exists in which a man can sit down to contemplate his own life, to compare its phases, to survey its development, and to penetrate its meanings. Every man can and surely ought to take stock of himself. But he cannot survey himself even in the present moment, any more than in the whole of his past.

KARL BARTH

INSIDE THE THIRD REICH

Foreword

"I SUPPOSE YOU'LL BE WRITING YOUR MEMOIRS NOW?" SAID ONE OF THE
first Americans I met in Flensburg in May 1945. Since then twenty-four
years have passed, of which I spent twenty-one in a prison cell. A long
time.

Now I am publishing my memoirs. I have tried to describe the past as
I experienced it. Many will think it distorted; many will find my perspective wrong. That may or may not be so: I have set forth what I experienced and the way I regard it today. In doing so I have tried not to
falsify the past. My aim has been not to gloss over either what was fasci-
nating or what was horrible about those years. Other participants will
criticize me, but that is unavoidable. I have tried to be honest.

One of the purposes of these memoirs is to reveal some of the
premises which almost inevitably led to the disasters in which that period
culminated. I have sought to show what came of one man's holding unrestricted power in his hands and also to clarify the nature of this man. In
court at Nuremberg I said that if Hitler had had any friends, I would have
been his friend. I owe to him the enthusiasms and the glory of my youth
as well as belated horror and guilt.

In the description of Hitler as he showed himself to me and to others,
a good many likable traits will appear. He may seem to be a man capable
and devoted in many respects. But the more I wrote, the more I felt that
these were only superficial traits.

For such impressions are countered by one unforgettable experience:
the Nuremberg Trial. I shall never forget the account of a Jewish family
going to their deaths: the husband with his wife and children on the way
to die are before my eyes to this day.

In Nuremberg I was sentenced to twenty years imprisonment. The
military tribunal may have been faulty in summing up history, but it
attempted to apportion guilt. The penalty, however poorly such penalties
measure historical responsibility, ended my civil existence. But that scene
had already laid waste to my life. It has outlasted the verdict of the court.

January 11, 1969   ALBERT SPEER

PART

ONE

I

Origins and Youth

SOME OF MY FOREFATHERS WERE SWABIANS, SOME CAME FROM POOR PEAS-
ants of the Westerwald, others from Silesia and Westphalia. They belonged to the great mass of those who live quiet, unnotable lives. There
was one exception: Hereditary Reich Marshal Count Friedrich Ferdinand
zu Pappenheim[1] (1702–93), who begot eight sons with my unmarried
ancestress Humelin. He does not, however, seem to have worried much
about their welfare.

Three generations later my grandfather Hermann Hommel, son of a
poor forester in the Black Forest, had become by the end of his life sole
owner of one of the largest machine-tool firms in Germany and of a pre-
cision-instrument factory. In spite of his wealth he lived modestly and
treated his subordinates well. Hard-working himself, he knew how to let
others work without interfering. A typical Black Forest brooder, he could
sit for hours on a bench in the woods without wasting a word.

My other grandfather, Berthold Speer, became a prosperous architect
in Dortmund about this same time. He designed many buildings in the
neoclassical style of the period. Though he died young, he left enough to
provide for the education of his four sons. The success of both my grand-
fathers was furthered by the rapid industrialization of Germany which
began in the second half of the nineteenth century. But then, many persons who had started out from a better basis did not necessarily flourish.

My father's mother, prematurely white-haired, inspired in me more respect than love in my boyhood. She was a serious woman, moored fast to simple notions about life and possessing an obstinate energy. She dominated everyone around her.

I came into the world in Mannheim at noon on Sunday, March 19, 1905. The thunder of a spring storm drowned out the bells of nearby Christ Church, as my mother often used to tell me.

In 1892, at the age of twenty-nine, my father had established his own architectural firm. He had since become one of the busiest architects in Mannheim, then a booming industrial town. He had acquired a considerable fortune by the time he married the daughter of a prosperous Mainz businessman in 1900.

The upper-middle-class style of our apartment in one of his Mannheim houses was commensurate with my parents' status. It was an imposing house, built around a courtyard guarded by elaborate wrought-iron gates. Automobiles would drive into this courtyard and stop in front of a flight of stairs which provided a suitable entrance to the richly furnished house. But the children—my two brothers and I—had to use the back stairs. These were dark, steep, and narrow and ended unimpressively in a rear corridor. Children had no business in the elegant, carpeted front hall.

As children our realm extended from our bedrooms in the rear wing to a vast kitchen. We had to pass through the kitchen to enter the elegant part of the fourteen-room apartment. From a vestibule with a sham fireplace faced with valuable Delft tiles guests were conducted into a large room full of French furniture and Empire upholstery. The glittering crystal chandelier particularly is so impressed on my memory that I can see it to this day. So is the conservatory, whose appointments my father had bought at the Paris World Exhibition in 1900: richly carved Indian furniture, hand-embroidered curtains, and a tapestry-covered divan. Palms and other exotic plants suggested an exotic world. Here my parents had their breakfast and here my father would make ham rolls for us children of the kind that were eaten in his native Westphalia. My recollection of the adjacent living room has faded, but the paneled, neo-Gothic dining room has kept its magic for me. The table could seat more than twenty. There my baptism was celebrated; there our family festivals take place to this day.

My mother took great pleasure and pride in seeing to it that we belonged socially to the leading families of Mannheim. There were surely no more—but no less—than twenty or thirty households in the city that enjoyed comparable luxuries. A large staff of servants helped meet the requirements of status. In addition to the cook—whom for obvious reasons we children were especially fond of—my parents employed a kitchen maid, a chambermaid, a butler frequently, and a chauffeur always, as well as a nanny to look after us. The maids wore white caps, black dresses, and white aprons; the butler, purple livery with gilt buttons. The chauffeur was dressed most magnificently of all.

My parents did their best to provide a happy childhood for us. But wealth and status—social obligations, the large household, the nanny, and the servants—stood in the way of their doing as they wished in this respect. To this day I can feel the artificiality and discomfort of that world. Moreover, I often had dizzy spells and sometimes fainted. The Heidelberg physician whom they consulted, a distinguished professor of medicine, diagnosed the cause as "weakness of the vascular nerves." This disability was a considerable psychological burden and early made me conscious of the pressure of external conditions. I suffered all the more because my playmates and my two brothers were more robust than I, so that I felt inferior to them. In their rough and tumble way they often made it clear that this was how they thought of me, too.

An inadequacy often calls forth compensating forces. In any case these difficulties made me learn how to adjust better to the world of other boys. If I later showed some aptitude in dealing with difficult circumstances and troublesome people, I suspect that the gift can be traced back to my boyhood physical weakness.

When we were taken out by our French governess, we had to be nattily dressed, in keeping with our social status. Naturally, we were forbidden to play in the city parks, let alone on the street. All we had for a playground was our courtyard—not much larger than a few of our rooms put together. It was surrounded by the backs of tall apartment houses. This yard contained two or three wretched plane trees, starved for air, and an ivy-covered wall. A mound of tufa rocks in one corner suggested a grotto. By early spring a thick layer of soot coated the greenery, and whatever we touched was bent on transforming us into dirty, disreputable big-city children. My favorite playmate, before my school days began, was Frieda Allmendinger, the concierge's daughter. The atmosphere of sparse simplicity and the close-knit quality of a family living in crowded quarters had a curious attraction for me.

I attended the primary grades at a distinguished private school where the children of leading families were taught reading and writing. After this sheltered environment, my first months in the public Oberrealschule (high school), amid rowdy fellow pupils, were especially hard for me. I had a friend named Quenzer, however, who soon introduced me to all sorts of fun and games. He also persuaded me to buy a soccer ball with my pocket money. This was a plebeian impulse which horrified my parents, all the more so since Quenzer came from a poor family. I think it was at this time that my bent for statistics first manifested itself. I recorded all the bad marks in the class book in my "Phoenix Calendar for Schoolchildren," and every month counted up who had received the most demerits. No doubt I would not have bothered if I had not had some prospect of frequently heading the list.

The office of my father's architectural firm was right next door to our apartment. That was where the large renderings for the builders were made. Drawings of all sorts were made on a bluish transparent paper whose smell is still part and parcel of my memories of that office. My father's buildings were influenced by the neo-Renaissance: they had by-passed Jugendstil. Later on, the quieter classicism of Ludwig Hoffmann, the influential city architect of Berlin, served him as a model.

In that office I made my first "work of art" at the age of twelve. A birthday present for my father, it was a drawing of a sort of allegorical "life clock," in a highly ornamented case complete with Corinthian columns and intricate scrollwork. I used all the watercolors I could lay hands on. With the help of the office employees, I produced a reasonable facsimile of an object in Late Empire style.

Before 1914 my parents kept a touring car for summer use as well as a sedan for driving around the city in winter. These automobiles were the focus of my technological passions. At the beginning of the war they had to be put upon blocks, to spare the tires; but if the chauffeur were well disposed to us, we children were allowed to sit at the steering wheel in the garage. At such times I experienced the first sensations of technical intoxication in a world that was yet scarcely technical. In Spandau prison I had to live like a man of the nineteenth century without a radio, television set, telephone, or car and was not even allowed to work the light switch myself. After ten years of imprisonment I experienced a similar rapture when I was allowed to run an electric floor polisher.

In 1915 I encountered another product of the technical revolution of those decades. One of the zeppelins used in the air raids on London was stationed in Mannheim. The captain and his officers were soon frequent guests in our house. They invited my two brothers and me to tour their airship. Ten years old, I stood before that giant product of technology, clambered into the motor gondola, made my way through the dim mysterious corridors inside the hull, and went into the control gondola. When the airship started, toward evening, the captain had it perform a neat loop over our house, and the officers waved a sheet they had borrowed from our mother. Night after night afterward I was in terror that the airship would go up in flames, and all my friends would be killed.*

My imagination dwelt on the war, on the advances and retreats at the front, on the suffering of the soldiers. At night we sometimes heard a distant rumble from the great battle of attrition at Verdun. With the ardent sympathies of childhood, I would often sleep for several nights running on the hard floor beside my soft bed in order to be sharing the privations of the soldiers at the front.

* In 1917 heavy losses made it necessary to call off the attacks.

We did not escape the food shortages in the city and what was then called the turnip winter. We had wealth, but no relatives or acquaintances in the countryside. My mother was clever at devising endless new variations on turnip dishes, but I was often so hungry that in secret I gradually consumed a whole bag of stone-hard dog biscuits left over from peacetime. The air raids on Mannheim, which by present-day standards were quite innocuous, became more frequent. One small bomb struck a neighboring house. A new period of my boyhood began.

Since 1905 we had owned a summer home in the vicinity of Heidelberg. It stood on the slope of a quarry that was said to have supplied the stone for the nearby Heidelberg Schloss. Back of the slope rose the hills of the Odenwald with hiking paths through the ancient woods. Strip clearings provided occasional glimpses of the Neckar Valley. Here everything was peaceful; we could have a fine garden and vegetables, and the neighbor owned a cow. We moved there in the summer of 1918.

My health soon improved. Every day, even in snowstorms and rain, I tramped for three-quarters of an hour to and from school, often at a steady run. Bicycles were not available in the straitened early postwar period.

My way to school led me past the clubhouse of a rowing association. In 1919 I became a member and for two years was coxswain of the racing fours and eights. In spite of my still frail constitution I soon became one of the most diligent oarsmen in the club. At the age of sixteen I advanced to stroke in the school shells and took part in several races. For the first time I had been seized by ambition and was spurred to performances I would not have thought myself capable of. What excited me was more the chance to direct the crew by my own rhythm than the prospect of winning respect in the small world of oarsmen.

Most of the time we were defeated, to be sure. But since a team performance was involved, each individual's flaws could not be weighed. On the contrary, a sense of common action arose. There was another benefit to such training: the requirement of self-discipline. At the time I despised those among my schoolmates who were finding their first pleasures in dancing, wine, and cigarettes.

On my way to school, at the age of seventeen, I met the girl who was to become my wife. Falling in love made me more studious, for a year later we agreed that we would be married as soon as I completed my university studies. I had long been good at mathematics; but now my marks in other subjects also improved, and I became one of the best in the class.

Our German teacher, an enthusiastic democrat, often read aloud to us from the liberal *Frankfurter Zeitung*. But for this teacher I would have remained altogether nonpolitical in school. For we were being educated in terms of a conservative bourgeois view of the world. In spite of the Revolution which had brought in the Weimar Republic, it was still impressed upon us that the distribution of power in society and the traditional authorities were part of the God-given order of things. We remained largely untouched by the currents stirring everywhere during the early twenties. In school, there could be no criticism of courses or subject matter, let alone of the ruling powers in the state. Unconditional faith in the authority of the school was required. It never even occurred to us to doubt the order of things, for as students we were subjected to the dictates of a virtually absolutist system. Moreover, there were no subjects such as sociology which might have sharpened our political judgments. Even in our senior year, German class assignments called solely for essays on literary subjects, which actually prevented us from giving any thought to the problems of society. Nor did all these restrictions in school impel us to take positions on political events during extracurricular activities or outside of school. One decisive point of difference from the present was our inability to travel abroad. Even if funds for foreign travel had been available, no organizations existed to help young people undertake such travel. It seems to me essential to point out these lacks, as a result of which a whole generation was without defenses when exposed to the new techniques for influencing opinion.

At home, too, politics were not discussed. This was all the odder since my father had been a convinced liberal even before 1914. Every morning he waited impatiently for the *Frankfurter Zeitung* to arrive; every week he read the critical magazines *Simplicissimus* and *Jugend*. He shared the ideas of Friedrich Naumann, who called for social reforms in a powerful Germany. After 1923 my father became a follower of Coudenhove-Kalergi and zealously advocated his pan-European ideas. Father would surely have been glad to talk about politics with me, but I tended to dodge such discussions and he did not insist. This political indifference was characteristic of the youth of the period, tired and disillusioned as they were by a lost war, revolution, and inflation; but it prevented me from forming political standards, from setting up categories on which political judgments could be based. I was much more inclined to detour on my way to school across the park of the Heidelberg Schloss and to linger on the terrace looking dreamily at the ruins of the castle and down at the old city. This partiality for tumbledown citadels and tangles of crooked old streets remained with me and later found expression in my passion for collecting landscape paintings, especially the works of the Heidelberg Romantics. On the way to the Schloss I sometimes met the poet Stefan George, who radiated dignity and pride and a kind of priestliness. The great religious preachers must have had such an effect upon people, for there was something magnetic about him. When my elder brother was in his senior year, he was admitted to the Master's inner circle.

Music meant a good deal to me. Up to 1922, I was able to hear the young Furtwängler in Mannheim and after him, Erich Kleiber. At that time I found Verdi more impressive than Wagner and thought Puccini "frightful." On the other hand, I was ravished by a symphony of Rimsky-Korsakov and judged Mahler's *Fifth Symphony* "rather complicated, but I liked it." After a visit to the Playhouse, I observed that Georg Kaiser was "the most important modern dramatist who in his works wrestles with the concept of the value and power of money." And upon seeing Ibsen's *The Wild Duck,* I decided that we could not find the characteristics of the leaders of society as other than ridiculous. These people were "farcical," I wrote. Romain Rolland's novel *Jean Christophe* heightened my enthusiasm for Beethoven.[2]

It was, therefore, not only in a burst of youthful rebelliousness that I found the luxurious life at home not to my liking. There was a more basic opposition involved when I turned to what were then the advanced writers and looked for friends in a rowing club or in the huts of the Alpine Club. The custom in my circles was for a young man to seek his companions and his future wife in the sheltered class to which his parents belonged. But I was drawn to plain, solid artisan families for both. I even felt an instinctive sympathy for the extreme left—though this inclination never assumed any concrete form. At the time I was allergic to any political commitments. That continued to be so, even though I felt strong nationalistic feelings—as for example, at the time of the French occupation of the Ruhr in 1923.

To my amazement my *Abitur* essay was judged the best in my class. Nevertheless I thought, "That's hardly likely for you," when the head of the school in his farewell address told the graduates that now "the way to highest deeds and honors" was open to us.

Since I was the best mathematician in the school, I had intended to study that subject. But my father presented sound reasons against this choice, and I would not have been a mathematician familiar with the laws of logic if I had not yielded to his arguments. The profession of architecture, which I had been absorbing naturally since my boyhood, seemed the obvious choice. I therefore decided, to my father's delight, to become an architect, like him and his father before him.

During my first semester I studied at the Institute of Technology in nearby Karlsruhe. Financial reasons dictated this choice, for the inflation was growing wilder with each passing day. I had to draw my allowance weekly; by the end of the week the fabulous sum had melted away to nothing. From the Black Forest where I was on a bicycle tour in the middle of September 1923, I wrote: "Very cheap here! Lodgings 400,000 marks and supper 1,800,000 marks. Milk 250,000 marks a pint." Six weeks later, shortly before the end of the inflation, a restaurant dinner cost ten to twenty billion marks, and even in the student dining hall over a billion.

I had to pay between three and four hundred million marks for a theater ticket.

The financial upheaval finally forced my family to sell my deceased grandfather's firm and factory to another company at a fraction of its value in return for "dollar treasury bills." Afterward, my monthly allowance amounted to sixteen dollars—on which I was totally free of cares and could live splendidly.

In the spring of 1924, with the inflation now over, I shifted to the Institute of Technology in Munich. Although I remained there until the summer of 1925 and Hitler, after his release from prison, was again making a stir in the spring of 1925, I took no notice of him. In my long letters to my fiancée I wrote only of how I was studying far into the night and of our common goal: getting married in three or four years.

During the holidays my future wife and I with a few fellow students frequently went on tramps from shelter to shelter in the Austrian Alps. Hard climbs gave us the sense of real achievement. Sometimes, with characteristic obstinacy, I managed to convince my fellow hikers not to give up a tour we had started on, even in the worst weather—in spite of storms, icy rains, and cold, although mists spoiled the view from the peak when we finally reached it. Often, from the mountain tops, we looked down upon a deep gray layer of cloud over the distant plain. Down there lived what to our minds were wretched people; we thought we stood high above them in every sense. Young and rather arrogant, we were convinced that only the finest people went into the mountains. When we returned from the peaks to the normal life of the lowlands, I was quite confused for a while by the bustle of the cities.

We also sought "closeness with nature" on trips with our folding boats. In those days this sport was still new; the streams were not filled with craft of all kinds as they are today. In perfect quiet we floated down the rivers, and in the evenings we could pitch our tent at the most beautiful spot we could find. This leisurely hiking and boating gave us some of that happiness that had been a matter of course to our forefathers. Even my father had taken a tour on foot and in horse carriages from Munich to Naples in 1885. Later, when he would drive through all of Europe in his car, he used to speak of that tour as the finest travel experience he had ever had.

Many of our generation sought such contact with nature. This was not merely a romantic protest against the narrowness of middle-class life. We were also escaping from the demands of a world growing increasingly complicated. We felt that the world around us was out of balance. In nature, in the mountains and the river valleys, the harmony of Creation could still be felt. The more virginal the mountains, the lonelier the river valleys, the more they drew us. I did not, however, belong to any youth movement, for the group quality of these movements would have negated the very isolation we were seeking.

In the autumn of 1925, I began attending the Institute of Technology in Berlin-Charlottenburg, along with a group of Munich students of architecture. I wanted Professor Poelzig for my teacher, but he had set limits to the number of students in his drafting seminar. Since my talent for drawing was inadequate, I was not accepted. In any case, I was beginning to doubt that I would ever make a good architect and took this verdict without surprise. Next semester Professor Heinrich Tessenow was appointed to the institute. He was a champion of the spirit of simple craftsmanship in architecture and believed in architectonic expressiveness by severely delimited means. "A minimum of pomp is the decisive factor." I promptly wrote to my fiancée:

> My new professor is the most remarkable, most clear-headed man I
> have ever met. I am wild about him and am working with great eagerness.
> He is not modern, but in a certain sense more modern than all the others.
> Outwardly he seems unimaginative and sober, just like me, but his build-
> ings have something about them that expresses a profound experience. His
> intelligence is frighteningly acute. I mean to try hard to be admitted to his
> "master school" in a year, and after another year will try to become his
> assistant. Of course all this is wildly optimistic and is merely meant to trace
> what I'd like to do in the best of cases.

Only half a year after completing my examination I became his assistant. In Professor Tessenow I had found my first catalyst—and he remained that for me until seven years later when he was replaced by a more powerful one.

I also had great respect for our teacher of the history of architec-ture, Professor Daniel Krenkler. An Alsatian by birth, he was a ded-icated archaeologist and a highly emotional patriot as well. In the course of one lecture he burst into tears while showing us pictures of Strassburg Cathedral and had to suspend the lecture. For him I delivered a report on Albrecht Haupt's book on Germanic architecture, *Die Baukunst der Germanen*. But at the same time I wrote to my fiancée:

> A little racial mixture is always good. And if today we are on the down-
> ward path, it is not because we are a mixed race. For we were already that
> in the Middle Ages when we still had a vigorous germ in us and were
> expanding, when we drove the Slavs out of Prussia, or later transplanted
> European culture to America. We are going downhill because our energies
> have been consumed; it is the same thing that happened in the past to the
> Egyptians, Greeks, and Romans. There is nothing to be done about that.

The twenties in Berlin were the inspiring backdrop to my student years. Many theatrical performances made a deep impression upon me— among others Max Reinhardt's staging of *A Midsummer Night's Dream*,

Elisabeth Bergner in Shaw's *Saint Joan,* Pallenberg in Piscator's version of *Schweik.* But Charell's lavishly mounted revues also fascinated me. On the other hand, I took no pleasure in Cecil B. De Mille's bombastic pomp —never suspecting that ten years later I myself would be going his movie architecture one better. As a student I thought his films examples of "American tastelessness."

But overshadowing all such impressions was the poverty and unemployment all around me. Spengler's *Decline of the West* had convinced me that we were living in a period of decay strongly similar to the late Roman Empire: inflation, decline of morals, impotence of the German Reich. His essay "Prussianism and Socialism" excited me especially because of the contempt for luxury and comfort it expressed. On this score, Spengler's and Tessenow's doctrines coincided. But my teacher, in contrast to Spengler, saw hope for the future. He took an ironic tone toward the "cult of heroes" fashionable at the period.

Perhaps there are really uncomprehended "super" heroes all around us who because of their towering aims and abilities may rightly smile at even the greatest of horrors, seeing them as merely incidental. Perhaps, before handicraft and the small town can flourish again, there must first come something like a rain of brimstone. Perhaps nations which have passed through infernos will then be ready for their next age of flowering.[3]

In the summer of 1927, after nine semesters, I passed the architect's license examination. The following spring, at twenty-three, I became one of the youngest assistants at the institute. In the last year of the war, I had gone to a fortuneteller at a fair, and she had prophesied: "You will win early fame and retire early." Now I had reason to think of this prediction; for it seemed evident that if only I wanted to I could some day teach at the Institute of Technology like my professor.

This post as assistant made it possible for me to marry. We did not go to Italy for our honeymoon, but took faltboats and tent through the solitary, forested chain of lakes in Mecklenburg. We launched our boats in Spandau, a few hundred yards from the prison where I would be spending twenty years of my life.

2

Profession and Vocation

I VERY NEARLY BECAME AN OFFICIAL COURT ARCHITECT AS EARLY AS 1928. Aman Ullah, ruler of the Afghans, wanted to reform his country and was hiring young German technicians with that end in view. Joseph Brix, Professor of Urban Architecture and Road Building, organized the group. It was proposed that I would serve as city planner and architect and in addition as teacher of architecture at a technical school which was to be founded in Kabul. My wife and I pored over all available books on remote Afghanistan. We considered how a style natural to the country could be developed out of the simple existing structures, and the pictures of wild mountains filled us with dreams of ski tours. Favorable contractual conditions were worked out. But no sooner was everything virtually settled—the King had just been received with great honors by President Hindenburg—than the Afghans overthrew their ruler in a coup d'état.

The prospect of continuing to work with Tessenow consoled me. I had been having some misgivings anyhow, and I was glad that the fall of Aman Ullah removed the need to make a decision. I had to look after my seminar only three days a week; in addition there were five months of academic vacation. Nevertheless I received 300 Reichsmark—about the equivalent in value of 800 Deutsche Mark* [$200] today. Tessenow de-

---

* All figures in DM do not take into account the 1969 revaluation of the mark. The reader can easily reckon the amounts in U.S. dollars by dividing DM figures by four.

livered no lectures; he came to the large seminar room only to correct the papers of his fifty-odd students. He was around for no more than four to six hours a week; the rest of the time the students were left in my care for instruction and correction.

The first months in particular were very strenuous for me. The students assumed a highly critical attitude toward me and tried to trap me into a show of ignorance or weakness. It took a while before my initial nervousness subsided. But the commissions for buildings, which I had hoped to spend my ample free time on, did not come my way. Probably I struck people as too young. Moreover, the construction industry was very slow because of the economic depression. One exception was the commission to build a house in Heidelberg for my wife's parents. It proved to be a modest building which was followed by two others of no great consequence—two garage annexes for Wannsee villas—and the designing of the Berlin offices of the Academic Exchange Service.

In 1930 we sailed our two faltboats from Donaueschingen, which is in Swabia, down the Danube to Vienna. By the time we returned, there had been a Reichstag election on September 14 which remains in my memory only because my father was greatly perturbed about it. The NSDAP (National Socialist Party) had won 107 seats and was suddenly the chief topic of political discussion.

My father had the darkest forebodings, chiefly in view of the NSDAP's socialist tendencies. He was already disturbed enough by the strength of the Social Democrats and the Communists.

Our Institute of Technology had in the meanwhile become a center of National Socialist endeavors. The small group of Communist architecture students gravitated to Professor Poelzig's seminar, while the National Socialists gathered around Tessenow, even though he was and remained a forthright opponent of the Hitler movement, for there were parallels, unexpressed and unintended, between his doctrine and the ideology of the National Socialists. Tessenow was not aware of these parallels. He would surely have been horrified by the thought of any kinship between his ideas and National Socialist views.

Among other things, Tessenow taught: "Style comes from the people. It is in our nature to love our native land. There can be no true culture that is international. True culture comes only from the maternal womb of a nation."[1]

Hitler, too, denounced the internationalization of art. The National Socialist creed held that the roots of renewal were to be found in the native soil of Germany.

Tessenow decried the metropolis and extolled the peasant virtues: "The metropolis is a dreadful thing. The metropolis is a confusion of old and new. The metropolis is conflict, brutal conflict. Everything good should be left outside of big cities. . . . Where urbanism meets the peasantry, the spirit of the peasantry is ruined. A pity that people can no longer think in peasant terms." In a similar vein, Hitler cried out against the erosion of morals in the big cities. He warned against the ill effects of civilization which, he said, damaged the biological substance of the people. And he emphasized the importance of a healthy peasantry as a mainstay for the state.

Hitler was able to sense these and other currents which were in the air of the times, though many of them were still diffuse and intangible. He was able to articulate them and to exploit them for his own ends.

In the process of my correcting their papers, the National Socialist students often involved me in political discussions. Naturally, Tessenow's ideas were passionately debated. Well trained in dialectics, these students easily crushed the feeble objections I could make, borrowed as they were from my father's vocabulary.

The students were chiefly turning to the extremists for their beliefs, and Hitler's party appealed directly to the idealism of this generation. And after all, was not a man like Tessenow also fanning these flames? About 1931 he had declared: "Someone will have to come along who thinks very simply. Thinking today has become too complicated. An un-cultured man, a peasant as it were, would solve everything much more easily merely because he would still be unspoiled. He would also have the strength to carry out his simple ideas."[2] To us this oracular remark seemed to herald Hitler.

Hitler was delivering an address to the students of Berlin University and the Institute of Technology. My students urged me to attend. Not yet convinced, but already uncertain of my ground, I went along. The site of the meeting was a beer hall called the Hasenheide. Dirty walls, narrow stairs, and an ill-kept interior created a poverty-stricken atmosphere. This was a place where workmen ordinarily held beer parties. The room was overcrowded. It seemed as if nearly all the students in Berlin wanted to see and hear this man whom his adherents so much admired and his opponents so much detested. A large number of professors sat in favored places in the middle of a bare platform. Their presence gave the meeting an importance and a social acceptability that it would not otherwise have had. Our group had also secured good seats on the platform, not far from the lectern.

Hitler entered and was tempestuously hailed by his numerous fol-lowers among the students. This enthusiasm in itself made a great im-pression upon me. But his appearance also surprised me. On posters and in caricatures I had seen him in military tunic, with shoulder straps, swastika armband, and hair flapping over his forehead. But here he was wearing a well-fitted blue suit and looking markedly respectable. Everything about him bore out the note of reasonable modesty. Later I learned that he had a great gift for adjusting—consciously or intuitively—to his surroundings.

As the ovation went on for minutes he tried, as if slightly pained, to check it. Then, in a low voice, hesitantly and somewhat shyly, he began a kind of historical lecture rather than a speech. To me there was something engaging about it—all the more so since it ran counter to everything the propaganda of his opponents had led me to expect: a hysterical demagogue, a shrieking and gesticulating fanatic in uniform. He did not allow the bursts of applause to tempt him away from his sober tone.

It seemed as if he were candidly presenting his anxieties about the future. His irony was softened by a somewhat self-conscious humor; his South German charm reminded me agreeably of my native region. A cool Prussian could never have captivated me that way. Hitler's initial shyness soon disappeared; at times now his pitch rose. He spoke urgently and with hypnotic persuasiveness. The mood he cast was much deeper than the speech itself, most of which I did not remember for long.

Moreover, I was carried on the wave of the enthusiasm which, one could almost feel this physically, bore the speaker along from sentence to sentence. It swept away any skepticism, any reservations. Opponents were given no chance to speak. This furthered the illusion, at least momentarily, of unanimity. Finally, Hitler no longer seemed to be speaking to convince; rather, he seemed to feel that he was expressing what the audience, by now transformed into a single mass, expected of him. It was as if it were the most natural thing in the world to lead students and part of the faculty of the two greatest academies in Germany submissively by a leash. Yet that evening he was not yet the absolute ruler, immune from all criticism, but was still exposed to attacks from all directions.

Others may afterward have discussed that stirring evening over a glass of beer. Certainly my students pressed me to do so. But I felt I had to straighten things out in my own mind, to master my confusion. I needed to be alone. Shaken, I drove off into the night in my small car, stopped in a pine forest near the Havel, and went for a long walk.

Here, it seemed to me, was hope. Here were new ideals, a new understanding, new tasks. Even Spengler's dark predictions seemed to me refuted, and his prophecy of the coming of a new Roman emperor simultaneously fulfilled. The peril of communism, which seemed inexorably on its way, could be checked, Hitler persuaded us, and instead of hopeless unemployment, Germany could move toward economic recovery. He had mentioned the Jewish problem only peripherally. But such remarks did not worry me, although I was not an anti-Semite; rather, I had Jewish friends from my school days and university days, like virtually everyone else.

A few weeks after this speech, which had been so important to me, friends took me to a demonstration at the Sportpalast. Goebbels, the Gauleiter of Berlin, spoke. How different my impression was: much phrase-making, careful structure, and incisive formulations; a roaring crowd whom Goebbels whipped up to wilder and wilder frenzies of enthusiasm and hatred; a witches' cauldron of excitement such as I had hitherto witnessed only at six-day bike races. I felt repelled; the positive effect Hitler had had upon me was diminished, though not extinguished.

Both Goebbels and Hitler had understood how to unleash mass instincts at their meetings, how to play on the passions that underlay the veneer of ordinary respectable life. Practiced demagogues, they succeeded in fusing the assembled workers, petits bourgeois, and students into a homogeneous mob whose opinions they could mold as they pleased. . . . But as I see it today, these politicians in particular were in fact molded by the mob itself, guided by its yearnings and its daydreams. Of course Goebbels and Hitler knew how to penetrate through to the instincts of their audiences; but in the deeper sense they derived their whole existence from these audiences. Certainly the masses roared to the beat set by Hitler's and Goebbels's baton; yet they were not the true conductors. The mob determined the theme. To compensate for misery, insecurity, unemployment, and hopelessness, this anonymous assemblage wallowed for hours at a time in obsessions, savagery, license. This was no ardent nationalism. Rather, for a few short hours the personal unhappiness caused by the breakdown of the economy was replaced by a frenzy that demanded victims. And Hitler and Goebbels threw them the victims. By lashing out at their opponents and villifying the Jews they gave expression and direction to fierce, primal passions.

The Sportpalast emptied. The crowd moved calmly down Potsdamer Strasse. Their self-assurance fed by Goebbels's speech, they challengingly took up the whole width of the street, so that automobile traffic and the streetcars were blocked. At first the police took no action; perhaps they did not want to provoke the crowd. But in the side streets mounted squads and trucks with special patrols were held in readiness. At last the mounted police rode into the crowd, with raised truncheons, to clear the street. Indignantly, I watched the procedure; until that moment I had never witnessed such use of force. At the same time I felt a sense of partisanship, compounded of sympathy for the crowd and opposition to authority, take possession of me. My feelings probably had nothing to do with political motives. Actually, nothing extraordinary had happened. There had not even been any injuries.

The following day I applied for membership in the National Socialist Party and in January 1931 became Member Number 474,481.

It was an utterly undramatic decision. Then and ever afterward I scarcely felt myself to be a member of a political party. I was not choosing the NSDAP, but becoming a follower of Hitler, whose magnetic force had reached out to me the first time I saw him and had not, thereafter, released me. His persuasiveness, the peculiar magic of his by no means pleasant voice, the oddity of his rather banal manner, the seductive simplicity with which he attacked the complexity of our problems—all that bewildered and fascinated me. I knew virtually nothing about his program. He had taken hold of me before I had grasped what was happening.

I was not even thrown off by attending a meeting of the racist Kampfbund Deutscher Kultur (League of Struggle for German Culture), although I heard many of the aims advocated by our teacher Tessenow roundly condemned. One of the speakers called for a return to old-fashioned forms and artistic principles; he attacked modernism and finally berated Der Ring, the society of architects to which Tessenow, Gropius, Mies van der Rohe, Scharoun, Mendelsohn, Taut, Behrens, and Poelzig belonged. Thereupon one of our students sent a letter to Hitler in which he took exception to this speech and spoke with schoolboyish ardor of our admired master. Soon afterward he received a routine letter from party headquarters to the effect that National Socialists had the greatest respect for the work of Tessenow. We laid great weight on that. However, I did not tell Tessenow at the time about my membership in the party.*

It must have been during these months that my mother saw an SA parade in the streets of Heidelberg. The sight of discipline in a time of chaos, the impression of energy in an atmosphere of universal hopelessness, seems to have won her over also. At any rate, without ever having heard a speech or read a pamphlet, she joined the party. Both of us seem to have felt this decision to be a breach with a liberal family tradition. In any case, we concealed it from one another and from my father. Only years later, long after I had become part of Hitler's inner circle, did my mother and I discover by chance that we shared early membership in the party.

Quite often even the most important step in a man's life, his choice of vocation, is taken quite frivolously. He does not bother to find out enough about the basis and the various aspects of that vocation. Once he has chosen it, he is inclined to switch off his critical awareness and to fit himself wholly into the predetermined career.

My decision to enter Hitler's party was no less frivolous. Why, for

---

* After 1933 all the accusations made against Tessenow at this meeting, as well as his connection with the publisher Cassirer and his circle, were cited as incriminating. He became politically suspect and was barred from teaching. But thanks to my privileged position, I was able to persuade the Minister of Education to have him reinstated. He kept his chair at the Berlin Institute of Technology until the end of the war. After 1945 his reputation soared; he was elected one of the first rectors of Berlin's Technical University. "After 1933, Speer soon became a total stranger to me," Tessenow wrote to my wife in 1950, "but I have never thought of him as anything but the friendly, good-natured person I used to know."

example, was I willing to abide by the almost hypnotic impression Hitler's speech had made upon me? Why did I not undertake a thorough, systematic investigation of, say, the value or worthlessness of the ideologies of *all* the parties? Why did I not read the various party programs, or at least Hitler's *Mein Kampf* and Rosenberg's *Myth of the Twentieth Century*? As an intellectual I might have been expected to collect documentation with the same thoroughness and to examine various points of view with the same lack of bias that I had learned to apply to my preliminary architectural studies. This failure was rooted in my inadequate political schooling. As a result, I remained uncritical, unable to deal with the arguments of my student friends, who were predominantly indoctrinated with the National Socialist ideology.

For had I only wanted to, I could have found out even then that Hitler was proclaiming expansion of the Reich to the east; that he was a rank anti-Semite; that he was committed to a system of authoritarian rule; that after attaining power he intended to eliminate democratic procedures and would thereafter yield only to force. Not to have worked that out for myself; not, given my education, to have read books, magazines, and newspapers of various viewpoints; not to have tried to see through the whole apparatus of mystification—was already criminal. At this initial stage my guilt was as grave as, at the end, my work for Hitler. For being in a position to know and nevertheless shunning knowledge creates direct responsibility for the consequences—from the very beginning.

I did see quite a number of rough spots in the party doctrines. But I assumed that they would be polished in time, as has often happened in the history of other revolutions. The crucial fact appeared to me to be that I personally had to choose between a future Communist Germany or a future National Socialist Germany since the political center between these antipodes had melted away. Moreover, in 1931, I had some reason to feel that Hitler was moving in a moderate direction. I did not realize that there were opportunistic reasons for this. Hitler was trying to appear respectable in order to seem qualified to enter the government. The party at that time was confining itself—as far as I can recall today—to denouncing what it called the excessive influence of the Jews upon various spheres of cultural and economic life. It was demanding that their participation in these various areas be reduced to a level consonant with their percentage of the population. Moreover, Hitler's alliance with the old-style nationalists of the Harzburg Front led me to think that a contradiction could be detected between his statements at public meetings and his political views. I regarded this contradiction as highly promising. In actuality Hitler only wanted to thrust his way to power by whatever means he could.

Even after joining the party I continued to associate with Jewish acquaintances, who for their part did not break relations with me although they knew or suspected that I belonged to this anti-Semitic organization. At that time I was no more an anti-Semite than I became in the following years. In none of my speeches, letters, or actions is there any trace of anti-Semitic feelings or phraseology.

Had Hitler announced, before 1933, that a few years later he would burn down Jewish synagogues, involve Germany in a war, and kill Jews and his political opponents, he would at one blow have lost me and probably most of the adherents he won after 1930. Goebbels had realized that, for on November 2, 1931, he wrote an editorial in the *Angriff* entitled "Septemberlings" concerning the host of new members who joined the party after the September election of 1930. In this editorial he warned the party against the infiltration of more bourgeois intellectuals who came from the propertied and educated classes and were not as trustworthy as the Old Fighters. In character and principles, he maintained, they stood abysmally far below the good old party comrades, but they were far ahead in intellectual skills: "They are of the opinion that the Movement has been brought to greatness by the talk of mere demagogues and are now prepared to take it over themselves and provide it with leadership and expertise. That's what they think!"

In making this decision to join the accursed party, I had for the first time denied my own past, my upper-middle-class origins, and my previous environment. Far more than I suspected, the "time of decision" was already past for me. I felt, in Martin Buber's phrase, "anchored in responsibility in a party." My inclination to be relieved of having to think, particularly about unpleasant facts, helped to sway the balance. In this I did not differ from millions of others. Such mental slackness above all facilitated, established, and finally assured the success of the National Socialist system. And I thought that by paying my party dues of a few marks a month I had settled with my political obligations.

How incalculable the consequences were!

The superficiality of my attitude made the fundamental error all the worse. By entering Hitler's party I had already, in essence, assumed a responsibility that led directly to the brutalities of forced labor, to the destruction of war, and to the deaths of those millions of so-called undesirable stock—to the crushing of justice and the elevation of every evil. In 1931 I had no idea that fourteen years later I would have to answer for a host of crimes to which I subscribed beforehand by entering the party. I did not yet know that I would atone with twenty-one years of my life for frivolity and thoughtlessness and breaking with tradition. Still, I will never be rid of that sin.

3

Junction

I WOULD BE GIVING A MORE ACCURATE PICTURE OF THOSE YEARS IF I WERE to speak chiefly of my professional life, my family, and my inclinations. For my new political interests played a subsidiary part in my thinking. I was above all an architect.

As owner of a car I became a member of the newly founded Motorists Association of the National Socialist Party (NSKK), and since it was a new organization I promptly started as head of the Wannsee Section—Wannsee was the Berlin suburb where we lived. For the time being, any serious political activity for the party was far from my thoughts. I was, incidentally, the only member in Wannsee, and therefore in my section, who had a car; the other members only expected to have one after the "revolution" they dreamed of took place. By way of preparation they were finding out where in that rich suburb the right cars were available for X Day.

This party office sometimes led to my calling at Kreisleitung West (District Headquarters of the West End), which was headed by an uncomplicated but intelligent and highly energetic young journeyman miller named Karl Hanke. He had just leased a villa in elegant Grunewald as the future quarters for his district organization. For after its success in the elections of September 14, 1930, the party was trying hard to establish its respectability. He offered me the job of redecorating the villa—naturally without fee.

We conferred on wallpapers, draperies, and paints. The young district leader chose Bauhaus wallpapers at my suggestion, although I had hinted that these were "Communistic" wallpapers. He waved that warning aside with a grand gesture: "We will take the best of everything, even from the Communists." In saying this he was expressing what Hitler and his staff had already been doing for years: picking up anything that promised success without regard for ideology—in fact, determining even ideological questions by their effect upon the voters.

I had the vestibule painted bright red and the offices a strong yellow, further sparked by scarlet window hangings. For me this work was the fulfillment of a long unrealized urge to try my hand at practical architecture, and no doubt I wanted to express a revolutionary spirit. But my décor met with a divided reception.

Early in 1932 the salaries of professors' assistants were reduced—a small gesture toward balancing the strained budget of the State of Prussia. Sizable building projects were nowhere in sight; the economic situation was hopeless. Three years of working as an assistant were enough for us. My wife and I decided that I would give up my post with Tessenow and we would move to Mannheim. I would manage the buildings owned by my family and that would give us financial security and allow me to start seriously on my career as an architect, which so far had been distinctly inglorious.

In Mannheim I sent innumerable letters to the companies in the vicinity and to my father's business friends offering my services as an "independent architect." But of course I waited in vain for a builder who was willing to engage a twenty-six-year-old architect. Even well-established architects in Mannheim were not getting any commissions in those times. By entering prize competitions I tried to attract some attention to myself. But I did no better than win third prizes and have a few of my plans purchased. Rebuilding a store in one of my parents' buildings was my sole architectural activity in this dreary period.

The party here was marked by the easygoing atmosphere typical of Baden. After the exciting party affairs in Berlin, into which I had gradually been drawn, I felt in Mannheim as if I were a member of a bowling club. There was no Motorists Association, so Berlin assigned me to the Motorized SS. At the time I thought that meant I was a member, but apparently I was only a guest; for in 1942 when I wanted to renew my membership it turned out that I had not belonged to the Motorized SS at all.

When the preparations for the election of July 31, 1932, started, my wife and I went to Berlin in order to feel a little of the exciting election atmosphere and—if possible—to help somewhat. For the persistent stagnation of my professional life had greatly intensified my interest, or what I thought was that, in politics. I wanted to do my bit to contribute to

Hitler's electoral victory. This stay in Berlin was meant to be merely a few days' break, for from there we planned to go on to make a long-planned faltboat tour of the East Prussian lakes.

I reported along with my car to my NSKK chief of the Berlin Kreis-leitung West, Will Nagel, who used me for courier duty to a wide variety of local party headquarters. When I had to drive into the parts of the city dominated by the "Reds," I often felt distinctly uncomfortable. In those areas, Nazi bands were quartered in cellar apartments that rather resembled holes in the ground and were subject to a good deal of har-rassment. The Communist outposts in the areas dominated by the Nazis were in a similar situation. I cannot forget the careworn and anxious face of a troop leader in the heart of Moabit, one of the most dangerous areas at the time. These people were risking their lives and sacrificing their health for an idea, never imagining that they were being exploited in behalf of the fantastic notions of a power-hungry man.

On July 27, 1932, Hitler was to arrive at the Berlin-Staaken airport from a morning meeting in Eberswalde. I was assigned to drive a courier from Staaken to the site of the next meeting, the Brandenburg Stadium. The three-motored plane rolled to a stop. Hitler and several of his associates and adjutants got out. Aside from myself and the courier, there was scarcely anyone at the airport. I kept at a respectful distance, but I saw Hitler reproving one of his companions because the cars had not yet arrived. He paced back and forth angrily, slashing at the tops of his high boots with a dog whip and giving the general impression of a cross, un-controlled man who treats his associates contemptuously.

This Hitler was very different from the man of calm and civilized manner who had so impressed me at the student meeting. Although I did not give much thought to it, what I was seeing was an example of Hitler's remarkable duplicity—indeed, "multiplicity" would be a better word. With enormous histrionic intuition he could shape his behavior to chang-ing situations in public while letting himself go with his intimates, ser-vants, or adjutants.

The cars came. I took my passenger into my rattling roadster and drove at top speed a few minutes ahead of Hitler's motorcade. In Branden-burg the sidewalks close to the stadium were occupied by Social Demo-crats and Communists. With my passenger wearing the party uniform, the temper of the crowd grew ugly. When Hitler with his entourage arrived a few minutes later, the demonstrators overflowed into the street. Hitler's car had to force its way through at a snail's pace. Hitler stood erect beside the driver. At that time I felt respect for his courage, and still do. The negative impression that his behavior at the airport had made upon me was wiped out by this scene.

I waited outside the stadium with my car. Consequently I did not hear the speech, only the storms of applause that interrupted Hitler for minutes at a time. When the party anthem indicated the end, we started out again. For that day Hitler was speaking at still a third meeting in the Berlin Stadium. Here, too, the stands were jammed. Thousands who had not been able to obtain admission stood outside in the streets. For hours the crowd waited patiently; once more Hitler was very late. My report to Hanke that Hitler was on his way was promptly announced over the loudspeaker. A roar of applause burst out—incidentally the first and only applause that I myself was ever the cause of.

The following day decided my future. The faltboats were already at the railroad station and our tickets to East Prussia purchased. We were planning to take the evening train. But at noon I received a telephone call. NSKK Chief Nagel informed me that Hanke, who had now risen to organization leader of the Berlin District, wanted to see me.

Hanke received me joyfully. "I've been looking everywhere for you. Would you like to rebuild our new district headquarters?" he asked as soon as I entered. "I'll propose it to the Doctor* today. We're in a great hurry."

A few hours later I would have been sitting in the train and on the lonely East Prussian lakes would have been out of reach for weeks. The district would have had to find another architect. For years I regarded this coincidence as the luckiest turning point in my life. I had reached the junction.

Two decades later, in Spandau, I read in Sir James Jeans:

> The course of a railway train is uniquely prescribed for it at most points of its journey by the rails on which it runs. Here and there, however, it comes to a junction at which alternative courses are open to it, and it may be turned on to one or the other by the quite negligible expenditure of energy involved in moving the points.

The new district headquarters was situated on imposing Voss Strasse, cheek by jowl with the legations of the German states. From the rear windows I could see eighty-five-year-old President von Hindenburg strolling in the adjacent park, often in the company of politicians or military men. As Hanke said to me, even in visual terms the party wanted to advance to the immediate vicinity of political power and thus make a political impression. My assignment was not so impressive; once again it came down to repainting the walls and making minor alterations. The furnishing of a conference room and the Gauleiter's office likewise turned out to be a fairly plain affair, partly for lack of funds, partly because I was still under Tessenow's influence. But this modesty was offset by the ornate carved woods and molded plaster of the *Gründerzeit,* the boom period

* This was how Goebbels was always referred to in party circles. The party simply did not have many doctors of philosophy among its members in those days.

of the early eighteen-seventies. I worked day and night because the district was anxious to have the place ready as soon as possible. I seldom saw Gauleiter Goebbels. The campaign for the forthcoming elections of November 6, 1932, was taking up all his time. Harried and hoarse, he deigned to be shown the rooms several times, but without evincing much interest.

The renovations were finished, the estimate of costs far exceeded, and the election was lost. Membership shrank; the treasurer wrung his hands over the unpaid bills. To the workmen he could show only his empty cashbox. As party members they had to consent to wait for their pay, in order not to bankrupt the party.

A few days after the dedication Hitler also inspected the district headquarters, which was named after him. I heard that he liked what he saw, which filled me with pride, although I was not sure whether he had praised the architectural simplicity I had striven for or the ornateness of the original Wilhelmine structure.

Soon afterward I returned to my Mannheim office. Nothing had changed; the economic situation and therefore the prospect of commissions had grown worse, if anything. Political conditions were becoming even more confused. One crisis followed on the heels of another, and we paid no attention. For us, things went on as before. On January 30, 1933, I read of Hitler's appointment as Chancellor, but for the time being that did not affect me. Shortly afterward I attended a membership meeting of the Mannheim local party group. I was struck by the low personal and intellectual level of the members. "A country cannot be governed by such people," I briefly thought. My concern was needless. The old bureaucratic apparatus continued to run the affairs of state smoothly under Hitler, too.*

Then came the election of March 5, 1933, and a week later I received a telephone call from District Organization Leader Hanke in Berlin:

---

* Particularly in the early years Hitler achieved his successes largely by using the existing organizations that he had taken over. In the administrative bureaucracy the old civil servants carried on as before. Hitler found his military leaders among the elite of the old Imperial Army and the Reichswehr. Practical matters concerning labor were still partially in the hands of the old union officials. And later, of course (after I introduced the principle of industrial self-responsibility), the directors who helped to achieve the extraordinary increase in armaments production from 1942 on were ones who had already made names for themselves before 1933. Significantly, great successes resulted from combining these old, proven organizations and carefully selected officials from them with Hitler's new system. But undoubtedly this harmonious phase would have been only transitional. After a generation at most, the old leadership would have been replaced by a new one trained in Adolf Hitler Schools and Ordensburgen [Order Castles, special training schools for Nazi leaders] according to the new educational principles. Even in party circles the products of such schools were occasionally regarded as too ruthless and arrogant.

"Would you come to Berlin? There is certainly work for you here. When can you come?" he asked. I had the oil changed in our small BMW sports car, packed a suitcase, and we drove all night to Berlin. On little sleep, I called on Hanke at headquarters in the morning. "You're to drive over with the Doctor right away. He wants to have a look at his new Ministry."

The result was that I made a ceremonial entrance along with Goebbels into the handsome building on Wilhelmsplatz, the work of the well-known nineteenth-century architect Karl Friedrich Schinkel. A few hundred people who were waiting there for something, perhaps for Hitler, waved to the new Minister of Propaganda. I felt—and not only here—that new life had been infused into Berlin. After the long crisis people seemed more vigorous and hopeful. Everyone knew that this time more than another of the usual cabinet shifts was involved. Everyone seemed to sense that an hour of decision had arrived. Groups of people stood around in the streets. Strangers exchanged commonplaces, laughed with one another, or expressed approval of the political events—while somewhere, unnoticed, the party machinery was relentlessly settling accounts with the opponents of years of political struggles, and hundreds of thousands of people were trembling because of their descent, their religion, or their convictions.

After inspecting the Ministry, Goebbels commissioned me to rebuild it and to furnish various important rooms, such as his office and the meeting halls. He gave me a formal assignment to begin at once, without waiting for an estimate of costs and without troubling to find out whether funds were available. That was, as subsequently developed, rather autocratic, for no appropriations had yet been made for the newly created Propaganda Ministry, let alone for these renovations. I tried to carry out my assignment with due deference for Schinkel's interior. But Goebbels thought what I had done insufficiently impressive. After some months he commissioned the Vereinigte Werkstätten (United Workshops) in Munich to redo the rooms in "ocean-liner style."

Hanke had secured the influential post of "Minister's Secretary" in the Ministry and ruled over the new minister's anterooms with great skill. I happened to see a sketch on his desk of the decorations for the night rally that was to be held at Tempelhof Field on May 1. The designs outraged both my revolutionary and my architectural feelings. "Those look like the decorations for a rifle club meet," I exclaimed. Hanke replied: "If you can do better, go to it."

That same night I sketched a large platform and behind it three mighty banners, each of them taller than a ten-story building, stretched between wooden struts: two of the banners would be black-white-red with the swastika banner between them. (A rather risky idea, for in a strong wind those banners would act like sails.) They were to be illuminated by powerful searchlights. The sketch was accepted immediately, and once more I had moved a step ahead.

Full of pride, I showed my drawings to Tessenow. But he remained fixed in his ideal of solid craftsmanship. "Do you think you have created something? It's showy, that's all." But Hitler, as Hanke told me, was enthusiastic about the arrangement—although Goebbels claimed the idea for himself.

A few weeks later Goebbels moved into the official residence of the Minister of Nutrition. He took possession of it more or less by force, for Hugenberg insisted that it ought to remain at his disposal, the portfolio of Minister of Nutrition being then assigned to his German Nationalist Party. But this dispute soon ended, for Hugenberg left the cabinet on June 26.

I was given the assignment to redo the minister's house and also to add a large hall. Somewhat recklessly I promised to have house and annex ready within two months. Hitler did not believe it would be possible to keep this deadline, and Goebbels, in order to spur me on, told me of his doubts. Day and night I kept three shifts at work. I took care that various aspects of the construction were synchronized down to the smallest detail, and in the last few days I set a large drying apparatus to work. The building was finally handed over, furnished, punctually on the promised date.

To decorate the Goebbels house I borrowed a few watercolors by Nolde from Eberhard Hanfstaengl, the director of the Berlin National Gallery. Goebbels and his wife were delighted with the paintings—until Hitler came to inspect and expressed his severe disapproval. Then the Minister summoned me immediately: "The pictures have to go at once; they're simply impossible!"

During those early months after the taking of power, a few, at least, of the schools of modern painting, which in 1937 were to be branded as "degenerate" along with the rest, still had a fighting chance. For Hans Weidemann, an old party member from Essen who wore the gold party badge, headed the Art Section in the Propaganda Ministry. Knowing nothing about this episode with Nolde's watercolors, he assembled an exhibition of pictures more or less of the Nolde-Munch school and recommended them to the Minister as samples of revolutionary, nationalist art. Goebbels, having learned better, had the compromising paintings removed at once. When Weidemann refused to go along with this total repudiation of modernity, he was reassigned to some lesser job within the Ministry. At the time this conjunction of power and servility on Goebbels's part struck me as weird. There was something fantastic about the absolute authority Hitler could assert over his closest associates of many years, even in matters of taste. Goebbels had simply groveled before Hitler. We were all in the same boat. I too, though altogether at home in modern art, tacitly accepted Hitler's pronouncement.

No sooner had I finished the assignment for Goebbels than I was summoned to Nuremberg. That was in July 1933. Preparations were being made there for the first Party Rally of what was now the government party. The victorious spirit of the party was to be expressed even in the architecture of the background, but the local architect had been unable to come up with satisfactory suggestions. I was taken to Nuremberg by plane and there made my sketches. They were not exactly overflowing with fresh ideas, for in fact they resembled the design for May 1. Instead of my great banners I provided a gigantic eagle, over a hundred feet in wingspread, to crown the Zeppelin Field. I spiked it to a timber framework like a butterfly in a collection.

The Nuremberg organization leader did not dare to decide on this matter by himself, and therefore sent me to headquarters in Munich. I had a letter of introduction with me, since I was still completely unknown outside of Berlin. It seemed that headquarters took architecture, or rather festival décor, with extraordinary seriousness. A few minutes after my arrival I stood in Rudolf Hess's luxuriously appointed office, my folder of drawings in my hand. He did not give me a chance to speak. "Only the Fuehrer himself can decide this sort of thing." He made a brief telephone call and then said: "The Fuehrer is in his apartment. I'll have you driven over there." For the first time I had an intimation of what the magic word "architecture" meant under Hitler.

We stopped at an apartment house in the vicinity of the Prinzregenten Theater. Two flights up I was admitted to an anteroom containing mementos or presents of low quality. The furniture, too, testified to poor taste. An adjutant came in, opened a door, said casually, "Go in," and I stood before Hitler, the mighty Chancellor of the Reich. On a table in front of him lay a pistol that had been taken apart; he seemed to have been cleaning it. "Put the drawings here," he said curtly. Without looking at me, he pushed the parts of the pistol aside and examined my sketches with interest but without a word. "Agreed." No more. Since he turned to his pistol again, I left the room in some confusion.

There was astonishment in Nuremberg when I reported that I had received the approval from Hitler in person. Had the organizers there known how spellbound Hitler was by any drawing, a large delegation would have gone to Munich and I would at best have been allowed to stand at the very back of the group. But in those days few people were acquainted with Hitler's hobby.

In the autumn of 1933 Hitler commissioned his Munich architect, Paul Ludwig Troost, who had designed the fittings for the ocean liner *Europa* and rebuilt the Brown House, to completely redo and refurnish the Chancellor's residence in Berlin. The job was to be completed as quickly as possible. Troost's building supervisor came from Munich and was thus not familiar with Berlin construction firms and practices. Hitler then recollected that a young architect had finished an annex for Goebbels in a remarkably brief time. He assigned me as an aide to the Munich supervisor; I was to choose the firms, to guide him through the mazes of the Berlin construction market, and to intervene wherever needed in the interests of speed.

This collaboration began with a careful inspection of the Chancellor's residence by Hitler, his building supervisor, and myself. In the spring of 1939, six years later, in an article on the previous condition of the place, Hitler wrote:

> After the 1918 Revolution the building gradually began to decay. Large parts of the roof timbers were rotted and the attics completely dilapidated. . . . Since my predecessors in general could count upon a term of office of only three to five months, they saw no reason to remove the filth of those who had occupied the house before them nor to see to it that those who came after would have better conditions than they themselves. They had no prestige to maintain toward foreign countries since these in any case took little notice of them. As a result the building was in a state of utter neglect. Ceilings and floors were moldy, wallpaper and floors rotting, the whole place filled with an almost unbearable smell.[1]

That was certainly exaggerated. Still, the condition of this residence was almost incredible. The kitchen had little light and was equipped with long-outmoded stoves. There was only one bathroom for all the inhabitants, and its fixtures dated from the turn of the century. There were also innumerable examples of bad taste: doors painted to imitate natural wood and marble urns for flowers which were actually only marbleized sheet-metal basins. Hitler exclaimed triumphantly: "Here you see the whole corruption of the old Republic. One can't even show the Chancellor's residence to a foreigner. I would be embarrassed to receive even a single visitor here."

During this thorough tour, which lasted perhaps three hours, we also went into the attic. The janitor explained: "And this is the door that leads to the next building."

"What do you mean?"

"There's a passage running through the attics of all the ministries as far as the Hotel Adlon."

"Why?"

"During the riots at the beginning of the Weimar Republic it turned out that the rioters could besiege the residence and cut the Chancellor off from the outside world. The passage was created so that in an emergency he could clear out."

Hitler had the door opened, and sure enough, we could walk into the adjacent Foreign Office. "Have the door walled up," he said. "We don't need anything like that."

After the repairs had begun, Hitler came to the site at noon almost every day, followed by an adjutant. He studied the progress that had been made and took pleasure in the rooms as they came into being. Soon the band of construction workers were greeting him in a friendly and easy way. In spite of the two SS men in civilian dress who stood unobtrusively in the background, these scenes had an idyllic air. You could see from Hitler's behavior that he felt "at home" amid construction. Yet he avoided any cheap popularity-chasing.

The supervisor and I accompanied him on these tours. In a terse but not unfriendly manner, he addressed his questions to us: "When is this room to be plastered? . . . When are the windows coming? . . . Have the detail drawings arrived from Munich? Not yet? I'll ask the Professor [that was the way he usually referred to Troost] about them myself." Another room was inspected: "Ah, this has already been plastered. That hadn't been done yesterday. Why, this ceiling molding is very handsome. The Professor does that sort of thing wonderfully. . . . When do you think you'll be finished? I'm in a great hurry. All I have now is the small state secretary's apartment on the top floor. I can't invite anyone there. It's ridiculous, how penny-pinching the Republic was. Have you seen the entrance? And the elevator? Any department store has a better one." The elevator in fact would get stuck from time to time and was rated for only three persons.

That was the tone Hitler took. It is easy to imagine how this naturalness of his impressed me—after all, he was not only the Chancellor but also the man who was beginning to revive everything in Germany, who was providing work for the unemployed and launching vast economic programs. Only much later, and on the basis of tiny clues, did I begin to perceive that a good measure of propagandist calculation underlay all this simplicity.

I had already accompanied him some twenty or thirty times when he suddenly invited me, in the course of a tour: "Will you come to dinner with me today?" Naturally this unexpected gesture made me happy—all the more so since I had never expected it, because of his impersonal manner.

I was used to clambering around building sites, but that particular day I unluckily had a hod of plaster fall on me from a scaffolding. I must have looked at my stained jacket with a rueful expression, for Hitler commented: "Just come along; we'll fix that upstairs."

In his apartment the guests were already waiting, among them Goebbels, who looked quite surprised to see me appear in this circle. Hitler took me into his private rooms. His valet was sent off for Hitler's own dark-blue jacket. "There, wear that for the while." And so I entered the dining room behind Hitler and sat at his side, favored above all the other guests. Evidently he had taken a liking to me. Goebbels noticed something that had entirely escaped me in my excitement. "Why, you're wearing the Fuehrer's badge.* That isn't your jacket, then?" Hitler spared me the reply: "No, it's mine."

On this occasion Hitler for the first time addressed a few personal questions to me. Only now did he discover that I had designed the May 1 decorations. "I see, and you did the ones in Nuremberg too? There was an architect who came to see me with the plans! Right, that was you! . . . I never would have thought you could have got Goebbels's building finished by the deadline." He did not ask about my membership in the party. In the case of artists, it seemed to me, he did not care one way or the other. Instead of political questions, he wanted to find out as much as possible about my origins, my career as an architect, and my father's and grandfather's buildings.

Years later Hitler referred to this invitation:

> You attracted my notice during our rounds. I was looking for an architect to whom I could entrust my building plans. I wanted someone young; for as you know these plans extend far into the future. I need someone who will be able to continue after my death with the authority I have conferred on him. I saw you as that man.

After years of frustrated efforts I was wild to accomplish things—and twenty-eight years old. For the commission to do a great building, I would have sold my soul like Faust. Now I had found my Mephistopheles. He seemed no less engaging than Goethe's.

* Hitler was the only party member to wear a gold "badge of sovereignty"—an eagle with a swastika in its talons. Everyone else wore the round party badge. But Hitler's jacket did not differ from ordinary civilian jackets.

4

My Catalyst

————

I WAS BY NATURE HARDWORKING, BUT I ALWAYS NEEDED A SPECIAL IMPULSE to develop new talents and rally fresh energy. Now I had found my catalyst; I could not have encountered a more effective one. At an ever quickening pace and with ever greater urgency, all my powers were summoned forth.

In responding to this challenge I gave up the real center of my life: my family. Completely under the sway of Hitler, I was henceforth possessed by my work. Nothing else mattered. Hitler knew how to drive his associates to the greatest efforts. "The higher he aims, the more a man grows," he would say.

During the twenty years I spent in Spandau prison I often asked myself what I would have done if I had recognized Hitler's real face and the true nature of the regime he had established. The answer was banal and dispiriting: My position as Hitler's architect had soon become indispensable to me. Not yet thirty, I saw before me the most exciting prospects an architect can dream of.

Moreover, the intensity with which I went at my work repressed problems that I ought to have faced. A good many perplexities were smothered by the daily rush. In writing these memoirs I became increasingly astonished to realize that before 1944 I so rarely—in fact almost never—found the time to reflect about myself or my own activities, that I never gave my own existence a thought. Today, in retrospect, I often have the feeling that something swooped me up off the ground at the time, wrenched me from all my roots, and beamed a host of alien forces upon me.

In retrospect, what perhaps troubles me most is that my occasional spells of uneasiness during this period were concerned mainly with the direction I was taking as an architect, with my growing estrangement from Tessenow's doctrines. On the other hand I must have had the feeling that it was no affair of mine when I heard the people around me declaring an open season on Jews, Freemasons, Social Democrats, or Jehovah's Witnesses. I thought I was not implicated if I myself did not take part.

The ordinary party member was being taught that grand policy was much too complex for him to judge it. Consequently, one felt one was being represented, never called upon to take personal responsibility. The whole structure of the system was aimed at preventing conflicts of conscience from even arising. The result was the total sterility of all conversations and discussions among these like-minded persons. It was boring for people to confirm one another in their uniform opinions.

Worse still was the restriction of responsibility to one's own field. That was explicitly demanded. Everyone kept to his own group—of architects, physicians, jurists, technicians, soldiers, or farmers. The professional organizations to which everyone had to belong were called chambers (Physicians' Chamber, Art Chamber), and this term aptly described the way people were immured in isolated, closed-off areas of life. The longer Hitler's system lasted, the more people's minds moved within such isolated chambers. If this arrangement had gone on for a number of generations, it alone would have caused the whole system to wither, I think, for we would have arrived at a kind of caste society. The disparity between this and the *Volksgemeinschaft* (community of the people) proclaimed in 1933 always astonished me. For this had the effect of stamping out the promised integration, or at any rate of greatly hindering it. What eventually developed was a society of totally isolated individuals. For although it may sound strange today, for us it was no empty slogan that "the Fuehrer proposes and disposes" for all.

We had been rendered susceptible to such ideas from our youth on. We had derived our principles from the *Obrigkeitsstaat,* the authoritarian though not totalitarian state of Imperial Germany. Moreover, we had learned those principles in wartime, when the state's authoritarian character had been further intensified. Perhaps the background had prepared us like soldiers for the kind of thinking we encountered once again in Hitler's system. Tight public order was in our blood; the liberalism of the Weimar Republic seemed to us by comparison lax, dubious, and in no way desirable.

In order to be available to my client at any time, I had rented a painter's studio on Behrenstrasse, a few hundred yards from the Chancellery, for my office. My assistants, all of them young, worked from morning until late at night without regard for their private lives. For lunch we generally had a few sandwiches. It would be nearly ten o'clock at night before we would quit and, exhausted, end our working day with a bite at the nearby Pfälzer Weinstube—where we would once more discuss the day's labors.

Major assignments did not come our way at once. I continued to receive a few occasional rush jobs from Hitler, who apparently thought that what I was chiefly good for was the speedy completion of commissions. The previous Chancellor's office on the second floor of the office building had three windows overlooking Wilhelmsplatz. During those early months of 1933 a crowd almost invariably gathered there and chanted their demand to see the Fuehrer. As a result, it had become impossible for Hitler to work in the room, and he did not like it anyhow. "Much too small. Six hundred and fifty square feet—it might do for one of my assistants. Where would I sit with a state visitor? In this little corner here? And this desk is just about the right size for my office manager."

Hitler had me refurbish a hall overlooking the garden as his new private office. For five years he contented himself with this room, although he considered it only temporary. But even after he moved into his office in the new Chancellery built in 1938, he soon came to feel that this too was unsatisfactory. By 1950, according to his instructions and my plans, a final new Chancellery was to be built. It was to include a palatial office for Hitler and his successors in coming centuries, which would measure ten thousand square feet—sixteen times larger than the original Chancellor's office. But after talking the matter over with Hitler, I tucked in a private office to supplement this vast hall; it again measured about six hundred square feet.

As things worked out, the old office was not to be used. For Hitler wanted to be able to show himself to the crowd and therefore had me build a new "historic balcony" in great haste. "The window was really too inconvenient," Hitler remarked to me with satisfaction. "I could not be seen from all sides. After all, I could not very well lean out." But the architect of the first reconstruction of the Chancellery, Professor Eduard Jobst Siedler of the Berlin Institute of Technology, made a fuss about our doing violence to his work, and Lammers, chief of the Reich Chancery, agreed that our addition would constitute an infringement on an artist's copyright. Hitler scornfully dismissed these objections: "Siedler has spoiled the whole of Wilhelmsplatz. Why, that building looks like the headquarters of a soap company, not the center of the Reich. What does he think? That I'll let him build the balcony too?" But he propitiated the professor with another commission.

A few months later I was told to build a barracks camp for the workmen of the autobahn, construction of which had just begun. Hitler was displeased with the kind of quarters hitherto provided and instructed me to develop a model which could be used for all such camps: with decent kitchens, washrooms, and showers, with a lounge and cabins containing only two beds each. These quarters were indeed a great improvement over the building site barracks commonly used up to that time. Hitler took an interest in these model buildings and asked me to give him a report on their effect on the workers. This was just the attitude I had imagined the National Socialist leader would have.

Until the remodeling of his Chancellor's residence was done, Hitler stayed in the apartment of State Secretary Lammers, on the top floor of the office building. Here I frequently had lunch or dinner with him. Evenings he usually had some trusty companions about: Schreck, his chauffeur of many years; Sepp Dietrich, the commander of his SS bodyguard; Dr. Otto Dietrich, the press chief; Brückner and Schaub, his two adjutants; and Heinrich Hoffmann, his official photographer. Since the table held no more than ten persons, this group almost completely filled it. For the midday meal, on the other hand, Hitler's old Munich comrades foregathered, such as Amann, Schwarz, and Esser or Gauleiter Wagner. Frequently, Werlin was present also; he was head of the Munich branch of Daimler-Benz and supplier of Hitler's personal cars. Cabinet ministers seemed seldom present; I also saw very little of Himmler, Roehm, or Streicher at these meals, but Goebbels and Goering were often there. Even then all regular officials of the Chancellery were excluded. Thus it was noticeable that even Lammers, although the apartment was his, was never invited—undoubtedly with good reason.

For in this circle Hitler often spoke his mind on the day's developments. He used these sociable hours to work off the nervous strain of his office. He liked to describe the way he had broken the grip of the bureaucracy, which threatened to strangle him in his capacity as Reich Chancellor:

> In the first few weeks every petty matter was brought to me for decision. Every day I found heaps of files on my desk, and however much I worked there were always as many again. Finally, I put an end to that nonsense. If I had gone on that way, I would never have accomplished anything, simply because that stuff left me no time for thinking. When I refused to see the files they told me that important decisions would be held up. But I decided that I had to clear the decks so I could give my mind to the important things. That way I governed the course of development instead of being governed by the officials.

Sometimes he talked about his drivers:

> Schreck was the best driver you can imagine, and our supercharger is good for over a hundred. We always drove very fast. But in recent years

I've told Schreck not to drive over fifty. How terrible if something had happened to me. What fun we had teasing the big American cars. We kept right behind them until they tried to lose us. Those Americans are junk compared to a Mercedes. Their motor couldn't take it; after a while it would overheat, and they'd have to pull over to the side of the road, looking glum. Served them right!

Every evening a crude movie projector was set up to show the newsreel and one or two movies. In the early days the servants were extremely inept at handling the apparatus. Frequently, the picture was upside down or the film strip broke. In those days Hitler took such accidents with more good humor than his adjutants, who were fond of using the power they derived from their chief to bawl out underlings.

The choice of films was a matter Hitler discussed with Goebbels. Usually they were the same ones being shown in the Berlin movie houses at the time. Hitler preferred light entertainment, love, and society films. All the films with Emil Jannings and Heinz Rühmann, with Henny Porten, Lil Dagover, Olga Tschechowa, Zarah Leander, or Jenny Jugo had to be procured as quickly as possible. Revues with lots of leg display were sure to please him. Frequently we saw foreign films, including those that were withheld from the German public. Sports and mountaineering films were shown very rarely, animal and landscape movies and travelogues never. Hitler also had no feeling for the comedies of the kind I loved at the time, those featuring Buster Keaton or Charlie Chaplin. German movie production was not nearly sufficient to fill the quota of two new movies every day. Many were therefore shown twice or even more often—interestingly enough, never those with tragic plots. The ones we saw more than once were frequently spectaculars or movies with his favorite actors. His preferences, and the habit of seeing one or two films every evening, continued until the beginning of the war.

At one of these dinners, in the winter of 1933, I happened to be seated beside Goering. "Is Speer doing your residence, my Fuehrer? Is he your architect?" I wasn't, but Hitler said I was. "Then permit me to have him remodel my house too." Hitler gave his consent, and Goering, scarcely inquiring what I thought of the proposal, put me into his big open limousine after the meal was over and dragged me off to his residence like a piece of booty. He had picked out for himself the former official residence of the Prussian Minister of Commerce, a palace that the Prussian state had built with great lavishness before 1914. It was situated in one of the gardens behind Leipziger Platz.

Only a few months before, this residence had been expensively redone according to Goering's own instructions, with Prussian state funds. Hitler had come to see it and commented deprecatingly: "Dark! How can anyone live in such darkness! Compare this with my professor's work.

Everything bright, clear, and simple!" I did in fact find the place a romantically tangled warren of small rooms gloomy with stained-glass windows and heavy velvet hangings, cluttered with massive Renaissance furniture. There was a kind of chapel presided over by the swastika, and the new symbol had also been reiterated on ceilings, walls, and floors throughout the house. There was the feeling that something terribly solemn and tragic would always be going on in this place.

It was characteristic of the system—and probably of all authoritarian forms of society—that Hitler's criticism and example produced an instant change in Goering. For he immediately repudiated the decorative scheme he had just completed, although he probably felt fairly comfortable in it, since it rather corresponded to his disposition. "Don't look at this," he said to me. "I can't stand it myself. Do it any way you like. I'm giving you a free hand; only it must turn out like the Fuehrer's place." That was a fine assignment. Money, as was always the case with Goering, was no object. And so walls were ripped out, in order to turn the many rooms on the ground floor into four large rooms. The largest of these, his study, measured almost fifteen hundred square feet, thus approaching the size of Hitler's. An annex was added, mostly of glass framed in bronze. Bronze was in short supply; it was treated as a scarce metal and there were high penalties for using it for nonessential purposes, but that did not bother Goering in the least. He was rapturous every time he made an inspection; he beamed like a child on its birthday, rubbed his hands, and laughed.

Goering's furniture suited his bulk. An old Renaissance desk was of enormous proportions, as was the desk chair whose back rose far above his head; it had probably been a prince's throne. On the desk he had two silver candelabra with enormous parchment shades to illuminate an oversized photograph of Hitler; the original, which Hitler had given him, had not seemed impressive enough. He had had it tremendously enlarged, and every visitor wondered at this special honor that Hitler had seemingly conferred on him, since it was well known in party and government circles that Hitler presented his portrait to his paladins always in the same size, inside a silver frame specially designed for it by Frau Troost.

There was an immense painting in the hall which could be drawn up to the ceiling in order to expose openings to a projection room behind the wall. The painting struck me as familiar. In fact, as I subsequently learned, Goering had in his unabashed fashion simply ordered "his" director of the Kaiser Friedrich Museum to deliver the famous Rubens, *Diana at the Stag Hunt*, considered one of the museum's prize possessions, to his residence.

During the reconstruction, Goering lived in the mansion of the President of the Reichstag, opposite the Reichstag itself, an early twentieth-century building with strong elements of *nouveau riche* rococo. Here our discussions about his future residence took place. Frequently present at these talks was one of the directors of the Vereinigte Werkstätten, Herr Paepke, a gray-haired elderly gentleman full of best intentions to please Goering, but cowed by the brusque manner Goering used with subordinates.

One day we were sitting with Goering in a room whose walls were done in the Wilhelmine neorococo style, adorned from top to bottom with roses in bas-relief—quintessential atrociousness. Even Goering knew that when he asked: "How do you like this decoration, *Herr Direktor?* Not bad, is it?" Instead of saying, "It's ghastly," the old gentleman became unsure of himself. He did not want to disagree with his prominent employer and customer and answered evasively. Goering immediately scented an opportunity for a joke and winked at me: "But, *Herr Direktor,* don't you think it's beautiful? I mean to have you decorate all my rooms this way. We were talking about just that, weren't we, Herr Speer?" "Yes, of course, the drawings are already being made." "There you are, *Herr Direktor.* You see, this is the style we're going to follow. I'm sure you like it." The director writhed; his artistic conscience brought beads of sweat to his forehead and his goatee quivered with distress. Goering had taken it into his head to make the old man forswear himself. "Now look at this wall carefully. See how wonderfully those roses twine their way up. Like being in a rose arbor out in the open. And you mean to say you can't feel enthusiastic about this sort of thing?" "Oh yes, yes," the desperate man concurred. "But you should be enthusiastic about such a work of art—a well-known connoisseur like you. Tell me, don't you think it's beautiful?" The game went on for a long time until the director gave in and voiced the praise Goering demanded.

"They're all like that!" Goering afterward said contemptuously. And it was true enough: They were all like that, Goering included. For at meals he now never tired of telling Hitler how bright and expansive his home was now, "just like yours, my Fuehrer."

If Hitler had had roses climbing the walls of his room, Goering would have insisted on roses.

By the winter of 1933, only a few months after that decisive invitation to dinner, I had been taken into the circle of Hitler's intimates. There were very few persons besides myself who had been so favored. Hitler had undoubtedly taken a special liking to me, although I was by nature reticent and not very talkative. I have often asked myself whether he was projecting upon me his unfulfilled youthful dream of being a great architect. But given the fact that Hitler so often acted in a purely intuitive way, why he took to me so warmly remains a mystery.

I was still a long way from my later neoclassical manner. By chance some plans which I drew up in the autumn of 1933 have been preserved. They were for a prize competition for a party school in Munich-Grün-wald. All German architects were invited to participate. My design already relied heavily on melodrama and a dominant axis, but I was still using the austere vocabulary I had learned from Tessenow.

Hitler, along with Troost and myself, looked at the entries before the judging. The sketches were unsigned, as is mandatory in such competitions. Of course I did not win. After the verdict, when the incognitos were lifted, Troost in a studio conversation praised my sketch. And to my astonishment Hitler remembered it in detail, although he had looked at my plans for only a few seconds among a hundred others. He silently ignored Troost's praise; probably in the course of it he realized that I was still far from being an architect after his own heart.

Hitler went to Munich every two or three weeks. More and more often, he took me along on these trips. In the train he would usually talk animatedly about which drawings "the professor" would probably have ready. "I imagine he's redone the ground-floor plan of the House of Art. There were some improvements needed there. . . . I wonder whether the details for the dining room have been drafted yet? And then perhaps we'll be able to see the sketches for Wackerle's sculptures."

On arrival he usually went directly from the railroad station to Professor Troost's studio. It was situated in a battered backyard off Theresienstrasse, fairly near the Institute of Technology. We would go up two flights of a dreary stairway that had not been painted for years. Troost, conscious of his standing, never came to meet Hitler on the stairs, nor ever accompanied him downstairs when he left. In the anteroom, Hitler would greet him: "I can't wait, *Herr Professor*. Is there anything new—let's see it!" And we would plunge right in—Hitler and I would stand in the studio itself while Troost, composed and quiet as always, spread out his plans and the sketches of his ideas. But Hitler's foremost architect had no better luck than I later did; Hitler seldom showed his enthusiasm.

Afterward Troost's wife, *Frau Professor,* would show samples of the textiles and wall colors to be used for the Munich Fuehrer Building. These were subtle and restrained, actually too understated for Hitler's taste, which inclined toward the gaudy. But he liked what he saw. The balanced bourgeois atmosphere which was then the fashion in wealthy society had about it a muted luxury that obviously appealed to him. Two or more hours would pass; then Hitler would take his leave, tersely but very cordially, to go to his own Munich apartment. He would throw a few quick words to me: "But come for lunch in the Osteria."

At the usual time, around half past two, I went to the Osteria Bavaria, a small artists' restaurant which rose to unexpected fame when it became Hitler's regular restaurant. In a place like this, one could more easily imagine a table of artists gathered around Lenbach or Stuck, with long hair and huge beards, than Hitler with his neatly dressed or uniformed retinue. But he felt at ease in the Osteria; as a "frustrated artist" he obviously liked the atmosphere he had once sought to attain to, and now had finally both lost and surpassed.

Quite often the select group of guests had to wait for hours for Hitler. There would be an adjutant, also Bavarian Gauleiter Wagner if by this time he had slept off last night's drinking bout, and of course Hitler's constant companion and court photographer, Hoffmann, who by this time was quite often slightly tipsy. Very often the likable Miss Unity Mitford was present, and sometimes, though rarely, a painter or a sculptor. Then there would be Dr. Dietrich, the Reich press chief, and invariably Martin Bormann, Rudolf Hess's secretary, who seemed utterly inconspicuous. On the street several hundred people would be waiting, for our presence was indication enough that *he* would be coming.

Shouts of rejoicing outside. Hitler headed toward our regular corner, which was shielded on one side by a low partition. In good weather we sat in the small courtyard where there was a hint of an arbor. Hitler gave the owner and the two waitresses a jovial greeting: "What's good today? Ravioli? If only you didn't make it so delicious. It's too tempting!" Hitler snapped his fingers: "Everything would be perfect in your place, Herr Deutelmoser, if I did not have to think of my waistline. You forget that the Fuehrer cannot eat whatever he would like to." Then he would study the menu for a long time and order ravioli.

Everyone ordered whatever he liked: cutlets, goulash, Hungarian wine from the cask. In spite of Hitler's occasional jokes about "carrion eaters" and "wine drinkers," everyone ate and drank with zest. In this circle there was a sense of privacy. One tacit agreement prevailed: No one must mention politics. The sole exception was Lady Mitford, who even in the later years of international tension persistently spoke up for her country and often actually pleaded with Hitler to make a deal with England. In spite of Hitler's discouraging reserve, she did not abandon her efforts through all those years. Then, in September 1939, on the day of England's declaration of war, she tried to shoot herself with a small pistol in Munich's Englischer Garten. Hitler had the best specialists in Munich care for her, and as soon as she could travel sent her home to England by a special railroad car through Switzerland.

The principal topic during these meals was, regularly, the morning visit to Professor Troost. Hitler would be full of praise for what he had seen; he effortlessly remembered all the details. His relationship to Troost was somewhat that of a pupil to his teacher; it reminded me of my own uncritical admiration of Tessenow.

I found this trait very engaging. I was amazed to see that this man, although worshiped by the people around him, was still capable of a kind of reverence. Hitler, who felt himself to be an architect, respected the superiority of the professional in this field. He would never have done that in politics.

He talked frankly about how the Bruckmanns, a highly cultivated publishing family of Munich, had introduced him to Troost. It was, he said, "as if scales fell from my eyes" when he saw Troost's work. "I could no longer bear the things I had drawn up to then. What a piece of good luck that I met this man!" One could only assent; it is ghastly to think what his architectural taste would have been like without Troost's influence. He once showed me his sketchbook of the early twenties. I saw attempts at public buildings in the neobaroque style of Vienna's Ringstrasse—products of the eighteen-nineties. Curiously enough, such architectural sketches often shared the page with sketches of weapons and warships.

In comparison to that sort of thing, Troost's architecture was actually spare. Consequently, his influence upon Hitler remained marginal. Up to the end Hitler lauded the architects and the buildings which had served him as models for his early sketches. Among these was the Paris Opera (built 1861–74) by Charles Garnier: "The stairwell is the most beautiful in the world. When the ladies stroll down in their costly gowns and uniformed men form lanes—Herr Speer, we must build something like that too!" He raved about the Vienna Opera: "The most magnificent opera house in the world, with marvelous acoustics. When as a young man I sat up there in the fourth gallery. . . ." Hitler had a story to tell about van der Nüll, one of the two architects of this building: "He thought the opera house was a failure. You know, he was in such despair that on the day before the opening he put a bullet through his head. At the dedication it turned out to be his greatest success; everyone praised the architect." Such remarks quite often led him to observations about difficult situations in which he himself had been involved and in which some fortunate turn of events had again and again saved him. The lesson was: You must never give up.

He was especially fond of the numerous theaters built by Hermann Helmer (1849–1919) and Ferdinand Fellner (1847–1916), who had provided both Austria-Hungary and Germany at the end of the nineteenth century with many late-baroque theaters, all in the same pattern. He knew where all their buildings were and later had the neglected theater in Augsburg renovated.

But he also appreciated the stricter architects of the nineteenth century such as Gottfried Semper (1803–79), who built the Opera House and the Picture Gallery in Dresden and the Hofburg and the court museums in Vienna, as well as Theophil Hansen (1803–83), who had designed several impressive classical buildings in Athens and

Vienna. As soon as the German troops took Brussels in 1940, I was dispatched there to look at the huge Palace of Justice by Poelaert (1817–79), which Hitler raved about, although he knew it only from its plans (which was also true of the Paris Opera). After my return he had me give him a detailed description of the building.

Such were Hitler's architectural passions. But ultimately he was always drawn back to inflated neobaroque such as Kaiser Wilhelm II had also fostered, through his court architect Ihne. Fundamentally, it was decadent baroque, comparable to the style that accompanied the decline of the Roman Empire. Thus, in the realm of architecture, as in painting and sculpture, Hitler really remained arrested in the world of his youth: the world of 1880 to 1910, which stamped its imprint on his artistic taste as on his political and ideological conceptions.

Contradictory impulses were typical of Hitler. Thus he would sing the praises of the Viennese examples that had impressed him in his youth, and in the same breath would declare:

> I first learned what architecture is from Troost. When I had some money, I bought one piece of furniture after the other from him. I looked at his buildings, at the appointments of the *Europa,* and always gave thanks to fate for appearing to me in the guise of Frau Bruckmann and leading this master to me. When the party had greater means, I commissioned him to remodel and furnish the Brown House. You've seen it. What trouble I had on account of it! Those philistines in the party thought it was a waste of money. And how much I learned from the Professor in the course of that remodeling!

Paul Ludwig Troost was a Westphalian, extremely tall and spare, with a close-shaven head. Restrained in conversation, eschewing gestures, he belonged to a group of architects such as Peter Behrens, Joseph M. Olbrich, Bruno Paul, and Walter Gropius who before 1914 led a reaction against the highly ornamented Jugendstil and advocated a lean approach, almost devoid of ornament, and a spartan traditionalism with which they combined elements of modernity. Troost had occasionally won prizes in competitions, but before 1933 he was never able to advance into the leading group of German architects.

There was no "Fuehrer's style," for all that the party press expatiated on this subject. What was branded as the official architecture of the Reich was only the neoclassicism transmitted by Troost; it was multiplied, altered, exaggerated, and sometimes distorted to the point of ludicrousness. Hitler appreciated the permanent qualities of the classical style all the more because he thought he had found certain points of relationship between the Dorians and his own Germanic world. Nevertheless, it would be a mistake to try to look within

Hitler's mentality for some ideologically based architectural style. That would not have been in keeping with his pragmatic way of thinking.

Undoubtedly Hitler had something in mind when he regularly took me along on those architectural consultations in Munich. He must have wanted me in my turn to become a disciple of Troost. I was eager to learn and actually did learn a good deal from Troost. The elaborate but restrained architecture of my second teacher decisively influenced me.

The prolonged table talk in the Osteria was brought to an end: "The Professor told me that the stairwell in the Fuehrer House is being paneled today. I can hardly wait to see it. Brückner, send for the car—we'll drive right over." And to me: "You'll come along?"

He would hurry straight from the car to the stairwell in the Fuehrer House, inspect it from downstairs, from the gallery, from the stairs, then go upstairs again, full of enthusiasm. Finally he would look over the entire building. He would once again demonstrate his familiarity with every detail of the plans and sufficiently astonish everyone concerned with the building. Satisfied with the progress, satisfied with himself because he was the cause and prime mover of these buildings, he went to his next destination: The home of his photographer in Munich-Bogenhausen.

In good weather coffee would be served in the Hoffmanns' little garden. Surrounded by the gardens of other villas, it was hardly more than two thousand feet square. Hitler tried to resist the cake, but finally consented, with many compliments to Frau Hoffmann, to have some put on his plate. If the sun were shining brightly the Fuehrer and Reich Chancellor might even take off his coat and lie down on the grass in shirtsleeves. At the Hoffmanns' he felt at home; once he sent for a volume of Ludwig Thoma and read a passage aloud.

Hitler particularly looked forward to the paintings which the photographer had brought to his house for the Fuehrer to choose from. At first I was stunned at what Hoffmann showed Hitler and what met with his approval. Later I grew accustomed to Hitler's taste in art, though I myself still went on collecting early romantic landscapes by such painters as Rottmann, Fries, or Kobell.

One of Hitler's as well as Hoffmann's favorite painters was Eduard Grützner, whose pictures of tipsy monks and inebriated butlers seemed hardly the right sort of thing for a teetotaler like Hitler. But Hitler regarded these paintings solely from their "artistic" aspect: "What, that one is priced at only five thousand marks?" The painting's market value could not have been more than two thousand marks. "Do you know, Hoffmann, that's a steal! Look at these details. Grützner is greatly underrated." The next work by this painter cost him considerably more. "It's simply that he hasn't been discovered yet. Rembrandt also counted for nothing for many decades after his death. His pictures were practically given away. Believe me, this Grützner will some day be worth as much as a Rembrandt. Rembrandt himself couldn't have painted that better."

For all departments of art Hitler regarded the late nineteenth century as one of the greatest cultural epochs in human history. That it was not yet recognized as such, he said, was only because we were too close to it in time. But his appreciation stopped at Impressionism, whereas the naturalism of a Leibl or a Thoma suited his activistic approach to art. Makart ranked highest; he also thought highly of Spitzweg. In this case I could understand his feeling, although what he admired was not so much the bold and often impressionistic brushwork as the staunch middle-class genre quality, the affable humor with which Spitzweg gently mocked the small-town Munich of his period.

Later, to the consternation of the photographer, it turned out that a forger had exploited this fondness for Spitzweg. Hitler began to be uneasy about which of his Spitzwegs were genuine, but quickly repressed these doubts and commented maliciously: "You know, some of the Spitzwegs that Hoffmann has hanging are fake. I can tell at a glance. But let's not take away his pleasure in them." He said that last with the Bavarian intonation he liked to fall into while in Munich.

He frequently visited Carlton's Tearoom, a bogus luxurious place with reproduction furniture and fake crystal chandeliers. He liked it because the people there left him undisturbed, did not bother him with applause or requests for autographs, as was generally the case elsewhere in Munich.

Frequently, I would receive a telephone call late at night from Hitler's apartment: "The Fuehrer is driving over to the Café Heck and has asked that you come too." I would have to get out of bed and had no prospect of returning before two or three o'clock in the morning.

Occasionally Hitler would apologize. "I formed the habit of staying up late during our days of struggle. After rallies I would have to sit down with the old fighters, and besides my speeches usually stirred me up so much that I would not have been able to sleep before early morning."

The Café Heck, in contrast to Carlton's Tearoom, was furnished with plain wooden chairs and iron tables. It was the old party café where Hitler used to meet his comrades. But any such meetings stopped after 1933. The Munich group had shown him such devotion over so many years that I had expected him to have a group of close Munich friends; but there was nothing of the sort. On the contrary, Hitler tended to become sulky when one of the old comrades wanted to speak to him and almost always managed to refuse or delay such requests on all sorts of pretexts. No doubt the old party comrades did not always assume the tone of respectful distance that Hitler, for all the geniality he outwardly displayed, now thought proper. Frequently, they adopted an air of unseemly familiarity; what they supposed was their well-earned right to such intimacy no longer comported with the historical role Hitler by now attributed to himself.

On extremely rare occasions he might still pay a visit to one or another of them. They had meanwhile acquired lordly mansions; most of them held important offices. Their one annual meeting was the anniversary of the putsch of November 9, 1923, which was celebrated in the Bürgerbräukeller. Surprisingly, Hitler did not at all look forward to these reunions; it was clear that he found it distasteful to have to be present.

After 1933 there quickly formed various rival factions that held divergent views, spied on each other, and held each other in contempt. A mixture of scorn and dislike became the prevailing mood within the party. Each new dignitary rapidly gathered a circle of intimates around him. Thus Himmler associated almost exclusively with his SS following, from whom he could count on unqualified respect. Goering also had his band of uncritical admirers, consisting partly of members of his family, partly of his closest associates and adjutants. Goebbels felt at ease in the company of literary and movie people. Hess occupied himself with problems of homeopathic medicine, loved chamber music, and had screwy but interesting acquaintances.

As an intellectual Goebbels looked down on the crude philistines of the leading group in Munich, who for their part made fun of the conceited academic's literary ambitions. Goering considered neither the Munich philistines nor Goebbels sufficiently aristocratic for him, and therefore avoided all social relations with them; whereas Himmler, filled with the elitist missionary zeal of the SS (which for a time expressed itself in a bias for the sons of princes and counts), felt far superior to all the others. Hitler, too, had his retinue, which went everywhere with him. Its membership, consisting of chauffeurs, the photographer, his pilot, and secretaries, remained always the same.

Hitler held these divergent circles together politically. But after a year in power, neither Himmler nor Goering nor Hess appeared frequently enough at his dinner table or movie showings for there to be any semblance of a "society" of the new regime. When they did come their interest was so completely concentrated upon wooing Hitler's favor that no cross-connections to the other groups sprang up.

To be sure, Hitler did not foster any social ties among the leaders.

In fact, as his situation grew increasingly critical in later years, he watched any efforts at rapprochement with keen suspicion. Not until it was all over did the still surviving heads of these isolated miniature worlds meet all together in a Luxemburg hotel—and then only because they had no choice in the matter, for they were all prisoners.

During these stays in Munich, Hitler paid little attention to government or party business, even less than in Berlin or at Obersalzberg. Usually only an hour or two a day remained available for conferences. Most of his time he spent marching about building sites, relaxing in studios, cafés, and restaurants, or hurling long monologues at his associates who were already amply familiar with the unchanging themes and painfully tried to conceal their boredom.

After two or three days in Munich, Hitler usually ordered preparations for the drive to "the mountain"—Obersalzberg. We rode over dusty highways in several open cars; the autobahn to Salzburg did not exist in those days, although it was being built on a priority basis. Usually the motorcade stopped for coffee in a village inn at Lambach am Chiemsee, which served delicious pastries that Hitler could scarcely ever resist. Then the passengers in the following cars once more swallowed dust for two hours, for the column rode in close file. After Berchtesgaden came the steep mountain road full of potholes, until we arrived at Hitler's small, pleasant wooden house on Obersalzberg. It had a wide overhanging roof and modest interior: a dining room, a small living room, and three bedrooms. The furniture was bogus old-German peasant style and gave the house a comfortable petit-bourgeois look. A brass canary cage, a cactus, and a rubber plant intensified this impression. There were swastikas on knickknacks and pillows embroidered by admiring women, combined with, say, a rising sun or a vow of "eternal loyalty." Hitler commented to me with some embarrassment: "I know these are not beautiful things, but many of them are presents. I shouldn't like to part with them."

Soon he emerged from his bedroom, having changed out of his jacket into a Bavarian sports coat of light-blue linen, which he wore with a yellow tie. Usually he fell to talking about his building plans.

A few hours later a small Mercedes sedan would drive up with his two secretaries, Fräulein Wolf and Fräulein Schröder. A simple Munich girl would usually be with them. She was pleasant and fresh-faced rather than beautiful and had a modest air. There was nothing about her to suggest that she was a ruler's mistress: Eva Braun.

This sedan was never allowed to drive in the official motorcade, for no one was to connect it with Hitler. The secretaries also served the function of disguising the mistress's presence. I could only wonder at the way Hitler and Eva Braun avoided anything that might suggest an intimate relationship—only to go upstairs to the bedrooms together late at night. It has always remained incomprehensible to me why this needless, forced practice of keeping their distance was continued even in this inner circle whose members could not help being aware of the truth.

Eva Braun kept her distance from every one of Hitler's intimates. She was the same toward me too; that changed only in the course of years. When we became more familiar with one another I realized that her reserved manner, which impressed many people as haughty, was merely embarrassment; she was well aware of her dubious position in Hitler's court.

During those early years of our acquaintanceship Hitler, Eva Braun, an adjutant, and a servant were the only persons who stayed in the small house; we guests, five or six of us, including Martin Bormann and Press Chief Dietrich, as well as the two secretaries, were put up in a nearby pension.

Hitler's decision to settle on Obersalzberg seemed to point to a love of nature. But I was mistaken about that. He did frequently admire a beautiful view, but as a rule he was more affected by the awesomeness of the abysses than by the harmony of a landscape. It may be that he felt more than he allowed himself to express. I noticed that he took little pleasure in flowers and considered them entirely as decorations. Some time around 1934, when a delegation of Berlin women's organizations was planning to welcome Hitler at Anhalter Station and hand him flowers, the head of the organization called Hanke, then the Propaganda Minister's secretary, to ask what Hitler's favorite flower was. Hanke said to me: "I've telephoned around, asked the adjutants, but there's no answer. He hasn't any." He reflected for a while: "What do you think, Speer? Shouldn't we say edelweiss? I think edelweiss sounds right. First of all it's rare and then it also comes from the Bavarian mountains. Let's simply say edelweiss!" From then on the edelweiss was officially "the Fuehrer's flower." The incident shows how much liberty party propaganda sometimes took in shaping Hitler's image.

Hitler often talked about mountain tours he had undertaken in the past. From a mountain climber's point of view, however, they did not amount to much. He rejected mountain climbing or alpine skiing: "What pleasure can there be in prolonging the horrible winter artificially by staying in the mountains?" His dislike for snow burst out repeatedly, long before the catastrophic winter campaign of 1941–42. "If I had my way I'd forbid these sports, with all the accidents people have doing them. But of course the mountain troops draw their recruits from such fools."

Between 1934 and 1936 Hitler still took tramps on the public forest paths, accompanied by his guests and three or four plainclothes detectives belonging to his SS bodyguard. At such times Eva Braun was permitted to accompany him, but only trailing along with the two secretaries at the end of the file. It was considered a sign of favor when he called someone up to the front, although conversation with him flowed rather thinly. After perhaps half an hour Hitler would change partners: "Send the press chief to me," and the companion of the moment would be demoted back to the rear. Hitler set a fast pace. Frequently other walkers met us; they would pause at the side of the path, offering reverent greetings. Some would take up their courage, usually women or girls, and address Hitler, whereupon he would respond with a few friendly words.

The destination was often the Hochlenzer, a small mountain inn, on the Scharitzkehl, about an hour's walk, where we sat outside at plain wooden tables and had a glass of milk or beer. On rare occasions there would be a longer tour; I remember one with General von Blomberg, the Commander in Chief of the army. We had the impression that weighty military problems were being discussed, since everyone had to stay far enough behind to be out of hearing. Even when we rested for a while in a clearing in the woods, Hitler had his servant spread his blankets at a considerable distance from the rest of us, and he stretched out on them with the general—a peaceful and innocent-seeming sight.

Another time we drove by car to the Königssee and from there by motorboat to the Bartholomä Peninsula; or else we took a three-hour hike over the Scharitzkehl to the Königssee. On the last part of this walk we had to thread our way through numerous strollers who had been lured out by the lovely weather. Interestingly enough, these many people did not immediately recognize Hitler in his rustic Bavarian clothes, since scarcely anyone imagined that he would be among the hikers. But shortly before we reached our destination, the Schiffmeister restaurant, a band of enthusiasts began excitedly following our group; they had belatedly realized whom they had encountered. Hitler in the lead, almost running, we barely reached the door before we were overtaken by the swelling crowd. We sat over coffee and cake while the big square outside filled. Hitler waited until police reinforcements had been brought up before he entered the open car, which had been driven there to meet us. The front seat was folded back, and he stood beside the driver, left hand resting on the windshield, so that even those standing at a distance could see him. Two men of the escort squad walked in front of the car, three more on either side, while the car moved at a snail's pace through the throng. I sat as usual in the jump seat close behind Hitler and shall never forget that surge of rejoicing, the ecstasy reflected in so many faces. Wherever Hitler went during those first years of his rule, wherever his car stopped for a short time, such scenes were repeated. The mass exultation was not called forth by rhetoric or suggestion, but solely by the effect of Hitler's presence. Whereas individuals in the crowd were subject to this influence only for a few seconds at a time, Hitler himself was eternally exposed to the worship of the masses. At the time I admired him for nevertheless retaining his informal habits in private.

Perhaps it is understandable that I was carried along by these tempests of homage. But it was even more overwhelming for me to speak with the idol of a nation a few minutes or a few hours later, to discuss building plans with him, sit beside him in the theater, or eat ravioli with him in the Osteria. It was this contrast that overcame me.

Only a few months before I had been carried away by the prospect of drafting and executing buildings. Now I was completely under Hitler's spell, unreservedly and unthinkingly held by him. I was ready to follow him anywhere. Yet his ostensible interest in me was only to launch me on a glorious career as an architect. Years later, in Spandau, I read Ernst Cassirer's comment on the men who of their own accord threw away man's highest privilege: to be an autonomous person.*

Now I was one of them.

Two deaths in 1934 delimited the private and the political realms. After some weeks of severe illness, Hitler's architect Troost died on January 21; and on August 2, Reich President von Hindenburg passed away. His death left the way clear for Hitler to assume total power.

On October 15, 1933, Hitler had solemnly laid the cornerstone for the House of German Art in Munich. He delivered the ceremonial hammer blows with a fine silver hammer Troost had designed specially for this day. But the hammer broke. Now, four months later, Hitler remarked to us: "When that hammer shattered I knew at once it was an evil omen. Something is going to happen, I thought. Now we know why the hammer broke. The architect was destined to die." I have witnessed quite a few examples of Hitler's superstitiousness.

But for me Troost's death meant a grave loss. A close relationship had just become established between us, and I counted on profiting, both humanly and artistically, from it. Funk, then state secretary in Goebbels's Propaganda Ministry, took a different view. On the day of Troost's death I met him in Goebbels's anteroom, a long cigar in his round face. "Congratulations! Now you're the first!" he said to me.

I was twenty-eight years old.

---

* In *The Myth of the State* (New Haven: Yale University Press, 1946), p. 286, Ernst Cassirer writes: "But here are men, men of education and intelligence, honest and upright men who suddenly give up the highest human privilege. They have ceased to be free and personal agents." And earlier: "Man no longer questions his environment; he accepts it as a matter of course."

5

Architectural Megalomania

FOR A WHILE IT LOOKED AS IF HITLER HIMSELF INTENDED TO TAKE OVER Troost's office. He worried lest the plans be carried out without the necessary sympathy with the deceased architect's vision. "I'd best take that in hand myself," he remarked. This notion, after all, was no stranger than his later assuming supreme command of the army.

No doubt he had several weeks enjoyment out of imagining himself as the head of a smoothly functioning studio. On the trip to Munich he sometimes prepared himself for the role by discussing designs or making sketches, and a few hours later he would be sitting at the bureau manager's drawing board correcting plans. But Bureau Manager Gall, a simple, straightforward Bavarian, defended Troost's work with unexpected tenacity. He did not accept the highly detailed suggestions Hitler drafted and showed that he could do better.

Hitler acquired confidence in him and soon tacitly dropped his plan. He acknowledged the man's ability. After some time he made Gall chief of the studio and gave him additional assignments.

Hitler also remained close to the deceased architect's widow, with whom he had been friendly for a long time. She was a woman of taste and character who defended her frequently idiosyncratic views more obstinately than a good many men in high office. She came to the defense of her husband's work with a determination and sometimes a heatedness that made her much feared. Thus, she lashed out at Bonatz when he was so imprudent as to object to Troost's design for Königsplatz in Munich. She violently attacked the modern architects Vorhoelzer and Abel. In all these cases her views were the same as Hitler's. In addition she introduced her favorite Munich architects to him, made deprecatory or favorable remarks about artists and artistic events, and because Hitler frequently listened to her, became a kind of arbiter of art in Munich. But unfortunately not on questions of painting. For Hitler had given his photographer, Hoffmann, the job of first sifting through the paintings submitted for the annual Grand Art Show. Frau Troost frequently protested against the one-sided selection, but in this field Hitler would not give way to her, so that she soon stopped going to the shows.

If I myself wanted to give paintings to associates, I chose them from among the excluded pictures stored in the cellars of the House of German Art. Nowadays, when I see these paintings here and there in the homes of acquaintances, I am struck by the fact that they can scarcely be distinguished from the pictures that were actually shown at the time. The differences, once the subject of such violent controversies, have melted away in the interval.

I was in Berlin during the Roehm putsch.* Tension hung over the city. Soldiers in battle array were encamped in the Tiergarten. Trucks full of police holding rifles cruised the streets. There was clearly an air of "something cooking," similar to that of July 20, 1944, which I would likewise experience in Berlin.

The next day Goering was presented as the savior of the situation in Berlin. Late on the morning of July 1, Hitler returned after making a series of arrests in Munich, and I received a telephone call from his adjutant: "Have you any new designs? If so, bring them here!" That suggested that Hitler's entourage was trying to distract him by turning his mind to his architectural interests.

Hitler was extremely excited and, as I believe to this day, inwardly convinced that he had come through a great danger. Again and again he described how he had forced his way into the Hotel Hanselmayer in Wiessee—not forgetting, in the telling, to make a show of his courage: "We were unarmed, imagine, and didn't know whether or not those swine might have armed guards to use against us." The homosexual atmosphere had disgusted him: "In one room we found two naked boys!" Evidently he believed that his personal action had averted a disaster at the last minute: "I alone was able to solve this problem. No one else!"

His entourage tried to deepen his distaste for the executed SA leaders by assiduously reporting as many details as possible about the intimate

---

* The Blood Purge of June 30, 1934. The official version was that Ernst Roehm, leader of the SA, was planning a putsch; hence the name.—*Translators' note.*

life of Roehm and his following. Brückner showed Hitler the menus of banquets held by the Roehm clique, which had purportedly been found in the Berlin SA headquarters. The menus listed a fantastic variety of courses, including foreign delicacies such as frogs' legs, birds' tongues, shark fins, seagulls' eggs, along with vintage French wines and the best champagnes. Hitler commented sarcastically: "So, here we have those revolutionaries! And our revolution was too tame for them."

After paying a call on the President he returned overjoyed. Hindenburg had approved his operation, he said, saying something like: "When circumstances require it, one must not shrink from the most extreme action. One must be able to spill blood also." The newspapers concurrently reported that President von Hindenburg had officially praised Chancellor Hitler and Prussian Prime Minister Hermann Goering* for their action.

The leadership became frenziedly busy justifying the operation. A day of great activity ended with a speech by Hitler to a special session of the Reichstag. His feelings of guilt were audible in his protestations of innocence. A Hitler defending himself was something we would not encounter again in the future, not even in 1939, at the beginning of the war. Even Minister of Justice Gürtner was dragged into the proceedings. Since he was nonpartisan and consequently did not appear to be dependent on Hitler, his support carried special weight with all doubters. The fact that the army silently accepted General Schleicher's death seemed highly significant. But what most impressed me, as well as many of my unpolitical acquaintances, was the attitude of Hindenburg. The field marshal of the First World War was held in reverence by people of middle-class origins. Even in my school days he epitomized the strong, steadfast hero of modern history, and as such seemed to belong to a somewhat legendary realm. During the last year of the war, we children were allowed to take part in the nationwide ceremony of driving nails into huge statues of Hindenburg—each nail representing a contribution of a mark. Thus for as long as I could remember he had been for me the symbol of authority. That Hitler's action was approved by this supreme judge was highly reassuring.

It was no accident that after the Roehm putsch the Right, represented by the President, the Minister of Justice, and the generals, lined up behind Hitler. These men were free of radical anti-Semitism of the sort Hitler advocated. They in fact despised that eruption of plebeian hatreds. Their conservatism had nothing in common with racist delusions. Their open display of sympathy for Hitler's intervention sprang from quite different causes: in the Blood Purge of June 30, 1934, the strong

* While in prison I learned from Funk that Hindenburg had made a similar remark to him. The inside story of Hindenburg's congratulatory telegram remains an unfathomable mystery.

left wing of the party, represented chiefly by the SA, was eliminated. That wing had felt cheated of the fruits of the revolution. And not without reason. For the majority of the members of the SA, raised in the spirit of revolution before 1933, had taken Hitler's supposedly socialist program seriously. During my brief period of activity in Wannsee I had been able to observe, on the lowest plane, how the ordinary SA man sacrificed himself for the movement, giving up time and personal safety in the expectation that he would some day receive tangible compensation. When nothing came of that, anger and discontent built up. It could easily have reached the explosive point. Possibly Hitler's action did indeed avert that "second revolution" Roehm was supposed to have been plotting.

With such arguments we soothed our consciences. I myself and many others snatched avidly at excuses; the things that would have offended us two years before we now accepted as the standard of our new environment. Any troublesome doubts were repressed. At a distance of decades I am staggered by our thoughtlessness in those years.[1]

These events led the very next day to a new commission for me. "You must rebuild the Borsig Palace as quickly as possible. I want to transfer the top SA leadership from Munich to Berlin, so that I can have them nearby in the future. Go over there and start at once." To my objection that the offices of the Vice Chancellor were in the Borsig Palace, Hitler merely replied: "Tell them to clear out right away! Don't give that a second thought!"

With these orders, I promptly went over to Papen's office. The office manager of course knew nothing about the plan. He proposed that I wait for a few months until new quarters had been found and prepared. When I returned to Hitler, he flew into a rage. He again ordered that the building be immediately evacuated and told me to begin on my project without consideration for the presence of the officials.

Papen remained invisible. His officials wavered but promised to arrange their files and transfer them to a provisional home in a week or two. I thereupon ordered the workmen to move into the building without further ado and encouraged them to knock the heavy plaster decorations from the walls and ceilings in halls and anterooms, creating the maximum noise and dust. The dust wafted through the cracks of the doors into the offices, and the racket made all work impossible. Hitler was delighted. Along with his expressions of approval he made jokes about the "dusty bureaucrats."

Twenty-four hours later they moved out. In one of the rooms I saw a large pool of dried blood on the floor. There, on June 30, Herbert von Bose, one of Papen's assistants, had been shot. I looked away and from then on avoided the room. But the incident did not affect me any more deeply than that.

On August 2, Hindenburg died. That same day Hitler personally commissioned me to take care of the background for the funeral ceremonies at the Tannenberg Monument in East Prussia.

I had a high wooden stand built in the inner courtyard. Decorations were limited to banners of black crepe hung from the high towers that framed the inner courtyard. Himmler turned up for a few hours with a staff of SS leaders and had his men explain the security measures to me. He retained his aloofness while I set forth my sketch. He gave me the impression of cold impersonality. He did not seem to deal with people but rather to manipulate them.

The benches of fresh, light-colored wood disturbed the intended impression. The weather was good, and so I had the structure painted black; but unfortunately toward evening it began to rain. The rain continued for the next few days and the paint remained wet. We had bales of black cloth flown by special plane from Berlin and covered the benches with it. Nevertheless the wet paint soaked through, and a good many of the funeral guests must have ruined their clothes.

On the eve of the funeral the coffin was brought on a gun carriage from Neudeck, Hindenburg's East Prussian estate, to one of the towers of the monument. Torchbearers and the traditional flags of German regiments of the First World War accompanied it; not a single word was spoken, not a command given. This reverential silence was more impressive than the organized ceremonial of the following days.

In the morning Hindenburg's coffin was placed on a bier in the center of the Court of Honor. The speaker's lectern was set up right beside it, rather than at a discreet distance. Hitler stepped forward. Schaub took the manuscript of his funeral oration from a briefcase and laid it on the lectern. Hitler began to speak, hesitated, and shook his head angrily in a manner quite out of keeping with the solemnity of the occasion. The adjutant had given him the wrong manuscript. After the mistake was corrected, Hitler read a surprisingly cool, formal memorial address.

Hindenburg had long—much too long for Hitler's impatience—made difficulties for him. The old man had been rigid and thick-headed on many matters; Hitler had often had to resort to cunning, cleverness, or intrigue to win him over. One of Hitler's shrewd moves had been to send Funk, then still Goebbels's state secretary and an East Prussian by birth, to the President's morning press briefing. As a fellow countryman, Funk was often able to take the sting out of a bit of news that Hindenburg found objectionable or to present the matter so that the President did not take offense.

Hindenburg and many of his political allies had expected the new regime to reinstate the monarchy. Any such step, however, was far from Hitler's mind. He was apt to make such remarks as:

I've permitted the Social Democratic ministers like Severing to continue receiving their pensions. Think whatever you like about them, you have to grant there is one thing to their credit: They did away with the monarchy. That was a great step forward. To that extent they prepared the way for us. And now we're supposed to bring back this monarchy? Am I to divide my power? Look at Italy! Do they think I'm that dumb? Kings have always been ungrateful to their foremost associates. We need only remember Bismarck. No, I'm not falling for that. Even though the Hohenzollerns are being so friendly right now.

Early in 1934 Hitler surprised me with my first major commission. The temporary bleachers on the Zeppelin Field in Nuremberg were to be replaced by a permanent stone installation. I struggled over those first sketches until, in an inspired moment, the idea came to me: a mighty flight of stairs topped and enclosed by a long colonnade, flanked on both ends by stone abutments. Undoubtedly it was influenced by the Pergamum altar. The indispensable platform for honored guests presented problems; I tried to place it as unobtrusively as possible midway in the flight of stairs.

With some trepidation I asked Hitler to look at the model. I was worried because the design went far beyond the scope of my assignment. The structure had a length of thirteen hundred feet and a height of eighty feet. It was almost twice the length of the Baths of Caracalla in Rome.

Hitler took his time looking at the plaster model from all sides, professionally assuming the proper eye level, silently studying the drawings, and remaining totally impassive through it all. I was beginning to think he would reject my work. Then, just as he had done that time at our first meeting, he tersely said, "Agreed," and took his leave. To this day I am not sure why, given as he was to long-winded comments, he remained so terse about such decisions.

Where other architects were concerned, Hitler usually rejected the first draft. He liked an assignment to be worked over several times and even during construction would insist on changes in detail. But after this first test of my ability he let me go on without interference. Henceforth he respected my ideas and treated me, as an architect, as if I were his equal.

Hitler liked to say that the purpose of his building was to transmit his time and its spirit to posterity. Ultimately, all that remained to remind men of the great epochs of history was their monumental architecture, he would philosophize. What had remained of the emperors of Rome? What would still bear witness to them today, if their buildings had not survived? Periods of weakness are bound to occur in the history of nations, he argued; but at their lowest ebb, their architecture will speak to them of former power. Naturally, a new national consciousness could not be awakened by architecture alone. But when after a long spell of inertia a sense of national grandeur was born anew, the monuments of men's ancestors were the most impressive exhortations. Today, for example, Mussolini could point to the buildings of the Roman Empire as symbolizing the heroic spirit of Rome. Thus he could fire his nation with the idea of a modern empire. Our architectural works should also speak to the conscience of a future Germany centuries from now. In advancing this argument Hitler also stressed the value of a permanent type of construction.

The building on the Zeppelin Field was begun at once, in order to have at least the platform ready for the coming Party Rally. To clear ground for it, the Nuremberg streetcar depot had to be removed. I passed by its remains after it had been blown up. The iron reinforcements protruded from concrete debris and had already begun to rust. One could easily visualize their further decay. This dreary sight led me to some thoughts which I later propounded to Hitler under the pretentious heading of "A Theory of Ruin Value." The idea was that buildings of modern construction were poorly suited to form that "bridge of tradition" to future generations which Hitler was calling for. It was hard to imagine that rusting heaps of rubble could communicate these heroic inspirations which Hitler admired in the monuments of the past. My "theory" was intended to deal with this dilemma. By using special materials and by applying certain principles of statics, we should be able to build structures which even in a state of decay, after hundreds or (such were our reckonings) thousands of years would more or less resemble Roman models.[2]

To illustrate my ideas I had a romantic drawing prepared. It showed what the reviewing stand on the Zeppelin Field would look like after generations of neglect, overgrown with ivy, its columns fallen, the walls crumbling here and there, but the outlines still clearly recognizable. In Hitler's entourage this drawing was regarded as blasphemous. That I could even conceive of a period of decline for the newly founded Reich destined to last a thousand years seemed outrageous to many of Hitler's closest followers. But he himself accepted my ideas as logical and illuminating. He gave orders that in the future the important buildings of his Reich were to be erected in keeping with the principles of this "law of ruins."

In the course of an inspection of the Party Rally area Hitler turned to Bormann and in a few good-natured words said that I must henceforth appear in party uniform. Those who were with him constantly, his doctor, the photographer, even the director of Daimler-Benz, had already received a uniform. The sight of a single civilian therefore struck a jarring note. But this little gesture also meant that Hitler now counted me as a member of his intimate circle. He had never said a word of reproof when one of his acquaintances in the Chancellery or at the Berghof appeared in civilian dress, for Hitler himself preferred such dress whenever possible. But on his journeys and inspections he was appearing in an official capacity, and to his mind such occasions called for a uniform. Thus, at the beginning of 1934, I was appointed Abteilungsleiter (department chief) on the staff of his deputy, Rudolf Hess. A few months later Goebbels conferred the same rank upon me within his staff for my contribution toward the Party Rally, the Harvest Festival, and the May 1 celebration.

After January 30, 1934, at the suggestion of Robert Ley, head of the Labor Front, a leisure-time organization was created. I was supposed to take over the section called Beauty of Labor; the name had provoked a good deal of mockery, as had the title Strength through Joy itself. A short while before, on a trip through the Dutch province of Limburg, Ley had seen a number of mines conspicuous for their neatness and cleanliness and surrounded by beautifully tended gardens. By temperament Ley always tended to generalize, and he now wanted to have all of German industry follow this example. The project turned out to be an extremely gratifying one, at least for me personally. First we persuaded factory owners to modernize their offices and to have some flowers about. But we did not stop there. Lawn was to take the place of asphalt. What had been wasteland was to be turned into little parks where the workers could sit during breaks. We urged that window areas within factories be enlarged and workers' canteens set up. What was more, we designed the necessary artifacts for these reforms, from simple, well-shaped flatware to sturdy furniture, all of which we had manufactured in large quantities. We provided educational movies and a counseling service to help businessmen on questions of illumination and ventilation. We were able to draw former union leaders and some members of the dissolved Arts and Crafts Society into this campaign. One and all devoted themselves to the cause of making some improvements in the workers' living conditions and moving closer to the ideal of a classless People's Community. However, it was somewhat dismaying to discover that Hitler took hardly any interest in these ideas. He who could lose himself in the details of an architectural project proved remarkably indifferent when I came to him with reports of my progress in this social area. The British ambassador in Berlin, at any rate, thought better of it than Hitler.*

* Sir Neville Henderson, *Failure of a Mission* (New York, 1940), p. 15: "There are, in fact, many things in the Nazi organization and social institutions, as distinct from its rabid nationalism and ideology, which we might study and adapt to our own use with great profit both to the health and happiness of our own nation and old democracy."

It was due to my new party rank that in the spring of 1934 I received my first invitation to an official evening reception that Hitler gave as party chief, one to which wives were also invited. We were seated in groups of six to eight persons at round tables in the large dining hall of the Chancellor's residence. Hitler went from table to table, said a few friendly words, and made the acquaintance of the ladies. When he came up to us I introduced my wife, whom I had hitherto not mentioned to him. "Why have you deprived us of your wife for so long?" he commented privately a few days later, obviously much taken with her. In fact one reason I had avoided introducing her earlier was my dislike for the way Hitler treated his mistress. Moreover, it seemed to me that it should have been the business of the adjutants to invite my wife or to call Hitler's attention to her existence. But you could not expect any sense of etiquette from them. In the final analysis Hitler's own petit-bourgeois origins were reflected in the behavior of the adjutants.

That first evening they met, Hitler said to my wife with a certain solemnity: "Your husband is going to erect buildings for me such as have not been created for four thousand years."

Every year a rally was held at the Zeppelin Field for the assemblage of middle and minor party functionaries, the so-called *Amtswalter*, who were in charge of the various organizations affiliated with the NSDAP. While the SA, the Labor Front, and, of course, the army tried to make a good showing at its mass meetings and impress Hitler and visitors by their bearing and discipline, it proved a rather difficult task to present the Amtswalter in a favorable fashion. For the most part they had converted their small prebends into sizable paunches; they simply could not be expected to line up in orderly ranks. There were conferences about this problem in the Organization Section for Party Rallies, for the appearance of the Amtswalter had already provoked some sarcastic comments on Hitler's part. The saving idea came to me: "Let's have them march up in darkness."

I explained my plan to the organization leaders of the Party Rally. The thousands of flags belonging to all the local groups in Germany were to be held in readiness behind the high fences surrounding the field. The flagbearers were to divide into ten columns, forming lanes in which the Amtswalter would march up. Since all this was to take place at evening, bright spotlights would be cast on these banners, and the great eagle crowning them all. That alone would have a dramatic effect. But even this did not seem sufficient to me. I had occasionally seen our new anti-aircraft searchlights blazing miles into the sky. I asked Hitler to let me have a hundred and thirty of these. Goering made a fuss at first, since these hundred and thirty searchlights represented the greater part of the strategic reserve. But Hitler won him over: "If we use them in such large numbers for a thing like this, other countries will think we're swimming in searchlights."

The actual effect far surpassed anything I had imagined. The hundred and thirty sharply defined beams, placed around the field at intervals of forty feet, were visible to a height of twenty to twenty-five thousand feet, after which they merged into a general glow. The feeling was of a vast room, with the beams serving as mighty pillars of infinitely high outer walls. Now and then a cloud moved through this wreath of lights, bringing an element of surrealistic surprise to the mirage. I imagine that this "cathedral of light" was the first luminescent architecture of this type, and for me it remains not only my most beautiful architectural concept but, after its fashion, the only one which has survived the passage of time. "The effect, which was both solemn and beautiful, was like being in a cathedral of ice," British Ambassador Henderson wrote.[3]

When it came to cornerstone layings, there seemed no way to blot out the dignitaries, ministers, Reichsleiters, and Gauleiters, although these too were a less than impressive bunch. The parade marshals had all they could do to teach them to line up properly. When Hitler appeared they stiffened to attention and raised their arms in salute. At the cornerstone laying of the Nuremberg Kongresshalle, Hitler saw me standing in the second rank. He interrupted the solemn ceremonial to extend his hand to me. I was so overwhelmed by this unusual sign of favor that I let my own hand, raised in salute, fall with a loud smack on the bald head of Julius Streicher, the Gauleiter of Franconia, who stood just front of me.

During the Nuremberg Party Rallies, Hitler remained out of sight most of the time, as far as his intimates were concerned. He withdrew either to prepare his speeches or to attend one of the numerous functions. He took special satisfaction in the foreign visitors and delegations who came each year in growing numbers, especially when these were from the democratic West. During his hasty lunches he asked to have their names read and was obviously pleased at the interest shown by the world at large in National Socialist Germany.

I too had a strenuous time of it in Nuremberg, having been made responsible for all the buildings in which Hitler would appear in the course of the rally. As "chief decorator" I had to check on the arrangements shortly before the beginning of the function, then rush along to see to the next. At that time I dearly loved flags and used them wherever I could. They were a way of introducing a play of color into somber architecture. I found it a boon that the swastika flag Hitler had designed proved more amenable to these uses than a flag divided into three stripes of color. Of course it was not altogether consonant with the flag's dignity to use it mostly for decorative effect, for accenting the pleasing harmonies of certain façades or covering ugly nineteenth-century buildings from eaves to sidewalks. Quite often I added gold ribbons to the flag to intensify the effect of the red. But it was always scenic drama I was after. I arranged for veritable orgies of flags in the narrow streets of Goslar and Nuremberg, with banners stretched from house to house, so that the sky was almost blotted out.

With all this to attend to, I missed most of Hitler's rallies except for his "cultural speeches," as he himself called these major oratorical flights. He used to draft these while he was at Obersalzberg. At the time I admired the speeches not so much, I thought, for their rhetorical brilliance as for what I felt to be their incisive content, their intellectual level. In Spandau I decided I would reread them, once my prison term was over, on the theory that I would find in them one element in my former world which would not repel me. But my expectations were disappointed. In the context of that time they had said a great deal to me; now they seemed empty, without tension, shallow and useless. What was more, in them Hitler openly aired his intention to pervert the very meaning of the concept of culture by mobilizing it for his own power goals. I found it incomprehensible that these tirades should once have impressed me so profoundly. What had done it?

I also never missed the first event of the Party Rally, a performance of *Die Meistersinger* with the ensemble of the Berlin State Opera under Furtwängler. One might have expected that such a gala night, which could be matched only by the performances in Bayreuth, would have been jammed. Over a thousand leaders of the party received invitations and tickets, but they apparently preferred to investigate the quality of Nuremberg beer or Franconian wine. Each of them probably assumed that the others would do their duty for the party and sit out the opera— indeed, legend has it that the top leadership of the party was interested in music. But in fact the leading men in the party were on the whole diamonds in the rough who had as little bent for classical music as for art and literature in general. Even the few representatives of the intelligentsia in Hitler's leadership, such as Goebbels, did not bother with such functions as the regular concerts of the Berlin Philharmonic under Furtwängler. Of all the prominent personalities of the Third Reich, only Minister of the Interior Frick could be met at these concerts. Hitler, too, who seemed partial to music, went to the Berlin Philharmonic concerts only on rare official occasions after 1933.

Given this background, it is understandable that the Nuremberg Opera House was almost empty in 1933 when Hitler entered the central box to hear *Die Meistersinger*. He reacted with intense vexation. Nothing he said, was so insulting and so difficult for an artist as playing to an empty house. He ordered patrols sent out to bring the high party functionaries from their quarters, beer halls, and cafés to the opera house; but even so the seats could not be filled. The following day many jokes were told about where and how the missing leaders had been picked up.

Next year Hitler explicitly ordered the party chiefs to attend the festival performance. They showed their boredom; many were visibly overpowered by sleep. Moreover, to Hitler's mind the sparse applause did not do justice to the brilliant performance. From 1935 on, therefore, the indifferent party audience was replaced by members of the public who had to buy their tickets for hard cash. Only then was the "atmosphere" as encouraging and the applause as hearty as Hitler required.

Late at night I would return from my rounds to the Hotel Deutscher Hof, which had been reserved for Hitler's staff and for the Gauleiters and Reichsleiters. In the hotel restaurant I usually found a group of old Gauleiters waxing boisterous over their beer as they denounced the party's betrayal of the principles of the revolution and betrayal of the workers. Here was a sign that the ideas of Gregor Strasser, who had once led the anticapitalist wing within the NSDAP, were still alive, though reduced to mere bombast. Only in alcohol could these fellows resurrect their old revolutionary élan.

In 1934 some military exercises were performed for the first time at the Party Rally, in Hitler's presence. That same evening Hitler officially visited the soldiers' bivouac. As a former corporal, he seemed thrown back into a world that was familiar to him. He mingled with the soldiers at the campfires, was surrounded by them, tossed jokes back and forth with them. He returned from this episode in a relaxed mood, and during a late snack, described it all with a good many telling details.

The high command of the army, however, was by no means overjoyed. Army Adjutant Hossbach spoke of the soldiers' "breaches of discipline." He insisted that such familiarities must be prevented in the future, since they infringed upon the dignity of the Chief of State. Hitler privately expressed annoyance with this criticism, but was ready to comply. I was astonished at his almost timid attitude in the face of these demands. But he must have felt he had to be careful of the army and have been still shaky in his role as Chief of State.

During the preparations for the Party Rallies I met a woman who had impressed me even in my student days: Leni Riefenstahl, who had starred in or had directed well-known mountain and skiing movies. Hitler appointed her to make films of the rallies. As the only woman officially involved in the proceedings, she had frequent conflicts with the party organization, which was soon up in arms against her. The Nazis were by tradition antifeminist and could hardly brook this self-assured woman, the more so since she knew how to bend this men's world to her purposes. Intrigues were launched and slanderous stories carried to Hess, in order to have her ousted. But after the first Party Rally film, which convinced even the doubters of her skill as a director, these attacks ceased.

When I was first introduced to her, she took a yellowed newspaper clipping from a little chest. "Three years ago, when you reconstructed the Gau headquarters, I clipped your picture from the newspaper," she said. Why in the world had she done that, I asked in astonishment. "I thought at the time that with your head you might well play a part. . . . In one of my movies, of course."

I recall, incidentally, that the footage taken during one of the solemn sessions of the 1935 Party Congress was spoiled. At Leni Riefenstahl's suggestion Hitler gave orders for the shots to be refilmed in the studio. I was called in to do a backdrop simulating a section of the Kongresshalle, as well as a realistic model of the platform and lectern. I had spotlights aimed at it; the production staff scurried around—while Streicher, Rosenberg, and Frank could be seen walking up and down with their manuscripts, determinedly memorizing their parts. Hess arrived and was asked to pose for the first shot. Exactly as he had done before an audience of 30,000 at the Party Congress, he solemnly raised his hand. With his special brand of ardor, he turned precisely to the spot where Hitler would have been sitting, snapped to attention and cried: "My Leader, I welcome you in the name of the Party Congress! The congress will now continue. The Fuehrer speaks!"

He did it all so convincingly that from that point on I was no longer so sure of the genuineness of his feelings. The three others also gave excellent performances in the emptiness of the studio, proving themselves gifted actors. I was rather disturbed; Frau Riefenstahl, on the other hand, thought the acted scenes better than the original presentation.

By this time I thoroughly admired the art with which Hitler would feel his way during his rallies until he had found the point to unleash the first great storm of applause. I was by no means unaware of the demagogic element; indeed I contributed to it myself by my scenic arrangements. Nevertheless, up to this time I had believed that the feelings of the speakers were genuine. It was therefore an upsetting discovery, that day in the studio, when I saw that all this emotion could be represented "authentically" even without an audience.

For the buildings in Nuremberg I had in mind a synthesis between Troost's classicism and Tessenow's simplicity. I did not call it neoclassicist, but neoclassical, for I thought I had derived it from the Dorian style. I was deluding myself, deliberately forgetting that these buildings had to provide a monumental backdrop such as had already been attempted on the Champs de Mars in Paris during the French Revolution, although the resources at that time were more modest. Terms like "classical" and "simple" were scarcely consonant with the gigantic proportions I employed in Nuremberg. Yet, to this day I still like my Nuremberg sketches best of all, rather than many others that I later prepared for Hitler and that turned out considerably more practical.

Because of my fondness for the Doric, when I went on my first trip abroad in May 1935, I did not go to Italy to see the Renaissance palaces and the colossal buildings of Rome, although these might have served me better as prototypes for what was wanted. Instead, I turned to Greece— a sign of where I considered my architectural allegiance to lie. My wife and I sought out chiefly examples of Doric buildings. I shall never forget how overwhelmed we were by the reconstructed stadium of Athens. Two years later, when I myself had to design a stadium, I borrowed its basic horseshoe form.

In Delphi I thought I discerned how the purity of Greek artistic creativeness was speedily contaminated by the wealth won in the Ionian colonies in Asia. Didn't this prove how sensitive a high artistic consciousness was and how little it took to distort the ideal conception to the point of unrecognizability? I happily played with such theories; it never occured to me that my own works might be subject to these same laws.

When we came back in June 1935 my own house in Berlin-Schlachtensee was completed. It was of modest dimensions, 1345 square feet of living space comprising one dining room, one living room, and minimal bedrooms—in deliberate contrast to the recent habit among the leaders of the Reich, who were moving into huge villas or acquiring palaces. We wanted to avoid all that, for we had observed that in surrounding themselves with pomp and stiff officialism, these people were condemning themselves to a slow process of "petrifaction"—which involved their private lives as well.

In any case I could not have built on any greater scale, since I lacked the means. My house cost seventy thousand marks; in order to swing it I had to ask my father to take a mortgage of thirty thousand marks. Although I was acting as a free-lance architect for the party and the state, my income remained low. For in an idealistic spirit which seemed to accord with the temper of the time, I had renounced any architect's fees for all my official buildings.

This attitude, however, caused some amazement in party circles. One day in Berlin, Goering said to me in high good humor: "Well, Herr Speer, you have a great deal to do now, of course. You must be earning plenty." When I said that was not the case, he stared incredulously at me. "What's that? An architect as busy as you? I figured you for a couple of hundred thousand a year. That's all nonsense, this idealistic business. You must make money!" Thereafter I accepted the architect's fee, except for my Nuremberg buildings, for which I received a thousand marks a month. But it was not only on financial grounds that I clung to my professional independence and fended off an official post. Hitler had, I knew, much greater confidence in nonofficial architects—his prejudice against bureaucrats colored his views in everything. At the end of my career as an architect my fortune had increased to about one and a half million marks, and the Reich owed me another million that I did not collect.

My family lived happily in this house. I wish I could write that I had a share in this familial happiness, as my wife and I had once dreamed. But by the time I arrived home, it would be late in the evening and the children would have long since been put to bed. I would sit with my wife for a while—silent from exhaustion. This kind of rigidity became more and more the norm, and when I consider the matter in retrospect, what was happening to me was no different from what was happening to the party bigwigs, who ruined their family life by their ostentatious style of living. They froze into poses of officialism. My own rigidity sprang from excessive work.

In the autumn of 1934 Otto Meissner, state secretary in the Chancellery, who had served under Ebert and Hindenburg and now was working for his third Chief of State, telephoned me. I was to come to Weimar the next day in order to accompany Hitler to Nuremberg.

I sat up until the wee hours sketching out ideas that had been exciting me for some time. More major construction for the Party Rallies was wanted: a field for military exercises, a large stadium, a hall for Hitler's cultural addresses and for concerts as well. Why not concentrate all that, together with what already existed, into a great center? I thought. Until then I had not ventured to take the initiative on such questions, for Hitler kept this sort of decision for himself. I therefore went about drafting this plan with some hesitation.

In Weimar, Hitler showed me a sketch for a "Party Forum" by Professor Paul Schultze-Naumburg. "It looks like an oversized marketplace for a provincial town," he commented. "There's nothing distinctive about it, nothing that sets it off from former times. If we are going to build a party forum, we want people centuries hence to be able to see that our times had a certain building style, like Königsplatz in Munich, for example." Schultze-Naumburg, a pillar of the League of Struggle for German Culture, was given no chance to defend his proposal; he was not even called into Hitler's presence. With total disregard for the man's reputation, Hitler threw away the plans and ordered a new competition among various architects of his choice.

We went on to Nietzsche's house where his sister, Frau Förster-Nietzsche, was expecting Hitler. This solitary, eccentric woman obviously could not get anywhere with Hitler; an oddly shallow conversation at cross-purposes ensued. The principle purpose of the meeting, however, was settled to the satisfaction of all parties: Hitler undertook to finance an annex to the old Nietzsche house, and Frau Förster-Nietzsche was willing to have Schultze-Naumburg design it. "He's better at that sort of thing, doing something in keeping with the old house," Hitler remarked. He was plainly pleased to be able to offer the architect some small sop.

Next morning we drove by car to Nuremberg, although Hitler pre-ferred the railroad at that period, for reasons that I was to learn that very day. As always he sat beside his driver in the dark-blue open seven-liter supercharged Mercedes; I was behind him on one jump seat, on the other his servant, who on request produced from a pouch automobile maps, crusty rolls, pills, or eyeglasses; in the rear sat his adjutant Brückner and Press Chief Dietrich. In an accompanying car of the same size and color were five strong men of his bodyguard squad and Hitler's personal physician, Dr. Brandt.

As soon as we had traversed the Thuringian Forest and come into more thickly settled areas, the difficulties began. Riding through a village, we were recognized; but before the people could recover from their astonishment we had passed them. "Now watch," Hitler said. "In the next village it won't be so easy. The local party group will certainly have telephoned ahead by now." Sure enough, when we arrived, the streets were full of cheering people. The village policeman was doing his best, but the car could advance no faster than a walk. Even after we had worked our way out, a few enthusiasts on the open highway let down the railroad barrier in order to keep Hitler among them a while longer.

In this way we made slow progress. When it was time for lunch, we stopped at a small inn in Hildburghausen where years before Hitler had had himself appointed police commissioner in order to acquire Ger-man citizenship. But no one mentioned this. The innkeeper and his wife were beside themselves with excitement. After some difficulty, the adjutant managed to elicit from them what they could serve: spaghetti with spinach. We waited for a long time; finally the adjutant went to take a look in the kitchen. "The women are in such a state that they can't tell whether the spaghetti is done."

Meanwhile, thousands of people were gathering outside chanting calls for Hitler. "If only we were out of this," he commented when we emerged from the inn. Slowly, under a rain of flowers, we reached the medieval gate. Juveniles closed it before our eyes; children climbed on the running boards of the car. Hitler had to give autographs. Only then would they open the gate. They laughed, and Hitler laughed with them.

Everywhere in the countryside farmers left their implements, women waved. It was a triumphal procession. As the car rolled along, Hitler leaned back to me and exclaimed: "Heretofore only one German has been hailed like this: Luther. When he rode through the country, people gathered from far and wide to cheer him. As they do for me today!"

This enormous popularity was only too easy to understand. The public credited Hitler and no one else with the achievements in economics and foreign policy of the period. They more and more regarded him as the leader who had made a reality of their deeply rooted longings for a powerful, proud, united Germany. Very few were mistrustful at this time. And those who occasionally felt doubts rising reassured themselves with thoughts of the regime's accomplishments and the esteem it enjoyed even in critical foreign countries.

During these stormy scenes of homage by the populace, which certainly affected me as well, there was one person in our car who refused to be carried away: Hitler's chauffeur of many years, Schreck. I heard some of his mutterings: "Folks are dissatisfied because . . . party people swellheaded . . . proud, forget where they come from. . . ." After his early death an oil painting of Schreck hung in Hitler's private office at Obersalzberg side by side with one of Hitler's mother[4]—there was none of his father.

Shortly before we reached Bayreuth, Hitler shifted over to a small Mercedes sedan which was driven by his photographer Hoffmann and rode to Villa Wahnfried, where Frau Winifred Wagner was expecting him. We others went on to Berneck, the nearby spa where Hitler regularly spent the night on the drive from Munich to Berlin. In eight hours we had covered only a hundred and thirty miles.

When I learned that Hitler would be staying at Wahnfried until quite late, I was in some embarrassment, for next morning we were to drive on to Nuremberg where Hitler might very possibly agree to the building program proposed by the municipal administration, which had its own axes to grind. If so, there was little prospect that my design would even be considered, for Hitler never liked to rescind a decision. Under the circumstances, I turned to Schreck. I explained my plan for the Party Rally area. He promised to tell Hitler about it during the drive and to show him the sketch if he reacted favorably.

Next morning, shortly before we set out, I was called to Hitler's suite: "I agree to your plan. We'll discuss it today with Mayor Liebel."

Two years later Hitler would have come directly to the point in dealing with a mayor: "Here is the plan for the Party Rally area; this is how we're going to do it." But at that time, in 1935, he did not yet feel so completely in command and so spent almost an hour in prefatory explanations, before he finally placed my sketch on the table. Naturally the mayor found the design excellent, for as an old party man he had been trained to concur.

After my plan had been properly praised, Hitler again began feeling his way: The design called for moving the Nuremberg zoo. "Can we ask the people of Nuremberg to accept that? They're very attached to it, I know. Of course we'll pay for a new and even more beautiful zoo."

The mayor, who was equally alert to protect the interests of his city, suggested: "We would have to call a stockholders' meeting, perhaps try to buy their shares. . . ." Hitler proved amenable to everything. Outside, Liebel, rubbing his hands, said to one of his aides: "I wonder why the Fuehrer spent so much time persuading us? Of course he can have the old zoo, and we'll get a new one. The old one was no good anyhow. We'll have the finest in the world. They're paying for it, after all." Thus the people of Nuremberg at least got their new zoo—the only thing in the plan which was ever carried to completion.

That same day we took the train to Munich. That evening Adjutant Brückner telephoned me: "You and your goddamned plans! Couldn't they keep? The Fuehrer didn't close an eye last night, he was so excited. Next time have the goodness to ask me first!"

To build this giant complex an Association for the Nuremberg Party Rally Site was created. The Finance Minister of the Reich reluctantly assumed the duty of funding the project. Out of some whimsical impulse Hitler appointed Minister of Churches Kerrl to take charge of the association, and as the latter's deputy, Martin Bormann, who thus received his first important assignment outside the party secretariat.

The plan called for an expenditure of between seven and eight hundred million marks on building, which today would cost three billion marks [$750,000,000]—eight years later I would be spending such a sum every four days on armaments.[5] Including the camping grounds for participants, the tract embraced an area of 16.5 square kilometers (about 6.5 square miles). Under Kaiser Wilhelm II, incidentally, there had been plans for a "Center for German National Festivals" with an area 6600 by 2000 feet.

Two years after Hitler had approved it, my design was exhibited as a model at the Paris World's Fair of 1937 and won the Grand Prix. At the southern end of the complex was the Marchfield; the name was intended not only as a reference to the war god Mars, but also to the month in which Hitler introduced conscription.* Within this enormous tract, an area of 3400 by 2300 feet was set aside where the army could practice minor maneuvers. By contrast, the grandiose area of the palace of Kings Darius I and Xerxes in Persepolis (fifth century B.C.) had embraced only 1500 by 900 feet. Stands 48 feet high were to surround the entire area, providing seats for a hundred and sixty thousand spectators. Twenty-four towers over a hundred and thirty feet in height were to punctuate these stands; in the middle was a platform for guests of honor which was to be crowned by a sculpture of a woman. In A.D. 64 Nero erected on the Capitol a colossal figure 119 feet high. The Statue of Liberty in New York is 151 feet high; our statue was to be 46 feet higher.

To the north, in the direction of the old Nuremberg castle of the Hohenzollerns, which could be seen in the distance, the Marchfield

* It probably also referred to the National Assembly of the Franks, which was likewise called the Marchfield.

opened out into a processional avenue a mile and a quarter long and 264 feet wide. The army was to march down this avenue in ranks 165 feet wide. This avenue was finished before the war and paved with heavy granite slabs, strong enough to bear the weight of tanks. The surface was roughened to provide a secure footing for the goose-stepping soldiers. On the right rose a flight of stairs from which Hitler, flanked by his generals, would review such parades. Opposite was a colonnade where the flags of the regiments would be displayed.

This colonnade with its height of only sixty feet was to serve as a foil for the "Great Stadium" towering up behind it. Hitler had stipulated that the stadium was to hold four hundred thousand spectators. History's largest precedent was the Circus Maximus in Rome, built for between one hundred and fifty and two hundred thousand persons. Modern stadiums in those days contained about a hundred thousand seats.

The pyramid of Cheops, with a base of 756 feet and a height of 481 feet, measured 3,277,300 cubic yards. The Nuremberg stadium would have been 1815 feet long and 1518 wide and could have enclosed a volume of over 11,100,000 cubic yards, some three times more than the pyramid of Cheops.[6] The stadium was to be by far the largest structure on the tract and one of the hugest in history. Calculations showed that in order to hold the required number of spectators the stands would have to be over three hundred feet high. An oval would really have been out of the question; the resultant bowl would not only have intensified the heat, but produced psychological discomfort. I therefore turned my thoughts to the Athenian horseshoe shape. We took a hillside of approximately the same shape and smoothed out its irregularities by temporary wooden structures; the question was whether sporting events would be visible from the upper rows. The results of our study were more positive than I had expected.

Our rough estimate of the costs of the Nuremberg stadium came to between two hundred and two hundred and fifty million marks—approximately a billion marks [$250,000,000] at present-day construction costs. Hitler took this calmly. "That is less than two battleships of the *Bismarck* class. How quickly a warship can be destroyed, and if not, it is scrap-iron anyhow in ten years. But this building will stand for centuries. When the Finance Minister asks what it will cost, don't give him any answer. Say that nobody has any experience with building projects of such size." Granite to the value of several million marks was ordered, pink for the exteriors, white for the stands. At the site a gigantic pit for the foundation was dug; during the war it became a picturesque lake, which suggested the proportions of the structure.

Farther to the north of the stadium the processional avenue crossed an expanse of water in which the buildings would be reflected. Then, concluding the complex, came a square, bounded on the right by the

Kongresshalle, which still stands, and on the left by a "Kulturhalle" meant specifically for Hitler's speeches on cultural matters.

Hitler had appointed me the architect for all these buildings except the Kongresshalle, which had been designed in 1933 by Ludwig Ruff. He gave me a free hand with plans and execution and participated every year in a ceremonial cornerstone laying. However, these cornerstones were subsequently moved to the municipal buildings and grounds yard to wait until the building had made further progress and they could be incorporated in the wall. At the laying of the cornerstone for the stadium on September 9, 1937, Hitler solemnly shook hands with me before the assembled party bigwigs. "This is the greatest day of your life!" Perhaps I was something of a skeptic even then, for I replied: "No, not today, my Fuehrer, but only when the building is finished."

Early in 1939 Hitler, in a speech to construction workers, undertook to justify the dimensions of his style: "Why always the biggest? I do this to restore to each individual German his self-respect. In a hundred areas I want to say to the individual: We are not inferior; on the contrary, we are the complete equals of every other nation."[7]

This love for vast proportions was not only tied up with the totalitarian cast of Hitler's regime. Such tendencies, and the urge to demonstrate one's strength on all occasions, are characteristic of quickly acquired wealth. Thus we find the largest buildings in Greek antiquity in Sicily and Asia Minor. It is an interesting corollary that those cities were generally ruled by despots. But even in Periclean Athens the statue of Athena Parthenos by Phidias was forty feet high. Moreover, most of the Seven Wonders of the World won their repute by their excessive size: the Temple of Diana at Ephesus, the Mausoleum at Halicarnassus, the Colossus of Rhodes, and the Olympian Zeus of Phidias.

Hitler's demand for huge dimensions, however, involved more than he was willing to admit to the workers. He wanted the biggest of everything to glorify his works and magnify his pride. These monuments were an assertion of his claim to world dominion long before he dared to voice any such intention even to his closest associates.

I, too, was intoxicated by the idea of using drawings, money, and construction firms to create stone witnesses to history, and thus affirm our claim that our works would survive for a thousand years. But I found Hitler's excitement rising whenever I could show him that at least in size we had "beaten" the other great buildings of history. To be sure, he never gave vent to these heady feelings. He was sparing in his use of high-sounding words to me. Possibly at such moments he actually felt a certain awe; but it was directed toward himself and toward his own greatness, which he himself had willed and projected into eternity.

At the same Party Rally of 1937 at which Hitler laid the cornerstone of the stadium, his last speech ended with the ringing words: "The German nation has after all acquired its Germanic Reich." At dinner afterward Hitler's adjutant, Brückner, reported that at these words Field Marshal von Blomberg had burst into tears from sheer emotion. Hitler took this as evidence of the army's assent to what was being promised in this slogan.

At the time there was a great deal of talk to the effect that this mysterious dictum would be ushering in a new era in foreign policy; that it would bear much fruit. I had an idea of what it meant, for shortly before the speech was given, Hitler one day abruptly stopped me on the stairs to his apartment, let his entourage go on ahead, and said: "We will create a great empire. All the Germanic peoples will be included in it. It will begin in Norway and extend to northern Italy. I myself must carry this out. If only I keep my health!"

That was still a relatively restrained formulation. In the spring of 1937 Hitler visited me at my Berlin showrooms. We stood alone in front of the nearly seven-foot high model of the stadium for four hundred thousand people. It had been set up precisely at eye level. Every detail had been rendered, and powerful spotlights illuminated it, so that with only a little imagination we could conceive the effect of this structure. Alongside the model were the plans, pinned up on boards. Hitler turned to these. We talked about the Olympic Games, and I pointed out, as I had done several times before, that my athletic field did not have the prescribed Olympic proportions. Without any change of tone, as if it were a matter settled beyond the possibility of discussion, Hitler observed: "No matter. In 1940 the Olympic Games will take place in Tokyo. But thereafter they will take place in Germany for all time to come, in this stadium. And then we will determine the measurements of the athletic field."

According to our carefully worked out schedule this stadium was supposed to be completed in time for the Party Rally of 1945. . . .

6

The Greatest Assignment

HITLER WAS PACING BACK AND FORTH IN THE GARDEN AT OBERSALZBERG. "I really don't know what I should do. It is a terribly difficult decision. I would by far prefer to join the English. But how often in history the English have proved perfidious. If I go with them, then everything is over for good between Italy and us. Afterward the English will drop me, and we'll sit between two stools." In the autumn of 1935 he made frequent remarks of this sort to his intimate circle, which as always had accompanied him to Obersalzberg. At this point Mussolini had begun his invasion of Abyssinia, accompanied by massive air raids; the Negus had fled and a new Roman Empire proclaimed.

Ever since Hitler had made his unfortunate visit to Italy in June 1934, he distrusted the Italians and Italian policy, though not Mussolini. Now that he saw his doubts reinforced, Hitler recalled an item in Hindenburg's political testament, to the effect that Germany should never again ally herself with Italy. Under England's leadership the League of Nations imposed economic sanctions on Italy. This was the moment, Hitler remarked, when he had to decide whether he should ally himself with the English or the Italians. The decision must be taken in terms of the long view, he said. He spoke of his readiness to guarantee England's empire in return for a global arrangement—a favorite idea of his, which he was to voice often. But circumstances left him no choice. They forced him to decide in favor of Mussolini. In spite of the ideological relationship and the developing personal tie, that was no easy decision. For days afterward Hitler would remark in somber tones that the situation had forced him to take this step. He was all the more gratified when it turned out a few weeks later that the sanctions as ultimately voted were relatively mild. From this Hitler concluded that both England and France were loath to take any risks and anxious to avoid any danger. Actions of his which later seemed reckless followed directly from such observations. The Western governments had, as he commented at the time, proved themselves weak and indecisive.

He found this view confirmed when the German troops marched into the demilitarized Rhineland on March 7, 1936. This was an open breach of the Treaty of Locarno and might have provoked military counter-measures on the part of the Allies. Nervously, Hitler waited for the first reactions. The special train in which we rode to Munich on the evening of that day was charged, compartment after compartment, with the tense atmosphere that emanated from the Fuehrer's section. At one station a message was handed into the car. Hitler sighed with relief: "At last! The King of England will not intervene. He is keeping his promise. That means it can all go well." He seemed not to be aware of the meager influence the British Crown has upon Parliament and the government. Nevertheless, military intervention would have probably required the King's approval, and perhaps this was what Hitler meant to imply. In any case, he was intensely anxious, and even later, when he was waging war against almost the entire world, he always termed the remilitarization of the Rhineland the most daring of all his undertakings. "We had no army worth mentioning; at that time it would not even have had the fighting strength to maintain itself against the Poles. If the French had taken any action, we would have been easily defeated; our resistance would have been over in a few days. And what air force we had then was ridiculous. A few Junkers 52's from Lufthansa, and not even enough bombs for them." After the abdication of King Edward VIII, later the Duke of Windsor, Hitler frequently referred to his apparent friendliness toward National Socialist Germany: "I am certain that through him permanent friendly relations with England could have been achieved. If he had stayed, everything would have been different. His abdication was a severe loss for us." Whereupon he would launch into remarks about sinister anti-German forces who were deciding the course of British policy. His regret at not having made an ally out of England ran like a red thread through all the years of his rule. It increased when the Duke of Windsor and his wife visited Hitler at Obersalzberg on October 22, 1937, and allegedly had good words to say about the achievements of the Third Reich.

A few months after the uncontested remilitarization of the Rhineland, Hitler exulted over the harmonious atmosphere that prevailed during the Olympic Games. International animosity toward National Socialist

Germany was plainly a thing of the past, he thought. He gave orders that everything should be done to convey the impression of a peace-minded Germany to the many prominent foreign guests. He himself followed the athletic contests with great excitement. Each of the German victories—and there were a surprising number of these—made him happy, but he was highly annoyed by the series of triumphs by the marvelous colored American runner, Jesse Owens. People whose antecedents came from the jungle were primitive, Hitler said with a shrug; their physiques were stronger than those of civilized whites. They represented unfair competition and hence must be excluded from future games. Hitler was also jolted by the jubilation of the Berliners when the French team filed solemnly into the Olympic Stadium. They had marched past Hitler with raised arms and thereby sent the crowd into transports of enthusiasm. But in the prolonged applause Hitler sensed a popular mood, a longing for peace and reconciliation with Germany's western neighbor. If I am correctly interpreting Hitler's expression at the time, he was more disturbed than pleased by the Berliners' cheers.

In the spring of 1936 Hitler took me with him to inspect a stretch of the autobahn. In conversation he dropped the remark: "I have one more building assignment to give out. The greatest of all." There was only this one hint. He did not explain.

Occasionally, it was true, he outlined a few of his ideas for the rebuilding of Berlin, but it was not until June that Hitler showed me a plan for the center of the city. "I patiently explained to the mayor why this new avenue must be a hundred and thirty yards wide, and now he presents me with one only a hundred yards wide." A few weeks later Mayor Lippert, an old party member and editor in chief of the Berlin *Angriff*, was summoned again; but nothing had changed; the avenue was still a hundred yards in width. Lippert could not work up any enthusiasm for Hitler's architectural ideas. At first Hitler was merely annoyed, remarking that Lippert was petty, incapable of governing a metropolis, and even more incapable of understanding the historical importance he planned to give it. As time wore on, these remarks mounted in intensity: "Lippert is an incompetent, an idiot, a failure, a zero." What was astonishing, however, was that Hitler never showed his dissatisfaction in the mayor's presence and never tried to win him over to his views. Even in this early period he sometimes shied away from the wearisome business of explaining reasons. After four years of this sort of thing, and right after a walk from the Berghof to the teahouse, during which he once more brooded over Lippert's stupidity, he telephoned Goebbels and categorically ordered him to replace his mayor.

Until the summer of 1936 Hitler had evidently meant to have his plans for Berlin carried out by the municipal government. Now he sent for me and tersely gave me the assignment: "There's nothing to be done with the Berlin city government. From now on you make the plans. Take this drawing along. When you have something ready, show it to me. As you know, I always have time for such things."

As Hitler told me, his conception of an enormously wide avenue went back to the early twenties, when he began to study the various plans for Berlin, found them all inadequate, and was impelled to develop his own ideas.* Even then, he said, he had decided to shift the Anhalter and Potsdam railroad stations to the south of Tempelhof Field. This would release broad strips of trackage in the center of the city, so that with only a little further clearing, starting from the Siegesallee, a magnificent avenue lined with impressive buildings could be built, three miles long.

To be sure, all the architectural proportions of Berlin would be shattered by two buildings that Hitler envisaged on this new avenue. On the northern side, near the Reichstag, he wanted a huge meeting hall, a domed structure into which St. Peter's Cathedral in Rome would have fitted several times over. The diameter of the dome was to be eight hundred twenty-five feet. Beneath it, in an area of approximately four hundred and ten thousand square feet, there would be room for more than a hundred and fifty thousand persons to assemble standing.

During these first discussions, when our general views on the city plan were still fluid, Hitler thought it necessary to explain to me that the size of meeting halls should be governed by medieval conceptions. The cathedral of Ulm, for example, had thirty thousand square feet of area; but when the building was begun in the fourteenth century only fifteen thousand people lived in Ulm, including children and the aged. "Therefore they could never fill the space. Compared to that, a hall for a hundred fifty thousand persons could be called small for a city of millions like Berlin."

To balance this structure Hitler wanted an arch of triumph four hundred feet high. "At least that will be a worthy monument to our dead of the world war. The names of our dead, all 1,800,000 of them, will be chiseled in the granite. What a paltry affair the Berlin monument put up by the Republic is. How wretched and undignified for a great nation." He handed me two sketches drawn on small cards. "I made these drawings ten years ago. I've always saved them, because I never doubted that some day I would build these two edifices. And this is how we will carry it out now."

---

* He was probably referring to the plans by Martin Mächler which were shown in 1927 at a major art exhibit in Berlin. As a matter of fact these bear a striking resemblance to Hitler's ideas. I did not become acquainted with them until I read Alfred Schinz's book, *Berlin: Stadtschicksal und Städtebau* (Braunschweig, 1964) in Spandau prison.

The proportions of the drawings showed, Hitler explained, that even then he had intended a diameter of more than six hundred and fifty feet for the dome and a height of more than three hundred thirty feet for the arch of triumph. What is startling is less the grandiosity of the project than the obsessiveness with which he had been planning triumphant monumental buildings when there was not a shred of hope that they could ever be built. And today it strikes me as rather sinister that in the midst of peacetime, while continually proclaiming his desire for international reconciliation, he was planning buildings expressive of an imperial glory which could be won only by war.

"Berlin is a big city, but not a real metropolis. Look at Paris, the most beautiful city in the world. Or even Vienna. Those are cities with grand style. Berlin is nothing but an unregulated accumulation of buildings. We must surpass Paris and Vienna." These were some of the points he made during the series of discussions that now began. Most of the time we conferred in his apartment in the Chancellery. As a rule, he would have all other guests leave, so we could talk seriously.

At an earlier stage in his life he had carefully studied the plans of Vienna and Paris, and he revealed an amazing memory for these. In Vienna he admired the architectural complex of Ringstrasse with its great buildings, the Rathaus, the Parliament, the Concert Hall, or the Hofburg and the twin museums. He could draw this part of the city in correct proportions and had absorbed the lesson that impressive public buildings, like monuments, must be planned to be freely visible from all sides. He admired these buildings even if they did not directly coincide with his views, like the neo-Gothic Rathaus. "Here Vienna is worthily represented. By contrast, consider the Berlin Rathaus. We will give Berlin a more beautiful one than Vienna's, no doubt about that."

He was even more impressed by the vast rebuilding project and the new boulevards that Georges E. Haussmann had built in Paris between 1853 and 1870 at an expenditure of 2.5 million gold francs. He regarded Haussmann as the greatest city planner in history, but hoped that I would surpass him. The struggles that Haussmann had waged for years led him to expect that the plans for Berlin would also encounter opposition. Only his authority, he believed, would successfully put the work across.

Initially, however, he found a cunning way to bring the municipal administration around; for the city was less than eager to accept Hitler's plans when it became evident that the considerable expense of clearing ground and building the avenues, the public gardens, and the rapid-transit railways would fall to the city. "We'll let them think we're considering building our new capital on the Müritzsee in Mecklenburg. You'll see how the Berliners come to life at the threat that the federal government may move out," he remarked. And in fact a few hints of this sort sufficed; the city fathers soon proved ready to foot the costs of the architectural planning. Nevertheless, for a few months Hitler was rather taken with this plan for a German Washington, and liked to talk about creating an ideal city out of nothingness. In the end, however, he rejected the idea: "Artificially created capitals always remain lifeless. Think of Washington or Canberra. In our own Karlsruhe, too, no life springs up because the dull bureaucrats are left to themselves there." In connection with this episode, I am not certain to this day whether Hitler was play-acting as well, or whether for a while he was not somewhat converted to this idea of a new city.

His plans for Berlin were inspired by the Champs Elysées with its Arc de Triomphe, a hundred and sixty feet high, begun by Napoleon I in 1805. This was the model for his great arch and for the width of his avenue as well: "The Champs Elysées is three hundred and thirty feet wide. In any case we'll make our avenue seventy-odd feet wider. When the far-sighted Great Elector laid out Unter den Linden in the seventeenth century with a width of two hundred feet, he could no more have fore-seen present-day traffic than Haussmann when he designed the Champs Elysées."

To carry out this project, Hitler had State Secretary Lammers issue an ordinance giving me extensive powers and making me his direct subordi-nate. Neither the Minister of the Interior nor the Mayor of Berlin nor the Gauleiter of Berlin, Goebbels, had any authority over me. In fact, Hitler explicitly exempted me from having to inform the city government or the party of my plans.[1] When I told Hitler that I preferred to carry out this commission also as a free-lance architect, he immediately consented. State Secretary Lammers invented a legal device which took account of my distaste for a bureaucratic position. My office was not treated as a part of the government, but as a large, independent research institute.

On January 30, 1937, I was officially commissioned to carry out Hit-ler's "greatest architectural task." For a long time he searched for a re-sounding enough title for me. Finally Funk hit on a good one: "Inspector General of Buildings for the Renovation of the Federal Capital." In pre-senting me with the certification of my appointment, Hitler manifested a kind of shyness which sometimes came over him. After lunch he pressed the document into my hand: "Do a good job." By a generous interpreta-tion of my contract I thereafter held the formal rank of a state secretary of the Reich government. At the age of thirty-two I could sit beside Dr. Todt in the third row of the government benches, was entitled to a place at the lower end of the table at official state dinners and automatically re-ceived from every foreign state visitor a decoration of fixed rank. I also received a monthly salary of fifteen hundred marks, an insignificant sum compared to my architect's fees.

In February, moreover, Hitler bluntly ordered the Minister of Education to clear out the venerable Academy of Arts on Pariser Platz, so that my offices—called GBI for *Generalbauinspektor* (Inspector General of Buildings)—could be installed there. He chose this building because he could reach it through the intervening ministerial gardens without being seen by the public. Soon he made ample use of this convenience.

Hitler's city plan had one major fault: It had not been thought through to the end. He had become so set on the notion of a Berlin Champs Elysées two and a half times the length of the original in Paris that he entirely lost sight of the structure of existing Berlin, a city of four million people. For a city planner such an avenue could only have a meaning and function as the core of a general reorganization of the city. For Hitler, however, it was a display piece and an end in itself. Moreover, it did not solve the Berlin railroad problem. The huge wedge of tracks which divided the city into two parts would merely be shifted a few miles to the south.

Ministerial Director Leibbrand of the Reich Traffic Ministry, the chief planner for the German railroads, saw in Hitler's plans an opportunity for a large-scale reorganization of the entire railroad network in the capital. Together, we found an almost ideal solution. The capacity of the Berlin suburban railroad, the Ringbahn, would be expanded by two tracks, so that long-distance traffic could also be funneled into it. We could thus have a central station in the north and another in the south, which would do away with the need for the various Berlin terminals. The cost of the new arrangement was estimated at between one and two billion marks.[2]

This would give us the old tracks to the south for a prolongation of our avenue and a large open area in the heart of the city for new housing for four hundred thousand persons.[3] We could do the same to the north as well, and by eliminating the Lehrter Station open up new residential districts. The only trouble with this plan was that neither Hitler nor I wanted to give up the domed hall, which was to form the terminus of the magnificent avenue. The vast square in front of the hall was to remain free of traffic. So the plan, which would also have been a boon to traffic, was sacrificed on the altar of ostentation, and the flow of north-south traffic considerably hampered by a detour.

It was an obvious idea to continue the existing two hundred foot wide thoroughfare to the west, Heerstrasse, with the same width in an easterly direction—a project that was partly realized after 1945 by the extension of the former Frankfurter Allee. This axis, like the north-south axis, would be continued to its natural terminus, the ring formed by the autobahn, so that new urban areas could also be opened up in the eastern part of Berlin. In this way, even though we were razing the heart of the city, we would be able to provide room for almost double the city's population.[4]

Both axes were to be lined by tall office buildings which would be scaled down at either end, passing by degrees into lower and lower buildings until an area was reached of private homes surrounded by considerable greenery. By this system I hoped to avoid the usual strangulation of the city center. This plan, which arose necessarily out of my axial structure, led the areas of greenery along the radii deep into the heart of the city.

Beyond the autobahn, at the four terminal points of the two great spokes, land was reserved for airports. In addition, the Rangsdorfer Lake was expected to serve as landing field for a water airport, for in those days a greater future was envisaged for the seaplane. Tempelhof Airfield, situated much too close to the prospective new center of the city, would be turned into an amusement park in the style of Copenhagen's Tivoli. In years to come, we considered, the intersecting axes would be supplemented by five rings and seventeen radial thoroughfares, each of which was to be two hundred feet wide. For the present, however, we limited ourselves to determining where the new rows of buildings were to go. To connect the midpoint of the axes and part of the rings and to relieve traffic in the streets, rapid-transit subways were planned. In the west, bordering on the Olympic Stadium, we planned a new university quarter, for most of the buildings of the old Friedrich Wilhelm University on Unter den Linden were antiquated and in deplorable condition. To the north of the new university district a new medical quarter was to be established, with hospitals, laboratories, and medical schools. The banks of the Spree between the museum island and the Reichstag—a neglected area full of junkyards and small factories— were also to be reconstructed and additions and new buildings for the Berlin museums undertaken.

The land beyond the ring formed by the autobahn was to be set aside for recreation purposes. The typical Brandenburg pine forest of the area had been given into the charge of a high official in the Forestry Bureau who took his orders from me. Instead of pines, a woodland of deciduous trees was to be established here. After the model of the Bois de Boulogne, Grunewald was to be provided with hiking paths, rest areas, restaurants, and athletic fields for the capital's millions. The work had already begun. I had tens of thousands of deciduous trees planted, in order to restore the old mixed forest which Frederick the Great had cut for lumber to finance the Silesian War. Of the whole vast project for the reshaping of Berlin, these deciduous trees are all that have remained.

In the course of the work a new urban concept emerged from Hitler's initially pointless plan for a grand avenue. In the light of all this, his original idea seemed relatively insignificant. At least where urban renewal was concerned, I had gone far beyond Hitler's megalomaniacal notions. I imagine that this had rarely happened to him in the course of his life. He went along with all these expansions of the original idea and gave me a free hand, but he could not really work up much enthusiasm for this part of the project. He would look at the plans, but really only glance at them, and after a few minutes would ask with palpable boredom: "Where do you have the plans for the grand avenue?" Then he would revel in visions of ministries, office buildings and showrooms for major German corporations, a new opera house, luxury hotels, and amusement palaces—and I gladly joined in these visions. Nevertheless, I considered these official buildings as subsidiary to the total plan; Hitler did not. His passion for building for eternity left him without a spark of interest in traffic arrangements, residential areas, and parks. He was indifferent to the social dimension.

Hess, on the other hand, was interested only in the residential structures and scarcely took notice of the representational aspect of our plans. At the end of one of his visits he chided me for putting too much emphasis on the latter. I promised him that for every brick used for these ostentatious buildings, I would use one for a residential structure. Hitler was rather annoyed when he heard of this bargain; he spoke of the urgency of his requirements but did not cancel our arrangement.

It has been generally assumed that I was Hitler's chief architect, to whom all others were subordinate. This was not so. The architects for the replanning of Munich and Linz had similar powers bestowed upon them. In the course of time Hitler consulted an ever-growing number of architects for special tasks. Before the war began, there must have been ten or twelve.

When buildings were in question, Hitler repeatedly displayed his ability to grasp a sketch quickly and to combine the floor plan and renderings into a three-dimensional conception. Despite all his government business and although he was often dealing with anywhere from ten to fifteen large buildings in different cities, whenever the drawings were presented to him again—often after an interval of months—he immediately found his bearings and could remember what changes he had asked for. Those who assumed that a request or a suggestion had long since been forgotten quickly learned otherwise.

In these conferences he usually behaved with restraint and civility. He asked for changes amiably and without any note of insult—entirely in contrast to the domineering tone he took toward his political associates. Convinced that the architect should be responsible for his building, he encouraged the architect to do the talking, not the Gauleiter or Reichsleiter who accompanied him. For he did not want any nonprofessional higher authority snarling up the explanations. If the architect's ideas ran counter to his own, Hitler was not stubborn: "Yes, you're right, that's better."

The result was that I too was left with the feeling of creative independence. I frequently had differences of opinion with Hitler, but I cannot recall a single case in which he forced me as the architect to adopt his view. This comparatively equal relationship is the reason why later on, as Minister of Armaments, I assumed greater initiative than the majority of ministers and field marshals.

Hitler reacted obstinately and ungraciously only when he sensed a mute opposition based on antagonistic principles. Thus Professor Bonatz, the teacher of a whole generation of architects, received no more commissions after he had criticized Troost's new buildings on Munich's Königsplatz. Bonatz was in such disfavor that even Todt did not dare consult him for the building of a few bridges on the autobahn. Only my intervening with Frau Troost brought Bonatz back into currency. "Why shouldn't he build bridges?" she remarked to Hitler. "He's very good on technical structures." Her word was weighty enough, and thereafter Bonatz built autobahn bridges.

Hitler declared again and again: "How I wish I had been an architect." And when I responded: "But then I would have no client," he would say: "Oh, you, you would have made your way in any case!" I sometimes ask myself whether Hitler would have forsaken his political career if in the early twenties he had met a wealthy client willing to employ him as architect. But at bottom, I think, his sense of political mission and his passion for architecture were always inseparable. It seems to me that this theory is borne out by the two sketches he made around 1925, when at the age of thirty-six his political career had been virtually wrecked—for certainly it must then have seemed a wild absurdity that he would ever be a political leader who could crown his success with a triumphal arch and a domed hall.

The German Olympic Committee was thrown into a quandary when State Secretary Pfundtner of the Ministry of the Interior showed Hitler its first plans for the rebuilding of the Olympic Stadium. Otto March, the architect, had designed a concrete structure with glass partition walls, similar to the Vienna Stadium. Hitler went to inspect the site and came back in a state of anger and agitation. Having been summoned to discuss some plans with him, I was present when he curtly informed State Secretary Pfundtner to cancel the Olympic Games. They could not take place without his presence, he said, since the Chief of State must open them. But he would never set foot inside a modern glass box like that.

Overnight I made a sketch showing how the steel skeleton already built could be clad in natural stone and have more massive cornices added. The glass partitions were eliminated, and Hitler was content. He saw to the financing of the increased costs; Professor March agreed to the changes, and the Olympic Games were held in Berlin after all—although I was never sure whether Hitler would actually have carried out his threat or whether it was merely a flash of pique, which he often used to get his way.

Hitler also abruptly threatened withdrawal from the Paris World's Fair of 1937, although the invitation had already been accepted and the site for the German pavilion fixed. He strongly disliked all the sketches he was shown. The Ministry of Economics thereupon asked me for a design. The Soviet Russian and German pavilions were to be placed directly opposite one another on the fairgrounds; the French directors of the fair had deliberately arranged this confrontation. While looking over the site in Paris, I by chance stumbled into a room containing the secret sketch of the Soviet pavilion. A sculptured pair of figures thirty-three feet tall, on a high platform, were striding triumphantly toward the German pavilion. I therefore designed a cubic mass, also elevated on stout pillars, which seemed to be checking this onslaught, while from the cornice of my tower an eagle with the swastika in its claws looked down on the Russian sculptures. I received a gold medal for the building; so did my Soviet colleague.

At the dedication dinner for our pavilion I met the French ambassador to Berlin, André François-Poncet. He proposed that I exhibit my works in Paris in exchange for a show of modern French painting in Berlin. French architecture was lagging, he commented, "but in painting you can learn from us." At the next opportunity I told Hitler of this proposal, which might open the way for me to win an international reputation. Hitler passed over the ambassador's unwelcome comment in silence, but for the moment said neither yes nor no. The upshot was that I could never bring up the subject again.

During those days in Paris I saw the Palais de Chaillot and the Palais des Musées d'Art Moderne, as well as the Musée des Travaux Publics, then still being built, which had been designed by the famous avant-gardist August Perret. It surprised me that France also favored neo-classicism for her public buildings. It has often been asserted that this style is characteristic of the architecture of totalitarian states. That is not at all true. Rather, it was characteristic of the era and left its impress upon Washington, London, and Paris as well as Rome, Moscow, and our plans for Berlin.[5]

We had obtained some extra French currency. My wife and I drove by car through France with some friends. Slowly, we toured southward, stopping at castles and cathedrals on the way. We reached Carcassonne and found it highly stirring and romantic, although it was merely one of the most utilitarian fortifications of the Middle Ages, as typical of its time as an atomic shelter is of ours. In the citadel hotel we enjoyed an old French red wine and decided to linger in the region for a few days more. In the evening I was called to the telephone. I had thought myself safe in this remote corner of France from Hitler's adjutants, all the more so since nobody knew our destination.

For reasons of security and control, however, the French police had checked our movements. At any rate, in response to an inquiry from Obersalzberg they were able to say at once where we were. Adjutant Brückner was on the phone: "You're to come to the Fuehrer by tomorrow noon." I objected that it would take me two and a half days to drive back. "A conference has been set for tomorrow afternoon," Brückner replied, "and the Fuehrer insists on your presence." I tried one more feeble protest. "Just a moment . . . . Yes, the Fuehrer knows where you are, but you must be here tomorrow."

I was wretched, angry, and perplexed. Lengthy telephone calls with Hitler's pilot produced the news that the Fuehrer's private plane could not land in France. But a place would be obtained for me on a German cargo plane that was due for a stopover in Marseilles, on a flight from Africa, at six o'clock in the morning. Hitler's special plane would then take me from Stuttgart to Ainring Airport near Berchtesgaden.

That same night we set out on the drive to Marseilles. For a few minutes we looked at the Roman buildings in Arles, which had been the actual goal of our journey, by moonlight. At two o'clock in the morning we reached a hotel in Marseilles. Three hours later I was off to the airport, and in the afternoon I presented myself, as ordered, to Hitler in Obersalzberg. "Oh yes, I'm sorry, Herr Speer, I've postponed the conference. I wanted to have your opinion on a suspension bridge for Hamburg." Dr. Todt had been supposed to show him the design for a mammoth bridge that would surpass San Francisco's Golden Gate Bridge. Since construction was not due to begin until the nineteen-forties, Hitler might easily have let me have another week's vacation.

Another time I had fled to the Zugspitze with my wife when the usual telephone call from the adjutant reached me: "You're to come to the Fuehrer. Dinner tomorrow afternoon in the Osteria." He cut off my objections: "No, it's urgent." In the Osteria, Hitler greeted me with: "Why, how nice that you've come to dine with us. What, you were sent for? I merely asked yesterday: I wonder where Speer is? But you know, it serves you right. What's this about going skiing with all you have to do?"

Von Neurath displayed more backbone. Once when Hitler told his adjutant late one evening: "I'd like to talk to the Foreign Minister," he received the reply: "The Foreign Minister has already gone to bed."— "Tell them he's to be waked when I want to talk to him." Another telephone call; the adjutant returned discomfited: "The Foreign Minister says he will be available in the morning; he's tired now and wants to sleep."

Faced with such resolution, Hitler could only give up, but he was in bad humor for the rest of the evening. Moreover, he could never forget such defiance and took revenge at the first opportunity.

7

Obersalzberg

THERE IS A SPECIAL TRAP FOR EVERY HOLDER OF POWER, WHETHER THE director of a company, the head of a state, or the ruler of a dictatorship. His favor is so desirable to his subordinates that they will sue for it by every means possible. Servility becomes endemic among his entourage, who compete among themselves in their show of devotion. This in turn exercises a sway upon the ruler, who becomes corrupted in his turn.

The key to the quality of the man in power is how he reacts to this situation. I have observed a number of industrialists and military men who knew how to fend off this danger. Where power has been exercised over generations, a kind of hereditary incorruptibility grows up. Only a few individuals among those around Hitler, such as Fritz Todt, withstood the temptation to sycophancy. Hitler himself put up no visible resistance to the evolution of a court.

The special conditions of his style of rule led Hitler, especially after 1937, into increasing isolation. Added to that was his inability to make human contacts. Among his intimates we sometimes spoke of the change which was more and more marked in him. Heinrich Hoffmann had just put out a new edition of his book, *Hitler, wie ihn keiner kennt* (*The Hitler Nobody Knows*). The old edition had to be withdrawn because of a picture showing Hitler amicably together with Roehm, whom he was shortly afterward to kill. Hitler himself selected the new photos. They showed a casual, good-natured private individual in leather shorts, in a rowboat, stretched out on meadows, hiking, surrounded by enthusiastic young people, or in artists' studios. He was always seen relaxed, friendly, and accessible. The book proved to be Hoffmann's greatest success. But it was already out of date by the time it was published. For the genial, relaxed Hitler whom I too had known in the early thirties had become, even to his intimate entourage, a forbidding despot with few human relationships.

In the Ostertal, a remote mountain valley in the Bavarian Alps, I had located a small hunting lodge, big enough to set up drawing boards, which with a bit of crowding could accommodate my family and a few associates. There, in the spring of 1935, we worked away at my plans for Berlin. That was a happy period for my work and for the family. But one day I made a crucial error; I told Hitler about this idyll. His response was: "Why, you can have all that and more near me. I'll put the Bechstein house* at your disposal. There's ample room for your office there in the conservatory." (At the end of May 1937 we moved from the Bechstein house into a studio building which Hitler had Bormann build from my design.) Thus I became the fourth "Obersalzberger," along with Hitler, Goering, and Bormann.

Naturally I was happy to be granted so obvious a distinction and be admitted to the most intimate circle. But I soon came to realize that the change had not been exactly advantageous. From the solitary mountain valley we passed into an area guarded by a high barbed-wire fence which could be entered only after identity checks at two gates. It was reminiscent of an open-air enclosure for wild animals. Curiosity-seekers were always trying to catch a glimpse of some of the prominent inhabitants of the mountain.

Bormann was the real master of Obersalzberg. He forcibly bought up centuries-old farms and had the buildings torn down. The same was done to the numerous votive chapels, despite the objections of the parishes. He also confiscated state forests, until the private area reached from the top of the mountain, which was some sixty-four hundred feet high, to the valley at an altitude of two thousand feet, and embraced an area of 2.7 square miles. The fence around the inner area was almost two miles long, around the outer area nine miles long.

With total insensitivity to the natural surroundings, Bormann laid out a network of roads through this magnificent landscape. He turned forest paths, hitherto carpeted by pine needles and penetrated by roots, into paved promenades. A barracks, a vast garage building, a hotel for Hitler's guests, a new manor house, a complex for the constantly growing number of employees, sprang up as rapidly as in a suddenly fashionable resort. Dormitory barracks for hundreds of construction workers clung

* A villa near Hitler's residence at Obersalzberg, formerly owned by his friends, the Bechsteins.

to the slopes; trucks loaded with building materials rumbled along the roads. At night the various building sites glowed with light, for work went on in two shifts, and occasionally detonations thundered through the valley.

On the top of Hitler's private mountain Bormann erected a house that was luxuriously furnished in a somewhat rusticated ocean-liner style. You reached it by a precipitous road that ended in an elevator blasted into the rock. Bormann squandered between twenty and thirty million marks merely on the access route to this eyrie, which Hitler visited only a few times. Cynics in Hitler's entourage remarked: "Bormann has created a gold-rush town atmosphere. Only he doesn't find any, he spends it." Hitler regretted the hubbub but commented: "It's Bormann's doing; I don't want to interfere." Another time he said: "When it's all finished I'll look for a quiet valley and build another small wooden house there like the first." It never was finished. Bormann conceived a never-ending succession of new roads and buildings, and when the war finally broke out he began building underground quarters for Hitler and his entourage.

The gigantic installations on the mountain were, in spite of Hitler's occasional sarcasms about the tremendous effort and expenditure, characteristic of the change in the Fuehrer's style of life and also indicative of his tendency to withdraw more and more from the wider world around him. Fear of assassination cannot explain it, for almost daily he allowed thousands of people to enter the protected area to pay homage to him. His entourage considered such behavior more dangerous than spontaneous strolls on public forest paths.

In the summer of 1935 Hitler had decided to enlarge his modest country house into one more suitable for his public duties, to be known as the Berghof. He paid for the project out of his own money, but that was nothing but a gesture, since Bormann drew upon other sources for the subsidiary buildings, sums disproportionately greater than the amount Hitler himself provided.

Hitler did not just sketch the plans for the Berghof. He borrowed drawing board, T-square, and other implements from me to draw the ground plan, renderings, and cross sections of his building to scale, refusing any help with the matter. There were only two other designs on which Hitler expended the personal care that he applied to his Obersalzberg house: that of the new Reich war flag and his own standard as Chief of State.

Most architects will put a wide variety of ideas down on paper, and see which lends itself best to further development. It was characteristic of Hitler that he regarded his first inspiration as intuitively right and drew it with little hesitation. Afterward, he introduced only small retouchings to eliminate glaring defects.

The old house was preserved within the new one, whose living room joined the old through a large opening. The resultant ground plan was most impractical for the reception of official visitors. Their staffs had to be content with an unprepossessing entry hall which also led to the toilets, stairwell, and the large dining room.

During official conferences Hitler's private guests were banished to the upper floor. But since the stairs led down to the entry hall, private visitors had to be cleared by a guard before being allowed to go through the room and leave the house for a walk.

A huge picture window in the living room, famous for its size and the fact that it could be lowered, was Hitler's pride. It offered a view of the Untersberg, Berchtesgaden, and Salzburg. However, Hitler had been inspired to situate his garage underneath this window; when the wind was unfavorable, a strong smell of gasoline penetrated into the living room. All in all, this was a ground plan that would have been graded D by any professor at an institute of technology. On the other hand, these very clumsinesses gave the Berghof a strongly personal note. The place was still geared to the simple activities of a former weekend cottage, merely expanded to vast proportions.

All the cost estimates were exceeded by far, and Hitler was somewhat embarrassed:

> I've completely used up the income from my book, although Amann's given me a further advance of several hundred thousand. Even so there's not enough money, so Bormann has told me today. The publishers are after me to release my second book, the 1928 one, for publication.* But I'm certainly glad this volume hasn't been published. What political complications it would make for me at the moment. On the other hand it would relieve me of all financial pressures at one stroke. Amann promised me a million just as an advance, and beyond that it would bring in millions. Perhaps later, when I'm further along. Now it's impossible.

There he sat, a voluntary prisoner with his view of the Untersberg where, legend has it, the Emperor Charlemagne still sleeps, but will one day arise to restore the past glory of the German Empire. Hitler naturally appropriated this legend for himself: "You see the Untersberg over there. It is no accident that I have my residence opposite it."

Bormann was linked to Hitler not only by his vast building projects on the Obersalzberg. He contrived at the same time to take over administration of Hitler's personal finances. Not only were Hitler's adjutants tied to the purse strings that Bormann controlled, but even Hitler's mistress was dependent upon him, as she candidly confessed to me. Hitler left it to Bormann to attend to her modest needs.

* Hitler's so-called second book was not published until 1961.

Hitler praised Bormann's financial skill. Once I heard him relate how Bormann had performed a significant service for the party during the difficult year of 1932 by introducing compulsory accident insurance for all party members. The income from this insurance fund considerably exceeded the expenditures, Hitler said, and the party was able to use the surplus for other purposes. Bormann also did his bit to eliminate Hitler's financial anxieties permanently after 1933. He found two sources of ample funds. Together with Hitler's personal photographer Hoffmann and Hoffmann's friend Ohnesorge, the Minister of Posts, he decided that Hitler had rights to the reproduction of his picture on postage stamps and was therefore entitled to payments. The percentage royalty was infinitesimal, but since the Fuehrer's head appeared on all stamps, millions flowed into the privy purse administered by Bormann.

Bormann developed another source by founding the Adolf Hitler Endowment Fund of German Industry. Entrepreneurs who were profiting by the economic boom were bluntly requested to show their appreciation by voluntary contributions to the Fuehrer. Since other party bigwigs had had the same notion, Bormann obtained a decree assuring him a monopoly on such contributions. But he was clever enough to return a part of the donations to various party leaders "in behalf of the Fuehrer." Almost all of the top party functionaries received gifts from this fund. This power to set the living standards of the Gauleiters and Reichsleiters did not attract attention; but fundamentally it conferred on Bormann more power than many other positions within the hierarchy.

With his typical perseverance, from 1934 on Bormann followed the simple principle of always remaining in closest proximity to the source of all grace and favor. He accompanied Hitler to the Berghof and on trips, and in the Chancellery never left his side until Hitler went to bed in the early morning hours. In this way Bormann became Hitler's hardworking, reliable, and ultimately indispensable secretary. He pretended to be obliging to everyone, and almost everyone availed himself of Bormann's services—all the more so since he obviously served Hitler with utter selflessness. Even his immediate superior, Rudolf Hess, found it convenient to have Bormann close to Hitler at all times.

The powerful men under Hitler were already jealously watching one another like so many pretenders to the throne. Quite early there were struggles for position among Goebbels, Goering, Rosenberg, Ley, Himmler, Ribbentrop, and Hess. Only Roehm had been left by the wayside, and before long Hess was to lose all his influence. But none of them recognized a threat in the shape of trusty Bormann. He had succeeded in representing himself as insignificant while imperceptibly building up his bastions. Even among so many ruthless men, he stood out by his brutality and coarseness. He had no culture, which might have put some restraints on him, and in every case he carried out whatever Hitler had ordered or what he himself had gathered from Hitler's hints. A sub-ordinate by nature, he treated his own subordinates as if he were dealing with cows and oxen. He was a peasant.

I avoided Bormann; from the beginning we could not abide each other. We treated each other with formal correctness, as the private atmosphere at Obersalzberg required. With the exception of my own studio, I never designed a building for him to execute.

Hitler's stays on "the mountain" provided him, as he often stressed, with the inner calm and assurance for his surprising decisions. He also composed his most important speeches there, and it is worth noting how he wrote them. Thus, before the Nuremberg Party Rally he regularly retreated to Obersalzberg for several weeks in order to work out his long speeches on basic principles. As the deadline drew nearer, his adjutants kept urging him to begin the dictation and kept everyone and everything away from him, even architectural plans and visitors, so that he would not be distracted from the work. But Hitler postponed the task from week to week, then from day to day, and would reluctantly set to work on it only under extreme time pressure. By then it was usually too late to finish all the speeches, and during the Rally, Hitler usually had to stay up nights to make up for the time he had squandered at Obersalzberg.

I had the impression that he needed this pressure in order to be able to work, that in the bohemian manner of the artist he despised discipline and could not or would not force himself to work regularly. He let the content of his speeches or his thoughts ripen during these weeks of apparent idling until all that had accumulated poured out like a stream bursting its bounds upon followers or negotiators.

Our move from our secluded valley to the bustle of Obersalzberg was ruinous to my work. The very sameness of the day's routine was tiring, the unchanging group around Hitler—the same coterie who regularly met in Munich and in Berlin—was boring. The only difference from Berlin and Munich was that wives were present on the mountain, and also two or three women secretaries and Eva Braun.

Hitler usually appeared in the lower rooms late in the morning, around eleven o'clock. He then went through the press summaries, received several reports from Bormann, and made his first decisions. The day actually began with a prolonged afternoon dinner. The guests assembled in the anteroom. Hitler chose the lady he would take in to dinner, while Bormann, from about 1938 on, had the privilege of escorting Eva Braun, to the table; she usually sat on Hitler's left. That in itself was proof of Bormann's dominant position in the court. The dining room was a mixture of artistic rusticity and urban elegance of a sort which was often characteristic of country houses of the wealthy. The walls and ceilings were paneled in pale larchwood, the chairs covered with bright red morocco leather. The china was a simple white; the silver bore Hitler's monogram and was the same as that used in Berlin. Hitler always took pleasure in its restrained floral decoration. The food was simple and substantial: soup, a meat course, dessert, with either Fachinger mineral water or wine. The waiters, in white vests and black trousers, were members of the SS bodyguard. Some twenty persons sat at the long table, but because of its length no general conversation could arise. Hitler sat in the middle, facing the window. He talked with the person opposite him, who was different every day, or with the ladies to either side of him.

Shortly after dinner the walk to the teahouse began. The width of the path left room for only two abreast, so that the file resembled a procession. Two security men walked at the head. Then came Hitler with one other person, with whom he conversed, followed in any order by the dinner company, with more guards bringing up the rear. Hitler's two police dogs roamed about the area and ignored his commands— the only oppositionists at his court. To Bormann's vexation, Hitler was addicted to this particular walk, which took about half an hour, and disdained using the mile-long paved forest roads.

The teahouse had been built at one of Hitler's favorite lookout points above the Berchtesgaden valley. The company always marveled at the panorama in the same phrases. Hitler always agreed in much the same language. The teahouse itself consisted of a round room about twenty-five feet in diameter, pleasing in its proportions, with a row of small-paned windows and a fireplace along the interior wall. The company sat in easy chairs around the round table, with Eva Braun and one of the other ladies again at Hitler's side. Those who did not find seats went into a small adjoining room. According to taste, one had tea, coffee, or chocolate, and various types of cake and cookies, followed by liqueurs. Here, at the coffee table, Hitler was particularly fond of drifting into endless monologues. The subjects were mostly familiar to the company, who therefore listened absently, though pretending attention. Occasionally Hitler himself fell asleep over one of his monologues. The company then continued chatting in whispers, hoping that he would awaken in time for the evening meal. It was all very familial.

After about two hours the teatime ended, generally around six. Hitler stood up, and the procession moved on to the parking area, about twenty minutes' walk, where a column of cars waited. After returning to the Berghof, Hitler usually withdrew to the upper rooms, while the retinue scattered. Bormann frequently disappeared into the room of one of the younger stenographers, which elicited spiteful remarks from Eva Braun.

Two hours later the company met again for supper, with repetition

of the afternoon ritual. Afterward, Hitler went into the salon, again followed by the still unchanged company.

The Troost studio had furnished the salon sparsely, but with oversize furniture: a sideboard over ten feet high and eighteen feet long
which housed phonograph records along with various certificates of
honorary citizenship awarded to Hitler; a monumental classicist china
closet; a massive clock crowned by a fierce bronze eagle. In front of the
large picture window stood a table twenty feet long, which Hitler used
for signing documents or, later, for studying military maps. There were
two sitting areas: one a sunken nook at the back of the room, with the
red upholstered chairs grouped around a fireplace; the other, near the
window, dominated by a round table whose fine veneer was protected by
a glass top. Beyond this sitting area was the movie projection cabinet, its
openings concealed by a tapestry. Along the opposite wall stood a massive chest containing built-in speakers, and adorned by a large bronze
bust of Richard Wagner by Arno Breker. Above this hung another tapestry which concealed the movie screen. Large oil paintings covered the
walls: a lady with exposed bosom ascribed to Bordone, a pupil of Titian; a
picturesque reclining nude said to be by Titian himself; Feuerbach's
Nana in a very handsome frame; an early landscape by Spitzweg; a landscape with Roman ruins by Pannini; and, surprisingly, a kind of altar
painting by Eduard von Steinle, one of the Nazarene group, representing
King Henry, founder of cities. But there was no Grützner. Hitler occasionally let it be known that he had paid for these paintings out of his
own income.

We found places on the sofas or in one of the easy chairs in either of
the sitting areas; the two tapestries were raised; and the second part of
the evening began with a movie, as was also the custom when Hitler was
in Berlin. Afterward the company gathered around the huge fireplace—
some six or eight persons lined up in a row on the excessively long and
uncomfortably low sofa, while Hitler, once more flanked by Eva Braun
and one of the ladies, ensconced himself in one of the soft chairs. Because
of the inept arrangement of the furniture the company was so scattered
that no common conversation could arise. Everyone talked in low voices
with his neighbor. Hitler murmured trivialities with the two women at his
side, or whispered with Eva Braun; sometimes he held her hand. But
often he fell silent or stared broodingly into the fire. Then the guests fell
silent also, in order not to disturb him in important thoughts.

Occasionally the movies were discussed, Hitler commenting mainly
on the female actors and Eva Braun on the males. No one took the trouble
to raise the conversation above the level of trivialities by, for example,
remarking on any of the new trends in directing. Of course the choice of
films scarcely allowed for any other approach, for they were all standard
products of the entertainment industry. Such experiments of the period

as Curt Ortel's Michelangelo film were never shown, at least not when I was there. Sometimes Bormann used the occasion to take some swipes at Goebbels, who was responsible for German film production. Thus, he would remark that Goebbels had made all kinds of trouble for the movie based on Kleist's *The Broken Jug* because he thought Emil Jannings's portrayal of the lame village magistrate, Adam, was a caricature of himself. Hitler gleefully watched the film, which had been withdrawn from circulation, and gave orders that it be shown again in the largest Berlin movie theater. But—and this is typical of Hitler's sometimes amazing lack of authority—for a long time this simply was not done. Bormann, however, kept bringing up the matter until Hitler showed serious irritation and let Goebbels know that his orders had better be obeyed.

Later, during the war, Hitler gave up the evening showings, saying that he wanted to renounce his favorite entertainment "out of sympathy for the privations of the soldiers." Instead records were played. But although the record collection was excellent, Hitler always preferred the same music. Neither baroque nor classical music, neither chamber music nor symphonies, interested him. Before long the order of the records became virtually fixed. First he wanted a few bravura selections from Wagnerian operas, to be followed promptly with operettas. That remained the pattern. Hitler made a point of trying to guess the names of the sopranos and was pleased when he guessed right, as he frequently did.

To animate these rather barren evenings, sparkling wine was handed around and, after the occupation of France, confiscated champagne of a cheap brand; Goering and his air marshals had appropriated the best brands. From one o'clock on some members of the company, in spite of all their efforts to control themselves, could no longer repress their yawns. But the social occasion dragged on in monotonous, wearing emptiness for another hour or more, until at last Eva Braun had a few words with Hitler and was permitted to go upstairs. Hitler would stand up about a quarter of an hour later, to bid his company goodnight. Those who remained, liberated, often followed those numbing hours with a gay party over champagne and cognac.

In the early hours of the morning we went home dead tired, exhausted from doing nothing. After a few days of this I was seized by what I called at the time "the mountain disease." That is, I felt exhausted and vacant from the constant waste of time. Only when Hitler's idleness was interrupted by conferences was I free to put myself and my associates to work on designs. As a favored permanent guest and inhabitant of Obersalzberg I could not withdraw from these evenings, agonizing as they were, without appearing impolite. Dr. Otto Dietrich, the press chief, ventured to slip away to performances at the Salzburg Festival a few times, but in doing so he incurred Hitler's anger. During Hitler's longer stays at Obersalzberg the only way to save oneself was to flee to Berlin.

Sometimes familiars of Hitler's old Munich or Berlin circles, such as Goebbels, Franz Schwarz, the party treasurer, or Hermann Esser, State Secretary for Tourism in the Ministry of Propaganda, put in an appearance. But this happened rarely and then only for a day or two. Even Hess, who should have had every reason to check the activities of his deputy, Bormann, turned up only two or three times, at least while I was there. These close associates, who could frequently be met at afternoon dinners in the Chancellery, obviously avoided Obersalzberg. Their absence was particularly noticeable because Hitler showed considerable pleasure when they turned up and frequently asked them to come often and to stay longer. But they had meanwhile become the centers of their own circles, and it was therefore rather uncomfortable for them to submit to Hitler's altogether different routine and to his manner, which in spite of all his charm was painfully self-assertive.

Eva Braun was allowed to be present during visits from old party associates. She was banished as soon as other dignitaries of the Reich, such as cabinet ministers, appeared at table. Even when Goering and his wife came, Eva Braun had to stay in her room. Hitler obviously regarded her as socially acceptable only within strict limits. Sometimes I kept her company in her exile, a room next to Hitler's bedroom. She was so intimidated that she did not dare leave the house for a walk. "I might meet the Goerings in the hall."

In general Hitler showed little consideration for her feelings. He would enlarge on his attitude toward women as though she were not present: "A highly intelligent man should take a primitive and stupid woman. Imagine if on top of everything else I had a woman who interfered with my work! In my leisure time I want to have peace. . . . I could never marry. Think of the problems if I had children! In the end they would try to make my son my successor. Besides, the chances are slim for someone like me to have a capable son. That is almost always how it goes in such cases. Consider Goethe's son—a completely worthless person! . . . Lots of women are attracted to me because I am unmarried. That was especially useful during our days of struggle. It's the same as with a movie actor; when he marries he loses a certain something for the women who adore him. Then he is no longer their idol as he was before."

Hitler believed that he had a powerful sexual appeal to women. But he was also extremely wary about this; he never knew, he used to say, whether a woman preferred him as the Chancellor or as Adolf Hitler, and as he often remarked ungallantly, he certainly did not want witty and intelligent women about him. In making such remarks he was apparently not aware of how offensive they must have been to the ladies present. On the other hand Hitler could sometimes behave like a good head of a family. Once, when Eva Braun was skiing and came to tea rather late, he looked uneasy, kept glancing nervously at the clock, and was plainly worried that she might have had an accident.

Eva Braun came of a family of modest circumstances. Her father was a schoolteacher. I never met her parents; they never appeared and continued to live as befitted their station until the end. Eva Braun, too, remained simple; she dressed quietly and wore the inexpensive jewelry* that Hitler gave her for Christmas or her birthdays: usually semiprecious stones worth a few hundred marks at most and actually insulting in their modesty. Bormann would present a selection, and Hitler would choose these trinkets with what seemed to me petit-bourgeois taste.

Eva Braun had no interest in politics. She scarcely ever attempted to influence Hitler. With a good eye for the facts of everyday life, however, she did sometimes make remarks about minor abuses in conditions in Munich. Bormann did not like that, since in such cases he was instantly called to account. She was sports-loving, a good skier with plenty of endurance with whom my wife and I frequently undertook mountain tours outside the enclosed area. Once Hitler actually gave her a week's vacation —when he himself was not at Obersalzberg, of course. She went to Zürs with us for a few days. There, unrecognized, she danced with great passion into the wee hours of the morning with young army officers. She was very far from being a modern Madame Pompadour; for the historian she is interesting only insofar as she set off some of Hitler's traits.

Out of sympathy for her predicament I soon began to feel a liking for this unhappy woman, who was so deeply attached to Hitler. In addition, we were linked by our common dislike for Bormann, although at that time what we resented most was the coarseness with which he was raping the beauty of nature at Obersalzberg and betraying his wife. When I heard at the Nuremberg Trial that Hitler had married Eva Braun in the last day and a half of his life, I felt glad for her—even though I could sense even in this act the cynicism with which Hitler had treated her and probably women in general.

I have often wondered whether Hitler felt anything like affection for children. He certainly made an effort when he met them, whether they were the children of acquaintances or unknown to him. He even tried to deal with them in a paternally friendly fashion, but never managed to be very convincing about it. He never found the proper easy manner of treating them; after a few benign words he would soon turn to others. On the whole he regarded children as representatives of the next

---

* N. E. Gun's *Eva Braun: Hitler's Mistress* (Meredith, 1968) gives a list of valuable jewelry. So far as I remember she did not wear anything of the sort, nor does any appear in the many photographs of her. Perhaps the list refers to the objects of value which Hitler saw to it that she received through Bormann during the war.

generation and therefore took more pleasure in their appearance (blond, blue-eyed), their stature (strong, healthy), or their intelligence (brisk, aggressive) than in their nature as children. His personality had no effect whatsoever upon my own children.

What remains in my memory of social life at Obersalzberg is a curious vacuity. Fortunately, during my first years of imprisonment, while my recollections were still fresh, I noted down a few scraps of conversations which I can now regard as reasonably authentic.

In those hundreds of teatimes questions of fashion, of raising dogs, of the theater and movies, of operettas and their stars were discussed, along with endless trivialities about the family lives of others. Hitler scarcely ever said anything about the Jews, about his domestic opponents, let alone about the necessity for setting up concentration camps. Perhaps such topics were omitted less out of deliberate intention than because they would have been out of place amidst the prevailing banality. On the other hand, Hitler made fun of his closest associates with striking frequency. It is no accident that these particular remarks have remained in my mind, for after all they involved persons who were officially immune from all criticism. Hitler's private circle was not held to these rules, and in any case Hitler considered it pointless to attempt to keep women from gossiping. Was it self-aggrandizement when he spoke disparagingly of everything and everyone? Or did such talk spring from his general contempt for all persons and events?

Thus Hitler had little sympathy with Himmler in his mythologizing of the SS.

What nonsense! Here we have at last reached an age that has left all mysticism behind it, and now he wants to start that all over again. We might just as well have stayed with the church. At least it had tradition. To think that I may some day be turned into an SS saint! Can you imagine it? I would turn over in my grave. . . .

Himmler has made another speech calling Charlemagne the "butcher of the Saxons." Killing all those Saxons was not a historical crime, as Himmler thinks. Charlemagne did a good thing in subjugating Widukind and killing the Saxons out of hand. He thereby made possible the empire of the Franks and the entry of Western culture into what is now Germany.

Himmler had scientists undertake excavations of prehistoric sites. Hitler commented:

Why do we call the whole world's attention to the fact that we have no past? It isn't enough that the Romans were erecting great buildings when our forefathers were still living in mud huts; now Himmler is starting to dig up these villages of mud huts and enthusing over every potsherd and stone axe he finds. All we prove by that is that we were still throwing stone hatchets and crouching around open fires when Greece and Rome had already reached the highest stage of culture. We really should do our best to keep quiet about this past. Instead Himmler makes a great fuss about it all. The present-day Romans must be having a laugh at these revelations.

Amid his political associates in Berlin, Hitler made harsh pronouncements against the church, but in the presence of the women he adopted a milder tone—one of the instances where he adapted his remarks to his surroundings.

"The church is certainly necessary for the people. It is a strong and conservative element," he might say at one time or another in this private circle. However, he conceived of the church as an instrument that could be useful to him. "If only Reibi [this was his nickname for Reich Bishop Ludwig Müller] had some kind of stature. But why do they appoint a nobody of an army chaplain? I'd be glad to give him my full support. Think of all he could do with that. Through me the Evangelical [Protestant] Church could become the established church, as in England."

Even after 1942 Hitler went on maintaining that he regarded the church as indispensable in political life. He would be happy, he said in one of those teatime talks at Obersalzberg, if someday a prominent churchman turned up who was suited to lead one of the churches—or if possible both the Catholic and Protestant churches reunited. He still regretted that Reich Bishop Müller was not the right man to carry out his far-reaching plans. But he sharply condemned the campaign against the church, calling it a crime against the future of the nation. For it was impossible, he said, to replace the church by any "party ideology." Undoubtedly, he continued, the church would learn to adapt to the political goals of National Socialism in the long run, as it had always adapted in the course of history. A new party religion would only bring about a relapse into the mysticism of the Middle Ages. The growing SS myth showed that clearly enough, as did Rosenberg's unreadable *Myth of the Twentieth Century*.

If in the course of such a monologue Hitler had pronounced a more negative judgment upon the church, Bormann would undoubtedly have taken from his jacket pocket one of the white cards he always carried with him. For he noted down all Hitler's remarks that seemed to him important; and there was hardly anything he wrote down more eagerly than deprecating comments on the church. At the time I assumed that he was gathering material for a biography of Hitler.

Around 1937, when Hitler heard that at the instigation of the party and the SS vast numbers of his followers had left the church because it was obstinately opposing his plans, he nevertheless ordered his chief associates, above all Goering and Goebbels, to remain members of the church. He too would remain a member of the Catholic Church, he said, although he had no real attachment to it. And in fact he remained in the church until his suicide.

Hitler had been much impressed by a scrap of history he had learned from a delegation of distinguished Arabs. When the Mohammedans attempted to penetrate beyond France into Central Europe during the eighth century, his visitors had told him, they had been driven back at the Battle of Tours. Had the Arabs won this battle, the world would be Mohammedan today. For theirs was a religion that believed in spreading the faith by the sword and subjugating all nations to that faith. The Germanic peoples would have become heirs to that religion. Such a creed was perfectly suited to the Germanic temperament. Hitler said that the conquering Arabs, because of their racial inferiority, would in the long run have been unable to contend with the harsher climate and conditions of the country. They could not have kept down the more vigorous natives, so that ultimately not Arabs but Islamized Germans could have stood at the head of this Mohammedan Empire.

Hitler usually concluded this historical speculation by remarking: "You see, it's been our misfortune to have the wrong religion. Why didn't we have the religion of the Japanese, who regard sacrifice for the Fatherland as the highest good? The Mohammedan religion too would have been much more compatible to us than Christianity. Why did it have to be Christianity with its meekness and flabbiness?" It is remarkable that even before the war he sometimes went on: "Today the Siberians, the White Russians, and the people of the steppes live extremely healthy lives. For that reason they are better equipped for development and in the long run biologically superior to the Germans." This was an idea he was destined to repeat in far more drastic tones during the last months of the war.

Rosenberg sold his seven-hundred page *Myth of the Twentieth Century* in editions of hundreds of thousands. The public regarded the book as the standard text for party ideology, but Hitler in those teatime conversations bluntly called it "stuff nobody can understand," written by "a narrow-minded Baltic German who thinks in horribly complicated terms." He expressed wonderment that such a book could ever have attained such sales: "A relapse into medieval notions!" I wondered if such private remarks were carried back to Rosenberg.

Hitler believed that the culture of the Greeks had reached the peak of perfection in every field. Their view of life, he said, as expressed in their architecture, had been "fresh and healthy." One day a photograph of a beautiful woman swimmer stirred him to enthusiastic reflections: "What splendid bodies you can see today. It is only in our century that young people have once again approached Hellenistic ideals through sports.

How the body was neglected in earlier centuries. In this respect our times differ from all previous cultural epochs since antiquity." He personally, however, was averse to any kind of sports. Moreover, he never mentioned having practiced any sport at all as a young man.

By the Greeks he meant the Dorians. Naturally his view was affected by the theory, fostered by the scientists of his period, that the Dorian tribe which migrated into Greece from the north had been of Germanic origin and that, therefore, its culture had not belonged to the Mediterranean world.

Goering's passion for hunting was one of his favorite topics.

How can a person be excited about such a thing. Killing animals, if it must be done, is the butcher's business. But to spend a great deal of money on it in addition. . . . I understand, of course, that there must be professional hunters to shoot sick animals. If only there were still some danger connected with hunting, as in the days when men used spears for killing game. But today, when anybody with a fat belly can safely shoot the animal down from a distance. . . . Hunting and horse racing are the last remnants of a dead feudal world.

Hitler also took delight in having Ambassador Hewel, Ribbentrop's liaison man, transmit the content of telephone conversations with the Foreign Minister. He would even coach Hewel in ways to disconcert or confuse his superior. Sometimes he stood right beside Hewel, who would hold his hand over the mouthpiece of the telephone and repeat what Ribbentrop was saying, while Hitler whispered what to answer. Usually these were sarcastic remarks intended to fan the nervous Foreign Minister's suspicions that unauthorized persons might be influencing Hitler on questions of foreign policy, thus infringing on his domain.

After dramatic negotiations Hitler was apt to deride his opposites. Once he described Schuschnigg's visit to Obersalzberg on February 12, 1938. By a pretended fit of passion he had made the Austrian Chancellor realize the gravity of the situation, he said, and finally forced him to yield. Many of those hysterical scenes that have been reported were probably carefully staged. In general, self-control was one of Hitler's most striking characteristics. In those early days he lost control of himself only a very few times, at least in my presence.

Some time around 1936 Schacht had come to the salon of the Berghof to report. We guests were seated on the adjacent terrace and the large window of the salon was wide open. Hitler was shouting at his Finance Minister, evidently in extreme excitement. We heard Schacht replying firmly in a loud voice. The dialogue grew increasingly heated on both sides and then ceased abruptly. Furious, Hitler came out on the terrace and ranted on about this disobliging, limited minister who was holding up the rearmament program. He had another such fit of rage at Pastor Niemöller in 1937. Niemöller had once again delivered a rebellious sermon in Dahlem; at the same time transcripts of his tapped telephone conversations were presented to Hitler. In a bellow Hitler ordered Niemöller to be put in a concentration camp and, since he had proved himself incorrigible, kept there for life.

Another incident refers back to his early youth. On a trip from Budweis to Krems in 1942 I noticed a large plaque on a house in the village of Spital, close to the Czech border. In this house, according to the plaque, "the Fuehrer lived in his youth." It was a handsome house in a prosperous village. I mentioned this to Hitler. He instantly flew into a rage and shouted for Bormann, who hurried in much alarmed. Hitler snarled at him: How many times had he said that this village must never be mentioned. But that idiot of a Gauleiter had gone and put up a plaque there. It must be removed at once. At the time I could not explain his excitement, since he was usually pleased when Bormann told him about the refurbishing of other sites connected with his youth around Linz and Braunau. Apparently he had some motive for erasing this part of his youth. Today, of course, these chapters of family history lost in the mists of this Austrian forest region are well known.*

Sometimes Hitler sketched one of the towers of the historic fortifications of Linz. "Here was my favorite playground. I was a poor pupil in school, but I was the leader of our pranks. Someday I am going to have this tower made into a large youth hostel, in memory of those days." He would also frequently speak of the first important political impressions of his youth. Almost all of his fellow pupils in Linz, he said, had distinctly felt that the immigration of the Czechs into German Austria should be stopped. This had made him conscious of the problem of nationalities for the first time. But then, in Vienna, he said, the danger of Judaism had abruptly dawned on him. Many of the workers with whom he was thrown together had been intensely anti-Semitic. In one respect, however, he had not agreed with the construction workers: "I rejected their Social Democratic views. Moreover, I never joined a union. This attitude brought me into my first political difficulties." Perhaps this was one of the reasons he did not have good memories of Vienna—altogether in contrast to his time in Munich before the war. For he would go on and on in praise of Munich and—with surprising frequency—in praise of the good sausages to be had in its butcher shops.

He spoke with unqualified respect about the Bishop of Linz in his early days, who in the face of many obstacles insisted on the unusual proportions of the cathedral he was building in Linz. The bishop had had

* The reference is to the illegitimacy of Hitler's father, Alois Schicklgruber.— *Translators' note.*

difficulties with the Austrian government, Hitler said, because he wanted to surpass St. Stephan's Cathedral and the government did not wish to see Vienna outstripped.[1] Such remarks were usually followed by comments on the way the Austrian central government had crushed all independent cultural impulses on the part of cities like Graz, Linz, or Innsbruck. Hitler could say these things apparently without being aware that he was imposing the same kind of forcible regimentation upon whole countries. Now that he was giving the orders, he said, he would help his native city win its proper place. His program for the transformation of Linz into a "metropolis" envisioned a number of impressive public buildings on both sides of the Danube. A suspension bridge was to connect the two banks. The apex of his plan was a large Gau House (District Headquarters) for the National Socialist Party, with a huge meeting hall and a bell tower. There would be a crypt in this tower for his own burial place. Other impressive monuments along the shore were to be a town hall, a large theater, a military headquarters, a stadium, a picture gallery, a library, a museum of armaments, and an exhibition building, as well as a monument celebrating the liberation of Austria in 1938 and another glorifying Anton Bruckner.* The design for the picture gallery and the stadium was to be assigned to me. The stadium would be situated on a hill overlooking the city. Hitler's residence for his old age would be located nearby, also on a height.

Hitler sometimes went into raptures over the shorelines in Budapest which had grown up on both sides of the Danube in the course of centuries. It was his ambition to transform Linz into a German Budapest. Vienna was oriented all wrong, he would comment in this connection, since it merely turned its back to the Danube. The planners had neglected to incorporate the river in their design. Thanks to what he would be doing with the river in Linz, the city might some day rival Vienna. No doubt he was not altogether serious in making such remarks; he would be tempted into them by his dislike for Vienna, which would spontaneously break out from time to time. But there were many other times when he would exclaim over the brilliant stroke of city planning accomplished in Vienna by the use of the former fortifications.

Before the war Hitler was already talking about the time when, his political goals accomplished, he would withdraw from the affairs of state and finish out his life in Linz. When this time came, he would say, he would no longer play any political part at all; for only if he withdrew completely could his successor gain authority. He would not interfere in any way. People would turn to his successor quickly enough once it became evident that power was now in those hands. Then he himself would be soon forgotten. Everyone would forsake him. Playing with this idea,

---

* Hitler himself had done sketches for all these structures.

with a good measure of self-pity, he continued: "Perhaps one of my former associates will visit me occasionally. But I don't count on it. Aside from Fräulein Braun, I'll take no one with me. Fräulein Braun and my dog. I'll be lonely. For why should anyone voluntarily stay with me for any length of time? Nobody will take notice of me any more. They'll all go running after my successor. Perhaps once a year they'll show up for my birthday." Naturally everyone at the table protested and assured him that they would remain faithful and always stay by him. Whatever Hitler's motives may have been for these allusions to an early retirement from politics, he at any rate seemed to assume at such times that the source of his authority was not the magnetism of his personality but his position of power.

The nimbus that surrounded Hitler for those of his collaborators who did not have any intimate association with him was incomparably greater than for his immediate entourage. Members of the "retinue" did not speak respectfully of the "Fuehrer," but of the "Chief." They were sparing in their use of *"Heil Hitler"* and greeted one another with an ordinary *"Guten Tag."* They even openly made fun of Hitler, without his taking offense. Thus, his standard phrase, "There are two possibilities," would be used by one of his secretaries, Fräulein Schröder, in his presence, often in the most banal of contexts. She would say: "There are two possibilities. Either it is going to rain or it is not going to rain." Eva Braun in the presence of his table companions might pertly call Hitler's attention to the fact that his tie did not go with his suit, and occasionally she gaily referred to herself as "Mother of the Country."

Once, when we were seated at the round table in the teahouse, Hitler began staring at me. Instead of dropping my eyes, I took it as a challenge. Who knows what primitive instincts are involved in such staring duels. I had had others, and always used to win them, but this time I had to muster almost inhuman strength, seemingly forever, not to yield to the ever-mounting urge to look away—until Hitler suddenly closed his eyes and shortly afterward turned to the woman at his side.

Sometimes I asked myself: Why can't I call Hitler my friend? What is missing? I spent endless time with him, was almost at home in his private circle and, moreover, his foremost associate in his favorite field, architecture.

Everything was missing. Never in my life have I met a person who so seldom revealed his feelings, and if he did so, instantly locked them away again. During my time in Spandau I talked with Hess about this peculiarity of Hitler's. Both of us agreed that there had been moments when we felt we had come close to him. But we were invariably disillusioned. If either of us ventured a slightly more personal tone, Hitler promptly put up an unbreakable wall.

Hess did think there had been one person with whom Hitler had

had a closer bond: Dietrich Eckart. But as we talked about it, we decided that the relationship had been, on Hitler's side, more a matter of admiration for the older man, who was regarded chiefly in anti-Semitic circles as a leading writer, than a friendship. When Eckart died in 1923 there remained four men with whom Hitler used the *Du* of close friendship: Hermann Esser, Christian Weber, Julius Streicher, and Ernst Roehm.*
In Esser's case he found a pretext after 1933 to reintroduce the formal *Sie;* Weber he avoided; Streicher he treated impersonally; and Roehm he had killed. Even toward Eva Braun he was never completely relaxed and human. The gulf between the leader of the nation and the simple girl was always maintained. Now and then, and it always struck a faintly jarring note, he would call her *Tschapperl,* a Bavarian peasant pet name with a slightly contemptuous flavor.

Hitler must already have realized the immense drama that his life was, the high stakes he was playing for, by the time he had a long conversation with Cardinal Faulhaber at Obersalzberg in November 1936. Afterward Hitler sat alone with me in the bay window of the dining room, while the twilight fell. For a long time he looked out of the window in silence. Then he said pensively: "There are two possibilities for me: To win through with all my plans, or to fail. If I win, I shall be one of the greatest men in history. If I fail, I shall be condemned, despised, and damned."

---

* Hermann Esser was one of the very first party members and later became the state secretary for tourism. Christian Weber, also one of the earliest party members, was reduced to a rather limited role after 1933; among other things he was in charge of the horse races at Riem. Ernst Roehm was head of the SA and was murdered by Hitler in 1934. Julius Streicher was Germany's foremost anti-Semite, editor of *Der Stürmer* and Gauleiter of Franconia.

8

The New Chancellery

To PROVIDE THE PROPER BACKGROUND FOR HIS RISE TO THE RANK OF "ONE of the greatest men in history," Hitler now demanded an architectural stage set of imperial majesty. He described the Chancellery into which he had moved on January 30, 1933, as "fit for a soap company." It would not do for the headquarters of a now powerful Reich, he said.

At the end of January 1938 Hitler called me to his office. "I have an urgent assignment for you," he said solemnly, standing in the middle of the room. "I shall be holding extremely important conferences in the near future. For these, I need grand halls and salons which will make an impression on people, especially on the smaller dignitaries. For the site I am placing the whole of Voss Strasse at your disposal. The cost is immaterial. But it must be done very quickly and be of solid construction. How long do you need? For plans, blueprints, everything? Even a year and a half or two years would be too long for me. Can you be done by January 10, 1939? I want to hold the next diplomatic reception in the new Chancellery." I was dismissed.

Hitler later described the rest of that day in his speech for the raising of the ridgepole of the building: "My *Generalbauinspektor* (Inspector General of Buildings) asked for a few hours time for reflection, and in the evening he came to me with a list of deadlines and told me: 'On such-and-such a date in March the old buildings will be gone, on August 1 we will celebrate the raising of the ridgepole, and on January 9, my Leader,

I shall report completion to you.' I myself have been in the business, in building, and know what such a schedule means. This has never happened before. It is a unique achievement."[1] Actually, it was the most thoughtless promise of my life. But Hitler seemed satisfied.

I had the razing of the houses on Voss Strasse begun at once in order to clear the site. Simultaneously, I plunged ahead with plans for the exterior of the building. The underground air-raid shelter had in fact to be started from crude sketches. But even at a later stage of the work I had to order many components before the architectural data had been definitely settled. For example, the longest delivery times were required for the enormous hand-knotted rugs which were to be used in several large salons. I decided their colors and size before I knew what the rooms they were meant for would look like. In fact the rooms were more or less designed around these rugs. I decided to forgo any complicated organizational plan and schedule, since these would only have revealed that the project could not possibly be carried out within the time limit. In many respects this improvised approach resembled the methods I was to apply four years later in directing the German war economy.

The oblong site was an invitation to string a succession of rooms on a long axis. I showed Hitler my design: From Wilhelmsplatz an arriving diplomat drove through great gates into a court of honor. By way of an outside staircase he first entered a medium-sized reception room from which double doors almost seventeen feet high opened into a large hall clad in mosaic. He then ascended several steps, passed through a round room with domed ceiling, and saw before him a gallery four hundred eighty feet long. Hitler was particularly impressed by my gallery because it was twice as long as the Hall of Mirrors at Versailles. Deep window niches were to filter the light, creating that pleasant effect I had seen in the Salle de Bal at the Palace of Fontainebleau.

As a whole, then, it was to be a series of rooms done in a rich variety of materials and color combinations, in all some seven hundred twenty-five feet long. Only then came Hitler's reception hall. To be sure, it was architecture that reveled in ostentation and aimed at startling effects. But that sort of thing existed in the baroque period, too—it has always existed.

Hitler was delighted: "On the long walk from the entrance to the reception hall they'll get a taste of the power and grandeur of the German Reich!" During the next several months he asked to see the plans again and again but interfered remarkably little in this building, even though it was destined for him personally. He let me work freely.

The haste with which Hitler was urging the building of the new Chancellery had a deeper cause in his anxiety about his health. He seriously feared that he did not have much longer to live. Since 1935 his imagination had dwelt increasingly on a stomach ailment which he tried to cure by a self-imposed regimen. He thought he knew what foods harmed him and in the course of time was prescribing a starvation diet for himself. A little soup, salad, small quantities of the lightest food— he no longer ate anything substantial. He sounded desperate when he pointed to his plate: "A man is supposed to keep alive on that! Look at it. It's easy for the doctors to say that people ought to eat what they have an appetite for.[2] Hardly anything is good for me nowadays. After every meal the pain begins. Leave out still more? Then how am I going to exist?"

He often interrupted a conference because of his gastric pains and withdrew for half an hour or more, or did not return at all. He also suffered, so he said, from excessive formation of gas, cardiac pains, and insomnia. Eva Braun once confided that he had said to her—this before he was fifty: "I'll soon have to give you your freedom. Why should you be tied to an old man?"

His physician, Dr. Brandt, was a young surgeon who tried to persuade Hitler to undergo a thorough examination by a first-class specialist in internal medicine. All of us supported this proposal. The names of celebrated doctors were mentioned, and plans made for carrying out an examination without creating any stir, for instance at a military hospital, since secrecy could be most easily maintained there. But in the end, again and again, Hitler repulsed all such suggestions. He simply could not afford to be regarded as sick, he said. It would weaken his political position, especially abroad. He even refused to have a specialist come to his home for a preliminary examination. To my knowledge he was never seriously examined at the time, but experimented with treating his symptoms by his own theories—which accorded, incidentally, with his inveterate bent for amateurish activities.

On the other hand, when he suffered from increasing hoarseness he consulted the famous Berlin throat specialist Professor von Eicken. He underwent a thorough examination in his apartment in the Chancellery and was relieved when no cancer was detected. For months he had been referring to the fate of Emperor Frederick III, who died of cancer of the throat. The surgeon removed a harmless node. This minor operation also took place in Hitler's apartment.

In 1935 Heinrich Hoffmann fell critically ill. Dr. Theodor Morell, an old acquaintance, tended him and cured him with sulfanilamides[3] which he obtained from Hungary. Hoffmann was forever telling Hitler about the wonderful doctor who had saved his life. Undoubtedly Hoffmann meant well, though one of Morell's talents was his ability to exaggerate immoderately any illness he cured, in order to cast his skill in the proper light.

Dr. Morell alleged that he had studied under the famous bacteriologist Ilya Mechnikov (1845–1916), Nobel Prize winner and professor at the Pasteur Institute.[4] Mechnikov, he claimed, had taught him the art of combating bacterial diseases. Later, Morell had taken long voyages on passenger liners as a ship's doctor. Undoubtedly he was not an out-and-out quack—rather a bit of a screwball obsessed with making money.

Hitler was persuaded to undergo an examination by Morell. The result surprised us all, for Hitler for the first time became convinced of a doctor's importance. "Nobody has ever before told me so clearly and precisely what is wrong with me. His method of cure is so logical that I have the greatest confidence in him. I shall follow his prescriptions to the letter." The chief finding, so Hitler said, was that he suffered from complete exhaustion of the intestinal flora, which Morell attributed to the overburdening of his nervous system. If that were cured, all the other complaints would fade away. Morell, however, wished to accelerate the restorative process by injections of vitamins, hormones, phosphorus, and dextrose. The cure would take a year; only partial results could be expected in any shorter period.

The most discussed medicine Hitler received henceforth consisted of capsules of intestinal bacteria, called "Multiflor" which were, Morell assured him, "raised from the best stock of a Bulgarian peasant." The other injections and drugs he gave to Hitler were not generally known; they were only hinted at. We never felt entirely easy about these methods. Dr. Brandt asked around among his specialist friends, and they all pronounced Morell's methods risky and unproved and foresaw dangers of addiction. And in fact the injections had to be given more and more frequently, and biologicals obtained from the testicles and intestines of animals, as well as from chemical and plant sources, were poured into Hitler's bloodstream. One day Goering deeply offended Morell by addressing him as "Herr Reich Injection Master."

Soon after the beginning of the treatment, however, a foot rash vanished that had long caused Hitler much concern. After a few weeks Hitler's stomach also improved; he ate considerably more, and heavier dishes, felt better, and fervently declared: "What luck that I met Morell! He has saved my life. Wonderful, the way he has helped me!"

If Hitler had the faculty for placing others under his spell, in this case the reverse relationship developed: Hitler was completely convinced of his personal physician's genius and soon forbade any criticism of the man. From then on Morell belonged to the intimate circle and became—when Hitler was not present—the butt of humor, since he could talk of nothing but strepto- and other cocci, of bulls' testicles and the newest vitamins.

Hitler kept urging all his associates to consult Morell if they had the slightest ailments. In 1936, when my circulation and stomach rebelled against an irrational working rhythm and adjustment to Hitler's abnormal habits, I called at Morell's private office. The sign at the entrance read: "Dr. Theodor Morell. Skin and Venereal Diseases." Morell's office and home were situated in the smartest part of Kurfürstendamm, near the Gedächtniskirche. The walls were hung with inscribed photographs of well-known actors and film stars. The time I was there, I shared the waiting room with the Crown Prince. After a superficial examination Morell prescribed for me his intestinal bacteria, dextrose, vitamin, and hormone tablets. For safety's sake I afterward had a thorough examination by Professor von Bergmann, the specialist in internal medicine of Berlin University. I was not suffering from any organic trouble, he concluded, but only nervous symptoms caused by overwork. I slowed down my pace as best I could, and the symptoms abated. To avoid offending Hitler, I pretended that I was carefully following Morell's instructions, and since my health improved I became for a time Morell's showpiece. Hitler also had him examine Eva Braun. Afterward she told me that he was disgustingly dirty and vowed that she would not let Morell treat her again.

Hitler's health improved only temporarily. But he would no longer part with his personal physician. On the contrary, Morell's country house on Schwanenwerder Island near Berlin became the goal of Hitler's teatime visits more and more frequently. It was the only place outside the Chancellery that continued to attract him. He visited Dr. Goebbels's very rarely and came to my place at Schlachtensee only once, to see the house I had built for myself.

From the end of 1937 on, when Morell's treatments began to fail, Hitler resumed his old laments. Even as he gave assignments and discussed plans, he would occasionally add: "I don't know how long I am going to live. Perhaps most of these buildings will be finished only after I am no longer here. . . ."[5] The date for the completion of many of the major buildings had been fixed between 1945 and 1950. Evidently Hitler was counting on only a few more years of life. Another example: "Once I leave here . . . I shall not have much more time."[6] In private one of his standard remarks became: "I shall not live much longer. I always counted on having time to realize my plans. I must carry them out myself. None of my successors will have the force to. I must carry out my aims as long as I can hold up, for my health is growing worse all the time."

On May 2, 1938, Hitler drew up his personal will. He had already outlined his political testament on November 5, 1937, in the presence of the Foreign Minister and the military heads of the Reich. In that speech, he referred to his extensive plans for conquest as a "testamentary bequest in case of my decease."[7] With his intimate entourage, who night after night had to watch trivial operetta movies and listen to endless tirades on the Catholic Church, diet recipes, Greek temples, and police dogs, he did not reveal how literally he took his dream of world dominion.

Many of Hitler's former associates have since attempted to establish the theory that Hitler changed in 1938. They attribute the change to his deteriorated health resulting from Morell's treatment. It seems to me, on the contrary, that Hitler's plans and aims never changed. Sickness and the fear of death merely made him advance his deadlines. His aims could only have been thwarted by superior counterforces, and in 1938 no such forces were visible. Quite the opposite: The successes of that year encouraged him to go on forcing the already accelerated pace.

The feverish haste with which Hitler pushed our building work seemed also connected with this inner unrest. At the Chancellery ridgepole celebration he said to the workmen: "This is no longer the American tempo; it has become the German tempo. I like to think that I also accomplish more than other statesmen accomplish in the so-called democracies. I think we are following a different tempo politically, and if it is possible to annex a country to the Reich in three or four days, why it must be possible to erect a building in one or two years." Sometimes, however, I wonder whether his excessive passion for building did not also serve the purpose of camouflaging his plans and deceiving the public by means of building schedules and cornerstone layings.

I remember one occasion in 1938 when we were sitting in the Deutscher Hof in Nuremberg. Hitler spoke of the need to keep to oneself things not meant for the ears of the public. Among those present was Reichsleiter Philip Bouhler and his young wife. She objected that such restrictions surely did not apply to this group, since all of us knew how to keep any secret he confided to us. Hitler laughed and answered: "Nobody here knows how to keep his mouth shut, except for one person." And he indicated me. But there were things that happened in the next several months of which he breathed no word to me.

On February 2, 1938, I saw the Commander in Chief of the Navy, Erich Raeder, crossing the main salon of the apartment, coming from a conference with Hitler. He looked utterly distraught. He was pale, staggering, like someone on the verge of a heart attack. On the day after next I learned from the newspapers that Foreign Minister von Neurath had been replaced by Ribbentrop and Army Commander in Chief von Fritsch by von Brauchitsch. Hitler personally had assumed the post of Commander in Chief of the Armed Forces, replacing Field Marshal von Blomberg, and had made General Wilhelm Keitel his chief of staff.

I was acquainted with Colonel General von Blomberg from Obersalzberg; he was a pleasant, aristocratic looking man who enjoyed Hitler's esteem and had been treated with unusual amiability until his dismissal. In the autumn of 1937, at Hitler's suggestion, he had called at my office on Pariser Platz and looked over the plans and models for the rebuilding of Berlin. He listened calmly and with interest for about an hour. At the time he was accompanied by a general who seconded his chief's every word by an approving nod of his head. This was Wilhelm Keitel, who had now become Hitler's closest military assistant in the High Command of the Armed Forces. Ignorant of military hierarchy, I had taken him for Blomberg's adjutant.

About the same time Colonel General von Fritsch, whom I had not met up to then, asked me to call at his office on Bendlerstrasse. It was not curiosity alone that prompted him to ask to see the plans for Berlin. I spread them out on a large map table. Coolly and aloofly, with a military curtness that verged on unfriendliness, he listened to my explanations. From his questions, it appeared he was considering whether Hitler's vast building projects, extending over long periods of time, betokened any interest in preserving peace. But perhaps I was mistaken.

I also did not know the Foreign Minister, Baron von Neurath. One day in 1937 Hitler decided that Neurath's villa was not adequate for the Foreign Minister's official duties and sent me to Frau von Neurath to offer to have the house significantly enlarged at government expense. She showed me through but stated in a tone of finality that in her opinion and that of the Foreign Minister it fully served its purpose; would I tell the Chancellor: "No, thank you." Hitler was annoyed and did not repeat the offer. Here for once a member of the old nobility was demonstrating confident modesty and deliberately abstaining from the craving for ostentation on the part of the new masters. The same was certainly not true of Ribbentrop, who in the summer of 1936 had me come to London where he wanted the German Embassy enlarged and modernized. He wished to have it finished in time for the coronation of George VI in the spring of 1937. There would no doubt be many parties given then, and he meant to impress London society by the sumptuousness of the embassy. Ribbentrop left the details to his wife, who indulged herself in such splendors with an interior decorator from Munich's United Workshops that I felt my services were superfluous. Toward me Ribbentrop took a conciliatory tone. But in those days in London he was always in a bad temper upon receiving cabled instructions from the Foreign Minister. This he regarded as pure meddling and would irritably and loudly declare that he cleared his actions with Hitler personally; the Fuehrer had directly assigned him to London.

Even this early many of Hitler's political associates who hoped for good relations with England were beginning to think Ribbentrop was not the man for the job. In the autumn of 1937, Dr. Todt made an inspection trip of the various building sites for the autobahn, taking Lord Wolton along as guest. Afterward, it appeared that Lord Wolton expressed the wish, unofficially, to have Todt himself sent as ambassador to London in Ribbentrop's place. So long as Ribbentrop remained, relations would never improve, Lord Wolton said. We took care that Hitler heard of these remarks. He did not react.

Soon after Ribbentrop's appointment as Foreign Minister, Hitler suggested that the old Foreign Minister's villa be torn down entirely, and the former palace of the Reich President be renovated for his official residence. Ribbentrop accepted the offer.

I was in the salon of Hitler's Berlin apartment when the second event of this year, and one which testified to the acceleration in Hitler's political plans, began to unfold. The day was March 9, 1938. Hitler's adjutant, Schaub, sat at the radio listening to the Innsbruck speech of Dr. Schuschnigg, the Austrian Chancellor. Hitler had withdrawn to his private study on the second floor. Apparently Schaub was waiting for something in particular. He was taking notes. Schuschnigg spoke more and more plainly, finally presenting his plan for a plebiscite in Austria. The Austrian people themselves would decide for or against independence. And then Schuschnigg sounded the watchword to his fellow countrymen: "Austrians, the time has come!"

The time had come for Schaub too; he rushed upstairs to Hitler. A short while later, Goebbels in full dress and Goering in gala uniform hustled in. They were coming from some party, for the Berlin season for balls was in full swing, and vanished upstairs for some mysterious conference.

Once more enlightenment came to me several days later and via the newspapers. On March 13, German troops marched into Austria. Some three weeks later I too drove to Vienna by car to prepare the hall of the Northwest Railroad Station for a grand rally. Everywhere in towns and villages German cars were cheered. At the Hotel Imperial in Vienna I encountered the sordid hidden side of the rejoicing over the *Anschluss*. Many bigwigs from the Reich, such as Berlin Police Commissioner Count Helldorf, had hurried there, lured by the well-stocked shops. "They still have good underclothing. . . . Wool blankets, as many as you like. . . . I've discovered a place for foreign liqueurs. . . ." Scraps of the conversations in the hotel lobby. I felt repelled and limited myself to buying a Borsalino. Did any of this concern me?

Shortly after the annexation of Austria, Hitler sent for a map of Central Europe and showed his reverently listening entourage how Czechoslovakia was now caught in a "pincers." For years to come he would recall how magnanimously Mussolini had given his consent to the invasion of Austria. He would remain eternally grateful to the Duce for that, Hitler said. For Austria had been an invaluable buffer zone for Italy. To have German troops standing at the Brenner Pass would in the long run cause a certain strain. Hitler's Italian journey of 1938 was partly intended as an assurance of friendship. But he was also eager to see the monuments and art treasures of Rome and Florence. Resplendent uniforms were designed for the entourage and shown to Hitler. He loved such pomp; that his own dress was modest was a matter of careful strategy. "My surroundings must look magnificent. Then my simplicity makes a striking effect." About a year later Hitler turned to the stage designer Benno von Arent, known for his sets for opera and operettas, and had him design new uniforms for diplomats. He was pleased by the frock coats laden with gold braid. But wits remarked: "They look like a scene from *Die Fledermaus*." Arent also designed medals for Hitler; those too would have looked great on the stage. Thereafter I used to call Arent: "Tinsmith of the Third Reich."

Back from Italy, Hitler summed up his impressions: "How glad I am that we have no monarchy and that I have never listened to those who have tried to talk me into one. Those court flunkies and that etiquette! It's awful. And the Duce always in the background. The best places at all the dinners and on the platforms are taken by the royal family. The Duce was always kept at a remove, and yet he is the one who really runs the government." By diplomatic protocol Hitler, as Chief of State, was treated as of equal rank with the King, Mussolini only as Prime Minister.

Even after the visit, Hitler felt obliged to do something special to honor Mussolini. He decided that Berlin's Adolf Hitler Platz would bear Mussolini's name after it had been incorporated into the major urban renewal project for Berlin.[8] Privately, he thought this square appalling, disfigured as it was by "modern" buildings of the Weimar Republic. But: "If we rename it Mussolini Platz, I am rid of it, and besides it seems like an exceptional honor to cede my own square to the Duce. I already have designed a Mussolini monument for it!" Nothing came of the project, since the rebuilding plans were never carried out.

The dramatic year 1938 led finally to Hitler's wresting the consent of the Western powers for the partition of Czechoslovakia. A few weeks before Hitler had put on an exceptionally effective performance at the Nuremberg Party Rally, playing the enraged leader of his nation; and supported by the frenzied applause of his followers, he tried to convince the contingent of foreign observers that he would not shrink from war. That was, judged with benefit of hindsight, intimidation on a grand scale. He had already tested this technique in his conference with Schuschnigg. On the other hand, he loved to sharpen his mettle by such audacities, going so far that he could no longer retreat without risking his prestige.

This time he wanted even his closest associates to believe in his feint. He explained the various considerations to them and stressed the inevitability of a military showdown, whereas his usual behavior was to veil his basic intentions. What he said about his resolve for war impressed even Brückner, his chief adjutant of many years. In September 1938, during the Party Rally, I was sitting with Brückner on a wall of Nuremberg Castle. Wreathed in smoke, the old city lay before us, in the mild September sunshine. Downcast, Brückner remarked: "We may be seeing this peaceful scene for the last time. Probably we shall soon be at war."

The war Brückner was predicting was averted again more because of the compliance of the Western powers than because of any reasonableness on Hitler's part. The surrender of the Sudetenland to Germany took place before the eyes of a frightened world and of Hitler's followers, now completely convinced of their leader's invincibility.

The Czech border fortifications caused general astonishment. To the surprise of experts a test bombardment showed that our weapons would not have prevailed against them. Hitler himself went to the former frontier to inspect the arrangements and returned impressed. The fortifications were amazingly massive, he said, laid out with extraordinary skill and echeloned, making prime use of the terrain. "Given a resolute defense, taking them would have been very difficult and would have cost us a great many lives. Now we have obtained them without loss of blood. One thing is certain: I shall never again permit the Czechs to build a new defense line. What a marvelous starting position we have now. We are over the mountains and already in the valleys of Bohemia."

On November 10, driving to the office, I passed by the still smoldering ruins of the Berlin synagogues. That was the fourth momentous event that established the character of this last of the prewar years. Today, this memory is one of the most doleful of my life, chiefly because what really disturbed me at the time was the aspect of disorder that I saw on Fasanenstrasse: charred beams, collapsed façades, burned-out walls— anticipations of a scene that during the war would dominate much of Europe. Most of all I was troubled by the political revival of the "gutter." The smashed panes of shop windows offended my sense of middle-class order.

I did not see that more was being smashed than glass, that on that night Hitler had crossed a Rubicon for the fourth time in his life, had taken a step that irrevocably sealed the fate of his country. Did I sense, at least for a moment, that something was beginning which would end with the annihilation of one whole group of our nation? Did I sense that this outburst of hoodlumism was changing my moral substance? I do not know.

I accepted what had happened rather indifferently. Some phrases of Hitler's, to the effect that he had not wanted these excesses, contributed to this attitude. Later, in private, Goebbels hinted that he had been the impresario for this sad and terrible night, and I think it very possible that he confronted a hesitant Hitler with a *fait accompli* in order to force him to take the initiative.

It has repeatedly surprised me, in later years, that scarcely any anti-Semitic remarks of Hitler's have remained in my memory. Out of the scraps that remain, I can reconstruct what crossed my mind at the time: dismay over the deviation from the image I wanted to have of Hitler, anxiety over the increasing deterioration of his health, hope for some letup of the struggle against the churches, a certain puzzlement at his partiality for utopian-sounding remote goals, all sorts of odd feelings —but Hitler's hatred for the Jews seemed to me so much a matter of course that I gave it no serious thought.

I felt myself to be Hitler's architect. Political events did not concern me. My job was merely to provide impressive backdrops for such events. And this view was reinforced daily, for Hitler consulted me almost exclusively on architectural questions. Moreover, it would have been regarded as self-importance on the part of a man who was pretty much of a latecomer in the party had I attempted to participate in the political discussions. I felt that there was no need for me to take any political positions at all. Nazi education, furthermore, aimed at separatist thinking; I was expected to confine myself to the job of building. The grotesque extent to which I clung to this illusion is indicated by a memorandum of mine to Hitler as late as 1944: "The task I have to fulfill is an unpolitical one. I have felt at ease in my work only so long as my person and my work were evaluated solely by the standard of practical accomplishments."[9]

But fundamentally the distinction was inconsequential. Today it seems to me that I was trying to compartmentalize my mind. On the one hand there was the vulgar business of carrying out a policy proclaimed in the anti-Semitic slogans printed on streamers over the entrances to towns. On the other hand there was my idealized picture of Hitler. I wanted to keep these two apart. Actually, it did not matter, of course, who mobilized the rabble of the gutter to attack synagogues and Jewish businesses, it did not matter whether this happened at Hitler's direct instigation or merely with his approval.

During the years after my release from Spandau I have been repeatedly asked what thoughts I had on this subject during my two decades alone in the cell with myself; what I actually knew of the persecution, the deportation, and the annihilation of the Jews; what I should have known and what conclusions I ought to have drawn.

I no longer give the answer with which I tried for so long to soothe the questioners, but chiefly myself: that in Hitler's system, as in every totalitarian regime, when a man's position rises, his isolation increases and he is therefore more sheltered from harsh reality; that with the application of technology to the process of murder the number of murderers is reduced and therefore the possibility of ignorance grows; that the craze for secrecy built into the system creates degrees of awareness, so it is easy to escape observing inhuman cruelties.

I no longer give any of these answers. For they are efforts at legalistic exculpation. It is true that as a favorite and later as one of Hitler's most influential ministers I was isolated. It is also true that the habit of thinking within the limits of my own field provided me, both as architect and as Armaments Minister, with many opportunities for evasion. It is true that I did not know what was really beginning on November 9, 1938, and what ended in Auschwitz and Maidanek. But in the final analysis I myself determined the degree of my isolation, the extremity of my evasions, and the extent of my ignorance.

I therefore know today that my agonized self-examinations posed the question as wrongly as did the questioners whom I have met since my release. Whether I knew or did not know, or how much or how little I knew, is totally unimportant when I consider what horrors I ought to have known about and what conclusions would have been the natural ones to draw from the little I did know. Those who ask me are fundamentally expecting me to offer justifications. But I have none. No apologies are possible.

The New Chancellery was supposed to be finished on January 9. On January 7, Hitler came to Berlin from Munich. He came in a mood of great suspense and obviously expecting to find teams of workmen and cleaning squads rushing about. Everyone knows the frantic atmosphere at a building site shortly before the building is to be handed over to the occupant: scaffoldings being dismantled, dust and rubbish being removed, carpets being unrolled and pictures hung. But his expectations were deceived. From the start we had given ourselves a few days reserve. We did not need them and therefore were finished forty-eight hours before the official handing over of the building. Hitler could have sat down at his desk right then and there and begun working on the affairs of government.

The building greatly impressed him. He highly praised the "genius of the architect" and, quite contrary to his habit, said so to me. But the fact that I had managed to finish the task two days early earned me the reputation of being a great organizer.

Hitler especially liked the long tramp that state guests and diplomats would now have to take before they reached the reception hall. Unlike me, he was not worried about the polished marble floor, which I was reluctant to cover with a runner. "That's exactly right; diplomats should have practice in moving on a slippery surface."

The reception hall struck him as too small; he wanted it tripled in size. The plans for this were ready at the beginning of the war. His study, on the other hand, met with his undivided approval. He was particularly pleased by an inlay on his desk representing a sword half drawn from its sheath. "Good, good. . . . When the diplomats sitting in front of me at this desk see that, they'll learn to shiver and shake."

From the gilded panels I had installed over the four doors of his study, four Virtues looked down on him: Wisdom, Prudence, Fortitude, and Justice. I don't know what suggested this idea to me. I had put two sculptures by Arno Breker in the Round Salon, flanking the portal to the Great Gallery. One of them represented Daring, the other Caring.[10] This rather pathetic hint on the part of my friend Breker that audacity should be tempered with responsibility, as well as my own allegorical reminder that bravery was a virtue but that the other virtues should not be forgotten, showed how naïvely we overestimated the influence of art. But it also betrayed a certain uneasiness on our part over the course things were taking.

A large marble-topped table stood by the window, useless for the time being. From 1944 on, military conferences were held at it. Here outspread strategic maps showed the rapid advance of the western and eastern enemies into the territory of the German Reich. This was Hitler's penultimate military headquarters; the ultimate one was located five hundred feet away, under many feet of concrete. The hall for cabinet meetings, completely paneled in wood for acoustic reasons, found favor with Hitler, but he never used it for the intended purpose. Every so often a cabinet minister asked me whether I could arrange for him at least to see "his" room. Hitler gave permission, and so now and then a minister would stand for a few minutes at the place he had never taken, where a large blue leather desk pad, with his name embossed in gold letters, lay on the conference table.

Forty-five hundred workers had labored in two shifts to meet the deadline. There were several thousand more scattered over the country who had produced components. The whole work force, masons, carpenters, plumbers, and so on, were invited to inspect the building and filed awestruck through the finished rooms. Hitler addressed them in the Sportpalast:

> I stand here as representative of the German people. And whenever I receive anyone in the Chancellery, it is not the private individual Adolf Hitler who receives him, but the Leader of the German nation—and therefore it is not I who receive him, but Germany through me. For that reason I want these rooms to be in keeping with their high mission. Every individual has contributed to a structure that will outlast the centuries and will speak to posterity of our times. This is the first architectural creation of the new, great German Reich!

After meals he frequently asked which of his guests had not yet seen the Chancellery, and he was delighted whenever he could show one of them through. On such occasions he liked to show off his ability to store up data. Thus, he would begin by asking me: "How large is this room? How high?" I would shrug my shoulders in embarrassment, and he would give the measurements. They were exactly right. Gradually this developed into a prearranged game, since I too became adept at rattling off the figures. But since it obviously gave him pleasure, I played along.

Hitler's honors to me increased. He arranged a dinner in his residence for my closest associates; he wrote an essay for a book on the Chancellery, conferred the Golden Party Badge on me, and with a few shy words gave me one of the watercolors he had done in his youth. A Gothic church done in 1909, it is executed in an extremely precise, patient, and pedantic style. No personal impulses can be felt in it; not a stroke has any verve. But it is not only the brush strokes that lack all character; by its choice of subject, the flat colors, the conventional perspective, the picture seems a candid witness to this early period of Hitler. All his watercolors from the same time have this quality, and even the watercolors done while he was an orderly in the First World War lack distinctiveness. The transformation in Hitler's personality, the growth of self-assurance, came later. It is evident in the two pen sketches for the great hall in Berlin and for the triumphal arch, which he drew about 1925. Ten years later he would often sketch with a vigorous hand, using red and blue pencil, sometimes going over and over his drawing until he had forced his way through to the conception he had dimly in mind. Nevertheless he still thought well enough of the modest watercolors of his youth to give them away occasionally as a special distinction.

For decades a marble bust of Bismarck by Reinhold Begas had stood in the Chancellery. A few days before the dedication of the new building, while workmen were moving the bust to the new headquarters, it dropped and broke off at the neck. I felt this as an evil omen. And since I had heard Hitler's story that right at the beginning of the First World War the Reich eagle had toppled from the post-office building, I kept the accident a secret and had Arno Breker make an exact copy. We gave it some patina by steeping it in tea.

In the aforementioned speech Hitler made the following pronouncement: "This is the special and wonderful property of architecture: When the work has been done, a monument remains. That endures; it is something different from a pair of boots, which also can be made, but which the wearer wears out in a year or two and then throws away. This remains, and through the centuries will bear witness to all those who helped to create it." On January 10, 1939, the new building destined to last for centuries was dedicated: Hitler received the diplomats accredited to Berlin in the Grand Salon and delivered his New Year address to them.

Sixty-five days after the dedication, on March 15, 1939, the President of Czechoslovakia was ushered into Hitler's new study. This room was the scene of the tragedy which ended at night with Hacha's submission and early in the morning with the occupation of his country. "At last," Hitler reported later, "I had so belabored the old man that his nerves gave way completely, and he was on the point of signing; then he had a heart attack. In the adjoining room Dr. Morell gave him an injection, but in this case it was too effective. Hacha regained too much of his strength, revived, and was no longer prepared to sign, until I finally wore him down again."

On July 16, 1945, seventy-eight months after the dedication, Winston Churchill was shown through the Chancellery. "In front of the Chancellery there was a considerable crowd. When I got out of the car and walked among them, except for one old man who shook his head disapprovingly, they all began to cheer. My hate had died with their surrender, and I was much moved by their demonstrations." Then the party walked for a good while through the shattered corridors and halls of the Chancellery.

Soon afterward the remains of the building were removed. The stone and marble supplied the materials for the Russian war monument in Berlin-Treptow.

9

A Day in the Chancellery

BETWEEN FORTY AND FIFTY PERSONS HAD ACCESS TO HITLER'S AFTERNOON dinner table in the Chancellery. They needed only to telephone his adjutant and say they would be coming. Usually they were the Gauleiters and Reichsleiters of the party, a few cabinet ministers, the members of the inner circle, but no army officers except for Hitler's Wehrmacht adjutant. More than once this adjutant, Colonel Schmundt, urged Hitler to allow the leading military men to dine with him; but Hitler would not have it. Perhaps he realized that the quality of his regular associates was such that the officers' corps would soon be looking down on them.

I too had free admission to Hitler's residence and often availed myself of it. The policeman at the entrance to the front garden knew my car and opened the gate without making inquiries; I would park my car in the yard and enter the apartment that Troost had rebuilt. It extended along the right side of the new Chancellery and was connected with it by a hall.

The SS member of Hitler's escort squad greeted me familiarly. I would hand him my roll of drawings and then, unaccompanied, like someone who belonged to the household, step into the spacious entrance hall: a room with two groups of comfortable seats, the white walls adorned with tapestries, the dark-red marble floor richly covered with rugs. There would usually be several guests there conversing, while others might be making private telephone calls. In general this room was favored because it was the only one where smoking was permitted.

It was not at all customary to use the otherwise mandatory *"Heil Hitler"* in greeting; a *"Guten Tag"* was far more common. The party lapel badge was also little flaunted in this circle, and uniforms were relatively seldom seen. Those who had penetrated as far as this privileged group could allow themselves a certain informality.

Through a square reception salon, which thanks to its uncomfortable furniture remained unused, you reached the actual living room, where the guests would be chatting, usually standing. This room, about a thousand square feet in area, was the only one in the entire apartment furnished with a measure of *Gemütlichkeit*. Out of respect for its Bismarckian past it had been preserved during the major reconstruction of 1933-34 and had a beamed ceiling, wood wainscoting, and a fireplace adorned by a Florentine Renaissance coat of arms which Chancellor von Bülow had once brought back from Italy. This was the only fireplace on the lower floor. Around it were grouped a sofa and chairs upholstered in dark leather; behind the sofa stood a largish table with a marble top on which several newspapers usually lay. A tapestry and two paintings by Schinkel hung on the walls. They had been lent by the National Gallery for the Chancellor's apartment.

Hitler was royally unreliable about the time of his appearance. The dinner was usually set for about two o'clock, but it was apt to be three or later before Hitler arrived, sometimes from the upper private rooms of the apartment, often from a conference in the Chancellery. His entrance was as informal as that of any private individual. He greeted his guests by shaking hands; everyone gathered in a circle around him. He would express his opinion on one or another problem of the day; with a few favored guests he inquired, usually in a conventional tone, about the well-being of "your spouse." Then he took the news excerpts from his press chief, sat down off to one side, and began to read. Sometimes he would pass an excerpt on to one of the guests because the news seemed especially interesting to him, and would throw out a few casual remarks about it.

The guests would continue to stand around for another fifteen or twenty minutes, until the curtain was drawn away from a glass door that led to the dining room. The house steward, a man with the encouraging bulk of a restaurateur, would inform Hitler quietly, in a tone in keeping with the whole unpublic atmosphere, that dinner was ready. The Fuehrer would lead the way; the others followed him into the dining room without any order of rank.

Of all the rooms in the Chancellor's apartment that Professor Troost had redecorated, this large square dining room (forty by forty feet) was the most harmonious. A wall with three glass doors led out to the garden. Opposite was a large buffet of palisander wood; above it hung a painting by Kaulbach which had a certain charm because it was unfinished; at any rate it was without some of the embarrassing aspects of that eclectic painter. Each of the two other walls was marked by a shallow recess in which, on pedestals of marble, stood nude studies by the Munich sculptor Josef Wackerle. To either side of the recesses were more glass doors which led to the pantry, to a large salon, and into the living room from which we had come. Smoothly plastered walls, painted ivory, and equally light-colored curtains, produced a feeling of openness and brightness. Slight jogs in the walls carried out the clean, austere rhythm; a molding held it all together. The furnishing was restrained and restful: a large round table for about fifteen persons, ringed by simple chairs with dark red leather seats. The chairs were all alike, the host's no more elaborate than the rest. At the corners of the room stood four more small tables, each with from four to six similar chairs. The tableware consisted of light, plain china and simple glasses; both had been selected by Professor Troost before his death. A few flowers in a bowl formed the centerpiece.

Such was the "Merry Chancellor's Restaurant," as Hitler often called it in speaking to his guests. He had his seat on the window side of the room, and before entering would select which of the guests would be seated at his side. All the rest sat down around the table wherever they found a place. If many guests came, the adjutants and persons of lesser importance, among whom I belonged, took seats at the side tables—an advantage, I always thought, since there we could talk with less constraint.

The food was emphatically simple. A soup, no appetizer, meat with vegetables and potatoes, a sweet. For beverage we had a choice between mineral water, ordinary Berlin bottled beer, or a cheap wine. Hitler was served his vegetarian food, drank Fachinger mineral water, and those of his guests who wished could imitate him. But few did. It was Hitler himself who insisted on this simplicity. He could count on its being talked about in Germany. Once, when the Helgoland fishermen presented him with a gigantic lobster, this delicacy was served at table, much to the satisfaction of the guests, but Hitler made disapproving remarks about the human error of consuming such ugly monstrosities. Moreover, he wanted to have such luxuries forbidden, he declared.

Goering seldom came to these meals. Once, when I left him to go to dinner at the Chancellery, he remarked: "To tell the truth, the food there is too rotten for my taste. And then, these party dullards from Munich! Unbearable."

Hess came to table about once every two weeks; he would be followed by his adjutant in a rather weird getup, carrying a tin vessel containing a specially prepared meal which was to be rewarmed in the kitchen. For a long time it was hidden from Hitler that Hess had his own special vegetarian meal served to himself. When someone finally gave the secret away, Hitler turned irritably to Hess in the presence of the assembled company and blustered: "I have a first-class diet cook here. If your doctor has prescribed something special for you, she will be glad to prepare it. But you cannot bring your food with you." Hess, even then inclining to obstinate contrariness, began explaining that the components of his meals had to be of special biodynamic origin. Whereupon Hitler bluntly informed him that in that case he should take his meals at home. Thereafter Hess scarcely ever came to the dinners.

When, at the instance of the party, word was sent out that all households in Germany should eat a one-dish meal on Sundays, thereby promoting guns instead of butter, only a tureen of soup was served at Hitler's table too. The number of Sunday guests thereafter shrank to two or three, which provoked some sarcastic remarks from Hitler about the spirit of sacrifice among his associates. For there would also be a list passed around the table, with every guest pledging his donation to the war effort. Every one-dish meal cost me fifty or a hundred marks.

Goebbels was the most prominent guest at table; Himmler seldom came; Bormann of course never missed a meal, but like me he belonged to the inner group of courtiers and could not be considered a guest.

Here, too, Hitler's conversation at table did not go beyond the very narrow range of subjects and the limited point of view that made the Obersalzberg talk so wearisome. In Berlin he tended to phrase his opinions more harshly, but the repertory remained the same; he neither extended nor deepened it, scarcely ever enriched it by new approaches and insights. He did not even try to cover up the frequent repetitions which were so embarrassing to his listeners. I cannot say that I found his remarks impressive, even though I was still captivated by his personality. What he said rather sobered me, for I had expected opinions and judgments of higher quality.

In these monologues he frequently asserted that his political, artistic, and military ideas formed a unity which he had developed in detail between the ages of twenty and thirty. That had been intellectually his most fertile period, he said; the things he was now planning and doing were only the execution of the ideas of that period.

In the table talk much weight was given to experiences in the First World War. Most of the guests had served during the war. For a time Hitler had been in the trenches opposite the British forces, whose bravery and determination had won his respect, although he also often made fun of their idiosyncrasies. Thus he liked to relate with heavy irony that they were in the habit of stopping their artillery fire exactly at teatime, so that he as a courier was always able to carry out his errands safely at that hour.

In 1938 he expressed no ideas of revenge upon the French; he did not want a rerun of the war of 1914. It was not worth waging another war, he said, over that insignificant strip of territory constituting Alsace-Lorraine. Besides, he would add, the Alsatians had become so characterless due to the constant shifting of their nationality that it would be a gain to neither side to have them. They ought to be left where they were. In saying this, of course, Hitler was assuming that Germany could expand to the east. The bravery of the French soldiers had impressed him in the First World War; only the officer corps was morally enfeebled. "With German officers the French would be a splendid army."

He did not exactly repudiate the alliance with Japan—from the racist point of view a dubious affair—but he took a tone of reserve toward it as far as the more distant future was concerned. Whenever he touched on this theme, he implied that he was somewhat sorry about having made an alliance with the so-called yellow race. But then he would remind himself that England, too, had mobilized Japan against the Central Powers in the World War. Hitler considered Japan an ally that ranked as a world power, whereas he was not convinced that Italy was in the same class.

The Americans had not played a very prominent part in the war of 1914–18, he thought, and moreover had not made any great sacrifices of blood. They would certainly not withstand a great trial by fire, for their fighting qualities were low. In general, no such thing as an American people existed as a unit; they were nothing but a mass of immigrants from many nations and races.

Fritz Wiedemann, who had once been regimental adjutant and superior to Hitler in his days as a courier and whom Hitler had now with signal lack of taste made his own adjutant, thought otherwise and kept urging Hitler to have talks with the Americans. Vexed by this offense against the unwritten law of the round table, Hitler finally sent him to San Francisco as German consul general. "Let him be cured of his notions there."

Those who took part in these table conversations were almost to a man without cosmopolitan experience. Most had never been outside Germany; if one of them had taken a pleasure trip to Italy, the matter was discussed at Hitler's table as if it were an event and the person in question was considered a foreign affairs expert. Hitler, too, had seen nothing of the world and had acquired neither knowledge nor understanding of it. Moreover, the average party politician lacked higher education. Of the fifty Reichsleiters and Gauleiters, the elite of the leadership, only ten had completed a university education, a few had attended university classes for a while, and the majority had never gone beyond secondary school. Virtually none of them had distinguished himself by any notable achievement in any field whatsoever. Almost all displayed an astonishing intellectual dullness. Their educational standard certainly did not correspond to what might be expected of the top leadership of a nation with a traditionally high intellectual level. Basically, Hitler preferred to have people of the same origins as himself in his immediate entourage; no doubt he felt most at ease among them. In general he was pleased if his associates showed some "flaw in the weave," as we called it at the time. As Hanke commented one day: "It is all to the good if associates have faults and know that the superior is aware of them. That is why the Fuehrer so seldom changes his assistants. For he finds them easiest to work with. Almost every one of them has his defect; that helps keep them in line." Immoral conduct, remote Jewish ancestors, or recent membership in the party were counted as flaws in the weave.

Hitler would often theorize to the effect that it was a mistake to export ideas such as National Socialism. To do so would only lead to a strengthening of nationalism in other countries, he said, and thus to a weakening of his own position. He was glad to see that the Nazi parties of other countries produced no leader of his own caliber. He considered the Dutch Nazi leader Mussert and Sir Oswald Mosley, chief of the British Nazi party, mere copyists who had had no original or new ideas. They only imitated us and our methods slavishly, he commented, and would never amount to anything. In every country you had to start from different premises and change your methods accordingly, he argued. He had a better opinion of Degrelle, but did not expect much of him either.

Politics, for Hitler, was purely pragmatic. He did not except his own book of confessions and professions, *Mein Kampf,* from this general rule. Large parts of it were no longer valid, he said. He should not have let himself be pinned down to definite statements so early. After hearing that remark I gave up my fruitless efforts to read the book.

When ideology receded into the background after the seizure of power, efforts were made to tame down the party and make it more respectable. Goebbels and Bormann were the chief opponents of that tendency. They were always trying to radicalize Hitler ideologically. To judge by his speeches, Ley must also have belonged to the group of tough ideologists, but lacked the stature to gain any significant influence. Himmler, on the other hand, obviously was going his own absurd way, which was compounded of beliefs about an original Germanic race, a brand of elitism, and an assortment of health-food notions. The whole thing was beginning to assume far-fetched pseudoreligious forms. Goebbels, with Hitler, took the lead in ridiculing these dreams of Himmler's, with Himmler himself adding to the comedy by his vanity and obsessiveness. When, for example, the Japanese presented him with a samurai sword, he at once discovered kinships between Japanese and Teutonic cults and called upon scientists to help him trace these similarities to a racial common denominator.

Hitler was particularly concerned with the question of how he could assure his Reich a new generation of followers committed to his ideas. The general outlines of a plan were drafted by Ley, to whom Hitler had also entrusted the organization of the educational system. Adolf Hitler Schools were established for the elementary grades and Ordensburgen (Order Castles) for higher education. These were meant to turn out a technically and ideologically trained elite. To be sure, all this elite would have been good for was positions in a bureaucratic party administration, since thanks to their isolated and specialized education the young people knew nothing about practical life, while on the other hand their arrogance and conceit about their own abilities were boundless. It was significant that the high party functionaries did not send their own children into these schools; even so fanatical a party member as Gauleiter Sauckel refrained from launching a single one of his many boys on such a course. Conversely, Bormann sent one of his sons to an Adolf Hitler School as punishment.

In Bormann's mind, the *Kirchenkampf*, the campaign against the churches, was useful for reactivating party ideology which had been lying dormant. He was the driving force behind this campaign, as was time and again made plain to our round table. Hitler was hesitant, but only because he would rather postpone this problem to a more favorable time. Here in Berlin, surrounded by male cohorts, he spoke more coarsely and bluntly than he ever did in the midst of his Obersalzberg entourage. "Once I have settled my other problems," he occasionally declared, "I'll have my reckoning with the church. I'll have it reeling on the ropes."

But Bormann did not want this reckoning postponed. Brutally direct himself, he could ill tolerate Hitler's prudent pragmatism. He therefore took every opportunity to push his own projects. Even at meals he broke the unspoken rule that no subjects were to be raised which might spoil Hitler's humor. Bormann had developed a special technique for such thrusts. He would draw one of the members of the entourage into telling him about seditious speeches a pastor or bishop had delivered, until Hitler finally became attentive and demanded details. Bormann would reply that something unpleasant had happened and did not want to bother Hitler with it during the meal. At this Hitler would probe further, while Bormann pretended that he was reluctantly letting the story be dragged from him. Neither the angry looks from his fellow guests nor Hitler's gradually flushing face deterred him from going on. At some point he would take a document from his pocket and begin reading passages from a defiant sermon or a pastoral letter. Frequently Hitler became so worked up that he began to snap his fingers—a sure sign of his anger—pushed away his food and vowed to punish the offending clergyman eventually. He could much more easily put up with foreign indignation and criticism than opposition at home. That he could not immediately retaliate raised him to a white heat, though he usually managed to control himself quite well.

Hitler had no humor. He left joking to others, although he could laugh loudly, abandonedly, sometimes literally writhing with laughter. Often he would wipe tears from his eyes during such spasms. He liked laughing, but it was always laughter at the expense of others.

Goebbels was skilled at entertaining Hitler with jokes while at the same time demolishing any rivals in the internal struggle for power. "You know," he once related, "the Hitler Youth asked us to issue a press release for the twenty-fifth birthday of its staff chief, Lauterbacher. So I sent along a draft of the text to the effect that he had celebrated this birthday 'enjoying full physical and mental vigor.' We heard no more from him." Hitler doubled up with laughter, and Goebbels had achieved his end of cutting the conceited youth leader down to size.

To the dinner guests in Berlin, Hitler repeatedly talked about his youth, emphasizing the strictness of his upbringing. "My father often dealt me hard blows. Moreover, I think that was necessary and helped me." Wilhelm Frick, the Minister of the Interior, interjected in his bleating voice: "As we can see today, it certainly did you good, *mein Führer.*" A numb, horrified silence around the table. Frick tried to save the situation: "I mean, *mein Führer*, that is why you have come so far." Goebbels, who considered Frick a hopeless fool, commented sarcastically: "I would guess you never received a beating in your youth, Frick."

Walther Funk, who was both Minister of Economics and president of the Reichsbank, told stories about the outlandish pranks that his vice president, Brinkmann, had gone on performing for months, until it was finally realized that he was mentally ill. In telling such stories Funk not only wanted to amuse Hitler but to inform him in this casual way of events which would sooner or later reach his ears. Brinkmann, it seemed, had invited the cleaning women and messenger boys of the Reichsbank to a grand dinner in the ballroom of the Hotel Bristol, one of the best hotels in Berlin, where he played the violin for them. This sort of thing rather fitted in with the regime's propaganda of all Germans forming one "folk community." But as everyone at table laughed, Funk continued: "Recently he stood in front of the Ministry of Economics on Unter den Linden, took a large package of newly printed banknotes from his briefcase—as you know, the notes bear my signature—and gave them out to passers-by, saying: 'Who wants some of the new Funks?' "* Shortly afterward, Funk continued, the poor man's insanity had become plain for all to see. He called together all the employees of the Reichsbank. " 'Everyone older than fifty to the left side, the younger employees to the right.' " Then, to one man on the right side: " 'How old are you?'—'Forty-nine sir.'—'You go to the left too. Well now, all on the left side are dismissed at once, and what is more with a double pension.' "

Hitler's eyes filled with tears of laughter. When he had recovered, he launched into a monologue on how hard it sometimes is to recognize a madman. In this roundabout way Funk was also accomplishing another end. Hitler did not yet know that the Reichsbank vice president in his irresponsible state had given Goering a check for several million marks.

* A pun in German; *Funken* = sparks.—*Translators' note.*

Goering cashed the check without a qualm. Later on, of course, **Goering** vehemently objected to the thesis that Brinkmann did not know what he was doing. Funk could expect him to present this point of view to Hitler. Experience had shown that the person who first managed to suggest a particular version of an affair to Hitler had virtually won his point, for Hitler never liked to alter a view he had once expressed. Even so, Funk had difficulties recovering those millions of marks from Goering.

A favorite target of Goebbels's jokes and the subject of innumerable anecdotes was Rosenberg, whom Goebbels liked to call "the Reich philosopher." On this subject Goebbels could be sure that Hitler agreed with him. He therefore took up the theme so frequently that the stories resembled carefully rehearsed theatrical performances in which the various actors were only waiting for their cues. Hitler was almost certain to interject at some point: "The *Völkischer Beobachter* is just as boring as its editor, Rosenberg. You know, we have a so-called humor sheet in the party, *Die Brennessel*. The dreariest rag imaginable. And on the other hand the *VB* is nothing but a humor sheet." Goebbels also made game of the printer Müller, who was doing his best both to keep the party and not to lose his old customers, who came from strictly Catholic circles in Upper Bavaria. His printing program was certainly versatile, ranging from pious calendars to Rosenberg's antichurch writings. But Müller was allowed considerable leeway; in the twenties he had gone on printing the *Völkischer Beobachter* no matter how large the bill grew.

Many jokes were carefully prepared, tied up as they were with actual events, so that Hitler was kept abreast of interparty developments under the guise of foolery. Again, Goebbels was far better at this than all the others, and Hitler gave him further encouragement by showing that he was very much amused.

An old party member, Eugen Hadamowski, had obtained a key position as Reichssendeleiter (Head of Broadcasting for the Reich), but now he was longing to be promoted to Leiter des Reichsrundfunks (Head of the Reich Radio System). The Propaganda Minister, who had another candidate, was afraid that Hitler might back Hadamowski because he had skillfully organized the public address systems for the election campaigns before 1933. He had Hanke, state secretary in the Propaganda Ministry, send for the man and officially informed him that Hitler had just appointed him Reichsintendant (General Director) for radio. At the table Hitler was given an account of how Hadamowski had gone wild with joy at this news. The description was, no doubt, highly colored and exaggerated, so that Hitler took the whole affair as a great joke. Next day Goebbels had a few copies of a newspaper printed reporting on the sham appointment and praising the new appointee in excessive terms. He outlined the article for Hitler, with all its ridiculous phrases, and acted out Hadamowski's rapture upon reading these things about himself. Once more Hitler and the whole table with him was convulsed. That same day Hanke asked the newly appointed Reichsintendant to make a speech into a dead microphone, and once again there was endless merriment at Hitler's table when the story was told. After this, Goebbels no longer had to worry that Hitler would intervene in favor of Hadamowski. It was a diabolic game; the ridiculed man did not have the slightest opportunity to defend himself and probably never realized that the practical joke was carefully plotted to make him unacceptable to Hitler. No one could even know whether what Goebbels was describing was true or whether he was giving his imagination free rein.

From one point of view, Hitler was the real dupe of these intrigues. As far as I could observe, Hitler was in fact no match for Goebbels in such matters; with his more direct temperament he did not understand this sort of cunning. But it certainly should have given one pause that Hitler allowed this nasty game to go on and even encouraged it. One word of displeasure would certainly have stopped this sort of thing for a long while to come.

I often asked myself whether Hitler was open to influence. He surely could be swayed by those who knew how to manage him. Hitler was mistrustful, to be sure. But he was so in a cruder sense, it often seemed to me; for he did not see through clever chess moves or subtle manipulation of his opinions. He had apparently no sense for methodical deceit. Among the masters of that art were Goering, Goebbels, Bormann, and, within limits, Himmler. Since those who spoke out in candid terms on the important questions usually could not make Hitler change his mind, the cunning men naturally gained more and more power.

Let me conclude my account of afternoon dinners in the Chancellery by relating another joke of this perfidious type. This time the target was the foreign press chief, Putzi Hanfstaengl, whose close personal ties with Hitler were a source of uneasiness to Goebbels. Goebbels began casting aspersions on Hanfstaengl's character, representing him as miserly, money grubbing, and of dubious honesty. He once brought in a phonograph record of an English song and attempted to prove that Hanfstaengl had stolen its melody for a popular march he had composed.

The foreign press chief was already under a cloud when Goebbels, at the time of the Spanish Civil War, told the table company that Hanfstaengl had made adverse remarks about the fighting spirit of the German soldiers in combat there. Hitler was furious. This cowardly fellow who had no right to judge the courage of others must be given a lesson, he declared. A few days later Hanfstaengl was informed that he must make a plane trip; he was given sealed orders from Hitler which were not to be opened until after the plane had taken off. Once in the air, Hanfstaengl read, horrified, that he was to be put down in "Red Spanish territory" where he was to work as an agent for Franco. At the table Goebbels told Hitler every detail: How Hanfstaengl pleaded with the pilot to turn back; it must all be a misunderstanding, he insisted. But the plane, Goebbels related, continued circling for hours over German territory, in the clouds. The passenger was given false location reports, so that he believed he was approaching closer and closer to Spanish territory. Finally the pilot announced that he had to make an emergency landing and set the plane down safely at Leipzig airport. Hanfstaengl, who only then realized that he had been the victim of a bad joke, began asserting that there was a plot against his life and soon afterward vanished without a trace.

All the chapters in this story elicited great merriment at Hitler's table —all the more so since in this case Hitler had plotted the joke together with Goebbels. But when word came a few days later that the missing press chief had sought asylum abroad, Hitler became afraid that Hanfstaengl would collaborate with the foreign press and profit by his intimate knowledge of the Third Reich. But for all his reputation for money grubbing, Hanfstaengl did nothing of the sort.

I, too, found myself going along with this streak in Hitler, who seemed to enjoy destroying the reputation and self-respect of even his close associates and faithful comrades in the struggle for power. But although I was still under Hitler's spell, my feeling had evolved considerably from what it had been during the early years of our association. Seeing him daily as I did, I acquired some perspective and occasionally a capacity for critical observation.

My close relation with him, moreover, centered increasingly around architecture. To be able to serve him with all my ability and to translate his architectural ideas into reality still filled me with enthusiasm. In addition, the larger and more important my building assignments became, the more respect others paid me. I was on the way, I thought at the time, to creating a body of work that would place me among the most famous architects of history. My sense of this also made me feel that I was not just the recipient of Hitler's favor. Rather, I was offering him a return of equal value for having established me as an architect. What is more, Hitler treated me like a colleague and often made it clear that I stood above him where architecture was concerned.

Dining with Hitler regularly meant a considerable loss of time, for we sat at table until half past four in the afternoon. Naturally, hardly anyone could afford to squander so much time every day. I too went to the meals no more than once or twice a week, for otherwise I would have had to neglect my work.

Yet it was important for one's prestige to attend these dinners. Moreover, it was important to most of the guests to be kept abreast of Hitler's daily opinions. The round table was useful to Hitler himself as well, for in this way he could casually and effortlessly hand down a political line or slogan. On the other hand, Hitler was apt to speak little about his own work, say about the outcome of an important conference. Whenever he did allude to such matters, it was usually for the purpose of commenting critically upon an interlocutor.

Some of the guests would throw out their bait during the meal itself, in hopes of being granted a special interview with Hitler. They would mention that they had brought along photographs of the latest stage of a building project. Other favorite baits were photographs of the sets for some newly staged work, preferably a Wagner opera or an operetta. But the infallible attraction was always: "*Mein Führer,* I have brought you new building plans." The guest who said that could be fairly certain that Hitler would reply: "Oh, good, show them to me right after dinner." To be sure, the other diners frowned on such direct approaches. But otherwise one might wait for months before receiving an official appointment to see Hitler.

When the meal was over, Hitler rose, the guests said brief good-bys, and the favored guest was led into the adjacent salon, which for some inexplicable reason was called the "conservatory." On such occasions Hitler would often say to me: "Wait a moment. There's something I'd like to discuss with you." The moment often turned into an hour or more. Then Hitler would have me called in. Now he behaved quite informally, sat opposite me in one of the comfortable chairs and inquired about the progress of my buildings.

By this time it was often six o'clock. Hitler went to his rooms on the upper floor, while I drove to my office, frequently for only a short time. The adjutant might telephone to say that Hitler had asked me to come to supper, which meant I had to return to the Chancellor's apartment two hours later. But often, when I had plans to show, I went unasked.

From six to eight persons would assemble on those evenings: his adjutants, his doctor, the photographer Hoffmann, one or two Munich acquaintances, quite often Hitler's pilot Bauer along with his radio man and onboard mechanic, and the inevitable Bormann. This was the most private circle in Berlin, for political associates such as Goebbels were usually not wanted in the evenings. The level of the conversations was a distinct stage lower than at the afternoon affairs. The talk wandered off into trivialities. Hitler liked to hear about the theater. Scandals also interested him. The pilot talked about flying; Hoffmann contributed anecdotes about Munich artistic circles and reported on his art collecting. But usually Hitler would tell stories about his life and development.

The meal again consisted of simple dishes. Kannenberg, the house steward, did try a few times to serve better food for these rather private meals. For a few weeks Hitler actually ate caviar by the spoonful with gusto, and praised the taste, which was new to him. But then he asked Kannenberg about the price, was horrified, and gave strict orders against having that again. Thereupon the cheaper red caviar was served him, but that too he rejected as an extravagance. To be sure, these expenses were insignificant in comparison with the total outlay for the Chancellor's household. But the idea of a caviar-eating Leader was incompatible with Hitler's conception of himself.

After supper the company moved into the salon, which was otherwise reserved for official occasions. Everyone settled into easy chairs; Hitler unbuttoned his jacket and stretched out his legs. The lights slowly dimmed, while household employees, including some of the women, and members of Hitler's bodyguard were admitted through a rear door. The first movie began. There we sat, as at Obersalzberg, mute for some three or four hours, and when these films came to an end at about one in the morning, we stood up stiff and dazed. Hitler alone seemed sprightly; he discoursed on the actors' performances, spoke appreciatively of the art of one of his favorite actors, then went on to other subjects. The conversation was continued at a sluggish pace in the small drawing room. Beer, wine, and sandwiches were handed around, until Hitler at last said good night at about two o'clock in the morning. I frequently reflected that this mediocre group was assembling at the same spot where Bismarck used to talk brilliantly with friends and political associates.

A few times I suggested inviting a famous pianist or a scientist, in order to introduce a new element into the monotony of these evenings. But Hitler always fended off anything of this sort. "The artists would not be so eager to come as they say." In fact many of them would have regarded such an invitation as a distinction. Probably Hitler did not want to have the sluggish, banal conclusion of his daily routine disturbed; he was fond of it. Moreover, I often observed that Hitler felt a certain shyness toward people of high standing in some professional field. He did receive them occasionally, but in the reserved atmosphere of an official audience. Perhaps that was one of the reasons he had picked out so very young an architect as myself. He did not feel such an inferiority complex toward me.

During the early years after 1933 the adjutants were permitted to invite ladies, some of them screen stars selected by Goebbels. But as a rule only married women were admitted, usually with their husbands. Hitler followed this rule in order to forestall rumors which might harm the image shaped by Goebbels of a Leader whose style of life was absolutely respectable. Toward these women Hitler behaved rather like the graduate of a dance class at the final dance. He displayed a shy eagerness to do nothing wrong, to offer a sufficient number of compliments, and to welcome them and bid them good-by with the Austrian kissing of the hand. When the party was over, he usually sat around for a while with his private circle to rave a bit about the women. He spoke more about their figures than their charm or cleverness, and always there was something in his tone of the schoolboy who is convinced that his wishes are unattainable. Hitler loved tall, full-figured women; Eva Braun, who was rather small and delicate of build, was actually not at all his type.

Abruptly, some time in 1935, as I recall, this practice ceased from one day to the next. I never learned the reason for this; perhaps it was due to some gossip. Whatever the reason, Hitler suddenly announced that henceforth the invitations to women were to stop. From then on he contented himself with the stars in the nightly movies.

Around 1939 Eva Braun was assigned a bedroom in the Berlin residence. It adjoined his; the windows looked out on a narrow courtyard. Here even more than in Obersalzberg she led a completely isolated life, stealing into the building through a side entrance and going up a rear staircase, never descending into the lower rooms, even when there were only old acquaintances in the apartment, and she was overjoyed whenever I kept her company during her long hours of waiting.

In Berlin, Hitler very seldom went to the theater, except to see operettas. He would never miss a new production of the by now classical operettas such as *Die Fledermaus* and *The Merry Widow*. I am certain that I saw *Die Fledermaus* with him at least five or six times in cities all over Germany. He customarily contributed considerable sums from Bormann's privy purse to have the operetta put on in lavish style.

In addition he liked revues. He went to the Wintergarten several times to attend a Berlin variety show and would certainly have gone more frequently but for the fact that he was embarrassed to be seen there. Sometimes he sent his house steward in his place and then late in the evening would look over the program and ask for an account of what had gone on. Several times he also went to the Metropol Theater which put on insipid musicals with plenty of scantily clad girls.

During the Bayreuth Festival every year he attended every single performance of the first cycle. It seemed to a musical layman like myself that in his conversations with Frau Winifred Wagner he displayed knowledge about musical matters in detail; but he was even more concerned about the directing.

Aside from Bayreuth, however, he very seldom attended performances of operas, and his initially rather keen interest in theater also dwindled. Even his enthusiasm for Bruckner never seemed very marked and imposed no obligations on others. Although a movement from a Bruckner symphony was played before each of his "cultural speeches" at the Nuremberg Party Rallies, for the rest he merely took care that Bruckner's works continued to be fostered at St. Florian. He saw to it, however, that his public image of a man passionately devoted to art was cultivated.

I never found out whether and to what extent Hitler had an interest in literature. Mostly he talked about books on military science, naval matters and architecture, which he would pore over with great interest during the night hours. On other books he made no comment.

I myself threw all my strength into my work and was baffled at first by the way Hitler squandered his working time. I could understand that he might wish his day to trail off in boredom and pastimes; but to my notion this phase of the day, averaging some six hours, proved rather long, whereas the actual working session was by comparison relatively short. When, I would often ask myself, did he really work? Little was left of the day; he rose late in the morning and conducted one or two official conferences; but from the subsequent dinner on he more or less wasted time until the early hours of the evening.[1] His rare appointments in the late afternoon were imperiled by his passion for looking at building plans. The adjutants often asked me: "Please don't show any plans today." Then the drawings I had brought with me would be left by the telephone switchboard at the entrance, and I would reply evasively to Hitler's inquiries. Sometimes he saw through this game and would himself go to look in the anteroom or the cloakroom for my roll of plans.

In the eyes of the people Hitler was the Leader who watched over the nation day and night. This was hardly so. But Hitler's lax scheduling could be regarded as a life style characteristic of the artistic temperament. According to my observations, he often allowed a problem to mature during the weeks when he seemed entirely taken up with trivial matters. Then, after the "sudden insight" came, he would spend a few days of intensive work giving final shape to his solution. No doubt he also used his dinner and supper guests as sounding boards, trying out new ideas, approaching these ideas in a succession of different ways, tinkering with them before an uncritical audience, and thus perfecting them. Once he had come to a decision, he relapsed again into his idleness.

IO

Our Empire Style

I WENT TO HITLER'S EVENINGS ONCE OR TWICE A WEEK. AROUND MIDNIGHT, after the last movie had been run, he sometimes asked to see my roll of drawings and studied every detail until two or three o'clock in the morning. The other guests withdrew for a glass of wine, or went home, aware that there would be little chance to have a word with Hitler once he was caught up in his ruling passion.

Hitler's favorite project was our model city, which was set up in the former exhibition rooms of the Berlin Academy of Arts. In order to reach it undisturbed, he had doors installed in the walls between the Chancellery and our building and a communicating path laid out. Sometimes he invited the supper guests to our studio. We would set out armed with flashlights and keys. In the empty halls spotlights illuminated the models. There was no need for me to do the talking, for Hitler, with flashing eyes, explained every single detail to his companions.

There was keen excitement when a new model was set up and illuminated by brilliant spots from the direction in which the sun would fall on the actual buildings. Most of these models were made on a scale of 1:50; cabinetmakers reproduced every small detail, and the wood was painted to simulate the materials that would actually be used. In this way whole sections of the grand new avenue were gradually put together, and we could have a three-dimensional impression of the building intended to be a reality in a decade. This model street went on for about a hundred feet through the former exhibition rooms of the Academy of Arts.

Hitler was particularly excited over a large model of the grand boulevard on a scale of 1 : 1000. He loved to "enter his avenue" at various points and take measure of the future effect. For example, he assumed the point of view of a traveler emerging from the south station or admired the great hall as it looked from the heart of the avenue. To do so, he bent down, almost kneeling, his eye an inch or so above the level of the model, in order to have the right perspective, and while looking he spoke with unusual vivacity. These were the rare times when he relinquished his usual stiffness. In no other situation did I see him so lively, so spontaneous, so relaxed, whereas I myself, often tired and even after years never free of a trace of respectful constraint, usually remained taciturn. One of my close associates summed up the character of this remarkable relationship: "Do you know what you are? You are Hitler's unrequited love!"

These rooms were kept under careful guard and no one was allowed to inspect the grand plan for the rebuilding of Berlin without Hitler's express permission. Once, when Goering had examined the model of the grand boulevard, he had his escort walk on ahead, then said in a deeply moved tone: "A few days ago the Fuehrer spoke to me about my mission after his death. He leaves me free to handle everything as I think best. But he made me promise one thing, that I would never replace you by anyone else after his death; that I would not tamper with your plans, but let you take complete charge. And that I must place the money for the buildings at your disposal, all the money you ask for." Goering made an emotional pause. "I solemnly took the Fuehrer's hand and promised him that, and I now make the same promise to you." Whereupon, he gave me a long and sentimental handshake.

My father, too, came to see the work of his now famous son. He only shrugged his shoulders at the array of models: "You've all gone completely crazy." The evening of his visit we went to the theater and saw a comedy in which Heinz Rühmann was appearing. By chance Hitler was at the same performance. During the intermission he sent one of his adjutants to ask whether the old gentleman sitting beside me was my father; then he asked us both to his box. When my father—still erect and self-controlled in spite of his seventy-five years—was introduced to Hitler, he was overcome by a violent quivering such as I had never seen him exhibit before, nor ever did again. He turned pale, did not respond to Hitler's lavish praise of his son, and then took his leave in silence. Later, my father never mentioned this meeting, and I too avoided asking him about the fit of nerves that the sight of Hitler had produced in him.

"You've all gone completely crazy." Nowadays, when I leaf through the numerous photos of models of our one-time grand boulevard, I see that it would have turned out not only crazy, but also boring.

We had, of course, recognized that lining the new avenue solely with public buildings would lead to a certain lifelessness and had therefore reserved two-thirds of the length of the street for private buildings. With Hitler's support we fended off efforts by various government agencies to displace these business buildings. We had no wish for an avenue consisting solely of ministries. A luxurious movie house for premières, another cinema for the masses accommodating two thousand persons, a new opera house, three theaters, a new concert hall, a building for congresses, the so-called House of the Nations, a hotel of twenty-one stories, variety theaters, mass and luxury restaurants, and even an indoor swimming pool, built in Roman style and as large as the baths of Imperial Rome, were deliberately included in the plans with the idea of bringing urban life into the new avenue.[1] There were to be quiet interior courtyards with colonnades and small luxury shops set apart from the noise of the street and inviting strollers. Electric signs were to be employed profusely. The whole avenue was also conceived by Hitler and me as a continuous sales display of German goods which would exert a special attraction upon foreigners.

Whenever, nowadays, I look through the plans and the photos of the models, even these varied parts of the avenue strike me as lifeless and regimented. When on the morning after my release from imprisonment I passed one of these buildings on the way to the airport,[2] I saw in a few seconds what I had been blind to for years: our plan completely lacked a sense of proportion. We had set aside block units of between five hundred feet and six hundred and sixty feet even for private businesses. A uniform height had been imposed on all the buildings, as well as on all the store fronts. Skyscrapers, however, were banished from the foreground. Thus we deprived ourselves of all the contrasts essential for animating and loosening the pattern. The entire conception was stamped by a monumental rigidity that would have counteracted all our efforts to introduce urban life into this avenue.

Our happiest concept, comparatively speaking, was the central railroad station, the southern pole of Hitler's grand boulevard. The station, its steel ribbing showing through sheathings of copper and glass, would have handsomely offset the great blocks of stone dominating the rest of the avenue. It provided for four traffic levels linked by escalators and elevators and was to surpass New York's Grand Central Station in size.

State visitors would have descended a large outside staircase. The idea was that as soon as they, as well as ordinary travelers, stepped out of the station they would be overwhelmed, or rather stunned, by the urban scene and thus the power of the Reich. The station plaza, thirty-three hundred feet long and a thousand feet wide, was to be lined with captured weapons, after the fashion of the Avenue of Rams which leads from Karnak to Luxor. Hitler conceived this detail after the campaign in France and came back to it again in the late autumn of 1941, after his first defeats in the Soviet Union.

This plaza was to be crowned by Hitler's great arch or "Arch of Triumph," as he only occasionally called it. Napoleon's Arc de Triomphe on the Place de l'Etoile with its one-hundred-sixty-foot height certainly presents a monumental appearance and provides a majestic terminus to the Champs Elysées. Our triumphal arch, five hundred and fifty feet wide, three hundred and ninety-two feet deep, and three hundred and eighty-six feet high, would have towered over all the other buildings on this southern portion of the avenue and would literally have dwarfed them.

After trying a few times in vain, I no longer had the courage to urge any changes on Hitler. This was the heart of his plan; he had conceived it long before encountering the purifying influence of Professor Troost, and the arch was the classic example of the architectural fantasies he had worked out in his lost sketchbook of the twenties. He remained impervious to all my hints that the monument might be improved by a change of proportions or a simplification of lines and did not demur when on the plans I delicately indicated the architect by three X's. Everyone would know who the "anonymous" architect was.

Sighting through the two hundred sixty foot opening of the great arch, the arriving traveler would see at the end of a three-mile vista the street's second great triumphal structure rearing out of the haze of the metropolis: the great hall with its enormous dome, described in an earlier chapter.

Eleven separate ministry buildings adorned the avenue between the triumphal arch and the great hall. I had already designed quarters for the ministries of the Interior, Transportation, Justice, Economics, and Food when, after 1941, I was told to include a Colonial Ministry in my plans.[3] In other words, even after the invasion of Russia, Hitler was dreaming of acquiring German colonies. The ministers, who hoped that our program would result in concentration of their offices, now distributed throughout Berlin, were disappointed. For by Hitler's decree the new buildings were to serve chiefly for purposes of prestige, not for the housing of the bureaucratic apparatus.

After the monumental central section, the avenue once more resumed its business and entertainment character for a distance of more than half a mile and ended with the round plaza at the intersection with Potsdamer Strasse. Proceeding northward it once more began to be ceremonial. On the right rose Soldiers' Hall, designed by Wilhelm Kreis: a huge cube whose purpose Hitler had never stated frankly, but was probably to be a combination of armory and veterans' memorial. At any rate, after the armistice with France he gave orders that the dining car in which the surrender of Germany had been signed in 1918 and the surrender of France in 1940 was to be brought here as the hall's first exhibit. A crypt was planned for the tombs of celebrated German field marshals of the past, present, and future.[4] Stretching westward behind the hall as far as Bendlerstrasse were to be the buildings for a new High Command of the Army.[5]

After inspecting these plans Goering felt that his Air Ministry had been demoted. He asked me to be his architect,* and opposite the soldiers' hall, on the edge of the Tiergarten, we found an ideal building site for his purposes. Goering was enraptured by my plans for his new building (which after 1940 went by the name of Office of the Reich Marshal, in order to do justice to the multitude of positions he held), but Hitler was less so. "The building is too big for Goering," he commented. "He's puffing himself up too much. All in all, I don't like his taking my architect for that purpose." Although he privately grumbled a good deal over Goering's plans, he never found the courage to speak out on the matter. Goering knew Hitler and reassured me: "Just let the matter be and don't worry about it. We'll build it that way, and in the end the Fuehrer will be delighted."

Hitler often showed similar forbearance in personal matters. Thus he overlooked the marital misdemeanors of his entourage—unless, as in the Blomberg case,[6] the scandal could be made to serve a political purpose. He could also smile at someone's craving for pomp and make acid remarks in private without so much as hinting to the person concerned that he disapproved of his conduct.

The design for Goering's headquarters provided for extensive series of stairways, halls, and salons which took up more room than the offices themselves. The heart of the building was to be an imposing hall with a great flight of stairs rising through four stories, which would never have been used since everyone would of course have taken the elevator. The whole thing was pure spectacle. This was a decisive step in my personal development from the neoclassicism I had first espoused, and which was perhaps still to be seen in the new Chancellery, to a blatant *nouveau riche* architecture of prestige. An entry for May 5, 1941, in my office journal records that the Reich Marshal was highly pleased with the model of his building. The staircase especially delighted him. Here he would stand, he declared, when he proclaimed the watchword of the year for the officers of the air force. The office journal preserves more of his magnil-

* Despite my official position as General Inspector of Buildings, Hitler allowed me to design major buildings as a private architect. The general procedure for the reconstruction of Berlin was to call in private architects to design the official buildings as well as the commercial buildings.

oquence. "In tribute to this, the greatest staircase in the world," Goering continued, "Breker must create a monument to the Inspector General of Buildings. It will be installed here to commemorate forever the man who so magnificently shaped this building."

This part of the ministry, with its eight hundred feet of frontage on the grand boulevard, was supplemented by a wing of equal size, on the Tiergarten side, which contained the ballrooms Goering had stipulated as well as his private apartment. I situated the bedrooms on the top story. Alleging the need for air-raid protection, I decided to cover the roof with thirteen feet of garden soil, which meant that even large trees would have been able to strike root there. Thus I envisioned a two and a half acre roof garden, with swimming pools and tennis courts, fountains, ponds, colonnades, pergolas, and refreshment rooms, and finally a summer theater for two hundred and forty spectators above the roofs of Berlin. Goering was overwhelmed and began raving about the parties he would hold there. "I'll illuminate the great dome with Bengal lights and provide grand fireworks for my guests."

Without the basements, Goering's building would have had a volume of seven hundred and fifty-four thousand cubic yards; the volume of Hitler's newly built Chancellery was only five hundred and twenty thousand cubic yards. Nevertheless, Hitler did not feel that Goering had outstripped him. In that speech of August 1, 1938, in which he disclosed so many of his theories on architecture, Hitler let it be known that according to the great plan for the rebuilding of Berlin the newly completed Chancellery would be used for ten or twelve years. The plan, he said, provided for a residence and seat of government many times larger. After an inspection of Hess's party headquarters in Berlin, Hitler had abruptly decided on the final destiny of the Voss Strasse Chancellery. At Hess's headquarters Hitler was unpleasantly impressed by a stairwell painted a fiery red and furnishings that were considerably plainer and more austere than the ocean-liner style he and the other party and government leaders inclined toward. Back at the Chancellery, Hitler criticized his deputy's taste in no uncertain terms: "Hess is totally unartistic. I must never let him build anything new. After a while he'll receive the present Chancellery as his headquarters, and he won't be allowed to make the slightest changes in it, because he's completely ignorant on such matters." This kind of criticism, especially of a man's aesthetic judgment, could sometimes spell an end to a career, and in the case of Rudolf Hess it was generally so taken. But Hitler never said a word of this to Hess. Hess could only observe that his standing must have fallen by the courtiers' reserved attitude toward him thereafter.

There was to be a huge railroad station to the north as well as to the south of the city. Emerging from it, the visitor would face a basin of water thirty-three hundred feet long and eleven hundred and fifty-five feet wide, across which the great dome was to be seen a mile away. We did not intend to take our water from the Spree, polluted as it was by the filth of the city. As a lover of water sports, I wanted this artificial lake to be clean enough for swimming. Dressing cabins, boathouses, and refreshment terraces were to line this vast open-air pool in the heart of the city; presumably it would have presented a remarkable contrast to the massive buildings that were to be reflected in the lake. The reason for my lake was very simple: The marshy subsoil made the land unfit for building purposes.

Three enormous buildings were to stand on the western side of the lake. In the middle would be the new Berlin Town Hall, some fifteen hundred feet in length. Hitler and I favored different designs; after many discussions my arguments prevailed, even against Hitler's persistent opposition. The Town Hall was flanked by the new High Command of the Navy and the new Berlin Police Headquarters. On the eastern side of the lake, in the midst of gardened areas, a new German War Academy was to be built. The plans for all these buildings were completed.

This avenue between the two central railroad stations was meant to spell out in architecture the political, military, and economic power of Germany. In the center sat the absolute ruler of the Reich, and in his immediate proximity, as the highest expression of his power, was the great domed hall which was to be the dominant structure of the future Berlin. At least the planning would reflect Hitler's statement: "Berlin must change its face in order to adapt to its great new mission."[7]

For five years I lived in this world of plans, and in spite of all their defects and absurdities I still cannot entirely tear myself away from it all. When I look deep into myself for the reasons for my present hatred of Hitler, I sometimes think that in addition to all the terrible things he perpetrated I should perhaps include the personal disappointment his warmaking brought to me; but I also realize that these plans could only have sprung from his unscrupulous game of power.

Designs of such scale naturally indicate a kind of chronic megalomania, which is reason enough to dwell on these grandiose plans. Yet that broad boulevard, those new central railroad stations with their underground communications, are not so excessive by present-day standards when skyscrapers and public buildings all over the world have reached similar proportions. Perhaps it was less their size than the way they violated the human scale that made them abnormal. The great domed hall, Hitler's future Chancellery, Goering's grandiose ministry, the Soldiers' Hall, and the triumphal arch—I saw all these buildings with Hitler's political eyes. Once, when we were contemplating the model city, he took my arm and with moist eyes confided: "Now do you understand why we are building all this on such a scale? The capital of the Germanic Empire—if only my health were good. . . ."

Hitler was in a hurry for work to start on the five-mile-long core of his plan. After involved calculations I promised him that all the buildings would be completed by 1950. This was the spring of 1939. I had imagined that in setting such an early date, based as it was on a nonstop work program, I would give him special pleasure, so I was somewhat dashed when he merely accepted this deadline. Perhaps he was thinking about his military plans, which of course made a mockery of my calculations.

At other times, however, he was so intent upon finishing within the intended period and seemed to be looking forward to 1950 with such eagerness, that if his architectural fantasies were only meant to conceal his imperialistic aims they would have been the best of all his deceits. His frequent allusions to the political importance of this project should have alerted me to the real nature of his plans; but the way he seemed to assume that my building operations in Berlin would go forward undisturbed offset these suspicions. I was accustomed to his occasionally saying things that sounded hallucinatory; in retrospect it is easier to find the thread between this trancelike state and the building projects.

Hitler was extremely concerned that our designs should not be publicized. Only parts were made known, since we could not work entirely in secret; too many persons were engaged on preliminary jobs. Thus we occasionally permitted glimpses of aspects of the plan that seemed innocuous, and Hitler even let me publish an article outlining the basic idea of our urban renewal.[8] But when the cabaret humorist Werner Fink made fun of these projects he was sent off to a concentration camp, although this may not have been his only sin. His arrest took place, incidentally, just the day before I meant to attend his show as proof that I was not offended.

Our caution extended even to details. When we were considering tearing down the tower of the Berlin Town Hall, we launched a trial balloon by having State Secretary Karl Hanke insert a "reader's letter" in a Berlin newspaper. When angry protests from the populace poured in, I postponed the matter. Our aim in general was to spare the feelings of the public in carrying out our plans. Thus we considered, for example, what to do about charming Monbijou Palace, since a museum was planned for the site. We decided to reconstruct it in the park of Charlottenburg Palace.[9] Even the radio tower was to be preserved for similar reasons. The Victory Column, while it would break the line of our projected avenue, was also not to be razed. Hitler regarded it as a monument of German history. In fact, he was going to make the column more impressive by adding a tambour to increase its height. He drew a sketch of the improvement; the drawing has been preserved. In discussing the matter he made fun of the thrift practiced by the State of Prussia even at the height of its triumph, pinching pennies by saving on the height of its column.

I estimated the total cost of the Berlin rebuilding at between **four** and six billion Reichsmark, which at present-day building costs would have been between 16 and 24 billion Deutsche Mark (DM). Spread over eleven years, this meant about five hundred million Reichsmark to be allocated annually to the project. This was by no means a utopian proposal, for it amounted to only one twenty-fifth of the total volume of the German construction industry.* To further reassure myself, I proposed another comparison, though a highly dubious one. I calculated what percentage of the total tax revenues of the Prussian state the notably thrifty King Frederick William I of Prussia, the father of Frederick the Great, had expended on his buildings in Berlin. It was many times our projected expenditures, which amounted to only 3 per cent of the 15 billion, 700 million Reichsmark tax revenues. But the parallel was questionable because the revenues of the early eighteenth century cannot be compared with the taxation of the present day.

Professor Hettlage, my budgetary adviser, commented sardonically about our approach to the matter: "For the municipality of Berlin expenditures have to be governed by income; for us it is the other way around."[10] As Hitler and I saw it, our annual 500 million should not be represented as a single appropriation. Rather, it was to be divided among as many budgets as possible. Every ministry and every government office was to pay for its new quarters out of its individual budget, just as the government railroad system would pay for the modernization of its Berlin installations, and the city of Berlin for streets and subways. Private industry would of course cover its own costs.

By 1938 we had settled these details, and Hitler took some glee in the cunning of it all: "Distributed this way," he commented, "the cost of the whole thing won't attract attention. All that we'll finance ourselves will be the great hall and the triumphal arch. We'll call on the people to make contributions. In addition the Finance Minister is to place 60 million annually at the disposal of your office. Whatever we don't use of this can be put aside for the future." By 1941 I had already accumulated 218 million marks.[11] In 1943—the sum had meanwhile increased to three hundred twenty million—the Finance Minister proposed, and I agreed, that the account be quietly dissolved. We never said a word to Hitler about this.

Finance Minister von Schwerin-Krosigk, aghast at this squandering of public funds, repeatedly made objections. Lest these disturb me, Hitler fetched up counter arguments:

If the Finance Minister could realize what a source of income to the state my buildings will be in fifty years! Remember what happened with

* According to Rolf Wagenführ, *Die deutsche Industrie im Kriege 1939–1945* (Berlin, 1954), 12.8 billion Reichsmarks were spent on building projects in 1939.

Ludwig II. Everyone said he was mad because of the cost of his palaces. But today? Most tourists go to Upper Bavaria solely to see them. The entrance fees alone have long since paid for the building costs. Don't you agree? The whole world will come to Berlin to see our buildings. All we need do is tell the Americans how much the Great Hall cost. Maybe we'll exaggerate a bit and say a billion and a half instead of a billion. Then they'll be wild to see the most expensive building in the world.

Each time he sat over the plans he was apt to repeat: "My only wish, Speer, is to live to see these buildings. In 1950 we'll organize a world's fair. Until then the buildings will remain empty, and then they'll serve as exhibition buildings. We'll invite the entire world." That was the way Hitler talked; it was difficult to guess his real thoughts. To console my wife, who saw the next eleven years devoted entirely to work with no prospect of any family life, I promised her a trip around the world in 1950.

Hitler's idea of distributing the cost of the project over as many shoulders as possible actually worked out. For Berlin, wealthy, prospering and increasingly the center of national authority, attracted more and more government officials. Industries responded to this by making impressive additions to their Berlin headquarters. So far there had been only one avenue which functioned as "Berlin's show window": Unter den Linden. Big companies were lured to the broad new boulevard partly in the expectation of avoiding the traffic jams of the old prestige streets, partly because building lots were relatively cheap in this still undeveloped area. At the outset of my work I received many applications for building projects which would otherwise have been scattered at random throughout the city. Thus, soon after Hitler's accession to power the large new building of the Reichsbank had been put up in an out-of-the-way quarter; several blocks had been torn down to make room for it. Incidentally, one day after dinner Himmler pointed out that the longitudinal and transverse wings had the shape of a Christian cross. This, he maintained, was obviously a veiled attempt on the part of the Catholic architect Wolf to glorify the Christian religion. Hitler knew enough about building to be merely amused by such points.

Within a few months after the plans were finally drafted and even before the shifting of the railroad tracks had been completed, the first available section of the avenue, three quarters of a mile long, was assigned to the various builders. Applications from ministries, private companies, and government departments for some of the other building sites, which would not be available for several years, increased to such an extent that all the sites along the entire four and a half miles were taken. What is more, we had to begin allocating sites south of the south station. With some difficulty we restrained Dr. Robert Ley, head of the German Labor Front, from using the enormous funds he collected from workmen's contributions to buy up a fifth of the entire length of the boulevard for his own purposes. Even so, he obtained a block a thousand feet in length, which he planned to make into a huge amusement area.

Among the motives for this burst of building fever was, of course, the desire to curry favor with Hitler by erecting important edifices. Since the expenses for such buildings were higher than they would have been on ordinary sites, I suggested to Hitler that he commend the people who commissioned the buildings for all the additional millions they were spending. The idea appealed to him immediately. "Why not have a medal for those who have rendered service to art? We'll award it very rarely and chiefly to those who have financed a major building. A lot can be done with medals." Even the British Ambassador thought (and he was not wrong) that he was ingratiating himself with Hitler when he proposed building a new embassy within the framework of the Berlin renewal plan. Mussolini, too, was extremely interested in the project.*

Although Hitler did not reveal the full extent of his ambitions in the realm of architecture, there was plenty of discussion about what he did make public. As a result, there was a boom in architecture. Had Hitler been interested in breeding horses, a passion for horse breeding would undoubtedly have sprung up among the leading men in the Reich. As it was, there was a veritable flood of designs with a Hitlerian cast. True, no such thing as a style of the Third Reich developed, but buildings took a definite cast, marked by certain eclectic elements. Soon this mode became almost universal. Yet Hitler was by no means doctrinaire. He realized full well that an autobahn restaurant or a Hitler Youth home in the country should not look like an urban building. Nor would it ever have occurred to him to build a factory in his public-display style; in fact, he could become enthusiastic over an industrial building in glass and steel. But any public building in a nation that was on the point of creating an empire must, he thought, have a particular stamp.

The plans for Berlin inspired a host of designs for other urban programs. Every Gauleiter henceforth wanted to immortalize himself in

---

* Sir Neville Henderson in *Failure of a Mission* (New York, 1940), p. 48, wrote:

My idea, therefore, was to exchange the Embassy, which the German Government would have been glad to use for government offices, for some large site on a corner of one of Hitler's new thoroughfares. . . . I spoke both to Goering and Ribbentrop of this plan and asked them to let Hitler know that I contemplated it. I suggested that they might inform him and that I meant one day to talk to him about it and hoped it would form part of a general understanding with Germany.

According to the *Office Journal*, August 20, 1941, Alfieri mentioned that "the Duce takes an extraordinary interest in German architecture and has already asked him if he knows Speer."

his own city. Almost every one of the plans provided, as did my Berlin design, for intersecting axes; they imitated my design even to the orientation. The Berlin model had become a rigid pattern.

In conferring with me over plans, Hitler perpetually drew sketches of his own. They were casually tossed off but accurate in perspective; he drew outlines, cross sections, and renderings to scale. An architect could not have done better. Some mornings he would show me a well-executed sketch he had prepared overnight, but most of his drawings were done in a few hasty strokes during our discussions.

I kept these quick sketches of Hitler's, noting their dates and subjects, and have preserved them to this day. It is interesting that of a total of one hundred and twenty-five such drawings, a good fourth of them relate to the Linz building project, which was always closest to his heart. Equally frequent are sketches for theaters. One morning he surprised me with a neatly drawn design for a commemorative shaft for Munich, which was to be a new symbol of the city dwarfing the towers of the Frauenkirche. He regarded this project, like the Berlin triumphal arch, as his very own, and did not hesitate to make revisions, based on his own sketch, in the design of a Munich architect. Even today these changes strike me as real improvements, providing better for the transition between the static elements of the base and the dynamic thrust of the column.

Hermann Giessler, whom Hitler commissioned to draw up the plans for Munich, could do marvelous imitations of Dr. Ley, the stammering Labor Front leader. Hitler was so delighted with this sort of comedy that he would ask Giessler again and again to tell the story of a visit by the Leys to the showrooms where the models for the Munich city plan were on exhibition. First, Giessler described how the leader of the German workers appeared at the studio in an elegant summer suit, with white stitched gloves and straw hat, accompanied by his wife, who was dressed with equal ostentation. Giessler showed him the Munich plan until Ley interrupted: "I'll build on this entire block. What will that cost? A few hundred millions? Yes, we want to build solidly. . . ."

"And what will be the purpose of the building?"

"A large fashion house. We'll set all the fashions. My wife will take care of that end. We need a whole building for it. Let's! My wife and I will set the German fashions. . . . And . . . and . . . and we'll need whores too! Lots of them, a whole house full, with the most modern furnishings. We'll take everything in hand; a few hundred millions for the building, that's nothing." Hitler laughed until the tears came over the depraved notions of his "labor leader." Giessler, who had had to act out this scene innumerable times, was sick to death of it.

My own building plans were not the only ones Hitler was energetically promoting. He was constantly approving forums for provincial capitals and urging his corps of leaders to officiate as patrons of public edifices. He liked to see a good deal of ruthless competition, since he assumed that this was the only road to outstanding achievement. This attitude of his often irritated me. He could not understand that there were limits to what we could do. Thus, he passed over my objection that before long it would be impossible for me to keep any deadlines because his Gauleiters were using up the available quarry materials for their own buildings.

Himmler came to Hitler's aid. When he heard of the threatening shortage of brick and granite, he offered to employ his prisoners to increase production. He proposed to Hitler that an extensive brickworks be set up in Sachsenhausen, near Berlin, under SS direction and as SS property. Since Himmler was extremely receptive to innovations, some- one soon turned up with a new system for manufacturing brick. But the promised production did not follow, for the technique proved a failure.

Another promise made by Himmler, who was constantly pursuing futuristic projects, ended similarly. He offered to supply granite blocks for the buildings in Nuremberg and Berlin using the labor of concentra- tion camp prisoners. He immediately started a firm with a noncommital name and set the prisoners to breaking stone. Because of the incredible ignorance of the SS entrepreneurs, the blocks developed cracks, and the SS was finally forced to admit that it could supply only a small part of the promised granite. Dr. Todt's road-building organization took the rest of the material produced and used it for cobblestones. Hitler, who had placed great hopes in Himmler's promises, was more and more annoyed. Finally, he commented sarcastically that the SS had better devote itself to making felt slippers and paper bags, the traditional prison products.

Out of the multitude of projects, I myself was to design the square in front of the great hall, at Hitler's request. In addition I had taken over Goering's new building and the south station. That was more than enough, for I was also to design the Nuremberg Party Rally buildings. But since these various projects were to be carried out over a decade I was able to manage if I turned the technical details over to others, with a studio of eight to ten associates. It was still possible for me to keep personal control of a group that size. My private office was on Lindenallee in the West End, near Adolf Hitler Platz, which had formerly been Reichs- kanzler Platz. But my afternoons, until the late hours of the evening, were regularly reserved for my city-planning office in Pariser Platz. Here I assigned major commissions to those men I considered Germany's best architects. Paul Bonatz, after many designs for bridges, was given his first high-rise commission: the High Command of the Navy. Hitler was especially pleased with the grand scale of the design. German Bestelmeyer was assigned the new Town Hall, Wilhelm Kreis the High Command of the Army, the Soldiers' Hall, and various museums. Peter Behrens, the teacher of Walter Gropius and Mies van der Rohe, who had long worked for the AEG electrical company, was entrusted with building the firm's new administrative building on the grand boulevard. This naturally called forth objections from Rosenberg and his cultural watch-and-ward society; they were outraged that this forerunner of architectural radicalism should be allowed to win immortality on "the Fuehrer's avenue." Hitler, who thought well of Peter Behrens's embassy in Leningrad (built when the city was still St. Petersburg), backed up my decision. Several times I also pressed my teacher, Tessenow, to take part in the design competitions. But he did not want to abandon his simple small-town craftsman's style and stubbornly resisted the temptation to design big buildings.

For sculpture I employed chiefly Josef Thorak and Arno Breker, the pupil of Maillol. In 1943, Breker acted as my intermediary in commissioning a sculpture by Maillol to be set up in Grunewald.

Historians have commented that in my private associations I kept away from the party.* It might also be said that the party bigwigs kept away from me, whom they regarded as an interloper. But I was not especially interested in what the Reichsleiters and Gauleiters felt, since I had Hitler's confidence. Aside from Karl Hanke, who had "discovered" me, I was not on familiar terms with any of them. None of them visited me at home. Instead, I found my circle of friends among the artists I gave employment to and among their friends. What time I had in Berlin for socializing I spent with Arno Breker and Wilhelm Kreis; we also frequently saw Wilhelm Kempff, the pianist. In Munich I was on friendly terms with Josef Thorak and Hermann Kaspar, the painter. Late in the night Kaspar could seldom be restrained from loudly proclaiming his preference for the Bavarian monarchy.

I was also close to my first client, Dr. Robert Frank, for whom I had rebuilt a manor house back in 1933, before I became involved with the buildings for Hitler and Goebbels. It was situated near Wilsnack some eighty miles from Berlin, and I frequently spent weekends there with my family. Until 1933, Frank had been general manager of the Prussian Electricity Works, but after the Nazis took power he was relieved of his post and had since lived in retirement. Occasionally bothered by the party, he was protected by my friendship. In 1945, I entrusted my family to him; there, in Schleswig, they were as far as possible from the center of the collapse.

Shortly after my appointment I managed to persuade Hitler that party members of any quality had long since been assigned leading posts, so that only members of the second rank were available for my tasks.

---

* For example, Trevor-Roper, Fest, and Bullock.

He therefore gave me permission to choose my associates as I pleased. Gradually word went round that a sanctuary for nonparty people could be found in my office, and so more and more architects thronged to join us.

Once one of my associates asked me for a reference for admission to the party. My answer went the rounds of the Inspectorate General of Building: "Why? It's enough for all of us that I'm in the party." We took Hitler's building plans seriously but were not so reverential as others about the solemnity of this Hitlerian Reich.

I also continued to absent myself from party meetings, had scarcely any contact with party circles even in the Berlin district, and neglected the party duties turned over to me, although I could have built them up into positions of power. If only from sheer lack of time, I turned over the "Beauty of Work" office to a permanent deputy. I could plead my total incapacity for making public speeches as an excuse for this sort of lack of zeal.

In March 1939, I took a trip with a group of close friends through Sicily and southern Italy. Wilhelm Kreis, Josef Thorak, Hermann Kaspar, Arno Breker, Robert Frank, Karl Brandt, and their wives, formed the party. Magda Goebbels, the Propaganda Minister's wife, came along at our invitation; she used a false name for the journey.

There were certainly a good many love affairs in Hitler's entourage, and he tolerated them. Thus Bormann, with a crudeness that might be expected from this unfeeling and amoral man, had his movie-actress mistress visit him at Obersalzberg and actually stay in his house in the midst of his family. Frau Bormann put up with this situation in a way I found incomprehensible.

Goebbels, too, had many love affairs. Half amused, half revolted, his state secretary, Hanke, would tell how the all-powerful Minister of Culture would blackmail young movie actresses. But Goebbels's intimacy with the Czech film star Lida Baarova was more than an affair. At the time, his wife broke with him and demanded that he live separately from her and the children. Hanke and I were entirely on the wife's side, but Hanke himself complicated this marital crisis when he fell in love with his minister's wife, who was so many years his senior. In order to extricate her from this embarrassment, I proposed that she accompany us on the trip. Hanke wanted to follow her; during our travels he bombarded her with love letters; but she was firm in her refusal.

Throughout this trip, Frau Goebbels proved a pleasant and sensible woman. In general the wives of the regime's bigwigs resisted the temptation of power far more than their husbands. They did not lose themselves in the latters' fantasy world. They looked on at the often grotesque antics of their husbands with inner reservations and were not caught up in the political whirlwind in which their men were carried steeply upward.

Frau Bormann remained a modest, somewhat browbeaten housewife, although blindly devoted both to her husband and the party ideology. I had the impression that Frau Goering was inclined to smile at her husband's mania for pomp. And in the final analysis Eva Braun, too, proved her inner superiority. At any rate she never used for personal ends the power which lay within her grasp.

Sicily, with its Doric temple ruins in Segesta, Syracuse, Selinus, and Agrigentum, provided a valuable supplement to the impressions of our earlier journey to Greece. At the sight of the temples of Selinus and Agrigentum, I observed once again, and with some satisfaction, that even classical antiquity had not been free of megalomaniacal impulses. The Greeks of the colonies were obviously departing from the principle of moderation so praised in the motherland. Compared to these temples, all the examples of Saracen-Norman architecture we encountered paled, except for Frederick II's wonderful hunting castle, the octagonal Castel del Monte. Paestum was another high point of our trip; Pompeii, on the other hand, seemed to me further away from the pure forms of Paestum than were our buildings from the world of the Dorians.

On the return journey we stayed in Rome for a few days. The Fascist government discovered the real identity of our illustrious traveling companion, and Italian Propaganda Minister Alfieri invited us all to the opera. But we found it hard to give a plausible explanation for the fact that the second lady of the German Reich was traveling abroad without her husband and therefore set out for home as quickly as possible.

While we had been dreaming our way through Greek antiquity, Hitler occupied Czechoslovakia and annexed it to the Reich. Back in Germany we found a general mood of depression. Apprehensions about the future filled all of us. To this day I find it strange that a nation can have so right a sense of what is to come, so much so that all the massive propaganda by the government does not banish this feeling.

Nevertheless, it seemed a better sign that Hitler stood up to Goebbels one day when, at lunch in the Chancellery, the Propaganda Minister attacked former Foreign Minister von Neurath, who a few weeks earlier had been appointed Reich Protector of Bohemia and Moravia. Goebbels said: "Everyone knows von Neurath is a weak sneak. But what is needed in the Protectorate is a strong hand to keep order. This man has nothing in common with us; he belongs to an entirely different world." Hitler took issue with this. "Von Neurath was the only man for the job. In the Anglo-Saxon world he is considered a man of distinction. The international effect of his appointment will be reassuring because people will see in it my decision not to deprive the Czechs of their racial and national life."

Hitler asked me to report on my impressions of Italy. I had been most struck by the fact that the walls of even the villages were painted with militant propaganda slogans. "We don't need that," Hitler commented. "If it comes to a war, the German people are tough enough. This kind of propaganda may be all right for Italy. Whether it does any good is another question."*

Hitler had already asked me several times to deliver the opening address at the Munich Architectural Exhibition in his stead. Hitherto I had always been able to avoid such duties by a variety of pretexts. In February 1938 my evasions resulted in a kind of deal: I agreed to design the picture gallery and the stadium for Linz, if I did not have to make a speech.

But now, on the eve of Hitler's fiftieth birthday, a part of the "East-West axis" in Berlin was to be opened to traffic, with Hitler present at the dedication. That maiden speech could no longer be fended off— and to make matters worse in the presence of the Chief of State. At dinner Hitler announced: "A great event: Speer is making a speech. I can hardly wait to hear what he will say."

In the middle of the roadway, at the Brandenburg Gate, the dignitaries of the city had lined up, with me on the right wing and with the crowd massed behind ropes on the distant sidewalks. From the distance came cheers, swelling as Hitler's motorcade approached and becoming a steady roar. Hitler's car stopped right in front of me; he got out and greeted me by shaking hands, while responding to the welcome of the dignitaries merely by raising his arm briefly. Portable movie cameras began filming the scene from close up, while Hitler expectantly took up a position six feet away from me. I took a deep breath, then spoke these exact words: *Mein Führer,* I herewith report the completion of the East-West axis. May the work speak for itself!" There was a protracted pause before Hitler replied with a few sentences. Then I was invited into his car and drove with him down the five-mile lane of Berliners who were paying tribute to him on his fiftieth birthday. No doubt it had taken an energetic effort by the Propaganda Ministry to bring this crowd here; but the applause seemed to me genuine.

After we had reached the Chancellery and were waiting to be called to dinner, Hitler commented good-humoredly: "You put me in a fine fix with your two sentences. I was expecting a long speech and meant to use the time while you were talking to frame my answer, the way I usually do. But since you were finished so quickly, I didn't know what to say. Still I must grant you that it was a good speech. One of the best I have ever

* In his speech to the editors in chief of the German press Hitler described what he considered to be the proper method of propaganda for creating war readiness: "Certain events should be presented in such a light that unconsciously the masses will automatically come to the conclusion: If there's no way to redress this matter pleasantly then it will have to be done by force; we can't possibly let things go on this way."

heard." In the following years this anecdote became part of his regular repertory, and he told it often.

At midnight the diners offered Hitler the proper congratulations. But when I told him that to celebrate the day I had set up a thirteen-foot model of his triumphal arch in one of the salons, he immediately left the party and hurried to the room. For a long time he stood contemplating with visible emotion the dream of his younger years, realized in this model. Overwhelmed, he gave me his hand without a word, and then, in a euphoric mood, lectured his birthday guests on the importance of this structure for the future history of the Reich. That night he returned to look at the model several times. On the way back and forth we would pass the former cabinet room where Bismarck had presided over the Congress of Berlin in 1878. Here Hitler's birthday presents were heaped up on long tables—pretty much a collection of kitsch sent by his Reichsleiters and Gauleiters: white marble nudes, small bronze casts of such well-known works as the Roman boy extracting a thorn from his foot, and oil paintings whose level matched the stuff exhibited in the House of Art. Hitler spoke well of some of the presents, made fun of others, but there was in fact not much difference between them.

Meanwhile matters had progressed between Hanke and Frau Goebbels to such a point that, to the horror of everyone in the know, they wished to marry. An ill-matched couple: Hanke was young and awkward, she was considerably older and a polished society woman. Hanke petitioned Hitler for his approval, but Hitler refused to allow the Goebbelses to divorce for *raison d'état!* At the beginning of the 1939 Bayreuth Festival, Hanke arrived at my house one morning in a state of despair. Magda and Joseph Goebbels had had a reconciliation, he reported, and gone to Bayreuth together. For my part I thought this was the happiest outcome for Hanke, too. But you cannot console a desperate lover with felicitations on his escape. I therefore promised him to find out what had happened in Bayreuth and left at once.

The Wagner family had added a spacious wing to Haus Wahnfried, where Hitler and his adjutants stayed during the festival, while Hitler's guests were put up in private homes in Bayreuth. Incidentally, Hitler selected these guests more carefully than he did at Obersalzberg, or even at the Chancellery. Aside from the adjutants he invited only a few other persons with their wives, those he could be sure would be welcome to the Wagner family. Actually, these guests were almost always only Dr. Dietrich, Dr. Brandt, and myself.

On these festival days Hitler seemed more relaxed than usual. He obviously felt at ease in the Wagner family and free of the compulsion to represent power, which he sometimes thought himself obliged to do even with the evening group in the Chancellery. He was gay, paternal to the children, friendly and solicitous toward Winifred Wagner. Without Hitler's financial aid, the festival could scarcely have been kept going. Every year Bormann produced hundreds of thousands of marks from his funds in order to make the festival productions the glory of the German opera season. As patron of the festival and as the friend of the Wagner family, Hitler was no doubt realizing a dream which even in his youth he perhaps never quite dared to dream.

Goebbels and his wife had arrived in Bayreuth on the same day as myself and, like Hitler, had moved into the Wahnfried annex. Frau Goebbels looked very drawn. She spoke quite candidly with me: "It was frightful, the way my husband threatened me. I was just beginning to recuperate at Gastein when he turned up at the hotel. For three days he argued with me incessantly, until I could no longer stand it. He used the children to blackmail me; he threatened to take them away from me. What could I do? The reconciliation is only for show. Albert, it's terrible! I've had to swear never to meet Karl privately again. I'm so unhappy, but I have no choice."

What could have been more appropriate for this marital tragedy than, of all operas, *Tristan und Isolde?* Hitler, Herr and Frau Goebbels, Frau Winifred Wagner, and I heard it sitting in the big central box. Frau Goebbels, on my right, cried silently throughout the performance. During the intermission she sat, bowed and sobbing uncontrollably, in a corner of the salon, while Hitler and Goebbels went to the window to show themselves to the audience, both of them strenuously pretending to be unaware of the embarrassing episode.

Next morning I was able to explain to Hitler, who could not understand Frau Goebbels's conduct, the background of the so-called reconciliation. As Chief of State he welcomed this turn of events, but in my presence he sent for Goebbels at once and in a few dry words informed him that it would be better if he left Bayreuth immediately with his wife. Without allowing him to reply, or even shaking hands with him, he dismissed the Propaganda Minister and then turned to me: "With women Goebbels is a cynic." He too was one, though in a different way.

I I

The Globe

WHENEVER HE CAME TO SEE MY MODELS OF THE BERLIN BUILDINGS, HITLER
would particularly brood over one part of the plan: the future headquarters of the Reich which was meant to manifest for hundreds of years
to come the power that had been attained in the era of Hitler. Just as the
Champs Elysées finds its dramatic focus in the residence of the French
kings, so the grand boulevard was to culminate in a group of buildings
which Hitler regarded as central to his political activities. These were
the Chancellery, where the affairs of government were conducted; the
High Command of the Armed Forces, where the power of command over
the three branches of the services was concentrated; and a secretariat
for the party (Bormann), for protocol (Meissner), and for Hitler's personal affairs (Bouhler). The Reichstag building also formed part of this
complex, but this in no way signified that Hitler meant the German parliament to play any important part in the exercise of power. It was mere
chance that the old Reichstag building happened to be situated there.

I proposed to Hitler that Paul Wallot's Reichstag, built in Wilhelmine
Germany, be razed. But here I met unexpected resistance. Hitler liked the
structure. However, he intended to use it merely for social purposes.
Hitler was usually taciturn about his ultimate goals. When on this
and some other occasions he spoke rather candidly to me about the background of his building plans, he did so out of that intimacy that almost
always crops up in the relationship between an architect and his client.

"In the old building we can set up reading rooms and lounges for the deputies. For all I care the chamber can be turned into a library. With its five hundred and eighty seats it's much too small for us. We'll build a new one right beside it. Provide a chamber for twelve hundred deputies!"[1] That assumed a population of one hundred and forty million, and so in saying this Hitler was revealing the scale on which he was thinking. Partly he had in mind a rapid natural increase of the Germans, partly the incorporation into the Reich of other Germanic peoples—but he was not including the population of subjugated nations, for these would not have any voting rights. I proposed that he simply increase the number of voters whom each deputy represented, and thereby make the old Reichstag chamber still usable. But Hitler did not want to alter the proportion of sixty thousand voters for each deputy which had been set by the Weimar Republic. He never explained his reasons; but he was as firm on this matter as he was firm about nominal retention of the traditional electoral system with its fixed dates for elections, rules of franchise, ballot boxes, and secret ballot. On this matter he evidently wanted to preserve a tradition which had brought him to power, even though his introduction of the one-party system had made the whole thing pointless.

The buildings which were intended to frame the future Adolf Hitler Platz lay in the shadow of the great domed hall. But as if Hitler wanted by architecture alone to denigrate the whole process of popular representation, the hall had a volume fifty times greater than the proposed Reichstag building. He had asked me to work out the designs for this hall as early as the summer of 1936.[2] On April 20, 1937, his birthday, I gave him the renderings, ground plans, cross sections, and a first model of the building. He was delighted and only quarreled with my having signed the plans: "Developed on the basis of the Fuehrer's ideas." I was the architect, he said, and my contribution to this building must be given greater credit than his sketch of the idea dating from 1925. I stuck to this formula, however, and Hitler was probably gratified at my refusal to claim authorship for this building. Partial models were prepared from the plans, and in 1939 a detailed wooden model of the exterior some ten feet high and another model of the interior were made. The floor could be removed in order to test the future effect at eye level. In the course of his many visits to the exhibit Hitler would unfailingly spend a long time contemplating these two models. He would point triumphantly to them as an idea that must have struck his friends fifteen years ago as a fantastic quirk. "In those days who was prepared to believe me when I said that this would be built some day!"

This structure, the greatest assembly hall in the world ever conceived up to that time, consisted of one vast hall that could hold between one hundred fifty and one hundred eighty thousand persons standing. In spite of Hitler's negative attitude toward Himmler's and Rosenberg's mystical notions, the hall was essentially a place of worship. The idea was that over the course of centuries, by tradition and venerability, it would acquire an importance similar to that St. Peter's in Rome has for Catholic Christendom. Without some such essentially pseudoreligious background the expenditure for Hitler's central building would have been pointless and incomprehensible.

The round interior was to have the almost inconceivable diameter of eight hundred and twenty-five feet. The huge dome was to begin its slightly parabolic curve at a height of three hundred and twenty-three feet and rise to a height of seven hundred and twenty-six feet.

In a sense the Pantheon in Rome had served as our model. The Berlin dome was also to contain a round opening for light, but this opening alone would be one hundred and fifty-two feet in diameter, larger than the entire dome of the Pantheon (142 feet) and of St. Peter's (145 feet). The interior would contain sixteen times the volume of St. Peter's.

The interior appointments were to be as simple as possible. Circling an area four hundred sixty-two feet in diameter, a three-tier gallery rose to a height of one hundred feet. A circle of one hundred rectangular marble pillars—still almost on a human scale, for they were only eighty feet high—was broken by a recess opposite the entrance. This recess was one hundred and sixty-five feet high and ninety-two feet wide, and was to be clad at the rear in gold mosaic. In front of it, on a marble pedestal forty-six feet in height, perched the hall's single sculptural feature: a gilded German eagle with a swastika in its claws. This symbol of sovereignty might be said to be the very fountainhead of Hitler's grand boulevard. Beneath this symbol would be the podium for the Leader of the nation; from this spot he would deliver his messages to the peoples of his future empire. I tried to give this spot suitable emphasis, but here the fatal flaw of architecture that has lost all sense of proportion was revealed. Under that vast dome Hitler dwindled to an optical zero.

From the outside the dome would have loomed against the sky like some green mountain, for it was to be roofed with patinated plates of copper. At its peak we planned a skylight turret one hundred and thirty-two feet high, of the lightest possible metal construction. The turret would be crowned by an eagle with a swastika.

Optically, the mass of the dome was to have been set off by a series of pillars sixty-six feet high. I thought this effect would bring things back to scale—undoubtedly a vain hope. The mountainous dome rested upon a granite edifice two hundred and forty-four feet high with sides ten hundred and forty feet long. A delicate frieze, four clustered, fluted pillars on each of the four corners, and a colonnade along the front facing the square were to dramatize the size of the enormous cube.[3]

Two sculptures each fifty feet high would flank the colonnade. Hitler had already decided on the subjects of these sculptures when we were preparing our first sketches of the building. One would represent Atlas bearing the vault of the heavens, the other Tellus supporting the globe of the world. The spheres representing sky and earth were to be enamel coated with constellations and continents traced in gold.

The volume of this structure amounted to almost 27.5 million cubic yards;[4] the Capitol in Washington would have been contained many times in such a mass. These were dimensions of an inflationary sort.

Yet the hall was by no means an insane project which could in fact never be executed. Our plans did not belong to that supergrandiose category envisioned by Claude Nicolas Ledoux as the swan song of the Bourbon dynasty of France, or by Etienne L. Boullée to glorify the Revolution—projects which were never meant to be carried out. Their scale, however, was by no means vaster than Hitler's.[5] But we were seriously going ahead with our plans. As early as 1939 many old buildings in the vicinity of the Reichstag were razed to make room for our Great Hall and the other buildings that were to surround the future Adolf Hitler Platz. The character of the underlying soil was studied. Detail drawings were prepared and models built. Millions of marks were spent on granite for the exterior. Nor were the purchases confined to Germany. Despite the shortage of foreign exchange, Hitler had orders placed with quarries in southern Sweden and Finland. Like all the other edifices on Hitler's long grand boulevard, the great hall was also scheduled to be completed in eleven years, by 1950. Since the hall would take longer to build than all the rest, the ceremonial cornerstone laying was set for 1940.

Technically, there was no special problem in constructing a dome over eight hundred feet in diameter.* The bridge builders of the thirties had no difficulty with similar spans of steel or reinforced concrete. Leading German engineers had even calculated that it would be possible to build a massive vault with such a span. In keeping with my notion of "ruin value" I would rather have eschewed the use of steel; but in this case Hitler expressed doubts. "You know, an aerial bomb might strike the dome and damage the vaulting. If there were danger of collapse, how would you go about making repairs?" He was right, and we therefore had a steel skeleton constructed, from which the inner shell of the dome would be suspended. The walls, however, were to be of solid stone like the Nuremberg buildings. Their weight, along with that of the dome, would exert tremendous pressure and would demand an unusually strong foundation. The engineers decided on an enormous concrete footing which would have had a content of 3.9 million cubic yards. According to our calculations, this would sink only a few centimeters into the sandy soil; but

* A special problem connected with every dome is the acoustics. But to our relief prominent acoustical experts calculated that if we observed a few precautions there would be no need to worry.

to test this a sample section was built near Berlin.[6] Except for drawings and photographs of models, it is the only thing that has remained of the projected structure.

In the course of the planning I had gone to see St. Peter's in Rome. It was rather dashing for me to realize that its size had little to do with the impression it creates. In work on such a scale, I saw, effectiveness is no longer proportionate to the size of the building. I began to be afraid that our great hall would turn out disappointingly.

Ministerial Councilor Knipfer, who was in charge of air-raid protection in the Reich Air Ministry, had heard rumors about this gigantic structure. He had just issued directives providing that all future buildings be as widely dispersed as possible in order to diminish the effect of air raids. Now, here in the center of the city and of the Reich, a building was to be erected which would tower above low clouds and act as an ideal navigational guide to enemy bombers. It would be virtually a signpost for the government center. I mentioned these considerations to Hitler. But he was sanguine. "Goering has assured me," he said, "that no enemy plane will enter Germany. We will not let that sort of thing stand in the way of our plans."

Hitler was obsessed with the idea for this domed building. We had already drawn up our designs when he heard that the Soviet Union was also planning an enormous assembly building in Moscow in honor of Lenin. He was deeply irked, feeling himself cheated of the glory of building the tallest monumental structure in the world. Along with this was an intense chagrin that he could not make Stalin stop by a simple command. But he finally consoled himself with the thought that his building would remain unique. "What does one skyscraper more or less amount to, a little higher or a little lower. The great thing about our building will be the dome!" After the war with the Soviet Union had begun, I now and then saw evidence that the idea of Moscow's rival building had preyed on his mind more than he had been willing to admit. "Now," he once said, "this will be the end of their building for good and all."

The domed hall was to be surrounded on three sides by water which would reflect it and enhance its effect. For this purpose we intended to widen the Spree into a kind of lake. The normal river traffic, however, would have to bypass this area through a set of underground canals. On its south side, the building would be flanked by the great plaza, the future Adolf Hitler Platz. Here the annual May 1 rallies would take place; these had previously been held on Tempelhof Field.[7]

The Propaganda Ministry had worked out a pattern for managing such mass rallies. In 1939, Karl Hanke told me of the variants of such demonstrations; which manner of demonstration was wanted depended on political and propagandistic factors. From the gathering of school-children to cheer a foreign guest all the way to the mobilizing of millions of workers to express the will of the people, the Propaganda Ministry had a prepared scenario. Ironically, Hanke spoke of "cheering levies." Had the future gone according to plan, it would have taken the ultimate of all "cheering levies" to fill Adolf Hitler Platz, since it would hold a million people.

One side of the square was to be bounded by the new High Command of the Armed Forces, the other by the Chancellery office building. The fourth side was open, permitting an enormous vista down the grand boulevard. This would be the only opening in the gigantic square, otherwise hemmed in completely by buildings.

Aside from the great hall, the most important and psychologically the most interesting of the buildings was to be Hitler's palace. It is no exaggeration to speak of a palace rather than the Chancellor's residence. As the preserved sketches show, Hitler had been thinking about this building as early as November 1938.[8] The architecture made plain his craving for status, which had increased by leaps and bounds since his accession to power. From the Chancellor's residence of Bismarck's day into which he originally moved to this projected palace, the proportions had multiplied by a factor of one hundred and fifty. Even Nero's legendary palace area, the Golden House, with its expanse of more than eleven million square feet, would be outstripped by Hitler's palace. Right in the center of Berlin, it was to occupy, with the attached grounds, twenty-two million square feet. Reception rooms led through several series of salons into a dining hall which could have accommodated thousands. Eight vast entertainment halls were available for gala receptions.[*] The most modern stage equipment was to be provided for a theater of four hundred seats, an imitation of the ducal theaters of the baroque and rococo eras.

From his own quarters Hitler could reach the great dome by a series of covered galleries. His offices, on the other hand, were conveniently adjacent to the private apartment, and his personal office located at the very center of this official sector. Its measurements far exceeded the reception room of the President of the United States.[9] Hitler was so well pleased with the long hike the diplomats had to take in the recently completed new Chancellery that he wanted a similar device in the new building. I therefore doubled the distance visitors would have to traverse, making it somewhat more than a quarter of a mile.

From the former Chancellery, built in 1931, Hitler's aspirations had

---

[*] The eight public rooms would have had a total area of 161,400 square feet. The theater was to contain four hundred comfortable seats. Following the normal practice of allowing about two and a half square feet per seat in a theater, the 3,442 square feet would have provided easily for eight hundred persons in the orchestra and another hundred and fifty in the balcony. Hitler planned to have a special box for himself in the theater.

by now multiplied seventy-fold.[10] That gives some idea of the proportions by which his megalomania had evolved.

And in the midst of all this splendor Hitler would have set up his white enameled bedstead in a bedroom of fairly modest dimensions. He once said to me: "I hate all show in a bedroom. I feel most comfortable in a simple ordinary bed."

In 1939, when these plans were assuming tangible form, Goebbels's propaganda went on fostering the German people's belief in Hitler's modesty and simplicity. In order not to imperil this image, Hitler said scarcely a word about the plans for his palatial private residence and the future Chancellery. But once, when we were tramping through the snow, he gave me justification for his soaring demands:

> You see, I myself would find a simple little house in Berlin quite suffi-
> cient. I have enough power and prestige; I don't need such luxury to sustain
> me. But believe me, those who come after me will find such ostentation an
> urgent necessity. Many of them will be able to hold on only by such means.
> You would hardly believe what power a small mind acquires over the people
> around him when he is able to show himself in such imposing circumstances.
> Such rooms, with a great historical past, raise even a petty successor to
> historical rank. You see, that is why we must complete this construction in
> my lifetime—so that I shall have lived there and my spirit will have con-
> ferred tradition upon the building. If I live in it only for a few years, that
> will be good enough.

In his speeches to the construction workers of the Chancellery in 1938, Hitler had made similar remarks, though of course without revealing any of his plans, which by then were already quite far advanced. As Leader and Chancellor of the German nation, he had said, he did not enter former palaces; that was why he had refused to move into the palace of the Reich President, for he was not going to live in a former Lord Chamberlain's residence. But in this area, too, he would see to it that the German state was provided with a public building that matched the prestigious edifices of any foreign king or emperor.[11]

Even at that time, Hitler ruled that we were not to worry about the costs of these buildings, and we therefore obediently omitted volume calculations. I have drawn them up for the first time only now, after a quarter of a century. The result is the following table:

1. Domed hall	27,468,000	cubic yards
2. Residential palace	2,485,000	
3. Office suite and Chancellery	1,569,000	
4. Appendant secretariats	261,000	
5. High Command of the Armed Forces	784,000	
6. New Reichstag	457,000	
	33,024,000	cubic yards

Although the immense scale would have reduced the price per cubic yard, the total costs were almost inconceivable. For these vast structures would need enormous walls and correspondingly deep foundations. Moreover, the exterior walls were to be clad in expensive granite, the interior walls in marble. The very best materials were likewise to be employed for doors, windows, ceilings, and so on. A cost of five billion present-day marks for the buildings of Adolf Hitler Platz alone probably represents far too low an estimate.[12]

The shift in the mood of the population, the drooping morale which began to be felt throughout Germany in 1939, was evident in the necessity to organize cheering crowds where two years earlier Hitler had been able to count on spontaneity. What is more, he himself had meanwhile moved away from the admiring masses. He tended to be angry and impatient more often than in the past when, as still occasionally happened, a crowd on Wilhelmsplatz began clamoring for him to appear. Two years before he had often stepped out on the "historic balcony." Now he sometimes snapped at his adjutants when they came to him with the request that he show himself: "Stop bothering me with that!"

This seemingly small point had a certain bearing on the conception of the new Adolf Hitler Platz, for one day he said to me: "You know it is not out of the question that I shall some day be forced to take unpopular measures. These might possibly lead to riots. We must provide for that eventuality. All the buildings on this square must be equipped with heavy steel bulletproof shutters over their windows. The doors, too, must be of steel, and there should be heavy iron gates for closing off the square. It must be possible to defend the center of the Reich like a fortress."

This remark betrayed a nervousness he had not had before. The same feeling emerged when we discussed the location of the barracks for the bodyguard, which had meanwhile grown into a fully motorized regiment armed with the most modern equipment. He shifted its head-quarters to the immediate vicinity of the grand southern axis. "Suppose there should be some disturbances!" he said. And pointing to the four hundred foot wide avenue: "If they come rolling up here in their armored vehicles the full width of the street—nobody will be able to put up any resistance." I do not know whether the army heard of this arrangement and wanted to be on the spot before the SS, or whether Hitler himself gave the order—but in any case, at the request of the army command and with Hitler's approval a barracks site was prepared even closer to the center for the Grossdeutschland guards regiment.[13]

I unwittingly gave expression to this separation of Hitler from his people—a Hitler who was ready to have soldiers fire upon the populace —in my design for the façade of his palace. There was no opening in it except for the great steel entrance gate and a door to a balcony from which Hitler could show himself to the crowd. But this balcony was now suspended five stories high above the street. This frowning façade still seems to me to communicate an accurate image of the remote Leader who had in the meantime moved into realms of self-idolatry.

During my imprisonment, this design, with its red mosaics, its pillars, its bronze lions and gilded silhouettes, had assumed in my memory a bright, almost pleasant character. But when I once again saw the color photographs of the model, after a lapse of more than twenty-one years, I was struck by the resemblance to a Cecil B. De Mille set. Along with its fantastic quality I also became aware of the cruel element in this architecture. It had been the very expression of a tyranny.

Before the war, I had laughed at an inkwell which the architect Brinckmann (who like Troost had originally designed steamship décor) had presented Hitler as a surprise gift. Brinckmann had made a solemn construction out of this simple utensil. It was a mass of ornamentation, scrolls and steps—and then, alone and forlorn amid all the magnificence of this "inkwell for the Chief of State," there was a tiny pool of ink. I thought I had never seen anything so abnormal. But contrary to my expectations Hitler did not disdain the object. In fact he praised this bronze inkwell immoderately. Brinckmann was no less successful with a desk chair he had designed for Hitler. It was veritably of Goeringesque proportions, a kind of throne with two oversized gilded pine cones topping the back. These two items, with their inflated bombast, seemed to me to reek of the parvenu. But from about 1937 on Hitler furthered this tendency toward pomposity by showing increasing approval of it. He had come round again to Vienna's Ringstrasse, where he had once begun. Slowly but steadily he moved even further away from the doctrines of Troost.

And I moved with him. For my designs of this period owed less and less to what I regarded as "my style." This estrangement from my beginnings was revealed in other ways besides the wildly excessive size of my buildings. For they also no longer had any of the Dorian character I had originally tried to achieve. They had become pure "art of decadence." Wealth, the inexhaustible funds at my disposal, but also Hitler's party ideology, had led me along the path to a style which drew its inspiration rather from the show palaces of Oriental despots.

At the beginning of the war, I had formed a theory which I explained at a dinner in Maxim's in Paris to a group of German and French artists. Cocteau and Despiau were among the latter. The French Revolution, I said, had developed a new sense of style which was destined to replace the late rococo. Even its simplest furniture was beautifully proportioned. This style, I argued, had found its purest expression in the architectural designs of Boullée. The Directoire that followed this revolutionary style had still treated their more abundant means with lightness and good taste. The turning point, I said, had come with the Empire style. From year to year new elements were introduced; elaborate ornamentation had been lavished upon the still classical basic forms until, at the end, Late Empire had achieved a resplendence and wealth that could scarcely be surpassed. Late Empire had expressed the end point of a stylistic evolution which had begun so promisingly with the Consulate. It had also expressed the transition from Revolution to the Napoleonic Empire. Within it were revealed signs of decay which were a forecast of the end of the Napoleonic era. Compressed within the span of twenty years, I said, we could observe a phenomenon that ordinarily took place only over centuries: the development from the Doric buildings of early antiquity to the fissured baroque façades of Late Hellenism, such as was to be seen in, say, Baalbek; or the Romanesque buildings at the beginning of the medieval period and the playful Late Gothic at its end.

Had I been able to think the matter out consistently, I ought to have argued further that my designs for Hitler were following the pattern of the Late Empire and forecasting the end of the regime; that, therefore, Hitler's downfall could be deduced from these very designs. But this was hidden from me at the time. Probably Napoleon's entourage saw in the ornate salons of the Late Empire only the expression of grandeur. Probably only posterity beholds the symptoms of downfall in such creations. Hitler's entourage, at any rate, felt the towering inkwell to be a suitable prop for his genius as a statesman, and similarly accepted my hulking dome as the symbol of Hitler's power.

The last buildings we designed in 1939 were in fact pure neo-Empire, comparable to the style that prevailed a hundred and twenty-five years before, shortly before Napoleon's fall. They were marked by excessive ornamentation, a mania for gilding, a passion for pomp, and total decadence. And not only the style but the excessive size of these buildings plainly revealed Hitler's intention.

One day in the early summer of 1939, he pointed to the German eagle with the swastika in its claws which was to crown the dome nine hundred fifty-seven feet in the air. "That has to be changed. Instead of the swastika, the eagle is to be perched above the globe. To crown this greatest building in the world the eagle must stand above the globe."*
There are photos of the models in which this revision is plainly to be seen.

A few months later the Second World War began.

---

* As late as May 8, 1943, Goebbels noted in his diary: "The Fuehrer expresses his unshakable conviction that the Reich will one day rule all of Europe. We will have to survive a great many conflicts, but they will doubtless lead to the most glorious triumphs. And from then on the road to world domination is practically spread out before us. For whoever rules Europe will be able to seize the leadership of the world."

12

The Descent Begins

ABOUT THE BEGINNING OF AUGUST 1939 WE, AN UNTROUBLED GROUP, DROVE with Hitler up to the Eagle's Nest. The long motorcade wound along the road which Bormann had blasted into the rock. Through a high bronze portal we entered a marble hall, damp from the moisture in the heart of the mountain, and stepped into the elevator of polished brass.

As we rode up the hundred and sixty-five feet of shaft, Hitler said abruptly, as if he were talking to himself: "Perhaps something enormously important will happen soon. Even if I should have to send Goering. . . . But if need be I would even go myself. I am staking everything on this card." There was no more beyond this hint.

Barely three weeks later, on August 21, 1939, we heard that the German Foreign Minister was in Moscow for some negotiations. During supper a note was handed to Hitler. He scanned it, stared into space for a moment, flushed deeply, then banged on the table so hard that the glasses rattled, and exclaimed in a voice breaking with excitement: "I have them! I have them!" Seconds later he had already regained control of himself. No one dared ask any question, and the meal continued.

After supper Hitler called his entourage together. "We are going to conclude a nonaggression pact with Russia. Here, read this. A telegram from Stalin." It briefly acknowledged the agreement that had been reached. To see the names of Hitler and Stalin linked in friendship on a piece of paper was the most staggering, the most exciting turn of events

I could possibly have imagined. Immediately afterward we were shown a movie depicting Stalin watching a Red army parade; a tremendous number of troops marched past him. Hitler expressed his gratification that this military might was now neutralized. He turned to his military adjutants, evidently wanting to hear their estimate of the mass display of weapons and troops. The ladies were still excluded, but of course they soon heard the news from us, and shortly afterward it was announced on the radio.

Goebbels held an evening press conference on August 23 in which he offered commentary on the pact. Hitler telephoned him immediately afterward. He wanted to know how the foreign correspondents had reacted. With eyes glistening feverishly, he told us what Goebbels had said. "The sensation was fantastic. And when the church bells simultaneously began ringing outside, a British correspondent fatalistically remarked: 'That is the death knell of the British Empire.'" These words made the strongest impression upon Hitler in his euphoria that night. He thought he now stood so high as to be out of the reach of fate.

In the course of the night we stood on the terrace of the Berghof with Hitler and marveled at a rare natural spectacle. Northern lights[1] of unusual intensity threw red light on the legend-haunted Untersberg across the valley, while the sky above shimmered in all the colors of the rainbow. The last act of *Götterdämmerung* could not have been more effectively staged. The same red light bathed our faces and our hands. The display produced a curiously pensive mood among us. Abruptly turning to one of his military adjutants, Hitler said: "Looks like a great deal of blood. This time we won't bring it off without violence."[2]

Weeks before, the center of Hitler's interests had already shifted to the military area. In long talks with his four military adjutants—Colonel Rudolf Schmundt for the High Command of the Armed Services (OKW); Captain Gerhard Engel for the Army, Captain Nikolaus von Below for the air force, and Captain Karl-Jesko von Puttkamer for the navy—Hitler tried to arrive at definitive plans. He seemed to especially like these young and unbiased officers, all the more since he was always seeking approval, which they were more likely to give him than the perhaps better informed but skeptical generals.

During these days immediately after announcement of the German-Russian pact, however, he saw less of the adjutants than of the political and military heads of the German Reich, among them Goering, Goebbels, Keitel, and Ribbentrop. Goebbels above all spoke openly and anxiously about the danger of war. Surprisingly, the usually radical Propaganda Minister considered the risk excessively large. He tried to recommend a peaceful line to Hitler's entourage and was particularly acrid toward Ribbentrop, whom he regarded as the chief representative of the war party. We who were members of Hitler's personal circle considered him as well as Goering, who also counseled peace, weaklings who had degenerated in the luxury of power and did not want to risk the privileges they had acquired.

Even though my future as an architect was also at stake, I thought that the solution of national questions must take precedence over personal interests. Any doubts I might have had were quelled by the self-assurance Hitler showed. In those days he seemed to me like a hero of ancient myth who unhesitantly, in full consciousness of his strength, could enter upon and masterfully meet the test of the wildest undertakings.*

Whoever did belong to the actual war party, aside from Hitler and Ribbentrop, had worked out arguments more or less as follows:

Let us assume that because of our rapid rearmament we hold a four to one advantage in strength at the present time. Since the occupation of Czechoslovakia the other side has been rearming vigorously. They need at least one and a half to two years before their production will reach its maximum yield. Only after 1940 can they begin to catch up with our relatively large headstart. If they produce only as much as we do, however, our proportional superiority will constantly diminish, for in order to maintain it we would have to go on producing four times as much. We are in no position to do so. Even if they reach only half of our production, the proportion will constantly deteriorate. Right now, on the other hand, we have new weapons in all fields, the other side obsolete types.[3]

Considerations of this sort probably did not govern Hitler's decisions, but they undoubtedly influenced his choice of the time to strike. For the present, however, he remarked: "I shall stay at Obersalzberg as long as possible, in order to keep myself fresh for the difficult days to come. I'll go to Berlin only when decisions become essential."

Only a few days later Hitler's motorcade was moving along the autobahn to Munich. There were ten cars at long distances from one another, for security. My wife and I were in one of the cars. It was a beautiful, cloudless sunny day at the end of summer. The populace remained unusually silent as Hitler drove by. Hardly anyone waved. In Berlin, too, it was strikingly quiet in the vicinity of the Chancellery. Usually, when Hitler's private standard was raised to indicate his presence, the building was besieged by people who cheered him as he drove out and in.

In the nature of things I was excluded from the further course of events—all the more so because the normal routine of Hitler's day was turned topsy-turvy during this tumultuous spell. After the court moved

---

* And, in fact, nine months previously I had had bas-reliefs portraying the Hercules legend installed on the new Chancellery.

to Berlin, an incessant series of conferences fully occupied Hitler's time. Our common meals were for the most part canceled. Memory can be peculiarly arbitrary, and among my most vivid recollections is the somewhat comic picture of Bernardo Attolico, the Italian Ambassador, rushing breathlessly into the Chancellery a few days before the attack upon Poland. He was bringing word that for the present Italy could not keep its obligations under the alliance. The Duce cloaked this bad news in impossible demands for immediate delivery of a vast quantity of military and economic goods. Granting such demands could have resulted in a disastrous weakening of the German armed forces. Hitler had a high regard for the fighting strength of the Italian fleet in particular, with its modern units and large number of submarines. He was equally convinced of the effectiveness of the big Italian air force. For a moment he thought his plans had been ruined, for he assumed that Italy's bellicosity would help frighten the Western powers. In some dismay, he postponed the assault on Poland, which had already been ordered.

But this temporary retreat soon yielded to new hopes; his instincts told him that even with Italy defaulting, the West might still shrink from declaring war. He therefore rejected Mussolini's offer to mediate; he would hold back no longer, he said, for if the army were held in suspense too long it would grow nervous. Besides, the period of good autumn weather would soon pass, and during the later rainy season there was danger of the troops bogging down in the Polish mud.

Notes on the Polish question were exchanged with England. Out of the rush of events I particularly remember one evening in the conservatory of the Chancellor's residence. I had the impression that Hitler looked exhausted from overwork. He spoke with deep conviction to his intimate circle: "This time the mistake of 1914 will be avoided. Everything depends on making the other side accept responsibility. In 1914 that was handled clumsily. And now again the ideas of the Foreign Office are simply useless. The best thing is for me to compose the notes myself." As he spoke he held a page of manuscript in his hand, probably the draft of a note from the Foreign Office. He hastily took his leave, not joining us for dinner, and vanished into the upper rooms. Later, in prison, I read that exchange of notes; it did not seem to me that Hitler had carried out his intent very well.

Hitler's view that the West would once more give in to his demands as it had done at Munich was supported by intelligence information: An officer on the British General Staff was said to have evaluated the strength of the Polish army and come to the conclusion that Polish resistance would soon collapse. Hitler thus had reason to hope that the British General Staff would do everything in its power to advise its government against so hopeless a war. When, on September 3, the Western powers followed up their ultimatum with declarations of war,

Hitler was initially stunned, but quickly reassured himself and us by saying that England and France had obviously declared war merely as a sham, in order not to lose face before the whole world. In spite of the declarations there would be no fighting; he was convinced of that, he said. He therefore ordered the Wehrmacht to remain strictly on the defensive. He felt that this decision of his showed remarkable political acumen.

During those last days of August Hitler was in an unwonted state of nerves and at times completely lost the reassuring air of infallible leader. The hectic activities were followed by an uneasy period of quiet. For a short time Hitler resumed his customary daily routine. Even his interest in architectural plans revived. To his round table he explained: "Of course we are in a state of war with England and France, but if we on our side avoid all acts of war, the whole business will evaporate. As soon as we sink a ship and they have sizable casualties, the war party over there will gain strength." Even when German U-boats lay in a favorable position near the French battleship *Dunkerque* he refused to authorize an attack. But the British air raid on Wilhelmshaven and the sinking of the *Athenia* soon called for a reconsideration of this policy.

He stuck unswervingly to his opinion that the West was too feeble, too worn out, and too decadent to begin the war seriously. Probably it was also embarrassing for him to admit to his entourage and above all to himself that he had made so crucial a mistake. I still remember his consternation when the news came that Churchill was going to enter the British War Cabinet as First Lord of the Admiralty. With this ill-omened press report in his hand, Goering stepped out of the door of Hitler's salon. He dropped into the nearest chair and said wearily: "Churchill in the Cabinet. That means that the war is really on. Now we shall have war with England." From these and other observations I deduced that this initiation of real war was not what Hitler had projected.

His illusions and wish-dreams were a direct outgrowth of his unrealistic mode of working and thinking. Hitler actually knew nothing about his enemies and even refused to use the information that was available to him. Instead, he trusted his inspirations, no matter how inherently contradictory they might be, and these inspirations were governed by extreme contempt for and underestimation of the others. In keeping with his classic phrase that there were always two possibilities, he wanted to have the war at this supposedly most favorable moment, while at the same time he failed to adequately prepare for it. He regarded England, as he once stressed, as "our enemy Number One,"[4] while at the same time hoping to come to an arrangement with that enemy.

I do not think that in those early days of September, Hitler was fully aware that he had irrevocably unleashed a world war. He had merely meant to move one step further. To be sure, he was ready to accept the risk associated with that step, just as he had been a year before during the Czech crisis; but he had prepared himself only for the risk, not really for the great war. His naval rearmament was obviously planned for a later date; the battleships as well as the first large aircraft carriers were still under construction. He knew that they would not attain full military value until they could face the enemy on more or less even terms. Moreover, he had spoken so often of the neglect of the submarine arm in the First World War that he probably would not have knowingly begun the Second without preparing a strong fleet of U-boats.

But all his anxieties seemed to be scattered to the winds in early September, when the campaign in Poland yielded such successes for the German troops. Hitler seemed to recover his assurance swiftly, and later, at the climax of the war, I frequently heard him say that the Polish campaign had been a necessary thing.

> Do you think it would have been good fortune for our troops if we had taken Poland without a fight, after obtaining Austria and Czechoslovakia without fighting? Believe me, not even the best army can stand that sort of thing. Victories without loss of blood are demoralizing. Therefore it was not only fortunate there was no compromise; at the time we would have had to regard it as harmful, and I therefore would have struck in any case.[5]

It may be, nevertheless, that by such remarks he was trying to gloss over his diplomatic miscalculations of August 1939. On the other hand, toward the end of the war Colonel General Heinrici told me about an early speech of Hitler's to the generals which points in the same direction. I noted down Heinrici's remarkable story as follows: "Hitler said that he was the first man since Charlemagne to hold unlimited power in his own hand. He did not hold this power in vain, he said, but would know how to use it in a struggle for Germany. If the war were not won, that would mean that Germany had not stood the test of strength; in that case she would deserve to be and would be doomed."[6]

From the start the populace took a far more serious view of the situation than did Hitler and his entourage. Because of the general nervousness a false air-raid alarm was sounded in Berlin early in September. Along with many other Berliners I sat in a public shelter. The atmosphere was noticeably depressed; the people were full of fear about the future.[7]

None of the regiments marched off to war decorated with flowers

Near Oberammergau, 1925. Albert Speer with his fiancée, Margarete Weber, both at the age of nineteen. (SPEER-ARCHIV)

Nationalsozialiftische Deutsche Arbeiterpartei

Gauleitung   Groß-Berlin.

Abschrift

Berlin, den 10. November 1932

Sehr geehrter Herr Speer

Nach Fertigstellung unserer neuen Geschäftsstelle in der Vossstrasse spreche ich Ihnen für die von
Ihnen geleistete Arbeit meine volle Anerkennung und wärm-
sten Dank aus.

Wir haben es ganz besonders angenehm empfunden,
dass Sie trotz der sehr knapp bemessenen Zeit den Umbau
so rechtzeitig fertigstellten, dass wir die Wahlarbeit
bereits in der neuen Geschäftsstelle in Angriff nehmen
konnten. Ihr reibungsloses Zusammenarbeiten mit allen
Parteidienststellen und vor allen Dingen mit den Handwer-
kern hat uns den Wechsel von unserer Geschäftsstelle
kaum spürbar werden lassen.

Ganz besonders wird von mir die handwerklich
einfache, ruhige Linie der von Ihnen entworfenen und
ausgeführten Inneneinrichtung des Hauses, besonders meines Arbeitszimmers, der Arbeitszimmer meiner engeren Mit-
arbeiter und insbesondere der beiden Sitzungssäle gewertet.

gez. Dr. Goebbels

LEFT: *Goebbels's letter of commendation to Speer for completing new party office in record time.* (SPEER-ARCHIV)

BELOW: *Goebbels at the Sportpalast in Berlin, 1932.* (ASSOCIATED PRESS PHOTO)

Hitler greeting crowds from window of the Chancellery, spring 1933.
(SPIEGEL-ARCHIV)

The new balcony at the Chancellery.
(SPIEGEL-ARCHIV)

*Hitler and Troost examining model of the
Haus der Kunst, 1933.*
(HEINRICH HOFFMANN)

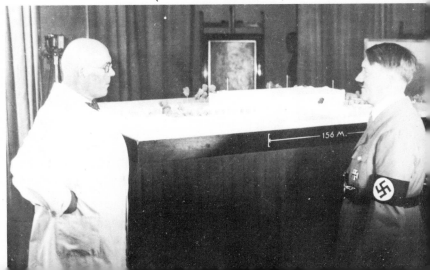

*Hitler looking at Speer's architectural plans at
Obersalzberg, spring 1934.*
(HEINRICH HOFFMANN)

ABOVE: *Hitler asleep in his Mercedes, 1934.*
(HEINRICH HOFFMANN)

RIGHT: *Cheering crowd stops Hitler's car, 1935.*
(HEINRICH HOFFMANN)

BELOW: *Clearing the way for Hitler's car, 1935.*
(HEINRICH HOFFMANN)

Hitler welcomed by Bavarian peasants, 1935. Behind Hitler an adjutant (Martin Bormann's brother Albert). In background, Heinrich Hoffmann, Hitler's photographer, and SS bodyguards. (MAX EHLERT)

Wooden model of Nuremberg Stadium (400,000 seats), designed by Albert Speer. Although the model was completed in 1936, the stadium was never begun. (HEINRICH HOFFMANN)

Hitler in Nuremberg with SS Obergruppenführer Jüttner and his trusty adjutant, Julius Schaub. (HEINRICH HOFFMANN)

Trial section of Nuremberg Stadium. Left to right: Mayor Liebel of Nuremberg, *Liebermann, architectural engineer for the Stadium, Brugmann, head of the Nuremberg building administration, and Albert Speer.* (SPEER-ARCHIV)

Speer's eagle—over one hundred feet in wingspread, crowning the temporary stands at the Zeppelin airfield. "I spiked it to timber framework like a butterfly in a collection."
(ASSOCIATED PRESS PHOTO)

*Speer's dramatic lighting effect at the Nuremberg Party Rally,
creating what Sir Neville Henderson called "a cathedral of ice."*
(SPIEGEL-ARCHIV)

Hitler sound asleep amid his entourage at the teahouse, Obersalzberg. On his right, Eva Braun. (BLICK + BILD)

LEFT: *Hitler inspecting the newly completed long gallery in the Chancellery designed by Speer (January 7, 1939). First row, left to right: Martin Bormann, Hitler, Speer, Theodor Morell, Heinrich Hoffmann. Second row: Albert Bormann, Kramer (Hitler's valet), unknown SS adjutant, Dr. Haase (surgeon), unknown.*
(HEINRICH HOFFMANN)

ABOVE: *Garden façade of the New Chancellery.*
(SPIEGEL-ARCHIV)

BELOW: *The new Cabinet Room, never used by Hitler.*
(BILDERDIENST SÜDDEUTSCHER VERLAG)

ABOVE: *Hitler's Obersalzberg residence.* (SPEER-ARCHIV)

RIGHT: *Albert Speer with Eva Braun, 1940.* (BLICK + BILD)

BELOW: *Hitler's own sketch of his Obersalzberg house.* (SPEER-ARCHIV)

as they had done at the beginning of the First World War. The streets remained empty. There was no crowd on Wilhelmsplatz shouting for Hitler. It was in keeping with the desolate mood that Hitler had his bags packed into the cars one night to drive east, to the front. Three days after the beginning of the attack on Poland he had his adjutant summon me to the provisionally blacked-out residence in the Chancellery to bid me good-by. I found a man who lost his temper over trivialities. The cars drove up, and he tersely took his leave of the "courtiers" who were remaining behind. Not a soul on the street took notice of this historic event: Hitler driving off to the war he had staged. Obviously Goebbels could have provided a cheering crowd of any size, but he was apparently not in the mood to do it.

Even during the mobilization Hitler did not forget his artists. In the late summer of 1939, orders were given that their draft records be sent to Hitler's adjutant by the various army districts. He then tore up the papers and threw them away. By this original device, the men ceased to exist for the draft boards. On the list drawn up by Hitler and Goebbels, however, architects and sculptors occupied little space. The overwhelming majority of those thus exempted were singers and actors. The fact that young scientists were also important for the future was not discovered until 1942, and then with my help.

While still at Obersalzberg I had telephoned Will Nagel, my former superior and now head of my staff, and asked him to begin forming a technical assistance group under my leadership. We wanted to put our well-coordinated team of construction supervisors to use in rebuilding bridges, extending or widening roads, and similar areas of the war effort. However, our notions about what we could do immediately were extremely vague. For the time being it consisted of no more than getting sleeping bags and tents ready, and painting my car field-gray. On the day of general mobilization I went to the High Command of the Army on Bendlerstrasse. As might be expected in a Prusso-German organization, General Fromm, who was responsible for the army mobilization, sat idle in his office while the machinery ran according to plan. He readily accepted my offer of assistance; my car was given an army number, and I myself army identification papers. For the present, that was the extent of my wartime activity.

It was Hitler who tersely forbade me to undertake any missions for the army. My duty, he told me, was to continue working at his plans. Thereupon I at least placed the workmen and the technical staffs employed on my buildings in Berlin at the disposal of the army and industry. We took charge of the Peenemünde site for the development of rockets and of some urgent buildings for the aircraft industry.

I informed Hitler of these commitments, which seemed to me the least I could do. I was confident of his approval. But to my surprise there came an unusually rude letter from Bormann. What was I doing choosing new assignments, he demanded. I had received no such orders. Hitler had asked him to let me know that all building projects were to proceed unchecked.

This order provides another example of how unrealistically and dividedly Hitler thought. On the one hand he repeatedly asserted that Germany was now being challenged by fate and had to wage a life-and-death struggle; on the other hand he did not want to give up his grandiose toys. In making such choices, moreover, he was disregarding the mood of the masses, who were inevitably baffled by the construction of such luxury buildings, now that Hitler's expansionism was beginning to demand sacrifices. This order of his was the first one I shirked. It was true that I saw Hitler far more rarely during this first year of the war. But whenever he came to Berlin for a few days, or to Obersalzberg for a few weeks, he still asked to be shown the building plans and urged me to go on developing them. But I think he soon tacitly accepted the cessation of actual work on the buildings.

Around the beginning of October the German Ambassador in Moscow, Count von Schulenburg, informed Hitler that Stalin was personally interested in our building plans. A series of photographs of our models was exhibited in the Kremlin, but on Hitler's instructions our largest buildings were kept secret in order, as he said, "not to give Stalin any ideas." Schulenburg had proposed that I fly to Moscow to explain the plans. "He might keep you there," Hitler commented half jokingly, and refused to let me take the trip. A short while afterward, Schnurre, a member of the embassy staff, informed me that Stalin had liked my sketches.

On September 29, Ribbentrop returned from his second Moscow conference with a German-Soviet frontier and friendship treaty which was to seal the fourth partition of Poland. At Hitler's table he recounted that he had never felt so much at ease as among Stalin's associates: "As if I were among old party comrades of ours, *mein Führer!*" Hitler listened without a flicker of expression to this burst of enthusiasm on the part of the normally impassive Foreign Minister. Stalin, so Ribbentrop declared, seemed satisfied with the border arrangements, and when it was all settled drew in his own hand on the map along the border of the zone assigned to Russia an area which he presented to Ribbentrop as a vast hunting preserve. At this Goering's hackles rose; he insisted that Stalin could hardly have meant this gift to apply to the Foreign Minister personally. On the contrary, it was a grant to the German Reich and consequently to himself as Reich Master of the Hunt. A hot dispute broke out between the two passionate hunters which ended with the Foreign Minister sulking, for Goering proved more forceful in argument and better able to get his way.

In spite of the war the renovation of the former palace of the Reich President, which was to be the Foreign Minister's new official residence, had to proceed. Hitler inspected the nearly completed building and showed dissatisfaction. Hastily and recklessly, Ribbentrop thereupon ordered the new annex torn down and rebuilt. Probably in order to please Hitler he insisted on clumsy marble doorways, huge doors, and moldings which were quite unsuitable for rooms of middling size. Before the second inspection I begged Hitler to refrain from making negative comments, or else the Foreign Minister would order a third rebuilding. Hitler actually held his tongue, and only later in his intimate circle did he make fun of the building, which to his mind was an utter failure.

In October, Hanke told me something which had been learned when German troops met Soviet troops on the demarcation line in Poland: that Soviet equipment appeared extremely deficient, in fact wretched. Hanke had reported this to Hitler. Army officers confirmed this point; Hitler must have listened to this piece of intelligence with the keenest interest, for thereafter he repeatedly cited this report as evidence that the Russians were weak and poorly organized. Soon afterward, the failure of the Soviet offensive against Finland confirmed him in this view.

In spite of all the secrecy I obtained some light on Hitler's further plans when he gave me the assignment, still in 1939, to fit out a head-quarters for him in western Germany. Ziegenberg, a manorial estate of Goethe's time, situated near Nauheim in the foothills of the Taunus range, was modernized by us for this purpose, and provided with shelters.

When the arrangements were completed, millions of marks squandered on building, telephone cables laid over hundreds of miles, and the most modern communications equipment installed, Hitler abruptly decided that the place was too luxurious for him. In wartime he must lead a simple life, he said, and therefore quarters conceived in this spirit were to be built for him in the Eifel hills. This may have made an impression upon those who did not know how many millions of marks had already been expended and how many more millions would now have to be spent. We pointed this out to Hitler, but he would not be swayed, for he saw his reputation for "modesty" imperiled.

After the swift victory in France, I was firmly convinced that Hitler had already become one of the great figures in German history. Yet I wondered at the apathy I thought I observed in the public despite all the grand triumphs. Hitler's self-confidence was obviously growing by leaps and bounds. He had found a new theme for his monologues at table. His great concept, he declared, had not run afoul of the inade-quacies which had caused Germany to lose the First World War. In those days there had been dissension between the political and the military leadership, he said. The political parties had been given leeway to undermine the unity of the nation and even to engage in treasonous activities. For reasons of protocol incompetent princes of the ruling houses had to be commanders of their armies; they were supposed to earn military laurels in order to increase the glory of their dynasties. The only reason that enormous disasters had been averted was that these incompetent scions of decadent royal families had been assigned excellent General Staff officers to aid them. Moreover, at the top as supreme war lord had been the incompetent Wilhelm II. Today, on the other hand, Germany was united. The states had been reduced to unimportance, the army commanders were selected from among the best officers without regard to their descent, the privileges of the nobility had been abolished, political life and the army as well as the nation as a whole had been forged into a unity. Moreover, he, Hitler, stood at the head. His strength, his determination, his energy would overcome all future difficulties.

Hitler claimed total credit for the success of the campaign in the West. The plan for it came from him, he said. "I have again and again," he told us, "read Colonel de Gaulle's book on methods of modern warfare employing fully motorized units, and I have learned a great deal from it."

Shortly after the end of the campaign in France, I received a telephone call from the office of the Fuehrer's adjutant: I was to come to headquarters for a few days for a special purpose. Hitler had set up temporary headquarters in the small village of Bruly le Peche near Sedan. The village had been cleared of all inhabitants. The generals and adjutants were established in the small houses that lined the single village street. Hitler's own quarters in no way differed from those of the others. At my arrival he greeted me in the best of humors. "In a few days we are flying to Paris. I'd like you to be with us. Breker and Giessler are coming along also." With that I was dismissed for the present, astonished that the victor had sent for three artists to accompany him on his entry into the French capital.

That same evening I was invited to dine with Hitler's military circle. Details of the trip to Paris were discussed. This was not to be an official visit, I learned, but a kind of "art tour" by Hitler. This was the city, as he had so often said, which had fascinated him from his earliest years, so that he thought he would be able to find his way about the streets and important monuments as if he had lived there, solely from his endless studies of its plans.

The armistice was to go into effect at 1:35 A.M. on June 25, 1940. That night we sat with Hitler around a deal table in the simple room of a peasant house. Shortly before the agreed time Hitler gave orders to turn out the light and open the windows. Silently, we sat in the darkness, swept by the sense of experiencing a historic moment so close to the author of it. Outside, a bugler blew the traditional signal for the end of fighting. A thunderstorm must have been brewing in the distance, for as in a bad novel occasional flashes of heat lightning shimmered through the dark room. Someone, overcome by emotion, blew his nose. Then Hitler's voice sounded, soft and unemphatic: "This responsibility . . ." And a few minutes later: "Now switch the light on." The trivial conversation continued, but for me it remained a rare event. I thought I had for once seen Hitler as a human being.

Next day I set out from headquarters for Rheims, to see the cathedral. A ghostly looking city awaited me, almost deserted, ringed by military police protecting the champagne cellars. Casement windows banged in the wind, newspapers of several days ago blew through the streets, open front doors revealed interiors. It was as if ordinary life had stood still for a foolish moment. Glasses, dishes, and half-eaten meals could be seen on the tables. En route we had encountered innumerable refugees along the roads; they used the sides of the roads, for the middle was taken up by columns of German army units. These self-assured troops between the worn-looking people transporting their worldly goods in baby carriages, wheelbarrows, and other primitive vehicles made a striking contrast. Three and a half years later I saw similar scenes in Germany.

Three days after the beginning of the armistice we landed at Le Bourget airfield. It was early in the morning, about five-thirty. Three large Mercedes sedans stood waiting. Hitler as usual sat in the front seat beside the chauffeur, Breker and I on the jump seats behind him, while Giessler and the adjutants occupied the rear seats. Field-gray uniforms had been provided for us artists, so that we might fit into the military framework. We drove through the extensive suburbs directly to the Opera, Charles Garnier's great neobaroque building. It was Hitler's favorite and the first thing he wanted to see. Colonel Speidel, assigned by the German Occupation Authority, was waiting at the entrance for us.

The great stairway, famous for its spaciousness, notorious for its excessive ornamentation, the resplendent foyer, the elegant, gilded parterre, were carefully inspected. All the lights glowed as they would on a gala night. Hitler had undertaken to lead the party. A white-haired attendant accompanied our small group through the deserted building. Hitler had actually studied the plans of the Paris opera house with great care. Near the proscenium box he found a salon missing, remarked on it, and turned out to be right. The attendant said that this room had been eliminated in the course of renovations many years ago. "There, you see how well I know my way about," Hitler commented complacently. He seemed fascinated by the Opera, went into ecstasies about its beauty, his eyes glittering with an excitement that struck me as uncanny. The attendant, of course, had immediately recognized the person he was guiding through the building. In a businesslike but distinctly aloof manner, he showed us through the rooms. When we were at last getting ready to leave the building, Hitler whispered something to his adjutant, Brückner, who took a fifty-mark note from his wallet and went over to the attendant standing some distance away. Pleasantly, but firmly, the man refused to take the money. Hitler tried a second time, sending Breker over to him; but the man persisted in his refusal. He had only been doing his duty, he told Breker.

Afterward, we drove past the Madeleine, down the Champs Elysées, on to the Trocadéro, and then to the Eiffel Tower, where Hitler ordered another stop. From the Arc de Triomphe with its tomb of the Unknown Soldier we drove on to the Invalides, where Hitler stood for a long time at the tomb of Napoleon. Finally, Hitler inspected the Panthéon, whose proportions greatly impressed him. On the other hand he showed no special interest in some of the most beautiful architectural works in Paris: the Place des Vosges, the Louvre, the Palace of Justice, and Sainte-Chapelle. He became animated again only when he saw the unitary row of houses on the Rue de Rivoli. The end of our tour was the romantic, insipid imitation of early medieval domed churches, the church of Sacré Coeur on Montmartre—a surprising choice, even given Hitler's taste. Here he stood for a long time surrounded by several powerful men of his escort squad, while many churchgoers recognized him but ignored him. After a last look at Paris we drove swiftly back to the airport. By nine o'clock in the morning the sightseeing tour was over. "It was the dream of my life to be permitted to see Paris. I cannot say how happy I am to have that dream fulfilled today." For a moment I felt something like pity for him: three hours in Paris, the one and only time he was to see it, made him happy when he stood at the height of his triumphs.

In the course of the tour Hitler raised the question of a victory parade in Paris. But after discussing the matter with his adjutants and Colonel Speidel, he decided against it after all. His official reason for calling off the parade was the danger of its being harassed by English air raids. But later he said: "I am not in the mood for a victory parade. We aren't at the end yet."

That same evening he received me once more in the small room in the peasant house. He was sitting alone at table. Without more ado he declared: "Draw up a decree in my name ordering full-scale resumption of work on the Berlin buildings. . . . Wasn't Paris beautiful? But Berlin must be made far more beautiful. In the past I often considered whether we would not have to destroy Paris," he continued with great calm, as if he were talking about the most natural thing in the world. "But when we are finished in Berlin, Paris will only be a shadow. So why should we destroy it?" With that, I was dismissed.

Although I was accustomed to hearing Hitler make impulsive remarks, I was nevertheless shocked by this cool display of vandalism. He had reacted in a similar fashion to the devastation of Warsaw. At the time he had announced that he was not going to allow the city to be rebuilt, in order to deprive the Polish people of their political and cultural center. Warsaw, however, had been devastated by acts of war. Now Hitler was showing that he could entertain the thought of wantonly and without cause annihilating the city which he himself had called the most beautiful in Europe, with all its priceless artistic treasures. Within a few days some of the contradictions in Hitler's nature had been revealed to me, although at the time I certainly did not perceive them in anything like their full intensity. He contained a multitude of selves, from a person deeply aware of his responsibilities all the way to a ruthless and mankind-hating nihilist.

The effect of this experience however was quickly obscured for me. I was once again seduced by Hitler's brilliant victories and by the prospect of soon resuming work on my building projects. Now it was up to me to surpass Paris. Nothing more was said of razing her monuments. Instead, Hitler gave orders that our own be erected with maximum urgency. As he himself reworded the decree: "Berlin is to be given the style commensurate with the grandeur of our victory," and he further declared: "I regard the accomplishment of these supremely vital constructive tasks for the Reich as the greatest step in the preservation of our victory." He antedated this decree to June 25, 1940, the day of the armistice and of his greatest triumph.

Hitler was pacing back and forth on the gravel path in front of his house, accompanied by Generals Jodl and Keitel, when an adjutant came to tell him that I wished to take my leave. I was summoned, and as I approached the group I heard a snatch of the conversation: "Now we have shown what we are capable of," Hitler was saying. "Believe me, Keitel, a campaign against Russia would be like a child's game in a sandbox by comparison." In radiant good humor, he bade me goodby, sent his warmest regards to my wife, and promised that he would soon be discussing new plans and models with me.

13

Excess

EVEN WHILE HITLER WAS DEEP IN THE PLANS FOR THE RUSSIAN CAMPAIGN, his mind was already dwelling on theatrical effects for the victory parades of 1950, once the grand boulevard and the great triumphal arch had been completed.[1] But while he dreamed of new wars, new victories and celebrations, he suffered one of the greatest defeats of his career. Three days after a talk with me in which he had outlined more of his conceptions of the future, I was called to Obersalzberg with my sketches. Waiting in the anteroom at the Berghof, pale and agitated, were Leitgen and Pintsch, two of Hess's adjutants. They asked if I would let them see Hitler first; they had a personal letter from Hess to transmit to him. At this moment Hitler descended from his room upstairs. One of the adjutants was called into the salon. While I began leafing through my sketches once more, I suddenly heard an inarticulate, almost animal outcry. Then Hitler roared: "Bormann, at once! Where is Bormann?" Bormann was told to get in touch with Goering, Ribbentrop, Goebbels, and Himmler by the fastest possible means. All private guests were confined to the upper floor. Many hours passed before we learned what had happened: Hitler's deputy had flown to hostile England.

Superficially, Hitler soon appeared to have regained his usual composure. What bothered him was that Churchill might use the incident to pretend to Germany's allies that Hitler was extending a peace feeler. "Who will believe me when I say that Hess did not fly there in my name, that the whole thing is not some sort of intrigue behind the backs of my allies?" Japan might even alter her policy because of this, he fretted. He put through a phone call to Ernst Udet, the famous First World War fighter pilot and now technical chief of the air force, and wanted to know whether the two-motored plane Hess was using could reach its goal in Scotland and what weather conditions it would encounter. After a brief interval Udet called back to say that Hess was bound to fail for navigational reasons alone; because of the prevailing side winds he would probably fly past England and into empty space. For a moment Hitler regained hope: "If only he would drown in the North Sea! Then he would vanish without a trace, and we could work out some harmless explanation at our leisure." But after a few hours his anxieties returned, and in order to anticipate the British in any case he decided to announce over the radio that Hess had gone mad. The two adjutants, however, were arrested—as the harbingers of bad news used to be at the courts of ancient despots.

A rush of activity began at the Berghof. Aside from Goering, Goebbels, and Ribbentrop, Ley, various Gauleiters, and other party leaders arrived. Ley, as organizational chief of the party, made a bid to take over Hess's duties. In organizational terms this was no doubt what should have happened. But Bormann now showed for the first time how much influence he had over Hitler. He made short work of fending off Ley's proposal, and took the post for himself. Churchill commented at the time that this flight showed the presence of a worm in the German apple. He could not possibly have guessed how literally this phrase applied to Hess's successor.

Henceforth, Hess was scarcely ever mentioned in Hitler's entourage. Bormann alone looked into the affairs of his former superior and showed great zeal in visiting the sins of her husband on Frau Hess. Eva Braun tried to intercede with Hitler on her behalf, but unsuccessfully; later she gave her a small allowance behind Hitler's back. A few weeks later I heard from my doctor, Professor Chaoul, that Hess's father was dying. I sent him flowers, though without disclosing myself as the sender.

At the time it appeared to me that Bormann's ambition had driven Hess to this desperate act. Hess, also highly ambitious, could plainly see himself being excluded from access to and influence over Hitler. Thus, for example, Hitler said to me some time in 1940, after a conversation with Hess lasting many hours: "When I talk with Goering, it's like a bath in steel for me; I feel fresh afterward. The Reich Marshal has a stimulating way of presenting things. With Hess every conversation becomes an unbearably tormenting strain. He always comes to me with unpleasant matters and won't leave off." By his flight to England, Hess was probably trying, after so many years of being kept in the background, to win prestige and some success. For he did not have the qualities necessary for survival in the midst of a swamp of intrigues and struggles for power. He was too sensitive, too receptive, too unstable, and often told all factions they were in the right, in the order of their appearance. As a type he undoubtedly corresponded to the majority of the high party leaders; like him, most of them had great difficulty keeping the ground of reality under their feet.

Hitler put the blame for Hess's flight on the corrupting influence of Professor Haushofer.* Twenty-five years later, in Spandau prison, Hess assured me in all seriousness that the idea had been inspired in him in a dream by supernatural forces. He said he had not at all intended to oppose or embarrass Hitler. "We will guarantee England her empire; in return she will give us a free hand in Europe." That was the message he took to England—without managing to deliver it. It had also been one of Hitler's recurrent formulas before and occasionally even during the war.

If I judge correctly, Hitler never got over this "disloyalty" on the part of his deputy. Some while after the assassination attempt of July 20, 1944, he mentioned, in the course of one of his fantastic misreadings of the real situation, that among his conditions for peace was the extradition of the "traitor." Hess would have to be hanged, he said. When I told Hess about this later, he commented: "He would have made it up with me. I'm certain of it. And don't you believe that in 1945, when everything was going to smash, he sometimes thought: 'Hess was right after all'?"

Hitler went even further than insisting that the Berlin buildings be pushed forward at full speed in the midst of war. Under the influence of his Gauleiters he also wildly lengthened the list of cities slated for reconstruction. Originally they had been only Berlin, Nuremberg, Munich, and Linz. Now, by personal decrees, he declared another twenty-seven cities, including Hanover, Augsburg, Bremen, and Weimar, to be "reconstruction cities."[2] Neither I nor anyone else was ever asked about the feasibility of such decisions. Instead, after each such conference I merely received a copy of the decree Hitler had informally issued. According to my estimate at the time the costs for party buildings alone in those reconstruction cities would be, as I wrote to Bormann on November 26, 1940, between 22 and 25 billion marks.

I thought that my own deadlines were being imperiled by these requirements. At first I tried to secure a decree from Hitler placing all building plans throughout the Reich under my authority. But when this

* Hess had first introduced Hitler to Professor Karl Haushofer, a former general and founder of the theories of "geopolitics." His ideas strongly influenced Hitler's early thinking, but Haushofer evidently did not go all the way with Nazism. His son, Albrecht Haushofer, was arrested for participation in the July 20, 1944, conspiracy, and was shot in the closing days of the war. Professor Haushofer committed suicide after his son's death.

effort was blocked by Bormann, I told Hitler on January 17, 1941—after a long illness that had given me time to reflect on many problems—that it would be better if I were to concentrate only upon the buildings in Nuremberg and Berlin which had been assigned to me. Hitler instantly agreed: "You're right. It would be a pity if you threw away your energies on general matters. If necessary you can declare in my name that I, the Fuehrer, do not wish you to become involved in these other matters lest you be led away from your proper artistic tasks."[3]

I availed myself generously of this exemption, and during the next few days resigned all my party offices. If I can sort out my motives at the time, this step was probably also directed against Bormann, who had been hostile to me from the start. I knew I was in no danger, however, since Hitler had frequently referred to me as irreplaceable.

Occasionally I was caught amiss, at which times Bormann could deliver a sharp reproof to me from headquarters, undoubtedly with satisfaction. Thus, for example, I had consulted with the Protestant and Catholic authorities on the location of churches in our new section of Berlin.* Bormann curtly informed me that churches were not to receive building sites.

Hitler's decree of June 25, 1940, for the "preservation of our victory" was tantamount to an order for work to go forward on the buildings in Berlin and Nuremberg. A few days later, however, I made it clear to Reich Minister Lammers that of course we did not "intend to proceed at once with the practical reconstruction of Berlin . . . as long as the war was going on." But Hitler remonstrated and commanded continuance of the building operations even though to do so ran against public feeling. Again on his insistence I set up a "Fuehrer's immediate program," in the light of which Goering—this was in the middle of April 1941—assigned the necessary quantity of iron to me. It amounted to eighty-four thousand tons annually. To camouflage the operation from the public, the program was given the code name "War program for waterways and Reich railways, Berlin section." On April 18, Hitler and I again discussed deadlines: for the completion of the great hall, the High Command of the Armed Forces, the Chancellery, the Fuehrer's building—in short, for his power centers around Adolf Hitler Platz. He was still determined to have that complex erected as quickly as possible. Simultaneously, an association of seven of the best German construction firms was organized for the purpose of speeding the work.

With his characteristic obstinacy and in spite of the impending campaign against the Soviet Union, Hitler personally continued to take a hand in the selection of paintings for the Linz gallery. He sent his

* As yet we had only agreed to compensate the churches for those of their buildings situated in parts of the inner city which were slated for demolition.

art dealers into the occupied areas to comb the picture market there, with the result that there was soon a bitter contest between his dealers and Goering's. The picture war had begun to take a nasty turn when Hitler finally reproved his Reich Marshal and thereby once and for all restored the order of rank even in regard to art dealers.

In 1941 large catalogues bound in brown leather arrived at Obersalzberg. They contained photographs of hundreds of paintings which Hitler personally distributed among his favorite galleries: Linz, Königsberg, Breslau, and other eastern cities. At the Nuremberg Trials, I saw these volumes again as evidence for the prosecution. The majority of the paintings had been seized from Jewish owners by Rosenberg's Paris office.

Hitler made no inroads on the famous state art collections of France. However, this restraint was not so unselfish as it seemed, for he occasionally remarked that in a peace treaty the best pieces from the Louvre would have to be delivered to Germany as part of war reparations. But Hitler did not utilize his authority for his private ends. He did not keep in his own possession a single one of the paintings acquired or confiscated in the occupied territories.

Goering, on the other hand, went about increasing his art collection during the war by any means whatsoever. The halls and rooms of Karinhall were sheathed with valuable paintings hung one above the other in three and four tiers. He even had a life-size nude representing Europa mounted above the canopy of his magnificent bed. He himself also dabbled in art dealing: The walls of one large hall of his country estate were covered with paintings. They had been the personal property of a well-known Dutch art dealer who after the occupation had been compelled to turn over his collection to Goering for a ridiculous price. In the middle of the war Goering sold these pictures to Gauleiters, as he told me with a childlike smile, for many times what he had paid—adding, moreover, an extra something to the price for the glory of the paintings having come "from the famous Goering collection."

One day—it must have been sometime in 1943—I heard from a French intermediary that Goering was pressing the Vichy government to exchange a famous painting belonging to the Louvre for several of the worthless pictures in his own collection. Knowing Hitler's views about the inviolability of the Louvre's collection, I was able to advise the French informant not to yield to this pressure; if Goering should persist in the matter, he was to let me know. Goering, however, let it drop. On the other hand, one day at Karinhall he showed me the Sterzing Altar, which had been presented to him by Mussolini after the agreement on South Tyrol in the winter of 1940. Hitler was often outraged by the way the "Second Man in the State" appropriated valuable works of art, but he never dared call Goering to account.

Toward the end of the war Goering invited my friend Breker and me to afternoon dinner at Karinhall—this was a rare and exceptional occasion. The meal was not too lavish, but I was rather taken aback when at its end an ordinary brandy was poured for us, while Goering's servant poured his, with a certain solemnity, from a dusty old bottle. "This is reserved for me alone," he commented without embarrassment to his guests and went on about the particular French palace in which this rare find had been confiscated. Afterward, in an expansive mood, he showed us the treasures stowed away in the Karinhall cellar. Among them were some priceless classical pieces from the Naples Museum; these had been removed before the evacuation of Naples at the end of 1943. With the same pride of ownership he had his cupboards opened to allow us a glimpse of his hoard of French soaps and perfumes, a stock that would have sufficed for years. At the conclusion of this display he sent for his collection of diamonds and other precious stones, obviously worth hundreds of thousands of marks.

Hitler's purchases of paintings stopped after he had appointed the head of the Dresden Gallery, Dr. Hans Posse, as his agent for building the Linz collection. Until then Hitler had chosen his purchases himself from the auction catalogues. In the course of this he had occasionally been victimized by his habit of appointing two or three rivals to carry out a particular assignment. There were times when he would have separately instructed both his photographer, Heinrich Hoffmann, and one of his art dealers, to bid without limit. The result was that Hitler's two emissaries kept fearlessly outbidding one another long after all other bidders had dropped out. This went on until one day Hans Lange, the Berlin auctioneer, called my attention to this state of affairs.

Shortly after the appointment of Posse, Hitler showed him his previous acquisitions, including the Grützner collection. The showing took place in Hitler's air-raid shelter, where he had stored these treasures for safety. Chairs were brought in for Posse, Hitler, and myself, and SS orderlies carried in picture after picture. Hitler went on about his favorite paintings in his usual way, but Posse refused to be overpowered either by Hitler's position or by his engaging amiability. Objective and incorruptible, he turned down many of these expensive acquistions: "Scarcely useful," or "Not in keeping with the stature of the gallery, as I conceive it." As was so often the case when Hitler was dealing with a specialist, he accepted the criticisms without demur. Posse rejected most of the pictures by painters of Hitler's beloved Munich School.

In the middle of November 1940, Molotov arrived in Berlin. Hitler and his dinner guests greatly relished the tale carried by his physician, Dr. Karl Brandt, that the Soviet Foreign Minister's staff had all plates and silverware boiled before use for fear of German germs.

In the salon at the Berghof stood a large globe on which, a few months later, I found traces of this unsuccessful conference. One of the army adjutants pointed out, with a significant look, an ordinary pencil line: a line running from north to south along the Urals. Hitler had drawn it to indicate the future boundary between his sphere of interest and that of the Japanese. On June 21, 1941, the eve of the attack on the Soviet Union, Hitler called me into his Berlin salon after dinner, had a record put on and a few bars from Liszt's *Les Préludes* played. "You'll hear that often in the near future, because it is going to be our victory fanfare for the Russian campaign. Funk chose it. How do you like it?* . . . We'll be getting our granite and marble from there, in any quantities we want."

Hitler was now openly manifesting his megalomania. What his building plans had been implying for years was now to be sealed "in blood," as he put it, by a new war. Aristotle once wrote in the *Politics:* "It remains true that the greatest injustices proceed from those who pursue excess, not from those who are driven by necessity."

For Ribbentrop's fiftieth birthday in 1943 several of his close associates presented him with a handsome casket, ornamented with semiprecious stones, which they intended to fill with photocopies of all the treaties and agreements concluded by the Foreign Minister. "We were thrown into great embarrassment," Ambassador Hewel, Ribbentrop's liaison man, remarked to Hitler at supper, "when we were about to fill the casket. There were only a few treaties that we hadn't broken in the meantime."

Hitler's eyes filled with tears of laughter.

As had happened at the beginning of the war, I was again oppressed by the idea of pushing forward with such vast building operations, drawing upon all available means, when the great war was obviously reaching a crucial stage. On July 30, 1941—while the German advance in Russia was still proceeding boldly—I proposed to Dr. Todt, who was in charge of the entire German construction industry, that work be suspended on all buildings not essential for the war effort.[4] Todt, however, thought that in view of the present favorable state of military operations we could wait a few weeks more before facing this question. The question was to be deferred altogether, for my arguments once again made no impression on Hitler. He would not hear of any restrictions and refused to divert the material and labor for his private buildings to war industries any more than he would consider calling a halt to his favorite projects, the autobahns, the party buildings, and the Berlin projects.

* For each of the previous campaigns Hitler had personally chosen a musical fanfare that preceded radio announcements of striking victories.

In the middle of September 1941, when the advance in Russia was already lagging considerably behind the overconfident forecasts, Hitler ordered sizable increases in our contracts for granite purchases from Sweden, Norway, and Finland for my big Berlin and Nuremberg buildings. Contracts to the value of thirty million Reichsmarks had been awarded to the leading companies in the Norwegian, Finnish, Italian, Belgian, Swedish, and Dutch stone industry.[5] In order to bring these vast quantities of granite to Berlin and Nuremberg, we founded (on June 4, 1941) a transport fleet of our own and set up our own shipyards in Wismar and Berlin, with plans to build a thousand boats with a cargo capacity of five hundred tons each.

My proposals that we cease peacetime building continued to be disregarded even when the outlines of the disaster of the winter of 1941 in Russia began to be apparent. On November 29, 1941, Hitler told me bluntly: "The building must begin even while this war is still going on. I am not going to let the war keep me from accomplishing my plans."[6]

After the initial successes in Russia, moreover, Hitler decided that we wanted even more martial accents for our boulevard. These were to be supplied by captured enemy armaments set up on granite pedestals. On August 20, 1941, on Hitler's orders, I informed an astonished Admiral Lorey, commander of the Berlin armory, that we intended to place thirty pieces of captured heavy artillery between the south station and the triumphal arch ("Structure T," as we privately called it). There were other points, I informed the admiral, on the grand boulevard and along the southern axis where Hitler wanted to place such guns, so that we would need about two hundred pieces of the heaviest type *in toto*. Any extra large tanks were to be reserved for setting up in front of important public buildings.

Hitler's ideas about the political constitution of his "Teutonic Empire of the German Nation" still seemed quite vague, but he had already made up his mind about one point: In the immediate vicinity of the Norwegian city of Trondheim, which offered a particularly favorable strategic position, the largest German naval base was to arise. Along with shipyards and docks a city for a quarter of a million Germans would be built and incorporated into the German Reich. Hitler had commissioned me to do the planning. On May 1, 1941, I obtained from Vice Admiral Fuchs of the High Command of the Navy the necessary data on the space required for a large state-owned shipyard. On June 21, Grand Admiral Raeder and I went to the Chancellery to report to Hitler on the project. Hitler then determined the approximate site of the city. As much as a year later, on May 13, 1942, he discussed this base in the course of a conference on armaments.[7] Special maps were prepared from which he studied the optimum position of the docks, and he decided that a large underground submarine base was to be blasted into the granite cliff. For the rest, Hitler assumed that St. Nazaire and Lorient in France, as well as the British Channel Islands, would be incorporated into a future naval base system. Thus he disposed at will of territories, interests, and rights belonging to others; by now he was totally convinced of his world dominion.

In this connection I must mention his plan for founding German cities in the occupied areas of the Soviet Union. On November 24, 1941, in the very midst of the winter catastrophe, Gauleiter Meyer, deputy of Alfred Rosenberg, the Reich Minister for the occupied eastern territories, asked me to take over the section on "new cities" and plan and build the settlements for the German garrisons and civil administrations. I finally refused this offer at the end of January 1942 on the grounds that a central authority for city planning would inevitably lead to a uniformity of pattern. I instead suggested that the great German cities each stand as sponsor for the construction of the new ones.[8]

Ever since I had begun, at the beginning of the war, to assume responsibilty for erecting buildings for the army and air force, I had considerably expanded the organization entrusted with this work. To be sure, by the standards of a few months hence, the twenty-six thousand construction workers employed on these military programs by the end of 1941 would be insignificant. But at this time I was proud of being able to make a small contribution to the war effort; it eased my conscience not to be engaged entirely on Hitler's peacetime plans. The most pressing task was the Ju 88 Program for the air force, which was to turn out the new two-motored, medium-range Junkers 88 dive bombers. Three big factories in Brünn, Graz, and Vienna, each of them larger than the Volkswagen plant, were completed within eight months. For the first time we used prefabricated concrete elements. From the autumn of 1941 on, however, our work was hampered by the shortage of fuel. Even though our programs had top priority, in September 1941 the amounts of fuel assigned to them had to be reduced by a third, and by January 1, 1942, to a sixth of our needs.[9] That is just one example of how greatly Hitler had overextended his resources by embarking on the Russian campaign.

Along with this, repair of the bomb damage in Berlin and the building of air-raid shelters had been turned over to me. Without suspecting it, I was thus preparing for my duties as Minister of Armaments. For one thing, this gave me some insight into the havoc wreaked on the mechanisms of production by the constant arbitrary shifts in programs and priorities. For another thing, it taught me a good deal about the power relationships and the dissensions within the leadership.

For example, I took part in a session with Goering in the course of which General Thomas expressed his anxieties about the vast demands the leadership was making upon the economy. Goering answered the respected general by roaring at him: "What business is that of yours? I am handling that—I am, do you hear. Or are you by any chance in charge of the Four-Year Plan? You have nothing to say in this matter; the Fuehrer has entrusted all these questions to me alone." In such disputes General Thomas could expect no support from his chief, General Keitel, who was only too glad to escape being bullied by Goering. The well-conceived economic plan of the Armaments Office of the High Command of the Armed Forces was never carried out. But as I had already realized by then, Goering did nothing about these problems. Whenever he did do anything, he usually created total confusion, since he never took the trouble to work through the problems but made his decisions on the basis of impulsive inspirations.

A few months later, around November 1941, in my capacity as chief of armaments construction I took part in a conversation between Field Marshal Milch and Dr. Todt. In the autumn of 1941, Hitler was convinced that the Russians were already defeated; he therefore wanted priority to be given to building up the air force in preparation for his next operation, the subjugation of England.* Milch now insisted on this priority, as was his duty—while Dr. Todt, who knew something about the military situation, was close to despair. For he too was responsible for increasing the equipment of the army as fast as possible, but lacked an order from Hitler which would have given his assignment the necessary priority. At the end of the conference Todt summed up his helplessness: "It would be best, sir, if you'd take me into your ministry and let me be your assistant."

It was again in the fall of 1941 that I visited the Junkers plant in Dessau to see General Manager Koppenberg and discuss how to coordinate our building programs with his production plans. After we had worked the matter out, he led me into a locked room and showed me a graph comparing American bomber production for the next several years with ours. I asked him what our leaders had to say about these depressing comparative figures. "That's just it, they won't believe it," he said. Whereupon he broke into uncontrollable tears. But Goering, the Commander in Chief of the then heavily engaged Luftwaffe, had plenty of leisure. On June 23, 1941, the day after the beginning of the

---

* This order of Hitler's was still in effect in December 1941, although the situation had changed radically. Hitler hesitated to withdraw such orders, partly because he had a general tendency to hesitate and partly because he was concerned about saving face. A new order consistent with the exigencies of the war, giving army equipment priority over air force equipment, as required by the circumstances, was not issued until January 10, 1942.

attack on the Soviet Union, he found time to dress in his gala uniform and come with me to see the models of his Reich Marshal's office, which were being exhibited in Treptow.

My last art tour for a quarter of a century took me to Lisbon, where on November 8 an exhibit of new German architecture was being opened. I was supposed to fly in Hitler's plane; but when it appeared that some of the alcoholic members of his entourage, such as Adjutant Schaub and the photographer Hoffmann, wanted to go along on the flight, I shook off their company by proposing to Hitler that I drive to Lisbon in my car. I saw ancient cities such as Burgos, Segovia, Toledo, and Salamanca; I visited the Escorial, a complex I could compare only to Hitler's Fuehrer palace in its proportions, although the underlying impulse was quite different and far more spiritual: Philip II had surrounded the palace nucleus with a monastery. What a contrast with Hitler's architectural ideas: in the one case, remarkable conciseness and clarity, magnificent interior rooms, their forms perfectly controlled; in the other case, pomp and disproportionate ostentation. Moreover, this rather melancholic creation by the architect Juan de Herrera (1530–97) more closely matched our ominous situation than Hitler's boastful program music. In hours of solitary contemplation it began to dawn on me for the first time that my recent architectural ideals were on the wrong track.

Because of this trip I missed the visit to Berlin of several Parisian acquaintances, among them Vlaminck, Derain, and Despiau,[10] who at my invitation had come to see the models of our plans for Berlin. They must have looked in dead silence at our project and at the buildings that were going up; the office journal does not record a word about the impression that our exhibit made on them. I had met them during my stays in Paris and through my office had several times helped them out with commissions. Curiously enough, they had more freedom than their German colleagues. For when I visited the Salon d'Automne in Paris during the war, the walls were hung with pictures which would have been branded degenerate art in Germany. Hitler, too, had heard of this show. His reaction was as surprising as it was logical: "Are we to be concerned with the intellectual soundness of the French people? Let them degenerate if they want to! All the better for us."

While I was on my trip to Lisbon, a transportation disaster had developed behind the fronts in the eastern theater of war. The German military organization had been unable to cope with the Russian winter. Moreover, the Soviet troops in the course of their retreat had systematically wiped out all locomotive sheds, watering stations, and other technical apparatus of their railroad system. In the intoxication of success during the summer and autumn when it seemed that "the Russian bear is already finished," no one had given sufficient thought to the repair of this equipment. Hitler had refused to understand that such technical measures must be taken well ahead of time, in view of the Russian winter.

I heard about these difficulties from high officials of the Reichsbahn (the government railroad system) and from army and air force generals. I thereupon proposed to Hitler that thirty thousand of the sixty-five thousand German construction workers I was employing be assigned under the direction of my engineers, to repair work on the railroads. Incredibly, it was two weeks before Hitler could bring himself to authorize this. On December 27, 1941, he at last issued the order. Instead of hurling construction crews into the breach at the beginning of November, he had gone on with his triumphal buildings, determined not to capitulate in any way to reality.

On that same December 27, I had a meeting with Dr. Todt in his modest house on Hintersee near Berchtesgaden. He assigned the entire Ukraine to me as my field of activity, while staffs and workmen who had all along been frivolously engaged in working on the autobahns were made responsible for the central and northern areas of Russia. Todt had just returned from a long tour of inspection in the eastern theater of war. He had seen stalled hospital trains in which the wounded had frozen to death and had witnessed the misery of the troops in villages and hamlets cut off by snow and cold. He had been struck by the discouragement and despair among the German soldiers. Deeply depressed himself, he concluded that we were both physically incapable of enduring such hardships and psychologically doomed to destruction in Russia. "It is a struggle in which the primitive people will prove superior," he continued. "They can endure everything, including the harshness of the climate. We are too sensitive and are bound to be defeated. In the end the victory will go to the Russians and the Japanese." Hitler too, obviously influenced by Spengler, had expressed similar ideas in peacetime when he spoke of the biological superiority of the "Siberians and Russians." But when the campaign in the east began, he thrust aside his own thesis, for it ran counter to his plans.

Hitler's passion for building, his blind attachment to his personal hobbies, stimulated the same sort of thing in his imitative paladins, so that most of them had assumed the life style of victors. Even at that time I felt that here was one dangerous flaw in Hitler's system. For unlike the democratic regimes, there could be no public criticism; no demand could arise that these abuses be corrected. On March 19, 1945, in my last letter to Hitler, I reminded him of this tendency: "I was sore at heart in the victorious days of 1940 when I saw how we were losing, among a broad spectrum of our leadership, our inner discipline. That was the very time when we ought to have proved our worthiness to Providence by decency and inner modesty."

Though these lines were written five years later, they confirm the fact that at the time I saw the mistakes, winced at the abuses, took a critical stand, and was tormented by doubts and skepticism. But I must admit that these feelings were born from my fear that Hitler and his leadership might gamble away the victory.

In the middle of 1941, Goering inspected our model city on Pariser Platz. In a moment of affability he made an unusual remark to me: "I have told the Fuehrer," he said, "that I consider you, after him, the greatest man Germany possesses." But as second man in the hierarchy he felt he had better qualify this statement: "In my eyes you are absolutely the greatest architect. I would like to say that I esteem you as highly for your architectural creativity as I do the Fuehrer for his political and military abilities."[11]

After nine years as Hitler's architect I had worked my way up to an admired and uncontested position. The next three years were to confront me with entirely different tasks which for a time actually made me the most important man after Hitler.

PART

TWO

14

Start in My New Office

Sepp Dietrich, one of Hitler's earliest followers and now the commander of an SS tank corps hard pressed by the Russians near Rostov
in the southern Ukraine, was flying to Dnepropetrovsk on January 30,
1942, in a plane of the Fuehrer's air squadron. I asked him to take me
along. My staff was already in the city, organizing the task of repairing
the railroads in southern Russia.* The obvious idea of having a plane
placed at my disposal had not occurred to me—a sign of how small a role
in the war effort I so far attributed to myself.

Huddled close together, we sat in a Heinkel bomber refitted as a
passenger plane. Beneath us the dreary, snow-covered plains of southern
Russia flowed by. On large farms we saw the burned sheds and barns.
To keep our direction, we flew along the railroad line. Scarcely a train
could be seen; the stations were burned out, the roundhouses destroyed.
Roads were rare, and they too were empty of vehicles. The great stretches
of land we passed over were frightening in their deathly silence, which
could be felt even inside the plane. Only gusts of snow broke the monotony of the landscape—or, rather, emphasized it. This flight brought home

* According to the *Office Journal*, beginning on January 28, 1942, a train left
Berlin every day carrying construction workers and building materials to the Ukraine.
Several hundred workers had already been sent ahead to Dnepropetrovsk to make
preparations.

to me the danger to the armies almost cut off from supplies. At dusk we landed in the Russian industrial city of Dnepropetrovsk.

My group of technicians was called the "Speer Construction Staff" —in keeping with the bent of the period to link assignments with the names of individuals. They had taken up emergency quarters in a sleeping car. From time to time a locomotive sent a whiff of steam through the heating coils to keep them from freezing. Working conditions were just as grim; for our office we had only a dining car. The assignment was proving more formidable than we had thought. The Russians had destroyed all the intermediate stations. Nowhere were repair sheds still standing, nowhere were water tanks protected from freezing, nowhere were there stations or intact switching yards. The simplest matters, which at home could have been settled by a telephone call, became a problem here. Even lumber and nails were hard to come by.

It snowed and snowed. Railroad and highway traffic had come to a total standstill. The airport runway was drifted over. We were cut off; my return had to be postponed. Socializing with our construction workmen filled the time; get-togethers were held, songs sung. Sepp Dietrich made speeches and was cheered. I stood by; with my awkwardness at speechmaking I did not dare say even a few words to my men. Among the songs distributed by the army corps were some very melancholy ones, expressing the longing for home and the dreariness of the Russian steppes. These songs were undisguised statements of inner stress, and significantly enough, they were the soldiers' favorite songs.

Meanwhile the situation was growing critical. A small Russian tank group had broken through and was approaching Dnepropetrovsk. We held conferences on what we could use to oppose them. Virtually nothing was available; a few rifles and an abandoned artillery piece without ammunition. The Russians advanced to within about twelve miles, then circled around aimlessly in the steppe. One of the mistakes so typical of war happened; they did not take advantage of their situation. A brief sortie to the long bridge over the Dnieper and destroying it by fire—it had been rebuilt in wood in months of toilsome work—would have cut off the German army southeast of Rostov from winter supplies for several mouths more.

I am not at all disposed to be a hero, and since the seven days of my stay had been of no use whatsoever and I was only eating into my engineers' scarce provisions, I decided to go along on a train that was going to attempt to break through the snowdrifts to the west. My staff gave me a friendly—and it seemed to me thankful—farewell. All night we went along at six or seven miles an hour, stopped, shoveled snow, rode again. I thought we were a good deal farther to the west at dawn, when the train pulled into a deserted station.

But everything looked oddly familiar to me: burned sheds, clouds of steam above a few dining cars and sleeping cars, patrolling soldiers. We were back in Dnepropetrovsk. The huge drifts had forced the train to turn back. Depressed, I tramped into my construction staff's dining car, where my associates received me with astonished and, I felt, rather irritated expressions. After all, they had pillaged their stocks of alcohol until the early morning hours drinking to their chief's departure.

On that same day, February 7, 1942, the plane that had flown Sepp Dietrich in was to start on the return flight. Air Captain Nein, who was soon to be pilot of my own plane, was willing to take me with him. Just getting out to the airfield involved considerable difficulty. Under a clear sky and at a temperature barely above zero, a violent wind was whipping masses of snow in all directions. Russians in padded jackets tried in vain to clear the many feet of snow from the road. After we had tramped along for about an hour, several of them surrounded me and addressed me excitedly. I did not understand a word. Finally one of them picked up some snow and began rubbing my face with it. "Frozen," I thought; I knew that much from my mountain tours. My astonishment grew when one of the Russians took from his filthy clothes a snow-white and neatly folded handkerchief to dry my face.

After some difficulty, around eleven o'clock we managed to take off from a runway poorly cleared of drifts. The plane's destination was Rastenburg in East Prussia, the headquarters of the squadron. My destination was Berlin, but it was not my plane and so I was glad that at least I would be taken a considerable part of the way. By this chance I for the first time came to Hitler's East Prussian headquarters.

In Rastenburg, I telephoned one of the adjutants in the hope that he would report my presence to Hitler and perhaps Hitler would want to talk with me. I had not seen him since the beginning of December, and it would have been a special distinction if he were at least to give me a brief greeting.

One of the Fuehrer's cars drove me to headquarters. There I at last had a good meal in the dining barracks where Hitler ate daily with his generals, political associates, and adjutants. Hitler himself was not present. Dr. Todt, the Minister of Armaments and Munitions, was reporting to him, and the two were dining alone in Hitler's private apartment. Meanwhile, I discussed our difficulties in the Ukraine with Army Transport Chief General Gercke and the commander of the railroad engineering troops.

After supper with a large group, Hitler and Todt continued their conference. It was late at night before Todt emerged, strained and fatigued, from a long and—it appeared—trying discussion. He wore a depressed air. I sat with him for a few minutes while he silently drank a glass of wine without speaking of the reason for his mood. By chance he mentioned, in the course of our rather lame conversation, that he was to fly back to Berlin next morning and that there was an unoccupied seat in his plane.* He said he would be glad to take me along, and I was relieved not to have to make that long trip by rail. We agreed to fly at an early hour, and Dr. Todt bade me good night, since he was going to try to get a little sleep.

An adjutant came in and requested me to join Hitler. It was then after one o'clock in the morning; in Berlin, too, we had often sat over our plans at this hour. Hitler seemed as exhausted and out of sorts as Todt. The furniture of his room stressed spareness; he had even renounced the comfort of an upholstered chair here at headquarters. We talked about the Berlin and Nuremberg building projects, and Hitler visibly brightened. Even his sallow complexion seemed to take on color. Finally he asked me to tell him what impressions I had gathered on my visit to southern Russia and helped me along by interjecting questions. The difficulties in restoring the railroad equipment, the blizzards, the incomprehensible behavior of the Russian tank force, the social evenings with their melancholy songs—bit by bit everything I had observed came out. When I mentioned the songs his attention sharpened, and he asked about the words. I produced the text I had in my pocket. He read it and said nothing. My opinion was that the songs were the natural response to a grim situation. Hitler, however, decided at once that some traitor was trying to undermine morale. He thought my story would enable him to track down this "oppositionist." Not until after the war did I learn that he had ordered a court-martial of the officer responsible for printing the songs.

This episode was characteristic of his perpetual suspiciousness. He closed his mind against the truth, but thought he could draw important conclusions from such random observations. Consequently he was always querying subordinates, even though they could not possibly have a view of the whole. Such distrust, usually without basis, had become a strong component in Hitler's character. It caused him to become obsessed with trivialities. Undoubtedly it was also to blame for his isolation from the events and the mood at the front; for his entourage tried as far as possible to fend off any informants who might stir up his suspicions that all was not well with the army in the east.

When I finally left Hitler at three o'clock in the morning, I sent word that I would not be flying with Dr. Todt. The plane was to start five hours later, I was worn out and wanted only to have a decent sleep. In my small bedroom I considered—who in Hitler's entourage did not do so after a two-hour conversation with him?—what impression I had probably left with him. I was content, my confidence restored that we would be able to carry out our building projects, a matter I had begun

---

* Todt was flying to Munich and expected to make a stopover in Berlin.

to doubt in view of the military situation. That night our dreams were transformed into realities; we had once again worked ourselves up to a hallucinatory optimism.

Next morning, the shrill clang of the telephone startled me out of a deep sleep. Dr. Brandt reported excitedly: "Dr. Todt's plane has just crashed, and he has been killed."

From that moment on my whole world was changed.

My relationship to Dr. Todt had become perceptibly closer in recent years. With his death I felt that I had lost an older, prudent colleague. We had much in common. Both of us came from prosperous, upper-middle-class circumstances; both of us were Badeners and had technological backgrounds. We loved nature, life in alpine shelters, ski tours—and shared a strong dislike for Bormann. Todt had repeatedly had serious run-ins with Bormann, protesting against his despoiling the landscape around Obersalzberg. My wife and I had frequently been Todt's house guests; the Todts lived in a small unpretentious place off the beaten track on Hintersee near Berchtesgaden. No one would have guessed that the famous road builder and creator of the autobahns lived there.

Dr. Todt was one of the very few modest, unassertive personalities in the government, a man you could rely on, and who steered clear of all the intrigues. With his combination of sensitivity and matter-of-factness, such as is frequently found in technicians, he fitted rather poorly into the governing class of the National Socialist state. He lived a quiet, withdrawn life, having no personal contacts with party circles —and even very rarely appeared at Hitler's dinners and suppers, although he would have been welcome. This retiring attitude enhanced his prestige; whenever he did appear he became the center of interest. Hitler, too, paid him and his accomplishments a respect bordering on reverence. Nevertheless, Todt had maintained his personal independence in his relations with Hitler, although he was a loyal party member of the early years.

In January 1941, when I was having difficulties with Bormann and Giessler, Todt wrote me an unusually candid letter which revealed his own resigned approach to the working methods of the National Socialist leadership:

> Perhaps my own experiences and bitter disappointments with all the men with whom I should actually be cooperating might be of help to you, enabling you to regard your experience as conditioned by the times, and perhaps the point of view which I have gradually arrived at after much struggle might somewhat help you psychologically. For I have concluded that in the course of such events . . . every activity meets with opposition,

everyone who acts has his rivals and unfortunately his opponents also. But not because people want to be opponents, rather because the tasks and relationships force different people to take different points of view. Perhaps, being young, you have quickly discovered how to cut through all such bother, while I only brood over it.[1]

At the breakfast table in the Fuehrer's headquarters there was lively discussion of who could possibly be considered for Dr. Todt's successor. Everyone agreed that he was irreplaceable. For he had held the positions of three ministers. Thus, he had been the supreme head of all road-building operations, in charge of all navigable waterways and improvements on them, as well as of all power plants. In addition, as Hitler's direct envoy, he was Minister of Armaments and Munitions. Within the framework of Goering's Four-Year Plan he headed the construction industry and had also created the Todt Organization which was building the West Wall and the U-boat shelters along the Atlantic, as well as the roads in the occupied territories all the way from northern Norway to southern France. Now he was also responsible for road building in Russia.

Thus in the course of the past several years Todt had gathered the major technical tasks of the Reich into his own hands. For the time being his operations were still nominally divided into various offices, but in essence he had set up the future technical ministry—all the more so since he was entrusted, within the party organization, with the Head Office for Technology, whose scope included all technical societies and associations.

During these first few hours I had already realized that an important portion of Todt's widely ranging tasks would surely fall to me. For as early as the spring of 1939, on one of his inspection tours of the West Wall, Hitler had remarked that if anything should happen to Todt, I would be the man to carry out his construction assignments. Later, in the summer of 1940, Hitler received me officially in the Chancellery office to inform me that Todt was overburdened. He had therefore decided, he said, to put me in charge of all construction, including the fortifications along the Atlantic. At the time I had been able to convince Hitler that it would be better if construction and armaments remained in one hand, since they were closely linked. Hitler had not referred to the matter again, and I had not spoken to anyone about it. The arrangement would not only have offended Todt but would surely have diminished his prestige.[2]

I was therefore prepared for some such assignment when I was summoned to Hitler as the first caller of the day at the usual late hour, around one o'clock in the afternoon. Even the face of Chief Adjutant Schaub expressed the importance of the occasion. In contrast to the night before, Hitler received me officially as Fuehrer of the Reich. Standing, earnest and formal, he received my condolences, replied very briefly, then said without more ado: "Herr Speer, I appoint you the successor to Minister Todt in all his capacities."

I was thunderstruck. He was already shaking hands with me and on the point of dismissing me. But I thought he had expressed himself imprecisely and therefore replied that I would try my best to be an adequate replacement for Dr. Todt in his construction assignments. "No, in all his capacities, including that of Minister of Armaments," Hitler corrected me.

"But I don't know anything about . . ." I protested.

"I have confidence in you. I know you will manage it," Hitler cut me off. "Besides, I have no one else. Get in touch with the Ministry at once and take over!"

"Then, *mein Führer,* you must put that as a command, for I cannot vouch for my ability to master this assignment."

Tersely, Hitler issued the command. I received it in silence.

Without a personal word, such as had been the usual thing between us, Hitler turned to other business. I took my leave, having experienced a first sample of our new relationship. Hitherto, Hitler had displayed a kind of fellowship toward me as an architect. Now a new phase was perceptibly beginning. From the first moment on he was establishing the aloofness of an official relationship to a minister who was his subordinate.

As I turned to the door, Schaub entered. "The Reich Marshal is here and urgently wishes to speak to you, *mein Führer.* He has no appointment."

Hitler looked sulky and displeased. "Send him in." He turned to me. "Stay here a moment longer."

Goering bustled in and after a few words of condolence stated his mind: "Best if I take over Dr. Todt's assignments within the framework of the Four-Year Plan. This would avoid the frictions and difficulties we had in the past as a result of overlapping responsibilities."

Goering had presumably come in his special train from his hunting lodge in Rominten, about sixty miles from Hitler's headquarters. Since the accident had taken place at half past nine he must have wasted no time at all.

Hitler ignored Goering's proposal. "I have already appointed Todt's successor. Reich Minister Speer here has assumed all of Dr. Todt's offices as of this moment."

The statement was so unequivocal that it excluded all possible argument. Goering seemed stunned and alarmed. But within a few seconds he recovered his composure. Coldly and ill-humoredly, he made no comment on Hitler's announcement. Instead he said: "I hope you will understand, *mein Führer,* if I do not attend Dr. Todt's funeral. You know what battles I had with him. It would hardly do for me to be present."

I no longer remember precisely what Hitler replied, since all this washing of dirty linen was naturally somewhat of a shock to me at this early moment in my new ministerial career. But I recall that Goering finally consented to come to the funeral, so that his disagreements with Todt would not become public knowledge. Given the importance assigned to such ceremonies by the system, it would have caused quite a stir if the second man in the state was absent from a formal act of state in honor of a dead cabinet minister.

There could be no doubt that Goering had tried to win his point by a surprise assault. I even surmised that Hitler had expected such a maneuver, and that this was the reason for the speed of my appointment.

As Minister of Armaments, Dr. Todt could carry out his assignment from Hitler only by issuing direct orders to industry. Goering, on the other hand, as Commissioner of the Four-Year Plan, felt responsible for running the entire war economy. He and his apparatus were therefore pitted against Todt's activities. In the middle of January 1942, about two weeks before his death, Todt had taken part in a conference on production matters. In the course of it Goering had so berated him that Todt informed Funk on the same afternoon that he would have to quit. On such occasions it worked to Todt's disadvantage that he wore the uniform of a brigadier general of the air force. This meant that in spite of his ministerial office he ranked as Goering's subordinate in the military hierarchy.

After this little episode one thing was clear to me: Goering would not be my ally, but Hitler seemed prepared to back me if I should encounter difficulties with the Reich Marshal.

At first Hitler seemed to treat Todt's death with the stoic calm of a man who must reckon with such incidents as part of the general picture. Without citing any evidence, he expressed the suspicion, during the first few days, that foul play might have been involved and that he was going to have the secret service look into the matter. This view, however, soon gave way to an irritable and often distinctly nervous reaction whenever the subject was mentioned in his presence. In such cases Hitler might declare sharply: "I want to hear no more about that. I forbid further discussion of the subject." Sometimes he would add: "You know that this loss still affects me too deeply for me to want to talk about it."

On Hitler's orders the Reich Air Ministry tried to determine whether sabotage might have been responsible for the plane crash. The investigation established the fact that the plane had exploded, with a sharp flame darting straight upward, some sixty-five feet above the ground. The report of the commission, which because of its importance was headed by an air force lieutenant general, nevertheless concluded with the curious statement: "The possibility of sabotage is ruled out. Further measures are therefore neither requisite nor intended."* Incidentally, not long before his death Dr. Todt had deposited a sizable sum of money in a safe, earmarked for his personal secretary of many years service. He had remarked that he was doing this in case something should happen to him.

One can only wonder at the recklessness and the frivolity with which Hitler appointed me to one of those three or four ministries on which the existence of his state depended. I was a complete outsider to the army, to the party, and to industry. Never in my life had I had anything to do with military weapons, for I had never been a soldier and up to the time of my appointment had never even used a rifle as a hunter. To be sure, it was in keeping with Hitler's dilettantism that he preferred to choose nonspecialists as his associates. After all, he had already appointed a wine salesman as his Foreign Minister, his party philosopher as his Minister for Eastern Affairs, and an erstwhile fighter pilot as overseer of the entire economy. Now he was picking an architect of all people to be his Minister of Armaments. Undoubtedly Hitler preferred to fill positions of leadership with laymen. All his life he respected but distrusted professionals such as, for example, Schacht.

As after the death of Professor Troost, my career was again being furthered by the death of another man. Hitler regarded it as a specially striking instance of Providence that I had arrived at headquarters the night before by sheer chance, and that I had canceled my projected flight with Todt. Later, when I was having my first successes, he liked to say

---

* The plane executed a normal takeoff, but while still within sight of the airport the pilot made a rapid turn which suggested that he was trying for an emergency landing. As he was coming down he steered for the landing strip without taking time to head into the wind. The accident occurred near the airport and at a low altitude. The plane was a Heinkel III, converted for passenger flight; it had been lent to Dr. Todt by his friend Field Marshal Sperrle, since Todt's own plane was undergoing repairs. Hitler reasoned that this Heinkel, like all the courier planes that were used at the front, had a self-destruct mechanism on board. It could be activated by pulling a handle located between the pilot's and the copilot's seats, whereupon the plane would explode within a few minutes. The final report of the military tribunal, dated March 8, 1943 (K 1 T.L. II/42) and signed by the commanding general and the commander of Air District I, Königsberg, stated: "Approximately twenty-three hundred feet from the airport and the end of the runway the pilot apparently throttled down, then opened the throttle again two or three seconds later. At that moment a long flame shot up vertically from the front of the plane, apparently caused by an explosion. The aircraft fell at once from an altitude of approximately sixty-five feet, pivoting around its right wing and hitting the ground almost perpendicularly, facing directly away from its flight direction. It caught fire at once and a series of explosions totally demolished it."

that the plane crash had been engineered by fate in order to bring about an increase in armaments production.

In contrast to the troublesome Dr. Todt, Hitler must have found me a rather willing tool at first. To that extent, this shift in personnel obeyed the principle of negative selection which governed the composition of Hitler's entourage. Since he regularly responded to opposition by choosing someone more amenable, over the years he assembled around himself a group of associates who more and more surrendered to his arguments and translated them into action more and more unscrupulously.

Nowadays, historians are apt to inquire into my activities as Armaments Minister and inclined to treat my building plans for Berlin and Nuremberg as of secondary importance. For me, however, my work as architect still remained my life task. I regarded my surprising appointment as an interim thing for the "duration," a form of wartime service. I saw the possibility of winning a reputation, and even fame, as Hitler's architect, whereas whatever even a prominent minister could accomplish would necessarily be absorbed in Hitler's glory. I therefore very soon extracted the promise from Hitler that he appoint me his architect again after the war.[3] The fact that I thought this necessary shows how dependent we all felt on Hitler's will, even in his most personal decisions. Hitler met my request without hesitation. He too thought that I would perform my most valuable services for him and his Reich as his foremost architect. When on occasion he spoke of his plans for the future, he frequently declared longingly: "Then both of us will withdraw from affairs for several months to go through all the building plans once more." But soon such remarks became rarer and rarer.

The first result of my appointment as a minister was the arrival by plane at the Fuehrer's headquarters of Oberregierungsrat Konrad Haasemann, Todt's personal assistant. There were more influential and more important associates of Todt. I was therefore vexed and interpreted the dispatch of Haasemann as an attempt to test my authority. Haasemann claimed that he had come to brief me on the qualities of my future associates. I told him sharply that I intended to form my own view. That same evening I took the night train to Berlin. For the time being I had lost any fondness I may have had for plane travel.

Next morning as I rode through the suburbs of the capital with their factories and railroad yards, I was overcome by anxiety. How would I be able to contend with this vast and alien field, I wondered. I had considerable doubts about my qualifications for this new task, for coping with either the practical difficulties or the personal demands that were made upon a minister. As the train pulled into the Schlesischer Station, I found my heart pounding and felt weak.

Here I was about to occupy a key position in the wartime organization, although I was rather shy in dealing with strangers, lacked the gift of speaking up easily at public meetings, and even in conferences found it hard to express my thoughts precisely and understandably. What would the generals of the army say when I, already marked as a nonsoldier and artist, was presented to them as their colleague? Actually, such questions of personal impression and of the extent of my authority worried me as much as the practical tasks.

A rather considerable problem awaited me in dealing with the administrative aspect of my new job. I was aware that Todt's old associates would regard me as an intruder. They knew me, of course, as a friend of their chief, but they also knew me as someone always petitioning them for supplies of building materials. And these men had been in close collaboration with Dr. Todt for many years.

Immediately after my arrival I paid a visit to all the important department heads in their offices, thus sparing them the necessity of coming to me to report. I also gave the order that nothing was to be changed in Dr. Todt's private office, although its furnishings did not suit my taste.*

On the morning of February 11, 1942, I had to be present at Anhalter Station to receive the coffin with Todt's remains. This ceremony was hard on my nerves, as was the funeral on the next day in my mosaic hall in the Chancellery—in the presence of a Hitler moved to tears. During the simple ceremony at the grave Xaver Dorsch, one of Todt's key men, solemnly assured me of his loyalty. Two years later, when I fell seriously ill, he entered into an intrigue against me led by Goering.

My work began immediately. Field Marshal Erhard Milch, state secretary of the Air Ministry, invited me to a conference in the great hall of the Ministry, to be held on Friday, February 13, at which armament questions were to be discussed with the three branches of the services and with representatives of industry. When I asked whether this conference could not be postponed, since I first had to get the feel of my job, Milch replied with a counterquestion typical of his free and easy manner and the good relations between us: The top industrialists from all over the Reich were already on their way to the conference, and was I going to beg off? I agreed to come.

On the day before, I was summoned to Goering. This was my first

---

* Not until the summer of 1943, when I moved, was I able to get rid of these ugly furnishings unobtrusively and replace them with furniture I had designed for my old study. In the process I also succeeded in parting company with a picture that had previously hung over my desk. It showed Hitler, who was hopeless on horseback, staring sternly from the saddle and decked out as a medieval knight with a lance. . . . Sensitive technicians do not always show the best taste in their interior decoration.

visit to him in my new capacity of minister. Cordially, he spoke of the harmony between us while I was his architect. He hoped this would not change, he said. When Goering wanted to, he could display a good deal of charm, hard to resist if somewhat condescending. But then he came down to business. He had had a written agreement with my predecessor, he said. A similar document had been prepared for me; he would send it to me for my signature. The agreement stipulated that in my procurement for the army I could not infringe on areas covered by the Four-Year Plan. He concluded our discussion by saying rather obscurely that I would learn more in the course of the conference with Milch and the others. I did not reply and ended the discussion on the same note of cordiality. Since the Four-Year Plan embraced the entire economy, I would have had my hands completely tied if I abided by Goering's arrangement.

I sensed that something unusual was awaiting me at Milch's conference. Since I still felt by no means secure and since Hitler was still in Berlin, I informed him of my anxieties. I knew, from the little episode with Goering at the time of my appointment, that I could count on his backing. "Very well," he said. "If any steps are taken against you, or if you have difficulties, interrupt the conference and invite the participants to the Cabinet Room. Then I'll tell those gentlemen whatever is necessary."

The Cabinet Room was regarded as a "sacred place"; to be received there would inevitably make a deep impression. And the fact that Hitler would be willing to address this group, with whom I would be dealing in the future, offered me the best possible prospects for my start.

The large conference hall of the Air Ministry was filled. There were thirty persons present: the most important men in industry, among them General Manager Albert Vögler; Wilhelm Zangen, head of the German Industry Association; General Ernst Fromm, chief of the Reserve Army, with his subordinate, Lieutenant General Leeb, chief of the army Ordnance Office; Admiral Witzell, armaments chief of the navy; General Thomas, chief of the War Economy and Armaments Office of the OKW; Walther Funk, Reich Minister of Economics; various officials of the Four-Year Plan; and a few more of Goering's important associates. Milch took the chair as representative of the conference host. He asked Funk to sit at his right and me at his left. In a terse introductory address he explained the difficulties that had arisen in armaments production due to the conflicting demands of the three services. Vögler of the United Steel Works followed with some highly intelligent explanations of how orders and counterorders, disputes over priority levels, and constant shifting of priorities interfered with industrial production. There were still unused reserves available, he said, but because of the tugging and hauling these did not come to light. Thus it was high time to establish clear relationships. There must be one man able to make all decisions. Industry did not care who it was.

Thereafter, General Fromm spoke for the army and Admiral Witzell for the navy. In spite of some reservations they expressed general agreement with Vögler's remarks. The other participants likewise were convinced of the necessity for having one person to assume authority in economic matters. During my own work for the air force I too had recognized the urgency of this matter.

Finally Economics Minister Funk stood up and turned directly to Milch. We were all in essential agreement, he said; the course of the meeting had revealed that. The only remaining question, therefore, was who the man should be. "Who would be better suited for the purpose than you, my dear Milch, since you have the confidence of Goering, our revered Reich Marshal? I therefore believe I am speaking in the name of all when I ask you to take over this office!" he exclaimed, striking a rather overemotional note for the occasion.

This had clearly been prearranged. Even while Funk was speaking, I whispered into Milch's ear: "The conference is to be continued in the Cabinet Room. The Fuehrer wants to speak about my tasks." Milch, quick-wittedly grasping the meaning of this, replied to Funk's proposal that he was greatly honored by such an expression of confidence, but that he could not accept.[4]

I spoke up for the first time, transmitting to the assembled group the Fuehrer's invitation and announcing that the discussion would be continued on Thursday, February 18, in my ministry, since it would probably deal with my assignment. Milch then adjourned the session.

Later Funk admitted to me that on the eve of the conference Billy Körner, Goering's state secretary and associate in the work of the Four-Year Plan, had urged him to propose Milch as the authority for final decisions. Funk took it for granted that Körner could not have made this request without Goering's knowledge.

Hitler's invitation alone must have made it clear to those familiar with the balance of power that I was starting from a stronger position than my predecessor had ever possessed.

Now Hitler had to make good on his promise. In his office he let me brief him on what had taken place and jotted down some notes. He then went into the Cabinet Room with me and immediately took the floor.

Hitler spoke for about an hour. Rather tediously, he expatiated on the tasks of war industry, emphasized the need for accelerated production, spoke of the valuable forces that must be mobilized in industry, and was astonishingly candid on the subject of Goering: "This man cannot look after armaments within the framework of the Four-Year Plan."

It was essential, Hitler continued, to separate this task from the Four-Year Plan and turn it over to me. A function was given to a man and then taken from him again; such things happened. The capacity for increased production was available, but things had been mismanaged.

(In prison Funk told me that Goering had asked for this statement of Hitler's—which amounted to stripping him of some of his powers—in writing so that he could use it as evidence against his use of forced labor.)

Hitler avoided touching on the problem of a single head for all armaments production. Similarly, he spoke only of supplies for the army and navy, deliberately excluding the air force. I too had glossed over this contested point in my words with him, since the matter involved a political decision and would have brought in all sorts of ambiguities. Hitler concluded his address with an appeal to the participants. He first described my great feats in construction—which could scarcely have made much of an impression on these people. He went on to say that this new job represented a great sacrifice on my part—a statement which did not have much meaning in view of the critical situation. He expected not only cooperation on their part but also fair treatment. "Behave toward him like gentlemen!" he said, employing the English word, which he rarely used. What exactly my assignment was, he did not clearly state, and I preferred it that way.

Heretofore Hitler had never introduced a minister in this way. Even in a less authoritarian system such a debut would have been of assistance. In our state the consequences were astonishing, even to me. For a considerable time I found myself moving in a kind of vacuum that offered no resistance whatsoever. Within the widest limits I could practically do as I pleased.

Funk, who then walked Hitler back to his apartment in the Chancellery along with me, promised emotionally on the way that he would place everything at my disposal and do all in his power to help me. Moreover he kept the promise, with minor exceptions.

Bormann and I stood chatting with Hitler in the salon for a few minutes longer. Before Hitler withdrew to his upstairs rooms, he once again recommended that I avail myself of industry as far as possible, since I would find the most valuable assistants there. This idea was not new to me, for Hitler had in the past often emphasized that one did best to let industry handle major tasks directly, for government bureaucracy only hampered initiative—this aversion to bureaucrats remained a standing point with him. I took this favorable moment with Bormann present to assure him that I would indeed be drawing chiefly on technicians from industry. But there would have to be no questions raised as to their party membership, since many of them kept aloof from the party, as was well known. Hitler agreed; he instructed

Bormann to go along with this; and so my ministry was—at least until the attempted assassination of July 20, 1944—spared the unpleasant probings of Bormann's party secretariat.

That same evening I had a full discussion with Milch, who pledged an end to that rivalry the air force had hitherto practiced toward the army and navy in matters of procurement. Especially during the early months his advice became indispensable; out of our official relationship there grew a cordial friendship which has lasted to the present.

15

Organized Improvisation

I HAD FIVE DAYS BEFORE THE CONFERENCE IN MY MINISTRY. BY THEN I would have to have some plan of action. Surprising though it may seem, the principles were clear to me from the start. From the first day on I headed, with a sleepwalker's sureness, toward the one system that could possibly achieve success in armaments production. Of course I had a certain advantage, for during my two years of construction work for the armaments industry on a lower plane I had caught glimpses of "many fundamental errors which would have remained hidden from me if I had been at the top."[1]

I prepared a plan of organization whose vertical lines represented individual items, such as tanks, planes, or submarines. In other words, the armaments for the three branches of the service were included. These vertical columns were enclosed in numerous rings, each of which was to stand for a group of components needed for all guns, tanks, planes, and other armaments. Within these rings I considered, for example, the production of forgings or ball bearings or electrical equipment as a whole. Accustomed as an architect to three-dimensional thinking, I drew this new organizational scheme in perspective.

On February 18 the top figures in war industry and in the government bureaus having to do with armaments met once again, in the former conference room of the Academy of Arts. After I had spoken for an hour, they accepted my organizational scheme without cavil and gave their endorsement to a statement reviewing the demands for unitary leadership made at the February 13 conference and announcing that I was herewith being given a mandate for full authority. I prepared to pass this paper around the table for signature—a most unusual procedure in relations among government boards.

Hitler's injunctions had had their effect. Milch was the first to declare himself in full agreement with the proposal and signed the paper without more ado. Some of the other participants raised formal objections, but Milch used his authority to override them. Only Admiral Witzell, the representative of the navy, continued his opposition to the last and finally gave his consent only under protest.

Next day, February 19, I went to the Fuehrer's headquarters accompanied by Field Marshal Milch, General Thomas, and General Olbricht (as General Fromm's representative) to present my organizational plans to Hitler and report to him on the results of the conference. Hitler approved of all I had done.

Immediately after my return Goering summoned me to his hunting lodge, Karinhall, more than forty-five miles north of Berlin. After Goering had seen Hitler's new Berghof in 1935, he had had his modest old hunting lodge rebuilt into a manor that exceeded Hitler's in size. The salon was just as large as Hitler's, but with an even bigger picture window. At the time Hitler was annoyed by this pomp. But it must be admitted that Goering's architect had created a suitable frame for Goering's craving for magnificence. It now served as his headquarters.

Such conferences usually meant the loss of a valuable working day. This time, too, when I arrived punctually toward eleven o'clock after a long automobile ride, I spent an hour in Goering's reception hall looking at pictures and tapestries. For in contrast to Hitler, Goering took a large view of the appointed time. Finally he emerged from his private apartment on the upper floor, dressed in a flowing green-velvet dressing gown, a picturesque note, and descended the stairs. We greeted each other rather coolly. With tripping steps he preceded me into his office and took his seat at a gigantic desk. I modestly sat down facing him. Goering was extremely angry; he complained bitterly that I had not invited him to the conference in the Cabinet Room and pushed toward me across the vast expanses of the desk an opinion by Erich Neumann, his ministerial director for the Four-Year Plan, on the legal implications of my own paper. With an agility I would not have thought so fat a man capable of, he leaped to his feet and began pacing the big room, frantic with agitation. His deputies were all spineless wretches, he declared. By giving their signatures they had made themselves my underlings for all time to come, and this without even asking him. Of course, this bluster was directed against me as well; but the fact that he did not dare storm at me signified a weakened position. He could not accept such nibbling away at his power, he declared in conclusion. He would go to Hitler at once and resign his office as boss of the Four-Year Plan.[2]

At the time such a resignation would certainly have been no loss. For although at the start Goering had pushed the Four-Year Plan with great energy, by 1942 he was generally regarded as sluggish and distinctly averse to work. Increasingly, he gave an impression of instability; he took up too many ideas, changed course all the time, and was consistently unrealistic.

Hitler would probably not have permitted Goering to resign because of the political backlash. Instead, he would have sought a compromise. I saw that this was something I had to head off, for Hitler's compromises were merely evasions and of a sort everyone in the government feared. They did not eliminate difficulties but instead made all administrative interrelationships more opaque and complicated.

I knew that I had to do something to build up Goering's prestige. For the time being, I assured him that the new arrangement desired by Hitler and approved by the representatives of industry and the services would in no way infringe on his position as head of the Four-Year Plan. At this, Goering seemed mollified. I went on to say that I was ready to become his subordinate and carry out my work within the framework of the Four-Year Plan.

Three days later I called on Goering again and showed him a draft agreement appointing me "Chief Representative for Armaments within the Four-Year Plan." Goering seemed satisfied, although he pointed out that I had undertaken much too much and would be wiser to limit my goals. Two days later, on March 1, 1942, he signed the decree. It author-ized me "to give armaments . . . within the whole of the economy the priority which is appropriate for them in wartime."[3] This was more power than had been given me by the document of February 18, which Goering had been so furious about.

On March 16, shortly after Hitler had approved the matter—he was glad to be relieved of all personal difficulties with Goering—I informed the German press of my appointment. To make my point more vividly, I had dug up an old photograph showing Goering, delighted with my design for his Reich Marshal's office building, clapping his hands on my shoulders. This was supposed to show that the crisis, which had begun to be talked about in Berlin, was now over. However, there was a protest from Goering's press agency: I was told that the photo and the decree should by rights have been released by Goering alone.

There were more problems of this sort. His sensitivities aroused, Goering complained of having heard from the Italian Ambassador that the foreign press was intimating that he had been downgraded. Such re-ports were bound to undermine his prestige in industry, he protested. Now it was an open secret that Goering's high style of living was financed by industry, and I had the feeling that he feared a reduction in his prestige would result in a reduction in these subsidies. I therefore suggested that he invite the chief industrialists to a conference in Berlin, in the course of which I would declare formally my subordination to him. This proposal gratified him enormously; his good humor returned instantly.

Goering thereupon ordered some fifty industrialists to come to Berlin. The conference began with a very brief address by me, saying what I had promised, while Goering delivered a long discourse on the importance of armaments. He exorted all those present to make the maximum effort, and other such commonplaces. On the other hand he did not mention my assignment in either a favorable or an unfavorable sense. Thereafter, thanks to Goering's lethargy, I was able to work freely and unhampered. No doubt he was often jealous of my successes with Hitler; but during the next two years he scarcely ever tried to interfere with anything I was doing.

Goering's own powers seemed to me, given his now reduced authority, not quite sufficient for my own work. Soon afterward, therefore —on March 21—I had Hitler sign another decree: "The requirements of the German economy as a whole must be subordinated to the necessities of armaments production." Given the usages of the authoritarian system, this decree of Hitler's amounted to dictatorial powers over the economy.

The constitutional forms of our organization were just as improvised and vague as all these arrangements. There was no precise statement of my assignments or jurisdiction. My feeling was that I was better off without such definitions. I did my best to keep the situation fluid. Consequently, we were able to determine our jurisdiction from case to case, depending on need and the impetuosity of my associates. A legalistic formulation of our rights, which given Hitler's favorable attitude toward me could have been used to acquire a position of almost unlimited power, would only have led to jurisdictional disputes with other ministries. It would not have achieved our purpose, which was to have everyone pull together satisfactorily.

These vaguenesses were a cancer in Hitler's mode of governing. But I was in accord with the system as long as it permitted me to function effectively and as long as Hitler signed all the decrees that I presented to him for signature. But when he no longer blindly granted my requests —and in certain areas he soon stopped doing so—I was condemned to either impotence or cunning.

On the evening of March 2, 1942, about a month after my appointment, I invited the architects employed on the rebuilding of Berlin to a farewell dinner at Horcher's. The very thing you have forcibly resisted, I said to them in a brief address, sooner or later overpowers you. I found it strange that my new work was not so alien, although at first sight it seemed so remote from what I had previously done. "I have known since my university days," I continued, "that if we wish to understand everything, we must do one thing thoroughly. I have therefore decided to take a keen interest in tanks for the moment, trusting that I thereby shall be better able to grasp the essence of many other tasks." As a cautious person, I said, I had for the time being drawn up my program for the next two years. I hoped, however, to be able to return to architecture sooner. My wartime assignment should prove of use later on, for we technicians would be called on to solve the problems of the future. "Moreover," I concluded somewhat grandiosely, "in the future architects will take over the leadership in technology."[4]

Equipped with Hitler's grant of full authority, with a peaceable Goering in the background, I could go forward with my comprehensive plan of "industrial self-responsibility," as I had sketched it in my outline. Today it is generally agreed that the astonishingly rapid rise in armaments production was due to this plan. Its principles, however, were not new. Both Field Marshal Milch and my predecessor Todt had already adopted the procedure of entrusting eminent technicians from leading industrial firms with the management of separate areas of armaments production. But Dr. Todt himself had borrowed this idea. The real creator of the concept of industrial self-responsibility was Walther Rathenau, the great Jewish organizer of the German economy during the First World War. He realized that considerable increases in production could be achieved by exchange of technical experiences, by division of labor from plant to plant, and by standardization. As early as 1917 he declared that such methods could guarantee "a doubling of production with no increase in equipment and no increase in labor costs."[5] On the top floor of Todt's Ministry sat one of Rathenau's old assistants who had been active in his raw materials organization during the First World War and had later written a memorandum on its structure. Dr. Todt benefited by his advice.

We formed "directive committees" for the various types of weapons and "directive pools" for the allocation of supplies. Thirteen such committees were finally established, one for each category of my armaments program. Linking these were an equal number of pools.[6]

Alongside these committees and pools I set up development commissions in which army officers met with the best designers in industry. These commissions were to supervise new products, suggest improvements in manufacturing techniques even during the design stage, and call a halt to any unnecessary projects.

The heads of the committees and the pools were to make sure—this was vital to our whole approach—that a given plant concentrated on producing only one item, but did so in maximum quantity. Because of Hitler's and Goering's continual restiveness, expressed in sudden shifts of program, the factories had hitherto tried to assure themselves of four or five different contracts simultaneously, and if possible, from different branches of the services, so that they could shift to alternative contracts in case of sudden cancellations. Moreover, the Wehrmacht frequently assigned contracts only for a limited time. Thus, for example, before 1942 the manufacture of ammunition was checked or increased depending on consumption, which came in sudden bursts because of the blitz campaigns. This state of affairs kept the factories from throwing all their productive energy into making ammunition. We provided contractual guarantees of continued procurement and assigned the types we needed among the various factories.

By dint of these changes, the armaments production of the early years of the war, which had been on a more or less piecework basis, was converted to industrial mass production. Amazing results were soon to show up; but significantly enough, not in those industries which had already been working along modern lines of efficiency, such as the automobile industry. These scarcely lent themselves to any increase in production. I regarded my task principally as one of tracking down and defining problems so far screened by long years of routine; but I left their solution to the specialists. Obsessed with my task, I did not try to keep down the extent of my responsibilities, but rather to take in more and more areas of the economy. Reverence for Hitler, a sense of duty, ambition, pride —all these elements were operative. After all, at thirty-six I was the youngest minister in the Reich. My Industry Organization soon comprised more than ten thousand assistants and aides, but in our Ministry itself there were only two hundred and eighteen officials at work.[7] This proportion was in keeping with my view of the Ministry as merely a steering organization, with the chief thrust of our operation lying in "industrial self-responsibility."

The traditional arrangement provided that most matters would be submitted to the minister by his state secretary. The latter functioned as a kind of sieve, deciding the importance of things at his own discretion. I eliminated this procedure and made directly subordinate to myself more than thirty leaders of the Industry Organization and no less than ten department chiefs* in the Ministry. In principle they were all supposed to settle their interrelationships among themselves, but I took the liberty

---

* All department heads under my direction were empowered to sign orders as "deputized by" the minister rather than "in behalf of" the minister. This was a technical breach in the rules of the state bureaucracy, for it implied that they were authorized to act independently, a power usually reserved to state secretaries. I ignored the protests submitted by the Minister of the Interior, who was responsible for preserving the regular procedures of government administration.

I brought the head of the Planning Department, Willy Liebel, from Nuremberg, where he had been mayor. The director of the Technical Department, Karl Saur, had risen from the intermediate ranks of party functionaries, after previously occupying a subordinate position in industry. The head of the Supply Department, Dr. Walter Schieber, was a chemist by profession; he was typical of the older party member in the SS and party who had had previous experience as specialists. Xaver Dorsch, my deputy in the Todt Organization, was our oldest party member. The head of the department responsible for consumer goods production, Seebauer, had also joined the party long before 1933.

of intervening in important questions or whenever differences of opinion arose.

Our method of work was just as unusual as this form of organization. The old-line officials of the government bureaucracy spoke disdainfully of a "dynamic Ministry" or a "Ministry without an organization plan" and a "Ministry without officials." It was said that I applied rough-and-ready or "American" methods. My comment, "If jurisdictions are sharply separated, we are actually encouraging a limited point of view,"[8] was prompted by rebellion against the caste mentality of the system, but also bore some resemblance to Hitler's notions of improvised government by an impulsive genius.

Another principle of mine also gave offense. This had to do with personnel policy. As soon as I assumed my post I gave instructions, as the Fuehrer's Minutes of February 19, 1942, record, that the leading men in important departments who were "over fifty-five years old must be assigned a deputy who is no older than forty."

Whenever I explained my organizational plans to Hitler, he showed a striking lack of interest. I had the impression that he did not like to deal with these questions; indeed, in certain realms he was altogether incapable of distinguishing the important from the unimportant. He also did not like establishing clear lines of jurisdiction. Sometimes he deliberately assigned bureaus or individuals the same or similar tasks. "That way," he used to say, "the stronger one does the job."

Within half a year after my taking office we had significantly increased production in all the areas within our scope. Production in August 1942, according to the *Index Figures for German Armaments End-Products*, as compared with the February production, had increased by 27 percent for guns, by 25 percent for tanks, while ammunition production almost doubled, rising 97 percent. The total productivity in armaments increased by 59.6 percent.[9] Obviously we had mobilized reserves that had hitherto lain fallow.

After two and a half years, in spite of the beginning of heavy bombing, we had raised our entire armaments production from an average index figure of 98 for the year 1941 to a summit of 322 in July 1944. During the same period the labor force expanded by only about 30 percent. We had succeeded in doubling the output of labor and had achieved the very results Rathenau had predicted in 1917 as the effect of efficiency: doubling production without increasing equipment or labor costs.

It was not that any genius was at work here, though that has often been asserted. Many of the technicians in my office would undoubtedly have been more fit for the job, as far as knowledge of the fields involved is concerned. But none of them could have thrown the nimbus of Hitler into the balance as I could, and that made all the difference. The backing of the Fuehrer counted for everything.

Aside from all organizational innovations, things went so well because I applied the methods of democratic economic leadership. The democracies were on principle committed to placing trust in the responsible businessmen as long as that trust was justified. Thus they rewarded initiative, aroused an awareness of mission, and spurred decision making. Among us, on the other hand, all such elements had long ago been buried. Pressure and coercion kept production going, to be sure, but destroyed all spontaneity. I felt it necessary to issue a declaration to the effect that industry was not "knowingly lying to us, stealing from us, or otherwise trying to damage our war economy."[10]

The party felt acutely challenged by that attitude, as I was to find out after July 20, 1944. Exposed to sharp attacks, I had to defend my system of delegated responsibility in a letter to Hitler.[11]

Paradoxically, from 1942 on, the developments in the warring countries moved in an opposite direction. The Americans, for example, found themselves compelled to introduce an authoritarian stiffening into their industrial structure, whereas we tried to loosen the regimented economic system. The elimination of all criticism of superiors had in the course of years led to a situation in which mistakes and failures, misplanning, or duplication of effort were no longer even noted. I saw to the formation of committees in which discussion was possible, shortages and mistakes could be uncovered, and their elimination considered. We often joked that we were on the point of reintroducing the parliamentary system.[12] Our new system had created one of the prerequisites for balancing out the weaknesses of every authoritarian order. Important matters were not to be regulated solely by the military principle, that is by channels of command from top to bottom. But for such "parliamentarism" to work, of course, the committees mentioned above had to be headed by persons who allowed arguments and counterarguments to be stated before they made a decision.

Grotesquely enough, this system met with considerable reserve on the part of the factory heads. Early in my job I had sent out a circular letter asking them to inform me of their "fundamental needs and observations on a larger scale then previously." I expected a flood of letters, but there was no response. At first I suspected my office staff of withholding the mail from me. But actually none had come in. The factory heads, as I learned later, feared reprimands from the Gauleiters.

There was more than enough criticism from above to below, but the necessary complement of criticism from below to above was hard to come by. I often had the feeling that I was hovering in the air, since my decisions produced no critical response.

We owed the success of our programs to thousands of technicians with special achievements to their credit to whom we now entrusted the responsibility for whole segments of the armaments industry. This aroused their buried enthusiasm. They also took gladly to my unorthodox style of leadership. Basically, I exploited the phenomenon of the technician's often blind devotion to his task. Because of what seems to be the moral neutrality of technology, these people were without any scruples about their activities. The more technical the world imposed on us by the war, the more dangerous was this indifference of the technician to the direct consequences of his anonymous activities.

In my work I preferred "uncomfortable associates to compliant tools."[13] The party, on the other hand, had a deep distrust for nonpolitical specialists. Fritz Sauckel, always one of the most radical of the party leaders, once commented that if they had begun by shooting a few factory heads, the others would have reacted with better performances.

For two years my position was unassailable. After the generals' putsch of July 20, 1944, Bormann, Goebbels, Ley, and Sauckel prepared to cut me down to size. I quickly appealed to Hitler in a letter stating that I did not feel strong enough to go on with my job if it were going to be subjected to political standards.[14]

The nonparty members of my Ministry enjoyed a legal protection highly unusual in Hitler's state. For over the objections of the Minister of Justice I had established the principle, right at the beginning of my job, that there would be no indictments for sabotage of armaments except on my motion.[15] This proviso protected my associates even after July 20, 1944. Ernst Kaltenbrunner, the Gestapo chief, wanted to indict three general managers, Bücher of the AEG electrical company, Vögler of the United Steel Works, and Reusch of the Gutehoffnungshütte (the mining combine), for "defeatist" conversations. He came to me for authorization. I pointed out that the nature of our work compelled us to speak candidly about the situation and thus fended off the Gestapo. On the other hand, I applied severe penalties for abuse of our honor system —if, for example, someone furnished false data in order to hoard important raw materials. For actions of this sort would result in the withholding of arms from the front.[16]

From the first day on I considered our gigantic organization temporary. Just as I myself wanted to return to architecture after the war and had even asked Hitler for an assurance to that effect, I felt we had to promise the uneasy leaders of business that our system of organization was solely a war measure. In peacetime, industry could not be asked, I told them, to give up their best men or to share their knowledge with rival enterprises.[17]

Along with this, I also made an effort to preserve the style of improvisation. The idea that bureaucratic methods were now taking root inside my own organization depressed me. Again and again I called upon my associates to cut down on record keeping, to make agreements informally in conversation and by means of telephone calls, and to eschew the multiplication of "transactions," as bureaucratic jargon called filling a file. Moreover, the bombing raids on German cities forced us to constant ingenuities. There were times when I actually regarded these raids as helpful—witness my ironic reaction to the destruction of the Ministry in the air raid of November 22, 1943: "Although we have been fortunate in that large parts of the current files of the Ministry have burned and so relieved us for a time of useless ballast, we cannot really expect that such events will continually introduce the necessary fresh air into our work."[18]

In spite of this technical and industrial progress, even at the height of the military successes in 1940 and 1941 the level of armaments production of the First World War was not reached. During the first year of the war in Russia, production figures were only a fourth of what they had been in the autumn of 1918. Three years later, in the spring of 1944, when we were nearing our production maximum, ammunition production still lagged behind that of the First World War—considering the total production of Germany at that time together with Austria and Czechoslovakia.[19]

Among the causes for this backwardness I always reckoned excessive bureaucratization, which I fought in vain.[20] For example, the size of the staff of the Ordnance Office was ten times what it had been during the First World War. The cry for simplification of administration runs through all my speeches and letters from 1942 to the end of 1944. The longer I fought the typically German bureaucracy, whose tendencies were aggravated by the authoritarian system, the more my criticism assumed a political cast. This matter became something of an obsession with me, for on the morning of July 20, 1944, a few hours before the attempted assassination, I wrote to Hitler that Americans and Russians knew how to act with organizationally simple methods and therefore achieved greater results, whereas we were hampered by superannuated forms of organization and therefore could not match the others' feats. The war, I said, was also a contest between two systems of organization, the "struggle of our system of overbred organization against the art of improvisation on the opposing side." If we did not arrive at a different system of organization, I continued, it would be evident to posterity that our outmoded, tradition-bound, and arthritic organizational system had lost the struggle.

16

Sins of Omission

IT REMAINS ONE OF THE ODDITIES OF THIS WAR THAT HITLER DEMANDED FAR less from his people[1] than Churchill and Roosevelt did from their respective nations. The discrepancy between the total mobilization of labor forces in democratic England and the casual treatment of this question in authoritarian Germany is proof of the regime's anxiety not to risk any shift in the popular mood. The German leaders were not disposed to make sacrifices themselves or to ask sacrifices of the people. They tried to keep the morale of the people in the best possible state by concessions. Hitler and the majority of his political followers belonged to the generation who as soldiers had witnessed the Revolution of November 1918 and had never forgotten it. In private conversations Hitler indicated that after the experience of 1918 one could not be cautious enough. In order to anticipate any discontent, more effort and money was expended on supplies of consumer goods, on military pensions or compensation to women for the loss of earnings by their men in the services, than in the countries with democratic governments. Whereas Churchill promised his people only blood, sweat, and tears, all we heard during the various phases and various crises of the war was Hitler's slogan: "The final victory is certain." This was a confession of political weakness. It betrayed great concern over a loss of popularity which might develop into an insurrectionary mood.

Alarmed by the setbacks on the Russian front, in the spring of 1942

I considered total mobilization of all auxiliary forces. What was more, I urged that "the war must be ended in the shortest possible time; if not, Germany will lose the war. We must win it by the end of October, before the Russian winter begins, or we have lost it once and for all. Consequently, we can only win with the weapons we have now, not with those we are going to have next year." In some inexplicable way this situation analysis came to the knowledge of *The Times* (London), which published it on September 7, 1942.[2] *The Times* article actually summed up the points on which Milch, Fromm, and I had agreed at the time.

"Our feelings tell us that this year we are facing the decisive turning point in our history," I also declared publicly in April 1942,[3] without suspecting that the turning point was impending: with the encirclement of the Sixth Army in Stalingrad, the annihilation of the Africa Corps, the successful Allied land operations in North Africa, and the first massive air raids on German cities. We had also reached a turning point in our wartime economy; for until the autumn of 1941 the economic leadership had been basing its politics on short wars with long stretches of quiet in between. Now the permanent war was beginning.

As I saw it, a mobilization of all reserves should have begun with the heads of the party hierarchy. This seemed all the more proper since Hitler himself had solemnly declared to the Reichstag on September 1, 1939, that there would be no privations which he himself was not prepared to assume at once.

In actual fact he at last agreed to suspend all the building projects he was still engaged on, including those at Obersalzberg. I cited this noble gesture of the Fuehrer's two weeks after entering office when I addressed the group that gave us the most difficulties, the assembled Gauleiters and Reichsleiters: "Consideration of future peacetime tasks must never be allowed to influence a decision. I have instructions from the Fuehrer to report to him in the future on any such hindrances to our armaments production, which from now on can no longer be tolerated." That was a plain enough threat, even though I softened it somewhat by saying that up to the winter of this year each of us had cherished special wishes. But now, I said, the military situation demanded that all superfluous construction be halted, anywhere in the country. It was our duty to lead the way by presenting a good example, even if the savings in labor forces and materials were not significant.

I took it for granted that in spite of the monotonous tone in which I had read these exhortations, anyone there would see their logic and obey. After the speech, however, I was surrounded by party leaders who wanted some special building project of theirs to be exempted from the general rule.

Reichsleiter Bormann was the arch offender. He easily persuaded a vacillating Hitler that the Obersalzberg project need not be canceled. The large crew employed there, who had to be provided for, actually stayed right there on the site until the end of the war, even though three weeks after the meeting I had again wrested a suspension order from Hitler.*

Then Gauleiter Sauckel pressed forward to plead that his "Party Forum" in Weimar would not be affected. He too went on building undeterred until the end of the war. Robert Ley fought for a pigsty on his model farm. This was actually a war priority, he argued, since his experiments in hog raising were of great importance for food production. I turned down this request in writing but took gleeful delight in addressing the letter: "To the Reich Organization Chief of the National Socialist Party and Chief of the German Labor Front. Subject: Your pigsty."

Even after I had made this ringing appeal, Hitler went ahead and had the tumble-down castle of Klessheim near Salzburg rebuilt into a luxurious guest house at an expenditure of many millions of marks. Near Berchtesgaden, Himmler erected a country lodge for his mistress and did it so secretly that I did not hear of it until the last weeks of the war. Even after 1942, Hitler encouraged one of his Gauleiters to renovate a hotel and the Posen Castle, both projects drawing heavily on essential materials. The same Gauleiter had a private residence built for himself in the vicinity of the city. In 1942–43 new special trains were built for Ley, Keitel, and others, although this kind of thing tied down valuable raw materials and technicians. For the most part, however, these whims of the party functionaries were concealed from me. Given the enormous powers of the Reichsleiters and Gauleiters there was no way to check up on what they were doing. I therefore could rarely interpose a veto—which in any case was disregarded. As late as the summer of 1944 Hitler and Bormann were capable of informing their Minister of Armaments that a Munich manufacturer of picture frames must not be made to shift to war production. A few months before, on their personal order, the "rug factories and other producers of artistic materials," which were engaged in manufacturing rugs and tapestries for Hitler's postwar buildings, were given a special status.[4]

---

* *Führerprotokoll*, March 5–6, 1942, Point 17, 3: "The Fuehrer has ordered that work at Obersalzberg be halted. Compose appropriate memorandum to Reichsleiter Bormann." But two and a half years later, on September 8, 1944, construction there was still continuing. Bormann wrote to his wife: "Herr Speer who, as I see time and again, has not the slightest respect for me, simply went to Hagen and Schenk and asked for a report on the Obersalzberg construction. A crazy way to go about things! Instead of going through the proper channels and addressing himself to me, the God of Building, without any more ado he ordered my men to report directly to him! And since we are dependent on him for materials and labor, all I can do is put a good face on the matter." (Bormann, *Letters*, p. 103.)

After only nine years of rule the leadership was so corrupt that even in the critical phase of the war it could not cut back on its luxurious style of living. For "representational reasons" the leaders all needed big houses, hunting lodges, estates and palaces, many servants, a rich table, and a select wine cellar.* They were also concerned about their lives to an insane degree. Hitler himself, wherever he went, first of all issued orders for building bunkers for his personal protection. The thickness of their roofs increased with the caliber of the bombs until it reached sixteen and a half feet. Ultimately there were veritable systems of bunkers in Rastenburg, in Berlin, at Obersalzberg, in Munich, in the guest palace near Salzburg, at the Nauheim headquarters, and on the Somme. And in 1944 he had two underground headquarters blasted into mountains in Silesia and Thuringia, the project tying up hundreds of indispensable mining specialists and thousands of workmen.[5]

Hitler's obvious fear and his exaggeration of the importance of his own person inspired his entourage to go in for equally exaggerated measures of personal protection. Goering had extensive underground installations built not only in Karinhall, but even in the isolated castle of Veldenstein near Nuremberg, which he hardly ever visited.[6] The road from Karinhall to Berlin, forty miles long and leading mostly through lonely woods, had to be provided with concrete shelters at regular intervals. When Ley saw the effect of a heavy bomb on a public shelter, he was interested solely in comparing the thickness of the ceiling with that in his private bunker in the rarely attacked suburb of Grunewald. Moreover, the Gauleiters—on orders from Hitler, who was convinced of their indispensability—had additional shelters built outside the cities for their personal protection.

Of all the urgent questions that weighed upon me during my early weeks in office, solution of the labor problem was the most pressing. Late one evening in the middle of March, I inspected one of the leading Berlin armaments plants, Rheinmetall-Borsig, and found its workshops filled with valuable machinery, but unused. There were not enough workers to man a second shift. Similar conditions prevailed in

---

* For propaganda reasons, Goebbels tried to change the life style of the prominent men in government and the party, but in vain. See his diary, February 22, 1942: "Bormann has issued a directive to the party regarding the need for greater simplicity in the conduct of the leaders, particularly with respect to banquets—a reminder to the party that it should provide a good example for the people. This directive is most welcome. I hope it will be taken to heart. In this connection I have become rather skeptical." Bormann's directive had no effect. On May 22, 1943, more than a year later, Goebbels wrote in his diary: "Because of the tense situation domestically the people naturally have been keeping a sharp eye on the life style of our so-called celebrities. Unfortunately many of the prominent people pay no heed; some of them are living a life which can in no way be called suitable under current conditions."

other factories. Moreover, during the day we had to reckon with difficulties with the electricity supply, whereas during the evening and night hours the drain on the available supply was considerably smaller. Since new plants worth some 11 billion marks were being built which would be faced with shortages of machine tools, it seemed to me more rational to suspend most of the new building and employ the labor force thus released to establish a second shift.

Hitler seemed to accept this logic. He signed a decree ordering reduction of the volume of building to 3 billion marks. But then he balked when, in carrying out this edict, I wanted to suspend long-term building projects by the chemical industry involving about a billion marks.* For he always wanted to have everything at once and reasoned as follows: "Perhaps the war with Russia will soon be ended. But then I have more far-reaching plans, and for them I need more synthetic fuel than before. We must go on with the new factories, even though they may not be finished for years." A year later, on March 2, 1943, I again had to remonstrate that there was no point to "building factories which are intended to serve great future programs and will not begin to produce until after January 1, 1945."[7] Hitler's wrong-headed decision of the spring of 1942 was still a drag upon our armaments production in September 1944, in a military situation that had meanwhile become catastrophic.

Despite Hitler's countermanding of my plan, it had nevertheless freed several hundred thousand construction workers, who could have been transferred to armaments production. But then a new, unexpected trouble arose: the head of the "Business Department for Labor Assignment within the Four-Year Plan," Ministerial Director Dr. Mansfeld, told me frankly that he lacked authority to transfer the released construction workers from one district to another over the objections of the Gauleiters.[8] And in fact the Gauleiters, for all their rivalries and intrigues, closed ranks whenever any of their privileges were threatened. I realized that in spite of my strong position I could never deal with them alone. I needed someone from their number to act as my ally. I would also need special powers from Hitler.

The man I had in mind was my old friend Karl Hanke, longtime state secretary under Goebbels, who since January 1941 had been Gauleiter of Lower Silesia. Hitler proved willing to nominate a commissioner

---

* This construction project tied up high-grade steel and many specialists. I opposed Hitler's view, arguing that "it is better to get one hydrogenation plant built in a few months than to build several over a period three times as long employing a third of the necessary construction workers. The plant that is built quickly by concentrating all the labor on the one project will provide fuel for many months to come, whereas if the usual practice is followed, the first deliveries of additional fuel will not be ready until a much later date." (Speech, April 18, 1942.)

from among the Gauleiters who would be assigned to me. But Bormann was quick to parry. For Hanke was considered one of my adherents. His appointment would have meant not only a reinforcement of my power but also an infringement of Bormann's realm, the party hierarchy.

Two days after my first request, when I again approached Hitler on the matter, he was still acquiescent to the idea, but had objections to my choice. "Hanke hasn't been a Gauleiter long enough and doesn't command the necessary respect. I've talked with Bormann. We'll take Sauckel."*

Bormann had not only put in his own candidate but had managed to have him made his, Bormann's, direct subordinate. Goering rightly protested that what was involved was a task hitherto handled within the framework of the Four-Year Plan. With his usual indifference in administrative matters, Hitler thereupon appointed Sauckel "Commissioner General," but placed him in Goering's Four-Year Plan organization. Goering protested once more, since the way the thing was handled seemed to diminish his prestige. The appointment of Sauckel should have come from Goering himself. But Hitler had overlooked that nicety. Once again Bormann had struck a blow at Goering's position.

Sauckel and I were summoned to Hitler's headquarters. In giving us the document authorizing the appointment, Hitler pointed out that basically there could not be any such thing as a labor problem. He repeated, in effect, what he had already stated on November 9, 1941: "The area working directly for us embraces more than two hundred fifty million people. Let no one doubt that we will succeed in involving every one of these millions in the labor process."[9] The necessary labor force, therefore, was to come from the occupied territories. Hitler instructed Sauckel to bring the needed workers in by any means whatsoever. That order marked the beginning of a fateful segment of my work.

During the early weeks of our association we cooperated smoothly. Sauckel gave us his pledge to eliminate all labor shortages and to provide replacements for specialists drafted into the services. For my part, I helped Sauckel gain authority and supported him wherever I could. Sauckel had promised a great deal, for in every peacetime year the attrition of the labor force by age or death was balanced by the maturing of some six hundred thousand young men. Now, however, not only these

---

* I must share the responsibility for Sauckel's dire labor policies. Despite differences of opinion on other matters, I was always in basic agreement with his mass deportations of foreign labor to Germany. Since Edward L. Homse, *Foreign Labor in Nazi Germany* (Princeton, 1967) gives exhaustive details on the little war that soon developed between Sauckel and me, I can restrict myself to the salient points. I agree with Homse that these internal enmities and clashes were typical. Dr. Allan S. Milward's recent book, *The New Order and the French Economy* (London, 1969), also gives an accurate picture.

men but sizable segments of the industrial working class were being drafted. In 1942, consequently, the war economy was short far more than one million workers.

To put the matter briefly, Sauckel did not meet his commitments. Hitler's fine rhetoric about drawing labor out of a population of two hundred fifty million came to nought, partly because of the ineffectiveness of the German administration in the occupied territories, partly because of the preference of the men involved for taking to the forests and joining the partisans sooner than be dragged off for labor service in Germany.

No sooner had the first foreign workers begun arriving in the factories than I began hearing protests from our Industry Organization. They had a number of objections to make. The first was as follows: The technical specialists now being replaced by foreigners had occupied key posts in vital industries. Any sabotage in these plants would have far-reaching consequences. What was to prevent enemy espionage services from planting agents in Sauckel's contingents?

Another problem was that there were not enough interpreters to handle the various linguistic groups. Without adequate communication, these new workers were as good as useless.

It seemed far more practicable to all concerned to employ German women rather than assorted foreign labor. Businessmen came to me with statistics showing that the employment of German women during the First World War had been significantly higher than it was now. They showed me photographs of workers streaming out of the same ammunition factory at closing time in 1918 and 1942; in the earlier war they had been predominantly women; now they were almost entirely men. They also had pictures from American and British magazines which indicated to what extent women were pitching in on the industrial front in those countries.[10]

At the beginning of April 1942 I went to Sauckel with the proposition that we recruit our labor from the ranks of German women. He replied brusquely that the question of where to obtain which workers and how to distribute them was his business. Moreover, he said, as a Gauleiter he was Hitler's subordinate and responsible to the Fuehrer alone. But before the discussion was over, he offered to put the question to Goering, who as Commissioner of the Four-Year Plan should have the final say. Our conference with Goering took place in Karinhall. Goering showed plainly that he was flattered at being consulted. He behaved with excessive amiability toward Sauckel and was markedly cooler toward me. I was scarcely allowed to advance my arguments; Sauckel and Goering continually interrupted me. Sauckel laid great weight on the danger that factory work might inflict moral harm upon German womanhood; not only might their "psychic and emotional life" be affected but also their ability to bear. Goering totally concurred. But to be absolutely sure, Sauckel went to Hitler immediately after the conference and had him confirm the decision.

All my good arguments were thereby blown to the winds. Sauckel informed his fellow Gauleiters of his victory in a proclamation in which, among other things, he stated: "In order to provide the German housewife, above all mothers of many children . . . with tangible relief from her burdens, the Fuehrer has commissioned me to bring into the Reich from the eastern territories some four to five hundred thousand select, healthy, and strong girls."[11] Whereas by 1943 England had reduced the number of maidservants by two-thirds, nothing of the sort took place in Germany until the end of the war.[12] Some 1.4 million women continued to be employed as household help. In addition, half a million Ukrainian girls helped solve the servant problem for party functionaries—a fact that soon caused a good deal of talk among the people.

Armaments production is directly dependent on the supply of crude steel. During the First World War the German war economy drew on 46.5 percent of its crude steel production. One of the first facts I learned when I took office was that the parallel figure was only 37.5 percent.[13] In order to be able to gain more steel for armaments, I proposed to Milch that we jointly undertake the allocation of raw materials.

On April 2, therefore, we once again set out for Karinhall. Goering at first beat about the bush, talking on a wide range of subjects, but finally he agreed to our suggestions about establishing a central planning authority within the Four-Year Plan. Impressed by our firmness, he asked almost shyly: "Could you possibly take in my friend Körner? Otherwise, he'll feel sad at the demotion."*

This "Central Planning" soon became the most important institution in our war economy. Actually it was incomprehensible that a top board of this sort to direct the various programs and priorities had not been established long ago. Until about 1939 Goering had personally taken care of this matter; but afterward there was no one with authority who could grasp the increasingly complicated and increasingly urgent problems and who could have leaped into the breach when Goering began shirking.[14] Goering's decree creating the office of Central Planning did in fact provide that he would have the final say whenever he thought necessary. But as I expected, he never asked about anything and we for our part had no reason ever to bother him.[15]

The Central Planning meetings took place in the large conference hall in my Ministry. They dragged on endlessly, with a vast number of participants. Ministers and state secretaries would come in person. Sup-

---

* Körner was Goering's state secretary and confidant.

ported by their experts, they would fight for their shares in sometimes highly dramatic tones. The task was particulary tricky, for we had to trim the civilian branch of the economy, but not so much as to impair its efficiency in producing what would be needed for the war industries or in providing basic necessities for the population.[16]

I myself was trying to push through a sizable cut in consumer goods production—especially since the consumer industries at the beginning of 1942 were producing at a rate only 3 percent below our peacetime level. But in 1942 the utmost I could manage was a 12 percent cutback.[17] For after only three months of such austerity, Hitler began to regret this policy, and on June 28–29, 1942, decreed "that the fabrication of products for the general supply of the population must be resumed." I protested, arguing that "such a slogan today will encourage those who have all along been averse to our concentration on armaments to resume resistance to the present line."[18] By "those" I meant the party functionaries. But Hitler remained deaf to these reminders.

Once again my efforts to organize an effective war economy had been ruined by Hitler's vacillation.

In addition to more workers and more crude steel, we needed an expansion of the railroads. This was essential even though the Reichsbahn had not yet recovered from the disaster of the Russian winter. Deep into German territory the tracks were still clogged by paralyzed trains. Transports of important war materials were therefore subject to intolerable delays.

On March 5, 1942, Dr. Julius Dorpmüller, our Minister of Transportation and a spry man in spite of his seventy-three years, went to headquarters with me in order to report to Hitler on transportation problems. I explained the catastrophic predicament that we were in, but since Dorpmüller gave me only lame support, Hitler, as always, chose the brighter view of the situation. He postponed the important question, remarking that "conditions are probably not so serious as Speer sees them."

Two weeks later, on my urging, he consented to designate a young official as successor to the sixty-five-year-old state secretary in the Ministry of Transportation. But Dorpmüller would not hear of it. "My state secretary too old?" he exclaimed when I told him what we had in mind. "That young man? When I was president of one of the Reichsbahn boards of directors in 1922, he was just starting in railroad work as a Reichsbahn inspector." He succeeded in keeping things as they were.

Two months later, however, on May 21, 1941, Dorpmüller was forced to confess to me: "The Reichsbahn has so few cars and locomotives available for the German area that it can no longer assume responsibility for meeting the most urgent transportation needs." This description of the situation, as my official journal noted, "was tantamount to a declaration of bankruptcy by the Reichsbahn." That same day the Reich Minister of Transportation offered me the post of "traffic dictator," but I refused.[19]

Two days later Hitler let me bring a young Reichsbahn inspector named Dr. Ganzenmüller to meet him. During the past winter Dr. Ganzenmüller had restored railroad traffic in a part of Russia (on the stretch between Minsk and Smolensk) after it had totally broken down. Hitler was impressed: "I like the man; I'm going to make him state secretary at once." Shouldn't we speak with Dorpmüller about that first, I suggested. "Absolutely not!" Hitler exclaimed. "Don't let either Dorpmüller or Ganzenmüller know anything about it. I'll simply summon you, Herr Speer, to headquarters with your man. Then I'll have the Transportation Minister come here separately."

On Hitler's instructions both men were put up at headquarters in different barracks, and Dr. Ganzenmüller entered Hitler's office without knowing what awaited him. There are minutes of Hitler's remarks which were made the same day:

> The transportation problem is crucial; therefore it must be solved. All my life, but more so than ever in the past winter, I have confronted crucial questions that had to be solved. So-called experts and men who by rights should have been leaders repeatedly told me: "That isn't possible, that won't do!" I cannot resign myself to such talk! There are problems that absolutely have to be solved. Where real leaders are present, these problems always are solved and always will be solved. This cannot be done by pleasant methods. Pleasantness is not what counts for me; in the same way, it is a matter of complete indifference to me what posterity will say about the methods I have been compelled to use. For me there is only a single question that must be solved: We must win the war or Germany faces annihilation.

Hitler went on to recount how he had pitted his will against the disaster of the past winter and against the generals who urged retreat. From this, he made a slight jump to the transport problem and mentioned some of the measures which I had earlier recommended to him as necessary if order were to be restored to the railways. Without calling in the Minister of Transportation, who was now waiting outside, also ignorant of what this was all about, he appointed Ganzenmüller the new state secretary in the Transportation Ministry because "he has proved at the front that he possesses the energy to restore order to the muddled transportation situation." Only at this point were Minister of Transportation Dorpmüller and his assistant, Ministerial Director Leibbrandt, brought into the conference. He had decided, Hitler announced, to intervene in the transportation situation, since victory depended on it. Then he continued with one of his standard arguments: "In my day I started with nothing, an obscure soldier in the World War, and began my career only when all others, who seemed more destined to leadership than I, failed. The whole course of my life proves that I never capitulate. The tasks of the war must be mastered. I repeat: For me the word 'impossible' does not exist." And he repeated, almost screaming: "It does not exist for me!" Thereupon he informed the Minister of Transportation that he had appointed the former Reichsbahn inspector the new state secretary in the Ministry of Transportation—an embarrassing situation for the Minister, for the state secretary, and for me as well.

Hitler had always spoken with great respect of Dorpmüller's expertise. In view of that Dorpmüller could have expected that the question of his deputy would first be discussed with him. But apparently Hitler (as was so often the case when he confronted experts) wanted to avoid an awkward argument by presenting the Minister of Transportation with a *fait accompli*. And in fact Dorpmüller took this humiliation in silence.

Hitler now turned to Field Marshal Milch and me and instructed us to act temporarily as transportation dictators. We were to see to it that the requirements were "met to the largest extent and in the fastest time." With the disarming comment, "We cannot allow the war to be lost because of the transportation question; therefore it can be solved!"[20] Hitler adjourned the meeting.

In fact it was solved. The young state secretary found procedures for handling the backup of trains. He speeded traffic and was able to provide for the increased transportation needs of the war plants. A special committee for rolling stock took charge of the locomotives damaged by the Russian winter; repair techniques were much accelerated. Instead of the previous craft system of manufacturing locomotives, we went over to assembly-line methods and increased production many fold.[21] In spite of the steadily rising demands of the war, traffic continued to flow in the future, or at least until the systematic air raids of the fall of 1944 once again throttled traffic and made transportation, this time for good, the greatest bottleneck in our war economy.

When Goering heard that we intended to increase production of locomotives many times over, he summoned me to Karinhall. He had a suggestion to offer, which was that we build locomotives out of concrete, since we did not have enough steel available. Of course the concrete locomotives would not last as long as steel ones, he said; but to make up for that we would simply have to produce more of them. Quite how that was to be accomplished, he did not know; nevertheless, he clung for months to this weird idea for the sake of which I had squandered a two-hour drive and two hours of waiting time. And I had come home on an empty stomach, for visitors in Karinhall were seldom offered a meal. That was the only concession the Goering household made to the needs of a total war economy.

A week after Ganzenmüller's appointment, at which such heroic words had been spoken on the solution of the transportation crisis, I visited Hitler once more. In keeping with my view that in critical times the leadership must set a good example, I proposed to Hitler that the use of private railroad cars by government and party officials be discontinued for the time being. Naturally, I was not thinking of Hitler himself when I made this suggestion. But Hitler demurred; private cars were a necessity in the east, he said, because of the poor housing conditions. I corrected him: most of the cars were not being used in the east, I said, but inside the Reich. And I presented him with a long list of the prominent users of private cars. But I had no luck.[22]

I met regularly for lunch with General Friedrich Fromm in a *chambre séparée* at Horcher's Restaurant. In the course of one of these meetings, at the end of April 1942, he remarked that our only chance of winning the war lay in developing a weapon with totally new effects. He said he had contacts with a group of scientists who were on the track of a weapon which could annihilate whole cities, perhaps throw the island of England out of the fight. Fromm proposed that we pay a joint visit to these men. It seemed to him important, he said, at least to have spoken with them.

Dr. Albert Vögler, head of the largest German steel company and president of the Kaiser Wilhelm Gesellschaft, also called my attention at this time to the neglected field of nuclear research. He complained of the inadequate support fundamental research was receiving from the Ministry of Education and Science, which naturally did not have much influence during wartime. On May 6, 1942, I discussed this situation with Hitler and proposed that Goering be placed at the head of the Reich Research Council—thus emphasizing its importance.[23] A month later, on June 9, 1942, Goering was appointed to this post.

Around the same time the three military representatives of armaments production, Milch, Fromm, and Witzell, met with me at Harnack House, the Berlin center of the Kaiser Wilhelm Gesellschaft, to be briefed on the subject of German atomic research. Along with scientists whose names I no longer recall, the subsequent Nobel Prize winners Otto Hahn and Werner Heisenberg were present. After a few demonstration lectures on the matter as a whole, Heisenberg reported on "Atom-smashing and the development of the uranium machine [sic] and the cyclotron."[24] Heisenberg had bitter words to say about the Ministry of Education's neglect of nuclear research, about the lack of funds and materials, and the drafting of scientific men into the services. Excerpts from

American technical journals suggested that plenty of technical and financial resources were available there for nuclear research. This meant that America probably had a head start in the matter, whereas Germany had been in the forefront of these studies only a few years ago. In view of the revolutionary possibilities of nuclear fission, dominance in this field was fraught with enormous consequences.

After the lecture I asked Heisenberg how nuclear physics could be applied to the manufacture of atom bombs. His answer was by no means encouraging. He declared, to be sure, that the scientific solution had already been found and that theoretically nothing stood in the way of building such a bomb. But the technical prerequisites for production would take years to develop, two years at the earliest, even provided that the program was given maximum support. Difficulties were compounded, Heisenberg explained, by the fact that Europe possessed only one cyclotron, and that of minimal capacity. Moreover, it was located in Paris and because of the need for secrecy could not be used to full advantage. I proposed that with the powers at my disposal as Minister of Armaments we build cyclotrons as large as or larger than those in the United States. But Heisenberg said that because we lacked experience we would have to begin by building only a relatively small type.

Nevertheless, General Fromm offered to release several hundred scientific assistants from the services, while I urged the scientists to inform me of the measures, the sums of money, and the materials they would need to further nuclear research. A few weeks later they presented their request: an appropriation of several hundred thousand marks and some small amounts of steel, nickel, and other priority metals. In addition, they asked for the building of a bunker, the erection of several barracks, and the pledge that their experiments would be given highest priority. Plans for building the first German cyclotron had already been approved. Rather put out by these modest requests in a matter of such crucial importance, I suggested that they take one or two million marks and correspondingly larger quantities of materials. But apparently more could not be utilized for the present,[25] and in any case I had been given the impression that the atom bomb could no longer have any bearing on the course of the war.

I was familiar with Hitler's tendency to push fantastic projects by making senseless demands, so that on June 23, 1942, I reported to him only very briefly on the nuclear-fission conference and what we had decided to do.[26] Hitler received more detailed and more glowing reports from his photographer, Heinrich Hoffmann, who was friendly with Post Office Minister Ohnesorge. Goebbels, too, may have told him something about it. Ohnesorge was interested in nuclear research and was supporting —like the SS—an independent research apparatus under the direction of Manfred von Ardenne, a young physicist. It is significant that Hitler did not choose the direct route of obtaining information on this matter from responsible people but depended instead on unreliable and incompetent informants to give him a Sunday-supplement account. Here again was proof of his love for amateurishness and his lack of understanding of fundamental scientific research.

Hitler had sometimes spoken to me about the possibility of an atom bomb, but the idea quite obviously strained his intellectual capacity. He was also unable to grasp the revolutionary nature of nuclear physics. In the twenty-two hundred recorded points of my conferences with Hitler, nuclear fission comes up only once, and then is mentioned with extreme brevity. Hitler did sometimes comment on its prospects, but what I told him of my conference with the physicists confirmed his view that there was not much profit in the matter. Actually, Professor Heisenberg had not given any final answer to my question whether a successful nuclear fission could be kept under control with absolute certainty or might continue as a chain reaction. Hitler was plainly not delighted with the possibility that the earth under his rule might be transformed into a glowing star. Occasionally, however, he joked that the scientists in their unworldly urge to lay bare all the secrets under heaven might some day set the globe on fire. But undoubtedly a good deal of time would pass before that came about, Hitler said; he would certainly not live to see it.

I am sure that Hitler would not have hesitated for a moment to employ atom bombs against England. I remember his reaction to the final scene of a newsreel on the bombing of Warsaw in the autumn of 1939. We were sitting with him and Goebbels in his Berlin salon watching the film. Clouds of smoke darkened the sky; dive bombers tilted and hurtled toward their goal; we could watch the flight of the released bombs, the pull-out of the planes and the cloud from the explosions expanding gigantically. The effect was enhanced by running the film in slow motion. Hitler was fascinated. The film ended with a montage showing a plane diving toward the outlines of the British Isles. A burst of flame followed, and the island flew into the air in tatters. Hitler's enthusiasm was unbounded. "That is what will happen to them!" he cried out, carried away. "That is how we will annihilate them!"

On the suggestion of the nuclear physicists we scuttled the project to develop an atom bomb by the autumn of 1942, after I had again queried them about deadlines and been told that we could not count on anything for three or four years. The war would certainly have been decided long before then. Instead I authorized the development of an energy-producing uranium motor for propelling machinery. The navy was interested in that for its submarines.

In the course of a visit to the Krupp Works I asked to be shown parts of our first cyclotron and asked the technician in charge whether we could not go on and build a considerably larger apparatus. But he confirmed what Professor Heisenberg had previously said: We lacked the technical experience. At Heidelberg in the summer of 1944, I was shown our first cyclotron splitting an atomic nucleus. To my questions, Professor Walther Bothe explained that this cyclotron would be useful for medical and biological research. I had to rest content with that.

In the summer of 1943, wolframite imports from Portugal were cut off, which created a critical situation for the production of solid-core ammunition. I thereupon ordered the use of uranium cores for this type of ammunition.[27] My release of our uranium stocks of about twelve hundred metric tons showed that we no longer had any thought of producing atom bombs.

Perhaps it would have proved possible to have the atom bomb ready for employment in 1945. But it would have meant mobilizing all our technical and financial resources to that end, as well as our scientific talent. It would have meant giving up all other projects, such as the development of the rocket weapons. From this point of view, too, Peenemünde was not only our biggest but our most misguided project.*

Our failure to pursue the possibilities of atomic warfare can be partly traced to ideological reasons. Hitler had great respect for Philipp Lenard, the physicist who had received the Nobel Prize in 1920 and was one of the few early adherents of Nazism among the ranks of the scientists. Lenard had instilled the idea in Hitler that the Jews were exerting a seditious influence in their concern with nuclear physics and the relativity theory.** To his table companions Hitler occasionally referred to nuclear physics as "Jewish physics"—citing Lenard as his authority for this. This view was taken up by Rosenberg. It thus becomes clearer why the Minister of Education was not inclined to support nuclear research.

But even if Hitler had not had this prejudice against nuclear research and even if the state of our fundamental research in June 1942 could have

---

* From 1937 to 1940 the army spent five hundred and fifty million marks on the development of a large rocket. But success was out of the question, for Hitler's principle of scattering responsibility meant that even scientific research teams were divided and often at odds with one another. According to the *Office Journal*, August 17, 1944, not only the three branches of the armed forces but also other organizations, the SS, the postal system, and such, had separate research facilities. In the United States, on the other hand, all the atomic physicists—to take an example—were in one organization.

** According to L. W. Helwig, *Persönlichkeiten der Gegenwart* (1940), Lenard inveighed against "relativity theories produced by alien minds." In his four-volume work, *Die Deutsche Physik* (1935), Helwig considered physics "cleansed of the outgrowths which the by now well-known findings of race research have shown to be the exclusive products of the Jewish mind and which the German *Volk* must shun as racially incompatible with itself."

freed several billion instead of several million marks for the production of atom bombs, it would have been impossible—given the strain on our economic resources—to have provided the materials, priorities, and technical workers corresponding to such an investment. For it was not only superior productive capacity that allowed the United States to undertake this gigantic project. The increasing air raids had long since created an armaments emergency in Germany which ruled out any such ambitious enterprise. At best, with extreme concentration of all our resources, we could have had a German atom bomb by 1947, but certainly we could not beat the Americans, whose bomb was ready by August 1945. And on the other hand the consumption of our latest reserves of chromium ore would have ended the war by January 1, 1946, at the very latest.

Thus, from the start of my work as Minister of Armaments I discovered blunder after blunder, in all departments of the economy. Incongruously enough, Hitler himself used to say, during those war years: "The loser of this war will be the side that makes the greatest blunders." For Hitler, by a succession of wrong-headed decisions, helped to speed the end of a war already lost because of productive capacities—for example, by his confused planning of the air war against England, by the shortage of U-boats at the beginning of the war, and, in general, by his failure to develop an overall plan for the war. So that when many German memoirs comment on Hitler's decisive mistakes, the writers are completely right. But all that does not mean that the war could have been won.

17

Commander in Chief Hitler

AMATEURISHNESS WAS ONE OF HITLER'S DOMINANT TRAITS. HE HAD NEVER learned a profession and basically had always remained an outsider to all fields of endeavor. Like many self-taught people, he had no idea what real specialized knowledge meant. Without any sense of the complexities of any great task, he boldly assumed one function after another. Unburdened by standard ideas, his quick intelligence sometimes conceived unusual measures which a specialist would not have hit on at all. The victories of the early years of the war can literally be attributed to Hitler's ignorance of the rules of the game and his layman's delight in decision making. Since the opposing side was trained to apply rules which Hitler's self-taught, autocratic mind did not know and did not use, he achieved surprises. These audacities, coupled with military superiority, were the basis of his early successes. But as soon as setbacks occurred he suffered shipwreck, like most untrained people. Then his ignorance of the rules of the game was revealed as another kind of incompetence; then his defects were no longer strengths. The greater the failures became, the more obstinately his incurable amateurishness came to the fore. The tendency to wild decisions had long been his forte; now it speeded his downfall.

Every two or three weeks I traveled from Berlin to spend a few days in Hitler's East Prussian, and later in his Ukrainian, headquarters in order to have him decide the many technical questions of detail in which he was interested in his capacity as Commander in Chief of the army. Hitler knew all the types of ordnance and ammunition, including the calibers, the lengths of barrels, and the range of fire. He had the stocks of the most important items of armament in his head—as well as the monthly production figures. He was able to compare our quotas with our deliveries and draw conclusions.

Hitler naïve pleasure at being able to shine in the field of armaments, as previously in automobile manufacturing or in architecture, by reciting abstruse figures, made it plain that in this realm also he was working as an amateur. He seemed to be constantly endeavoring to show himself the equal of or even the superior of the experts. The real expert sensibly does not burden his mind with details that he can look up or leave to an assistant. Hitler, however, felt it necessary for his own self-esteem to parade his knowledge. But he also enjoyed doing it.

He obtained his information from a large book in a red binding with broad yellow diagonal stripes. It was a catalogue, continually being brought up to date, of from thirty to fifty different types of ammunition and ordnance. He kept it on his night table. Sometimes he would order a servant to bring the book down when in the course of military conferences an assistant had mentioned a figure which Hitler instantly corrected. The book was opened and Hitler's data would be confirmed, without fail, every time, while the general would be shown to be in error. Hitler's memory for figures was the terror of his entourage.

By tricks of this sort, Hitler could intimidate the majority of the officers who surrounded him. But on the other hand he felt uncertain when he was confronting an out-and-out technical expert. He did not insist on his opinion if a specialist objected.

My predecessor, Todt, had sometimes gone to conferences with Hitler accompanied by two of his closest associates, Xaver Dorsch and Karl Saur; occasionally, he would bring one of his experts along. But he thought it important to deliver his reports personally and to involve his associates only on difficult points of detail. From the very first I did not even take the trouble to memorize figures which Hitler in any case kept in his head better than I. But knowing Hitler's respect for specialists, I would come to conferences flanked by all those experts who had the best mastery of the various points under discussion.

I was thus saved from the nightmare of all "Fuehrer conferences"— the fear of being driven into a corner by a bombardment of figures and technical data. I consistently appeared at the Fuehrer's headquarters accompanied by approximately twenty civilians. Before long everybody in Restricted Area I, as the specially guarded area round the headquarters was known, was making fun of "Speer's invasions." Depending on the subjects to be discussed, from two to four of my experts were invited to the conferences which took place in the situation room of the headquarters, adjacent to Hitler's private apartment. It was a modestly furnished room about nine hundred square feet in area, the walls paneled in light-colored wood. The room was dominated by a heavy oak map table thirteen feet long next to a large window. In one corner was a smaller table surrounded by six armchairs. Here our conference group sat.

During these conferences I remained in the background as far as possible. I opened them with a brief reference to the subject and then asked one of the experts present to state his views. Neither the environment, with its innumerable generals, adjutants, guard areas, barriers, and passes, nor the aureole that this whole apparatus conferred upon Hitler, could intimidate these specialists. Their many years of successful practice of their professions gave them a clear sense of their rank and their responsibility. Sometimes the conversation developed into a heated discussion, for they quite often forgot whom they were addressing. Hitler took all this partly with humor, partly with respect. In this circle he seemed modest and treated my people with remarkable courtesy. With them, moreover, he refrained from his habit of killing opposition by long, exhaustive, and numbing speeches. He knew how to distinguish key matters from those of lesser importance, was adaptable, and surprised everyone by the swiftness with which he could choose among several possibilities and justify his choice. Effortlessly, he found his bearings when presented with technical processes, plans, and sketches. His questions showed that during the brief explanation period he could grasp the essentials of complicated subjects. However, there was a disadvantage to this which he was unaware of: He arrived at the core of matters too easily and therefore could not understand them with real thoroughness.

I could never predict what the result of our conferences would be. Sometimes he instantly approved a proposal whose prospects seemed exceedingly slight. Sometimes he obstinately refused to permit certain trivial measures which he himself had demanded only a short time before. Nevertheless, my system of circumventing Hitler's knowledge of detail by having experts confront him with even more detailed knowledge netted me more successes than failures. His other associates observed with astonishment and with some degree of envy that Hitler often changed his mind after hearing our counterproposals and would alter decisions which in the preceding military conferences he had called unalterable.[1]

Hitler's technical horizon, however, just like his general ideas, his views on art, and his style of life, was limited by the First World War. His technical interests were narrowly restricted to the traditional weapons of the army and the navy. In these areas he had continued to learn and steadily increased his knowledge, so that he frequently proposed convincing and usable innovations. But he had little feeling for such new developments as, for example, radar, the construction of an atom bomb, jet fighters, and rockets. On his rare flights in the newly developed Condor he showed concern that the mechanism which let down the retracted landing gear might not function. Warily, he declared that he preferred the old Junkers 52 with its rigid landing gear.

Very often, directly after one of these conferences Hitler would lecture his military advisers on the technical knowledge he had just acquired. He loved to present such pieces of information with a casual air, as if the knowledge were his own.

When the Russian T-34 appeared, Hitler was triumphant, for he could then point out that he had earlier demanded the kind of long-barreled gun it had. Even before my appointment as Minister of Armaments, I heard Hitler in the Chancellery garden, after a demonstration of the Panzer IV, inveighing against the obstinacy of the Army Ordnance Office which had turned down his idea for increasing the velocity of the missile by lengthening the barrel. The Ordnance Office had at the time presented counterarguments: The long barrel would overload the tank in front, since it was not built with such a gun in view. If so major a change were introduced, the whole design would be thrown out of balance.

Hitler would always bring up this incident whenever his ideas encountered opposition. "I was right at the time, and no one wanted to believe me. Now I am right again!" When the army felt the need for a tank which could outmaneuver the comparatively fast T-34 by greater speed, Hitler insisted that more would be gained by increasing the range of the guns and the weight of the armor. In this field, too, he had mastered the necessary figures and could recite penetration results and missile velocities by heart. He usually defended his theory by the example of warships:

> In a naval battle the side having the greater range can open fire at the greater distance. Even if it is only half a mile. If along with this he has stronger armor . . . he must necessarily be superior. What are you after? The faster ship has only one advantage: to utilize its greater speed for re-treating. Do you mean to say a ship can possibly overcome heavier armor and superior artillery by greater speed? It's exactly the same for tanks. Your faster tank has to avoid meeting the heavier tank.

My experts from industry were not direct participants in these discussions. Our business was to build the tanks according to the requirements set by the army, whether these were decided by Hitler, by the General Staff, or by the Army Ordnance Office. Questions of battle tactics were not our concern; such discussions were usually conducted by the army officers. In 1942, Hitler still encouraged such discussions. He was still listening quietly to objections and offering his arguments just as quietly. Nevertheless, his arguments carried special weight.

Since the Tiger had originally been designed to weigh fifty tons but as a result of Hitler's demands had gone up to seventy-five tons, we decided to develop a new thirty-ton tank whose very name, Panther, was to signify greater agility. Though light in weight, its motor was to be the same as the Tiger's, which meant it could develop superior speed. But in the course of a year Hitler once again insisted on clapping so much armor on it, as well as larger guns, that it ultimately reached forty-eight tons, the original weight of the Tiger.

In order to compensate for this strange transformation of a swift Panther into a slow Tiger, we made still another effort to produce a series of small, light, quick-moving tanks.[2] By way of pleasing and re-assuring Hitler, Porsche also undertook to design a superheavy tank which weighed over a hundred tons and hence could be built only in small numbers, one by one. For security purposes this new monster was as-signed the code name Mouse. In any case Porsche had personally taken over Hitler's bias for superheaviness and would occasionally bring the Fuehrer reports about parallel developments on the part of the enemy. Once, Hitler sent for General Buhle and demanded: "I have just heard that an enemy tank is coming along with armor far beyond anything we have. Have you any documentation of that? If it is true a new antitank gun must be developed instantly. The force of penetration must . . . the gun must be enlarged, or lengthened—to be brief, we must begin reacting immediately. Instantly."[3]

Thus, Hitler's decisions led to a multiplicity of parallel projects. They also led to more and more complicated problems of supply. One of his worst failings was that he simply did not understand the necessity for supplying the armies with sufficient spare parts.* General Guderian, the Inspector General of Tank Ordnance, frequently pointed out to me that if we could repair our tanks quickly, thanks to sufficient spare parts, we could have more available for battle, at a fraction of the cost, than by producing new ones. But Hitler insisted on the priority of new produc-tion, which would have had to be reduced by 20 percent if we made provision for such repairs.

General Fromm as Chief of the Reserve Army was deeply concerned about this kind of poor planning. I took him with me to see Hitler several times so that he could present the arguments of the military. Fromm knew how to state a problem clearly; he had presence and had diplomatic tact. Sitting there, his sword pressed between his knees, hand on the hilt, he looked charged with energy; and to this day I believe

---

* This disastrous tendency was evident as early as 1942: "Presented the Fuehrer with the monthly list of tank replacement parts and reported that despite the increase in production the demand is so high that to raise the production of spare parts we must decrease the production of new tanks." (*Führerprotokoll*, May 6–7, 1942, Point 38.)

that his great abilities might have prevented many a blunder at the Fuehrer's headquarters. After several conferences, in fact, his influence increased. But immediately opposition appeared, both on the part of Keitel, who saw his position threatened, and on the part of Goebbels, who tried to persuade Hitler that Fromm had a dangerous political record. Finally, Hitler clashed with Fromm over a question of reserve supplies. Curtly, he let me know that I was no longer to bring Fromm with me.

Many of my conferences with Hitler were concerned with establishing the armaments programs for the army. Hitler's point of view was: The more I demand, the more I receive. And to my astonishment programs which industrial experts considered impossible to carry out were in the end actually surpassed. Hitler's authority liberated reserves that nobody had taken into his calculations. From 1944 on, however, his programs became totally unrealistic. Our efforts to push these through in the factories were self-defeating.

It often seemed to me that Hitler used these prolonged conferences on armaments and war production as an escape from his military responsibilities. He himself admitted to me that he found in them a relaxation similar to our former conferences on architecture. Even in crisis situations he devoted many hours to such discussions, sometimes refusing to interrupt them even when his field marshals or ministers urgently wanted to speak with him.

Our technical conferences were usually combined with a demonstration of new weapons which took place in a nearby field. A few moments before we would have been sitting intimately with Hitler, but now everybody had to line up in rank and file, Field Marshal Keitel, chief of the OKW (High Command of the Armed Forces), on the right. Obviously, Hitler laid stress on the ceremonial aspect of the occasion, adding a further note of formality by entering his official limousine to cover the few hundred yards to the field. I took my place in the back seat. Hitler would then step out, and Keitel would report the presence of the waiting line of generals and technicians.

This ritual concluded, the group promptly broke up. Hitler looked into details, clambered over the vehicles on portable steps held in readiness for him, and continued his discussions with the specialists. Often Hitler and I would make appreciative remarks about the weapons, such as: "What an elegant barrel," or, "What a fine shape this tank has!"—a ludicrous relapse into the terminology of our joint inspections of architectural models.

In the course of one such inspection, Keitel mistook a 7.5 centimeter antitank gun for a light field howitzer. Hitler passed over the mistake at the time but had his joke on our ride back: "Did you hear that? Keitel and the antitank gun? And he's a general of the artillery!"

Another time the air force had lined up on a nearby airfield the multiple variants and types in its production program for Hitler's inspection. Goering had himself reserved the right to explain the planes to Hitler. His staff thereupon provided him with a cram sheet, in the order of the models on display, giving their names, flight characteristics, and other technical data. One type had not been brought up in time, and Goering had not been informed. From that point on he blandly misidentified everything, for he adhered strictly to his list. Hitler instantly perceived the error but gave no sign.

At the end of June 1942 I read in the newspapers, just like everyone else, that a great new offensive in the east had begun. There was a mood of exuberance at headquarters. Every evening Hitler's chief adjutant, Schmundt, traced the onrush of the troops on a wall map, for the edification of civilians at headquarters. Hitler was triumphant. Once again he had proved that he was right and the generals wrong—for they had advised against an offensive and called for defensive tactics, occasionally straightening out the front. Even General Fromm had brightened up, although at the beginning of the operation he had commented to me that any such offensive was a luxury in the "poor man's" situation we were in.

The left wing east of Kiev grew longer and longer. The troops were approaching Stalingrad. Feats were performed to maintain emergency railroad traffic in the newly won territories and thus keep supplies moving.

Barely three weeks after the beginning of the successful offensive Hitler moved to an advanced headquarters near the Ukrainian city of Vinnitsa. Since Russian air activity was as good as nonexistent and the west this time was too far away, even given Hitler's anxieties, he for once did not demand the building of any special air-raid shelters. Instead of the usual concrete buildings a pleasant-looking cluster of blockhouses scattered about a forest was established.

Whenever I had to fly to the new headquarters, I used what free time I had to drive around the country. Once I drove to Kiev. Immediately after the October Revolution avant-gardists like Le Corbusier, May, or El Lissitzky had influenced modern Russian architecture. But under Stalin at the end of the twenties it had all swung back to a conservative and classicist style. The conference building in Kiev, for example, could have been designed by a good pupil of the Ecole des Beaux-Arts. I toyed with the notion of searching out the architect and employing him in Germany. A classicist stadium in Kiev was adorned with statues of athletes in the fashion of classical antiquity—but touchingly, the figures were clad in bathing suits.

I found one of the most famous churches of Kiev a heap of rubble. A Soviet powder magazine had blown up inside it, I was told. Later, I learned from Goebbels that the church had been blown up deliberately on orders of Erich Koch, Reich Commissioner for the Ukraine; the idea had been to destroy this symbol of Ukrainian national pride. Goebbels told the story with displeasure; he was horrified by the brutal course being pursued in occupied sectors of the Soviet Union. In fact the Ukraine at that time was still so peaceable that I could drive through the extensive forests without an escort. Half a year later, thanks to the twisted policy of the eastern commissioners, the whole area was infested with partisans.

Other drives took me to the industrial center of Dnepropetrovsk. What most impressed me was a university complex under construction. Its facilities went far beyond anything in Germany and left no doubt of the Soviet Union's determination to become a technical power of the first rank. I also visited the power plant of Saporoshe, blown up by the Russians. A large construction crew closed the blast hole in the dam, but they also had to install new turbines. Before retreating, the Russians had thrown the oil switch, interrupting the oiling of their turbines while they were running at full speed. The machines ran hot and finally ground themselves into a useless tangle of parts—a feat which could be accomplished by a single man pulling a lever. The vision of that later gave me many a sleepless hour when I learned of Hitler's intention to make Germany a wasteland.

Even at the Fuehrer's headquarters, Hitler kept to his habit of taking his meals in the midst of his close associates. But whereas at the Chancellery party uniforms had dominated the scene, he was now surrounded by generals and officers of his staff. In contrast to the luxuriously furnished dining hall in the Chancellery, this dining room looked rather like the railroad station restaurant in a small town. Pine boarding formed the walls, and the windows were those of a standardized barracks. There was a long table for about twenty persons, flanked by plain chairs. Hitler's seat was on the window side in the middle of the long table; Keitel sat facing him, while the places of honor on either side of Hitler were reserved for the ever-changing visitors. As in past days in Berlin, Hitler talked long-windedly about his favorite subjects, while his dinner guests were reduced to silent listeners. It was apparent, however, that Hitler made an effort in the presence of these men, with whom he was not especially intimate and who moreover were his superiors by birth and education, to present his thoughts in as impressive a manner as possible.*
Thus the level of the table talk in the Fuehrer's headquarters differed from that at the Chancellery. It was considerably higher.

During the first weeks of the offensive we had discussed the rapid

---

* *Tischgespräche (Table Talk)* published by Picker gives a good idea of Hitler's topics of conversation. But we must remember that this collection includes only those passages in Hitler's monologues—they took up one to two hours every day—which struck Picker as significant. Complete transcripts would reinforce the sense of stifling boredom.

progress of the troops in the South Russian plains in an exultant mood. By contrast, after two months the faces of the diners grew increasingly doleful, and Hitler too began to lose his self-assurance.

Our troops had, it is true, taken the oil fields of Maikop. The leading tank columns were already fighting along the Terek and pushing on, over a roadless steppe near Astrakhan toward the southern Volga. But this advance was no longer maintaining the pace of the first weeks. Supplies could no longer keep up; the spare parts the tanks carried with them had long since been consumed, so that the fighting wedge was steadily thinning out. Moreover, our monthly armaments production lagged far behind the demands of an offensive over such enormous spaces. At that time we were manufacturing only a third of the tanks and a fourth of the artillery we were to be producing in 1944. Aside from that, normal wear and tear was extremely high over such distances. The tank testing station at Kummersdorf operated on the assumption that the treads or the motor of a heavy tank would need repairs after four to five hundred miles.

Hitler realized none of this. With the enemy supposedly too weak to offer any resistance, he wanted the exhausted German troops to thrust on to the southern side of the Caucasus, toward Georgia. He therefore detached considerable forces from the already weakened wedge and directed them to advance beyond Maikop toward Sochi. These contingents were supposed to reach Sukhumi by way of the narrow coastal road. This was where the main blow was to be delivered; he assumed that the territory north of the Caucasus would fall easily to him in any case.

But the units were done in. They could no longer push forward, however imperiously Hitler ordered it. In the situation conferences Hitler was shown aerial photos of the impenetrable walnut forests outside Sochi. Chief of Staff Halder warned Hitler that the Russians could easily render the coastal road impassable for a long time by blasting the steep slopes. In any case, he argued, the road was too narrow for the advance of large troop units. But Hitler remained unimpressed:

> These difficulties can be overcome as all difficulties can be overcome! First we must conquer the road. Then the way is open to the plains south of the Caucasus. There we can deploy our armies freely and set up supply camps. Then, in one or two years, we'll start an offensive into the underbelly of the British Empire. With a minimum of effort we can liberate Persia and Iraq. The Indians will hail our divisions enthusiastically.

When in 1944 we were combing through the printing trade for unnecessary assignments, we came upon a plant in Leipzig that was turning out Persian maps and language guides for the OKW in large quantities. The contract had been let and then forgotten.

Even a layman like myself could tell that the offensive had run itself into the ground. Then the report arrived that a detachment of German mountain troops had taken Mount Elbrus, nearly nineteen thousand feet high, the highest mountain in the Caucasus and surrounded by broad fields of glaciers. They had planted the German war flag there. To be sure, this was a superfluous action, certainly on the smallest scale,* which could be understood only as an adventure by a group of enthusiastic mountain climbers. All of us could sympathize with the impulse behind this act, but otherwise it seemed to us completely unimportant. I often saw Hitler furious but seldom did his anger erupt from him as it did when this report came in. For hours he raged as if his entire plan of campaign had been ruined by this bit of sport. Days later he went on railing to all and sundry about "these crazy mountain climbers" who "belong before a court-martial." There they were pursuing their idiotic hobbies in the midst of a war, he exclaimed indignantly, occupying an idiotic peak even though he had commanded that all efforts must be concentrated upon Sukhumi. Here was a clear example of the way his orders were being obeyed.

Urgent business called me back to Berlin. A few days later the commander of the army group operating in the Caucasus was relieved, although Jodl vigorously defended him. When I returned to headquarters again about two weeks later, I found that Hitler had quarreled with Keitel, Jodl, and Halder. He refused to shake hands with them or to dine with them at the common table. From then on until the end of the war he had his meals served in his bunker room, only occasionally inviting a few select persons to join him. The close relations that Hitler had with his military associates were shattered for good.

Was the cause merely the failure of the offensive on which he had placed so many hopes, or did he for the first time have an inkling that this was the turning point? The fact that from then on he stayed away from the officers' table may have been due to the fact that he would no longer be sitting among them as the invincible leader in peace and war, but as a man whose plans had come to grief. Moreover, he must by now have run through the stock of general ideas with which he had regaled this group. Perhaps he also felt that his magic was failing him for the first time.

For several weeks Keitel skulked about mournfully and displayed great devotion, so that Hitler soon began treating him somewhat more amicably. His relations with Jodl—who had characteristically remained impassive through it all—likewise straightened out. But General Halder,

---

* One mountain division tried to push through to Tiflis by way of the Caucasian mountain passes, following the old military road from Grozny. Hitler considered this road a poor one to use for sending reinforcements, since it was blocked for months at a time by snow and avalanches. One group from the mountain division had gone off to take Mount Elbrus.

the army chief of staff, had to go. He was a quiet, laconic man who was probably always thrown off by Hitler's vulgar dynamism and thus gave a rather hapless impression. His successor, Kurt Zeitzler, was just the opposite: a straighforward, insensitive person who made his reports in a loud voice. He was not the type of military man given to independent thinking and no doubt represented the kind of Chief of Staff that Hitler wanted: a reliable "assistant" who, as Hitler was fond of saying, "doesn't go off and brood on my orders, but energetically sees to carrying them out." With that in mind, too, Hitler probably did not pick him from the ranks of the higher generals. Zeitzler had up to that time held a subordinate place in the army hierarchy; he was promoted two grades at once.

After the appointment of the new Chief of Staff, Hitler permitted me—the only civilian for the time being*—to participate in the situation conferences. I could take this as a special proof of his satisfaction with me—for which he had every reason, given the constantly rising production figures. But this favor would probably not have been shown me if he had felt threatened by a loss of prestige in my presence because of opposition, vehement debates, and disputes. The storm had calmed down again; Hitler had regained his standing

Every day around noon the grand situation conference took place. It lasted two to three hours. Hitler was the only one who was seated—on a plain armchair with a rush seat. The other participants stood around the map table: his adjutants, staff officers of the OKW and the Army General Staff, and Hitler's liaison officers to the air force, the navy, the Waffen-SS, and Himmler. On the whole they were rather young men with likable faces, most of them holding the rank of colonel or major. Keitel, Jodl, and Zeitzler stood casually amongst them. Sometimes Goering came too. As a gesture of special distinction and perhaps in consideration of his corpulence, Hitler had an upholstered stool brought in for the Reich Marshal, on which he sat beside Hitler.

Desk lamps with long, swinging arms illuminated the maps. First the eastern theater was discussed. Three or four strategic maps, pasted together, each of them about five by eight feet, were laid out on the long table in front of Hitler. The discussion began with the northern part of the eastern theater of war. Every detail of the events of the previous day was entered on the maps, every advance, even patrols—and almost every entry was explained by the Chief of Staff. Bit by bit the maps were pushed farther up the table, so that Hitler always had a comprehensible segment within reading distance. Longer discussion was devoted to the more important events, Hitler noting every change from the

* Several months passed before Bormann and Ribbentrop received permission to attend.

status of the previous day. Just the daily preparation for this conference was a tremendous burden on the time of the Chief of Staff and his officers, who no doubt had more important things to do. As a layman I was astonished at the way Hitler in the course of hearing the reports made deployments, pushed divisions back and forth, or dealt with petty details.

At least during 1942 he received the news of grave setbacks calmly. Or perhaps this was already the beginning of the apathy he later displayed. Outwardly, at any rate, he showed no sign of despair. He seemed determined to present the image of the superior war lord whose composure nothing could shake. Frequently he stressed that his experiences in the trenches of the First World War had given him more insight into many details of military policy than all his military advisers had acquired in the General Staff school. This may well have been true, for certain restricted areas. In the opinion of many army officers, however, his very "trench perspective" had given him a false picture of the process of leadership. In this regard his knowledge of detail, the detailed knowledge of a corporal, rather hampered him. General Fromm commented in his laconic fashion that a civilian as commander in chief might have been better than, of all people, a corporal—moreover one who had never fought in the east and therefore could not conceive the special problems of warfare in this part of the world.

Hitler practiced a policy of patchwork of the pettiest sort. Moreover, he labored under the handicap that the nature of any given terrain cannot really be gathered adequately from maps. In the early summer of 1942 he personally ordered the first six of our Tiger tanks to be thrown into battle. As always, when a new weapon was ready, he expected it to turn the tide of battle. He regaled us with vivid descriptions of how the Soviet 7.7 centimeter antitank guns, which penetrated our Panzer IV front armor even at sizable distances, would fire shot after shot in vain, and how finally the Tiger would roll over the antitank gun nests. His staff remonstrated that the terrain he had chosen made tactical deployment of the tanks impossible because of the marshy subsurface on both sides of the road. Hitler dismissed these objections, not sharply, but with a superior air. And so the first Tiger assault started. Everybody was tensely awaiting the results, and I was rather anxious, wondering whether all would go well technically. There was no opportunity for a technical dress rehearsal. The Russians calmly let the tanks roll past an antitank gun position, then fired direct hits at the first and last Tiger. The remaining four thereupon could move neither forward nor backward, nor could they take evasive action to the side because of the swamps, and soon they were also finished off. Hitler silently passed over the debacle; he never referred to it again.

The situation in the western theater of war, at that time still centered in Africa, was taken up next by General Jodl. Here too Hitler tended to intervene in every detail. He was bitterly annoyed with Rommel, who would often give extremely unclear bulletins on the day's movements. In other words, he "veiled" them from headquarters, sometimes for days, only to report an entirely changed situation. Hitler liked Rommel personally but could ill brook this sort of conduct.

Properly speaking, Jodl as chief of the Wehrmacht Operations Staff ought to have coordinated the actions in the various theaters of war. But Hitler had claimed this task for himself, although he did not actually perform it. Basically, Jodl had no clearly defined field of activity. But in order to have something to do, his staff assumed independent leadership in certain theaters, so that in the end two rival general staffs existed for the army. Hitler acted as arbitrator between them —in keeping with that principle of divisiveness he favored. The more critical the situation became, the more vehemently the two rival staffs fought over the shifting of divisions from east to west and vice versa.

Once the "army situation" had been discussed, reports of the events of the last twenty-four hours in the "air situation" and the "naval situation"—as these areas were designated—were reviewed, usually by the liaison officer or the adjutant for this branch of the services, rarely by the commander himself. Attacks on England, the bombings of German cities, were reported briefly, as were the latest accomplishments in submarine warfare. On questions of air and naval warfare Hitler left his commanders in chief the broadest freedom of choice. At least at that period he rarely intervened, and then only in an advisory capacity.

Toward the end of the conference Keitel presented Hitler with various documents for signature. Usually these were the partly sneered-at, partly dreaded "covering orders"—in other words, orders intended to cover him or someone else against subsequent reprimands from Hitler. At the time I called this procedure an outrageous abuse of Hitler's signature, since it often meant that altogether incompatible ideas and plans were thereby given the form of orders, creating a confusing and impenetrable thicket of contradictions.

The presence of so large a company in the relatively small space made the air stale, which quickly tired me as well as most of the others. A ventilation system had been installed, but Hitler thought it produced "excessive pressure" which resulted in headaches and a feeling of giddiness. Therefore it was switched on only before and after the situation conference. Even in the finest weather the window usually remained closed, and even by day the curtains were drawn. These conditions created an extremely sultry atmosphere.

I had expected respectful silence during these situation conferences and was therefore surprised that the officers who did not happen to be participating in a report talked together freely, though in low voices. Frequently, the officers, showing no further consideration for Hitler's presence, would take seats in the group of chairs at the back of the room. The many marginal conversations created a constant murmur that would have made me nervous. But it disturbed Hitler only when the side conversations grew too excited and too loud. When he raised his head disapprovingly, however, the noise immediately subsided.

From about the autumn of 1942 on, it became almost impossible to oppose Hitler on important questions, unless one went about it very cautiously. Outsiders had a better chance to present objections; Hitler would not stand for them from the group which constituted his daily entourage. Whenever he himself was trying to convince someone, he went far afield and tried as long as possible to keep the discussion on the plane of generalities. He would hardly allow the other person to say a word. If a controversial point arose in the course of the discussion, Hitler usually evaded it skillfully, postponing clarification of it to a subsequent conference. He proceeded on the assumption that military men were shy about giving in on points in front of their staff officers. Probably he also expected his aura and his persuasiveness to operate better in a face-to-face discussion with an individual. Both these elements came across poorly over the telephone. Probably that was why Hitler always showed a distinct dislike for conducting important arguments on the telephone.

In the late evening hours there was a further situation conference in which a younger General Staff officer reported on the developments of the last few hours. Hitler would sit alone with the officer. If I had dined with Hitler, he sometimes took me along to these reports. Undoubtedly he found these occasions far more relaxing than the main situation conference, and the atmosphere and tone would be considerably less formal.

Hitler's entourage certainly bore a measure of the blame for his growing belief in his superhuman abilities. Early in the game, Field Marshal Blomberg, Hitler's first and last Minister of War, had been overfond of praising Hitler's surpassing strategic genius. Even a more restrained and modest personality than Hitler ever was would have been in danger of losing all standards of self-criticism under such a constant torrent of applause.

In keeping with his character, Hitler gladly sought advice from persons who saw the situation even more optimistically and delusively than he himself. Keitel was often one of those. When the majority of the officers would greet Hitler's decisions with marked silence, Keitel would frequently feel called upon to speak up in favor of the measure. Constantly in Hitler's presence, he had completely succumbed to his influence. From an honorable, solidly respectable general he had developed in the course of years into a servile flatterer with all the wrong instincts. Basically, Keitel hated his own weakness; but the hopelessness of any dispute with Hitler had ultimately brought him to the point of not even trying to form his own opinion. If, however, he had offered resistance and stubbornly insisted on a view of his own, he would merely have been replaced by another Keitel.

In 1943-44 when Schmundt, Hitler's chief adjutant and army personnel chief, tried, along with many others, to replace Keitel by the much more vigorous Field Marshal Kesselring, Hitler said that he could not do without Keitel because the man was "loyal as a dog" to him. Perhaps Keitel embodied most precisely the type of person Hitler needed in his entourage.

General Jodl, too, rarely contradicted Hitler openly. He proceeded diplomatically. Usually he did not express his thoughts at once, thus skirting difficult situations. Later he would persuade Hitler to yield, or even to reverse decisions already taken. His occasional deprecatory remarks about Hitler showed that he had preserved a relatively unbiased view.

Keitel's subordinates, such as, for example, his deputy General Warlimont, could not be more courageous than their superior; for Keitel would not stand up for them against Hitler's ire. Occasionally they tried to counter the effects of obviously absurd orders by adding little clauses that Hitler did not understand. Under the leadership of a man so submissive and irresolute as Keitel, the High Command often had to look for all sorts of crooked paths in order to arrive at its goals.

The subjugation of the generals might also be laid in part to their state of permanent fatigue. Hitler's work routine intersected the normal daily routine of the High Command. As a result, the generals often went without regular sleep. Such purely physical strains probably affect events more than is generally assumed, especially when high performance over a protracted span of time is required. In private associations, too, Keitel and Jodl gave the impression of being exhausted, burned out. In order to break through this ring of hollow men, I hoped to place —in addition to Fromm—my friend Field Marshal Milch within the Fuehrer's headquarters. I had taken him with me to headquarters several times, supposedly in order to report on activities of Central Planning. A few times all went well, and Milch was gaining ground with his plan of concentrating on a fighter-plane program instead of the proposed fleet of big bombers. But then Goering forbade him to pay any further visits to headquarters.

Goering too gave the impression of a worn-out man at the end of 1942, when I sat with him in the pavilion that had been built especially for his brief stays at headquarters. Goering still had comfortable chairs, not the spartan furnishings of Hitler's bunker office. Depressed, the Reich Marshal said: "We will have reason to be glad if Germany can keep the boundaries of 1933 after the war." He quickly tried to cover up this remark by adding a few confident banalities, but I had the impression that in spite of the bluffness he put on, he saw defeat coming closer.

After his arrival at the Fuehrer's headquarters, Goering usually withdrew to his pavilion for a few minutes while General Bodenschatz, his liaison officer to Hitler, left the situation conference in order to brief Goering by telephone, so we suspected, on certain disputed questions. Fifteen minutes later, Goering would enter the situation conference. Of his own accord he would emphatically advocate exactly the viewpoint that Hitler wished to put across against the opposition of his generals. Hitler would then look around at his entourage: "You see, the Reich Marshal holds exactly the same opinion as I do."

On the afternoon of November 7, 1942, I accompanied Hitler to Munich in his special train. These journeys were a favorable occasion to draw Hitler into the necessary but time-consuming consideration of general armaments questions. This special train was equipped with radio, teletype machines, and a telephone switchboard. Jodl and some members of the General Staff had joined Hitler.

The atmosphere was tense. We were already many hours late, for at every sizable station a prolonged stop was made in order to connect the telephone cable with the railroad telegraph system, so we could get the latest reports. From early morning on a mighty armada of transports, accompanied by large naval units, had been passing through the Strait of Gibralter into the Mediterranean.

In earlier years Hitler had made a habit of showing himself at the window of his special train whenever it stopped. Now these encounters with the outside world seemed undesirable to him; instead, the shades on the station side of the train would be lowered. Late in the evening we sat with Hitler in his rosewood-paneled dining car. The table was elegantly set with silver flatware, cut glass, good china, and flower arrangements. As we began our ample meal, none of us at first saw that a freight train was stopped on the adjacent track. From the cattle car bedraggled, starved, and in some cases wounded German soldiers, just returning from the east, stared at the diners. With a start, Hitler noticed the somber scene two yards from his window. Without as much as a gesture of greeting in their direction, he peremptorily ordered his servant to draw the shades. This, then, in the second half of the war, was how Hitler handled a meeting with ordinary front-line soldiers such as he himself had once been.

At every station along the way the number of reported naval units rose. An enterprise of vast proportions was obviously afoot. Finally the units passed through the Strait. All the ships reported by our air reconnaissance were now moving eastward in the Mediterranean. "This is the largest landing operation that has ever taken place in the history of the world," Hitler declared in a tone of respect, perhaps taking pride that he was the cause of enterprises of such magnitude. Until the following morning the landing fleet remained north of the Moroccan and Algerian coast.

In the course of the night Hitler proposed several different explanations for this mysterious behavior. He thought the most probable thing was that the enemy was undertaking a great supply operation to reinforce the offensive against the hard-pressed Africa Corps. The naval units were keeping together in this way, he concluded, in order to advance through the narrow strait between Sicily and Africa under cover of darkness, safe from German air attacks. Or else, and this second version corresponded more to his feeling for perilous military operations: "The enemy will land in central Italy tonight. There he would meet with no resistance at all. There are no German troops there, and the Italians will run away. That way they can cut northern Italy off from the south. What will become of Rommel in that case? He would be lost in a short time. He has no reserves and supplies will no longer come through."

Hitler intoxicated himself with thoughts of far-reaching operations, of a kind he had long been missing. He more and more put himself into the position of the enemy: "I would occupy Rome at once and form a new Italian government. Or, and this would be the third possibility, I would use this great fleet to land in southern France. We have always been too gentle. And now this is what we get for it! No fortifications and no German troops at all down there. A great mistake that we have nothing garrisoned there. The Pétain government won't put up a bit of resistance, of course." From moment to moment he seemed to forget that these forces were gathering against himself.

Hitler's guesses were wide of the mark. It would never have occurred to him not to associate such a landing operation with a coup. To put the troops on land in safe positions from which they could methodically spread out, to take no unnecessary risks—that was a strategy alien to his nature. But that night he clearly realized one thing: Now the second front was beginning to be a reality.

By the next day the Allied troops were pouring ashore in North Africa. Nevertheless, Hitler went ahead with his speech in commemoration of his failed putsch of 1923. I still remember how shocked we all were when, instead of at least referring to the gravity of the situation and calling for a mustering of energies, he adopted his usual "victory-is-certain" tone: "They've already become idiots," he digressed about our enemy, whose operations had only yesterday called forth his homage, "if they think that they can ever shatter Germany. . . . We will not fall; consequently, the others will fall."

In the late autumn of 1942, Hitler triumphantly stated in the course of a situation conference: "Now the Russians are sending their cadets into the struggle.[4] That's the surest proof they have reached the end. A country sacrifices the next generation of officers only when it has nothing left."

A few weeks later, on November 19, 1942, the first reports of the great Russian winter offensive reached Hitler, who had withdrawn to Obersalzberg days before. The offensive, which nine weeks later was to lead to the capitulation of Stalingrad,[5] began near Serafinov. There, after violent artillery preparations, strong Soviet forces had broken through the positions of Rumanian divisions. Hitler tried at first to explain and belittle this disaster by making slurring remarks on the fighting qualities of his allies. But shortly afterward the Soviet troops began overwhelming German divisions as well. The front was beginning to crumble.

Hitler paced back and forth in the great hall of the Berghof.

Our generals are making their old mistakes again. They always overestimate the strength of the Russians. According to all the front-line reports, the enemy's human material is no longer sufficient. They are weakened; they have lost far too much blood. But of course nobody wants to accept such reports. Besides, how badly Russian officers are trained! No offensive can be organized with such officers. We know what it takes! In the short or long run the Russians will simply come to a halt. They'll run down. Meanwhile we shall throw in a few fresh divisions; that will put things right.

In the peaceful atmosphere of the Berghof he simply did not understand what was brewing. But three days later, when the bad news kept pouring in, he rushed back to East Prussia.

A few days afterward at Rastenburg the strategic map showed the area from Voronezh to Stalingrad covered with red arrows across a front a hundred and twenty-five miles wide. These represented the thrust of the Soviet troops. Among all the arrows were small blue circles, pockets of resistance by the remnants of German and allied divisions. Stalingrad was already surrounded by red rings. Disturbed, Hitler now commanded units to be detached from all other sectors of the front and from the occupied territories and dispatched in all haste to the southern sector. No operational reserve was available, although General Zeitzler had pointed out long before the emergency that each of the divisions in southern Russia had to defend a frontal sector of unusual length* and would not be able to cope with a vigorous assault by Soviet troops.

Stalingrad was encircled. Zeitzler, his face flushed and haggard from lack of sleep, insisted that the Sixth Army must break out to the west. He deluged Hitler with data on all that the army lacked, both as regards to rations and fuel, so that it had become impossible to provide warm meals for the soldiers exposed to fierce cold in the snow-swept fields or the scanty shelter of ruins. Hitler remained calm, unmoved and deliberate, as if bent on showing that Zeitzler's agitation was a psychotic reaction in the face of danger. "The counterattack from the south that I have ordered will soon relieve Stalingrad. That will recoup the situation. We have been in such positions often before, you know. In the end we always had the problem in hand again." He gave orders for supply trains to be dispatched right behind the troops deploying for the counteroffensive, so that as soon as Stalingrad was relieved something could at once be done about alleviating the plight of the soldiers. Zeitzler disagreed, and Hitler let him talk without interrupting. The forces provided for the counterattack were too weak, Zeitzler said. But if they could unite successfully with a Sixth Army that had broken out to the west, they would then be able to establish new positions farther to the south. Hitler offered counterarguments, but Zeitzler held to his view. Finally, after the discussion had gone on for more than half an hour, Hitler's patience snapped: "Stalingrad simply must be held. It must be; it is a key position. By breaking traffic on the Volga at that spot, we cause the Russians the greatest difficulties. How are they going to transport their grain from southern Russia to the north?" That did not sound convincing; I had the feeling, rather, that Stalingrad was a symbol for him. But for the time being the discussion ended after this dispute.

Next day the situation had worsened. Zeitzler's pleas had grown even more urgent; the atmosphere in the situation conference was somber; and even Hitler looked exhausted and downcast. Once he too spoke of a breakout. Once more he asked for figures on how many tons of supplies were needed daily to maintain the fighting strength of over two hundred thousand soldiers.

Twenty-four hours later the fate of the encircled army was finally sealed. For Goering appeared in the situation room, brisk and beaming like an operetta tenor who is supposed to portray a victorious Reich Marshal. Depressed, with a beseeching note in his voice, Hitler asked him: "What about supplying Stalingrad by air?" Goering snapped to

* Establishing the new line of defense, Orel-Stalingrad-Terek River-Maikop, meant that the troops had to defend a line 2.3 times longer than the Orel-Black Sea position taken in the spring

attention and declared solemnly: "My leader! I personally guarantee the supplying of Stalingrad by air. You can rely on that." As I later heard from Milch, the Air Force General Staff had in fact calculated that supplying the pocket was impossible. Zeitzler, too, instantly voiced his doubts. But Goering retorted that it was exclusively the business of the air force to undertake the necessary calculations. Hitler, who could be so pedantic about erecting edifices of figures, on this day did not even ask for an accounting of how the necessary planes could be made available. He had revived at Goering's mere words, and had recovered his old staunchness. "Then Stalingrad can be held! It is foolish to go on talking any more about a breakout of the Sixth Army. It would lose all its heavy weapons and have no fighting strength left. The Sixth Army remains in Stalingrad!"*

Although Goering knew that the fate of the army encircled in Stalingrad hung on his promise, on December 12, 1942,[6] he issued invitations to his subordinates to attend a festive performance of Richard Wagner's *Die Meistersinger* to celebrate the reopening of the destroyed Berlin State Opera House. In gala uniforms or full dress we took our seats in the Fuehrer's big box. The jovial plot of the opera painfully contrasted with the events at the front, so that I kept chiding myself for having accepted the invitation.

A few days later I was back at the Fuehrer's headquarters. Zeitzler was now giving a daily report on the tons of rations and munitions the Sixth Army was receiving by air. They came to only a fraction of the promised quantities. Goering, repeatedly called to account by Hitler, had excuses: The weather was bad, fog, freezing rain, or snowstorms had so far prevented commitment of as many planes as planned. But as soon as the weather changed, Goering said, he would be able to deliver the promised tonnage.

Thereupon, food rations had to be reduced still further in Stalingrad. Zeitzler conspicuously had himself served the same rations in the General Staff casino, and visibly lost weight. After a few days of this Hitler informed him that he considered it improper for a chief of staff to wear out his nerves with such demonstrations of solidarity with the troops. He commanded Zeitzler to resume at once taking sufficient nourishment. However, for a few weeks Hitler prohibited the serving of champagne and cognac. The mood became blacker and blacker. Faces froze into masks. Often we stood about in silence. No one wanted to talk about the gradual destruction of what had been, only a few months before, a victorious army.

But Hitler went on hoping; he was still hoping when I once more

* Later experience with battles fought in winter by the retreating armies belies Hitler's theory, since adopted by some historians, that the Stalingrad pocket served its purpose because it tied up the Soviet forces for eight weeks.

was at headquarters from January 2 to 7. The counterattack he had ordered, which was supposed to break the ring around Stalingrad and bring fresh supplies to the dying army, had failed two weeks before. The sole remaining hope, and that a faint one, lay in a decision to evacuate the pocket.

One day, while I waited outside the situation room, I heard Zeitzler urging Keitel, literally begging him, on this day at least to support him in persuading Hitler to give the order for evacuation. This was the last moment to avert a fearful catastrophe, Zeitzler said. Keitel emphatically agreed and solemnly promised Zeitzler that he would help as requested. But at the situation conference, when Hitler once again stressed the necessity of holding out in Stalingrad, Keitel strode emotionally toward him, pointed to the map, where a small remnant of the city was surrounded by thick red rings, and declared: "*Mein Führer*, we will hold that!"

In this hopeless situation, on January 15, 1943, Hitler signed a special decree giving Field Marshal Milch the power to take all measures in the air force and the civilian air fleet that he considered necessary for supplying Stalingrad—without asking Goering's permission.* At the time I telephoned Milch several times, for he had promised me to rescue my brother, who was caught with the rest of the encircled troops in Stalingrad. In the general confusion, however, it proved impossible to locate him. Desperate letters came from him. He had jaundice and swollen limbs, was taken to a field hospital, but could not endure conditions there and dragged himself back to his comrades at an artillery observation post. After that nothing more was heard from him. What my parents and I went through was repeated by hundreds of thousands of families who for a time continued to receive airmail letters from the encircled city, until it was all over.** In the future Hitler never said another word about the catastrophe for which he and Goering were alone responsible. Instead, he commanded the immediate formation of a new Sixth Army which was supposed to restore the glory of the doomed one. A year and a half later, in the middle of August 1944, it too was encircled by the Russians and annihilated.

Our enemies rightly regarded this disaster at Stalingrad as a turning

---

* Milch directed this operation from the air force headquarters south of Stalingrad. He was able to increase the flights to Stalingrad appreciably, so that at least some of the wounded could be evacuated. After performing his mission, Milch was received by Hitler. Their conversation ended in a violent clash over the desperate military situation, whose seriousness Hitler still refused to acknowledge.

** Hitler could not have blocked delivery of these letters without causing wild rumors. But when the Soviet Army allowed German prisoners to send home postcards, Hitler ordered the cards destroyed. Because they were a sign of life from the relatives, they might have mitigated the Russophobia that was being so carefully cultivated by Hitler's propaganda apparatus. Fritzsche told me about this at Nuremberg.

point in the war. But at Hitler's headquarters the only reaction was a temporary numbness followed by a rush of feverish staff work in which the most trivial details were threshed over. Hitler began conceiving plans for new victories in 1943. The top leadership of the Reich, already torn by dissension and filled with envy and jealousy, did not close ranks in the face of the peril that was almost upon us. On the contrary, in that den of intrigue which Hitler had created by splitting all the centers of power, the gamblers began playing for higher stakes than ever before.

18

Intrigues

In the winter of 1942, during the Stalingrad crisis, Bormann, Keitel, and Lammers decided to close their own ring around Hitler more tightly. Henceforth, all orders to be signed by the Chief of State had to be cleared through these three men. This would supposedly prevent the unconsidered signing of decrees and therefore put a stop to the command confusion caused by this practice. Hitler was content so long as he retained the final decision. Henceforth, the divergent views of various branches of government would be "sifted" by this Committee of Three. In accepting this arrangement Hitler counted on objective presentation and a nonpartisan method of working.

The three-man committee divided up its jurisdictions. Keitel, who was to be in charge of all orders relating to the armed forces, came to grief right from the start, since the commanders in chief of the air force and the navy utterly refused to accept his authority. All changes in the powers of the ministries, all constitutional affairs, and all administrative questions were supposed to go through Lammers. As it turned out, however, he had to leave these decisions more and more to Bormann, since he himself had little access to Hitler. Bormann had reserved the field of domestic policy for himself. But he not only lacked the intelligence for these matters; he also had insufficient knowledge of the outside world. For more than eight years he had been little more than

Hitler's shadow. He had never dared go on any lengthy business trips, or even to allow himself a vacation, for fear that his influence might diminish. From his own days as Hess's deputy, Bormann knew the perils of ambitious deputies. For Hitler was all too ready to treat the second men in an organization, as soon as they were presented to him, as members of his staff and to make assignments directly to them. This quirk accorded with his tendency to divide power wherever he encountered it. Moreover, he loved to see new faces, to try out new persons. In order to avoid raising up such a rival in his own household, many a minister took care not to appoint an intelligent and vigorous deputy.

The plan of these three men to surround Hitler, to filter his information and thus control his power, might have led to an abridgement of Hitler's one-man rule—had the Committee of Three consisted of men possessing initiative, imagination, and a sense of responsibility. But since they had been trained always to act in Hitler's name, they slavishly depended on the expressions of his will. What is more, Hitler soon stopped abiding by this regulation. It became a nuisance to him, and was, moreover, contrary to his temperament. But it is understandable that those who stood outside this ring resented its stranglehold.

In fact Bormann was now assuming a role which could be dangerous to the top functionaries. He alone, with Hitler's compliance, drew up the appointments calendar, which meant that he decided which civilian members of the government or party could see, or more important, could not see, the Fuehrer. By now, hardly any of the ministers, Reichsleiters, or Gauleiters could penetrate to Hitler. They all had to ask Bormann to present their programs to him. Bormann was very efficient. Usually the official in question received an answer in writing within a few days, whereas in the past he would have had to wait for months. I was one of the exceptions to this rule. Since my sphere was military in nature, I had access to Hitler whenever I wished. Hitler's military adjutants were the ones who set up my appointments.

After my conferences with Hitler, it sometimes happened that the adjutant would announce Bormann, who would then come into the room carrying his files. In a few sentences he would report on the memoranda sent to him. He spoke monotonously and with seeming objectivity and would then advance his own solution. Usually Hitler merely nodded and spoke his terse, "Agreed." On the basis of this one word, or even a vague comment by Hitler, which was hardly meant as a directive, Bormann would often draft lengthy instructions. In this way ten or more important decisions were sometimes made within half an hour. De facto, Bormann was conducting the internal affairs of the Reich. A few months afterward, on April 12, 1943, Bormann obtained Hitler's signature to a seemingly unimportant piece of paper. He became "Secretary to the Fuehrer." Whereas previously his powers, strictly speaking, should have been restricted to party affairs, this new position now authorized him to act officially in any field he wished.

After my first major achievements in the field of armaments, Goebbels's hostility toward me, apparent ever since his affair with Lida Baarova, gave way to good will. In the summer of 1942, I had asked him to put his propaganda apparatus to work to speed armaments production. Newsreels, picture magazines, and newspapers were required to publish articles on the subject. My prestige rose. Thanks to this directive by the Propaganda Minister, I became one of the best-known personages in the Reich. This improvement in my status in its turn was useful to my associates in their daily bouts with government and party bureaus.

All of Goebbels's speeches sounded the note of stereotyped fanaticism, but it would be quite wrong to think of him as a hot-blooded man seething with temperament. Goebbels was a hard worker and something of a martinet about the way his ideas were carried out. But he never let the minutiae make him lose sight of the whole situation. He had the gift of abstracting problems from their surrounding circumstances so that, as it seemed to me then, he could arrive at objective judgments. I was impressed by his cynicism, but also by the logical arrangement of his ideas, which revealed his university training. Toward Hitler, however, he seemed extremely constrained.

During the first, successful phase of the war, Goebbels had shown no signs of ambition. On the contrary, as early as 1940 he expressed his intention of devoting himself to his many personal interests once the war was brought to a victorious conclusion. It would then be time for the next generation to assume responsibility, he would say.

In December 1942 the disastrous course of affairs prompted him to invite three of his colleagues to call on him more often: Walther Funk, Robert Ley, and myself. The choice was typical of Goebbels, for we were all men of academic background, university graduates.

Stalingrad had shaken us—not only the tragedy of the Sixth Army's soldiers, but even more, perhaps, the question of how such a disaster could have taken place under Hitler's orders. For hitherto there had always been a success to offset every setback; hitherto there had been a new triumph to compensate for all losses or at least make everyone forget them. Now for the first time we had suffered a defeat for which there was no compensation.

In one of our discussions at the beginning of 1943, Goebbels made the point that we had had great military successes at the beginning of the war while taking only half-measures inside the Reich. Consequently, we had thought we could go on being victorious without great efforts. The British, on the other hand, had been luckier in that Dunkirk had taken place right at the beginning of the war. This defeat had made them aware of the need to tighten up on the civilian economy. Now Stalingrad was our Dunkirk! The war could no longer be won simply by engendering confidence.

In speaking this way Goebbels was referring to the information he had from his band of correspondents concerning the uneasiness and dissatisfaction among the populace. The public was actually demanding a ban on all luxuries, which did not help the national struggle. In general, Goebbels said, he could sense a great readiness among the people to exert themselves to the utmost. In fact, significant restrictions were a real necessity if only to revive popular confidence in the leadership.

From the viewpoint of armaments, considerable sacrifices were certainly required. Hitler had demanded a step-up in production. What was more, in order to compensate for the tremendous casualties on the eastern front, eight hundred thousand of the younger skilled workers were going to be drafted.[1] Every subtraction of the German labor force would add to the difficulties all our factories were encountering.

On the other hand, the air raids had shown that life could continue on an orderly basis in the severely affected cities. Tax revenues for instance went on being paid even after bombs falling on Treasury offices had destroyed the documents. Taking my cue directly from the principle of self-responsibility in industry, I formulated a program which would substitute trust for distrust toward the populace and allow us to trim our supervisory and administrative agencies, which alone employed nearly three million persons. We considered ways in which the taxpayers could be made responsible for their own declarations, or the feasibility of not reassessing liability at all, or for withholding taxes from the payrolls. Given the billions being spent on the war every month, Goebbels and I argued, what did it matter if a few hundred millions were lost to the government due to the dishonesty of some individuals.

A considerably greater stir was created by my demands that the working time of all government officials be extended to match the hours of armaments workers. That alone, in purely arithmetical terms, would have freed some two hundred thousand administrative people for armaments work. Furthermore, I wanted to release several hundreds of thousands of workers by a drastic cut in the living standard of the upper classes. At a meeting of Central Planning, I made no attempt to gloss over the effect my radical proposals would have on the German scene: "This means that for the duration of the war, if it goes on for a long time, we shall be—to put it crudely—proletarianized."[2] Today, I am glad that my plan did not win acceptance. Had it, Germany would have faced the extraordinary burdens of the early postwar months economically even more weakened and administratively more disorganized. But I am also convinced that in England, for example—had she been facing the same situation—such proposals would have been consistently carried out.

We had a hard time persuading a hesitant Hitler that certain austerities were essential, that the administrative apparatus had to be enormously simplified, consumption checked, and cultural activities restricted. But my proposal that Goebbels handle all this was thwarted by an alert Bormann, who feared an increase in power on the part of this rival. Instead of Goebbels, Dr. Lammers, Bormann's ally in the Committee of Three, was assigned the task. He was a government official without initiative or imagination whose hair stood on end at the thought of such disregard for the sacred bureaucratic procedures.

It was also Lammers who from January 1943 on presided over the Cabinet meetings, which were then resumed, in Hitler's stead. Not all members of the Cabinet were invited, only those who were concerned with the subjects on the agenda. But the meeting place, the Cabinet Room, showed what power the Committee of Three had acquired or at any rate intended to acquire.

These meetings turned out quite heated. Goebbels and Funk supported my radical views. Minister of the Interior Frick, as well as Lammers himself, raised the anticipated doubts. Sauckel maintained that he could provide any number of workers requested of him, including skilled personnel, from abroad.[3] Even when Goebbels demanded that leading party members forgo their previous, almost limitless luxuries, he could change nothing. And Eva Braun, ordinarily so unassuming, had no sooner heard of a proposed ban on permanent waves as well as the end of cosmetic production when she rushed to Hitler in high indignation. Hitler at once showed uncertainty. He advised me that instead of an outright ban I quietly stop production of "hair dyes and other items necessary for beauty culture," as well as "cessation of repairs upon apparatus for producing permanent waves."*

After a few meetings in the Chancellery it was clear to Goebbels and me that armaments production would receive no spur from Bormann, Lammers, or Keitel. Our efforts had bogged down in meaningless details.

On February 18, 1943, Goebbels delivered his speech in the Sportpalast on "total war." It was not only directed to the population; it was

* Even Goebbels wavered on the question of cosmetics: "A whole series of individual points are still being debated [by the public], especially the question of feminine beauty care. . . . Perhaps in this case we ought to be somewhat more lenient." (Diary entry for March 12, 1943.) Hitler's recommendation may be found in the *Führerprotokoll*, April 25, 1943, Point 14.

obliquely addressed to the leadership which had ignored all our proposals for a radical commitment of domestic reserves. Basically, it was
an attempt to place Lammers and all the other dawdlers under the pressure of the mob.

Except for Hitler's most successful public meetings, I had never
seen an audience so effectively roused to fanaticism. Back in his home,
Goebbels astonished me by analyzing what had seemed to be a purely
emotional outburst in terms of its psychological effects—much as an
experienced actor might have done. He was also satisfied with his audience that evening. "Did you notice? They reacted to the smallest nuance and applauded at just the right moments. It was the politically
best-trained audience you can find in Germany." This particular crowd
had been rounded up out of the party organizations; among those present were popular intellectuals and actors like Heinrich George whose
applause was caught by the newsreel cameras for the benefit of the
wider public.

But this speech by Goebbels also had a foreign-policy aspect. It
was one of several attempts to supplement Hitler's purely military approach by introducing politics. Goebbels at any rate thought that he
was also pleading with the West to remember the danger which threatened all of Europe from the East. A few days later he expressed great
satisfaction that the Western press had commented favorably upon
these very sentences.

At the time, as a matter of fact, Goebbels seemed interested in becoming Foreign Minister. With all the eloquence at his command he
tried to turn Hitler against Ribbentrop and for a while seemed to be
succeeding. At least Hitler listened in silence to his arguments, without
shifting the conversation to a less unpleasant subject, as was his habit.
Goebbels already thought the game was won when Hitler unexpectedly
began praising Ribbentrop's excellent work and his talent for negotiations with Germany's "allies." He concluded finally with the remarkable statement: "You're altogether wrong about Ribbentrop. He is one
of the greatest men we have, and history will some day place him above
Bismarck. He is greater than Bismarck." Along with this, Hitler forbade Goebbels to extend any more feelers toward the West, as he had
done in his Sportpalast speech.

Nevertheless, Goebbels's speech on "total war" was followed up
by a gesture which was roundly applauded by the public: He had
Berlin's luxury restaurants and expensive places of amusement closed.
Goering, to be sure, promptly interposed his bulk to protect his favorite
restaurant, Horcher's. But when subsequently some demonstrators (set
on by Goebbels) appeared at the restaurant and smashed the windows,
Goering yielded. The result was a serious rift between him and Goebbels.

On the evening after the speech in the Sportpalast mentioned above, many prominent persons assembled in the palatial residence that Goebbels had built shortly before the beginning of the war near the Brandenburg Gate. Among those present were Field Marshal Milch, Minister of Justice Thierack, State Secretary Stuckart of the Ministry of the Interior, Goering's right-hand man, State Secretary Körner, and Funk and Ley. For the first time a motion proposed by Milch and myself was discussed: to use Goering's powers as "Chairman of the Council of Ministers for the Defense of the Reich" in order to stiffen the home front.

Nine days later Goebbels invited me to his home again, together with Funk and Ley. The huge building with its rich appointments now gave a gloomy appearance. In order to provide a good example of acting in the spirit of "total war," Goebbels had had the large public rooms closed and most of the electric bulbs removed in the remaining halls and rooms. We were asked into one of the smaller rooms, perhaps four hundred fifty square feet in area. Servants in livery served French cognac and tea; then Goebbels signaled to them to leave us undisturbed.

"Things cannot go on this way," he began. "Here we are sitting in Berlin. Hitler does not hear what we have to say about the situation. I cannot influence him politically, cannot even report the most urgent measures in my area. Everything goes through Bormann. Hitler must be persuaded to come to Berlin more often."

Domestic policy, Goebbels continued, had slipped entirely out of Hitler's hands. It was being controlled by Bormann, who managed to give Hitler the feeling that he was still directing things. Bormann, Goebbels said further, was guided only by ambition; with his rigidly doctrinaire approach, he represented a great danger to any sane evolution of policy. First and foremost his influence must be diminished!

Altogether contrary to his habit, Goebbels did not even except Hitler from his critical remarks. "We are not having a 'leadership crisis,' but strictly speaking a 'Leader crisis'!"[4] To Goebbels, a born politician, it was incomprehensible that Hitler should have abandoned politics, that most important of instruments, in favor of playing a superfluous role as Commander in Chief.

The rest of us could only agree; none of us could hold a candle to Goebbels where political instinct was concerned. His criticism showed what Stalingrad really meant. Goebbels had begun to doubt Hitler's star, and hence his victory—and we were doubting with him.

I repeated the proposal we had made: that Goering be reinstalled in the function that had been intended for him at the beginning of the war. Here was an organizational position equipped with the fullest powers, including the right to issue decrees even without Hitler's collaboration. From this post the power usurped by Bormann and Lammers could be shattered. Bormann and Lammers would have to bow to this existing authority whose potentialities had so far gone untapped because of Goering's indolence.

Since Goebbels and Goering were on bad terms because of the Horcher's Restaurant incident,* the group asked me to speak with Goering about the matter.

The present-day reader may well wonder why, when we were making a last effort to rally all our forces, our choice should have fallen on this man who had done nothing but loll about in apathetic luxury for years. Goering had not always been this way, and his reputation of an admittedly violent but also energetic and intelligent person still lingered on from the days when he had built up the air force and the Four-Year Plan. There seemed a chance that if a task appealed to him he might recover some of his old daring and energy. And if not, we reckoned, then the committee of the Reich Defense Council would in any case constitute an instrument that could make radical decisions.

Only in retrospect do I realize that stripping Bormann and Lammers of power would hardly have changed the course of events. For the shift in direction we wanted to bring about could not be achieved by overthrowing Hitler's secretaries but solely by turning against Hitler himself. For us, however, that was beyond imagination. Instead, if we had succeeded in restoring our personal positions which were endangered by Bormann, we would presumably have been ready to follow Hitler even more loyally than before, if possible; more so than we actually did under the cowardly Lammers and the scheming Bormann. The fact that we regarded minimal differences as so important merely shows in how closed a world we all moved.

This was the first time I emerged from my reserve as a specialist to plunge into political maneuvering. I had always carefully avoided such a step; but the fact that I took it now had a certain logic. I had decided that it was wrong to imagine I could concentrate exclusively upon my specialized work. In an authoritarian system anyone who wants to remain part of the leadership inevitably stumbles into fields of force where political battles are in progress.

Goering was staying in his summer house at Obersalzberg. As I learned from Field Marshal Milch, he had deliberately withdrawn there for a rather long vacation because he was offended by Hitler's criticisms of his leadership of the air force. I went to see him the day after our meeting, February 28, 1943. He was prepared at once to receive me.

The atmosphere of our discussion, which lasted for many hours, was friendly and unconstrained, in keeping with the intimate conditions of the relatively small house. I was astonished, though, by his lacquered fingernails and obviously rouged face, although the oversize ruby

---

* The dispute between Goebbels and Goering over the restaurant was resolved as follows: The restaurant remained closed as a public restaurant, but it reopened as a club for the Luftwaffe.

brooch on his green velvet dressing gown was already a familiar sight to me.

Goering listened quietly to our proposal and to my report of our Berlin conference. As he sat he occasionally scooped a handful of unset gems from his pocket and playfully let them glide through his fingers. It seemed to delight him that we had thought of him. He too saw the danger in the way things were going with Bormann and agreed with our plans. But he was still angry with Goebbels because of the Horcher incident, until I finally proposed that he personally invite the Propaganda Minister here, so that we could thoroughly discuss our plan with him.

Goebbels came to Berchtesgaden the very next day. I first informed him of the result of my discussion. Together, we drove to Goering's, where I soon withdrew to let the two men, whose relations had been almost continually strained, have it out. When I was called in again, Goering rubbed his hands with delight at the prospect of the struggle that was about to begin and showed his most engaging side. First of all, he said, the personnel of the Council of Ministers for the Defense of the Reich must be broadened. Goebbels and I ought to become members; the fact that we were not, by the way, indicated that the council was of little importance.

There was also talk about the necessity for replacing Ribbentrop. The Foreign Minister should be persuading Hitler to adopt a rational policy, but instead he was too much Hitler's mouthpiece to find a political solution for our sorry military predicament.

Growing more and more excited, Goebbels continued: "The Fuehrer has not seen through Lammers any more than he has seen through Ribbentrop."

Goering sprang to his feet. "He's always putting in a word edgewise, torpedoing me below the water line. But that's ending right now! I'm going to see to it, gentlemen!"

Goebbels was obviously relishing Goering's rage and deliberately trying to spur him on, while at the same time fearing some rash act on the part of the tactically unskilled Reich Marshal. "Depend on it, Herr Goering, we are going to open the Fuehrer's eyes about Bormann and Lammers. Only we mustn't risk going too far. We'll have to proceed slowly. You know the Fuehrer." His caution increased as he spoke: "At any rate we had better not talk too openly with the other members of the Council of Ministers. There's no need for them to know that we intend to slowly spike the Committee of Three. We're simply acting out of loyalty to the Fuehrer. We have no personal ambitions. But if each one of us supports the others to the Fuehrer we'll soon be on top of the situation and can form a solid fence around the Fuehrer."

Goebbels was highly pleased by the time he left. "This is going to work," he said to me. "Goering has really come to life again, don't you think?"

I too had not seen Goering so dynamic and bold in recent years. On a long walk in the peaceful vicinity of Obersalzberg, Goering and I discussed the course Bormann had taken. Goering maintained that Bormann was aiming at nothing less than the succession to Hitler, and that he would stop at nothing to outmaneuver him, Goering—in fact, all of us—in influencing Hitler. I took occasion to tell Goering how Bormann seized every opportunity to undermine the Reich Marshal's prestige. Goering listened with mounting feeling as I spoke of the tea-times with Hitler at Obersalzberg, from which Goering was excluded. There I had been able to observe Bormann's tactics at close vantage.

He never worked by direct attack, I said. Instead, he would weave little incidents into his conversation which were effective only in their sum. Thus, for example, in the course of the teatime chatter Bormann would tell unfavorable anecdotes from Vienna in order to damage Baldur von Schirach, the Hitler Youth leader. But Bormann carefully avoided agreeing with Hitler's subsequent negative remarks. On the contrary, he thought it prudent to praise Schirach afterward—the kind of praise, of course, which would leave an unpleasant aftertaste. After about a year of this sort of thing Bormann had brought Hitler to the point of disliking Schirach and often feeling outright hostility toward him. Then—when Hitler was not around—Bormann could venture to go a step further. With an air of casually dismissing the matter but in reality annihilating the man, he would remark contemptuously that of course Schirach belonged in Vienna since everybody there was always intriguing against everybody else. Bormann would be playing the same sort of game against Goering, I added in conclusion.

The trouble was that Goering was an easy mark for this sort of thing. In the course of these days at Obersalzberg, Goebbels himself spoke somewhat apologetically of the "baroque garments" Goering favored which did seem rather comical to anyone who did not know the Reich Marshal. And then Goering continued to comport himself with sovereign dignity, forgetful of his failures as Commander in Chief of the Air Force. Much later, in the spring of 1945, when Hitler publicly insulted his Reich Marshal in the most cutting manner before all the participants in the situation conference, Goering remarked to Below, Hitler's air force adjutant: "Speer was right when he warned me. Now Bormann has succeeded."

Goering was mistaken. Bormann had already done his work by the spring of 1943.

A few days later, on March 5, 1943, I flew to headquarters to obtain several decisions on armaments questions from Hitler. My chief purpose, however, was to promote our little plot. I found it easy to persuade Hitler to invite Goebbels to headquarters. Things were especially dreary, and he looked forward to a visit from the sprightly, clever Propaganda Minister.

Three days later Goebbels arrived at headquarters. He first took me aside. "What is the Fuehrer's mood, Herr Speer?" he asked. I had to tell him that Hitler was not feeling particularly warm toward Goering at this juncture and advised restraint. It would probably be better not to press the matter right now, I thought. Consequently, after briefly feeling my way, I had done nothing further. Goebbels agreed: "You're probably right. At the moment we had better not mention Goering to the Fuehrer. That would spoil everything."

The massed Allied air raids, which had been going on for weeks and meeting almost no opposition, had further weakened Goering's already imperiled position. If Goering's name was as much as mentioned, Hitler would start fuming at the mistakes and omissions in the planning for air warfare. That very day Hitler had repeatedly exclaimed that if the bombings went on not only would the cities be destroyed, but the morale of the people would crack irreparably. Hitler was succumbing to the same error as the British strategists on the other side who were ordering mass bombing.

Hitler invited Goebbels and me to lunch. Oddly enough, on such occasions he refrained from asking Bormann—who was otherwise indispensable—to join him. In this respect he treated Bormann entirely as a secretary. Enlivened by Goebbels, Hitler became considerably more talkative than I was accustomed to seeing him on my visits to headquarters. He used the opportunity to unburden his mind and as usual made disparaging remarks about almost all of his associates except those of us who were present.

After the meal I was dismissed, and Hitler spent several hours alone with Goebbels. The fact that Hitler courteously and amicably showed me out corresponded with his way of sharply separating individuals and areas. I did not return until it was time for the military situation conference. At supper we met again, this time all three of us. Hitler had a fire made in the fireplace; the orderly brought us a bottle of wine, and Fachinger mineral water for Hitler. We sat up until early morning in a relaxed, almost cozy atmosphere. I did not have a chance to say much, for Goebbels knew how to entertain Hitler: He spoke brilliantly, in polished phrases, with irony at the right place and admiration where Hitler expected it, with sentimentality when the moment and the subject required it, with gossip and love affairs. He mixed everything in a masterly brew: theater, movies, and old times. But Hitler also listened with eager interest —as always—to a detailed account of the children of the Goebbels family. Their childish remarks, their favorite games, their frequently pungent comments, distracted Hitler from his cares that night.

By recalling earlier periods of difficulty which one way or another had been overcome, Goebbels contrived to strengthen Hitler's self-assurance and to flatter his vanity, which the sober tone of the military men hardly pampered. Hitler, for his part, reciprocated by magnifying his Propaganda Minister's achievements and thus giving him cause for pride. In general the leaders of the Third Reich were fond of mutual praise and were continually reassuring one another.

In spite of certain qualms, Goebbels and I had agreed beforehand that somewhere in the course of the evening we would bring up our plans for activating the Council of Ministers for the Defense of the Reich, or at least drop some hints about it. The atmosphere certainly seemed favorable—though there was always the danger that Hitler might take such suggestions as a criticism of the way he was running things—when suddenly this idyll at the fireplace was interrupted by the report of a heavy air raid on Nuremberg. As if he had guessed our intention—perhaps, too, he had been warned by Bormann—Hitler put on a scene such as I had seldom witnessed. He immediately had Brigadier General Bodenschatz, Goering's chief adjutant, hauled out of bed and brought before him, where the poor man had to take a terrible tongue-lashing on behalf of the "incompetent Reich Marshal." Goebbels and I tried to soothe Hitler, and finally he did calm down. But all our spadework had obviously been in vain. Goebbels, too, thought it advisable to give the subject wide berth for the present. Nevertheless, after Hitler's many expressions of appreciation he felt that his political stock had risen considerably. Afterward, he no longer spoke of a "Leader crisis." On the contrary, it even seemed as if he had recovered his old confidence in Hitler. But we still had to go on with the struggle against Bormann, he decided.

On March 17, Goebbels, Funk, Ley, and I met with Goering in the latter's Berlin palace on Leipziger Platz. At first Goering received us in his office, adopting his most official manner—planted behind his enormous desk on his Renaissance throne. We sat facing him on uncomfortable chairs. Initially, there was no sign of the cordiality he had shown at Obersalzberg. It rather seemed as if Goering had repented of his candor.

But while the rest of us sat silent for the most part, Goering and Goebbels aroused each other by outlining the perils presented by that triumvirate around Hitler and by devising schemes for recapturing Hitler for ourselves. Goebbels seemed to have forgotten completely how Hitler had lashed into Goering only a few days earlier. Soon both of them saw their goal within reach. Goering, alternating as always between torpor and euphoria, was already beginning to discount the influence of the headquarters clique. "We mustn't overestimate it either, Herr Goebbels! Bormann and Keitel are nothing but the Fuehrer's secretaries, after all. Who do they think they are! As far as their own powers are concerned, they're nobodies."

What seemed to disturb Goebbels most was the possibility that

Bormann might utilize his direct contacts with the Gauleiters to build up bases against our efforts on the home front also. I recall the way Goebbels tried to enlist Ley against Bormann in his capacity of Organization Chief of the Party. Finally, Goebbels proposed that the Council of Ministers for the Defense of the Reich must be given the right to summon Gauleiters and call them to account. Fully aware that Goering would scarcely attend the sessions so often, he proposed weekly meetings. Casually, he added that probably it would be all right, wouldn't it, if he acted as deputy chairman if Goering were sometimes unable to attend.[5] Goering did not see through Goebbels's machinations and consented. Behind the fronts of the great struggle for power the old rivalries continued to smolder.

For a considerable time the numbers of workers whom Sauckel claimed to have sent into industry, statistics which he reported to Hitler, had ceased to correspond with the actual figures. The difference amounted to several hundred thousand. I proposed to our coalition that we join forces in compelling Sauckel, Bormann's outpost in our territory, as it were, to report truthful data.

At Hitler's request a large building in the rustic Bavarian style had been erected near Berchtesgaden to house the Berlin Chancellery secretariat. Whenever Hitler stayed at Obersalzberg for months at a time, Lammers and his immediate staff conducted the business of the Chancellery there. Goering arranged for Lammers as the host to invite our group, as well as Sauckel and Milch, to meet in the conference room of this building on April 12, 1943. Before the meeting Milch and I once more reminded Goering of what we wanted. He rubbed his hands: "That will soon be taken care of!"

We were surprised to find that Himmler, Bormann, and Keitel were also in the conference room. And to make matters worse, our ally Goebbels sent his apologies: On the way to Berchtesgaden he had suffered an attack of kidney colic and was lying ill in his special car. To this day I don't know whether this was true or whether he merely had an instinct for what was going to happen.

That session marked the end of our alliance. Sauckel simply challenged our demand for an additional two million, one hundred thousand workers for the entire economy, insisted that he had delivered the needed forces, and became furious when I charged that his figures could not be accurate.*

* Later we learned from General Roesch, our armaments inspector for Upper Bavaria, that Sauckel had directed his employment bureaus to list every worker who was assigned to a factory as placed, even if the worker turned out to be unqualified for the particular job and was sent back to the bureau. The factories, on the other hand, listed only those workers who were actually hired.

Milch and I expected that Goering would ask Sauckel for explanations and make him change his labor-assignment policy. Instead, to our horror Goering began with a violent attack upon Milch, and thus indirectly upon me. It was outrageous that Milch was making so many difficulties, he said. Our good party comrade Sauckel who was exerting himself to the utmost and had achieved such successes. . . . He at any rate felt a great debt of gratitude toward him. Milch was simply blind to Sauckel's achievements.

It was as though Goering had picked out the wrong phonograph record. In the ensuing prolonged discussion on the missing workers, each of the ministers present offered explanations, on entirely theoretical grounds, of the difference between the real and the official figures. Himmler commented with the greatest calm that perhaps the missing hundreds of thousands had died.

The conference proved a total failure. No light was thrown on the question of the missing labor force, and in addition our grand assault on Bormann had come to grief.

After this meeting Goering took me aside. "I know you like to work closely with my state secretary, Milch," he said. "In all friendship I'd like to warn you against him. He's unreliable; as soon as his own interests are in question, he'll trample over even his best friends."

I immediately passed this remark on to Milch. He laughed. "A few days ago Goering told me exactly the same thing about you."

This attempt on Goering's part to sow distrust was the very opposite of what we had agreed on: that we would form a bloc. The sad fact was that our circles were so infected by suspicion that friendship was felt to be a threat.

A few days after this affair Milch commented that Goering had switched sides because the Gestapo had proof of his drug addiction. Quite some time before Milch had suggested to me that I look closely at Goering's pupils. At the Nuremberg Trial my attorney, Dr. Flächsner, told me that Goering had been an addict long before 1933. Flächsner had acted as his lawyer once when he was sued for improperly administering a morphine injection.*

Our attempt to mobilize Goering against Bormann was probably doomed to failure from the start for financial reasons as well. For as was later revealed by a Nuremberg document, Bormann had made Goering a gift of six million marks from the industrialists' Adolf Hitler Fund.

After the collapse of our alliance, Goering actually bestirred himself for a while, but, surprisingly, his activity was directed against me. Contrary to his habit, a few weeks later he asked me to invite the leading

---

* A lady's dress caught fire in a night club. Goering gave her an injection of morphine to relieve the pain. But the injection left a scar and the woman sued Goering.

men in the steel industry to a conference at Obersalzberg. The meeting took place at the drafting tables in my studio and was memorable only because of Goering's behavior. He appeared in an euphoric mood, his pupils visibly narrowed, and delivered to the astonished specialists from the steel industry a long lecture on the manufacture of steel, parading all his knowledge of blast furnaces and metallurgy. There followed a succession of commonplaces: We had to produce more, must not shun innovations; industry was frozen in tradition, must learn to jump over its own shadow; and more of the like. At the end of his two-hour torrent of bombast, Goering's speech slowed and his expression grew more and more absent. Finally, he abruptly put his head on the table and fell peacefully asleep. We thought it politic to pretend to ignore the splendidly uniformed Reich Marshal and proceeded to discuss our problems until he awoke again and curtly declared the meeting over.

For next day Goering had announced a conference on radar problems which likewise ended with nothing accomplished. Once again, in the best of humor, he gave endless explanations in his Imperial Majesty style, telling the specialists what they already knew and he knew nothing about. Finally, there came a spate of directives and injunctions. After he had left the meeting, highly pleased with himself, I had my hands full undoing the damage he had done, while somehow avoiding an outright disavowal of Goering. Nevertheless, the incident was so serious that I was compelled to inform Hitler about it. He seized the next opportunity to summon the industrialists to headquarters on May 13, 1943, in order to restore the government's prestige.[*]

A few months after this setback to our plans I ran into Himmler at headquarters. Bluntly, in a threatening voice, he said to me: "I think it would be very unwise of you to try to activate the Reich Marshal again!"

But that was no longer possible in any case. Goering had relapsed into his lethargy, and for good. He did not wake up again until he was on trial in Nuremberg.

---

[*] In an unpublished diary passage, May 15, 1943, Goebbels wrote: "He [Hitler] spent the whole day conferring with the captains of the armaments industry on the measures that must be taken now. This conference with the Fuehrer was intended to salve the wounds left by Goering's latest, rather unfortunate conference. Goering's tactical blunders offended the armaments manufacturers. The Fuehrer has now straightened that out."

19

Second Man in the State

AROUND THE BEGINNING OF MAY 1943, A FEW WEEKS AFTER THE DEMISE OF our short-lived association, Goebbels was finding in Bormann the qualities he had ascribed to Goering a few weeks before. The two came to an arrangement—Goebbels promising to direct reports to Hitler through Bormann, in return for Bormann's extracting the right sort of decision from Hitler. It was clear that Goebbels had written Goering off; he would support him henceforth only as a prestige figurehead.

Thus actual power had shifted still more in Bormann's favor. Nevertheless, he had no way of knowing whether he might not need me some day. Although he must have heard of my ill-fated attempt to dethrone him, he behaved amiably toward me and hinted that I could come over to his camp as Goebbels had done. I did not avail myself of this offer, however. The price seemed to me too high: I would have become dependent upon him.

Goebbels, too, continued to remain in close contact with me, for both of us were still bent on making utmost use of our domestic reserves. Undoubtedly, I behaved much too trustfully in my relations with him. I was fascinated by his dazzling friendliness and perfect manners, as well as by his cool logic.

Outwardly, then, little had changed. The world in which we lived forced upon us dissimulation and hypocrisy. Among rivals an honest word was rarely spoken, for fear it would be carried back to Hitler in a distorted version. Everyone conspired, took Hitler's capriciousness into his reckonings, and won or lost in the course of this cryptic game. I played on this out-of-tune keyboard of mutual relations just as unscrupulously as all the others.

In the second half of May, Goering sent word to me that he wanted to make a speech on armaments, together with me, in the Sportpalast. I agreed. A few days later, however, Hitler to my surprise appointed Goebbels as the speaker. When we were coordinating our texts, the Propaganda Minister advised me to shorten my speech, since his would take an hour. "If you don't stay considerably under half an hour, the audience will lose interest." As usual, we sent both speeches to Hitler in manuscript, with a note to the effect that mine was going to be condensed by a third. Hitler ordered me to come to Obersalzberg. While I was sitting by, he read the drafts Bormann handed to him. With what seemed to me eagerness, he ruthlessly cut Goebbels's speech by half within a few minutes. "Here, Bormann, inform the Doctor and tell him that I think Speer's speech excellent." In the presence of the arch-intriguer Bormann, Hitler had thus helped me to increase my prestige vis-à-vis Goebbels. It was a way of letting both men know that I still stood high. I could count on Hitler's supporting me, if need be, against his closest associates.

My speech on June 5, 1943, in which I could for the first time announce a sizable increase in armaments production, was a failure on two scores. From the party hierarchy I heard such comments as: "So it can be done without big sacrifices! Then why should we upset the populace by drastic measures?" The General Staff and the frontline commanders, on the other hand, doubted the truth of my statistics whenever they had supply difficulties with ammunition or ordnance.

The Soviet winter offensive had ground to a halt. Our increased production enabled us to close the gap on the eastern front. What is more, the delivery of new weapons encouraged Hitler to make preparations for an offensive in spite of the winter's losses of matériel. The objective was to cut off a bend in the line near Kursk. The beginning of this offensive was prepared under the code name "Operation Citadel." It kept being postponed because Hitler counted heavily on the effectiveness of the new tanks. Above all he was expecting wonders from a new type of tank with electric drive constructed by Professor Porsche.

At a simple supper in a small back room of the Chancellery furnished in peasant style, I by chance heard from Sepp Dietrich, the commander of Hitler's bodyguard, that Hitler intended to issue an order that this time no prisoners were to be taken. In the course of advances by SS units it had been established, Dietrich said, that the Soviet troops had killed their German prisoners. Hitler had then and there announced that a thousandfold retaliation in blood must be taken.

I was thunderstruck. But I was also selfishly alarmed at the sheer wastefulness of such a step. Hitler was counting on hundreds of thousands of prisoners. For months we had been trying in vain to close a gap of hundreds of thousands in the supply of labor. I therefore took the first opportunity to reason with Hitler on this score. It was not difficult to persuade him to reconsider; he seemed rather relieved to be able to withdraw his pledge to the SS. That same day, July 8, 1943, he had Keitel prepare instructions to the effect that all prisoners must be sent into armaments production.[1]

The disagreement over the fate of prisoners proved to be unnecessary. The offensive began on July 5, but in spite of the formidable array of our most advanced weapons we were not able to encircle the Soviet forces. Hitler's confidence had been mistaken. After two weeks of battle he gave up. This failure was a sign that even in the summer the initiative had passed to the enemy.

After the second winter disaster at Stalingrad, the Army High Command had urged the establishing of a defensive position far to the rear, but Hitler would not hear of it. Now, after the thwarted offensive, even Hitler was ready to prepare defensive positions from twelve to fifteen miles behind the main line of battle.[2] The General Staff made a counterproposal: establishing the defensive line on the west bank of the Dnieper where the steep slope, over a hundred and fifty feet high, dominated the plain across the river. There would presumably have been sufficient time for building an extensive defensive line there, for the Dnieper was still some one hundred twenty-five miles behind the front. But Hitler flatly rejected this plan. Whereas during his successful campaigns he had always hailed the German soldiers as the best in the world, he now declared: "Building a position so far to the rear is not possible for psychological reasons. If the troops learn that there are fortified positions perhaps sixty miles behind the front line, no one will be able to persuade them to fight. At the first opportunity they'll fall back without resistance."[3]

In spite of this ban, on Manstein's orders and with the tacit consent of Zeitzler, the Todt Organization began building fortified positions on the Bug in December 1943. Hitler found out about this from my deputy, Dorsch. At this time the Soviet armies were still some one hundred to one hundred and twenty-five miles east of the Bug River. And once again Hitler commanded, in unusually strong language and on the same grounds as before, that the work be stopped at once.* This building of rear positions, he stormed, was proof again of the defeatist attitude of Manstein and his army group.

* Jodl's unpublished diary (entry for December 16, 1943) describes the outcome of this unauthorized action: "Dorsch reported the deployment of the Todt Organization along the Bug, something of which the Fuehrer had known nothing. . . . The Fuehrer spoke agitatedly to Minister Speer and me about the defeatist mood of Manstein's staff, which Gauleiter Koch had described to him."

Hitler's obstinacy made it easier for the Soviet troops to harass our armies. For in Russia digging became impossible once the ground froze in November. What time we had was squandered. The soldiers were exposed with no defenses to the weather; moreover our winter equipment was of poor quality compared to that of the enemy.

Such behavior was not the only indication that Hitler had refused to acknowledge the turn of affairs. In the spring of 1943 he had demanded that a three-mile-long road and railroad bridge be built across the Strait of Kerch, although we had long been building a cable railway there; it went into operation on June 14 with a daily capacity of one thousand tons. This amount of supplies just sufficed for the defensive needs of the Seventeenth Army. But Hitler had not forsaken his plan to push through the Caucasus to Persia. He justified his order for the bridge explicitly on the necessity to transport matériel and troops to the Kuban bridgehead for an offensive.* His generals, however, had long put any such ideas out of their heads. On a visit to the Kuban bridgehead the frontline generals expressed anxiety over whether the positions could be held at all in the face of the enemy's obvious strength. When I reported these fears to Hitler he said contemptuously: "Nothing but empty evasions! Jänicke is just like the General Staff; he hasn't faith in a new offensive."

Shortly afterward, in the summer of 1943, General Jänicke, commander of the Seventeenth Army, was forced to ask Zeitzler to recommend retreat from the exposed Kuban bridgehead. He wanted to take up a more favorable position in the Crimea to be ready for the expected Soviet winter offensive. Hitler, on the other hand, insisted even more obstinately than before that the building of the bridge for his offensive plans must be speeded. Even at that time it was clear that the bridge would never be completed. On September 4, the last German units began evacuating Hitler's bridgehead on the continent of Asia.

Just as we had met at Goering's house to discuss overcoming the crisis in political leadership, Guderian, Zeitzler, Fromm, and I were now talking about the military leadership crisis. In the summer of 1943, General Guderian, Inspector General of the Tank Forces, asked me to set up a meeting with army Chief of Staff Zeitzler. There had been some disputes between the two men, springing from unresolved jurisdictional questions. Since I had something approaching a friendly relationship with both generals, it was natural to ask me to play the part of go-between. But it turned out that Guderian had more in mind than the settlement of minor disputes.

* Because of the frequency of earth tremors, provision had to be made for extra-strength girders which would have required vast quantities of precious steel. In addition, as Zeitzler pointed out during the situation conference, if we transported building materials for the bridge over the inadequate railroad facilities of the Crimea, we would be forced to curtail the shipments needed to maintain our defensive positions.

He wanted to discuss common tactics in regard to the matter of a new Commander in Chief of the army. We met in my home at Obersalzberg.

The differences between Zeitzler and Guderian quickly dwindled to nothing. The conversation centered on the situation that had arisen from Hitler's assuming command of the army but not exercising it. The interests of the army as against the two other branches of the service and the SS must be represented more vigorously, Zeitzler thought. Hitler, as Commander in Chief of the armed forces, ought to remain non-partisan. A Commander in Chief of the army, Guderian added, had to maintain close personal contact with the army commanders. He should be looking out for the needs of his troops and deciding fundamental questions of supply. But Hitler, both men agreed, had neither the time nor the inclination to act on this practical level, nor to uphold the special interests of one branch of the service. He appointed and deposed generals whom he hardly knew. Only a Commander in Chief who associated with his higher-ranking officers on a personal basis could decide such questions of personnel. The army knew, Guderian said, that Hitler scarcely interfered in the personnel policies of his Commanders in Chief of the air force and the navy. Only the army was exposed to this sort of treatment.

We came to the conclusion that each of us would try to appeal to Hitler to appoint a new Commander in Chief of the army. But the very first hints that Guderian and I separately made to Hitler came to grief; he was obviously offended and rejected the idea in unusually sharp terms. I did not know that shortly before we spoke Field Marshals von Kluge and von Manstein had undertaken a similar probe on the same subject. Hitler must have assumed that we were all in collusion.

The time when Hitler readily granted all my personal and organizational requests was long since past. The triumvirate of Bormann, Lammers, and Keitel was doing its best to block any further extension of my power, even though concern for the armaments program might have dictated the opposite. However, there was little these three could do against the joint proposal by Admiral Doenitz and myself that we also assume control of naval armaments.

I had met Doenitz immediately after my appointment in June 1942. The then commander of the U-boat fleet received me in Paris in an apartment which struck me at once by its avant-garde severity. I was all the more taken with the plain surroundings since I had just come from an opulent lunch with many courses and expensive wines given by Field Marshal Sperrle, commander of the air forces stationed in France. He had set up headquarters in the Palais du Luxembourg, the former palace of Marie de Médicis. The Field Marshal's craving for luxury and public display ran a close second to that of his superior Goering; he was also his match in corpulence.

INSIDE THE THIRD REICH (272

During the next several months problems connected with the building of the large U-boat pens along the Atlantic brought Doenitz and me together several times. Admiral Raeder, Commander in Chief of the navy, seemed to be annoyed. He tartly forbade Doenitz to discuss technical questions directly with me.

At the end of December 1942, Captain Schütze, the successful U-boat commander, informed me of serious dissension between the Berlin navy command and Doenitz. From various signs and portents, Schütze said, the submarine fleet knew that their commander was going to be relieved in the near future. A few days later I heard from State Secretary Naumann that the navy censor in the Propaganda Ministry had stricken the name of Doenitz from the captions of all press photos showing an inspection tour undertaken jointly by Raeder and Doenitz.

When I was in headquarters at the beginning of January, Hitler was worked up over foreign press reports of a naval battle which the navy command had not informed him about in detail.* As if by chance, in our subsequent conference he raised the question of the feasibility of assembly-line building of U-boats, but soon he became more interested in the troubles I was having in my collaboration with Raeder. I told him of the stricture against my discussing technical questions with Doenitz, of the U-boat officers' fears that their commander was going to be replaced, and of the censorship of the photo captions. By now I had learned, from watching Bormann's tactics, that one had to plant suspicions very carefully and gradually for them to be effective with Hitler. Any direct attempt to influence him was hopeless, since he never accepted a decision which he thought had been imposed on him. Therefore I merely hinted that all obstacles standing in the way of our U-boat plans could be eliminated if Doenitz were given his head. Actually, what I wanted to achieve was the replacement of Raeder. But knowing the tenacity with which Hitler clung to his old associates I hardly hoped that I would succeed.

On January 30, Doenitz was named Grand Admiral and simultaneously appointed Commander in Chief of the navy, while Raeder was kicked upstairs: He became Admiral Inspector of the navy, which entitled him solely to the privilege of a state funeral.

By resolute expertise and technical arguments, Doenitz was able to protect the navy from Hitler's whims until the end of the war. I met with him frequently to discuss the problems of building submarines—despite the fact that this close cooperation began with a foul-up. Without consulting me, after hearing a report from Doenitz, Hitler raised all naval armament to the highest priority. This happened in the middle of April, but only three months before, on January 22, 1943, he had already classi-

* This was the naval battle that took place December 31, 1942. Hitler held that the *Lützow* and the *Hipper* had retreated in the face of weaker English forces. He accused the navy of lacking fighting spirit.

fied the expanded tank program as the task of highest priority. The upshot was that two programs would be competing. It was unnecessary for me to appeal to Hitler again. Before any controversy developed, Doenitz had already realized that cooperation with the massive apparatus of army procurement would be more useful than Hitler's favoritism. We soon agreed to transfer naval armaments production to my organization. In taking this on, I pledged myself to carry out the naval program Doenitz had envisaged. This meant, instead of the previous monthly production of twenty submarines of the smaller type totaling sixteen thousand tons displacement, producing forty U-boats per month with a displacement totaling more than fifty thousand tons. In addition I was to double the number of minesweepers and PT boats.

Doenitz had made it clear that only the production of a new type of U-boat could save our submarine warfare. The navy wanted to abandon the previous type of "surface ship" which occasionally moved under water. It wanted to give its U-boats the best possible streamlining and attain a higher underwater speed and a greater underwater range by doubling the power of the electric motors and simplifying the system of storage batteries.

As always in such cases, the chief problem was to find the right director for this assignment. I chose a fellow Swabian, Otto Merker, who had hitherto proved his talents in the building of fire engines. Here was a challenge to all marine engineers. On July 5, 1943, Merker presented his new construction system to the heads of the navy. As was being done in the production of Liberty ships in the United States, the submarines were to be built in inland factories, where the machinery and electrical equipment would also be installed. They were then to be transported in sections to the coast and quickly assembled there. We would thus avoid the problem of the shipyards, whose limited facilities had so far stood in the way of any expansion of our shipbuilding programs.[4] Doenitz sounded almost emotional when he declared, at the end of our conference: "This means we are beginning a new life."

For the time being, however, we had nothing but a vision of what the new U-boats would look like. In order to design them and to settle on the details, a development commission was established. Its chairman was not a leading engineer, as was customary, but Admiral Topp, whom Doenitz assigned to this task without our even attempting to clarify the complicated questions that arose as a result. The cooperation between Topp and Merker worked out as easily as that between Doenitz and myself.

Barely four months after the first session of the development commission—on November 11, 1943—all the drawings were finished. A month later Doenitz and I were able to inspect and even walk inside a wooden model of the large new sixteen hundred ton submarine. Even while the blueprints were being prepared, our Directive Committee for Shipbuilding was assigning contracts to industry—a procedure we had already used in speeding up the production of the new Panther tank. Thanks to all this, the first seaworthy U-boats of the new type were delivered to the navy for testing in 1944. We would have been able to keep our promise of delivering forty boats a month by early in 1945, however badly the war was going otherwise, if air raids had not destroyed a third of the submarines at the dockyards.[5]

At the time, Doenitz and I often asked ourselves why we had not begun building the new type of U-boat earlier. For no technical innovations were employed; the engineering principles had been known for years. The new boats, so the experts assured us, would have revolutionized submarine warfare. This fact seemed to be appreciated by the American navy, which after the war began building the new type for itself.

On July 26, 1943, three days after Doenitz and I signed our joint decree on the new naval program, I obtained Hitler's consent to placing all production under my Ministry. For tactical reasons I had asked for this on the grounds of the additional burdens which the naval program and other tasks required by Hitler were imposing upon industry. By transforming large consumer goods plants into armaments plants, I explained to Hitler, we would not only free half a million German workers but also enlist the industrial managers and the factory machinery in our urgent programs. Most of the Gauleiters, however, objected to such measures. The Ministry of Economics had proved too weak to enforce such shifts against the opposition of the Gauleiters. And, to jump a bit ahead in the story, I also was too weak, as I was soon forced to realize.

After an unusually protracted procedure, in which all the ministers involved and all the various boards of the Four-Year Plan were requested to hand in their objections, Lammers convoked the ministers for a meeting in the Cabinet Room on August 26. Thanks to the generosity of Funk, who at this meeting "delivered his own funeral oration with wit and humor," it was unanimously agreed that from now on all war production would be placed under the control of my Ministry. Willy-nilly, Lammers had to promise to communicate this result to Hitler via Bormann. A few days later Funk and I went to the Fuehrer's headquarters together to receive Hitler's final authorization.

Greatly to my surprise, however, Hitler, in Funk's presence, cut short my remarks, saying irritably that he would not listen to any further explanations. Only a few hours ago Bormann had warned him, he said, that I was going to lure him into signing something that had been discussed neither with Reich Minister Lammers nor with the Reich Marshal. He was not going to be drawn into our little rivalries. When I tried to explain that Reich Minister Lammers had properly obtained the consent of Goering's state secretary for the Four-Year Plan, Hitler again cut me off with unaccustomed curtness: "I am glad that in Bormann at least I have a faithful soul around me." The implication was clear: He was accusing me of trickery.

Funk informed Lammers of the incident. Then we went to meet Goering, who was on the way to Hitler's headquarters in his private car; he had just come from his personal hunting preserve, the Rominten Heath. Goering, too, was very huffy; undoubtedly he had been told only one side of the story and had been warned against us. Funk, amiable and persuasive, finally succeeded in breaking the ice and going over our decree point by point. And now Goering indicated full agreement, though not before we had inserted a sentence: "The powers of the Reich Marshal of the Greater German Reich as Commissioner General for the Four-Year Plan remain unaffected." In practice that was a very minor reservation—all the more so since most of the important functions of the Four-Year Plan were directed by me anyhow through the Central Planning Board.

As a sign of his approval, Goering signed our draft, and Lammers could report by teletype that there were no longer any objections. Thereupon Hitler, too, was ready to sign the draft when it was presented to him for signature a few days later, on September 2. From a Reich Minister of Armaments and Munitions I had now become Reich Minister of Armaments and War Production.

Bormann's intrigue had fallen through this time. I did not make remonstrances to Hitler; instead, I left it to him to consider whether Bormann had actually served him loyally in this case. After my recent experiences I knew it was wiser not to expose Bormann's machinations and to spare Hitler embarrassment.

But Bormann was surely the source of all the overt or covert opposition to an expansion of my Ministry. To Bormann it was all too clear that I was moving outside the reach of his power and accumulating more and more power myself. Moreover, my work had brought me into comradely contacts with the leadership of the army and navy: with Guderian, Zeitzler, Fromm, and Milch, and now lately with Doenitz. Even in Hitler's immediate entourage I was particularly close to the anti-Bormann forces: Hitler's army adjutant, General Engel; his air force adjutant, General von Below, and Hitler's armed forces adjutant, General Schmundt. In addition Hitler's physician, Dr. Karl Brandt, whom Bormann likewise considered a personal opponent of his, was quite close to me.

One evening when I had had a few glasses of Steinhäger with Schmundt, he came out with the declaration that I was the army's great hope. Wherever he went, he said, the generals had the greatest confidence in me, whereas they had nothing but derogatory opinions of Goering. With rather high-flown emotion he concluded: "You can always rely on the army, Herr Speer. It is behind you."

I have never quite fathomed what Schmundt had in mind, though I suspect that he was confusing the army with the generals. But it seems probable that Schmundt must have said something of the sort to others. Given the narrow confines of the headquarters, such remarks must surely have reached Bormann's ears.

Around this time, perhaps in the autumn of 1943, Hitler put me in some embarrassment when, just before the beginning of a situation conference, he greeted Himmler and me in the presence of several associates with the phrase: "You two peers." Whatever Hitler meant by it, the chief of the SS could scarcely have been pleased by this remark, given his special niche in the power structure. In those same weeks Zeitzler, too, told me with pleasure: "The Fuehrer is so pleased with you. He recently said that he placed the greatest hopes in you, that now a new sun has arisen after Goering."*

I asked Zeitzler not to quote this. But since the same words were reported to me by other persons within the headquarters area, there could be no doubt that Bormann also heard the tribute. Hitler's powerful secretary was forced to realize that he had not been able to turn Hitler against me that summer. Rather, the opposite had happened.

Since Hitler did not say such things often, Bormann must have taken the threat to heart. To him, it spelled danger. From now on he kept telling his closest associates that I was not only an enemy of the party but was actually bent on succeeding Hitler.** He was not entirely wrong in this assumption. I recall having had several conversations with Milch about the matter.

At the time Hitler must have been wondering whom he should select for his successor. Goering's reputation was undermined, Hess had ruled himself out, Schirach had been ruined by Bormann's intrigues, and Bormann, Himmler, and Goebbels did not correspond to the "artistic type" Hitler envisaged. Hitler probably thought he recognized kindred features in me. He considered me a gifted artist who within a short time had won an impressive position within the political hierarchy and finally, by achievements in the field of armaments, had also demonstrated special abilities in the military field. Only in foreign policy, Hitler's fourth domain, I had not come to the fore. Possibly he regarded me as an artistic genius who had successfully switched to politics, so that I thus indirectly served as a confirmation of his own career.

* It might be thought that after years of experience Hitler would know how such remarks were received and what reactions they inevitably evoked. I could not decide whether Hitler did think this far ahead or was even capable of doing so. Sometimes he struck me as a total innocent—or as a misanthrope who did not care what the effects were. Perhaps, too, he believed that he could set things right himself whenever he chose.

** Dr. G. Klopfer, Bormann's state secretary, testified in an affidavit dated July 7, 1947: "Bormann repeatedly stated that Speer was a confirmed opponent of the party and was in fact ambitious to become Hitler's successor."

Among friends I always called Bormann "the man with the hedge clippers." For he was forever using all his energy, cunning, and brutality to prevent anyone from rising above a certain level. From then on, Bormann devoted his full capacities to reducing my power. After October 1943 the Gauleiters formed a front against me. Before another year had passed, things became so difficult that I often wanted to give up and resign my post. Until the end of the war this struggle between Bormann and me remained undecided. Hitler did not want to lose me, even occasionally singled me out for a display of favor, but then again would turn on me rudely. Bormann could not wrest from me my successful industrial apparatus. This was so much my own creation that my fall would have meant the end of it and thus have endangered the war effort.

20

Bombs

———

THE EXUBERANCE I HAD FELT DURING THE BUILDING OF THE NEW ORGANIZATION
and the success and recognition of the early months soon gave way to
more somber feelings. The labor problem, unsolved raw materials questions, and court intrigues created constant worries. The British air raids
began to have their first serious effects on production and for a while
made me forget about Bormann, Sauckel, and the Central Planning Board.
However they also served to raise my prestige. For in spite of the losses
of factories we were producing more, not less.

These air raids carried the war into our midst. In the burning and
devastated cities we daily experienced the direct impact of the war. And
it spurred us to do our utmost.

Neither did the bombings and the hardships that resulted from them
weaken the morale of the populace. On the contrary, from my visits to
armaments plants and my contacts with the man in the street I carried
away the impression of growing toughness. It may well be that the estimated loss of 9 percent of our production capacity[1] was amply balanced
out by increased effort.

Our heaviest expense was in fact the elaborate defensive measures. In
the Reich and in the western theaters of war the barrels of ten thousand
antiaircraft guns were pointed toward the sky.[2] The same guns could have
well been employed in Russia against tanks and other ground targets. Had
it not been for this new front, the air front over Germany, our defensive

(278)

strength against tanks would have been about doubled, as far as equipment was concerned. Moreover, the antiaircraft force tied down hundreds of thousands of young soldiers. A third of the optical industry was busy producing gunsights for the flak batteries. About half of the electronics industry was engaged in producing radar and communications networks for defense against bombing. Simply because of this, in spite of the high level of the German electronics and optical industries, the supply of our frontline troops with modern equipment remained far behind that of the Western armies.*

We were given a foretaste of our coming woes as early as the night of May 30, 1942, when the British gathered all their forces for an attack on Cologne with ten hundred and forty-six bombers.

By chance Milch and I were summoned to see Goering on the morning after the raid. This time he was not residing in Karinhall, but at Veldenstein castle in Franconia. We found him in a bad humor, still not believing the reports of the Cologne bombing. "Impossible, that many bombs cannot be dropped in a single night," he snarled at his adjutant. "Connect me with the Gauleiter of Cologne."

There followed, in our presence, a preposterous telephone conversation. "The report from your police commissioner is a stinking lie!" Apparently the Gauleiter begged to differ. "I tell you as the Reich Marshal that the figures cited are simply too high. How can you dare report such fantasies to the Fuehrer!" The Gauleiter at the other end of the line was evidently insisting on his figures. "How are you going to count the fire bombs? Those are nothing but estimates. I tell you once more they're many times too high. All wrong! Send another report to the Fuehrer at once revising your figures. Or are you trying to imply that I am lying? I have already delivered my report to the Fuehrer with the correct figures. That stands!"

As though nothing had happened, Goering showed us through his house, his parents' former home. As if this were most serene peacetime, he had blueprints brought in and explained to us what a magnificent citadel he would be building to replace the simple Biedermeier house of his parents in the courtyard of the old ruin. But first of all he wanted to have a reliable air-raid shelter built. The plans for that were already drawn up.

Three days later I was at headquarters. The excitement over the air raid on Cologne had not yet died down. I mentioned to Hitler the curious telephone conversation between Goering and Gauleiter Grohé—naturally assuming that Goering's information must be more authentic than the

* Thus a serious shortage of army communications equipment developed—for instance, walkie-talkies for the infantry and sound-ranging apparatus for the artillery. In addition, further development of such devices had to be neglected in favor of antiaircraft weaponry.

Gauleiter's. But Hitler had already formed his own opinion. He presented Goering with the reports in the enemy newspapers on the enormous number of planes committed to the raid and the quantity of bombs they had dropped. These figures were even higher than those of the Cologne police commissioner.[3] Hitler was furious with Goering's attempt to cover up, but he also considered the staff of the air force command partly responsible. Next day Goering was received as usual. The affair was never mentioned again.

As early as September 20, 1942, I had warned Hitler that the tank production of Friedrichshafen and the ball-bearing facilities in Schweinfurt were crucial to our whole effort. Hitler thereupon ordered increased antiaircraft protection for these two cities. Actually, as I had early recognized, the war could largely have been decided in 1943 if instead of vast but pointless area bombing the planes had concentrated on the centers of armaments production. On April 11, 1943, I proposed to Hitler that a committee of industrial specialists be set to determining the crucial targets in Soviet power production. Four weeks later, however, the first attempt was made—not by us but by the British air force—to influence the course of the war by destroying a single nerve center of the war economy. The principle followed was to paralyze a cross section, as it were—just as a motor can be made useless by the removal of the ignition. On May 17, 1943, a mere nineteen bombers of the RAF tried to strike at our whole armaments industry by destroying the hydroelectric plants of the Ruhr.

The report that reached me in the early hours of the morning was most alarming. The largest of the dams, the Möhne dam, had been shattered and the reservoir emptied. As yet there were no reports on the three other dams. At dawn we landed at Werl Airfield, having first surveyed the scene of devastation from above. The power plant at the foot of the shattered dam looked as if it had been erased, along with its heavy turbines.

A torrent of water had flooded the Ruhr Valley. That had the seemingly insignificant but grave consequence that the electrical installations at the pumping stations were soaked and muddied, so that industry was brought to a standstill and the water supply of the population imperiled. My report on the situation, which I soon afterward delivered at the Fuehrer's headquarters, made "a deep impression on the Fuehrer. He kept the documents with him."[*]

The British had not succeeded, however, in destroying the three

---

[*] *Führerprotokoll*, May 30, 1943, Point 16. We immediately summoned experts from all over Germany who had the electrical insulation dried out and also confiscated other motors of this type from other factories, regardless of the consequences. Thus the Ruhr industries would be supplied with water within a few weeks.

other reservoirs. Had they done so, the Ruhr Valley would have been almost completely deprived of water in the coming summer months. At the largest of the reservoirs, the Sorpe Valley reservoir, they did achieve a direct hit on the center of the dam. I inspected it that same day. Fortunately the bomb hole was slightly higher than the water level. Just a few inches lower—and a small brook would have been transformed into a raging river which would have swept away the stone and earthen dam.[4] That night, employing just a few bombers, the British came close to a success which would have been greater than anything they had achieved hitherto with a commitment of thousands of bombers. But they made a single mistake which puzzles me to this day: They divided their forces and that same night destroyed the Eder Valley dam, although it had nothing whatsoever to do with the supply of water to the Ruhr.*

A few days after this attack seven thousand men, whom I had ordered shifted from the Atlantic Wall to the Möhne and Eder areas, were hard at work repairing the dams. On September 23, 1943, in the nick of time before the beginning of the rains, the breach in the Möhne dam was closed.[5] We were thus able to collect the precipitation of the late autumn and winter of 1943 for the needs of the following summer. While we were engaged in rebuilding, the British air force missed its second chance. A few bombs would have produced cave-ins at the exposed building sites, and a few fire bombs could have set the wooden scaffolding blazing.

After these experiences I wondered once again why our Luftwaffe, with its by now reduced forces, did not launch similar pinpoint attacks whose effects could be devastating. At the end of May 1943, two weeks after the British raid, I reminded Hitler of my idea of April 11 that a group of experts might pinpoint the key industrial targets in the enemy camp. But as so often, Hitler proved irresolute. "I'm afraid that the General Staff of the air force will not want to take advice from your industrial associates. I too have broached such a plan to General Jeschonnek several times. "But," he concluded in rather a resigned tone, "you speak to him about it sometime." Evidently Hitler was not going to do anything about this; he lacked any sense of the decisive importance of such operations. There is no question that once before he had thrown away his chance—between 1939 and 1941 when he directed our air raids against England's cities in-

---

* According to Charles Webster and Noble Frankland, *The Strategic Air Offensive against Germany* (London, 1961), Vol. II, the fifth plane succeeded in destroying the Möhne Valley dam. Subsequent attacks were directed against the Eder Valley dam, which served mainly to equalize the water level of the Weser and the Midland Canal during the summer months, thus maintaining navigation. Not until this dam had been destroyed did two planes attack the Sorpe Valley dam. In the meantime Air Marshal Bottomley had suggested on April 5, 1943, that the Möhne and Sorpe dams be attacked before the Eder dam. But the bombs that had been developed specifically for this purpose were considered unsuitable for the earthen dam of the Sorpe reservoir.

stead of coordinating them with the U-boat campaigns and, for example, attacking the English ports which were in any case sometimes strained beyond their capacity by the convoy system. Now he once again failed to see his opportunity. And the British, for their part, thoughtlessly copied this irrational conduct—aside from their single attack on the dams.

In spite of Hitler's skepticism and my own lack of influence upon air force strategy, I did not feel discouraged. On June 23, I formed a committee consisting of several industry experts to analyze prime bombing targets.[6] Our first proposal concerned the British coal industry, for British technical publications provided a complete picture of its centers, locations, capacities, and so on. But this proposal came two years too late; our air power no longer sufficed.

Given our reduced forces, one prime target virtually forced itself on our attention: the Russian electric power plants. To judge by our experiences, no systematically organized air defenses needed to be anticipated in Russia. Moreover, the electric power system in the Soviet Union differed structurally from that of the Western countries in one crucial point. Whereas the gradual industrial growth of the West had resulted in many middle-sized power plants connected in a grid, in the Soviet Union large power plants of gigantic dimensions had been built, usually in the heart of extensive industrial areas.[7] For example, a single huge power plant on the upper Volga supplied most of the energy consumption of Moscow. We had information, in fact, that 60 percent of the manufacturing of essential optical parts and electrical equipment was concentrated in the Soviet capital. Moreover, the destruction of a few gigantic power plants in the Urals would have put a halt to much of Soviet steel production as well as to tank and munitions manufacture. A direct hit on the turbines or their conduits would have released masses of water of a destructiveness greater than that of many bombs. Since many of the major Soviet power plants had been built with the assistance of German companies, we were able to obtain very good data on them.

On November 26, Goering gave the order to strengthen the Sixth Air Corps under Major General Rudolf Meister with long-range bombers. In December the units were assembled near Bialystok.[8] We had wooden models of the power plants made for use in training the pilots. Early in December I had informed Hitler.[9] Milch had relayed our plans to Günter Korten, the new Chief of Staff of the air force. On February 4, I wrote Korten that "even today the prospects are good . . . for an operative air campaign against the Soviet Union. . . . I definitely hope that significant effects on the fighting power of the Soviet Union will result from it." I was referring specifically to the attacks upon the power plants in the vicinity of Moscow and the upper Volga.

Success depended—as always in such operations—upon chance factors. I did not think that our action would decisively affect the war. But I hoped, as I wrote to Korten, that we would wreak enough damage on Soviet production so that it would take several months for American supplies to balance out their losses.

Once again we were two years too late. The Russian winter offensive forced our troops to retreat. The situation had grown critical. In emergencies Hitler was, as so often, amazingly short-sighted. At the end of February he told me that the "Meister Corps" had been ordered to destroy railroad lines in order to slow down Russian supplies. I objected that the soil in Russia was frozen hard and our bombs would have only a superficial effect. Moreover, according to our own experience and despite the fact that the German railroads were much more complex and hence more sensitive to destruction, damage to railroad sections could often be repaired in a matter of hours. But these objections were in vain. The "Meister Corps" came to grief in a senseless operation, and the Russians were in no way impeded.

Whatever interest Hitler might still have had in the idea of pinpoint bombing strategy was forgotten in his stubborn determination to retaliate against England. Even after the annihilation of the "Meister Corps," we would still have had enough bombers for limited targets. But Hitler succumbed to the unrealistic hope that a few massive air strikes on London might persuade the British to give up their pounding of Germany. That was the only reason he continued to demand, as late as 1943, the development and production of new heavy bombers. It made no impression upon him that such bombers could have been used with far greater effect in the east, although occasionally, even as late as the summer of 1944, he would seem to be swayed by my arguments.[10] He as well as our air force staff could not grasp the principle of aerial warfare in technological terms. Instead they proceeded along outmoded military lines. So did the other side at first.

While I was trying to convert Hitler and the General Staff of the air force to this policy, our Western enemies launched five major attacks on a single big city—Hamburg—within a week, from July 25 to August 2.[11] Rash as this operation was, it had catastrophic consequences for us. The first attacks put the water supply pipes out of action, so that in the subsequent bombings the fire department had no way of fighting the fires. Huge conflagrations created cyclone-like firestorms; the asphalt of the streets began to blaze; people were suffocated in their cellars or burned to death in the streets. The devastation of this series of air raids could be compared only with the effects of a major earthquake. Gauleiter Kaufmann teletyped Hitler repeatedly, begging him to visit the stricken city. When these pleas proved fruitless, he asked Hitler at least to receive a delegation of some of the more heroic rescue crews. But Hitler refused even that.

Hamburg had suffered the fate Goering and Hitler had conceived for London in 1940. At a supper in the Chancellery in that year Hitler had, in the course of a monologue, worked himself up to a frenzy of destructiveness:

> Have you ever looked at a map of London? It is so closely built up that one source of fire alone would suffice to destroy the whole city, as happened once before, two hundred years ago. Goering wants to use innumerable incendiary bombs of an altogether new type to create sources of fire in all parts of London. Fires everywhere. Thousands of them. Then they'll unite in one gigantic area conflagration. Goering has the right idea. Explosive bombs don't work, but it can be done with incendiary bombs—total destruction of London. What use will their fire department be once that really starts!

Hamburg had put the fear of God in me. At the meeting of Central Planning on July 29 I pointed out: "If the air raids continue on the present scale, within three months we shall be relieved of a number of questions we are at present discussing. We shall simply be coasting downhill, smoothly and relatively swiftly. . . . We might just as well hold the final meeting of Central Planning, in that case." Three days later I informed Hitler that armaments production was collapsing and threw in the further warning that a series of attacks of this sort, extended to six more major cities, would bring Germany's armaments production to a total halt.* "You'll straighten all that out again," he merely said.

In fact Hitler was right. We straightened it out again—not because of our Central Planning organization, which with the best will in the world could issue only general instructions, but by the determined efforts of those directly concerned, first and foremost the workers themselves. Fortunately for us, a series of Hamburg-type raids was not repeated on such a scale against other cities. Thus the enemy once again allowed us to adjust ourselves to his strategy.

We barely escaped a further catastrophic blow on August 17, 1943, only two weeks after the Hamburg bombings. The American air force launched its first strategic raid. It was directed against Schweinfurt where large factories of the ball-bearing industry were concentrated. Ball bearings had in any case already become a bottleneck in our efforts to increase armaments production.

---

* The next day I informed Milch's colleagues of similar fears (Conference with chief of Air Force Procurement, August 3, 1943): "We are approaching the point of total collapse . . . in our supply industry. Soon we will have airplanes, tanks, or trucks lacking certain key parts." Ten months later I said to a group of Hamburg dockworkers: "A while back we were saying to ourselves: If this goes on another few months we'll be washed up. Then armaments production will come to a standstill." (Office Journal.)

But in this very first attack the other side committed a crucial mistake. Instead of concentrating on the ball-bearing plants, the sizable force of three hundred seventy-six Flying Fortresses divided up. One hundred and forty-six of the planes successfully attacked an airplane assembly plant in Regensburg, but with only minor consequences. Meanwhile, the British air force continued its indiscriminate attacks upon our cities.

After this attack the production of ball bearings dropped by 38 percent.[12] Despite the peril to Schweinfurt we had to patch up our facilities there, for to attempt to relocate our ball-bearing industry would have held up production entirely for three or four months. In the light of our desperate needs we could also do nothing about the ball-bearing factories in Berlin-Erkner, Cannstatt, or Steyr, although the enemy must have been aware of their location.

In June 1946 the General Staff of the Royal Air Force asked me what would have been the results of concerted attacks on the ball-bearing industry. I replied:

Armaments production would have been crucially weakened after two months and after four months would have been brought completely to a standstill.

This, to be sure, would have meant:

One: All our ball-bearing factories (in Schweinfurt, Steyr, Erkner, Cannstatt, and in France and Italy) had been attacked simultaneously.

Two: These attacks had been repeated three or four times, every two weeks, no matter what the pictures of the target area showed.

Three: Any attempt at rebuilding these factories had been thwarted by further attacks, spaced at two-month intervals.[13]

After this first blow we were forced back on the ball-bearing stocks stored by the armed forces for use as repair parts. We soon consumed these, as well as whatever had been accumulated in the factories for current production. After these reserves were used up—they lasted for six to eight weeks—the sparse production was carried daily from the factories to the assembly plants, often in knapsacks. In those days we anxiously asked ourselves how soon the enemy would realize that he could paralyze the production of thousands of armaments plants merely by destroying five or six relatively small targets.

The second serious blow, however, did not come until two months later. On October 14, 1943, I was at the East Prussian headquarters discussing armaments questions with Hitler when Adjutant Schaub interrupted us: "The Reich Marshal urgently wishes to speak to you," he said to Hitler. "This time he has pleasant news."

Hitler came back from the telephone in good spirits. A new daylight raid on Schweinfurt had ended with a great victory for our defenses, he said.[14] The countryside was strewn with downed American bombers. Uneasy, I asked for a short recess in our conference, since I wanted to telephone Schweinfurt myself. But all communications were shattered; I could not reach any of the factories. Finally, by enlisting the police, I managed to talk to the foreman of a ball-bearing factory. All the factories had been hard hit, he informed me. The oil baths for the bearings had caused serious fires in the machinery workshops; the damage was far worse than after the first attack. This time we had lost 67 percent of our ball-bearing production.

My first measure after this second air raid was to appoint my most vigorous associate, General Manager Kessler, as special commissioner for ball-bearing production. Our reserves had been consumed; efforts to import ball bearings from Sweden and Switzerland had met with only slight success. Nevertheless, we were able to avoid total disaster by substituting slide bearings for ball bearings wherever possible.[15] But what really saved us was the fact that from this time on the enemy to our astonishment once again ceased his attacks on the ball-bearing industry.[16]

On December 23, the Erkner plant was heavily hit, but we were not sure whether this was a deliberate attack, since Berlin was being bombed in widely scattered areas. The picture did not change again until February 1944. Then, within four days, Schweinfurt, Steyr, and Cannstatt were each subjected to two successive heavy attacks. Then followed raids on Erkner, Schweinfurt, and again Steyr. After only six weeks our production of bearings (above 6.3 centimeters in diameter) had been reduced to 29 percent of what it had been before the air raids.[17]

At the beginning of April 1944, however, the attacks on the ball-bearing industry ceased abruptly. Thus, the Allies threw away success when it was already in their hands. Had they continued the attacks of March and April with the same energy, we would quickly have been at our last gasp.* As it was, not a tank, plane, or other piece of weaponry failed to be produced because of lack of ball bearings, even though such production had been increased by 19 percent from July 1943 to April 1944.[18] As far as armaments were concerned, Hitler's credo that the impossible could be made possible and that all forecasts and fears were too pessimistic, seemed to have proved itself true.

Not until after the war did I learn the reason for the enemy's error.

---

* Perhaps the enemy air staffs overrated the effects. Our Air Force General Staff also concluded from aerial photographs that an attack on a Soviet synthetic rubber factory in the fall of 1943 had completely wiped out production for many months to come. I showed these photos to our leading synthetic rubber specialist, Hoffmann, the manager of our plant in Hüls, which had undergone much more severe attacks. After pointing out various key sections of the plant which had not been hit, he explained that the plant would be in full production again within a week or two.

Hitler and Speer examining blueprints. (SPIEGEL-ARCHIV)

Hitler's sketch of the domed hall, 1925. (SPEER-ARCHIV)

The Great Hall planned for Berlin. (EDO KOENIG, BLACK STAR)

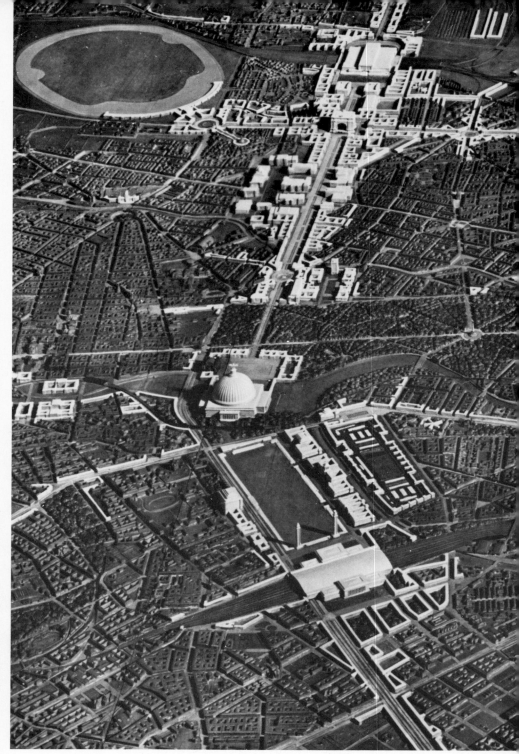

Model of Berlin's new center (Tempelhof Field, upper left). *1939.*
(SPEER-ARCHIV)

*View from the South Station: Arch of Triumph with
Great Hall at far end.* (SPEER-ARCHIV)

ABOVE LEFT: *Entrance hall of Goering's palace in Berlin, model.* (SPEER-ARCHIV)

BELOW LEFT: *Façade of Goering's palace.* (SPEER-ARCHIV)

ABOVE: *A small section of Goering's palace, erected in 1:1 scale, to control various details.* (SPEER-ARCHIV)

Hitler's design for monument to Mussolini. (SPEER-ARCHIV)

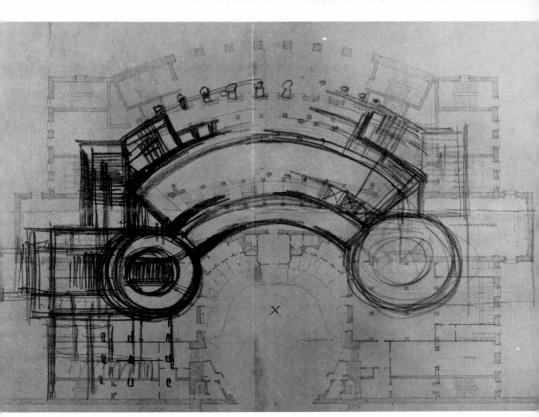

Hitler's rough sketch of a grand theater for Linz, which he hoped to convert into a metropolis.
(SPEER-ARCHIV)

The Soldiers Hall, a memorial building to be opposite Goering's palace, model, 1938 (Architect: Wilhelm Kreis).
(SPIEGEL-ARCHIV)

Model of entrance to Hitler's new palace. (SPEER-ARCHIV)

Façade of the palace (detail). (SPEER-ARCHIV)

Hitler's sketch of a triumphal arch (enormous domed hall in the background), 1925. (SPEER-ARCHIV)

Hitler examining Speer's model of the triumphal arch, presented upon the occasion of Hitler's fiftieth birthday in 1939. Left to right: Hitler, Colonel von Bülow, unknown SS adjutant, Martin Bormann, Dr. Karl Brandt, Philip Bouhler, Hitler's army adjutant, Speer. (HEINRICH HOFFMANN)

Hitler with his party returning from visit to Eiffel Tower (June 28, 1940). Front row, left to right: Unknown, Hermann Giessler, Speer, Hitler, Arno Breker. Second row: Unknown, two of Hitler's adjutants, Dr. Karl Brandt, Martin Bormann.
(SPIEGEL-ARCHIV)

Hitler visiting Paris Opera House. Speer on extreme right.
(HEINRICH HOFFMANN)

Margarete Speer with the pianist Alfred Cortot in Hotel Ritz, Paris, 1941. (SPEER-ARCHIV)

Bichelonne, the French Production Minister, and Speer inspecting the new steel works at Salzgitter, September 1943. (SPEER-ARCHIV)

ADOLF HITLER

Hauptquartier BERLIN, DEN *25/Juni 1940*

Berlin muß in kürzester Zeit durch seine bauliche Neugestaltung den ihm durch die Größe unseres Sieges zukommenden Ausdruck als Hauptstadt eines starken neuen Reiches erhalten.

In der Verwirklichung dieser nunmehr w i c h t i g s t e n   B a u a u f g a b e   d e s   R e i c h e s sehe ich den bedeutendsten Beitrag zur endgültigen Sicherstellung unseres Sieges.

Ihre Vollendung erwarte ich bis zum Jahre 1950.

Das Gleiche gilt auch für die Neugestaltung der Städte München, Linz, Hamburg und die Parteitagbauten in Nürnberg.

Alle Dienststellen des Reiches, der Länder und der Städte sowie der Partei haben dem Generalbauinspektor für die Reichshauptstadt bei der Durchführung seiner Aufgaben jede geforderte Unterstützung zu gewähren.

Hitler's decree ordering Speer to concentrate all his energies upon the reconstruction of Berlin, Munich, Linz and Hamburg as well as the party buildings in Nuremberg. Signed on June 28, Hitler deliberately pre-dated this decree to June 25, the day of the French capitulation. (BUNDESARCHIV KOBLENZ)

The air staffs assumed that in Hitler's authoritarian state the important factories would be quickly shifted from the imperiled cities. On December 20, 1943, Sir Arthur Harris declared his conviction that "at this stage of the war the Germans have long since made every possible effort to decentralize the manufacture of so vital a product [as ball bearings]." He considerably overestimated the strengths of the authoritarian system, which to the outside observer appeared so tightly knit.

As early as December 19, 1942, eight months before the first air raid on Schweinfurt, I had sent a directive to the entire armaments industry stating: "The mounting intensity of the enemy air attacks compels accelerated preparations for shifting manufactures important for armaments production." But there was resistance on all sides. The Gauleiters did not want new factories in their districts for fear that the almost peacetime quiet of their small towns would be disturbed. My band of directors, for their part, did not want to expose themselves to political infighting. The result was that hardly anything was done.

After the second heavy raid on Schweinfurt on October 14, 1943, we again decided to decentralize. Some of the facilities were to be distributed among the surrounding villages, others placed in small and as yet unendangered towns in eastern Germany.* This policy of dispersal was meant to provide for the future; but the plan encountered a great deal of opposition. As late as January 1944 the shifting of ball-bearing production to cave factories was still being discussed,[19] and in August 1944 my representative to the ball-bearing industry complained that he was having difficulties "pushing through the construction work for the shift of ball-bearing production."[20]

Instead of paralyzing vital segments of industry, the Royal Air Force began an air offensive against Berlin. I was having a conference in my private office on November 22, 1943, when the air-raid alarm sounded. It was about 7:30 P.M. A large fleet of bombers was reported heading toward Berlin. When the bombers reached Potsdam, I called off the meeting to drive to a nearby flak tower, intending to watch the attack from its platform, as was my wont. But I scarcely reached the top of the tower when I had to take shelter inside it; in spite of the tower's stout concrete walls, heavy hits nearby were shaking it. Injured antiaircraft gunners crowded down the stairs behind me; the air pressure from the exploding bombs had hurled them into the walls. For twenty minutes explosion followed explo-

* In the two months following the first attack on Schweinfurt nothing had been done. "The minister forcefully expressed his dissatisfaction with the measures previously taken, asserting that the urgency of the matter required all other considerations to be put aside. Deeply impressed by the damage and by the minister's account of the potential consequences for the armaments industry, everyone readily offered all assistance, even the neighboring Gauleiters who would have to accept the unwelcome intrusions into their domains that would accompany the transfer of operations from Schweinfurt to their territories." (*Office Journal*, October 18, 1943.)

sion. From above I looked down into the well of the tower, where a close-ly packed crowd stood in the thickening haze formed by cement dust fall-ing from the walls. When the rain of bombs ceased, I ventured out on the platform again. My nearby Ministry was one gigantic conflagration. I drove over there at once. A few secretaries, looking like Amazons in their steel helmets, were trying to save files even while isolated time bombs went off in the vicinity. In place of my private office I found nothing but a huge bomb crater.

The fire spread so quickly that nothing more could be rescued. But nearby was the eight-story building of the Army Ordnance Office, and since the fire was spreading to it and we were all nerved up from the raid and feeling the urge to do something, we thronged into the imperiled building in order at least to save the valuable special telephones. We ripped them from their wires and piled them up in a safe place in the base-ment shelter of the building. Next morning General Leeb, the chief of the Army Ordnance Office, visited me. "The fires in my building were extin-guished early in the morning hours," he informed me, grinning. "But un-fortunately we can't do any work now. Last night somebody ripped all the telephones from the walls."

When Goering, at his country estate Karinhall, heard about that noc-turnal visit to the flak tower, he gave the staff there orders not to allow me to step out on the platform again. But by this time the officers had al-ready formed a friendly relationship with me that was stronger than Goe-ring's command. My visits to the tower were not hampered by his order.

From the flak tower the air raids on Berlin were an unforgettable sight, and I had constantly to remind myself of the cruel reality in order not to be completely entranced by the scene: the illumination of the para-chute flares, which the Berliners called "Christmas trees," followed by flashes of explosions which were caught by the clouds of smoke, the in-numerable probing searchlights, the excitement when a plane was caught and tried to escape the cone of light, the brief flaming torch when it was hit. No doubt about it, this apocalypse provided a magnificent spectacle.

As soon as the planes turned back, I drove to those districts of the city where important factories were situated. We drove over streets strewn with rubble, lined by burning houses. Bombed-out families sat or stood in front of the ruins. A few pieces of rescued furniture and other posses-sions lay about on the sidewalks. There was a sinister atmosphere full of biting smoke, soot, and flames. Sometimes the people displayed that curi-ous hysterical merriment that is often observed in the midst of disasters. Above the city hung a cloud of smoke that probably reached twenty thou-sand feet in height. Even by day it made the macabre scene as dark as night.

I kept trying to describe my impressions to Hitler. But he would interrupt me every time, almost as soon as I began: "Incidentally, Speer, how many tanks can you deliver next month?"

On November 26, 1943, four days after the destruction of my Ministry, another major air raid on Berlin started huge fires in our most important tank factory, Allkett. The Berlin central telephone exchange had been destroyed. My colleague Saur hit on the idea of reaching the Berlin fire department by way of our still intact direct line to the Fuehrer's headquarters. In this way Hitler, too, learned of the blaze, and without making any further inquiries ordered all the fire departments in the vicinity of Berlin to report to the burning tank plant.

Meanwhile I had arrived at Allkett. The greater part of the main workshop had burned down, but the Berlin fire department had already succeeded in extinguishing the fire. As the result of Hitler's order, however, a steady stream of fire equipment from cities as far away as Brandenburg, Oranienburg, and Potsdam kept arriving. Since a direct order from the Fuehrer had been issued, I could not persuade the chiefs to go on to other urgent fires. Early that morning the streets in a wide area around the tank factory were jammed with fire engines standing around doing nothing—while the fires spread unchecked in other parts of the city.

In order to awaken my associates to the problems and anxieties about air armaments, Milch and I held a conference in September 1943 at the Air Force Experimental Center in Rechlin am Müritzsee. Among other things, Milch and his technical experts spoke on the future production of enemy aircraft. Graphs were presented for type after type of aircraft, with emphasis especially on American production curves as compared with our own. What alarmed us most were the figures on the future increase in four-motored daylight bombers. If these figures were accurate, what we were undergoing at the moment could be regarded only as a prelude.

Naturally, the question arose as to how aware Hitler and Goering were of these figures. Bitterly, Milch told me that he had been trying for months to have his experts on enemy armaments deliver a report to Goering. But Goering refused to hear anything about it. The Fuehrer had told him it was all propaganda, Milch said, and Goering was simply holding to this line. I too had no luck when I tried to force these production figures on Hitler's attention. "Don't let them fool you. Those are all planted stories. Naturally those defeatists in the Air Ministry fall for them." With similar remarks he had thrust aside all warnings in the winter of 1942. Now, when our cities were one after the next being blasted into rubble, he would not change his tune.

About this same time I witnessed a dramatic scene between Goering and General Galland, who commanded his fighter planes. Galland had reported to Hitler that day that several American fighter planes accompanying the bomber squadrons had been shot down over Aachen. He had added the warning that we were in grave peril if American fighters, thanks to improved fuel capacity, should soon be able to provide escort protection to the fleets of bombers on flights even deeper into Germany. Hitler had just relayed these points to Goering.

Goering was embarking for Rominten Heath on his special train when Galland came along to bid him good-by. "What's the idea of telling the Fuehrer that American fighters have penetrated into the territory of the Reich?" Goering snapped at him.

"*Herr Reichsmarschall,*" Galland replied with imperturbable calm, "they will soon be flying even deeper."

Goering spoke even more vehemently: "That's nonsense, Galland, what gives you such fantasies? That's pure bluff!"

Galland shook his head. "Those are the facts, *Herr Reichsmarschall!*" As he spoke he deliberately remained in a casual posture, his cap somewhat askew, a long cigar clamped between his teeth. "American fighters have been shot down over Aachen. There is no doubt about it!"

Goering obstinately held his ground: "That is simply not true, Galland. It's impossible."

Galland reacted with a touch of mockery: "You might go and check it yourself, sir; the downed planes are there at Aachen."

Goering tried to smooth matters over: "Come now, Galland, let me tell you something. I'm an experienced fighter pilot myself. I know what is possible. But I know what isn't, too. Admit you made a mistake."

Galland only shook his head, until Goering finally declared: "What must have happened is that they were shot down much farther to the west. I mean, if they were very high when they were shot down they could have glided quite a distance farther before they crashed."

Not a muscle moved in Galland's face. "Glided to the east, sir? If my plane were shot up . . ."

"Now then, Herr Galland," Goering fulminated, trying to put an end to the debate, "I officially assert that the American fighter planes did not reach Aachen."

The General ventured a last statement: "But, sir, they were there!"

At this point Goering's self-control gave way. "I herewith give you an official order that they weren't there! Do you understand? The American fighters were not there! Get that! I intend to report that to the Fuehrer."

Goering simply let General Galland stand there. But as he stalked off he turned once more and called out threateningly: "You have my official order!"

With an unforgettable smile the General replied: "Orders are orders, sir!"

Goering was not actually blind to reality. I would occasionally hear him make perceptive comments on the situation. Rather, he acted like a bankrupt who up to the last moment wants to deceive himself along with his creditors. Capricious treatment and blatant refusal to accept reality had already driven the first chief of Air Force Procurement, the famous fighter pilot Ernst Udet, to his death in 1941. On August 18, 1943, another of Goering's closest associates and the man who had been Air Force Chief of Staff for over four years, General Jeschonnek, was found dead in his office. He too had committed suicide. On his table, so Milch told me, a note was found stating that he did not wish Goering to attend his funeral. Nevertheless Goering showed up at the ceremony and deposited a wreath from Hitler.[21]

I have always thought it was a most valuable trait to recognize reality and not to pursue delusions. But when I now think over my life up to and including the years of imprisonment, there was no period in which I was free of delusory notions.

The departure from reality, which was visibly spreading like a contagion, was no peculiarity of the National Socialist regime. But in normal circumstances people who turn their backs on reality are soon set straight by the mockery and criticism of those around them, which makes them aware they have lost credibility. In the Third Reich there were no such correctives, especially for those who belonged to the upper stratum. On the contrary, every self-deception was multiplied as in a hall of distorting mirrors, becoming a repeatedly confirmed picture of a fantastical dream world which no longer bore any relationship to the grim outside world. In those mirrors I could see nothing but my own face reproduced many times over. No external factors disturbed the uniformity of hundreds of unchanging faces, all mine.

There were differences of degree in the flight from reality. Thus Goebbels was surely many times closer to recognizing actualities than, say, Goering or Ley. But these differences shrink to nothing when we consider how remote all of us, the illusionists as well as the so-called realists, were from what was really going on.

21

Hitler in the Autumn of 1943

BOTH HIS OLD ASSOCIATES AND HIS ADJUTANTS AGREED THAT HITLER HAD UN-
dergone a change in the past year. This could scarcely be surprising, for
during this period he had experienced Stalingrad, had looked on power-
lessly as a quarter of a million soldiers surrendered in Tunisia, and had
seen German cities leveled. Along with all this he had to approve the
navy's decision to withdraw the U-boats from the Atlantic, thus relinquish-
ing one of his greatest hopes for victory. Undoubtedly, Hitler could see the
meaning of this turn of affairs. And undoubtedly he reacted to it as human beings do, with disappointment, dejection, and increasingly forced
optimism.

In the years since then, Hitler may have become the object of sober
studies for the historian. But for me he possesses to this day a substan-
tiality and physical presence, as if he still existed in the flesh. Between
the spring of 1942 and the summer of 1943 he sometimes spoke despond-
ently. But, then, a curious transformation seemed to take place in him.
Even in desperate situations he displayed confidence in ultimate victory.
From this later period I can scarcely recall any remarks on the disastrous
course of affairs, although I was expecting them. Had he gone on for so
long persuading himself that he now firmly believed in victory? At any
rate, the more inexorably events moved toward catastrophe, the more
inflexible he became, the more rigidly convinced that everything he decided on was right.

His closest associates noted his growing inaccessibility. He deliberately made his decisions in isolation. At the same time he had grown intellectually more sluggish and showed little inclination to develop new ideas. It was as if he were running along an unalterable track and could no longer find the strength to break out of it.

Underlying all this was the impasse into which he had been driven by the superior power of his enemies. In January 1943 they had jointly issued a demand for Germany's unconditional surrender. Hitler was probably the only German leader who entertained no illusions about the seriousness of this statement. Goebbels, Goering, and the others would talk about exploiting the political antagonisms among the Allies. Still others imagined that Hitler would find some political device by which he could save the situation, even now. After all, had he not earlier, starting with the occupation of Austria up to the pact with the Soviet Union, contrived with apparent ease a succession of new tricks, new shifts, new finesses? But now, during the situation conferences, he more and more often declared: "Don't fool yourself. There is no turning back. We can only move forward. We have burned our bridges." In speaking this way Hitler was cutting his government off from any negotiation. The meaning of these words was first fully revealed at the Nuremberg Trial.

One of the causes for the changes in Hitler's personality, so I thought at the time, was the constant stress under which he labored. He was working in an unaccustomed way. Since the beginning of the Russian campaign he had abandoned his former staccato method of administering the affairs of government in flurries of activity, with spells of indolence in between. Instead, he regularly attended to an enormous daily mass of work. Whereas in the past he had known how to let others work for him, he now assumed more and more responsibility for details. As anxieties mounted, he made himself into a strictly disciplined worker. But such discipline ran counter to his nature, and this was inevitably reflected in the quality of his decisions.

It is true that even before the war Hitler had shown signs of overwork. At times he would be distinctly averse to making decisions, would appear absent-minded, and would relapse into painful spells of monologuing. Or else he would fall into a sort of muteness or would say nothing more than an occasional "yes" or "no." At such times it was not clear whether he still had his mind on the subject or was brooding on other thoughts. Earlier, however, these states of exhaustion did not usually last long. After staying at Obersalzberg for a few weeks he would appear more relaxed. His eyes would be brighter, his capacity for reaction would have increased, and he would recover his pleasure in state business.

In 1943, too, his entourage frequently urged him to take a vacation. At such times he would change the location of his headquarters and would go for weeks and sometimes even for months to Obersalzberg.* But these vacations did not involve any change in his daily routine. Bormann was always hovering nearby, with endless small questions which the Fuehrer had to settle. There was a stream of callers, Gauleiters or ministers who could not obtain admission to headquarters and who now insisted on seeing him. Along with all this the lengthy daily situation conferences went on, for the entire military staff came along to wherever Hitler happened to be staying. Hitler frequently said, when we expressed concern for his health: "It's easy to advise me to take a vacation. But it's impossible. I cannot leave current military decisions to others even for twenty-four hours."

The people in Hitler's military entourage had been used to concentrated daily work from their youth. They could not have realized how overstrained Hitler was. Bormann, likewise, seemed unable to understand that he was asking too much of Hitler. But even apart from this, Hitler neglected to do what every factory executive must do: appoint good deputies for each important phase of his work. He had neither a competent executive chief nor a vigorous head of the armed forces nor even a capable Commander in Chief of the army. He continually flouted the old rule that the higher his position the more free time a man should have available. Formerly, he had abided by this rule.

Overwork and isolation led to a peculiar state of petrifaction and rigor. He suffered from spells of mental torpor and was permanently caustic and irritable. Earlier, he had made decisions with almost sportive ease; now, he had to force them out of his exhausted brain.[1] As a former racing shell crewman I knew about the phenomenon of overtraining. I remembered how, when we reached such a state, our performance dropped, we became dull and irritable and lost all flexibility. We would become automatons to such an extent that a rest period seemed actually unwelcome and all we wanted was to go on training. Excessive intellectual strain can produce similar symptoms. During the difficult days of the war, I could observe in myself how my mind went on working mechanically, while at the same time my ability to absorb fresh impressions diminished and I made decisions in an apathetic way.

The fact that Hitler left the darkened Chancellery in silence and secrecy on the night of September 3, 1939, in order to go to the front, proved to be a step of high significance for the subsequent years. His

* During the twenty months from July 28, 1941, to March 20, 1943, Hitler interrupted his stay in Rastenburg four times, for a total of fifty-seven days. Beginning on March 20, 1943, on his doctor's urging, he went to Obersalzberg for a three-month vacation and then worked for the next nine months in Rastenburg. After this, completely exhausted, he spent the four months after March 16, 1944, at Obersalzberg and in Berlin. (Domarus, *Hitlers Reden*, Vol. IV [Munich, 1965].)

relationship to the people had changed. Even when he did come into contact with the populace—at intervals of many months—their enthusiasm and capacity to respond to him had faded and his magnetic power over them seemed likewise to have fled.

In the early thirties, during the final phases of the struggle for power, Hitler had driven himself as hard as during the second half of the war. But he probably drew more impetus and courage from those mass meetings than he himself had poured out upon the multitude. Even during the period between 1933 and 1939, when his position made life easier for him, he was visibly refreshed by the daily procession of admirers who came to pay homage to him at Obersalzberg. The rallies in the prewar period had also been a stimulant to Hitler. They were part of his life, and each one left him more incisive and self-assured than he had been before.

The private circle—his secretaries, doctors, and adjutants—in which he moved at headquarters was, if possible, even less stimulating than the prewar circle at Obersalzberg had been, or the circle in the Chancellery. Here there were no people so carried away by his aura that they could hardly speak. Daily association with Hitler, as I had already observed in the days when he and I dreamed together over building projects, reduced him from the demigod Goebbels had made of him to a human being with all ordinary human needs and weaknesses, although his authority remained intact.

Hitler's military entourage, too, must have been tiring to him. For in the matter-of-fact atmosphere of headquarters any touch of idolatry would have made a bad impression. On the contrary, the military officers remained distinctly dispassionate. Even had they not been so by nature, restrained etiquette was part of their training. For that reason the Byzantine flatteries of Keitel and Goering seemed all the more obtrusive. Moreover, they did not sound genuine. Hitler himself encouraged his military entourage not to be servile. In that atmosphere objectivity remained the dominant note.

Hitler would not listen to criticism about his own life pattern. Consequently, members of his entourage had to conceal their worries and accept his habits for what they were. More and more he avoided conversations of a personal nature, aside from the rare sentimental talks he had with a few of his comrades from the early days, such as Goebbels, Ley, or Esser. To me and others he spoke in an impersonal, rather aloof manner. Occasionally, Hitler still made decisions alertly and spontaneously, as he had in the past, and once in a long while he would even listen attentively to opposing arguments. But these times had become so unusual that we afterward made special note of them.

Schmundt and I hit on the idea of bringing young frontline officers to Hitler, in order to introduce a little of the mood of the outside world into the stale, hermetic atmosphere of the headquarters. But our efforts came to nought. For one thing Hitler seemed unwilling to spare the time for such things, and then we also realized that these interviews did more harm than good. For example, a young tank officer reported that during the advance along the Terek his unit had encountered hardly any resistance and had had to check the advance only because it ran out of ammunition. In his overwrought state of mind, Hitler kept brooding on the matter for days afterward. "There you have it! Too little ammunition for the 7.5 centimeter guns! What's the matter with production? It must be increased at once by every possible means." Actually, given our limited facilities there was enough of this ammunition available; but the supply lines were so overextended that the supplies had not caught up with the tempestuous advance of the tank troops. Hitler, however, refused to take this factor into account.

On such occasions the young frontline officers would disclose other details into which Hitler immediately read major errors of omission on the part of the General Staff. In reality most of the difficulties arose from the tempo of the advances, which Hitler insisted on. It was impossible for the army staff to discuss this matter with him, since he had no knowledge of the complicated logistics involved in such advances.

At long intervals Hitler still continued to receive officers and enlisted men on whom he was to confer high military decorations. Given his distrust in the competence of his staff, there were often dramatic scenes and peremptory orders after such visits. In order to avert such complications, Keitel and Schmundt did their best to neutralize the visitors beforehand, insofar as they could.

Hitler's evening tea, to which he invited guests even at headquarters, had in the course of time been shifted to two o'clock in the morning and did not end before three or four o'clock. The time when he went to bed had also been shifted more and more into the early morning, so that I once commented: "If the war goes on much longer we'll at least come around to the normal working hours of an early riser and take Hitler's evening tea as our breakfast."

Hitler unquestionably suffered from insomnia. He spoke of the agony of lying awake if he went to bed earlier. During the tea he would often complain that the day before he had only been able to snatch a few hours of rest in the morning, after many hours of sleeplessness.

Only the intimates were admitted to these teas: his doctors, his secretaries, his military and civilian adjutants, the press chief's deputy, the Foreign Ministry's representative, Ambassador Hewel, sometimes his Viennese diet cook, such visitors as were close to Hitler, and the inevitable Bormann. I too was welcome as a guest anytime. We sat stiffly in Hitler's dining room in uncomfortable armchairs. On these occasions Hitler still loved a *gemütlich* atmosphere, with, if possible, a fire in the fireplace. He passed cake to the secretaries with emphatic gallantry and tried to achieve a tone of friendliness with his guests like an easy-going host. I felt pity for him; there was always something misbegotten about his attempts to radiate warmth in order to receive it.

Since music was banned at headquarters, there remained only conversation, with Hitler himself doing most of the talking. His familiar jokes were appreciated as if they had been heard for the first time; his stories of his harsh youth or the "days of struggle" were listened to as raptly as if they were being told for the first time; but this circle could not whip up much liveliness or contribute to the conversation. It was an unwritten law that events at the front, politics, or criticism of leaders must be avoided. Naturally, Hitler, too, had no need to talk about such matters. Only Bormann had the privilege of making provocative remarks. Sometimes, too, a letter from Eva Braun would send Hitler into a fit, for she was apt to cite cases of blatant stupidity on the part of officials. When, for example, regulations were issued forbidding the people of Munich from going to the mountains for skiing, Hitler became extremely excited and launched into tirades about his everlasting struggle against the idiocy of the bureaucracy. In the end, Bormann would be ordered to look into such cases.

The banality of the subjects indicated that Hitler's threshold of irritability had become extremely low. On the other hand, such trivialities really had a kind of relaxing effect on him, since they led him back to a world in which he could still issue effective orders. For the moment at least he could forget the impotence that had plagued him since his enemies had begun to shape the course of events.

Even though he still played at being master of the situation and his circle did its best to abet him in his illusions, elements of the truth forced themselves upon his consciousness. At such moments, he would go back to his old litany that he had become a politician against his will, that basically he was an architect but that he had been out of luck: The kind of projects that would have suited his talents were not being built. Only when he himself was head of government was the right kind of building possible. He had only one remaining wish, he would say in one of those bursts of self-pity which became more and more frequent these days. "As soon as possible I want to hang the field-gray jacket on its nail again.* When I have ended the war victoriously, my life's task will be fulfilled, and I'll withdraw to the home of my old age, in Linz, across the Danube. Then my successor can worry about these problems." He had, it is true, sometimes spoken in this vein before the beginning of the war, during those

---

* Since the beginning of the war he had worn military dress rather than his old party uniform, and he had promised the Reichstag that he would not put it aside until the war was over—just as Isabella of Castile had once sworn not to take off her chemise until the country was liberated from the Moors.

more relaxed teatimes at Obersalzberg. But in those days, I suspect, all that was mere coquettishness. Now, he formulated such thoughts unsentimentally, in a normal conversational tone and with a credible note of bitterness.

His abiding interest in the plans for the city of his retirement years also gradually assumed an escapist character. Toward the end of the war, Hermann Giessler, the chief architect of Linz, was summoned to headquarters more and more frequently to present his designs, whereas Hitler scarcely ever asked for the Hamburg, Berlin, Nuremberg, or Munich plans, which had previously meant so much to him. When he considered the torments he now had to endure, he would say gloomily, death could only mean a release for him. In keeping with this mood, when he studied the Linz plans he would repeatedly turn to the sketches for his tomb, which was to be located in one of the towers of the Linz complex of party buildings. Even after a victorious war, he emphasized, he did not want to be buried beside his field marshals in the Soldiers Hall in Berlin.

During these nocturnal conversations in the Ukrainian or East Prussian headquarters, Hitler often gave the impression of being slightly unbalanced. The leaden heaviness of the early morning hours weighed on those few of us who participated. Only politeness and a sense of duty could induce us to attend the teas. For after the day of strenuous conferences, we could scarcely keep our eyes open during the monotonous conversations.

Before Hitler appeared, someone might ask: "Say, where is Morell this evening?"

Someone else would reply crossly: "He hasn't been here the past three evenings."

One of the secretaries: "He could stand staying up late once in a while. It's always the same. . . . I'd love to sleep too."

Another: "We really should arrange to take turns. It isn't fair for some to shirk and the same people have to be here all the time."

Of course Hitler was still revered by this circle, but his nimbus was distinctly wearing thin.

After Hitler had eaten breakfast late in the morning, the daily newspapers and press information sheets were presented to him. The press reports were crucially important in forming his opinions; they also had a great deal to do with his mood. Where specific foreign news items were concerned, he instantly formulated the official German position, usually highly aggressive, which he would then dictate word for word to his press chief, Dr. Dietrich, or to Dietrich's deputy, Lorenz. Hitler would boldly intrude on all areas of government, usually without consulting the ministers in question, such as Goebbels or Ribbentrop, or even bothering to inform them beforehand.

After that, Hewel reported on foreign events, which Hitler took more calmly than he did the press notices. In hindsight it seems to me that he considered the reverberations more important than the realities; that the newspaper accounts interested him more than the events themselves.

Schaub then brought in the reports of last night's air raids, which had been passed on from the Gauleiters to Bormann. Since I often went to look at the production facilities in the damaged cities a day or two later, I can judge that Hitler was correctly informed on the degree of destruction. It would in fact have been unwise of a Gauleiter to minimize the damage, since his prestige could only increase if, in spite of the devastation, he succeeded in restoring normal life and production.

Hitler was obviously shaken by these reports, although less by the casualties among the populace or the bombing of residential areas than by the destruction of valuable buildings, especially theaters. As in his plans for the "reshaping of German cities" before the war, he was primarily interested in public architecture and seemed to give little thought to social distress and human misery. Consequently, he was likely to demand that burned-out theaters be rebuilt immediately. Several times I tried to remind him of other strains upon the construction industry. Apparently the local political authorities were also less than eager to carry out these unpopular orders, and Hitler, in any case sufficiently taken up by the military situation, seldom inquired about the way the work was going. Only in Munich, his second home, and in Berlin did he insist that the opera houses be rebuilt at great expenditure of labor and money.[2]

Incidentally, Hitler betrayed a remarkable ignorance of the true situation and the mood of the populace when he answered all objections with: "Theatrical performances are needed precisely because the morale of the people must be maintained." The urban population certainly had other things to worry about. Once more, such remarks showed to what extent Hitler was rooted in a "bourgeois milieu."

While reading these reports, Hitler was in the habit of raging against the British government and the Jews, who were to blame for these air raids. We could force the enemy to stop by building a large fleet of bombers ourselves, he declared. Whenever I objected that we had neither the planes nor explosives for heavy bombing,[3] he always returned the same answer: "You've made so many things possible, Speer. You'll manage that too." It seems to me, in retrospect, that our ability to produce more and more in spite of the air raids must have been one of the reasons that Hitler did not really take the air battle over Germany seriously. Consequently, Milch's and my proposals that the manufacture of bombers be radically reduced in favor of increased fighter-plane production was rejected until it was too late.

I tried a few times to persuade Hitler to travel to the bombed cities and let himself be seen there.⁴ Goebbels, too, had tried to put over the same idea, but in vain. He lamented Hitler's obstinacy and referred enviously to the conduct of Churchill: "When I think of the propaganda value I could make of such a visit!" But Hitler regularly brushed away any such suggestion. During his drives from Stettin Station to the Chancellery, or to his apartment in Prinzregentenstrasse in Munich, he now ordered his chauffeur to take the shortest route, whereas he formerly loved long detours. Since I accompanied him several times on such drives, I saw with what absence of emotion he noted the new areas of rubble through which his car would pass.

Morell had advised Hitler to take long walks, and it would indeed have been very easy to lay out a few paths in the adjacent East Prussian woods. But Hitler vetoed any such project. The result was that his daily airing consisted of a small circuit barely a hundred yards long within Restricted Area I.

On these walks Hitler's interest was usually focused not on his companions but on his Alsatian dog Blondi. He used these intervals for training purposes. After a few exercises in fetching, the dog had to balance on a board about a foot wide and twenty-five feet long, mounted at a height of more than six feet. Hitler knew, of course, that a dog regards the man who feeds him as his master. Before the attendant opened the dog cage, Hitler usually let the excited dog leap up against the wire partitions for a few minutes, barking and whimpering with joy and hunger. Since I stood in special favor, I was sometimes allowed to accompany Hitler to this feeding, whereas all the others had to watch the process at a distance. The dog probably occupied the most important role in Hitler's private life; he meant more to his master than the Fuehrer's closest associates.

Hitler frequently took his meals alone when no guest he liked was at headquarters. In that case only the dog kept him company. As a matter of course, during my two- or three-day stays at headquarters I was asked to dine with the Fuehrer once or twice. People no doubt thought we were discussing important general matters or personal subjects during these meals. But even I found there was no talking with Hitler about broader aspects of the military situation, or even the economic situation. We stuck to trivial subjects or dreary production figures.

Initially, he remained interested in the matters that had absorbed both of us in the past, such as the future shaping of German cities. He also wanted to plan a transcontinental railroad network which would link his future empire together economically. After he decided on the size of the wide-gauge track he wanted for the railroad, he began considering various car types and plunging into detailed calculations on

freight tonnages. Such matters occupied him during his sleepless nights.*
The Transportation Ministry thought that the drawbacks of two railroad
systems more than outweighed the possible advantages, but Hitler had
become obsessed with this idea; he decided that it was even more important as a binding force in his empire than the autobahn system.

From month to month Hitler became more taciturn. It may also be
that he let himself go with me and made less of an effort at conversation
than he did with other guests. In any case, from the autumn of 1943 on,
a lunch with him became an ordeal. In silence, we spooned up our soup.
While we waited for the next course we might make a few remarks about
the weather, whereupon Hitler would usually say something acid about
the incompetence of the weather bureau. Finally the conversation would
revert to the quality of the food. He was highly pleased with his diet
cook and praised her skill at vegetarian cuisine. If a dish seemed to him
especially good, he asked me to have a taste of it.

He was forever worried about gaining weight. "Out of the question!
Imagine me going around with a potbelly. It would mean political ruin."
After making such remarks he would frequently call his orderly, to put
an end to temptation: "Take this away, please, I like it too much." Incidentally, even here at headquarters he would often make fun of meat-
eaters, but he did not attempt to sway me. He even had no objection to a
Steinhäger after fatty food—although he commented pityingly that he did
not need it, with his fare. If there were a meat broth I could depend on
his speaking of "corpse tea"; in connection with crayfish he brought out
his story of a deceased grandmother whose relations had thrown her body
into the brook to lure the crustaceans; for eels, that they were best fat-
tened and caught by using dead cats.

Earlier, during those evenings in the Chancellery, Hitler had never
been shy about repeating stories as often as he pleased. But now, in these
times of retreats and impending doom, such repetitions had to be regarded as signs that he was in an especially good humor. For most of the
time a deadly silence prevailed. I had the impression of a man whose life
was slowly ebbing away.

During conferences that often lasted for hours, or during meals,
Hitler ordered his dog to lie down in a certain corner. There the animal
settled with a protesting growl. If he felt that he was not being watched,
he crawled closer to his master's seat and after elaborate maneuvers finally
landed with his snout against Hitler's knee, whereupon a sharp command

---

* The idea behind this transcontinental service was that a single train would
transport as much as a freighter. Hitler felt that sea travel was never sufficiently safe
and was certainly unreliable in wartime. Even where plans for new railroad facilities
had already been completed, as in Berlin and Munich, an extra pair of tracks had to
be added for Hitler's new railroad system.

banished him to his corner again. I avoided, as did any reasonably prudent visitor to Hitler, arousing any feelings of friendship in the dog. That was often not so easy, especially when at meals the dog laid his head on my knee and in this position attentively studied the pieces of meat, which he evidently preferred to his master's vegetarian dishes. When Hitler noticed such disloyalty, he irritably called the dog back. But still the dog remained the only living creature at headquarters who aroused any flicker of human feeling in Hitler. Only—the dog was mute.

Hitler's deep estrangement from people proceeded slowly, almost imperceptibly. From about the autumn of 1943 on, he used to make one remark which was all too revealing of his unhappy isolation: "Speer, one of these days I'll have only two friends left, Fräulein Braun and my dog." His tone was so misanthropic, and the remark seemed to be wrung from such depths that it would not have done for me to assure him of my own loyalty. That was the one and only prediction of Hitler's that proved to be absolutely right. But that those two remained true to him was certainly no credit to Hitler, but rather to the staunchness of his mistress and the dependency of his dog.

Later, in my many years of imprisonment, I discovered what it meant to live under great psychological pressure. Only then did I realize that Hitler's life had borne a great resemblance to that of a prisoner. His bunker, although it did not yet have the tomblike proportions it was to assume in July 1944, had the thick walls and ceilings of a prison. Iron doors and iron shutters guarded the few openings, and even his meager walks within the barbed wire brought him no more fresh air and contact with nature than a prisoner's endless tramp around the prison yard.

Hitler's hour came when the main situation conference began after lunch, around two o'clock. Outwardly, the scene had not changed since the spring of 1942. Almost the same generals and adjutants gathered around the big map table. Only now all the participants seemed to have been aged and worn by the events of the past year and a half. Indifferent and rather resigned, they received his watchwords and commands.

Positive aspects were played up. From the testimony of prisoners and special reports from the Russian front, it might appear that the enemy would soon be exhausted. The Russian casualties seemed to be much higher than ours because of their offensives—higher even in proportion to the relative sizes of our populations. Reports of insignificant successes loomed larger and larger in the course of these discussions, until they had become for Hitler incontrovertible evidence that Germany would after all be able to delay the Soviet onslaught until the Russians had been bled white. Moreover, many of us believed that Hitler would end the war at the right time.

To forecast what we might expect in the next few months, Jodl prepared a report to Hitler. At the same time he tried to revive his real job as chief of the Armed Forces Operations Staff, which Hitler had more and more taken over. Jodl knew well Hitler's distrust for arguments based on calculations. Toward the end of 1943, Hitler was still speaking scornfully of a projection by General Georg Thomas which had rated the Soviet war potential as extremely high. Hitler was irate over this memorandum, and soon after its presentation he had forbidden Thomas and the OKW to undertake any further studies of this type. When around the autumn of 1944 my planning board, in an earnest effort to help the military operations staff make its decisions, worked out a memorandum on the enemy's armaments capacities, we received a reprimand from Keitel and were told not to transmit such documents to the OKW.

Thus, Jodl knew that there were serious barriers that prevented him from delivering his report. He therefore appointed a young air force colonel named Christian to give a quick sketch of the matter at one of the situation conferences. The colonel had the rather significant advantage of being married to one of Hitler's secretaries, one of those who belonged to the nightly teatime circle. The idea was to discern the enemy's possible long-run tactical plans and what the consequences would be for us. But aside from the scene of Colonel Christian's showing a completely silent Hitler various places on several large maps of Europe, I no longer recall what happened with this attempt. In any case, it failed miserably.

Without much fuss, and without any rebellion on the part of those concerned, Hitler continued to make all decisions himself, in total disregard of any technical basis. He dispensed with analyses of the situation and logistical calculations. He did not rely on any study group which would examine all aspects of offensive plans in terms of their effectiveness and possible countermeasures by the enemy. The headquarters staffs were more than competent to carry out these functions of modern warfare; it would only have been necessary to activate them. To be sure, Hitler would accept information about partial aspects of situations; but the grand synthesis was supposed to be born solely in his head. His field marshals as well as his closest associates had, therefore, merely advisory functions, for his decision had usually been forged beforehand and only minor aspects of it were subject to change. Moreover, whatever he had learned from the eastern campaign in the years 1942-43 was rigorously repressed. Decisions were made in a total vacuum.

At headquarters, where everyone lived under the tremendous pressure of responsibility, probably nothing was more welcome than a dictate from above. That meant being freed of a decision and simultaneously being provided with an excuse for failure. Only rarely did I hear of a member of the headquarters staff applying for frontline service in order to escape the permanent conflicts of conscience to which all at headquarters were exposed. To this day the whole thing remains an enigma for me. For in spite of a great deal of criticism hardly any one of us ever managed to put across our reservations. Actually, we were hardly conscious of them. In the stupefying world of the headquarters we remained unmoved by what Hitler's decisions must mean at the front, where men were fighting and dying. Yet time and again our men found themselves in emergencies that could have been avoided had Hitler not staved off a retreat proposed by the General Staff.

No one could expect the Chief of State to go to the front regularly. But as Commander in Chief of the army, who moreover decided on so many details himself, he was obliged to do so. If he were too ill, then he should have appointed someone else; if he were fearful for his life, he had no right to be Commander in Chief of the army.

A few trips to the front could easily have shown him and his staff the fundamental errors that were costing so much blood. But Hitler and his military advisers thought they could lead the army from their maps. They knew nothing of the Russian winter and its road conditions, nor of the hardships of soldiers who had to live in holes in the ground, without quarters, inadequately equipped, exhausted and half frozen. Their resistance had long since been shattered. At the situation conferences Hitler took these units as up to full strength, and under that delusion they were committed. He pushed about on the map divisions that had worn themselves out in previous fighting and now lacked arms and ammunition. Moreover, Hitler frequently set schedules that were completely unrealistic. Since he invariably ordered immediate action, the advance detachments came under fire before the task force could bring its full fire power to bear. The result was that the men were led piecemeal up to the enemy and slowly annihilated.

The communications apparatus at headquarters was remarkable for that period. It was possible to communicate directly with all the important theaters of war. But Hitler overestimated the merits of the telephone, radio, and teletype. For thanks to this apparatus the responsible army commanders were robbed of every chance for independent action, in contrast to earlier wars. Hitler was constantly intervening on their sectors of the front. Because of this communications apparatus individual divisions in all the theaters of war could be directed from Hitler's table in the situation room. The more fearful the situation, the greater was the gulf modern technology created between reality and the fantasies with which the man at this table operated.

Military leadership is primarily a matter of intelligence, tenacity, and iron nerves. Hitler thought he had all these qualities in far greater measure than his generals. Again and again he predicted, although only after the disaster of the winter of 1941-42, that even the worst situations could be overcome and, indeed, that only in such situations would he prove how firmly he stood and how sound his nerves were.*

Such remarks were scarcely complimentary toward the officers present; but Hitler was often capable of turning to the General Staff officers of his entourage and insulting them directly. He would tell them that they were not steadfast, that they were always wanting to retreat, that they were prepared to give up ground without any reason. These cowards on the General Staff would never have dared to start a war, he would say; they had always advised against it, always maintained that our forces were far too weak. But who had been proved right, if not himself! He would run down the usual list of earlier military successes and review the negative attitudes of the General Staff before these operations began—which produced a ghostly impression, given the situation that had meanwhile arisen. In going over the past that way he might lose his temper, flush deeply, and in a rapid, loud voice breaking with excitement burst out: "They aren't only notorious cowards, they're dishonest as well. They're notorious liars! The training of the General Staff is a school of lying and deception. Zeitzler, these figures are false! You yourself are being lied to. Believe me, the situation is deliberately being represented as unfavorable. That's how they want to force me to authorize retreats!"

Invariably, Hitler ordered the bends in the front to be held at all costs, and just as invariably the Soviet forces would overrun the position after a few days or weeks. Then there followed new rages, mingled with fresh denunciations of the officers and, frequently, complaints against the German soldiers: "The soldier of the First World War was much tougher. Think of all they had to go through, in Verdun, on the Somme. Today, they would run away from that kind of thing."

A good many of the officers who came in for these tongue-lashings later joined the July 20, 1944, conspiracy against Hitler. That plot cast its shadow before. In the past Hitler had had a fine sense of discrimination and was able to adapt his language to the people around him. Now he was unrestrained and reckless. His speech became an overflowing torrent like that of a prisoner who betrays dangerous secrets even to his prosecutor. In his talk Hitler seemed to me to be obeying an obsession.

In order to supply evidence for posterity that he had always issued the right orders, as early at the late autumn of 1942, Hitler sent for certified stenographers from the Reichstag who from then on sat at the table during the situation conference and took down every word.

Sometimes, when Hitler thought he had found the way out of a

---

* On July 26, 1944, Hitler boasted to the heads of industry: "All I know is that unprecedentedly strong nerves and unprecedented resolution are necessary if a leader is to survive in times such as these and make decisions which concern our very existence. . . . Any other man in my place would have been unable to do what I have done; his nerves would not have been strong enough."

dilemma, he would add: "Have you got that? Yes, someday people will see that I was right. But these idiotic General Staff officers refuse to believe me." Even when the troops were retreating, he would declare triumphantly: "Didn't I order so and so three days ago? Again my order hasn't been carried out. They don't carry out my orders and afterward they lie and blame the Russians. They lie when they say the Russians prevented them from carrying out the order." Hitler refused to admit that his failures were due to the weak position into which he had cast us by insisting on a war on many fronts.

Only a few months before, the stenographers who unexpectedly found themselves in this madhouse had probably envisioned Hitler as a superior genius, just as Goebbels had taught them. Here they were forced to catch a glimpse of the reality. I can still see them distinctly as they sat writing, sallow-faced, or in their free time pacing back and forth at headquarters with a downcast air. They seemed to me like envoys from the populace who were condemned to witness the tragedy from front-row seats.

At the beginning of the war in the east, Hitler, captive to his theory that the Slavs were subhuman, had called the war against them child's play. But the longer the war lasted, the more the Russians gained his respect. He was impressed by the stoicism with which they had accepted their early defeats. He spoke admiringly of Stalin, particularly stressing the parallels to his own endurance. The danger that hung over Moscow in the winter of 1941 struck him as similar to his present predicament. In a brief access of confidence,[5] he might remark with a jesting tone of voice that it would be best, after victory over Russia, to entrust the administration of the country to Stalin, under German hegemony, of course, since he was the best imaginable man to handle the Russians. In general he regarded Stalin as a kind of colleague. When Stalin's son was taken prisoner it was out of this respect, perhaps, that Hitler ordered him to be given especially good treatment. Much had changed since that day after the armistice with France when Hitler predicted that a war with the Soviet Union would be child's play.

In contrast to his ultimate realization that he was dealing with a formidable enemy in the east, Hitler clung to the end to his preconceived opinion that the troops of the Western countries were poor fighting material. Even the Allied successes in Africa and Italy could not shake his belief that these soldiers would run away from the first serious onslaught. He was convinced that democracy enfeebled a nation. As late as the summer of 1944 he held to his theory that all the ground that had been lost in the West would be quickly reconquered. His opinions on the Western statesmen had a similar bias. He considered Churchill, as he often stated during the situation conferences, an incompetent, alcoholic demagogue. And he asserted in all seriousness that Roosevelt was not a victim of infantile paralysis but of syphilitic paralysis and was therefore mentally unsound. These opinions, too, were indications of his flight from reality in the last years of his life.

Within Restricted Area I in Rastenburg a teahouse had been built. Its furnishings were a pleasant change from the general drabness. Here we occasionally met for a glass of vermouth; here field marshals waited before conferring with Hitler. He himself avoided this teahouse and thus escaped encounters with the generals and staff officers of the High Command and of the armed forces. But for a few days, after Fascism had ingloriously come to an end in Italy on July 25, 1943, and Badoglio had taken over the government, Hitler sat there over tea several afternoons with perhaps ten of his military and political associates, among them Keitel, Jodl, and Bormann. Suddenly, Jodl blurted out: "Come to think of it, Fascism simply burst like a soap bubble." A horrified silence followed, until someone launched another subject, whereupon Jodl, visibly alarmed, flushed beet red.

A few weeks afterward Prince Philip of Hesse was invited to the headquarters. He was one of the few followers whom Hitler always treated with deference and respect. Philip had often been useful to him, and especially in the early years of the Third Reich had arranged contacts with the heads of Italian Fascism. In addition he had helped Hitler purchase valuable art works. The Prince had been able to arrange their export from Italy through his connections with the Italian royal house, to which he was related.

When the Prince wanted to leave again after a few days, Hitler bluntly told him that he would not be allowed to leave headquarters. He continued to treat him with the greatest outward courtesy and invited him to his meals. But the members of Hitler's entourage, who until then had been so fond of talking with a "real prince," avoided him as if he had a contagious disease. On September 9, Prince Philip and Princess Mafalda, the Italian King's daughter, were taken to a concentration camp on Hitler's direct orders.

For weeks afterward Hitler boasted that he had begun suspecting early in the game that Prince Philip was sending information to the Italian royal house. He himself had kept an eye on him, Hitler said, and ordered his telephone conversations tapped. By methods such as these it had been discovered that the Prince was passing number codes to his wife. Nevertheless, Hitler had continued to treat the Prince with marked friendliness. That had been part of his tactics, he declared, obviously delighted with his gifts as a detective.

The arrest of the Prince and his wife reminded all those who were similarly close to Hitler that they had put themselves utterly into his hands. The feeling spread, unconsciously, that Hitler might be covertly and meanly keeping watch on anyone among his intimates and might deliver him up to a similar fate without giving him the slightest opportunity to justify himself.

Mussolini's relationship to Hitler had been for all of us, ever since the Duce's support during the Austrian crisis, the very symbol of amity. After the Italian Chief of State was overthrown and vanished without a trace, Hitler seemed to be inspired with a kind of Nibelungen loyalty. Again and again in the situation conferences he insisted that everything must be done to locate the missing Duce. He declared that Mussolini's fate was a nightmare that weighed on him day and night.

On September 12, 1943, a conference was held in headquarters to which the Gauleiters of Tyrol and Carinthia were invited, along with me. It was settled that not only South Tyrol but also the Italian territory as far as Verona would be placed under the administration of Gauleiter Hofer of Tyrol. Large parts of Venetia, including Trieste, were assigned to the territory of Gauleiter Rainer of Carinthia. I was given jurisdiction in all questions of armaments and production for the remaining Italian territory and powers over and above those of the Italian authorities. Then came a great surprise: A few hours after the signing of these decrees Mussolini's liberation was announced.

The two Gauleiters thought their newly acquired domains were lost again. So did I. "The Fuehrer won't expect the Duce to swallow that!" I said. Shortly afterward I met Hitler again and proposed that he cancel the new arrangement. I assumed that this was what he meant to do. To my surprise he fended off the suggestion. The decree would continue to be valid, he said. I pointed out to him that with a new Italian government formed under Mussolini, he could hardly infringe on Italy's sovereignty. Hitler reflected briefly, then said: "Present my decree to me for signature again, dated tomorrow. Then there will be no doubt that my order is not affected by the Duce's liberation."[6]

Undoubtedly Hitler had already been informed, a few days before this amputation of northern Italy, that the place where Mussolini was being held prisoner had been located. It seems a fair guess that we were called to headquarters so quickly precisely because of the impending liberation of the Duce.

The next day Mussolini arrived in Rastenburg. Hitler embraced him, sincerely moved. On the anniversary of the Three-Power Pact, Hitler sent to the Duce, with whom he declared himself "linked in friendship," his "warmest wishes for the future of an Italy once more led to honorable freedom by Fascism."

Two weeks before, Hitler had mutilated Italy.

22

Downhill

THE MOUNTING FIGURES FOR ARMAMENTS PRODUCTION STRENGTHENED MY position until the autumn of 1943. After we had virtually exhausted the industrial reserves of Germany, I tried to exploit the industrial potential of the other European countries we controlled.[1] Hitler was at first reluctant to make full use of the capacity of the West. And in years to come, he had decided, the occupied eastern territories were actually to be deindustrialized. For industry, he held, promoted communism and bred an unwanted class of intellectuals. But conditions quickly proved stronger than all such theories. Hitler was hardheaded enough to recognize how useful intact industries could be toward solving the problems of troop supply.

France was the most important of the occupied industrial countries. Until the spring of 1943, however, its industrial production scarcely helped us. Sauckel's forcible recruiting of labor had done more damage there than its results warranted. For in order to escape forced labor, the French workers fled their factories, quite a few of which were producing for our armaments needs. In May 1943, I remonstrated to Sauckel about this. That July at a conference in Paris I proposed that at least the factories in France that were working for us be immune from Sauckel's levies.*

* *Office Journal*, July 23, 1943: "The minister proposed to improve the situation by designating protected factories. These would be guaranteed against levying of workers and would thus be made more attractive to French labor."

(309)

My associates and I intended to have the factories in France particularly, but also in Belgium and Holland, produce large quantities of goods for the German civilian population, such as clothing, shoes, textiles, and furniture, in order to free similar factories in Germany for armaments. As soon as I was charged with all of German production at the beginning of September, I invited the French Minister of Production to Berlin. Minister Bichelonne, a professor at the Sorbonne, was reputed to be a capable and energetic man.

After some bickering with the Foreign Office, I ensured that Bichelonne would be treated as a state visitor. To win that point I had to appeal to Hitler, explaining to him that Bichelonne was not going to "come up the back stairs" to see me. As a result, the French Production Minister was quartered in the Berlin government guest house.

Five days before Bichelonne arrived I cleared the idea with Hitler that we would set up a production planning council on a pan-European basis, with France as an equal partner along with the other nations. The assumption was, of course, that Germany would retain the decisive voice in this planning.[2]

On September 17, 1943, I received Bichelonne, and before very long a distinctly personal relationship sprang up between us. We were both young, we believed the future was on our side, and both of us therefore promised ourselves that someday we would avoid the mistakes of the First World War generation that was presently governing. I was even prepared to prevent what Hitler had in mind in the way of carving up France, all the more so since in a Europe integrated economically it did not matter where the frontiers ran. Such were the utopian thoughts in which Bichelonne and I lost ourselves for a while at that time—a token of the world of illusions and dreams in which we were moving.

On the last day of the negotiations Bichelonne asked to have a private talk with me. At the instigation of Sauckel, he began, Premier Laval had forbidden him to discuss the question of the transportation of workers from France to Germany.[3] Would I nevertheless be willing to deal with the question? I said I would. Bichelonne explained his concern, and I finally asked him whether a measure protecting French industrial plants from deportations would help him. "If that is possible, then all my problems are solved, including those relating to the program we have just agreed on," Bichelonne said with relief. "But then the transfer of labor from France to Germany will virtually cease. I must tell you that in all honesty."

I was fully aware of that, but this seemed the only way I could harness French industrial production to our purposes. Both of us had done something unusual. Bichelonne had disobeyed an instruction from Laval, and I had disavowed Sauckel. Both of us, basically without the backing of our superiors, had come to a far-reaching agreement.*

* Sauckel pointed this out at the Central Planning meeting, March 1, 1944: "It is certainly difficult for me as a German to be confronted with a situation which all

Our production plan would offer benefits to both countries. I would gain armaments capacity, while the French appreciated the chance to resume peacetime production in the midst of war. In collaboration with the military commander in France, restricted factories would be established throughout the country. Placards posted in these factories would promise immunity from Sauckel's levies to all the workers employed in them. I personally would stand behind this pledge, since the placards would bear my signature in facsimile. But French basic industry also had to be strengthened, transportation guaranteed, food production assured—so that ultimately almost every important productive unit—in the end a total of ten thousand—would be shielded from Sauckel.

Bichelonne and I spent the weekend at the country house of my friend Arno Breker. On Monday, I informed Sauckel's associates of the new arrangements. I called upon them to direct their efforts from then on to inducing workers to go back to French factories. Their numbers, I pledged, would be reckoned in on the quota of "assignments to German armaments production."[4]

Ten days later I was at the Fuehrer's headquarters to beat Sauckel to the punch in reporting to Hitler. And in fact Hitler proved content; he approved my arrangements and was even ready to take into account possible production losses because of riots or strikes.[5]

In this way Sauckel's operations in France virtually came to an end. Instead of the previous monthly quota of fifty thousand, before long only five thousand workers a month were being taken to Germany.[*] A few months later (on March 1, 1944), Sauckel reported angrily: "I hear from my offices in France that everything is finished there. 'We might as well close down,' they tell me. It's the same story in every prefecture: Minister Bichelonne has made an agreement with Minister Speer. Laval has the nerve to say: 'I won't give you any more men for Germany.'"

A short while later I proceeded to apply the same principle to Holland, Belgium, and Italy.

On August 20, 1943, Heinrich Himmler had been appointed Minister of the Interior of the Reich. Until then, to be sure, he had been Reichsführer of the all-embracing SS, which was spoken of as a "state within the state." But in his capacity as chief of the police he had been, strangely, a subordinate of Minister of the Interior Frick.

The power of the Gauleiters, constantly furthered by Bormann, had

---

too plainly tells the French industries in France they have been placed under protection simply to keep them out of the grasp of Sauckel."

[*] See Nuremberg Document RF 22. On June 27, 1943, Sauckel wrote to Hitler: "Therefore I ask you, *mein Führer,* to accept my proposal that another half a million French men and women be imported into the Reich until the end of the war." According to a notation by his assistant, Dr. Strothfang, dated July 28, 1943, Hitler had already agreed to this measure.

led to a splintering of sovereignty in the Reich. There were two categories of Gauleiters. The old ones, those who had held their positions before 1933, were simply incompetent to run an administrative apparatus. Alongside these men there rose, in the course of the years, a new class of Gauleiters of Bormann's school. They were young administrative officials, usually with legal training, whose one thought was to strengthen the influence of the party within the state.

It was characteristic of Hitler's double-track way of running things that the Gauleiters in their capacity of party functionaries were under Bormann, while in their capacity as Reich Commissioners for Defense they were under the Minister of the Interior. Under the feeble Frick this double allegiance involved no danger to Bormann. Analysts of the political scene suspected, however, that with Himmler as Minister of the Interior, Bormann had acquired a serious counterpoise.

I too saw it this way and was looking forward hopefully to Himmler's reign. Above all I counted on his checking the progressive fragmentation of the government executive power. And, in fact, Himmler promptly gave me his promise that on administrative matters of the Reich government he would call the willful Gauleiters to account.[6]

On October 6, 1943, I addressed the Reichsleiters and the Gauleiters of the party. The reaction to my speech signaled a turning point. My purpose was to open the eyes of the political leadership to the true state of affairs, to dispel their illusion that a great rocket would soon be ready for use, and to make it clear that the enemy was calling all the turns. For us to regain the initiative, the economic structure of Germany, in part still on a peacetime basis, must be shaken up, I declared. Of the six million persons employed in our consumer goods industries, one and a half million must be transferred to armaments production. From now on consumer goods would be manufactured in France. I admitted that this would place France in a favorable starting position for the postwar era. "But my view is," I declared to my audience of top party executives who sat there as if petrified, "that if we want to win the war we are the ones who will primarily have to make the sacrifices."

I challenged the Gauleiters even more bluntly when I continued:

> You will please take note of this: The manner in which the various districts [Gaue] have hitherto obstructed the shutdown of consumer goods production can and will no longer be tolerated. Henceforth, if the districts do not respond to my requests within two weeks I shall myself order the shutdowns. And I can assure you that I am prepared to apply the authority of the Reich government at any cost! I have spoken with Reichsführer-SS Himmler, and from now on I shall deal firmly with the districts that do not carry out these measures.

The Gauleiters were less disturbed by the comprehensiveness of my program than by these two last sentences. I had barely finished my speech when several of them came rushing up to me. Led by one of the oldest among them, Joseph Bürkel, in loud voices and with waving arms they charged that I had threatened them with concentration camp. In order to correct that misapprehension, I asked Bormann if I could once more take the floor. But Bormann waved me aside. With hypocritical friendliness he said this was not necessary at all, for there were really no misunderstandings.

The evening after this meeting many of the Gauleiters drank so heavily that they needed help to get to the special train taking them to the Fuehrer's headquarters that night. Next morning I asked Hitler to say a few words about temperance to his political associates; but as always he spared the feelings of his comrades in arms of the early days. On the other hand, Bormann informed Hitler about my quarrel with the Gauleiters.* Hitler gave me to understand that all the Gauleiters were furious, without telling me any of the specific reasons. Bormann, it soon became plain, had at last found a way to undermine my standing with Hitler. He went on chipping away incessantly, and for the first time with some success. I myself had given him the means. From now on I could no longer count on Hitler's support as a matter of course.

I also soon found out what Himmler's promise to enforce my directives was worth. I had documents on serious disputes with Gauleiters sent to him, but I did not hear anything about them for weeks. Finally, Himmler's state secretary, Wilhelm Stuckart, informed me with some embarrassment that the Minister of the Interior had sent the documents directly to Bormann, whose reply had only now arrived. All the cases had been checked over by the Gauleiters, Stuckart said. As might have been expected, it had turned out that my orders were invalid and the Gauleiters were entirely justified in refusing to follow them. Himmler, Stuckart said, had accepted this report. So much for my hope of strengthening the government's as against the party's authority. Nothing came of the Speer-Himmler coalition either.

A few months passed before I found out why all these plans were doomed to failure. As I heard from Gauleiter Hanke of Lower Silesia, Himmler had actually tried to strike a blow against the sovereignty of some Gauleiters. He sent them orders through his SS commanders in their districts, a clear affront to their power. But he quickly learned that the Gauleiters had all the backing they needed in Bormann's party headquarters. Within a few days Bormann had Hitler prohibit any such steps by Himmler. Hitler might have contempt for his Gauleiters, but at crucial moments he always remained loyal to these comrades of his early days of

---

* I did not learn the particulars from Gauleiter Kaufmann until May 1944. Then, I immediately requested a meeting with Hitler. For further details, see Chapter 23.

struggle. Even Himmler and the SS could do nothing against this senti-mental cronyism.

Worsted in this one inept maneuver, the SS leader completely ac-knowledged the independence of the Gauleiters. The projected meeting of "Reich Defense Commissioners" was never called, and Himmler contented himself with making his power felt among the politically less influential mayors and governors. Bormann and Himmler, who were on a first-name basis anyhow, soon became good friends again. My speech had brought to light the strata of interest-groups, but in revealing these power-relation-ships I had endangered myself.

Within a few months I could chalk up a third failure in my efforts to activate the power and potentialities of the regime. Faced with a dilemma, I tried to escape it by taking the offensive. Only five days after my speech I had Hitler appoint me chief of future planning for all the cities damaged by bombing. Thus I was invested with full powers in a field which was much closer to the hearts of my opponents, including Bormann himself, than many of the problems concerned with the war. Some of them were already thinking of this reconstruction of the cities as their foremost future task. Hitler's decree reminded them that I would be standing over them in this.

I wanted this assignment not only as a counter in the power struggle. There was another threat, one springing from the quality of the Gauleiters, which I felt had to be headed off. For they saw the devastation of the cities as an opportunity to tear down historic buildings which to them had little meaning. Instances of this tendency of theirs were all too common. One day, for example, I was sitting on a roof terrace with the Gauleiter of Essen looking out over the ruins after a heavy air raid. He commented casually that now the Cathedral of Essen could be torn down entirely, since the bombing had damaged it anyhow and it was only a hindrance to modernization of the city. The Mayor of Mannheim appealed to me for help to prevent the demolition of the burned-out Mannheim Castle and the National Theater. From Stuttgart, I heard that the burned palace there was also to be torn down at the orders of the local Gauleiter.*

* Hitler found out about such plans too late. Besides, the Gauleiters were able to make it appear that the buildings had been on the point of collapse. Eight months later, on June 26, 1944, I protested to Bormann: "In various cities efforts are under way to tear down buildings of historical and artistic merit that have been damaged in the raids. The argument offered to justify these measures is that the buildings are either about to collapse or cannot be restored. It is also contended that demolition will provide a welcome opportunity for urban renewal. I would be very grateful if you would send a memorandum to all the Gauleiters pointing out that historical monuments, even in ruins, must be preserved at all costs. I must ask you also to inform the Gauleiters that such monuments cannot be torn down until the Fuehrer himself has definitely decided on reconstruction plans for the cities and thus also for

The reasoning in all these cases was the same: Away with castles and churches; after the war we'll build our own monuments! In part this impulse sprang from the feeling of inferiority toward the past that the party bigwigs had. But there was another element in this feeling, as one of the Gauleiters explained when he was justifying his demolition order to me: Castles and churches of the past were citadels of reaction that stood in the way of our revolution. Remarks of this sort revealed a fanaticism that belonged to the early days of the party, but that had gradually been lost in the compromises and arrangements of a party in power.

I myself placed such importance on the preservation of the historical fabric of the German cities and on a sane policy of reconstruction that even at the climax and turning point of the war, in November and December 1943, I addressed a letter to all Gauleiters in which I recast most of my prewar philosophy: no more pretentious artistic notions, but economy-mindedness; broad-scale transportation planning to save the cities from traffic congestion; mass production of housing, cleaning up the old quarters of the cities, and establishing businesses in the city centers.[7] There was no longer any talk of monumental buildings. My enthusiasm for them had faded, and so in all probability had Hitler's, for he let me describe this new planning concept to him without the least protest.

Early in November 1943, Soviet troops were approaching Nikopol, the center of manganese mining. At this time there occurred a curious incident in which Hitler behaved much as Goering had when he ordered his generals to tell a deliberate lie.

Chief of Staff Zeitzler phoned to tell me that he had just had a violent disagreement with Hitler. He himself was highly agitated. Hitler had insisted, he said, that all available divisions be massed for the defense of Nikopol. Without manganese, Hitler had declared excitedly, the war would be lost in no time. Three months later Speer would have to halt armaments production, for he has no reserve stocks of manganese.[8] Zeitzler begged me to help him. Instead of bringing in new troops, he said, the time had come to begin the retreat. This was our only chance to avert another Stalingrad.

After hearing this, I at once sat down with Röchling and Rohland, our steel industry experts, to clarify our situation in regard to manganese. Manganese was, of course, one of the principal constituents of high-strength steels. But it was equally clear after Zeitzler's telephone call that one way or another the manganese mines in southern Russia were lost to us. What I learned at my conferences was surprisingly favorable. On

---

these buildings." Despite the limited means, materials, and workmen available, I also ordered that many damaged monuments be patched up sufficiently to prevent further dilapidation. I tried to put this plan into effect in northern Italy and in France by giving similar instructions to the Todt Organization.

November 11, I informed Zeitzler and Hitler by teletype: "Manganese stocks sufficient for eleven to twelve months available in the Reich even if present procedures are maintained. The Reich Steel Association guarantees that in case Nikopol is lost introduction of other metals will enable us to stretch the manganese stocks without additional strain on other alloy materials for eighteen months."[9] I could moreover state that even the loss of neighboring Krivoi Rog—for the holding of which Hitler wanted to wage a great defensive battle—would not seriously affect the continued flow of German steel production.

When I arrived at the Fuehrer's headquarters two days later, Hitler snarled at me in a tone he had never used toward me before: "What was the idea of your giving the Chief of Staff your memorandum on the manganese situation?"

I had expected to find him well pleased with me, and managed only to reply, stunned: "But, *mein Führer,* it's good news after all!"

Hitler did not accept that. "You are not to give the Chief of Staff any memoranda at all! If you have some information, kindly send it to me. You've put me in an intolerable situation. I have just given orders for all available forces to be concentrated for the defense of Nikopol. At last I have a reason to force the army group to fight! And then Zeitzler comes along with your memo. It makes me out a liar! If Nikopol is lost now, it's your fault. I forbid you once and for all"—his voice rose to a scream at the end—"to address any memos to anybody but myself. Do you understand that? I forbid it!"

Nevertheless, my memorandum had done its work; for soon afterward Hitler stopped insisting on a battle for the manganese mines. But since the Soviet pressure in this area ceased at the same time, Nikopol was not lost until February 18, 1944.

In a second memorandum I gave to Hitler that day, I had drawn up an inventory of our stocks of all alloy metals. By the single sentence, "imports from the Balkans, Turkey, Nikopol, Finland, and northern Norway have not been considered," I alluded to the possibility that these areas might well be lost to us. The following table sums up the results:[*]

	Manganese	Nickel	Chromium	Wolframite	Molybdenum	Silicon
Home stocks	140,000 t	6,000 t	21,000 t	1,330 t	425 t	17,900 t
Imports	8,100 t	190 t	——	——	15.5 t	4,200 t
Consumption	15,500 t	750 t	3,751 t	160 t	69.5 t	7,000 t
Months reserve	19	10	5.6	10.6	7.8	6.4

From this table I drew the following conclusion:

Hence, the element in shortest supply is chromium. This is especially grave since chromium is indispensable to a highly developed armaments

[*] Figures given in metric tons.

industry. Should supplies from Turkey be cut off, the stockpile of chromium is sufficient only for 5.6 months. The manufacture of planes, tanks, motor vehicles, tank shells, U-boats, and almost the entire gamut of artillery would have to cease from one to three months after this deadline, since by then the reserves in the distribution channels would be used up.[10]

That meant no more or less than that the war would be over approximately ten months after the loss of the Balkans. Hitler listened to my report, whose import was that it would not be Nikopol but the Balkans that would determine the outcome of the war, in total silence. Then he turned away, out of sorts. He addressed my associate Saur, to discuss new tank programs with him.

Until the summer of 1943, Hitler used to telephone me at the beginning of every month to ask for the latest production figures, which he then entered on a prepared sheet. I gave him the figures in the customary order, and Hitler usually received them with exclamations such as: "Very good! Why, that's wonderful! Really a hundred and ten Tigers? That's more than you promised. . . . And how many Tigers do you think you'll manage next month? Every tank is important now. . . . " He generally concluded these conversations with a brief reference to the situation: "We've taken Kharkov today. It's going well. Well then, nice to talk to you. My regards to your wife. Is she still at Obersalzberg? Well then, my regards again."

When I thanked him and added the salutation, *"Heil, mein Führer!"* he sometimes replied, "Heil, Speer." This greeting was a sign of favor which he only rarely vouchsafed to Goering, Goebbels, and a few other intimates; underlying it was a note of faint irony at the mandatory, *"Heil, mein Führer."* At such moments I felt as if a medal had been conferred on me. I did not notice the element of condescension in this familiarity. Although the fascination of the early days and the excitement of being on an intimate footing with Hitler had long since passed, although I no longer enjoyed the unique special position of Hitler's architect, and although I had become one of many in the apparatus of government, a word from Hitler had lost none of its magical force. To be precise, all the intrigues and struggles for power were directed toward eliciting such a word, or what it stood for. The position of each and every one of us was dependent on his attitude.

The telephone calls gradually ceased. It is difficult to say just when, but from the autumn of 1943 on, at any rate, Hitler fell into the habit of calling Saur to ask for the monthly reports.[11] I did not oppose this, since I recognized Hitler's right to take away what he had given. But since Bormann had particularly good relations with Saur as well as Dorsch—both men were old party members—I gradually began to feel insecure in my own Ministry.

At first I tried to consolidate my position by assigning a representative from industry as a deputy to each of my ten department heads.[12] But

Dorsch and Saur succeeded in frustrating my intention in their own departments. Since it became ever more apparent that a faction was forming in the Ministry under the leadership of Dorsch, on December 21, 1943, I initiated a kind of "coup d'état," appointing two old, reliable associates from my days as Hitler's chief architect as chiefs of the Personnel and Organization Section,[13] and placed the previously independent Todt Organization under their direction.

The next day I escaped from the heavy burdens of the year 1943, with its multitudinous personal disappointments and intrigues, by seeking out the remotest and loneliest corner of the world within our sphere of power: northern Lapland. In 1941 and 1942, Hitler had refused to let me travel to Norway, Finland, and Russia because he considered such a journey too dangerous and me too indispensable. But this time he gave his approval with no more ado.

We started at dawn in my new plane, a four-motored Focke-Wulf Condor. It had unusually long range because of its built-in reserve tanks.[14] Siegfried Borries, the violinist, and an amateur magician who became famous after the war under the name of Kalanag, accompanied us. My idea was that instead of making speeches, we would provide some Christmas entertainment for the soldiers and Todt Organization workers in the north. Flying low, we looked down at Finland's chains of lakes, which my wife and I had longed to explore with faltboat and tent. Early in the afternoon, in the last glimmers of dusk in this northern region, we landed near Rovaniemi on a primitive snow-covered runway marked out by kerosene lamps.

The very next day we drove two hundred and seventy-five miles north in an open car until we reached the small Arctic port of Petsamo. The landscape had a certain high-alpine monotony, but the changes of light through all the intervening shades from yellow to red, produced by the sun moving below the horizon, had a fantastic beauty.

In Petsamo we held several Christmas parties for workers, soldiers and officers, and even more on the following evenings in the other barracks. The following night we slept in the personal blockhouse of the commanding general of the Arctic front. From here we visited advanced bases on Fisher Peninsula, our northernmost and the most inhospitable sector of the front, only fifty miles from Murmansk. It was an area of depressing solitude. A sallow, greenish light slanted down through a veil of fog and snow upon a treeless, deathly rigid landscape. Accompanied by General Hengl, we slowly worked our way on skis to the advance strongpoints. At one of these positions a unit demonstrated to me the effect of one of our 15 centimeter infantry howitzers on a Soviet dugout. It was the first "test-firing" with live ammunition I had really witnessed. For when one of the heavy batteries at Cape Griz-Nez was demonstrated to me, the commander said his target was Dover but then explained that in reality he had ordered his men to fire into the water. Here, on the other hand, the gunners scored a direct hit and the wooden beams of the Russian dugout flew into the air. Immediately afterward a lance corporal right beside me collapsed without a sound. A Soviet sharpshooter had hit him in the head through the observation slit. Oddly enough, this was the first time I had been confronted with the reality of the war. I had been acquainted with our infantry howitzers only as technical items to be demonstrated on a shooting range; now I suddenly saw how this instrument, which I had regarded purely theoretically, was used to destroy human beings.

During this inspection tour both our soldiers and officers complained about our lack of light infantry weapons. They particularly missed an effective submachine gun. The soldiers made do with captured Soviet weapons of this type.

Hitler was directly responsible for this situation. The former First World War infantryman still clung to his familiar carbine. In the summer of 1942 he decided against a submachine gun that had already been developed and ruled that the rifle better served the ends of the infantry. One lingering effect of his own experience in the trenches was, as I now saw in practice, that he promoted the heavy weapons and tanks he had then admired, to the neglect of infantry weapons.

Immediately after my return I tried to correct this unbalance. At the beginning of January our infantry program was supported with specific requests from the army General Staff and the Commander in Chief of the reserve army. But Hitler, as his own expert on matters of armaments, waited six months before approving our proposals, only afterward to hector us for any failure to meet our quotas on the deadlines. Within three-quarters of a year we achieved significant increases in this important area. In the case of the submachine gun we actually expanded production twenty-fold—though, to be sure, hardly any of these guns had been produced previously.[15] We could have achieved these increases two years earlier without being compelled to use any facilities involved in the production of heavy weapons.

The next day, I had a look at the nickel plant of Kolosjokki, our sole source of nickel and the real destination of this Christmas trip of mine. Its yards were filled with ore that had not been shipped out because our transport facilities were being employed on building a bombproof power plant. I assigned the power plant a lower priority rating and the supply of nickel began to move to our factories at a faster pace.

In a clearing in the heart of the primeval forest, some distance from Lake Inari, Lapp and German woodcutters had gathered around an artfully built wood fire, source of both warmth and illumination, while Siegfried Borries began the evening with the famous chaconne from Bach's

D-minor Partita. Afterward we took a nocturnal ski tour lasting for several hours to one of the Lapp encampments. Our expected idyllic night in a tent at twenty-two degrees below zero Fahrenheit came to naught, however; for the wind turned and filled our shelter halves with smoke. I fled outside and at three o'clock in the morning bedded down in my reindeer skin sleeping bag. The next morning I felt a darting pain in my knee.

A few days later I was back at Hitler's headquarters. At Bormann's instigation he had called a major conference at which, in the presence of the chief ministers, the labor program for 1944 was to be drafted and Sauckel was to lodge his complaints against me. On the day before I proposed to Hitler that we hold a prior meeting under the chairmanship of Lammers to discuss those differences which were better thrashed out beforehand. At this, Hitler became distinctly aggressive. He said in an icy voice that he would not put up with such attempts to influence the participants in the conference. He did not want to hear any preconceived opinions; he wanted to make the decisions himself.

After this reprimand I went to Himmler, accompanied by my technical advisers. Field Marshal Keitel was also present at my request.[16] I wanted to agree on joint tactics with these men at least, in order to prevent Sauckel from resuming his deportations from the occupied western areas. For Keitel, as superior to all the military commanders, and Himmler, who was responsible for the policing of the occupied territories, feared that such a step would bring about a rise in partisan activities. Both Himmler and Keitel, we agreed, were to declare at the conference that they did not have the necessary personnel for any new roundup of labor by Sauckel and that therefore public order would be imperiled. By this shift I hoped to achieve my aim of finally stopping the deportations. I would then push through intensified employment of the German reserves, especially German women.

But apparently Bormann had prepared Hitler on the problems involved just as I had Himmler and Keitel. Even as Hitler greeted us he showed, by his coldness and rudeness toward all the participants, that he was out of sorts. Seeing such omens, anyone who knew Hitler would be very careful about raising difficult questions. I, too, on such a day, would have left all my most important concerns in my briefcase and would have presented him only with minor problems. But the subject of the conference could no longer be dodged. Irritably, Hitler cut me off: "Herr Speer, I will not have you trying once again to force your ideas on a conference. I am chairing this meeting and I shall decide at the end what is to be done. Not you! Kindly remember that!"

No one ever opposed Hitler in these angry, ill-natured moods. My allies Keitel and Himmler no longer dreamed of saying their pieces, as agreed on. On the contrary, they stoutly assured Hitler that they would do all in their power to support Sauckel's program. Hitler began to ask the various ministers present about their need for workers in 1944. He carefully wrote down all these figures, added up the sum himself, and turned to Sauckel,[17] "Can you, Party Comrade Sauckel, obtain four million workers this year? Yes or no."

Sauckel puffed out his chest. "Of course, *mein Führer*. I give you my word on that. But to fill the quota I'll have to have a free hand again in the occupied territories."

I made a few objections to the effect that I thought the majority of these millions could be mobilized in Germany itself. Hitler cut me off sharply: "Are you responsible to me for the labor force or is Party Comrade Sauckel?"

In a tone that excluded all contradiction, Hitler now ordered Keitel and Himmler to instruct their organizations to push the program of obtaining workers. Keitel, as always, merely said: *"Jawohl, mein Führer!"* And Himmler remained mute. The battle seemed already lost. In order to save something out of it, I asked Sauckel whether in spite of his recruitments he could also guarantee the labor supply for the restricted factories. Boastfully, he replied that this would not cause any problems. I then attempted to settle the priorities and to extract some kind of pledge from Sauckel to transport workers to Germany only after the supply for the restricted factories had been guaranteed. Sauckel also consented to this with a wave of his hand. But Hitler promptly intervened: "What more do you want, Herr Speer? Isn't it enough if Party Comrade Sauckel assures you that? Your mind should be at ease about French industry."

Further discussion would only have strengthened Sauckel's position. The conference was over; Hitler became more cordial again and exchanged a few friendly words, even with me. But that was the end of it. Nevertheless, Sauckel's deportations never got started. That had little to do with my efforts to block him through my French offices and with the collusion of the army authorities.[18] Loss of authority in the occupied areas, the spreading rule of the maquis, and the growing reluctance of the German occupation administrators to increase their difficulties, prevented the execution of all these plans.

The outcome of the conference at the Fuehrer's headquarters had consequences only for me personally. From Hitler's treatment of me, it was clear to everyone that I was in disfavor. The victor in the struggle between Sauckel and me had been Bormann. From now on we had to deal with, at first covert, but soon with more and more overt, attacks upon my aides from industry. More and more frequently I had to defend them at the party secretariat against suspicions or even intervene with the secret police to protect them.[19]

Even the last scintillating assembly of the prominent leaders of the Reich could scarcely distract me from my cares. That was the gala celebration of Goering's birthday on January 12, 1944, which he held at Karinhall. We all came with expensive presents, such as Goering expected: cigars from Holland, gold bars from the Balkans, valuable paintings and sculptures. Goering had let me know that he would like to have a marble bust of Hitler, more than life size, by Breker. The overladen gift table had been set up in the big library. Goering displayed it to his guests and spread out on it the building plans his architect had prepared for his birthday. Goering's palace-like residence was to be more than doubled in size.

At the magnificently set table in the luxurious dining room flunkies in white livery served a somewhat austere meal, in keeping with the conditions of the time. Funk, as he did every year, delivered the birthday speech at the banquet. He lauded Goering's abilities, qualities, and dignities and offered the toast to him as "one of the greatest Germans." Funk's extravagant words contrasted grotesquely with the actual situation. The whole thing was a ghostly celebration taking place against a background of collapse and ruin.

After the meal the guests scattered through the spacious rooms of Karinhall. Milch and I had some words about where the money for this ostentation was probably coming from. Milch said that recently Goering's old friend Loerzer, the famous fighter pilot of the First World War, had sent him a carload of stuff from the Italian black market: women's stockings, soap, and other rare items. Loerzer had informed Milch that he could have these things sold on the black market. There had even been a price list with the shipment, probably with the intention of keeping black market prices uniform throughout Germany, and the considerable profit that would fall to Milch had already been computed. Instead, Milch had the goods from the car distributed among the employees of his Ministry. Soon afterward I heard that many other carloads had been sold for Goering's benefit. And a while after that the superintendent of the Reich Air Ministry, Plagemann, who had to carry out these deals for Goering, was removed from Milch's control and made a direct subordinate of Goering.

I had had my personal experiences with Goering's birthdays. Ever since I had been entitled to six thousand marks annually as a member of the Prussian Council of State, I had also been receiving every year, just before Goering's birthday, a letter informing me that a considerable portion of my fee would be withheld for the Council of State's birthday gift to Goering. I was not even asked for this contribution. When I mentioned this to Milch he told me that a similar procedure was followed with the Air Ministry's general fund. On every birthday a large sum from this fund was diverted to Goering's account, whereupon the Reich Marshal himself decided what painting was to be bought with this sum.

Yet we knew that such sources could cover only a small part of Goering's enormous expenditures. We did not know what men in industry provided the subsidies; but Milch and I now and again had occasion to find out that such sources existed—when Goering telephoned us because some man in our organizations had treated one of his patrons a bit roughly.

My recent experiences and encounters in Lapland had provided the greatest imaginable contrast to the hothouse atmosphere of this corrupt bogus world. Evidently, too, I was more depressed by the uncertainty of my relationship with Hitler than I cared to admit to myself. The nearly two years of continuous tension had been taking their toll. Physically, I was nearly worn out at the age of thirty-eight. The pain in my knee hardly ever left me. I had no reserves of strength. Or were all these symptoms merely an escape?

On January 18, 1944, I was taken to a hospital.

PART

THREE

23

Illness

DR. GEBHARDT, SS GROUP LEADER AND WELL KNOWN AS A KNEE SPECIALIST
in the European world of sports,* ran the Red Cross's Hohenlychen Hospital. It was situated on a lakeside in wooded country about sixty miles north of Berlin. Without knowing it, I had put myself into the hands of a doctor who was one of Heinrich Himmler's very few intimate friends. For more than two months I lived in a simply furnished sickroom in the private section of the hospital. My secretaries were quartered in other rooms in the building, and a direct telephone line to my Ministry was set up, for I wanted to keep on working.

Sickness on the part of a minister of the Third Reich involved some special difficulties. Only too often Hitler had explained the elimination of a prominent figure in the government or the party on grounds of ill health. People in political circles therefore pricked up their ears if any of Hitler's close associates was reported "sick." Since, however, I was really sick, it seemed advisable to remain as active as possible. Moreover, I could not let go on my apparatus, for like Hitler I had no suitable deputy at my disposal. Though friends and associates did their best to

---

* Gebhardt had also been consulted about a knee injury by Leopold III of Belgium and by the Belgian industrialist Danny Heinemann. During the Nuremberg Trial, I learned that Gebhardt had performed experiments on prisoners in concentration camps.

give me the opportunity to rest, the conferences, telephone calls, and dictation conducted from my bed often did not stop before midnight.

My absence unleashed certain elements, as the following incident will illustrate. Almost as soon as I arrived at the hospital, my newly appointed personnel chief, Erwin Bohr, telephoned me, quite excited. There was a locked filing case in his office, he said. Dorsch had ordered this case transported at once to the Todt Organization headquarters. I instantly countermanded this, saying that it was to stay where it was. A few days later representatives of the Berlin Gauleiter's headquarters appeared, accompanied by several moving men. They had orders, Bohr informed me, to take the filing case with them, for it was party property along with its contents. Bohr no longer knew what to do. I managed to postpone this action by telephoning one of Goebbels's closest associates, Naumann. The filing case was sealed by the party officials—but the seal was placed only on its door. I then had it opened by unscrewing the back. The next day Bohr came to the hospital with a bundle of photocopied documents. They contained dossiers on a number of my time-honored assistants—adverse reports almost without exception. Most of the men were charged with attitudes hostile to the party; in some cases it was recommended that they be watched by the Gestapo. I also discovered that the party had a liaison man in my Ministry: Xaver Dorsch. The fact surprised me less than the person.

Since the autumn I had been trying to have one of the officials in my Ministry promoted. But the clique which had recently taken shape in the Ministry did not like him. My then personnel chief had resorted to all sorts of evasions, until I finally forced him to nominate my man for promotion. Shortly before my illness I had received a sharp, unfriendly rejection from Bormann. Now we found a draft of that sharp note among the documents in this secret file, composed, as it turned out, by Dorsch and Personnel Chief Haasemann (whom I had replaced by Bohr). Bormann's text followed it word for word.*

From my sickbed I telephoned Goebbels. As Gauleiter of Berlin he was head of all the party representatives in the Berlin ministries. Goeb-

---

* According to the "Report to the Fuehrer," No. 5, January 29, 1944, Dorsch was the "Special Department Supervisor of the League of German Officials." From the letter to the party secretariat: "Birkenholz . . . displayed uncomradely behavior, arrogance, etc., conduct that cannot be condoned in a high official who ought to stand solidly behind the National Socialist State. In character also he seems unsuitable for promotion to the rank of Ministerialrat. . . . For these reasons I cannot support the promotion. Moreover, certain internal events in this office militate against it." The party secretariat had the right to decide on the promotion of all ministerial officials. I wrote to Hitler on January 29, 1944: "The devastating report which without my knowledge was sent as a political evaluation to the party secretariat and to the Gau was jointly composed by Herr Dorsch and the former director of my personnel

bels agreed at once that my old assistant Gerhard Fränk was the man for this post in my Ministry. "An impossible state of affairs! Every minister is a party member nowadays. Either we have confidence in him or he must go!" Goebbels said. But I could not find out who the Gestapo's agents in my Ministry were.

The effort to maintain my position during my illness proved almost too much for me. I had to ask Bormann's state secretary, Gerhard Klopfer, to instruct the party functionaries to stay within their bounds. Above all I asked him to look out for the industrialists working for me and to see that no obstacles were placed in their way. For I had no sooner fallen sick than the district [*Gau*] economic adviser of the party had begun making inroads into my system. I asked Funk and his assistant Otto Ohlendorf, whom he had borrowed from Himmler, to take a more affirmative attitude toward my principle of industrial self-responsibility and to back me against Bormann's district economic advisers.

Sauckel, too, had already taken advantage of my absence to "make a general appeal to the men involved in armaments for an ultimate commitment." Faced with these effronteries from all sides, I turned to Hitler to tell him of my woes and ask his help. My letters—twenty-three typewritten pages that took me four days—were a sign of the funk I was in. I protested against Sauckel's arrogation of power and against the thrusts of Bormann's district economic advisers, and I asked Hitler for a statement of my unconditional authority in all questions that fell within my jurisdiction. Basically, I was asking for the very thing I had unsuccessfully demanded in such drastic language at the conference in Posen, to the indignation of the Gauleiters. I further wrote that our total production could be carried out rationally only if the "many offices which give directions, criticism, and advice to the plant managements" were concentrated in my hands.[1]

Four days later I appealed to Hitler again, with a candor that really was no longer in keeping with our present relationship. I informed him about the camarilla in my Ministry which was undermining my program. I said there was treachery afoot; that a certain small clique of Todt's former assistants, led by Dorsch, had broken faith with me. I therefore considered myself forced, I wrote, to replace Dorsch by a man who had my confidence.[2]

This last letter, with its news that I was dismissing one of Hitler's favorites without asking him beforehand, was particularly imprudent.

---

section, Herr Haasemann. It is thus established that behind my back these two men tried to block an official order of mine. They underhandedly prejudiced the political branches of the Gau and the party secretariat against the proposed candidate by writing a devastating report. In this way they betrayed me as a Minister of the Reich." Because of its personal nature I had this memo for the Fuehrer sent directly to Hitler's adjutant corps.

For I was violating one of the rules of the regime: that personnel matters must be broached to Hitler at the right moment and by skillful insinuation. Instead, I had bluntly come at him with charges of disloyalty and questionable character in one of his men. That I also sent Bormann a copy of my letter was either foolish or challenging. In doing this I was running counter to all I knew about the nature of Hitler's intriguing entourage. I was probably acting out of a certain attitude of defiance, forced upon me by my isolated position.

My illness had removed me too far from the true focus of power: Hitler. He reacted neither negatively nor positively to all my suggestions, demands, and complaints. I was addressing the empty air; he sent me no answer. I was no longer counted as Hitler's favorite minister and one of his possible successors—a few whispered words by Bormann and a few weeks of illness had put me out of the running. This was partly due to Hitler's peculiarity, often noted by everyone around him, of simply writing off anyone who vanished from his sight for a considerable time. If the person in question reappeared in his entourage after a while, the picture might or might not change. It disillusioned me and snapped some of my ties of personal feeling toward Hitler. But most of the time I was neither angry nor in despair over my new situation. Physically weakened as I was, I felt only weariness and resignation.

In roundabout ways I finally heard that Hitler was unwilling to part with Dorsch, his party comrade of the twenties. During these weeks he therefore rather ostentatiously honored Dorsch by making time for confidential talks with him and thus strengthening Dorsch's position vis-à-vis me. Goering, Bormann, and Himmler understood how the center of gravity had shifted and took this occasion to destroy my position completely. Undoubtedly each of them was working for himself, each from different motives, and probably each without communicating with the others. But any chance for getting rid of Dorsch was scuttled.

For twenty days I lay on my back, my leg immovable in a plaster cast, and had plenty of time to brood over my resentment and disappointments. A few hours after I was allowed to stand again, I felt violent pains in my back and chest. The blood in my sputum suggested a pulmonary embolism. But Professor Gebhardt diagnosed muscular rheumatism and massaged my chest with bee venom (forapin), then prescribed sulfanilimide, quinine, and various pain killers.[3] Two days later I suffered a second violent attack. My condition seemed critical, but Gebhardt continued to insist on muscular rheumatism.

At this point my wife went to Dr. Brandt, who immediately sent Dr. Friedrich Koch, internist at Berlin University and one of Sauerbruch's assistants, to Hohenlychen. Brandt, who was not only Hitler's personal physician but also the commissioner for public health, explicitly charged Professor Koch with sole responsibility for my treatment and forbade

Dr. Gebhardt to issue any medical orders in my case. On Brandt's instructions Dr. Koch was assigned a room near mine and was to stay at my side day and night for the time being.*

For three days my condition remained, as Koch stated in his report, "distinctly critical: extreme respiratory difficulty, intense blue coloration, considerable acceleration of the pulse, high temperatures, painful cough, muscular pain, and bloody sputum. The development of the symptoms could be interpreted only as the result of an embolism."

The doctors prepared my wife for the worst. But in contrast to this pessimism, I myself was feeling a remarkable euphoria. The little room expanded into a magnificent hall. A plain wardrobe I had been staring at for three weeks turned into a richly carved display piece, inlaid with rare woods. Hovering between living and dying, I had a sense of well-being such as I had only rarely experienced.

When I had recovered somewhat, my friend Robert Frank told me about a confidential talk he had had one night with Dr. Koch. What he related sounded somewhat sinister: During my critical state Gebhardt kept recommending a small operation which in Koch's view would have been far too perilous. When Koch at first refused to see the need for the operation and then flatly forbade it, Gebhardt had clumsily backed out of the whole thing, alleging that he had only wanted to test his opinion.

Frank begged me to keep the matter confidential, since Dr. Koch was afraid he would vanish into a concentration camp and my informant would certainly have trouble with the Gestapo. And in fact the story had to be suppressed, since I could scarcely have gone to Hitler with it. His reaction was predictable: In an access of rage he would have called the whole thing absolutely impossible, would have pressed that special button of his summoning Bormann, and would have ordered the arrest of these slanderers of Himmler.

At the time this affair did not strike me as quite so much like a cheap spy novel as it may sound today. Even in party circles Himmler had a reputation for ruthless, icy consistency. No one dared quarrel with him seriously. Moreover, the opportunity was made to order: The slightest complication of my illness would have carried me off, so that there would have been no grounds for any suspicion. The episode has its place in a chapter on the struggles for the succession. My position was, it indicated plainly, still powerful, although already so imperiled that further intrigues could be expected.

When we were together in Spandau prison, Funk told me the details

---

* On February 11, 1944, Dr. Gebhardt tried to force Dr. Koch out of the case by writing to Hitler's personal physician, Brandt's rival, Dr. Morell. He invited Morell for a consultation as an internist. Morell could not be spared from his other duties, but he had the case described to him by telephone and, sight unseen, prescribed vitamin K injections to stop me from spitting blood. Dr. Koch rejected this suggestion and a few weeks later described Morell as a total incompetent.

of an incident which he had only dared hint at in 1944. Sometime in the autumn of 1943 the staff of Sepp Dietrich's SS army had held a drinking bout. Dr. Gebhardt was among the guests. Funk himself had heard about it through his friend and former adjutant Horst Walter, who at the time was Dietrich's adjutant. It seemed that Gebhardt had remarked to this circle of SS leaders that in Himmler's opinion Speer was dangerous; he would have to disappear.

My uneasiness in this hospital was mounting, and I wanted desperately to be out of it, though the state of my health was still far from encouraging. Rather precipitately, on February 19, I set my people to finding a new place to convalesce. Gebhardt tried to dissuade me with all sorts of medical reasons, and even after I got up again at the beginning of March he tried to prevent my departure. Ten days later, however, when a nearby hospital was struck in the course of a heavy attack by the American Eighth Air Force, Gebhardt became convinced that I was the target. Overnight he changed his mind about my ability to be moved, and on March 17 I was at last able to leave this oppressive place.

Shortly before the end of the war I asked Dr. Koch what had really gone on at the time. But he would only tell me what I already knew, that he had had an angry dispute with Gebhardt over my case, in the course of which Gebhardt had remarked that it was Koch's business to be not only a physician but a "political physician." The one thing that was really clear, Koch said, was that Gebhardt had done his utmost to keep me in his hospital as long as possible.[4]

On February 23, 1944, Milch visited me in my sickroom. He informed me that the American Eighth and Fifteenth Air Forces were concentrating their bombing on the German aircraft industry, with the result that our aircraft production would be reduced to a third of what it had been, at least for the month to come. Milch brought with him a proposal in writing: Inasmuch as the Ruhr Staff had successfully dealt with the bomb damage in the Ruhr area, we needed a "Fighter Aircraft Staff" which would pool the talents of the two ministries (Air Ministry and Ministry of Armaments) in order to overcome the crisis in aircraft production.

With things as they were, it would have been prudent of me to stave off such proposals. But I wanted to leave nothing untried which would help the hard-pressed Luftwaffe and therefore consented. Both of us, Milch and I, fully realized that this Fighter Aircraft Staff represented the first step toward incorporation into my Ministry of Armaments production for the one branch of the services whose armaments work I had not yet taken over.

From my bed I telephoned Goering, who for his part refused to enter into such a partnership. As he saw it, I would be interfering in his domain. I did not accept this veto. Instead, I telephoned Hitler, who thought the idea good, but he turned cool and negative as soon as I said we had been thinking of Gauleiter Hanke to head the new staff. "I made a great mistake when I appointed Sauckel to take charge of labor assignment," Hitler answered on the telephone. "As a Gauleiter he should be in a position to make irrevocable decisions, and instead he is always having to negotiate and make compromises. Never again will I let a Gauleiter become involved in such tasks!" As he spoke Hitler had grown steadily angrier. "The example of Sauckel has had the effect of diminishing the authority of all the Gauleiters. Saur is going to take over this job!" After this Hitler abruptly ended the conversation. For the second time in a short while he had overruled me on an appointment. I had also noticed how cold and unfriendly Hitler's voice had been throughout the latter part of our telephone conversation. Perhaps some other matter had put him in an ill humor. But since Milch also favored Saur, whose power had grown during my illness, I accepted Hitler's order without more ado.

From years of experience I knew the distinctions Hitler made when his adjutant Schaub reminded him of the birthday or illness of one of his numerous associates. A curt "flowers and letter" meant a letter with a fixed text which was presented to him only for signature. The choice of flowers was left to the adjutant. It counted as an honor if Hitler added a few words in his own hand to the letter. If he were particularly concerned, however, he would have Schaub hand him the card and a pen and would write a few lines. Sometimes he even specified what flowers were to be sent. In the past I had belonged among those who were most conspicuously honored, along with movie stars and singers. Therefore, when shortly after the crisis of my illness I received a bowl of flowers with a standard typewritten note, I realized that I had been dropped to the lowest rung in the hierarchy, even though I had meanwhile become one of the most important members of his government. As a sick man I undoubtedly reacted more sensitively than was necessary. For Hitler also telephoned me two or three times to ask about my health. But he blamed me for having brought about my own illness. "Why did you have to go skiing up there! I've always said it's madness. With those long boards on your feet! Throw the sticks into the fire!" he would add every time in a clumsy attempt to conclude the conversation with a joke.

Dr. Koch did not think I should expose my lung to the strain of Obersalzberg's mountain air. In the park of Klessheim Palace, Hitler's guest house near Salzburg, the prince-bishops of Salzburg had commissioned the great baroque architect Fischer von Erlach to build a charmingly curved pavilion now called the Cloverleaf Palace. On March 18 the renovated building was assigned to me for my convalescence. At the same time Admiral Horthy, the Regent of Hungary, was engaged in negotiations in the main palace which led to Hitler's last bloodless march into a foreign country, Hungary. On the evening of my arrival Hitler paid a visit to me during a pause in the negotiations.

Seeing him again after an interval of ten weeks, I was for the first time in all the years I had known him struck by his overly broad nose and sallow color. I realized that his whole face was repulsive—the first sign that I was beginning to attain some perspective and see him with unbiased eyes. For almost a quarter of a year I had not been exposed to his personal influence but instead to his insults and reprimands. After years of frenzy and fever I had for the first time begun to think about the course I was pursuing at his side. Previously, he only needed to say a few words or to make a gesture in order to banish my states of exhaustion and release extraordinary energies in me; now, I felt—in spite of this reunion and in spite of Hitler's cordiality—just as weary and done in as I had before. All I wanted, all I was longing for, was to go to Meran with my wife and children as soon as possible; I wanted to spend many weeks there, to recover my strength. But I did not really know what I wanted my strength for, because I no longer had a goal.

Nevertheless, my self-assertiveness stirred again when I was forced to realize, during those five days in Klessheim, that my enemies were using lies and intrigues to eliminate me once and for all. The day after Hitler's visit Goering telephoned to congratulate me on my birthday. When I took occasion, overstating somewhat, to give him a favorable report on my health, he answered me in a cheerful rather than regretful tone: "But come now, what you're saying isn't true at all. Dr. Gebhardt told me yesterday that you're suffering from serious heart disease. Without any prospects for improvement, let me tell you! Maybe you don't know that yet!" With many words of praise for my previous achievements, Goering went on to hint at my impending demise. I told him that X-rays and electrocardiograms had found nothing wrong with me.* Goering replied that I had obviously been misinformed and simply refused to accept my account. But it was Gebhardt who had misinformed Goering.

Hitler too, visibly downcast, told his cronies when my wife happened to be within hearing: "Speer won't be recovering!" He too had spoken to Gebhardt, who had pronounced me a wreck incapable of further work.

Perhaps Hitler was thinking of our joint architectural dreams which I now would be prevented from carrying out by an incurable cardiac defect; perhaps he was also thinking of the early death of his first architect,

* Dorsch also told Zeitzler: "Speer is incurably ill and will therefore not be coming back." (Jotting by Zeitzler, May 17, 1944.) Afterward, Zeitzler informed me of this as an interesting sidelight on all the intrigues. According to Dr. Koch's "Supplementary Report," May 14, 1944: "On May 5, X-ray and electrocardiographic examinations were undertaken. All three sections of the latter revealed no pathological conditions. The X-ray showed a completely normal heart."

Professor Troost. At any rate, that same day he dropped in on me at Klessheim with a surprise—a wreath of flowers so gigantic that his orderly could barely stagger in with it—a gesture really unusual for him. But a few hours after Hitler's departure Himmler called and officially informed me that Hitler had ordered Dr. Gebhardt to take over the responsibility for my safety in his capacity as an SS group leader and for my health as a physician. Thus Dr. Koch was excluded from my case. Instead I was now attended by an SS escort squad, which Gebhardt assigned to protect me.[5]

On March 23, Hitler came once again to pay a farewell visit, as if he sensed the estrangement which had taken place within me during my illness. And, in spite of his repeated evidences of the old cordiality, my feelings toward Hitler had altered by a distinctly perceptible nuance. I was lastingly stung by the fact that he recalled my former closeness to him only because he was now seeing me again, whereas my achievements as an architect and as a minister had not been important enough to bridge a separation of several weeks. Naturally, I understood that a man as overburdened as Hitler, working under the most extreme pressure, could be excused for neglecting those of his associates who were temporarily out of his sight. But his general conduct during the past weeks had demonstrated to me how little I really counted for in the group that formed his entourage and also how little he was prepared to accept reason and objective facts as the basis for his decisions. Perhaps because he sensed my coolness, perhaps also in order to console me, he said gloomily that his health too was in a bad way. In fact there were strong indications that he would soon be losing his eyesight. He had nothing to say to my remark that Dr. Brandt would inform him of the sound condition of my heart.

Castle Goyen was situated on a height of land above Meran. Here I spent the six loveliest weeks of my time as Minister of Armaments, the only weeks I had with my family. Dr. Gebhardt had taken up quarters in a distant part of the valley and scarcely made use of his right to regulate my appointments.

During these weeks I was staying in Meran, Goering, without asking me or even informing me, took my two assistants Dorsch and Saur to several conferences with Hitler. For Goering this was an altogether unusual outburst of activity. Evidently he felt this was his chance to establish himself once more as the second man after Hitler, after his many setbacks in the past few years. He was using my two assistants, who were not dangerous to him, to strengthen himself at my expense. Furthermore, he spread the word that my departure from office could be expected, and during these weeks he asked Gauleiter Eigruber of the Upper Danube District what the party thought of General Manager Meindl. Goering, who was friendly with Meindl, explained that he was thinking of mentioning Meindl to Hitler as a possible successor to me.[6] Ley, already a Reichsleiter saddled with many official duties, likewise put in his claim. If Speer were going, he volunteered, then he would take on this work as well; he'd manage somehow!

Meanwhile Bormann and Himmler were trying to undermine Hitler's confidence in the rest of my department heads by making grave accusations against them. By roundabout ways—Hitler did not think it necessary to inform me—I heard that he was so annoyed with three of them—Liebel, Waeger, and Schieber—that they were as good as ousted. All it had taken was a few weeks for Hitler to forget what had seemed to be a renewal of our intimacy at Klessheim. Aside from Fromm, Zeitzler, Guderian, Milch, and Doenitz, only Minister of Economics Funk remained among the small group of top people who had shown some friendliness toward me during my weeks of illness.

For months Hitler had been demanding that industry be transferred to caves and huge shelters so that production would continue despite the bombing. I had always answered that bombers could not be combated with concrete; it would have taken many years of work before our plants could be placed underground or behind massive concrete. Moreover, we were lucky in that the enemy's attacks on armaments production resembled strikes at the wide delta of a river which flowed into many subsidiary channels. If we started protecting this delta, we could only force him to attack where the industrial stream was concentrated in a deep narrow stream bed, I argued. In saying this I was thinking of the chemical industry, coal mines, power plants, and other of my nightmares. There is no doubt that at this time, in the spring of 1944, England and America could have completely shut off one of these production streams and thus made a mockery of all of our other efforts to protect industry.

On April 14, Goering seized the initiative and summoned Dorsch. The huge shelters Hitler was demanding could only be constructed by the Todt Organization, so far as he could see, he said significantly. Dorsch pointed out that the Todt Organization was specifically confined to the occupied territories; it had no right to operate within the territory of the Reich. Still, he did have on hand a design for the kind of shelter wanted, although it had been projected for construction in France.

That same evening Dorsch was summoned to Hitler. "You alone will be authorized to carry out the building of such major structures inside the Reich as well as outside," Hitler said to him. By the next day Dorsch was able to propose several suitable locations and to explain the administrative and technical requirements for erecting the six planned underground industrial sites, each with an area of over one million square feet. The structures would be finished in November 1944, Dorsch promised.[7]

In one of his dreaded impulsive decrees Hitler made Dorsch his direct subordinate and gave the big shelters so high a priority that all other construction projects would have to yield to them. Nevertheless it was fairly easy to predict that these six gigantic underground shelters would not be ready in the promised six months, in fact, that they could no longer even be started. It was not at all difficult to recognize the right course when the wrong one was so wrong.

Before this, Hitler had not thought it necessary to tell me anything about these measures which cut so sharply into my powers. My injured self-esteem, the sense of having been personally offended, was certainly operative on April 19 when I wrote him a letter frankly questioning these decisions. This was the first of a long series of letters and memoranda in which, frequently concealed behind disagreements on matters of fact, I began to show some independence. It had taken long to evolve, after years of subjugation to Hitler's suggestive powers, and my insights were still murky. Nevertheless I spoke out rather clearly on the matter at hand. To begin such major building projects now, I told Hitler, was sheer delusion, for "there is already difficulty enough in meeting the minimal require- ments for sheltering German industrial workers and the foreign labor force and in simultaneously restoring our armaments factories. Any plans for launching construction for the long run have had to be shelved. What is more, I must constantly stop work on armaments plants already under construction in order to provide the basic necessities for maintaining Ger- man armaments production during the months immediately to come."

Along with arguments of this sort, I also reproached Hitler for having acted behind my back. "I have always, even in the days when I was your architect, followed the rule of letting my assistants work independently. I grant that this principle has often brought me severe disappointments, for not everyone is worthy of such trust, and some men, after having acquired sufficient prestige, have been disloyal to me." Hitler would not find it difficult to gather from this sentence that I was referring to Dorsch. My tone became definitely chiding as I continued: "But be this as it may, I will go on following this principle with iron consistency. In my view it is the only one that permits a man to govern and create. The higher the position, the more true this is."

Construction and armaments, I pointed out, were at the present stage an indivisible whole. It would be well for Dorsch to remain in charge of construction work in the occupied territories, but in Germany itself we needed a separate director for these operations. I proposed one of Todt's former assistants, Willi Henne, for the job. Both men would have more than enough to do. They could administer their separate tasks under the direction of a loyal associate, Walter Brugmann.[8]

Hitler rejected this proposal. Five weeks later, on May 26, 1944, Brugmann was killed like my predecessor Todt in an unexplained plane crash.

The letter was handed to Hitler on the eve of his birthday by my old assistant Gerhard Fränk. I ended it with an offer to resign if my views were unacceptable to Hitler. As I learned from the best possible source in this case, Hitler's chief secretary Johanna Wolf, Hitler displayed extraordinary annoyance at my letter. Among other things he spluttered: "Even Speer has to find out that there is such a thing as politics."

He had had a similar reaction six weeks before when I called off the building of Berlin bunkers for prominent members of the regime in order to take care of severe damage from an air raid. Evidently, he had gained the impression that I was becoming headstrong. Or, at any rate, this is what he accused me of. In the affair of bunkers, he had Bormann inform me very sharply, without consideration for my illness, that "the commands of the Fuehrer are to be carried out by every German; they cannot be ignored or postponed or delayed at will." At the same time Hitler threatened "to have the Gestapo instantly arrest the responsible official for acting contrary to an order from the Fuehrer and taken to a concentration camp."[9]

No sooner had I learned of Hitler's reaction to my letter—again by roundabout ways—than Goering telephoned me from Obersalzberg. He had heard about my intention to resign, he said, but must inform me from the very highest source that the Fuehrer alone could dictate when a minister might depart from his service.

Our conversation went angrily back and forth for half an hour until we agreed on a compromise action: "Instead of resigning I shall prolong my illness and silently disappear as a minister."

Goering was in hearty agreement: "Yes, that's the solution. That's the way we can do it. The Fuehrer will surely accept that."

In unpleasant situations Hitler always tried to avoid confrontations. He did not dare send for me and tell me to my face that after all that had happened he would have to draw the necessary conclusions and request me to leave my post. Out of similar pusillanimity, a year later, when we had reached an open break, he again did not attempt to force my resignation. But in retrospect I must admit that it was certainly possible to make Hitler so angry that dismissal would inevitably result. In other words, those who remained members of his entourage did so voluntarily.

Whatever my motives may have been at the time, in any case, I liked the idea of resigning. For I could see omens of the war's end almost every day in the blue southern sky when, flying provocatively low, the bombers of the American Fifteenth Air Force crossed the Alps from their Italian bases to attack German industrial targets. Not a German fighter plane anywhere in sight; no antiaircraft fire. This scene of total defenselessness produced a greater impression upon me than any reports. Although we had so far succeeded time and again in replacing the weapons lost in our retreats, that would soon have to stop, I thought pessimistically, in the face of this air offensive. How tempting to follow the line suggested by Goering and, given the inexorably approaching disaster, not stand in a responsible position, but quietly disappear. But it did not occur to me to resign my post in order to put an end to my contribution and thus hasten the end of Hitler and his regime. In spite of all our dissensions that thought did not come to me then and in a similar situation probably would not come to me today.

My escapist notions were interrupted on April 20 by a visit from one of my closest associates, Walter Rohland. For in the meantime word had seeped through to industry about my intention to resign, and Rohland had come to plead with me. "You have no right to put industry, which has followed you loyally to this day, at the mercy of those who will come after you. We can well imagine what they will be like! For us, the thing that matters from now on is what can we hang on to which will carry us through the period after a lost war. To help us with that, you have to stay at your post!"

So far as I recollect, this was the first time that the specter of "scorched earth" loomed before me. For Rohland went on to speak of the fear that a desperate top leadership might order wholesale destruction. Then and there, on that day, I felt something stirring within me that was quite apart from Hitler: a sense of responsibility toward the country and the people to save as much as possible of our industrial potential, so that the nation could survive the period after a lost war. But for the present it was still a vague and shadowy sense.

Only a few hours later, toward one o'clock at night, Field Marshal Milch, Karl Saur, and Dr. Fränk called on me. They had been traveling since the late afternoon and had come directly from Obersalzberg. Milch had brought me a verbal message from Hitler: He wanted to tell me how highly he esteemed me and how unchanged his relationship to me was. It sounded almost like a declaration of love. But, as I heard from Milch twenty-three years later, the statement had been more or less extorted from Hitler by Milch himself.

Only a few weeks earlier I would have been touched and flooded with happiness to have received such a distinction. Now, however, my response to the declaration was: "No, I'm sick of it. I want nothing more to do with it all."* Milch, Saur, and Fränk argued with me. I fended them off for a long time. Hitler's conduct seemed to me foolish and unaccountable, but after all I did not want to abandon my ministerial post now that Rohland had pointed out where my new responsibility lay. After hours of argument I yielded on condition that Dorsch would be placed under me again and the previous order of command restored. On the question of the giant shelters, however, I was now prepared to give in, feeling that it no longer mattered.

The very next day Hitler signed a directive as I had drafted it that

---

* Field Marshal Milch maintains today that I used the famous rough quotation from Goethe's *Götz von Berlichingen*, "Kiss my ———."

night: Dorsch would now build the shelters under my authority, though with the highest priority rating.[10]

Three days later, however, I realized that I had been hurried into an untenable arrangement. There was nothing to do but write to Hitler again. The program, as it now stood, was bound to cast me in an altogether ungrateful role. For if I supported Dorsch in building those underground hangars by supplying him with materials and labor, I would be forever in difficulties with other enterprises whose needs I could not meet. If I stinted Dorsch, on the other hand, I would be involved in everlasting complaints and endless "covering letters." It would therefore be more consistent, I told Hitler, if Dorsch should also assume responsibility for the other construction projects which competed with the building of the underground hangars. Under present circumstances, I concluded, the best solution might be to divorce the entire construction area from armaments and war production. My new proposal was that Dorsch be appointed Inspector General for Building and made Hitler's direct subordinate. Any other arrangement, I said, would be complicated by the difficulties in my personal relationship with Dorsch.

At this point I broke off my letter, for in the course of it I began to feel that this was something which had to be threshed out with Hitler personally. I wanted to fly to Obersalzberg. But obstacles arose. Dr. Gebhardt reminded me that he was there to supervise my health and safety and would not permit me to leave. On the other hand Dr. Koch had already told me a few days before that I need have no worry about flying.* Gebhardt finally telephoned Himmler, who agreed to my flying provided that I saw him first, before my conference with Hitler.

Himmler spoke frankly, which in such cases is always preferable. It seemed that conferences had already been held on the matter, with Goering present, and the decision already sealed that a separate agency should be set up for construction, to be headed by Dorsch and to be quite independent of the Armaments Ministry. Himmler wanted to ask me to make no more difficulties. Everything he said was a piece of effrontery; but since I had already come to the same conclusion, the conversation went off pleasantly enough.

No sooner had I arrived in my house at Obersalzberg than Hitler's

---

* I had privately invited Dr. Koch to Meran. Gebhardt complained to Brandt that Koch was *persona non grata;* he would see and hear too many things that were supposed to be kept secret. Koch then left Meran on April 20. In his affidavit Koch wrote: "I had a second clash with Gebhardt when Speer was already in Meran. At that time Speer asked me whether I considered him well enough to fly to Obersalzberg—probably to see Hitler. I approved the trip, with the proviso that the airplane not fly above sixty to sixty-five hundred feet. When Gebhardt heard of my decision he made a scene. He again accused me of not being a 'political doctor.' Here, as in Hohenlychen, I had the impression that Gebhardt wanted to keep Speer in his clutches."

adjutant invited me to join the circle at teatime. But I wanted to talk with Hitler on an official plane. The intimate teatime atmosphere would undoubtedly have smoothed over the ill feeling which had been accumulating between us, but that was exactly what I wished to avoid. I therefore refused the invitation. Hitler understood this unusual gesture, and shortly afterward I was given an appointment to see him at the Berghof.

Hitler had donned his uniform cap and, gloves in hand, posted himself officially at the entrance to the Berghof. He conducted me into his salon like a formal guest. All this made a strong impression on me, because I had no idea what the psychological purpose of this little scene was. From this point on there began, on my part, a period of an extremely schizoid relationship to Hitler. On the one hand he conferred distinctions upon me, gave me all sorts of signs of special favor which could not fail to affect me; on the other hand I was slowly growing aware that his actions were proving more and more dire for the German nation. And although the old magic still had its potency, although Hitler continued to prove his instinct for handling people, it became increasingly hard for me to remain unconditionally loyal to him.

The fronts were curiously reversed not only during this cordial welcome but also in our subsequent conversation: It was he who was courting me. For instance, he would not hear of construction's being removed from my jurisdiction and turned over to Dorsch. "I am determined not to separate these fields. You know I have nobody I can turn building over to. Such a misfortune that Dr. Todt was killed. You know what building means to me, Herr Speer. Please understand! I will approve sight unseen all the measures you think necessary for the construction area."[11]

In saying this Hitler was flatly reversing himself, for as I knew from Himmler, he had decided only a few days before that Dorsch would be entrusted with this work. As so often, he brushed aside the view he had only recently expressed and ignored Dorsch's feelings as well. This inconsistency was still another proof of his profound contempt for people. Moreover, I had to take into consideration the possibility that this new change of mind would not last. Therefore, I replied that this was something which had to be settled on a long-term basis. "It will put me in an impossible position if this matter comes up for discussion again."

Hitler promised to remain firm: "My decision is final. I will no longer consider changing it." He even went on to make little of the charges against my three department heads who had been, I knew, already slated for dismissal.*

When we had finished our conversation, Hitler led me to the cloak-

---

* Hitler hinted that Himmler suspected Schieber, my department head, of planning to flee Germany, that Mayor Liebel had political enemies, and that General Waeger was considered unreliable.

room again, took his hat and gloves, and prepared to accompany me to the door. This seemed to me a little too much officiality, and in the informal tone of his intimate circle I said that I had made an appointment upstairs with Below, his air force adjutant. That evening I sat in the group at the fireplace as in the past, with him, Eva Braun, and his court. The conversation trickled along dully; Bormann proposed that records be played. A Wagner aria was put on, and soon afterward *Die Fledermaus*.

After the ups and downs, the tensions and agonies of the recent past, I felt cheerful that evening. All the woes and causes of conflicts seemed cleared away. The uncertainty of the past weeks had deeply depressed me. I could not work without friendliness and appreciation. I felt I had come out victorious in a power struggle with Goering, Himmler, and Bormann. They were no doubt grinding their teeth now, for they must surely have thought they had finished me off. Perhaps—I was already speculating—Hitler had just realized what sort of game was being played and recognized who had misled him and whom he could really trust.

When I analyzed the complex of motives which so surprisingly led me back to this intimate circle, I realized that the desire to retain the position of power I had achieved was unquestionably a major factor. Even though I was only shining in the reflected light of Hitler's power—and I don't think I ever deceived myself on that score—I still found it worth striving for. I wanted, as part of his following, to gather some of his popularity, his glory, his greatness, around myself. Up to 1942, I still felt that my vocation as an architect allowed me a measure of pride that was independent of Hitler. But since then I had been bribed and intoxicated by the desire to wield pure power, to assign people to this and that, to say the final word on important questions, to deal with expenditures in the billions. I thought I was prepared to resign, but I would have sorely missed the heady stimulus that comes with leadership. The deep misgivings I had been having lately were, moreover, put to rout by the appeal from the industrialists, as well as by Hitler's magnetic power, which he could still radiate with virtually undiminished force. To be sure, our relationship had developed a crack; my loyalty had become shaky, and I sensed that it would never again be what it had been. But for the present I was back in Hitler's circle—and content.

Two days later I went to see Hitler again, accompanied by Dorsch, to present him as the newly appointed head of my construction sector. Hitler treated this occasion as I had expected: "I leave it entirely to you, my dear Speer, what arrangements you wish to make in your Ministry. Whom you assign is your affair. Of course I agree about Dorsch, but the responsibility for construction remains entirely yours."[12]

It looked like victory; but I had learned that victories did not count for much. Tomorrow the whole picture might be changed.

I informed Goering of the new situation with deliberate coolness. I had actually gone over his head when I decided to appoint Dorsch my representative in construction matters within the Four-Year Plan because, as I wrote with a note of sarcasm, "I assumed you would unquestionably be fully in accord." Goering replied curtly and rather angrily: "Very much in accord with everything. Have already placed entire construction apparatus of the air force under Dorsch."[13]

Himmler showed no reaction; in such cases he could be as slippery as a fish. In the case of Bormann, however, the wind began visibly turning in my favor for the first time in two years. For he instantly realized that I had carried off a considerable coup and that all the deep-dyed plots of the past several months had failed. He was neither man enough nor powerful enough to cultivate his grudge against me in the face of such a reversal. Visibly pained by my conspicuous manner of ignoring him, he assured me at the first opportunity—on one of the group walks to the teahouse—with excessive cordiality that he had not had any part in the grand intrigue against me. Perhaps it was true, although I found it hard to believe him; and at any rate in so saying he was admitting that there had been a grand intrigue.

Soon afterward he invited Lammers and me to his home at Obersalzberg. I was at once struck by its lack of any personal character. Abruptly and rather importunately, he insisted on our drinking, and after midnight he offered to exchange the familiar *Du* of intimacy with Lammers and me. The very next day, however, I pretended that this attempt at rapprochement had never happened, while Lammers made a point of using the familiar form of address. That did not keep Bormann from ruthlessly driving Lammers into a corner shortly afterward, while he accepted my snub without any reaction, or rather with increasing cordiality—at any rate as long as Hitler was obviously well disposed toward me.

In the middle of May 1944, during a visit to the Hamburg shipyards, Gauleiter Kaufmann confidentially informed me that even after half a year the resentment over my speech to the Gauleiters had not yet subsided. Almost all the Gauleiters disliked me, he said; and Bormann was encouraging this attitude. Kaufmann warned me of the danger that threatened me from this side.

I thought this hint important enough to mention it to Hitler in the course of my next conversation with him. He had again conferred a distinction upon me by a little gesture, inviting me for the first time up to his wood-paneled study on the second floor of the Berghof, where he generally held only extremely personal and intimate discussions. In his private tone, almost like an intimate friend, he advised me to avoid doing anything that would arouse the Gauleiters against me. I should never underestimate their power, he said, for that would complicate things for me in the future. He was well aware of their shortcomings, he said; many were simple-hearted swashbucklers, rather rough, but loyal. I had to take them as they were. Hitler's whole tone suggested that he was not going to let Bormann influence him in his attitude toward me. "I certainly have received complaints, but the matter is settled as far as I am concerned," he said. Thus this part of Bormann's offensive had also failed.

Hitler, too, had probably become entangled in contradictory feelings. For he now informed me, as if asking me not to take it amiss, of his intention to confer the Reich's highest distinction upon Himmler. For the Reichsführer-SS deserved it for some very special services, he added almost apologetically.* I replied good-humoredly that I would wait until after the war when I hoped to receive the no less valuable decoration for art and science for my achievements as an architect. Nevertheless, Hitler seemed to have been worried about how I would react to this show of favor for Himmler.

What was really bothering me on that day was that Bormann might show Hitler an article from the British newspaper *The Observer* (of April 9, 1944) in which I was described as a foreign body in the party-doctrinaire works. I could easily imagine him doing so, and even the caustic remarks he would make. In order to anticipate Bormann, I myself handed Hitler the translation of this article, commenting jokingly on it as I did so. With considerable fuss Hitler put on his glasses and began to read:

> Speer is, in a sense, more important for Germany today than Hitler, Himmler, Goering, Goebbels, or the generals. They all have, in a way, become the mere auxiliaries of the man who actually directs the giant power machine—charged with drawing from it the maximum effort under maximum strain. . . . In him is the very epitome of the "managerial revolution."
>
> Speer is not one of the flamboyant and picturesque Nazis. Whether he has any other than conventional political opinions at all is unknown. He might have joined any other political party which gave him a job and a career. He is very much the successful average man, well dressed, civil, noncorrupt, very middle-class in his style of life, with a wife and six children. Much less than any of the other German leaders does he stand for anything particularly German or particularly Nazi. He rather symbolizes a type which is becoming increasingly important in all belligerent countries: the pure technician, the classless bright young man without background, with no other original aim than to make his way in the world and no other means than his technical and managerial ability. It is the lack of psycho-

---

* The decoration in question was the Teutonic Order, whose holders were supposed to form a confraternity. Hitler never carried out his plan; Himmler was not given the decoration, which had previously been awarded only posthumously. The decoration for which I had expressed my preference was the National Prize. It was thickly encrusted with diamonds and so heavy that the wearer had to have a pendant inside his dinner jacket to carry the weight.

logical and spiritual ballast, and the ease with which he handles the terrifying technical and organizational machinery of our age, which makes this slight type go extremely far nowadays. . . . This is their age; the Hitlers and Himmlers we may get rid of, but the Speers, whatever happens to this particular special man, will long be with us.

Hitler read the long commentary straight through, folded the sheet, and handed it back to me without a word but with great respect.

During the following weeks and months I became more and more aware, in spite of everything, of the distance that had grown up between Hitler and me. It increased steadily. Nothing is more difficult than to restore authority after it has been shaken. After my first experiment in opposing Hitler, I had become more independent in my thinking and acting. And Hitler, instead of being enraged, had seemed only rather perplexed by my new attitude and tried to propitiate me, even to the point of retracting a decision he had made with Himmler, Goering, and Bormann. Although I too had given way, I had learned the valuable lesson that a resolute stand against Hitler could achieve results.

Nevertheless, even this episode did not shake my faith in Hitler. At best it made me begin to doubt the rectitude of this system of rule. Thus, I was outraged that the leaders continued to exempt themselves from any of the sacrifices they expected of the people; that they recklessly expended lives and property; that they pursued their sordid intrigues, showing themselves as totally unethical even toward each other. Thoughts of this sort may have contributed to my slowly freeing myself. Still hesitantly, I was beginning to bid farewell, farewell to my previous life, tasks, ties, and to the thoughtlessness that had brought me to this pass.

24

The War Thrice Lost

ON MAY 8, 1944, I RETURNED TO BERLIN TO RESUME MY WORK. I SHALL
never forget the date May 12, four days later. On that day the technological war was decided.* Until then we had managed to produce
approximately as many weapons as the armed forces needed, in spite of
their considerable losses. But with the attack of nine hundred and thirty-
five daylight bombers of the American Eighth Air Force upon several fuel
plants in central and eastern Germany, a new era in the air war began.
It meant the end of German armaments production.

The next day, along with technicians of the bombed Leuna Works,
we groped our way through a tangle of broken and twisted pipe systems.
The chemical plants had proved to be extremely sensitive to bombing;
even optimistic forecasts could not envisage production being resumed
for weeks. After this attack our daily output of five thousand, eight hundred and fifty metric tons dropped to four thousand, eight hundred and
twenty metric tons. Still, together with our reserve of five hundred and
seventy-four thousand metric tons of aircraft fuel, that could see us
through more than nineteen months.

On May 19, 1944, after I had taken measure of the consequences of the
attack, I flew to Obersalzberg, where Hitler received me in the presence
of General Keitel. I described the situation in these words: "The enemy
has struck us at one of our weakest points. If they persist at it this time,
we will soon no longer have any fuel production worth mentioning. Our

one hope is that the other side has an air force General Staff as scatter-brained as ours!"

Keitel, who was always trying to please Hitler, hastened to say that he would be able to bridge the gap with his reserves. He concluded with Hitler's standard argument: "How many difficult situations we have already survived!" And turning to Hitler, he said: "We shall survive this one too, *mein Führer!*"

But this time Hitler did not seem to share Keitel's optimism. Along with Goering, Keitel, and Milch, four industrialists, Krauch, Pleiger, Büte-fisch, and E. R. Fischer, as well as Kehrl, chief of the Planning and Raw Materials Department, were called in for a further discussion of the situation.** Goering tried to keep out the representatives of the fuel in-dustry. Such important matters had better be discussed in privacy, he said. But Hitler had already settled on the participants.

Four days later we were all waiting in the inhospitable entrance hall of the Berghof for Hitler, who was conducting a conference in the salon. Beforehand, I had asked the fuel industry people to tell Hitler the unvar-nished truth. But Goering used the last few minutes before the beginning of the meeting to exhort the industrialists not to say anything too pessi-mistic. He was probably afraid that Hitler would place the blame for the debacle chiefly on him.

Several high-ranking military men, participants in the preceding meet-ing, hurried past us. We were immediately called in by one of the adju-tants. Although Hitler shook hands with each of us, his welcome was terse and absent-minded. He asked us all to sit down and declared that he had called this meeting in order to be informed about the consequences of the latest air raids. Then he asked the representatives of industry for their opinion. Speaking as sober, statistically minded businessmen, they all testified to the hopelessness of the situation if the raids were continued systematically. Hitler, to be sure, at first tried to dispel such pessimistic verdicts by stereotyped interjections such as: "You'll manage it some-how," or, "We've been through worse crises." And Keitel and Goering instantly seized upon these cues, going even beyond Hitler in their con-

---

* There had certainly been critical situations before this—the bombings of the Ruhr reservoirs, for instance, or of the ball-bearing plants. But the enemy had always demonstrated a lack of consistency; he switched from target to target or attacked in the wrong places. In February 1944 he bombed the enormous airframe plants of the aircraft industry rather than the engine factories, although the most important factor in airplane production was the number of engines we were able to turn out. Destruc-tion of the plants making these would have blocked any increase in aircraft manu-facture, especially since, in contrast to the airframe plants, engine factories could not be dispersed among forests and caves.

** Krauch was the director of the chemical industry, Pleiger was Reich Com-missioner for Coal and also the manager of important fuel plants, Bütefisch was head of the Leuna Works, and Fischer was Chairman of the Board of I. G. Farben.

fidence in the future and trying to blur the effect of our factual arguments. Keitel, in particular, harped upon his fuel reserve. But the industrialists were made of sterner stuff than Hitler's entourage. They held fast to their verdicts, supporting them by data and comparative figures.

All at once Hitler executed one of his sudden turns and began to urge them to evaluate the situation in the most objective terms. It seemed as if at last he wanted to hear the unpleasant truth, as if he were tired of all the concealments, the false optimism, and the lying servilities. He himself summed up the result of the conference: "In my view the fuel, Buna rubber, and nitrogen plants represent a particularly sensitive point for the conduct of the war, since vital materials for armaments are being manufactured in a small number of plants."[1]

Torpid and absent-minded though he had seemed at the beginning, Hitler left the impression of a sober, intense man of keen insight. The only trouble was that a few months later, when the worst had already happened, he no longer wanted to acknowledge these insights. On the other hand, Goering scolded us as soon as we were back in the anteroom for having burdened Hitler with anxieties and pessimistic nonsense.

The cars drove up. Hitler's guests went to the Berchtesgadener Hof for some refreshments. For on such occasions Hitler regarded the Berghof merely as a conference site; he felt no obligations as a host. But now, after the participants in the meeting had left, members of his private circle poured out of all the rooms on the upper story. Hitler had withdrawn for a few minutes; we waited in the vestibule. He took his cane, hat, and black cape; the daily tramp to the teahouse began. There we were served coffee and cake. The fire crackled in the fireplace; trivial talk was made. Hitler let himself be wafted into a friendlier world. It was all too clear how much he needed that. To me, too, he said not another word about the danger hanging over our heads.

After sixteen days of feverish repairs we had just reached the former production level when the second attack wave struck on May 28–29, 1944. This time a mere four hundred bombers of the American Eighth Air Force delivered a greater blow than twice that number in the first attack. Concurrently, the American Fifteenth Air Force struck at the principal refineries in the Rumanian oil fields at Ploesti. Now production was actually reduced by half.[2] Our pessimistic statements at Obersalzberg had thus been fully confirmed only five days later, and Goering's bold bluster had been refuted. Occasional remarks of Hitler's subsequently suggested that Goering's standing had sunk to a new low.

It was not only for utilitarian reasons that I moved quickly to take advantage of Goering's weakness. Having done so well in the production of fighter planes we had, to be sure, every reason to propose to Hitler that my Ministry take charge of all air armaments.[3] But my motive was largely a desire to pay Goering back for his treacheries during my illness.

On June 4, I requested Hitler, who was still directing the war from Obersalzberg, "to influence the Reich Marshal so that he will call upon me of his own accord, and the proposal to incorporate production of air armaments in my Ministry will proceed from him."

Hitler did not object to my challenging Goering in this way. Moreover, he understood that this little strategem of mine would spare Goering's pride and prestige. He therefore took up my suggestion, saying with considerable forcefulness: "Air armaments must be incorporated into your Ministry; that is beyond discussion. I'll send for the Reich Marshal at once and inform him of my intentions. You discuss the details of the transfer with him."[4]

Only a few months before Hitler had gone to great lengths to avoid saying anything outright to his old paladin. He had, for example, sent me to see Goering in his hideaway in the remote Rominten Heath to discuss some third-rate unpleasantness that I have long since forgotten. Goering must have guessed my assignment, for contrary to his usual custom he treated me like a highly honored guest, had horses and carriage readied for a tour of the huge hunting preserve that went on for hours, and chattered away without pause or point, so that in the end I returned to Hitler having accomplished nothing. I never had a chance to say a word about my mission. Hitler knew Goering well enough to sympathize with my plight.

This time Goering did not try to dodge the issue by pretending cordiality. Our discussion took place in the private study of his house at Obersalzberg. Hitler had already told him what was in question. Goering complained bitterly about Hitler's somersaults. Only two weeks ago, Goering said, Hitler had wanted to take the construction industry away from me; it had all been settled, and then, after a short talk with me, he had undone it all. That was how things always were. Unfortunately the Fuehrer was all too frequently not a man of firm decisions. Naturally, if that was how Hitler wanted it, he would turn air armaments production over to me, Goering said resignedly. But it was all very baffling, since only a short while ago Hitler had thought that I had too many jobs on my hands as it was.

Although I too had begun to notice these sudden alternations of favor and disfavor and recognized them as dangerous to my own future, I confess that I found a certain justice in seeing Goering's and my roles exchanged. On the other hand I did not try to humble Goering publicly. Instead of preparing a decree for Hitler, I arranged to have Goering himself transfer the responsibility for air armaments to my Ministry. He issued the decree.[5]

My takeover of the air armaments industry was a minor matter compared with the havoc being wrought in Germany by the enemy air forces. After a pause of only two weeks, during which their air strength was mostly used for supporting the invasion, the Allies staged a new series of attacks which put many fuel plants out of action. On June 22, nine-tenths of the production of airplane fuel was knocked out; only six hundred and thirty-two metric tons were produced daily. The attacks then lessened somewhat, and on July 17, we once more attained two thousand three hundred and seven metric tons, forty percent of our original production. But on July 21, only four days later, we were down to one hundred and twenty tons daily production—virtually done for. Ninety-eight percent of our aircraft fuel plants were out of operation.

Then, the enemy permitted us to restore the great Leuna chemical works partially, so that by the end of July our production of airplane fuel was up to six hundred and nine tons again. By now we considered it a triumph to reach at least a tenth of our former production. The many attacks had taken such a toll of the piping systems in the chemical plants that direct hits were no longer required to do extensive damage. Merely the shock of bombs exploding in the vicinity caused leaks everywhere. Repairs were almost impossible. In August we reached ten percent, in September five and a half percent, in October ten percent again—of our former capacity. In November 1944 we ourselves were surprised when we reached twenty-eight percent (one thousand six hundred and thirty-three metric tons daily).[6]

"In view of the highly colored reports from Wehrmacht sources, the Minister fears that the extent of our critical situation has not been fully recognized," my *Office Journal* for July 22, 1944, records. The "Minister" therefore sent a memorandum to Hitler six days later on the fuel situation. Passages of this memorandum agreed almost word for word with the first memorandum of June 30.* Both documents stated plainly that the outlook for July and August was such that we would have to consume most of our reserves of aircraft and other fuels, and that, afterward, there would be a gap we could no longer close, which would inevitably lead "to tragic consequences."[7]

Along with these grim predictions I proposed various alternatives which might help us avoid these consequences, or at least postpone them. Above all, I asked Hitler for power to declare a total mobilization of all our resources. I suggested that Edmund Geilenberg, the successful head of our munitions organization, be given every opportunity to restore fuel

---

* On May 22, I had obtained the appointment of my friend Colonel von Below, Hitler's air force adjutant, as my liaison man to Hitler. According to Point 8 of the *Führerprotokoll*, May 22–25, 1944, Below's assignment was "to keep me constantly informed about the Fuehrer's remarks." This system was intended to forestall any further surprises of the kind that had beset me during my illness. Von Below was also to deliver my memoranda to Hitler in the future. It was useless for me to hand them to Hitler in person because he usually demanded that I summarize them for him and then interrupted before I had finished. Von Below reported that Hitler read this memorandum and the succeeding ones carefully, even underlining certain points and writing marginal comments.

production by ruthlessly confiscating materials, cutting down on other manufacturing, and drawing on skilled workers. At first Hitler refused: "If I give him such powers, first thing you know we'll have fewer tanks. That won't do. I can't allow that under any condition."

Obviously he had still not grasped the gravity of the situation, even though in the meantime we had talked about the emergency often enough. Again and again, I had explained to him that it would be pointless to have tanks if we could not produce enough fuel. Hitler gave his consent only after I had promised him high tank production and Saur had confirmed this promise. Two months later a hundred and fifty thousand workers had been assigned to rebuilding the hydrogenation plants. A large percentage of these constituted skilled workers whose labor was indispensable for armaments production. By the late fall of 1944 the number had risen to three hundred and fifty thousand.

Even as I was dictating my memorandum, I was aghast at the incomprehension of our leadership. On my desk lay reports from my Planning Department on the daily production losses, on plants knocked out, and the time required for starting them up again. But all these projections were made on the clear premise that we would manage to prevent or at least reduce enemy air raids. On July 28, 1944, I implored Hitler in my memorandum to "reserve a significantly larger part of the fighter plane production for the home front."[8] I repeatedly asked him in the most urgent terms whether it would not be more useful "to give sufficiently high priority to protecting the home hydrogenation plants by fighter planes so that in August and September at least partial production will be possible, instead of following the previous method which makes it a certainty that in September or October the Luftwaffe both at the front and at home will be unable to operate because of the shortage of fuel."*

This was the second time I had addressed these questions to Hitler. After our Obersalzberg conference at the end of May he had agreed to a plan drawn up by Galland providing that out of our increased production of fighter planes an air fleet would be assembled which would be reserved for defense of the home industry. Goering, for his part—after a major conference at Karinhall where the representatives of the fuel industry had again described the urgency of the situation—had solemnly promised that this "Reich" air fleet would never be diverted to the front. But once the invasion began, Hitler and Goering had the planes committed in France. There the entire fleet was knocked out within a few weeks without having done any visible good. Now, at the end of July, Hitler and Goering renewed their promise. Once more a force of two thousand fighter planes was set up for home defense. It was to be ready

* According to Galland, at that time there were only about two hundred fighter planes on Reich territory available for repelling daytime attacks.

to start in September. But once again the basic failure to comprehend the situation made a farce of this provision.

With benefit of hindsight I stated to an armaments conference on December 1, 1944: "We must realize that the men on the enemy side who are directing the economic air raids know something about German economic life; that there—in contrast to our bombings—wise planning exists. Fortunately for us the enemy began following this strategy only in the last half or three-quarters of a year. . . . Before that he was, at least from his standpoint, committing absurdities." When I said that I did not know that as early as December 9, 1942, a good two years before, a working paper of the American Economic Warfare Division had stated that it was "better to cause a high degree of destruction in a few really essential industries or services than to cause a small degree of destruction in many industries." The effects of such selective bombing, the experts pointed out, were cumulative, and they argued that the plan once adopted should be pursued with unyielding resolution.[9]

The idea was correct, the execution defective.

As early as August 1942, Hitler had assured the naval leadership that the Allies could not make a successful invasion unless they were able to take a sizable port.[10] Without one, he pointed out, an enemy landing at any point on the coast could not receive sufficient supplies long enough to withstand counterattacks by the German forces. Given the great length of the French, Belgian, and Dutch coasts, a complete line of pillboxes spaced close enough to offer mutual protection would have far exceeded the capacity of the German construction industry. Moreover, there were not enough soldiers available to man such a large number of pillboxes. Consequently, the larger ports were ringed with pillboxes, while the intervening coastal areas were only protected by observation bunkers at long intervals. Some fifteen thousand smaller bunkers were intended to shelter the soldiers during the shelling prior to an attack. As Hitler conceived it, however, during the actual attack the soldiers would come out into the open, since a protected position undermines those qualities of courage and personal initiative which were essential for battle.

Hitler planned these defensive installations down to the smallest details. He even designed the various types of bunkers and pillboxes, usually in the hours of the night. The designs were only sketches, but they were executed with precision. Never sparing in self-praise, he often remarked that his designs ideally met all the requirements of a frontline soldier. They were adopted almost without revision by the general of the Corps of Engineers.

For this task we consumed, in barely two years of intensive building, seventeen million three hundred thousand cubic yards of concrete[11] worth 3.7 billion DM. In addition the armaments factories were deprived of 1.2 million metric tons of iron. All this expenditure and effort was sheer waste. By means of a single brilliant technical idea the enemy bypassed these defenses within two weeks after the first landing. For as is well known, the invasion troops brought their own port with them. At Arromanches and Omaha Beach they built loading ramps and other installations on the open coast, following carefully laid-out plans. Thus they were able to assure their supplies of ammunition, implements, and rations, as well as the landing of reinforcements.* Our whole plan of defense had proved irrelevant.

Rommel, whom Hitler had appointed inspector of the coastal defenses in the west at the end of 1943, showed more foresight. Shortly after his appointment Hitler had invited him to the East Prussian headquarters. After a long conference he had accompanied the Field Marshal outside his bunker, where I was waiting since I had the next appointment. Apparently the discussion they were having flared up once more when Rommel bluntly told Hitler: "We must repulse the enemy at his first landing site. The pillboxes around the ports don't do the trick. Only primitive but effective barriers and obstacles all along the coast can make the landing so difficult that our countermeasures will be effective."

Rommel went on in a succinct, firm manner: "If we don't manage to throw them back at once, the invasion will succeed in spite of the Atlantic Wall. Toward the end in Tripoli and Tunis the bombs were dropped in such concentrations that even our best troops were demoralized. If you cannot check the bombing, all the other methods will be ineffective, even the barriers."

Rommel spoke courteously, but aloofly; he noticeably avoided the formula, *"mein Führer."* He too had acquired the reputation of being a technical expert; in Hitler's eyes he had become a kind of specialist in combating Western offensives. That was the only reason Hitler received Rommel's criticism calmly. But he seemed to have been waiting for the last argument about the concentrated bombings. "Here is something I wanted to show you today in that connection, Field Marshal." Hitler led the two of us to an experimental vehicle, a completely armored truck on which an 8.8 centimeter antiaircraft gun was mounted. Soldiers demonstrated the speed with which it could be fired and the

---

* According to W. S. Roskill, *The War at Sea* (London, 1961), Vol. III, Part 2, the landing could never have been carried out without these harbors. Some four hundred ships with a total displacement of a million and a half tons were used; some of them were sunk to form a breakwater. The construction time was doubled because of storms; yet after ten days the harbors began to take shape, and from July 8 on the British harbor at Avranches handled six thousand tons daily, whereas the American harbor was not yet completed.

safeguards against side-sway when it was fired. "How many of these can you deliver in the next few months, Herr Saur?" Hitler asked. Saur promised a few hundred. "You see, with this armored flak weapon we can take care of the concentration of bombers over our divisions."

Had Rommel given up arguing against so much amateurishness? At any rate, he responded with a contemptuous, almost pitying smile. When Hitler saw that he could not draw out the expressions of confidence he had been hoping for, he curtly bade Rommel good-by and returned to his bunker, out of sorts, for the conference with Saur and me. He did not mention the episode. Later, after the invasion, Sepp Dietrich gave me a vivid account of the demoralizing effect of massed bombing on his elite divisions. The soldiers who had survived were thrown completely off balance, reduced to apathy. Even if they were uninjured, their fighting spirit was shattered for days.

On June 6, I was at the Berghof about ten o'clock in the morning when one of Hitler's military adjutants told me that the invasion had begun early that morning.

"Has the Fuehrer been awakened?" I asked.

He shook his head. "No, he receives the news after he has eaten breakfast."

In recent days Hitler had kept on saying that the enemy would probably begin with a feigned attack in order to draw our troops away from the ultimate invasion site. So no one wanted to awaken Hitler and be ranted at for having judged the situation wrongly.

At the situation conference in the Berghof salon a few hours later Hitler seemed more set than ever on his preconceived idea that the enemy was only trying to mislead him. "Do you recall? Among the many reports we've received there was one that exactly predicted the landing site and the day and hour. That only confirms my opinion that this is not the real invasion yet."

The enemy intelligence service had deliberately played this information into his hands, Hitler maintained, in order to divert him from the true invasion site and lure him into committing his divisions too soon and in the wrong place. Misled by a correct report, he now rejected his originally accurate view that the Normandy coast would probably be the focus of the invasion.

During the previous several weeks, Hitler had received contradictory predictions on the time and place of the invasion from the rival intelligence organizations of the SS, the Wehrmacht, and the Foreign Office. As in so many other fields, in this one too Hitler had taken over the task, difficult enough for the professionals, of deciding which report was the right one, which intelligence service deserved more confidence, which one had penetrated more deeply into the enemy's counsels. Now he scoffed at the various services, calling them all incompetent, and, growing more and more heated, attacked intelligence in general. "How many of those fine agents are paid by the Allies, eh? Then they deliberately plant confusing reports. I won't even pass this one on to Paris. We simply have to hold it back. Otherwise it will only make our staffs nervous."

It was noon before the most urgent question of the day was decided: to throw the OKW reserve in France against the Anglo-American bridgehead. For Hitler had the final say on the disposition of every division. He had even been inclined to ignore the demand of Field Marshal Rundstedt, the Commander in Chief of the western theater of war, that these divisions be held in reserve for the impending battle. Because of this delay two armored divisions were no longer able to use the night of June 6–7 for their advance. By daylight their deployment was held up by the enemy bombers, and even before they made contact with the enemy they suffered severe losses in men and matériel.

This day so crucial for the course of the war had not, as might have been expected, been at all a turbulent one. Especially in dramatic situations, Hitler tried to maintain his calm—and his staff imitated this self-control. It would have been an infraction of the usual tone of casual discourse to show nervousness or anxiety.

But during the following days and weeks, in characteristic but more and more absurd mistrust, Hitler remained convinced that the invasion was merely a feint whose purpose was to trick him into deploying his defensive forces wrongly. He continued to hold that the real invasion would take place at another spot which would have meanwhile been stripped of troops. The navy, too, considered the terrain unfavorable for large-scale landings, he declared. For the time being he expected the decisive assault to take place in the vicinity of Calais—as though he were determined that the enemy, too, would prove him to have been right. For there, around Calais, he had ever since 1942 been emplacing the heaviest naval guns under many feet of concrete to destroy an enemy landing fleet. This was the reason he did not commit the Fifteenth Army, stationed at Calais, to the battlefield on the coast of Normandy.*

Hitler had still other grounds for expecting an attack across the Straits of Dover. Fifty-five positions had been prepared along it, from which several hundred "flying bombs" were to be launched toward Lon-

---

* The enemy was counting on finding Hitler more determined. According to W. F. Craven and J. L. Cate, *The Army Air Forces in World War II*, Vol. III, on D-Day and the following days the twelve railroad bridges and the fourteen regular bridges over the Seine were destroyed by the American Ninth Air Force in order to prevent the German Fifteenth Army, drawn up near Calais, from regrouping.

don daily. Hitler assumed that the real invasion would be directed primarily against these launching ramps. He refused to admit that the Allies could take this part of France quite quickly from Normandy. Rather, he was counting on being able to restrict the enemy bridgehead and whittle it down in heavy battles.

Hitler and all of us hoped that this new weapon, the V-1, would sow horror, confusion, and paralysis in the enemy camp. We far overestimated its effects. I myself did have some doubts because of the low speed of these flying bombs and therefore advised Hitler to launch them only when there were low-lying clouds.[12] But he paid no attention. On June 22, in response to Hitler's premature command, the first V-1 pilotless jets were catapulted off their launch ramps in great haste. Only ten of them could be dispatched, and only five reached London. Hitler forgot that he himself had insisted on rushing matters and vented his fury at the bungled project upon the builders. At the situation conference Goering hastened to shift the blame to his opponent Milch, and Hitler was on the point of deciding to halt the production of the flying bomb on the grounds that it was a wasteful blunder. Then the press chief handed him some exaggerated, sensationalized reports from the London press on the effects of the V-1. Hitler's mood promptly changed. Now he demanded increased production; and Goering too declared that this great achievement of his air force had always been a favorite project of his. Nothing more was said about Milch, the previous day's scapegoat.

Before the invasion Hitler had emphasized that immediately after the landing he would go to France to conduct operations in person. In view of this, at an expense of countless millions of marks, hundreds of miles of telephone cables were laid and two headquarters built by the Todt Organization, employing large quantities of concrete and expensive installations. Hitler himself had fixed on the location and the size of the headquarters. He justified the tremendous outlay during this period, when he was losing France, by remarking that at least one of the headquarters was situated precisely at the future western border of Germany and therefore could serve as part of a system of fortifications.

On June 17, he visited this headquarters, called W 2, situated between Soissons and Laon. That same day he returned to Obersalzberg. He was sulky and cross: "Rommel has lost his nerve; he's become a pessimist. In these times only optimists can achieve anything."

After such remarks it was only a question of time when Rommel would be relieved of his command. For Hitler still regarded his defensive positions opposite the bridgehead as unconquerable. But that same evening he remarked to me that W 2 seemed to him too unsafe, situated as it was in the heart of partisan-ridden France.

On June 22, 1944, almost at the same time as the Anglo-American invasion was achieving its first great successes, a Soviet offensive was initiated—which was soon to lead to the loss of twenty-five German divisions. Now the Red Army's advance could no longer be halted even in the summer. There can be no question that during these weeks, when three fronts were collapsing—in the West, in the East, and in the air—Hitler demonstrated steady nerves and an astonishing capacity for perseverance. No doubt the long struggle for power, with its many setbacks, had hardened his will as it had that of Goebbels and other of his fellows of that period. Perhaps the experiences of the "time of struggle," as it was always called, had taught him not to show the slightest anxiety in the presence of his associates. His entourage admired the composure he displayed at critical moments. That alone contributed greatly to the confidence placed in his decisions. Obviously, he was always conscious of the many eyes watching him and knew what discouragement he would have set in motion if he had lost his composure even for a moment. This self-control remained an extraordinary act of will to the last. He wrung it from himself in spite of his rapid aging, in spite of illness, in spite of Morell's experiments, and in spite of the ever greater burdens under which he staggered. His will often seemed to me as heedless and crude as that of a six-year-old child whom nothing can discourage or tire. But although it was in some ways ridiculous, it also commanded respect.

This phenomenal confidence in victory in a period of repeated defeats cannot, however, be explained on the grounds of his energy alone. In Spandau prison, Funk confided to me that the one reason he, Funk, was able to deceive the doctors so consistently and credibly about his health was that he believed his own lies. He added that this attitude had been the basis of Goebbels's propaganda. Similarly, I can only explain Hitler's rigid attitude on the grounds that he made himself believe in his ultimate victory. In a sense he was worshiping himself. He was forever holding up to himself a mirror in which he saw not only himself but also the confirmation of his mission by divine Providence. His religion was based on the "lucky break" which must necessarily come his way; his method was to reinforce himself by autosuggestion. The more events drove him into a corner, the more obstinately he opposed to them his certainty about the intentions of Fate. Naturally, he also soberly understood the military facts. But he transmuted them by his own faith and regarded even defeat as a secret guarantee, offered by Providence, of the coming victory. Sometimes he could realize the hopelessness of a situation, but he could not be shaken in his expectation that at the last moment Fate would suddenly turn the tide in his favor. If there was any fundamental insanity in Hitler, it was this unshakable belief in his lucky star. He was by nature a religious man, but his capacity for belief had been perverted into belief in himself.[13]

Hitler's obsessive faith inevitably influenced his entourage. One part of my consciousness certainly acknowledged that now everything must be approaching the end. But despite that, I spoke all the more frequently—though to be sure I spoke only for my own specific area—of "restoration of the situation." Strangely, this confidence existed apart from the recognition of unavoidable defeat.

When on June 24, 1944, I still tried to impart confidence to others at an armaments conference in Linz, I ran into something of a stone wall. Rereading the text of my speech today, I am horrified by my recklessness. There was something grotesque about my effort to persuade serious men that supreme exertions might yet bring success. At the end of my remarks I voiced the conviction that in our field we would overcome the impending crisis, that in the coming year we would achieve as great an increase in armaments production as we had in the year just past. Speaking extemporaneously, I was carried away; I expressed hopes which in the light of reality were sheer fantasies. Events were in fact to prove that in the next few months we could increase our production. But why was I realistic enough at the same time to be sending a series of memoranda to Hitler on the impending, and finally on the imminent, end of all our efforts? The latter step was an act of intelligence, the former of pure faith. The complete separation between the two revealed that special kind of derangement with which everyone in Hitler's immediate entourage regarded the inevitable end.

Only the final sentence of my speech touched on the idea of a responsibility which went beyond personal loyalty, whether to Hitler or to my own associates. What I said may have sounded like a mere flourish, but I meant something by it: "We shall continue to do our duty so that our German people will be preserved." It was, moreover, what this group of industrialists wanted to hear. In saying it I was for the first time publicly accepting that higher responsibility to which Rohland had appealed when he visited me in April. The idea had steadily grown stronger in my mind. I was beginning to see that here was a task still worth working for.

But it was clear that I had not convinced the businessmen. After my talk, as well as during the succeeding days of the conference, I heard many expressions of hopelessness.

Ten days earlier Hitler had promised that he would address the industrialists. Now, after I myself had so signally failed, I hoped more than ever that his speech would lift the general morale.

Before the war Bormann, on Hitler's orders, had built the Hotel Platterhof in the vicinity of the Berghof so that the innumerable pilgrims to Obersalzberg would have a place to go for refreshment, or even the privilege of spending the night in Hitler's proximity. On June 26 about a hundred representatives of the armaments industry gathered in the coffee room of the Platterhof. During our sessions in Linz, I had noticed that their disgruntlement was also partly concerned with the increasing interference of the party apparatus in economic affairs. Actually, a kind of state socialism seemed to be gaining more and more ground, furthered by many of the party functionaries. They had already managed to have all plants owned by the state distributed among the various party districts and subordinated to their own district enterprises. In particular the numerous underground plants, which had been equipped and financed by the state, but whose directors, skilled workers, and machinery had been provided by private industry, seemed destined to fall under state control after the war.[14] Our very system of industrial direction in the interests of war production could easily become the framework for a state-socialist economic order. The result was that our organization, the more efficient it became, was itself providing the party leaders with the instruments for the doom of private enterprise.

I had asked Hitler to take these anxieties into consideration. He asked me for a few cue phrases for his speech, and I noted down the suggestion that he promise the industrialists that they would be helped in the critical period to come, and furthermore that they would be protected against interference by local party authorities. Finally, I suggested that he affirm the "inviolability of private property even though certain factories may have become state property due to the temporary shift to underground quarters." It would reassure his audience immensely if he were to speak about "a free economy after the war and a fundamental rejection of nationalized industry."

Hitler made this speech and, by and large, took up these points. Yet all the while he was speaking, he sounded as if he were suffering from some impediment. He made frequent slips of the tongue, fumbled for words, broke off sentences midway, neglected transitions, and sometimes became confused. The speech was testimony to his frightening state of exhaustion. This very day the situation on the invasion front had so deteriorated that nothing could any longer prevent the Allies from taking Cherbourg, the first big port. That would solve all their supply problems and would considerably increase the strength of the invading armies.

First of all, Hitler repudiated all ideological prejudices. "For there can be only one single rule, and this rule, put succinctly, is: That is correct which is useful in itself." In saying this he was upholding his own pragmatic way of thinking but undermining all his promises to industry.

Hitler gave free rein to his bent for historical philosophy and vague evolutionary theories. In muddled terms, he assured his audience that:

> . . . the creative force not only shapes but also takes what it has shaped under its wing and directs it. This is what we generally mean by such phrases

as private capital or private property or private possessions. Therefore the future will not belong, as the Communist holds, to the communist ideal of equality, but on the contrary, the farther humanity moves along the road of evolution, the more individualized achievements will be, from which it follows that the direction of what has been achieved will best be carried out by those who are themselves responsible for the achievements. . . . The basis for all real higher development, indeed for the further development of all mankind [will therefore be found], in the encouragement of private initiative. When this war has been decided by our victory, the private initiative of the German economy will enjoy the greatest era in its history. Think of all the creative work that will have to be done then! Don't imagine that all I shall do is set up a few state construction departments or a few state economic departments. . . . And when the great era of German peacetime business has dawned again, then I shall have only one interest, to put the greatest geniuses in German business to work. . . . I am grateful to you that you have helped me to meet our [wartime] tasks. But as the expression of my highest gratitude I want you to leave here with the assurance that I shall show my gratitude again and again and that no German will say that I harmed my own program. That is, when I tell you that after this war German business will experience its greatest boom, perhaps of all times, then you must take these words as a promise that will one day be redeemed.

During this uneasy and disordered speech Hitler received scarcely any applause. We all felt stunned. Perhaps this lack of response prompted him to change course and attempt to frighten the industrial leaders by depicting what awaited them if the war were lost:

There is no doubt that if we were to lose this war, German private business would not survive. Rather, with the destruction of the entire German people, business would naturally be wiped out also. Not only because our enemies do not want German competition—this is a superficial view—but because fundamental matters are involved. We are involved in a struggle which will decide between two points of view: Either humanity will be thrown back several thousand years to a primitive condition, with mass production directed exclusively by the state, or humanity will continue to develop through the furthering of private initiative.

A few minutes later he reverted to this idea:

If the war were lost, gentlemen, then you would not have to worry about shifting [to a peacetime economy]. Then all anyone will have to think about is how he himself will accomplish his shift from this world to the hereafter. Whether he wants to take care of it himself, or let himself be hanged, or whether he prefers to starve or to labor in Siberia—these are some of the questions which the individual will have to face.

Hitler had spoken these words somewhat mockingly, certainly with a faint undertone of contempt for these "cowardly bourgeois souls." The audience understood—which was enough to destroy my hope that this speech would spur the business leaders to new efforts.

Perhaps Hitler had been stirred up by Bormann's presence; perhaps warned by him. At any rate, the declaration in favor of a free peacetime economy, which is what I had asked of Hitler and what he had promised me,[15] had turned out a good deal less precise and unequivocal than I had expected. Still, several sentences in the speech were remarkable enough, I thought at the time, to be worth recording in our Ministry archives. Hitler, of his own accord, offered to let me have the recording of the speech and even asked me to make suggestions for editing it. Bormann, however, blocked publication, whereupon I reminded Hitler again of his offer. This time he put me off. He wanted to edit the text first, he said.[16]

25

Blunders, Secret Weapons, and the SS

As the situation deteriorated further, Hitler closed his mind more and more to any word against his decisions. He proved to be more autocratic than ever in this crisis. This hardening of his mental arteries had crucial consequences in the technical area as well; because of it the most valuable of our "secret weapons" was made worthless. That was the Me-262, our most modern fighter plane, with two jet engines, a speed of over five hundred miles per hour, and a fighting capability far superior to any plane the enemy had.

As early as 1941, while I was still an architect, I had paid a visit to the Heinkel aircraft plant in Rostock and heard the deafening noise of one of the first jet engines on a testing stand. The designer, Professor Ernst Heinkel, was urging that this revolutionary advance be applied to aircraft construction.[1] During the armaments congress at the air force test site in Rechlin (September 1943) Milch silently handed me a telegram which had just been brought to him. It contained an order from Hitler to halt preparations for large-scale production of the Me-262. We decided to circumvent the order. But still the work could not be continued on the priority level it should have had.

Some three months later, on January 7, 1944, Milch and I were urgently summoned to headquarters. Hitler had changed his mind, and this on the basis of an excerpt from the British press on the success of British experiments with jet planes. He was now impatient to have as many aircraft of this type as we could make in the shortest possible time. Since in the meantime Hitler had let everything lapse, we could promise to deliver no more than sixty planes a month from July 1944 on. From January 1945 on, however, we would be able to produce two hundred and ten aircraft a month.[2]

In the course of this conference Hitler indicated that he planned to use the plane, which was built to be a fighter, as a fast bomber. The air force specialists were dismayed, but imagined that their sensible arguments would prevail. What happened was just the opposite. Hitler obstinately ordered all weapons on board removed so that the aircraft could carry a greater weight of bombs. Jet planes did not have to defend themselves, he maintained, since with their superior speed they could not be attacked by enemy fighters. Deeply mistrustful of this new invention, he wanted it employed primarily for straight flight at great heights, to spare its wings and engines, and wanted the engineers to gear it to a somewhat reduced speed to lessen the strain on the still untried system.[3]

The effect of these tiny bombers, which could carry a load of little more than a thousand pounds of bombs and had only a primitive bomb-sight, was ridiculously insignificant. As fighter planes, on the other hand, each one of the jet aircraft would have been able, because of its superior performance, to shoot down several of the four-motored American bombers which in raid after raid were dropping thousands of tons of explosives on German cities.

At the end of June 1944, Goering and I once more tried to make Hitler see these points, but again in vain. Meanwhile air force pilots had tried out the new planes and were spoiling to use them against the American fleets of bombers. But here was one of these moments when Hitler's prejudices were insuperable. Planes of this sort, he said, seizing on any sophism, because of their speedy turns and rapid shifts of altitude, would expose the pilots to far greater physical strains than in the past; and, because of their higher speed the planes would be at a disadvantage against the slower and therefore more agile enemy fighters.[4] The fact that these planes could fly higher than the American escort fighters and could attack the relatively clumsy American bomber squadrons at will because of their immensely superior speed made no impression at all on Hitler. The more we tried to dissuade him from this notion, the more stubbornly he held to it. To mollify us somewhat he spoke of someday, far in the future, when he would let the aircraft be used, at least partially, as fighters.

It was true, of course, that the planes in question existed so far only in a few prototypes. Nevertheless, Hitler's order necessarily influenced long-range military planning, for the General Staff had been counting on this new type of fighter to bring about a decisive turning point in the air war. Desperate as we were over this aspect of the war, everyone who could claim any knowledge of the subject at all put in a word and tried to change Hitler's mind. Jodl, Guderian, Model, Sepp Dietrich, and of course the leading generals of the air force, persistently took issue with Hitler's layman's opinion. But they only brought his anger down on their heads, since he took all this as an attack on his military expertise and technical intelligence. In the autumn of 1944 he finally and characteristically brushed aside the whole controversy by flatly forbidding any further discussion of this subject.

When I telephoned General Kreipe, the new chief of staff of the air force, to inform him of what I wanted to write to Hitler in my mid-September report on the question of jet planes, he strongly advised me not even to allude to the matter. At the very mention of the Me-262, Hitler was likely to fly off the handle, he said. And I would only be making trouble for him, since Hitler would assume that the air force chief of staff had put me up to it.

In spite of this warning I still felt I had to tell Hitler once more that trying to make fighter planes serve as bombers would be pointless and, given our present military situation, a grave error. I emphasized that this opinion was shared by the pilots and by all the army officers.[5] But Hitler did not even discuss my recommendations, and after so many vain efforts I simply withdrew from the fray and confined myself to worrying over my own work. Actually, questions of how aircraft were to be used were no more my business than the choice of what type of plane to produce.

The jet plane was not the only effective new weapon that could have been slated for mass production in 1944. We possessed a remote-controlled flying bomb, a rocket plane that was even faster than the jet plane, a rocket missile that homed on an enemy plane by tracking the heat rays from its motors, and a torpedo that reacted to sound and could thus pursue and hit a ship fleeing in a zigzag course. Development of a ground-to-air missile had been completed. The designer Lippisch had jet planes on the drawing board that were far in advance of anything so far known, based as they were on the all-wing principle.

We were literally suffering from an excess of projects in development. Had we concentrated on only a few types we would surely have completed some of them sooner. At one point the various departments in charge of these matters held council and decided not so much to seek new ideas in the future as to select from the existing ideas those which we were in a position to develop and to push these vigorously.

Once again it was Hitler who, in spite of all the tactical mistakes of the Allies, ordained those very moves which helped the enemy air offensive in 1944 achieve its successes. After postponing the development of the jet fighter and later converting it into a light bomber, Hitler now decided to use our big new rockets to retaliate against England. From the end of July 1943 on tremendous industrial capacity was diverted to the huge missile later known as the V-2: a rocket forty-six feet long and weighing more than thirteen metric tons. Hitler wanted to have nine hundred of these produced monthly.

The whole notion was absurd. The fleets of enemy bombers in 1944 were dropping an average of three thousand tons of bombs a day over a span of several months. And Hitler wanted to retaliate with thirty rockets that would have carried twenty-four tons of explosives to England daily. That was equivalent to the bomb load of only twelve Flying Fortresses.[6]

I not only went along with this decision on Hitler's part but also supported it. That was probably one of my most serious mistakes. We would have done much better to focus our efforts on manufacturing a ground-to-air defensive rocket. It had already been developed in 1942, under the code name Waterfall, to such a point that mass production would soon have been possible, had we utilized the talents of those technicians and scientists busy with rocket development at Peenemünde under Wernher von Braun.*

Approximately twenty-five feet long, the Waterfall rocket was ca-

---

* Even aside from Hitler's objections, a rational course of action such as this would have been complicated by the fact that Peenemünde was developing weapons for the army, whereas air defense was a matter for the air force. Given the conflict of interests and the fierce ambitions of the army and the air force, the army would never have allowed its rival to take over the installations it had built up in Peenemünde. This rivalry made it impossible for even research and development to be conducted jointly (see footnote on p. 216 in Chapter 16). Project Waterfall could have gone into production even earlier had Peenemünde's full capacity been used in time. As late as January 1, 1945, there were 2210 scientists and engineers working on the long-range rockets A-4 and A-9, whereas only 220 had been assigned to Waterfall, and 135 to another antiaircraft rocket project, Typhoon.

Professor C. Krauch, the commissioner for chemical production, had sent me a detailed memorandum on June 29, 1943, barely two months before our unfortunate decision, offering this opinion:

> Those who advocate accelerated development of aerial weapons are proceeding on the principle that terror is best answered by terror and that rocket attacks against England will necessarily lead to a decrease in the missions flown against the Reich. Even assuming that the large long-distance rocket were available in unlimited quantities, which it so far is not, previous experience suggests that this reasoning is unjustified. On the contrary, those elements in England who formerly opposed the use of terror-bombing against Germany's civilian population . . . have been moved, since our rocket attacks, to urge their government to launch massive raids against our densely populated areas. We are still helplessly vulnerable to raids of this sort. . . . Such considerations point to the necessity of concentrating heavily on antiaircraft weaponry, on the C-2 device of Waterfall. We must be able to deploy it at once and on a large scale. . . . In other words, every expert, every worker, and every man-hour devoted to the speeding of this program will yield results proportionately far more effective for winning the war than the same resources invested in any other program. Delaying such a program can mean the difference between victory and defeat.

pable of carrying approximately six hundred and sixty pounds of explosives along a directional beam up to an altitude of fifty thousand feet and hit enemy bombers with great accuracy. It was not affected by day or night, by clouds, cold, or fog. Since we were later able to turn out nine hundred of the offensive big rockets monthly, we could surely have produced several thousand of these smaller and less expensive rockets per month. To this day I think that this rocket, in conjunction with the jet fighters, would have beaten back the Western Allies' air offensive against our industry from the spring of 1944 on. Instead, gigantic effort and expense went into developing and manufacturing long-range rockets which proved to be, when they were at last ready for use in the autumn of 1944, an almost total failure. Our most expensive project was also our most foolish one. Those rockets, which were our pride and for a time my favorite armaments project, proved to be nothing but a mistaken investment. On top of that, they were one of the reasons we lost the defensive war in the air.

Ever since the winter of 1939, I had been closely associated with the Peenemünde development center, although at first all I was doing was meeting its construction needs. I liked mingling with this circle of non-political young scientists and inventors headed by Wernher von Braun—twenty-seven years old, purposeful, a man realistically at home in the future. It was extraordinary that so young and untried a team should be allowed to pursue a project costing hundreds of millions of marks and whose realization seemed far away. Under the somewhat paternalistic direction of Colonel Walter Dornberger these young men were able to work unhampered by bureaucratic obstacles and pursue ideas which at times sounded thoroughly utopian.

The work, mere glimmerings of which were being sketched out in 1939, also exerted a strange fascination upon me. It was like the planning of a miracle. I was impressed anew by these technicians with their fantastic visions, these mathematical romantics. Whenever I visited Peenemünde I also felt, quite spontaneously, somehow akin to them. My sympathy stood them in good stead when in the late fall of 1939 Hitler crossed the rocket project off his list of urgent undertakings and thus automatically cut off its labor and materials. By tacit agreement with the Army Ordnance Office, I continued to build the Peenemünde installations without its approval—a liberty that probably no one but myself could have taken.

After my appointment as Minister of Armaments, I naturally took a keener interest in this great project. Hitler, however, continued to be exceedingly skeptical. He was filled with a fundamental distrust of all innovations which, as in the case of jet aircraft or atom bombs, went beyond the technical experience of the First World War generation and presaged an era he could not know.

On June 13, 1942, the armaments chiefs of the three branches of the armed forces, Field Marshal Milch, Admiral Witzell, and General Fromm, flew to Peenemünde with me to witness the first firing of a remote-controlled rocket. Before us in a clearing among the pines towered an unreal-looking missile four stories high. Colonel Dornberger, Wernher von Braun, and the staff were as full of suspense over this first launching as we were. I knew what hopes the young inventor was placing on this experiment. For him and his team this was not the development of a weapon, but a step into the future of technology.

Wisps of vapor showed that the fuel tanks were being filled. At the predetermined second, at first with a faltering motion but then with the roar of an unleashed giant, the rocket rose slowly from its pad, seemed to stand upon its jet of flame for the fraction of a second, then vanished with a howl into the low clouds. Wernher von Braun was beaming. For my part, I was thunderstruck at this technical miracle, at its precision and at the way it seemed to abolish the laws of gravity, so that thirteen tons could be hurtled into the air without any mechanical guidance.

The technicians were just explaining the incredible distance the projectile was covering when, a minute and a half after the start, a rapidly swelling howl indicated that the rocket was falling in the immediate vicinity. We all froze where we stood. It struck the ground only a half a mile away. The guidance system had failed, as we later learned. Nevertheless the technicians were satisfied, since the thorniest problem had been solved: getting it off the ground. Hitler, however, continued to have the "gravest doubts" and wondered whether a guidance capability could ever be developed.[7]

On October 14, 1942, I was able to inform him that his doubts could be over. The second rocket had successfully flown the prescribed course of one hundred and twenty miles and had struck within two and a half miles of the target. For the first time a product of man's inventive mind had grazed the frontiers of space at an altitude of sixty miles. It seemed like the first step toward a dream. Only at this point did Hitler, too, show lively interest. As usual, his desires underwent instant inflation. He insisted that before the rocket was put into action a flock of five thousand missiles was to be ready, "available for wholesale commitment."[*]

I now had to make arrangements for mass production. On December 22, 1942, I had Hitler sign an order to this effect, although the rocket still needed considerable development before it could lend itself to mass manufacture.[8] I thought I could risk rushing matters in this way. Based on the progress already made and the promises from Peenemünde, the

---

[*] See *Führerprotokoll*, October 13–14, 1942, Point 25. Even 5000 long-range rockets, that is more than five months' production, would have delivered only 3750 tons of explosives; a single attack by the combined British and American air forces delivered a good 8000 tons.

final technical data was to be available by July 1943, at which point we could go right into production.

On the morning of July 7, 1943, I invited Dornberger and von Braun to headquarters at Hitler's request. The Fuehrer wanted to be informed on the details of the V-2 project. After Hitler had finished with one of his conferences, we went together over to the movie hall, where some of Wernher von Braun's assistants were ready. After a brief introduction the room was darkened and a color film shown. For the first time Hitler saw the majestic spectacle of a great rocket rising from its pad and disappearing into the stratosphere. Without a trace of timidity and with a boyish sounding enthusiasm, von Braun explained his theory. There could be no question about it: From that moment on, Hitler had been finally won over. Dornberger explained a number of organizational questions, while I proposed to Hitler that von Braun be appointed a professor. "Yes, arrange that at once with Meissner," Hitler said impulsively. "I'll even sign the document in person."

Hitler bade the Peenemünde men an exceedingly cordial good-by. He was greatly impressed, and his imagination had been kindled. Back in his bunker he became quite ecstatic about the possibilities of this project. "The A-4 is a measure that can decide the war. And what encouragement to the home front when we attack the English with it! This is the decisive weapon of the war, and what is more it can be produced with relatively small resources. Speer, you must push the A-4 as hard as you can! Whatever labor and materials they need must be supplied instantly. You know I was going to sign the decree for the tank program. But my conclusion now is: Change it around and phrase it so that A-4 is put on a par with tank production. But," Hitler added in conclusion, "in this project we can use only Germans. God help us if the enemy finds out about the business."[9]

There was only one point on which he pressed me, when we were alone again. "Weren't you mistaken? You say this young man is thirty-one? I would have thought him even younger!" He thought it astonishing that so young a man could already have helped to bring about a technical breakthrough which would change the face of the future. From then on he would sometimes expatiate on his thesis that in our century people squandered the best years of their lives on useless things. In past eras an Alexander the Great had conquered a vast empire at the age of twenty-three and Napoleon had won his brilliant victories at thirty. In connection with this he would often allude, as if casually, to Wernher von Braun, who at so young an age had created a technical marvel at Peenemünde.

In the autumn of 1943 it turned out that our expectations had been premature. The final blueprints had not been delivered in July, as promised, so that we were not able to go into mass production immediately. A great many sources of error had been discovered. In particular, when the first rockets with warheads were fired, there were inexplicable premature explosions when the missile reentered the atmosphere.[10] There were still many questions unsolved, I warned in a speech on October 6, 1943, so that it would be premature "to count with certainty on this new weapon." I added that the technical difference between individual manufacture and mass production, considerable enough in itself, would involve special difficulties in the case of these highly complicated mechanisms.

Almost a year passed. At the beginning of September 1944 the first rockets were fired at England. Not, as Hitler had imagined, five thousand at one blow, but twenty-five, and then not at one blow but over a period of ten days.

After Hitler had become excited over the V-2 project, Himmler entered the picture. Six weeks later he came to Hitler to propose the simplest way to guarantee secrecy for this vital program. If the entire work force were concentration camp prisoners, all contact with the outside world would be eliminated. Such prisoners did not even have any mail, Himmler said. Along with this, he offered to provide all necessary technicians from the ranks of the prisoners. All industry would have to furnish would be the management and the engineers.

Hitler agreed to this plan. And Saur and I had no choice, especially since we could not offer a more persuasive arrangement.[11]

The result was that we had to work out guidelines for a joint undertaking with the SS leadership—what was to be called the Central Works. My assistants went into it reluctantly, and their fears were soon confirmed. Formally speaking, we remained in charge of the manufacturing; but in cases of doubt we had to yield to the superior power of the SS leadership. Thus, Himmler had put a foot in our door, and we ourselves had helped him do it.

Himmler had conferred an honorary rank in the SS upon almost every government minister whose personal or political weight he had to reckon with. He had reserved a particularly high distinction for me; he wanted to make me an SS Oberstgruppenführer, a rank corresponding to that of a full general in the army and one very rarely conferred. But although he let me know how unusual the honor was, I refused his offer with polite phrases. I pointed out that the army[12] as well as the SA and the NSKK had in vain offered me high titular ranks. In order to make my refusal sound less challenging, I volunteered to reactivate my former ordinary membership in the Mannheim SS—not suspecting that I had not even been listed as a member there.

By conferring such ranks Himmler of course meant to gain influence and thrust his way into areas not yet under his command. My suspicions proved only too justified: Himmler promptly made every effort to push his way into the field of armaments production. He readily offered countless prisoners and as early as 1942 began placing pressure on a number of my assistants. As far as we could make out, he wanted to turn the concentration camps into large modern factories, especially for armaments, with the SS continuing to have direct control of them. General Fromm at the time called my attention to the perils of this for orderly production of armaments, and Hitler made it clear he was on my side. After all, we had had certain dismal experiences before the war with such SS projects, which had promised us bricks and granite. On September 21, 1942, Hitler ruled on the matter. The prisoners were to work in factories under the direction of the industrial armaments organization. Himmler's expansionist drive had been curbed for the present, at least in this field.[13]

At first the factory managers complained that the prisoners arrived in a weakened condition and after a few months had to be sent back, exhausted, to the regular camps. Since their training time alone required several weeks and instructors were scarce, we could not afford to train a new group every few months. In response to our complaints the SS made considerable improvements in the sanitary conditions and rations of the camps. Soon, in the course of my rounds through the armaments plants, I saw more contented faces among the prisoners and better fed people.[14]

Our hard-won independence in matters of armaments was broken by Hitler's order to erect a large rocket-production plant dependent on the SS.

In a lonely valley in the Harz Mountains a widely ramified system of caves had been established before the war for the storage of vital military chemicals. Here, on December 10, 1943, I inspected the extensive underground installations where the V-2 was to be produced. In enormous long halls prisoners were busy setting up machinery and shifting plumbing. Expressionlessly, they looked right through me, mechanically removing their prisoners' caps of blue twill until our group had passed them.

I cannot forget a professor of the Pasteur Institute in Paris who testified as a witness at the Nuremberg Trial. He too was in the Central Works which I inspected that day. Objectively, without any dramatics, he explained the inhuman conditions in this inhuman factory. The memory is especially painful, the more so because he made his charge without hatred, sadly and brokenly and also astonished at so much human degeneracy.

The conditions for these prisoners were in fact barbarous, and a sense of profound involvement and personal guilt seizes me whenever I think of them. As I learned from the overseers after the inspection was over, the sanitary conditions were inadequate, disease rampant; the prisoners were quartered right there in the damp caves, and as a result the mortality among them was extraordinarily high.* That same day I allocated the necessary materials and set all the machinery in motion to build a barracks camp immediately on an adjacent hill. In addition, I pressed the SS camp command to take all necessary measures to improve sanitary conditions and upgrade the food. They pledged that they would do so.

Up to this time I had actually paid almost no attention to these problems, and the assurances of the camp commanders persuaded me that matters would be corrected. I did not take action again until January 14, 1944. On January 13, Dr. Poschmann, the medical supervisor for all the departments in my Ministry, described the hygienic conditions at the Central Works in the blackest colors. The next day I sent one of my department heads to the plant.[15] Simultaneously, Dr. Poschmann started taking various medical measures. A few days later my own illness partially put a halt to these actions. But on May 26, soon after I was back at my post, Dr. Poschmann told me that he had arranged for the assignment of civilian doctors to many of the labor camps. But there were difficulties. On the same day, I received a rude letter from Robert Ley in which he protested against Dr. Poschmann's interference on formal grounds. Medical treatment in camps was his province, he declared, and angrily demanded that I reprimand Dr. Poschmann, forbid him any further meddling, and discipline him for the steps he had already taken.

I answered immediately that I had no reason to meet his demands, that on the contrary we had the greatest interest in adequate medical treatment for the prisoners.[16] That same day I discussed further medical measures with Dr. Poschmann. Since I was making all these arrangements in cooperation with Dr. Brandt, and since apart from all humanitarian considerations, the rational arguments were on our side, I did not give a hang about Ley's reaction. I was confident that Hitler would rebuke the party bureaucracy which we had passed over and would even make scornful remarks about the bureaucrats.

I heard no more from Ley. And Himmler himself failed when he tried to show me that he could strike as he pleased even against important groups of individuals. On March 14, 1944, he had Wernher von Braun and two of his assistants arrested. The official reason, as given to the chief of the Central Office, was that these men had violated one of my regulations by giving peacetime projects precedence over their war-production tasks. Actually von Braun and his staff used to talk freely about their speculations, describing how in the distant future

* The shocking effect the camp had on us is indicated in the deliberately veiled phraseology of the *Office Journal* entry for December 10, 1943: "On the morning of December 10 the minister went to inspect a new plant in the Harz Mountains. Carrying out this tremendous mission drew on the leaders' last reserves of strength. Some of the men were so affected that they had to be forcibly sent off on vacations to restore their nerves."

a rocket could be developed and used for mail service between the United States and Europe. High-spiritedly and naively they indulged in their dreams and let a picture magazine prepare all sorts of fantastic drawings based on their visions. When Hitler visited me at my sickbed in Klessheim and treated me with such surprising benevolence, I took this occasion to intercede for the arrested specialists, and had Hitler promise that he would get them released. But a week was to pass before this was done, and as much as six weeks later Hitler was still grumbling about the trouble he had gone to. As he phrased it, von Braun was to be "protected from all prosecution as long as he is indispensable, difficult though the general consequences arising from the situation" were. Actually, Himmler had achieved one of his ends. From now on even the top men of the rocket staff no longer felt safe from his arbitrary hand. It was conceivable, after all, that I might not always be in a position to free them if they were arrested again.

Himmler had long been striving to set up a business firm which would be the property of the SS. Hitler, or so it seemed to me, was cool to the idea, and I did my best to reinforce him in this. Perhaps this conflict was one of the reasons for Himmler's strange conduct during my illness. For during those months he had at last managed to persuade Hitler that a large-scale SS business enterprise would offer numerous advantages. At the beginning of June 1944, Hitler asked me to assist the SS in its efforts to build up an economic empire extending from raw materials to manufacturing. He had a strange reason, now, for furthering this enterprise: The SS must be strong enough so that under his successors it would be able, for example, to oppose a Finance Minister who wanted to cut its funds.

What followed from this was precisely what I had feared at the beginning of my work as Minister of Armaments. At least I was able to put across the point that Himmler's manufacturing sites "must be subject to the same control as the rest of the armaments and war-production industry," lest "one part of the armed forces go its own independent way when I have managed by great effort over two years to coordinate armaments production for the other three branches of the armed forces."[17] Hitler promised to back me if I had trouble with Himmler, but I had great doubts about the strength of such backing. Significantly enough Himmler had had a report from Hitler on this conversation at the time the Reichsführer-SS asked me to his house near Berchtesgaden.

It is true that the Reichsführer-SS sometimes seemed to be a visionary whose intellectual flights struck even Hitler as ridiculous. But Himmler was also a sober-minded realist who knew exactly what his far-reaching political aims were. In our discussions he displayed a friendly courtesy that seemed slightly forced and never cordial. And he always made a point of having a witness from his staff present. He had the patience to listen to his visitors' arguments—a gift rare in those days. In the discussion he often seemed petty and pedantic and had apparently thought out beforehand everything he wanted to say. He was obviously not concerned with the impression this made, that he seemed slow-minded let alone of limited intelligence. His office worked with the precision of a well-oiled machine—which was probably an expression of his own impersonality. At any rate I always felt that his pallid character was reflected in the utterly matter-of-fact style of his secretariat. His stenographers, all young girls, could certainly not be called pretty, but they all seemed to be extremely hard-working and conscientious.

Himmler presented me with a well-thought-out and wide-ranging plan. During my illness the SS, in spite of all Saur's efforts to oppose it, had acquired the Hungarian concern of Manfred-Weiss, an important armaments company. With this as a core, Himmler explained, he wanted systematically to construct a steadily expanding cartel. Would I suggest a specialist to help with the construction of this giant enterprise? After reflecting briefly, I proposed Paul Pleiger, who had set up large steel mills for the Four-Year Plan. Pleiger was an energetic and independent man who, with his manifold ties to industry, would be able to ensure that Himmler did not expand his concern too vigorously and too unscrupulously. But Himmler did not like my nominee. That was the last time he asked me for advice.

Himmler's close associates Oswald Pohl, Hans Jüttner, and Gottlob Berger were tough and ruthless in negotiation, but moderately good-natured. They had that kind of banality which seems quite tolerable at first sight. But two of his other men were surrounded by an aura of iciness like that of their chief: Both Reinhard Heydrich and Hans Kammler were blond, blue-eyed, long-headed, always neatly dressed, and well bred. Both were capable of unexpected decisions at any moment, and once they had arrived at them they would carry them through with a rare obstinacy. Himmler had made a significant choice in picking Kammler as his aide. For in spite of all his ideological crankiness, in matters of personnel Himmler was not overly concerned about lengthy party membership. He was more interested in such qualities as energy, swift intelligence, and extreme zeal. In the spring of 1942, Himmler had appointed Kammler, who had previously been a high-ranking construction employee in the Air Ministry, to head the SS construction operations, and in the summer of 1943 he chose him to handle the rocket program. In the course of my enforced collaboration with this man, I discovered him to be a cold, ruthless schemer, a fanatic in the pursuit of a goal, and as carefully calculating as he was unscrupulous.

Himmler heaped assignments on him and brought him into Hitler's presence at every opportunity. Soon rumors were afloat that Himmler was trying to build up Kammler to be my successor.[18] At the time I had seen only the best side of Kammler, and I rather liked his objective coolness. In many jobs my partner, in his intentions possibly my rival, he was in his career as well as his manner of work in many ways my mirror image. He too came from a solid middle-class family, had gone through the university, had been "discovered" because of his work in construction, and had gone far and fast in fields for which he had not been trained.

During the war the supply of labor became the key factor in any industrial unit. At the beginning of the forties, and subsequently at a faster and faster pace, the SS began secretly building labor camps and making sure they were kept full. In a letter of May 7, 1944, Walter Schieber, one of my department heads, called my attention to the efforts of the SS to use its powers over labor in order to promote its economic expansion. Moreover, the SS was casting eyes on the foreign workers in our factories and became more and more zealous in arresting them for trivial violations of rules and transferring them to its own camps.* My assistants estimated that by this technique we were being deprived of thirty to forty thousand workers a month during the spring of 1944.

At the beginning of June 1944, I protested to Hitler that I could not "stand a loss of half a million workers a year. . . . all the more so because a majority of them were skilled workers trained with considerable effort." I said that they simply had to be "returned to their original occupations as quickly as possible." Hitler told me to discuss the problem with Himmler; he would then make a decision in my favor.[19] But in defiance of the facts Himmler denied both to me and to Hitler that any such practices were being pursued.

The prisoners themselves, as I sometimes had a chance to observe, also feared Himmler's growing economic ambitions. I recall a tour through the Linz steelworks in the summer of 1944 where prisoners were moving about freely among the other workers. They stood at the machines in the lofty workshops, served as helpers to trained workers, and talked unconstrainedly with the free workers. It was not the SS but army soldiers who were guarding them. When we came upon a group of twenty Russians, I had the interpreter ask them whether they were satisfied with their treatment. They made gestures of pas-

---

* Dr. Schieber states further: "The SS siphons off by now a significant number of the many foreign and especially Russian workers who man the armaments plants. This drain is caused by the constant growth of the extensive SS economic interests, which is being promoted with particular zeal by Obergruppenführer Pohl." At the meeting of the Armaments Staff on May 26, 1944, Kammler had boasted that he had "simply placed fifty thousand persons in protective custody in order to obtain the necessary labor" for the SS enterprises.

sionate assent. Their appearance confirmed what they said. In contrast to the people in the caves of the Central Works, who were obviously wasting away, these prisoners were well fed. And when I asked them, just to make conversation, whether they would prefer to return to the regular camp, they gave a start of fright. Their faces expressed purest horror.

But I asked no further questions. Why should I have done so; their expressions told me everything. If I were to try today to probe the feelings that stirred me then, if across the span of a lifetime I attempt to analyze what I really felt—pity, irritation, embarrassment, or indignation—it seems to me that the desperate race with time, my obsessional fixation on production and output statistics, blurred all considerations and feelings of humanity. An American historian has said of me that I loved machines more than people.[20] He is not wrong. I realize that the sight of suffering people influenced only my emotions, but not my conduct. On the plane of feelings only sentimentality emerged; in the realm of decisions, on the other hand, I continued to be ruled by the principles of utility. In the Nuremberg Trial the indictment against me was based on the use of prisoners in the armaments factories.

By the court's standard of judgment, which was purely numerical, my guilt would have been greater had I prevailed over Himmler and raised the number of prisoners in our labor force, thus increasing the chances of more people for survival. Paradoxically, I would feel better today if in this sense I had been guiltier. But what preys on my mind nowadays has little to do with the standards of Nuremberg nor the figures on lives I saved or might have saved. For in either case I was moving within the system. What disturbs me more is that I failed to read the physiognomy of the regime mirrored in the faces of those prisoners—the regime whose existence I was so obsessively trying to prolong during those weeks and months. I did not see any moral ground outside the system where I should have taken my stand. And sometimes I ask myself who this young man really was, this young man who has now become so alien to me, who walked through the workshops of the Linz steelworks or descended into the caverns of the Central Works twenty-five years ago.

One day, some time in the summer of 1944, my friend Karl Hanke, the Gauleiter of Lower Silesia, came to see me. In earlier years he had told me a great deal about the Polish and French campaigns, had spoken of the dead and wounded, the pain and agonies, and in talking about these things had shown himself a man of sympathy and directness. This time, sitting in the green leather easy chair in my office, he seemed confused and spoke falteringly, with many breaks. He advised me never to accept an invitation to inspect a concentration camp in

Upper Silesia. Never, under any circumstances. He had seen something there which he was not permitted to describe and moreover could not describe.

I did not query him, I did not query Himmler, I did not query Hitler, I did not speak with personal friends. I did not investigate—for I did not want to know what was happening there. Hanke must have been speaking of Auschwitz. During those few seconds, while Hanke was warning me, the whole responsibility had became a reality again. Those seconds were uppermost in my mind when I stated to the international court at the Nuremberg Trial that as an important member of the leadership of the Reich, I had to share the total responsibility for all that had happened. For from that moment on, I was inescapably contaminated morally; from fear of discovering something which might have made me turn from my course, I had closed my eyes. This deliberate blindness outweighs whatever good I may have done or tried to do in the last period of the war. Those activities shrink to nothing in the face of it. Because I failed at that time, I still feel, to this day, responsible for Auschwitz in a wholly personal sense.

26

Operation Valkyrie

SURVEYING A BOMBED HYDROGENATION PLANT FROM THE AIR, I WAS STRUCK by the accurate carpet bombing of the Allied bomber fleets. Suddenly the thought flashed through my mind that given such precision it should be easy for the Allies to destroy all the bridges over the Rhine in a single day. I had experts draw the Rhine bridges to scale on aerial photographs of bomb holes; they confirmed my fear. Hastily, I had steel girders brought to the bridges to be ready for swift repairs. In addition I ordered the construction of ten ferries and a pontoon bridge.[1]

On May 29, 1944, ten days later, I wrote to Jodl in some agitation:

> I am tormented by the thought that someday all the bridges over the Rhine will be destroyed. According to my observations of the density of the bombings recently, it should be possible for the enemy to do this. What would the situation be if the enemy, after cutting off all traffic to the armies in the occupied western territories, did not carry out his landings at the Atlantic Wall, but on the North Sea coast in Germany? Such a landing would probably be practicable, since he already possesses absolute air superiority which is surely the prime prerequisite for a successful landing on the north German coastal area. At any rate his casualties would certainly be less by such an approach than by a direct assault on the Atlantic Wall.

> In Germany itself we had scarcely any troop units at our disposal. If the airports at Hamburg and Bremen could be taken by parachute

units and the ports of these cities be seized by small forces, invasion armies debarking from ships would, I feared, meet no resistance and would be occupying Berlin and all of Germany within a few days. Meanwhile, the three armies in the West would be cut off by the Rhine, and the army groups in the East tied down in heavy defensive battles; in any case they were too far away to be able to intervene in time.

My fears had the same sensational cast as some of Hitler's errant notions. The next time I went to Obersalzberg, Jodl said ironically to me that he supposed I was now, on top of everything else, becoming an armchair strategist. But Hitler was struck by the idea. There is a note in Jodl's diary for June 5, 1944: "Skeletal divisions are to be created in Germany into which in an emergency the men on leave and the convalescents can be pumped. Speer will provide weapons by a crash program. There are always three hundred thousand men on furlough at home; that means ten to twelve divisions."[2]

Although neither Jodl nor I knew anything about it, the organizational framework for this operation had long been in existence. Ever since May 1942 a plan known by the code name Valkyrie detailed every step for quickly assembling the units and soldiers present in Germany in case of domestic disturbances or emergencies.[3] But now Hitler's interest in the matter had been aroused, and on June 7, 1944, a special conference on it took place at Obersalzberg. In addition to Keitel and Fromm, Colonel von Stauffenberg participated in the discussion.

General Schmundt, Hitler's chief adjutant, had picked Count Stauffenberg to serve as Fromm's chief of staff and to inject some force into the work of the flagging general. As Schmundt explained to me, Stauffenberg was considered one of the most dynamic and competent officers in the German army.[4] Hitler himself would occasionally urge me to work closely and confidentially with Stauffenberg. In spite of his war injuries (he had lost an eye, his right hand, and two fingers of his left hand), Stauffenberg had preserved a youthful charm; he was curiously poetic and at the same time precise, thus showing the marks of the two major and seemingly incompatible educational influences upon him: the circle around the poet Stefan George and the General Staff. He and I would have hit it off even without Schmundt's recommendation. After the deed which will forever be associated with his name, I often reflected upon his personality and found no phrase more fitting for him than this one of Hölderlin's: "An extremely unnatural, paradoxical character unless one sees him in the midst of those circumstances which imposed so strict a form upon his gentle spirit."

There were further sessions of these conferences on July 6 and 8. Along with Hitler, Keitel, Fromm, and other officers sat at the round table by the big window in the Berghof salon. Stauffenberg had taken his seat beside me, with his remarkably plump briefcase. He explained the Valkyrie plan for committing the Home Army. Hitler listened attentively and in the ensuing discussion approved most of the proposals. Finally, he decided that in military actions within the Reich the military commanders would have full executive powers, the political authorities—which meant principally the Gauleiters in their capacity of Reich Defense Commissioners—only advisory functions. The military commanders, the decree went, could directly issue all requisite instructions to Reich and local authorities without consulting the Gauleiters.[5]

Whether by chance or design, at this period most of the prominent military members of the conspiracy were assembled in Berchtesgaden. As I know now, they and Stauffenberg had decided only a few days before to attempt to assassinate Hitler with a bomb kept in readiness by Brigadier General Stieff. On July 8, I met General Friedrich Olbricht to discuss the drafting of deferred workers for the army; up to now Keitel and I had been at odds over this question. As so often, Olbricht complained again about the difficulties that inevitably arose from the armed forces being split into four services. Were it not for the jealousies of the different branches, the army could avail itself of hundreds of thousands of young soldiers now in the air force, he said.

The next day, I met Quartermaster General Eduard Wagner at the Berchtesgadener Hof, along with General Erich Fellgiebel of the Signal Corps, General Fritz Lindemann, aide to the chief of staff, and Brigadier General Helmut Stieff, chief of the Organizational Section in the High Command of the Army (OKH). They were all members of the conspiracy and none of them was destined to survive the next few months. Perhaps because the long-delayed decision to attempt the coup d'état had now been irrevocably taken, they were all in a rather reckless state of mind that afternoon, as men often are after some great resolution. My *Office Journal* records my astonishment at the way they belittled the desperate situation at the front: "According to the Quartermaster General, the difficulties are minor. . . . The generals treat the eastern situation with a superior air, as if it were of no importance."[6]

One or two weeks before, General Wagner had painted that same situation in the blackest colors. He had outlined the demands he would have to make upon our armaments industries in case of further retreat. These were so high that they could not possibly have been met, and I am inclined to think today that his only purpose was to show Hitler that the army could no longer be provided with weapons and that we therefore were heading straight toward disaster. I was not present at this conference and my associate Karl Saur had scolded the much older Quartermaster General like a schoolboy, with Hitler joining in. Now, I had called on him to demonstrate my unchanged friendliness, only to discover that the whole problem did not seem to worry him any longer.

We discussed in detail the wastefulness that sprang from inadequate organization. General Fellgiebel described the squandering of men and materials caused solely by the fact that each branch of the armed forces maintained a separate communications network. The air force and the army, for example, had laid separate cables all the way to Athens or Lapland. Aside from all questions of economy, collaboration on such projects would promote efficiency. But Hitler would not hear of any changes. I myself contributed a few illustrations of the advantages which would result from single direction of armaments production for all the services.

Although I had often had unusually frank conversations with the conspirators, I did not catch wind of their plans. Only once did I sense that something was brewing—but that was not from talking with them. It was rather because of a remark of Himmler's. Sometime in the late autumn of 1943, he was talking with Hitler in the headquarters area. I was standing nearby and thus inadvertently became a witness to this conversation.

"Then you are in agreement, *mein Führer,* that I am to talk with the Gray Eminence and pretend I am willing to go along with them?" Hitler nodded.

"There are some obscure plans afoot. Perhaps, if I can win his confidence, I'll learn more about them. But then if you, *mein Führer,* hear about this from some third party, you'll know my motives."

Hitler made a gesture of agreement. "Of course, I have every confidence in you."

I asked one of the adjutants whether he knew whose nickname was "the Gray Eminence." "Oh yes," he replied, "that's Popitz, the Prussian Minister of Finance."

Chance assigned the roles. For a time Fate seemed uncertain whether on July 20 I was to be at the center of the uprising in Bendlerstrasse* or the center of the regime's counterattack, Goebbels's house.

On July 17, Fromm had his chief of staff, Stauffenberg, ask me to come to lunch with him on July 20 in Bendlerstrasse so I could confer with him after lunch. Since I had a long-standing appointment late that morning to address a group of businessmen and government officials on armaments problems, I had to decline. Stauffenberg nevertheless repeated the invitation for July 20 more urgently. It was absolutely essential that I come, he informed me. But I imagined that the morning affair would probably take a good deal out of me and could not face a conference with Fromm afterward, so I declined once more.

My address began around eleven o'clock in the impressively ap-

---

* The High Command of the Armed Forces was located on Bendlerstrasse, and the street name was used as a synonym for the building, just as "Wilhelmstrasse" stood for the Chancellery.—*Translators' note.*

pointed hall of the Propaganda Ministry which Goebbels had placed at my disposal. Some two hundred persons, all the ministers present in Berlin, all the state secretaries, and other high officials had come. Practically all of political Berlin was assembled there. The audience heard me appeal first of all for intensified commitment on the home front. This was the pitch I had made so often I could recite it almost by heart. Then I went on to explicate a number of graphs showing the present state of our armaments.

Around the time that I ended my talk and Goebbels, as the host, spoke a few concluding words, Stauffenberg's bomb exploded at the Fuehrer's headquarters in Rastenburg. If the rebels had been more skillful and taken parallel action immediately, they could have had a lieutenant with ten men march into this assembly and arrest many important members of the Reich government. As it was, an unsuspecting Goebbels took Funk and me along into his office in the Ministry. We talked, as was our wont of late, about what more might still be done about mobilizing the home front. Suddenly a small loudspeaker reported: "An urgent call from headquarters for the Minister. Dr. Dietrich is on the phone."

Goebbels threw a switch: "Transfer it here." He went over to his desk and picked up the receiver: "Dr. Dietrich? Yes? This is Goebbels. . . . What! An attempt to assassinate the Fuehrer? Just now? . . . The Fuehrer is alive, you say? I see, in the Speer Barracks. Anything more known yet? . . . The Fuehrer thinks it may be one of the OT [Todt Organization] workers?"

Dietrich evidently had to be brief; the conversation ended there. Operation Valkyrie had begun, the plan for mobilization of the Home Army, which the conspirators had incorporated into their action and had for months been discussing openly, even with Hitler.

"That's all I needed," the thought flashed through my mind as Goebbels repeated what he had heard and once again mentioned that suspicion had fallen on the OT workers. For if this guess proved correct, my own position was endangered; Bormann could easily use my responsibility for the Todt Organization as a basis for fresh intrigues and insinuations. Even now, Goebbels was flaring up at me because I could not tell him what security checks we made before assigning OT workers to Rastenburg. All I could tell him was that hundreds of workers were admitted into Restricted Area I every day to work on the reinforcement of Hitler's bunker, and that for the time being Hitler had taken over the barracks which had been put up for me since it had the only sizable conference room at headquarters and was also empty during my absence. Under such circumstances, Goebbels said, shaking his head at such carelessness, it would have been easy for anyone to get into what was supposedly the most carefully restricted and secured area in the world. "What was the point of all the protective measures!" he tossed off, as if speaking to someone invisible who was to blame for it all.

Soon afterward, Goebbels bade me good-by; both he and I were taken up, even in such a time of emergency, with our ministerial routines. Colonel Engel, Hitler's former army adjutant who now commanded a frontline unit, was already waiting for me for a late lunch. I was interested to hear what he thought of a memorandum in which I called for the appointment of a "subdictator," that is, a man armed with unusual powers who without regard to questions of prestige would be able to cut through the tangled threefold and fourfold organization of the Wehrmacht and at last establish clear and effective organizational structures. This memorandum had been written days before, and it was only by chance that it bore the date July 20. Nevertheless, it drew on many ideas which had come up in discussions with the military people who were now participants in the uprising.*

The obvious idea, to telephone the Fuehrer's headquarters and ask for details, did not occur to me. Probably, I assumed that in view of the excitement such an episode had undoubtedly produced, a telephone call would only be a nuisance. Besides, I felt the awkwardness of the suspicion that the assassin might have come from my organization. After lunch I went on with my appointments for the day and saw Ambassador Clodius of the Foreign Office, who reported on the "safeguarding of Rumanian oil." But before the conference was over Goebbels telephoned me.[7]

His voice had changed remarkably since the morning; it sounded excited and hoarse. "Can you interrupt your work at once? Come over here. It's extremely urgent! No, I can't tell you anything on the telephone."

I broke off my meeting with Clodius at once. About five o'clock I arrived at Goebbels's residence, which was situated south of the Brandenburg Gate. He received me in his second-floor office. Hastily, he said: "I've just had word from headquarters that a military putsch

---

* In my memorandum of July 20, 1944, I applied the experience I had gained from working with industry to the problems of armed forces administration. I also drew on knowledge I had acquired in conversations with members of the General Staff, such as Olbricht, Stieff, Wagner, and others. I explained that figures were deceptive since of 10.5 million men conscripted, only 2.3 million ever saw service in the field. The German organizational method was based on having as many independent units as possible, every one of which was eager to achieve the greatest possible self-sufficiency in every area. The memorandum continues: "Thus in the armed forces we have set up subdivisions for the three main branches, for the Waffen-SS, for the Todt Organization, and for the Labor Service—and these subdivisions are all autonomous. Clothing, food, communications and intelligence, health, supplies, and transportation are all organized separately, have separate headquarters and are separately equipped." The result, I stated, was a waste of manpower and material.

is going on throughout the Reich. In this situation I'd like to have you with me. I sometimes go at things too hastily. You can balance that out by your calm. We must take considered action."

This bombshell threw me into a state of excitement as great as Goebbels's. All at once the conversations I had had with Fromm, Zeitzler, and Guderian, with Wagner, Stieff, Fellgiebel, Olbricht, and Lindemann, leaped into my mind—along with thoughts of the hopeless situation on all the fronts, the successful Allied invasion, the overwhelming power of the Red Army, the threatening breakdown in our efforts to supply fuel—along with all this came recollection of our frequently bitter criticism of Hitler's amateurishness, of his absurd decisions, of his constant insults to high-ranking officers, of the incessant stream of demotions and humiliations. It did not occur to me then, however, that Stauffenberg, Olbricht, Stieff, and their circle might be carrying out the revolt. I would rather have attributed such an act to a man of Guderian's choleric temperament.

Goebbels, as I later found out, must by this time have learned that suspicion was directed against Stauffenberg. But he said nothing to me about that. Nor did he tell me that he had talked with Hitler himself on the telephone just before my arrival.*

While I was ignorant of these strands in the web, I had already taken my stand. The fact was that I regarded a putsch in the present state of affairs as an utter disaster. I did not perceive the morality of it. Goebbels could count on my assistance.

The office windows looked out on the street. A few minutes after my arrival I saw fully equipped soldiers, in steel helmets, hand grenades at their belts and submachine guns in their hands, moving toward the Brandenburg Gate in small, battle-ready groups. They set up machine guns at the gate and stopped all traffic. Meanwhile, two heavily armed men went up to the door at the wall along the park and stood guard there. I summoned Goebbels. He understood the significance at once, vanished into his adjacent bedroom, took a few pills from a box, and put them into his coat pocket. "Well, just in case!" he said, with visible tension.

We sent an adjutant to find out what orders these sentries had. But we did not learn much. The soldiers at the wall proved to be uncommunicative. Finally, one of them said curtly: "No one is entering or leaving here."

---

* It can be assumed that Hitler had told Goebbels which way suspicion was pointing. By this time at the Rastenburg headquarters orders had already been issued to arrest Stauffenberg. Fromm, too, must have been under suspicion, for by 6 P.M. Hitler had dismissed Fromm and named Himmler to succeed him. The fact that Goebbels did not take me into his confidence probably indicates that he did not entirely trust me.

The telephone calls Goebbels was making indefatigably in all directions provided confusing news. Troops from Potsdam were already on the march toward Berlin; garrisons from the provinces were also moving up, we heard. In myself, in spite of my spontaneous repudiation of the uprising, was a curious feeling of merely being there as a non-participant, as if all this hectic activity on the part of a nervous and resolute Goebbels did not concern me. At times the situation seemed rather hopeless, and Goebbels showed extreme anxiety. But since the telephone was still functioning and the radio had not yet broadcast any proclamations by the rebels, Goebbels concluded that the other side was still uncertain.

It was incomprehensible that the conspirators failed to stop communications or to seize them for their own use. Weeks before they had worked out a detailed schedule which included the arrest of Goebbels, occupation of the Berlin long-distance telephone office, the main telegraph office, the SS communications center, the central post office, the major broadcasting facilities around Berlin, and the radio station in Charlottenburg.[8] Only a few soldiers would have been needed to break into Goebbels's office and arrest the minister without resistance; a few revolvers were all the protection and arms we had. Goebbels would probably have tried to escape capture by taking the potassium cyanide he had in readiness. Thus, the most competent antagonist to the conspirators would have been put out of action.

Amazingly enough, during these critical hours Goebbels could not reach Himmler, who alone possessed reliable units that might have suppressed the putsch. Himmler had quite obviously withdrawn, and Goebbels was all the more disturbed by that because he could not, try though he might, see any apparent motive for such conduct. Several times he expressed his distrust of the Reichsführer-SS and Minister of the Interior. It has always seemed to me a sign of the uncertainties of those few hours that Goebbels could have revealed doubt about the reliability of even such a man as Himmler.

Was Goebbels also suspicious of me when he banished me to an adjoining room during a telephone call? He hardly took the trouble to conceal his skepticism toward me. Afterward, the thought occurred to me that perhaps he had wanted me there with him so that he could keep watch on me—all the more so since suspicion was already directed toward Stauffenberg and therefore, inevitably, toward Fromm as his superior officer. After all, Goebbels was aware of my friendship with Fromm, whom he had long openly referred to as an "enemy of the party."

I also thought of Fromm immediately. When Goebbels sent me out of his room, I called the switchboard at Bendlerstrasse and asked for Fromm, thinking that I could most easily find out from him what was happening. "General Fromm is not available," I was informed. I did not know that at this time he was already locked up in a room at Bendler-strasse. "Then connect me with his adjutant." No one answered at the adjutant's telephone, I was told. "Then General Olbricht, please."

Olbricht came to the phone at once. "What is going on, General?" I asked him in that joking tone customary between us, which often cut through difficult situations. "I have work to do and am being kept here at Goebbels's office by soldiers."

Olbricht apologized. "Sorry, in your case it's a mistake. I'll put that right in a moment." He hung up before I could ask any more questions. I did not tell Goebbels about this phone call. The tone and the content of it suggested an understanding with Olbricht which might arouse further mistrust in Goebbels.

Meanwhile Schach, the deputy Gauleiter of Berlin, entered the room where I was waiting. Someone named Hagen had just spoken to him and vouched for the National Socialist principles of Major Remer, whose battalion had encircled the government quarter. Goebbels's first thought was to persuade Remer to come and talk with him. As soon as he learned that Remer was willing, Goebbels admitted me to his office again. He was sure he could win Remer over to his side and asked me to be present. Hitler, he said, had been informed of this impending conversation; he was awaiting the results at headquarters and would be prepared to talk with the major himself at any time.

Major Remer entered. Goebbels seemed controlled, but nervous. He seemed to sense that everything hung on this, the fate of the uprising, and thus his own fate as well. After a few remarkably undramatic minutes, it was all over and the putsch lost.

First, Goebbels reminded the major of his oath to the Fuehrer. Remer replied by vowing his loyalty to Hitler and the party. But, he added, Hitler was dead. Consequently, he must obey the orders of his commander, Major General von Haase. Goebbels retorted with the ringing words: "The Fuehrer is alive!" Seeing that Remer was at first taken aback and then became obviously unsure of himself, Goebbels added at once: "He's alive. I spoke to him a few minutes ago. An ambitious little clique of generals has begun this military putsch. A filthy trick. The filthiest trick in history."

The news that Hitler was still living was evidently an enormous relief to this perplexed young man, recipient of an incomprehensible order to cordon off the government quarter. Happy, but still incredulous, Remer stared at all of us. Goebbels now pointed out to Remer that this was an historic hour, that a tremendous responsibility before history rested on his shoulders. Rarely had destiny afforded a single man such a chance, Goebbels said; it was up to him whether to use it or throw it away.

You had only to see Remer now to observe the change in him that these words produced, to realize that Goebbels had already won. But now the Propaganda Minister played his highest card: "I am going to talk to the Fuehrer now, and you can speak with him too. The Fuehrer can give you orders that rescind your general's orders, can't he?" Goebbels concluded in a faintly sarcastic tone. Then he put through the connection to Rastenburg.

The telephone switchboard in his Ministry had a special line direct to the Fuehrer's headquarters. Within seconds Hitler was on the phone. After a few remarks about the situation Goebbels handed the receiver to the major. Remer immediately recognized Hitler's voice, and receiver in hand involuntarily snapped to attention. We could hear only the repeated phrases: "*Jawohl, mein Führer. . . . Jawohl!*"

Goebbels then took the receiver back, and Hitler told him what had been settled. In place of General Haase, the major had been entrusted with carrying out all the military measures in Berlin. Along with this, he was to obey all instructions from Goebbels.

The uprising had failed, but it had not yet been fully crushed by seven o'clock that evening when Goebbels had it announced on the radio that an assassination of Hitler had been attempted but that the Fuehrer was alive and had already returned to his work. Thus, Goebbels took instant advantage of one of the technical aids which the rebels had neglected during the hours just past with such dire consequences.

Goebbels's confidence was possibly excessive; all was thrown into question again when he learned shortly afterward that a tank brigade had arrived at Fehrbelliner Platz and was refusing to obey Remer's orders. General Guderian alone was their commander, they had told Remer, and with military terseness had warned him: "Anyone who doesn't obey will be shot." Their fighting strength was so superior to Remer's battalion that the fate of a good deal more than the next hour or two seemed to hang on their attitude.

In keeping with the general confusion, no one knew definitely whether this brigade belonged to the rebels or the government. Both Goebbels and Remer thought it likely that Guderian was a participant in the putsch.[9] The leader of the brigade was Colonel Bollbrinker. Since I knew him well, I tried to reach him by telephone. The message I received was reassuring: The tanks had come to crush the rebellion.

About a hundred and fifty members of the Berlin guards battalion, most of them older men, had assembled meanwhile in Goebbels's garden. Before the minister went to address them he commented: "Once I convince them, we've won the game. Just watch how I handle them!" Meanwhile night had fallen; the scene was illuminated only by the light falling through an open door to the garden. From Goebbels's very first words the men listened with the greatest attention to his basically rather insignificant speech. Nevertheless, he put on a show of being extraordinarily self-assured, very much the victor of the day. Precisely because his speech turned familiar platitudes into a personal summons, it had a mesmeric effect. Simply by reading the faces of the soldiers, I could see the impression Goebbels was making on the men gathered in a semicircle around him, and listening, not to commands and threats, but to a plea to their long-conditioned loyalty.

Toward eleven o'clock, Colonel Bollbrinker came into the room where Goebbels had installed me. The conspirators had been arrested, Bollbrinker said, and back at Bendlerstrasse, Fromm wanted to hold a summary court-martial of the lot of them. I realized at once that such an act would seriously incriminate Fromm. Moreover, it seemed to me that Hitler himself ought to decide what was to be done with the rebels. Shortly after midnight I hurriedly drove off to prevent the executions. Bollbrinker and Remer sat in my car. In totally blacked-out Berlin the Bendlerstrasse headquarters was illuminated by searchlights—an unreal and ghostly scene. It also seemed as theatrical as a movie backdrop brightly lit inside a dark studio. Long, sharp shadows made the building look exceedingly solid and sculptured.

As I was about to turn into Bendlerstrasse, an SS officer signaled to me to stop at the curb on Tiergartenstrasse. Almost unrecognizable in the darkness under the trees stood Kaltenbrunner, the Gestapo chief, and Skorzeny, the man who had liberated Mussolini, surrounded by numerous subordinates. These dark figures looked like phantoms and behaved as such. When we greeted them, no one clicked his heels; the usual paraded briskness had vanished. Everything seemed muted; even the conversation was conducted in lowered voices, as at a funeral. I explained to Kaltenbrunner that I had come to stop Fromm's summary court-martial. I had rather expected Kaltenbrunner and Skorzeny would execrate the army, which they had always regarded as their rival, or at any rate gloat over its moral defeat. But both men replied in a fairly indifferent tone that whatever happened was primarily the army's business. "We don't want to get involved and certainly will not interfere. In any case, the summary court-martial has probably taken place already."

Kaltenbrunner informed me that no SS forces would be used to suppress the rebellion or to carry out punishments. He had even forbidden his men to enter the Bendlerstrasse headquarters, he said. Any interference by the SS would inevitably produce fresh trouble with the army and increase the existing tensions.[10] But such tactical considerations, product of the moment, proved to be short-lived. Only a few hours later the pursuit and persecution of the participating army officers by various organs of the SS was in full swing.

Kaltenbrunner had scarcely finished talking when a massive shadow appeared against the brightly illuminated background of the Bendlerstrasse. In full uniform, all alone, Fromm approached us with leaden steps. I bade good-by to Kaltenbrunner and his followers and emerged from the darkness of the trees toward Fromm. "The putsch is finished," he began, controlling himself with stern effort. "I have just issued the necessary commands to all corps area headquarters. For a time I was prevented from exercising my command of the Home Army. They actually locked me in a room. My chief of staff, my closest associates!" Indignation and a measure of uneasiness were detectable as, his voice growing steadily louder, he justified his execution of his staff. "As their appointing authority, it was my duty to hold a summary court-martial immediately of all participants in the rebellion." His voice dropping to a pained murmur, he added: "General Olbricht and my chief of staff, Colonel Stauffenberg, are no longer living."

The first thing Fromm wanted to do was to telephone Hitler. In vain I asked him to come to my Ministry first. He insisted on seeing Goebbels, although he knew as well as I that the Propaganda Minister disliked and distrusted him.

At Goebbels's residence, General Haase, the city commandant of Berlin, was already under arrest. In my presence Fromm briefly explained the events and asked Goebbels to connect him with Hitler. Goebbels, instead of replying, asked Fromm to go into another room; then he put through the call to Hitler. At this point, he asked me to leave also. After about twenty minutes he came to the door and summoned a guard whom he posted in front of Fromm's room.

It was already after midnight when Himmler, whom nobody had been able to locate up to this point, arrived at Goebbels's residence. In detail, and before being asked, he justified his absence.* There was a tried and true rule for dealing with uprisings, he said. You had to keep away from the center and conduct the counteractions from outside. That was the proper strategy.

Goebbels seemed to accept this. He appeared to be in the best of humor and gave Himmler a detailed account of the events in which he dramatized how he had mastered the situation virtually by himself. "If they hadn't been so clumsy! They had an enormous chance. What dolts! What childishness! When I think how I would have handled such a thing. Why didn't they occupy the radio station and spread the wildest lies? Here they put guards in front of my door. But they let me go right ahead and telephone the Fuehrer, mobilize everything! They didn't even silence my telephone. To hold so many trumps and botch it—what beginners!"

Those military men, he continued, had relied too heavily on the

* Himmler apparently hesitated to obey Hitler's order, issued at 5 P.M., that he return to Berlin. At first Himmler stayed in his headquarters; he did not land in Berlin until late in the evening, and then avoided Tempelhof Airfield, choosing an obscure landing strip outside the city.

traditional concept of obedience and had taken it for granted that every order would be carried out by the subordinate officers and men. That alone had doomed the putsch to failure. For they had forgotten, he added with cool self-congratulation, that in recent years the National Socialist state had educated the Germans to think politically. "It's simply no longer possible nowadays to make them follow the orders of a clique of generals like so many puppets." Abruptly, Goebbels stopped. As though my presence had become an embarrassment he said: "I have several questions to discuss with the Reichsführer alone, my dear Herr Speer. Good night."

On the next day, July 21, the important ministers were invited to the Fuehrer's headquarters to present their congratulations. Appended to my invitation was the request that I bring Dorsch and Saur, my two principal assistants, along with me—an unusual request, since all the other ministers came without their deputies. At the reception Hitler greeted them with pronounced cordiality, whereas he passed by me with a careless handshake. Hitler's entourage also behaved with inexplicable coolness. As soon as I entered a room, the conversation ceased and those in the room left or turned away. Schaub, Hitler's civilian adjutant, said meaningfully to me: "Now we know who was behind the assassination attempt." Then he walked out on me. I could learn no more. Saur and Dorsch were even invited to the afternoon tea in the intimate circle without me. Everything was very strange. I was greatly disturbed.

Keitel, on the other hand, had at last emerged from the clouds which had been gathering about him in the past weeks, due to the criticism of him by members of the entourage. When he picked himself up out of the dust immediately after the explosion and saw Hitler standing there relatively uninjured, he had rushed at him, as Hitler now repeatedly related, exclaiming: "*Mein Führer*, you're alive, you're alive!" and ignoring all convention had wildly embraced him. It was clear that after that Hitler would never drop him—he was even more closely than ever attached to him since Keitel seemed the right person to take harsh vengeance upon the rebels. "Keitel was almost killed himself," Hitler declared. "He will show no mercy."

The next day Hitler was more friendly to me again, and his entourage followed his example. Under his chairmanship a conference took place in the teahouse with Keitel, Himmler, Bormann, Goebbels, and myself participating. Without crediting me with the idea, Hitler had taken up what I had urged two weeks before and appointed Goebbels Reich Commissioner for Total Mobilization of Resources for War.[11] His escape from death had made him more resolute; he was ready to implement measures which Goebbels and I had been calling for, for more than a year.

Hitler then turned to the events of the past several days. He was triumphant; now at last the great positive turning point in the war had come. The days of treason were over; new and better generals would assume the command. Today he had realized, he said, that in trying Tukhachevsky, Stalin had taken a decisive step toward successful conduct of the war. By liquidating his General Staff, Stalin had made room for fresh, vigorous men who did not date back to Tsarist days. He had always thought the charges in the 1937 Moscow trials were trumped up, he said; but now after the experience of July 20 he wondered whether there might not have been something to them. He still had no more evidence than before, Hitler continued, but he could no longer exclude the possibility of treasonous collaboration between the Russian and the German general staffs.

Everybody agreed. Goebbels poured buckets of scorn and contempt upon the generals. When I tried to temper some of this, he snapped sharply at me in an unfriendly manner. Hitler listened in silence.*

The fact that General Fellgiebel, the chief of the Signal Corps, had also been a member of the conspiracy, prompted Hitler to an outburst in which spite and fury were mingled with a sense of being vindicated:

> Now I know why all my great plans in Russia had to fail in recent years. It was all treason! But for those traitors, we would have won long ago. Here is my justification before history. Now we will find out whether Fellgiebel had a direct wire to Switzerland and passed all my plans on to the Russians. He must be interrogated by every means! . . . Once again I was right. Who wanted to believe me when I objected to any unification of the Wehrmacht leadership! Under one man, the Wehrmacht is a menace! Do you still think it was chance that I had so many divisions of the Waffen-SS raised? I knew why I had to have that, against all the opposition. . . . The Inspector General of the Armored Forces—that was all done to split up the army as much as possible.

Hitler had another outburst of murderous rage against the conspirators. He would "annihilate and exterminate" every one of them, he declared. Then the names of men who had opposed him at one time or another occurred to him. He now included them in the ranks of the conspirators. Schacht had been a saboteur of rearmament, he said. Unfortunately he, Hitler, had always been too soft. He ordered the immedi-

---

* On July 23, 1944, Ley wrote an editorial in *Angriff* which revealed that the regime had launched a campaign against the old military aristocracy: "Degenerate to their very bones, blue-blooded to the point of idiocy, nauseatingly corrupt, and cowardly like all nasty creatures—such is the aristocratic clique which the Jew has sicked on National Socialism. . . . We must exterminate this filth, extirpate it root and branch. . . . It is not enough simply to seize the offensive . . . we must exterminate the entire breed."

ate arrest of Schacht. "Hess, too, will be mercilessly hanged, just like these swine, these criminal officers. He was the one who started it, he gave the example of treason."

After each such eruption Hitler calmed down. With the gratefulness of a man who has just survived a great peril, he recapitulated the whole story of the assassination attempt and then spoke of the turning point it had inaugurated, of the victory which had now again moved within reach. Euphorically, he drew new confidence from the failure of the plot, and we all too willingly let ourselves be swayed by his optimism.

Soon afterward the main bunker, whose rebuilding had caused Hitler to be in my barracks on the fateful day of July 20, was completed. If ever a building can be considered the symbol of a situation, this bunker was it. From the outside it looked like an ancient Egyptian tomb. It was actually nothing but a great windowless block of concrete, without direct ventilation, in cross section a building whose masses of concrete far exceeded the usable cubic feet of space. It seemed as if the concrete walls sixteen and a half feet thick that surrounded Hitler separated him from the outside world in a figurative as well as literal sense, and locked him up inside his delusions.

Chief of Staff Zeitzler had already been dismissed on the night of July 20. I took advantage of my stay to pay a farewell visit to him at his headquarters nearby. Saur could not be dissuaded from keeping me company. During our talk Zeitzler's adjutant, Lieutenant Colonel Günther Smend—who was to be executed a few weeks later—reported back. Saur instantly became suspicious: "Did you see the look of understanding with which the two of them greeted each other?" he said to me. I reacted with an irritable, "No." Shortly afterward, when Zeitzler and I were alone, I learned that Smend had just come from Berchtesgaden, where he had cleaned out the General Staff's safe. But the very fact that Zeitzler commented so innocently on this strengthened my impression that the conspirators had not taken him into their confidence. I never found out whether Saur gave Hitler a detailed report on this meeting. After three days in the Fuehrer's headquarters, I flew back to Berlin early on the morning of July 24.

SS Obergruppenführer Kaltenbrunner, the Gestapo chief, had announced his impending arrival. He had never called on me before. I received him lying down, since my leg was once again troubling me. I had the impression that Kaltenbrunner was scrutinizing me sharply; he had that air of cordial menace I had noticed in him on the night of July 20. Without preface he began: "In the safe at the Bendlerstrasse we have found papers relating to the government the July 20 men intended to set up. You are down on the list as Armaments Minister."

He asked whether and what I had known about the position intended for me, but otherwise remained formal and polite as usual. Perhaps such an expression of consternation had flashed across my face when he made his revelation that he was ready to believe me. He soon stopped making any further inquiries and instead took a document from his pocket. It was an organizational plan for the postconspiracy government. Apparently it had been drawn up by a military officer, for the organization of the Wehrmacht was treated with particular care. A "Great General Staff" was to coordinate the three branches of the armed forces. Subordinate to it was the Commander in Chief of the Home Army, who was also to be supreme Armaments Chief. Next to that, in the midst of the many other small boxes, neatly printed in block letters, I found the legend: "Armaments: Speer." In pencil a skeptic had written alongside: "If possible"—and added a question mark. That unknown officer, and the fact that I had not accepted the invitation to the Bendlerstrasse on July 20, saved my life. Curiously, Hitler never said a word about it to me. *

Naturally, I considered at the time what I would have done had the July 20 insurrection succeeded and the conspirators asked me to continue in my post. I probably would have complied for a transitional period, but not without considerable inner conflict. Judging by all I know today about the individuals and the motives of the conspiracy, collaboration with them would within a short time have cured me of my loyalty to Hitler. They would quickly have won me over to their cause. But that in itself would have made my remaining in the government, doubtful enough for superficial reasons, quite impossible for psychological reasons. For if I had come to a moral understanding of the nature of the regime and of the part that I had played in it, I would have been forced to recognize that it was no longer conceivable for me to hold any position of leadership in a post-Hitler Germany.

The next day our Ministry, like all the others, held a loyalty meeting in our conference hall. The whole affair lasted no longer than twenty minutes. I delivered the feeblest and most insecure speech I had ever made. As a rule I had steered clear of the usual formulas, but this time I bellowed out our faith in Hitler and his greatness and for the first time in my life ended a speech with "*Sieg Heil!*" Previously, I had not felt any need for such Byzantine turns of phrase; they ran contrary both to my temperament and my pride. But now I felt insecure, compromised, and involved in mysterious, opaque processes.

* This organization plan conformed largely to the draft found in the Bendlerstrasse of a decree which Regent Beck was supposed to sign; it established "the provisional wartime leadership structure." In addition there was a list of ministers; the Armaments Ministry was to be placed under Goerdeler, the future Chancellor. I was included in this list, also with a question mark after my name and the notation that I should not be asked until after the coup had succeeded. (From *Der 20. Juli*, ed. Hans Royce [Berto Verlag, Bonn, 1961].)

My fears, incidentally, were not unfounded. Rumors had it that I had been arrested; other rumors reported that I had already been executed—a sign that public opinion, which still existed only beneath the surface, considered my position as imperiled.[12]

All my worries were wiped out, however, when Bormann sent me a request to address a conference of Gauleiters in Posen on the subject of armaments again. The July 20 events still hung over the group, and although I was officially rehabilitated by this invitation, I encountered an icy air of prejudice. I found myself entirely alone among all these assembled party bigwigs. Nothing could have better characterized the atmosphere than a remark that Goebbels made to the Gauleiters and Reichsleiters around him before my talk: "Now we at last know where Speer stands."[13]

As it happened, however, in July 1944 our armaments production had reached its peak. In order not to provoke the party leaders again and worsen my situation, I cautiously refrained from any general remarks and instead showered them with a cloudburst of statistics on the successes of our previous work and on the new programs Hitler had assigned to us. From the overfulfilled quotas, even the party leaders must have seen that I and my apparatus were indispensable at this of all times. I noticed that the atmosphere warmed considerably when I demonstrated, with many examples, what huge stocks of spare parts and accessories the Wehrmacht still had and was not using. Goebbels cried out loudly, "Sabotage, sabotage!" proving how determined the leadership was since July 20 to see treason, conspiracy, and treachery at work everywhere. The Gauleiters could not help being impressed by my progress report.

From Posen the participants in this meeting went to headquarters, where Hitler addressed them the next day. Although by rank I did not belong to this group,[14] Hitler had explicitly invited me to be present. I took a seat in the back row.

Hitler spoke of the consequences of July 20. Once again he attributed the bad record of the past years to treason by army officers and expressed great hopes for the future. Never before in his life had he felt such confidence, said Hitler.[15] For all his previous efforts had been sabotaged, but now the criminal clique had been exposed and purged. In the end this putsch may well have been the most fortunate of events for our future. Thus Hitler repeated almost word for word what he had already said to his intimates immediately after the putsch. I too was falling under the spell of his self-confidence, for all its lapses of logic, when he dropped a sentence that suddenly startled me out of my trance: "If the German nation is now defeated in this struggle, it has been too weak. That will mean it has not withstood the test of history and was destined for nothing but doom."[16]

Surprisingly and quite contrary to his usual way of not especially heaping praise on his assistants, Hitler pointed to my work and my achievements. Probably he knew or sensed that this was necessary. Because of the unfriendly attitude of the Gauleiters, I had to be given a special boost to make it possible for me to go on working successfully. He made it emphatically clear to the party audience that his relations to me had not cooled since July 20.

I utilized my newly strengthened position to help acquaintances and associates who had been caught in the wave of persecution following the events of July 20.* Saur, on the other hand, denounced two officers of the Army Ordnance Office, General Schneider and Colonel Fichtner, whose arrests Hitler ordered at once. In Schneider's case, Saur had merely quoted a remark of his to the effect that Hitler was incapable of judging technical questions. Fichtner's arrest was based solely on his not having supported vigorously the new types of tanks that Hitler wanted at the beginning of the war. This was now interpreted as deliberate sabotage. Still, Hitler was sufficiently tractable at this point so that when I interceded for the two officers he agreed to their release, though on the condition that they no longer be employed in the Army Ordnance Office.[17]

On August 18 at headquarters I observed the curious state of mind Hitler was now in concerning the reliability of the officer corps. Field Marshal Kluge, the Commander in Chief in the West, had set out on a trip to visit the Seventh Army three days before, and could not be reached for many hours. When the report came that the Field Marshal, accompanied only by his adjutant who had a radio transmitter with him, had approached close to the front, Hitler began to make more and more detailed surmises. Soon he had decided that Kluge must have gone to a predetermined place in order to conduct negotiations with the Western Allies on a capitulation of the German army in the West. And when no such negotiations occurred, he reasoned that this was only because an air raid had interrupted the Field Marshal's trip and frustrated his treasonous intentions. By the time I arrived at headquarters Kluge had already been relieved of his command and ordered to headquarters. The next report to arrive was that the Field Marshal had succumbed to a heart attack on the way. Hitler, invoking his famous sixth sense, ordered the Gestapo to examine the corpse thoroughly. He was triumphant when it turned out that Kluge's death had been caused by poison. Now he

---

* As Gregor Janssen explains in *Das Ministerium Speer*, I used my influence to have several persons released, among them General Speidel, the publisher Suhrkamp, the wife of General Seydlitz and his brother-in-law, Dr. Eberhardt Barth. I also helped Count Schwerin, General Zeitzler, General Heinrici, and the industrialists Vögler, Bücher, Meyer, Stinnes, Haniel, Reuter, Meinen, and Reusch, who were implicated through Goerdeler.

was completely convinced that Kluge had been engaged in treasonous activities, although the Field Marshal had left a letter assuring him of his loyalty unto death.

During this stay at headquarters I came across the reports of Kaltenbrunner's interrogations lying on the big map table in Hitler's bunker. One of the adjutants who was friendly to me let me have them to read for two nights straight, for I still felt far from safe. Many things I had said before July 20, which could all along have passed for justified criticism, seemed in retrospect incriminating. But none of the arrested men had in fact incriminated me. The one thing the rebels had done was to adopt my favorite phrase for the yes-men in Hitler's entourage: "nodding donkeys."

During these days a heap of photographs also lay on this table. Lost in thought, I picked one up, but quickly put it down. It was a picture of a hanged man in convict dress, a broad, colored stripe on his trousers. One of the SS leaders standing near me remarked, in explanation: "That's Witzleben. Don't you want to see the others too? These are all photos of the executions."

That evening the film of the execution of the conspirators was shown in the movie room. I could not and would not see it. But in order not to attract attention, I gave the excuse that I was far behind in my work. I saw many others going to this showing, mostly lower-ranking SS men and civilians. Not a single officer of the Wehrmacht attended.

27

The Wave from the West

WHEN AT THE BEGINNING OF JULY, I HAD PROPOSED TO HITLER THAT Goebbels instead of the incompetent Committee of Three take over the job of rallying all the forces of the home front behind the war effort, I could not foresee that a few weeks later the balance of power between Goebbels and me would shift very much against me. This was largely because the conspirators had my name down on their list of candidates. But, more and more of the party leaders argued that things had gone wrong because not enough scope had been given to party elements. If the party had had its way, it would have even provided the generals. The Gauleiters openly bewailed the fact that in 1934 the SA had succumbed to the Wehrmacht. They now regarded Roehm's bygone efforts to form a people's army as a missed opportunity. Such an army would have bred an officer corps imbued with the National Socialist spirit, they argued; and it was the lack of just this spirit that had produced the defeats of recent years. The party thought that it was high time it took over at least in the civilian sector and energetically issued its orders to the government and all the rest of us.

Only a week after the Gauleiter meeting in Posen, Arthur Tix, the head of my Ordnance Directive Committee, informed me that "Gauleiters, SA leaders, and other party authorities were suddenly, without previous consultation," trying to interfere with the work of the factories. Three weeks later, as a result of inroads by the party, "a double line

397) The Wave from the West

of command" had arisen. The armaments bureaus were "having to yield to pressure from the Gauleiters; their arbitrary interference is creating a confusion that stinks to heaven."[1]

All this ambition and enterprise on the part of the Gauleiters was encouraged by Goebbels, who was suddenly feeling himself not so much a government minister as a party leader. Supported by Bormann and Keitel, he was preparing large-scale call-ups to the services. Such ill-considered intervention would only mean major disruption in the factories. On August 30, 1944, I informed the heads of my departments of my intention to make the Gauleiters responsible for armaments production.[2] I was going to capitulate.

I was driven to this because I no longer had any support behind me. As had long been the case for the majority of the ministers, I could not go to Hitler with any such concerns, especially if they involved the party. As soon as a conversation took a troublesome turn, Hitler became evasive. It had become more sensible to communicate my complaints to him in writing.

On September 20, I wrote Hitler a lengthy letter in which I candidly described the party's ill-feeling toward me, its efforts to eliminate me or at any rate by-pass me, its accusations and bullying tactics.

The events of July 20, I wrote, had "magnified the existing distrust of the reliability of the many men from industry who constituted my group of associates." The party clung to the notion that my closest aides were "reactionary, tied down to one-sided economic views, and alien to the party." Goebbels and Bormann had frankly expressed their view that my Ministry and my organization for industrial self-responsibility were "a collection of reactionary captains of industry," if not outright "antiparty." I would not, I said, "feel strong enough to carry out the technical work assigned to me and my associates unhampered and with any promise of success if it were going to be evaluated by the standards of party policy."[3]

Only on two conditions, the letter continued, would I allow the party a voice in armaments matters: If both the Gauleiters and Bormann's economic representatives in the districts (Gau economic advisers) were directly subordinated to me on questions of armaments. There must be, I insisted, "clarity in the chain of command and on matters of jurisdiction."[4] In addition I demanded that Hitler once again approve my principles: "A plain decision is needed whether industry is to be guided by industrial self-responsibility built on confidence in the factory managers or by a different system. In my opinion responsibility of the factory managers for their plants must be preserved and emphasized as strongly as possible." I concluded this letter by urging that a system which had proved itself in practice ought not to be changed—but that one way or another we had to have a decision "which will plainly indicate what direction the guidance of the economy is to take in the future."

On September 21, I handed Hitler my letter at headquarters. He received it without a word and looked through it. Then, still without replying, he pressed the signal button and handed the document to his adjutant, telling him to pass it on to Bormann. Goebbels was present at headquarters also, and Hitler explained that Goebbels and Bormann would decide together what to do. I had lost for good. Hitler had evidently grown weary of intervening in these disputes, which made little sense to him.

A few hours later Bormann asked me to his office, which was a few steps from Hitler's bunker. He was in shirtsleeves and wore suspenders over his fat trunk; Goebbels was carefully dressed. Citing Hitler's decree of July 25, Goebbels flatly declared that he would now make full use of his new powers to command me. Bormann agreed: I was under Goebbels now. For the rest, he would not stand for any further attempts on my part to influence Hitler directly. Bormann told me off in his usual loutish fashion, while Goebbels listened menacingly, making cynical interjections. The unification I had so often demanded had come into being at last, although in the surprising form of an alliance between Goebbels and Bormann.

Hitler continued to say nothing about my written demands, but two days later he gave me another sign of his sympathy by signing a proclamation of mine to the factory directors. This could be construed as support of the principle I had set forth in my letter. Under normal circumstances it would have constituted a victory over Bormann and Goebbels. But Hitler's authority in the party was no longer what it had been. His closest paladins simply ignored it or went counter to Hitler's pronouncements whenever they wished to tamper with the economy. These were the first clear signs of disintegration; now the party apparatus and the loyalty of Hitler's leading men had been affected. The conflict, which continued to smolder during the following weeks and grew increasingly violent, intensified these symptoms.[5] Naturally, Hitler himself was partly to blame for this loss of sovereignty. He stood helplessly between Goebbels's demands for more soldiers and mine for increased armaments production. First he backed one of us, then the other, nodding assent to contradictory commands—until the bombs and the advancing enemy armies made both, one and then the other, wholly superfluous, finally wiping out the quarrel and the question of Hitler's authority.

Harried both by politics and the external enemy, I was always glad to get away from Berlin. I soon began undertaking longer and longer visits to the front. As far as armaments went, it was little help, for the experiences I gathered could no longer be put to use. But still I hoped by the observations I made and the information I received from the commanders to be able occasionally to influence decisions at headquarters.

Later on, when I took account of the results, I had to recognize that all my reports, whether oral or written, had had no useful effect. For example, many of the generals in command of forward sectors, with whom I talked, asked to have their old forces replenished and fitted out with arms and tanks which our factories were still supplying. Hitler, however, and Himmler, his new commander of the Reserve Army, now thought that troops thrown back by the enemy no longer possessed the morale to resist and that it was better to hastily set up new units, the so-called people's grenadier divisions. As they put it, the beaten divisions might just as well be allowed to "bleed to death" completely.

I was able to observe the results of this theory at the end of September 1944 when I visited a unit of an experienced tank division near Bitburg. Its commander, a man tried and tested by many years in warfare, showed me the battlefield where a few days before a newly formed, inexperienced tank brigade had met tragedy. Insufficiently trained, it had lost ten of its thirty-two new Panthers from bad driving while deploying. The remaining twenty-two tanks that had reached the deployment area had, as the commander demonstrated, been ranged so stupidly on an open field, without adequate reconnaissance, that an American antitank unit had shot up fifteen of them as if it were engaged in target practice. "To think of what my experienced troops could have done with these tanks!" the captain said bitterly. I described this incident to Hitler, concluding with the caustic comment that this example showed that "new levies often have considerable disadvantages as against providing replacements."[6] But Hitler remained unimpressed. In a situation conference he commented that from his experiences as an infantryman he knew that the troops took care of their weapons only when supplies were kept extremely meager.

Other visits showed me that efforts were being made on the Western front to arrive at understandings with the enemy on special problems. At Arnhem, I found General Bittrich of the Waffen-SS in a state of fury. The day before his Second Tank Corps had virtually wiped out a British airborne division. During the fighting the general had made an arrangement permitting the enemy to run a field hospital situated behind the German lines. But party functionaries had taken it upon themselves to kill British and American pilots, and Bittrich was cast in the role of a liar. His violent denunciation of the party was all the more striking since it came from an SS general.

But even Hitler's former army adjutant, Colonel Engel, who was now commanding the Twelfth Infantry Division near Düren, had on his own initiative made an agreement with the enemy for rescue of the wounded during pauses in battles. It was inadvisable to mention such pacts at headquarters, for experience had taught me that Hitler would consider them signs of "slackness." Actually, we had often heard him disparaging the so-called chivalric tradition of the Prussian officer class. In contrast to that, he would say, the toughness and inflexibility of the struggle waged in the East on both sides had the effect of strengthening the fighting spirit of the enlisted man, since humane considerations could not even arise under such conditions.

I recall just one single case in which Hitler tacitly, though reluctantly, consented to a deal with the enemy. Late in the autumn of 1944 the British fleet cut the German troops on the Greek islands off from all connection with the mainland. In spite of the total British control of the sea, the German units were permitted to embark and sail undisturbed to the mainland; in some cases the German vessels passed within visual range of British naval units. As a quid pro quo the German side had agreed to use these troops to hold Salonika against the Russians until the city could be taken over by British forces. When this operation was over—it had been proposed by Jodl—Hitler commented: "This is the only time we have consented to anything like that."

In September 1944 the generals at the front, the industrialists, and the Gauleiters of the western regions expected the American and British armies to exploit their superior power and roll right over our almost unarmed and worn-out troops in an offensive that would never pause.[7] No one any longer counted on being able to stop them; no one who had preserved any sense of reality believed in anything like a "Marne miracle" in our favor.

Preparations for the demolition of industrial installations of all kinds, at home and in the occupied territories, lay within the jurisdiction of my Ministry. During the retreats in the Soviet Union, Hitler had already given orders to negate whatever territorial gains the enemy made by following a scorched earth policy. As soon as the invasion armies began advancing from their bridgehead in Normandy, he issued a similar order. At the beginning, rational operational considerations underlay this policy of destruction. The idea was to make it difficult for the enemy to establish a foothold, to draw his supplies from the liberated country, to make use of technical repair services as well as electricity and gas, or in the longer run to build up an armaments industry. As long as the end of the war remained a distant eventuality, such actions seemed to me justified. But they lost all meaning the moment ultimate defeat drew inescapably close.

In view of the hopeless situation, I very naturally assumed that we wanted to end this war with the least possible devastation of the kind that would hamper future reconstruction. For I was not imbued by that special mood of total doom which was now beginning to spread visibly among Hitler's followers. Hitler himself was more and more ruthlessly determined to bring on total catastrophe. But I was able to outwit him with his own arguments, and this by a simple trick. Since in hopeless situations he also always insisted that the lost territories would soon be reconquered, I needed only to repeat this premise of his and point out that I would need the industries of these areas to maintain arms production as soon as we had reconquered them.

Just after the beginning of the invasion—on June 20, when the Americans had broken through the German defensive front and encircled Cherbourg—I used this argument to good effect. This is the basis for Hitler's pronouncement that "in spite of the present difficulties of transportation at the front, abandonment of the industrial capacities there is out of the question."[8] This new directive allowed the military commander to evade a previous order of Hitler's which called for a million Frenchmen working in the restricted factories to be transported to Germany in case of a successful invasion.[9]

Now Hitler was once again talking about the necessity for sweeping destruction of French industry. In spite of this I succeeded on August 19, when the Allied troops were still northwest of Paris, in making him consent to our merely paralyzing rather than destroying the industrial and power installations about to fall into enemy hands.* But I could not obtain any fundamental decision from Hitler; I had to work from case to case, on the pretense that all retreats were only temporary. As time passed, that argument gradually came to seem more and more ridiculous.

When the enemy troops were approaching the ore basin near Longwy and Briey toward the end of August, I faced a changed situation. Since this region of Lorraine had been practically incorporated into Reich territory in 1940, I found myself running up against the jurisdiction of a Gauleiter. Since persuading the Gauleiter to surrender the area to the enemy without destruction was hopeless, I appealed directly to Hitler and was authorized to preserve iron mines

---

* See *Führerprotokoll*, August 18-20, 1944, Point 8. The verdict delivered September 30, 1946, by the International Military Tribunal stated concerning this and future activities of mine: "In the closing stages of the war he [Speer] was one of the few men who had the courage to tell Hitler that the war was lost and to take steps to prevent the senseless destruction of production facilities both in Germany and the occupied territories. He carried out his opposition to Hitler's scorched earth policy by intentionally sabotaging it in certain Western countries and in Germany, at considerable personal danger to himself."

and industry, and to inform the Gauleiters involved of this decision.*

At Saarbrücken in mid-September, Hermann Röchling informed me that we had handed over the French mines in running condition. But by chance the power plant which kept the mine pumps going was still on our side of the front. Röchling sounded me out on whether he could continue to deliver current to the pumping stations over the still undamaged high-tension line. I agreed to that, as I did to the proposal of a troop commander to continue supplying current to the hospitals of Liège after the city had fallen to the Allies, and the front ran between the city and its power plants.

From about the middle of September on, I was also faced with the question of what was to be done with German industry. Naturally, the industrialists were not at all willing to have their factories destroyed. Surprisingly enough, some of the Gauleiters in the endangered areas shared their views. This was a curious phase, both of the war and our lives. In roundabout conversations, full of traps and detours, one man would probe another's views; groups of accomplices formed; and a candid remark on this subject might mean putting your life on the line.

By way of precaution, in case Hitler should hear of the nondestruction of plants in German frontline areas, I informed him—in a report on a trip I had made between September 10–14—that production continued on a relatively satisfactory basis even right behind the front. I made the point that if a factory in Aachen, so close to the front, could turn out four million rounds of infantry ammunition per month,

---

* The Gauleiter of Cologne (Grohé) had been placed in charge of Belgium by Hitler; the Gauleiter of Mosel (Simon) was assigned Luxembourg and the Minette region; and the Gauleiter of the Saar Palatinate (Bürkel) was assigned the area between the Meurthe and the Moselle. Assured of Hitler's consent, I could thus write to Gauleiter Simon on September 5, 1944:

> Plans must be made so that if the Minette, the Luxembourg area, and other industrial regions fall into enemy hands, the factories will only be crippled temporarily; this is to be achieved by removing various elements and taking them along on the retreat, particularly the electrical ones, without damaging the factories themselves. We must count on recovering the Minette region, since in the long run we would not be able to continue the war without it. Our experiences in Russia have shown that industrial plants can change owners several times without either side's inflicting damage; each side simply runs the factory according to its own needs. The coal and iron associations will receive the appropriate instructions.

These associations received the same orders with the additional request that "the same measures be applied to the endangered coal-producing areas in Belgium, Holland, and the Saar. The pumps for the mines must be kept in perfect working order."

the sensible thing was to keep making this ammunition for the immediate use of the troops right up to the last moment, even under artillery bombardment. It would not be sensible, I argued, to shut down coking works in Aachen if these could continue to assure the supply of gas to Cologne, as in the past, and if at the same time a few tons of fuel for the troops were produced every day. Furthermore, it would be a mistake to shut down the power plants in the immediate vicinity of the front since the telephone communications of the troops and civilian populace were dependent on the supply of electricity.

Simultaneously, I sent the Gauleiters a teletype message referring to earlier decisions by Hitler and warning that industrial installations must not be damaged.[10]

Suddenly all these efforts seemed nullified. For when I was back in Berlin the chief of our Central Office, Liebel, met me in our guesthouse for engineers at Wannsee and informed me that during my absence important orders from Hitler had gone out to all the ministries. According to these latest orders, the principle of scorched earth must be ruthlessly carried out on German territory.

Partly to be safe from eavesdroppers, we sprawled on the guesthouse lawn. It was a sunny, late summer day; sailboats moved slowly along the lake, as Liebel drew the picture of what the Fuehrer's latest edict meant. No German was to inhabit territory occupied by the enemy. Those wretches who did remain would find themselves in a desert devoid of all the amenities of civilization. Not only the industrial plants, and not only the gas, water, electrical works and telephone exchanges were to be completely smashed. Everything, simply everything essential to the maintenance of life would be destroyed: the ration card records, the files of marriage and resident registries, the records of bank accounts. In addition, food supplies were to be destroyed, farms burned down and cattle killed. Not even those works of art that the bombs had spared were to be preserved. Monuments, palaces, castles and churches, theaters and opera houses were also to be leveled. A few days earlier, at Hitler's command, an editorial had appeared in the *Völkischer Beobachter* (September 7, 1944) putting this surge of vandalism into rhetoric: "Not a German stalk of wheat is to feed the enemy, not a German mouth to give him information, not a German hand to offer him help. He is to find every footbridge destroyed, every road blocked—nothing but death, annihilation, and hatred will meet him."[11]

In my travel report I had tried to arouse Hitler's sympathy for the war victims: "In the vicinity of Aachen one sees the miserable processions of evacuees, setting out with small children and the old, exactly as in France in 1940. As more evacuations take place, scenes such as these will surely multiply, which should make for restraint in issuing evacuation orders." I called upon Hitler to "go to the West to see for yourself the conditions there. . . . The populace expects this of you."[12]

But Hitler did not go. On the contrary. As soon as he heard that Kreisleiter Schmeer of Aachen had not applied all means of coercion to evacuate the city, he stripped him of his various posts, expelled him from the party, and ordered him to the front as an ordinary soldier.

It would have been pointless to try to persuade Hitler to rescind this order. And my authority did not suffice for independent action. Nevertheless my anxiety was so great that I impulsively dictated a teletype message with the request that after Hitler had approved it Bormann transmit it to the eight Gauleiters of the western areas. It was a stratagem for getting Hitler to reverse himself. I therefore said nothing at all about the radical orders of recent days, but instead reviewed the previous decisions on various individual problems and asked for some over-all ruling. My text was once again psychologically attuned to Hitler's real or pretended faith in ultimate victory: Unless he canceled his order for destruction, he was admitting that the war was lost. By such an admission he undercut the whole basis of argument for total resistance. Incisively, I began:

> The Fuehrer has declared that he can shortly reconquer the territories now lost. Since the western areas are vital for the armaments and war production needed to continue fighting, all measures undertaken in connection with evacuation must have in view the possibility of restoring full functioning to the industry of these areas. . . . Not until the last moment are the industrial installations to be rendered useless for a considerable time by "disabling actions" in the factories. . . . The power plants in the mining districts must be preserved, so that the water levels in the mine shafts may be controlled. If pumps fail and the pits fill, it takes months before the shafts can be restored to functioning condition.

Shortly afterward I telephoned headquarters to ask whether this teletype message had been presented to Hitler. It had, and had actually been issued, although with one slight change. I had anticipated cuts here and there, and probably some stiffening of the passages on disabling actions. But to my surprise Hitler had left the text unaltered except for one place, where the change had been made in his own hand. He had toned down the expression of his confidence in victory. The first sentence now read: "Recapture of a part of the territories now lost in the West is by no means out of the question."

Bormann passed this teletype message on to the Gauleiters with the forceful addition: "In behalf of the Fuehrer I herewith transmit to you a communication from Reich Minister Speer. Its provisos are to be observed strictly and unconditionally."[13] Even Bormann had played along with me. He seemed to be more aware than Hitler of the fearful consequences of total devastation in all the areas from which we were retreating.

Basically, however, Hitler was merely trying to save face when he spoke of "recapture of a part of the territories now lost in the West." For it had finally been borne upon him that even if we succeeded in stabilizing the front, the war would be lost within a few months because of lack of matériel. Jodl had in the meantime supplemented my previous forecasts on armaments policy by pointing out the strategic considerations: The army was holding too large an area under occupation. He used the image of a snake that had lost its swiftness from swallowing too large a prey. He therefore proposed abandonment of Finland, northern Norway, upper Italy, and most of the Balkans. By so doing we would be able to establish geographically more favorable defensive positions along the Tisa and Sava rivers and the southern margin of the Alps. It would also release many divisions. At first Hitler was stubbornly opposed to this; but finally, on August 20, 1944, he gave me permission[14] at least to calculate where we would stand without the raw materials from these areas.

But three days before I had finished my memorandum—on September 2, 1944—an armistice was concluded between Finland and the Soviet Union, and German troops were asked to evacuate Finland by September 15. Jodl telephoned me at once and asked for my findings. Hitler's mood had again changed. He no longer showed the slightest signs of willingness to undertake a voluntary evacuation. Jodl, on the other hand, was pressing for an immediate withdrawal from Lapland while the weather was still good. We would inevitably suffer great loss of arms, he declared, if the retreat were caught in the blizzards which started there early in autumn. Once again Hitler made the point he had used a year before during the dispute over evacuation of the manganese mines of the southern Soviet Union: "If the sources of nickel in northern Lapland are lost, our armaments production will be finished in a few months."

That argument did not last long. On September 5, three days after the Russo-Finnish armistice, I sent my memorandum to Jodl and Hitler by courier. The war of matériel would be decided, I demonstrated, not by loss of the Finnish nickel mines, but by the ending of deliveries of chromium ores from Turkey. Assuming that full production of armaments would continue—which of course was highly hypothetical, given the air raids—the last distribution of chromium to industry would come on June

1, 1945. "Considering the time needed by the processing industries, the production dependent on chromium, which means the entire production of armaments, will cease on January 1, 1946."[15]

By now Hitler's reactions had long since become entirely unpredictable. I was prepared for an outburst of impotent fury; but in fact he received my information calmly, drew no conclusions, and against Jodl's advice put off the evacuation of Lapland until the middle of October. In the light of the general military situation, such forecasts as mine probably left him quite unmoved. Since the fronts had collapsed both in the West and the East, the date January 1, 1946, probably seemed even to Hitler a utopian deadline.

At the moment we were far more bothered by the consequences of the fuel shortage. In July, I had written to Hitler that by September all tactical movements would necessarily come to a standstill for lack of fuel. Now this prediction was being confirmed. At the end of September, I wrote to Hitler: "A fighter group stationed at Krefeld with more than thirty-seven planes must take two days enforced rest in spite of excellent weather. It receives its fuel allotment only on the third day and then only enough for a brief sortie as far as Aachen with twenty of its planes." A few days later, when I visited an airport in Werneuchen, east of Berlin, the commander of the training company informed me that his student pilots could have flight practice only for an hour every week. Only a fraction of the necessary fuel was being supplied to the unit.

Meanwhile the army, too, had become virtually immobile because of the fuel shortage. At the end of October, I reported to Hitler after a night journey to the Tenth Army south of the Po. There I encountered "a column of a hundred and fifty trucks, each of which had four oxen hitched to it. Many trucks were being pulled by tanks and tractors." Early in December, I expressed concern that "the training of tank drivers leaves much to be desired" because they "have no fuel for practicing."[16] General Jodl, of course, knew even better than I how great the emergency was. In order to free seventeen and a half thousand tons of fuel—formerly the production of two and a half days—for the Ardennes offensive, he had to begin withholding fuel from other army groups on November 10, 1944.[17]

In the meantime the attacks on the hydrogenation plants had indirectly affected the entire chemical industry. I was forced to inform Hitler that "the supply of salt has to be stretched in order to fill the existing shells with explosives. This process has already reached the limit of acceptability." Actually, from October 1944 on our explosives consisted of 20 percent rock salt, which reduced their effectiveness correspondingly.[18]

In this desperate situation Hitler now made matters worse by gambling away his last technological trump. Grotesquely enough, in these

Hitler returning from a short walk at his headquarters in the Ukraine, summer 1942. (HEINRICH HOFFMANN)

Goering and Speer after Speer's appointment to his post as Minister of Armaments. (HEINRICH HOFFMANN)

Goering at his birthday party, 1942.
(SÜDDEUTSCHER VERLAG)

*Speer testing new caterpillar
tread motorcycle at tank-testing
site in Thuringia.*
(ÜLLSTEIN BILDERDIENST)

*Hitler inspecting a new army
truck, Left to right: Speer,
unknown, Werlin (director of
Mercedes-Benz), Hitler.*
(HEINRICH HOFFMANN)

LEFT: *Porsche and Speer in prototype of the Tiger tank.*
(SPEER-ARCHIV)

ABOVE: *Conference after test drive. Ferdinand Porsche (wearing cap and goggles), behind him Hugo Eckener, builder of the Graf Zeppelin. On the right, Speer.*
(SPIEGEL-ARCHIV)

RIGHT: *Speer, Saur, and Hitler at a display of new tank models at Hitler's headquarters, 1943.*
(SPEER-ARCHIV)

Doenitz and Speer, October 1943. (SPEER-ARCHIV)

German industrialists during an evening of recreation, following a meeting on naval armaments, October 1943. (SPEER-ARCHIV)

Eighth Air Force bombing of Schweinfurt, October 14, 1943.
(UNITED PRESS INTERNATIONAL)

ABOVE: *In the trench at the Murmansk front.* Left, *General Hengl, commander of the northernmost German army, December 1943.* (SPEER-ARCHIV)

RIGHT: *June 1944: Speer and Milch.* (SPIEGEL-ARCHIV)

Bunker on the Atlantic coast.
(SPEER-ARCHIV)

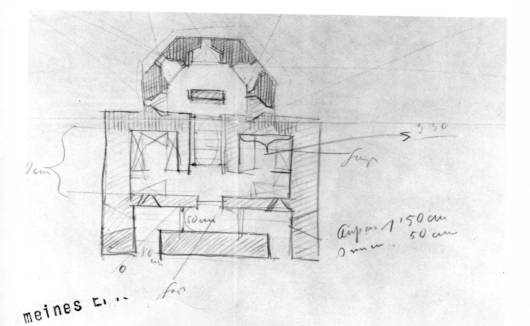

meines E. ..

massnahmen dienen

dem Gegner die

ABOVE: *Hitler's design for bunker, 1942.*
The drawing was executed neatly, the
legends highly readable. (SPEER-ARCHIV)

LEFT: *In March 1945 Hitler had the*
trembling handwriting of an old man.
(SPEER-ARCHIV)

Hitler, accompanied by Speer, on his daily walk from the Berghof to the teahouse, 1944. "We often walked in silence side by side, each dwelling on his own thoughts."
(HEINRICH HOFFMANN)

Silesia, February 1945: Heinrici, Malsacher, Speer meeting to control remaining destruction. (SPIEGEL-ARCHIV)

The Remagen bridgehead over the Rhine, March 1945. (UNITED PRESS INTERNATIONAL)

The great gallery in the last days of the war. (SPIEGEL-ARCHIV)

Soviet tanks roll into Berlin. (UNITED PRESS INTERNATIONAL)

The fallen emblem of Hitler's Reich.
(SPIEGEL-ARCHIV)

The wrecked hall of the Chancellery. (ACME)

Speer making his final speech before the Tribunal at Nuremberg, 1946. Front row, left to right: *Rosenberg, Frank, Frick, Streicher, Funk, Schacht.* Second row, left to right: *Seyss-Inquart, Speer, von Neurath, Fritzsche.*

Speer in his cell in Nuremberg, 1946. (ASSOCIATED PRESS PHOTO)

very months we were producing more and more fighter planes. Altogether, during this late phase of the war twelve thousand seven hundred and twenty fighters were delivered to the troops which had started the war in 1939 with only seven hundred and seventy-one fighter planes.[19] At the end of July, Hitler had for the second time agreed to assemble two thousand pilots for a special training course. We were still hoping that by intensive use of fighters we could inflict such heavy losses on the American air forces that we would force them to stop the bombing. For during their flights to their target and back to their bases, these bomber squadrons exposed a flank that was on the average six hundred miles long.

Fighter Commander General Adolf Galland and I had calculated that on the average one German fighter plane would be lost over Germany in order to shoot down a bomber, but that the expenditure of matériel on both sides would be in the proportion of one to six and the attrition of pilots one to two. Moreover, since half of our downed pilots could parachute safely to ground, while the enemy crew would be taken prisoner on German soil, the advantage was surely on our side, even given the enemy superiority in men, materials, and training potential.*

Around August 10, Galland, in extreme agitation, asked me to fly with him to headquarters at once. In one of his arbitrary decisions Hitler had issued new orders: The Reich air fleet, whose outfitting with two thousand fighter planes was nearing completion, was suddenly to be shifted to the western front. There, experience had long since shown us, it would be wiped out within a short time.

Hitler, of course, guessed why we were visiting him. He knew he had broken the promise he gave me in July to have the hydrogenation plants protected by fighter planes. But he forestalled a quarrel at the situation conference and agreed to receive us alone afterward.

I began by cautiously expressing doubts of the usefulness of his order and mastered my strong feelings by explaining as calmly as possible the catastrophic situation in armaments production. I cited figures and sketched the consequences that would follow from continued bombings. That alone made Hitler nervous and angry. Although he listened in silence, I could see by his expression, by the lively fluttering of his hands, the way he chewed his fingernails, that he was growing increasingly tense. When I finished, thinking I had amply proved that every available plane in the Reich should be employed to combat the bombers, Hitler was no longer in control of himself. His face had flushed deep red; his eyes had

---

* Central Planning announced on May 25, 1944: "The number of planes which will be completed in May is so large that the General Staff believes it will be eventually possible to inflict such losses on the enemy that he will no longer be able to afford flights over the Reich. If five fighters can be assigned to each enemy aircraft, the bomber is certain to be shot down. At the moment each bomber shot down costs us one of our fighter planes."

turned lifeless and fixed. Then he roared out at the top of his lungs: "Operative measures are my concern! Kindly concern yourself with your armaments! This is none of your business." Possibly he might have been more receptive had I talked to him privately. The presence of Galland made him incapable of understanding or flexibility.

Abruptly, he terminated the conference, cutting off all further argument. "I have no more time for you." Deeply perplexed, I returned to my barracks office with Galland.

The next day we were on the point of flying back to Berlin, our mission a failure, when Schaub informed us that we were to report to Hitler again. This time Hitler's rage was even more violent; he spoke faster and faster, stumbling over his own words:

> I want no more planes produced at all. The fighter arm is to be dissolved. Stop aircraft production! Stop it at once, understand? You're always complaining about the shortage of skilled workers, aren't you? Put them into flak production at once. Let all the workers produce antiaircraft guns. Use all the material for that too! Now that's an order. Send Saur to headquarters immediately. A program for flak production must be set up. Tell Saur that too. A program five times what we have now. . . . We'll shift hundreds of thousands of workers into flak production. Every day I read in the foreign press reports how dangerous flak is. They still have some respect for that, but not for our fighters.

Galland started to reply that the fighters would shoot down far more planes if they could be committed inside Germany, but he did not get beyond the first words. Again we were abruptly dismissed, actually thrown out.

In the teahouse I poured myself a glass of vermouth from the bottle that stood there for just such purposes; my stomach nerves had been affected by the scene. Galland, ordinarily so calm and controlled, looked distraught for the first time since I had known him. He could not grasp the fact that his fighter plane command was going to be dissolved, and what was more, on grounds of cowardice in the face of the enemy. For my part, I was acquainted with such tantrums on Hitler's part and knew that his decisions would usually be rescinded or revised by cautious change of course. I reassured Galland. The industrial facilities being used to build fighter planes could not be applied to the production of gun barrels, I told him. Our problem was not any shortage of flak guns, I pointed out, but the ammunition for them, and above all our lack of explosives.

Saur too, who also felt that Hitler was making unfulfillable demands, pointed out discreetly to Hitler the next day that increased production of antiaircraft guns depended mainly on the supply of special machine tools for drilling long tubes.

Soon afterward I went to headquarters again, this time accompanied by Saur, to discuss the details of his order—which to our sorrow had been made more official by being sent in writing. After a long struggle, Hitler lowered his original demand for a fivefold increase by half. He gave us a deadline of December 1945 to meet this quota and also demanded that the ammunition for these guns be doubled. [20] We were able to deal with more than twenty-eight points on the agenda, with a minimum of excitement on his part. But when I once more referred to our need to have the fighter planes committed to defense of the home front, he again interrupted me angrily, repeated his command to increase flak production at the expense of the fighter plane, and declared the meeting over.

That was the first command from Hitler that neither Saur nor I obeyed. I was acting on my own initiative and judgment when, on the following day, I stated to the Armaments Staff: "We must in any case maintain the production of fighter planes at a maximum." Three days later I called a meeting of the representatives of the air industry and explained to them, in Galland's presence, the importance of their assignment: "By sending the production of fighter aircraft soaring we can meet the greatest danger we face: the crushing of our armaments manufacture on the home front."* Meanwhile, however, Hitler had calmed down and suddenly, without another word on the subject, approved my proposal that a limited fighter aircraft program be assigned to the category of highest priority.

At the very time we were being forced to cut production in various fields, and actually to abandon new developments, Hitler began more and more pointedly alluding to future new weapons which would decide the war, thus arousing hopes among the generals and the political leaders. On my visits to divisions, I was frequently asked, with a mysterious smile, when the secret weapons would be coming along. I did not like such illusions, for sooner or later the hope would have to be dashed. In the middle of September, therefore, I addressed the following lines to Hitler:

> Belief in the imminent commitment of new, decisive weapons is widespread among the troops. They are expecting such commitment within days or weeks. This opinion is also seriously shared by high-ranking officers. It is questionable whether it is right, in such difficult times, to arouse hopes which cannot be fulfilled in so short a time and therefore must necessarily produce a disappointment which could have unfavorable effects upon morale. Since the population, too, is daily waiting for the miracle of the new weapons, wondering whether we know that the eleventh hour is already

---

* Quotations from the *Office Journal*, August 21 and 24, 1944. Despite Hitler's order that fighter plane production be cut in half, production remained at almost the same level: 2305 in July, 2352 in December.

upon us and that holding back these new—stockpiled—weapons can no longer be justified, the question arises whether this propaganda serves a useful purpose.*

In a private talk Hitler admitted that I was right. Nevertheless, as I soon heard, he continued to dangle the prospect of the secret weapons. On November 2, 1944, therefore, I wrote to Goebbels that "it seems to me unwise to arouse hopes in the public which cannot possibly be fulfilled for a considerable time. . . . I would therefore request you to take measures so that the daily press and technical journals refrain from alluding to future successes in our armaments production."

Goebbels actually put an end to these reports on new weapons. But strangely enough, the rumors increased. It was only at the Nuremberg Trial that I learned from Hans Fritzsche, one of the Propaganda Minister's foremost associates, that Goebbels had set up a special department for spreading such rumors. Then, too, I realized why these rumors were often so uncannily close to what indeed we projected for the future. How often at our armaments conferences we had sat together in the evening telling each other about the newest technological developments. Even the possibilities of an atom bomb were discussed on such occasions. One of Goebbels's chief assistants had often participated in these meetings as a reporter and thus been present at the evening gatherings.

In those turbulent times in which everyone was eager to find reason for hope, rumors found fertile soil. On the other hand, the populace had

* See travel report, September 10–14, 1944. A few days before, on August 31, 1944, I had told my colleagues that "I do not intend to succumb to the psychosis of attaching too much importance to the new weapons. Nor am I responsible for the extremely prominent place they are being given in our propaganda." On December 1, 1944, after a display of new weapons in Rechlin, I said to my associates: "You have seen that we do not have a miraculous secret weapon and probably never will have one. We for our part, speaking as technicians, have always made it perfectly clear to anyone who cared to listen that technical miracles of the sort that the layman expects are not really possible. . . . During my tours of the front I have time and again observed that the divisional and regimental commanders are concerned because their men are more and more clinging to a faith in these miracle weapons. I consider such delusions ominous."

A few weeks later, on January 13, 1945, I was asked by a group of generals and corps commanders: "Can we still count on the introduction of new weapons, now that there has been so much propaganda about them for the past three months?" I replied: "For my part I can only say that I am firmly opposed to these rumors. After all, I am not the author of this propaganda. . . . I have repeated again and again that we cannot expect miraculous secret weapons, and I have also notified the Fuehrer several times that I consider this entire propaganda campaign utterly wrong-headed, not only because it is misleading but also because it underrates the German soldier's fighting powers. . . . We will never have a secret weapon that will end the war in one blow. There is simply no such thing in the offing."

long since stopped believing the newspapers. There was one exception: During the closing months of the war a growing band of desperate people began pinning their hopes on the astrological sheets. Since these were dependent on the Propaganda Ministry, for a variety of reasons they were, as I learned from Fritzsche at Nuremberg, used as a tool for influencing public opinion. Fake horoscopes spoke of valleys of darkness which had to be passed through, foretold imminent surprises, intimated happy outcomes. Only in the astrological sheets did the regime still have a future.

28

The Plunge

THE ARMAMENTS INDUSTRY, WHICH FROM THE SPRING OF 1944 HAD BEEN unified in my Ministry, began to disintegrate by the late autumn. For one thing, the big rocket project had, as I have already related, been transferred to the SS. Then again, several Gauleiters had contrived to take over responsibility for armaments within their own districts. Hitler supported such enterprises. For example, he gave his consent when Sauckel as Gauleiter of Thuringia volunteered to set up a large underground factory for mass production of a single-motored jet fighter which Hitler dubbed the "people's fighter." But by then we were already entering our economic death throes, so that this splintering no longer had serious effects.

Along with such last-ditch efforts hopes arose, which could be construed as signs of increasing confusion, that we would win through even with primitive weapons and thus compensate for our technological predicament. The courage of the individual soldier was to take the place of technological efficiency in arms. In April 1944, Doenitz had put the ingenious Vice Admiral Heye in charge of building one-man submarines and other small fighting craft. But it was August before the piecework production reached sizable numbers, and by then the invasion had succeeded and it was really too late for such projects. Himmler, for his part, wanted to set up a "suicide squad" piloting manned rocket planes which would destroy the enemy bombers by ramming them. Another primitive weapon was the Panzerfaust (tank destroyer), a small rocket shot from the hand, which was to substitute for the antitank guns we did not have.*

In the late autumn of 1944, Hitler abruptly intervened in the matter of gas masks and appointed a special commissioner directly responsible to him. With great haste a program was set up to protect the entire population from the effects of gas warfare. Although gas mask production rose to more than two million three hundred thousand per month, it was evident that it would take a while before the entire urban population could be properly equipped. The party organs therefore published advice on primitive gas protection methods, such as the use of paper masks.

At the time, it is true, Hitler spoke of the danger of an enemy gas attack on German cities.** But Dr. Karl Brandt, whom he entrusted with the protective measures, thought it not unlikely that these hectic preparations were intended to serve the ends of gas warfare that we would begin. Among our "secret weapons" we possessed a poison gas called tabun; it penetrated the filters of all known gas masks and contact with even very small lingering quantities had fatal effects.

Robert Ley, by profession a chemist, took me along in his special railroad car to a meeting in Sonthofen held in the autumn of 1944. As usual, our conversation took place over glasses of strong wines. His increased stammering betrayed his agitation: "You know we have this new poison gas—I've heard about it. The Fuehrer must do it. He must use it. Now he has to do it! When else! This is the last moment. You too must make him realize that it's time." I remained silent. But apparently Ley had had a similar conversation with Goebbels, for the Propaganda Minister asked some of my associates in the chemical industry about the substance and its effect, and then urged Hitler to employ this novel gas. Hitler, to be sure, had always rejected gas warfare; but now he hinted at a situation conference

---

* Modeled on the American bazooka, 997,000 were produced in November 1944, 1,253,000 in December, and 1,200,000 in January 1945.

** In fact on August 5, 1944, Churchill called for a report on England's capability for waging poison-gas war against Germany. According to the report, the available 32,000 tons of mustard and phosgene gas would effectively poison 965 square miles of German territory, more than Berlin, Hamburg, Cologne, Essen, Frankfurt, and Kassel combined. See David Irving, *Die Geheimwaffen des Dritten Reiches* (Hamburg, 1969). According to my letter of October 11, 1944, to Keitel (RLA 1302/44), our production—until the chemical industry was bombed during the summer of 1944—amounted to 3100 tons of mustard gas and 1000 tons of tabun per month. Our side must thus have accumulated large quantities of poison gas during the five war years, more than the British supplies, even assuming that our production capacity was considerably extended during the war.

in headquarters that the use of gas might stop the advance of the Soviet troops. He went on with vague speculations that the West would accept gas warfare against the East because at this stage of the war the British and American governments had an interest in stopping the Russian advance. When no one at the situation conference spoke up in agreement, Hitler did not return to the subject.

Undoubtedly the generals feared the unpredictable consequences. I myself wrote to Keitel on October 11, 1944, that because of the blows to the chemical industry we were quite out of such basic materials as cyanide and methanol.* On November 1, therefore, the production of tabun had to be stopped and that of mustard gas limited to a quarter of capacity. Keitel, to be sure, obtained an order from Hitler not to reduce poison-gas production under any circumstances. But such orders no longer bore any relation to realities. I did not respond and merely allotted the basic chemical materials as I pleased.

On November 11 a new note of alarm entered my frequent memoranda on shutdowns in the fuel industry. For more than six weeks, traffic to and from the Ruhr area had been blocked. "It is self-evident, given the whole nature of the Reich's economic structure," I wrote to Hitler, "that cessation of production in the Rhine-Westphalian industrial area is intolerable for the entire German economy and for a successful conduct of the war. . . . The most important armaments plants are reported on the verge of going under. Under existing conditions there is no way to avoid these shutdowns."

Denied fresh supplies of Ruhr coal, I continued, the railroads were rapidly exhausting their stocks of coal, as were the gas works; oil and margarine plants were on the verge of shutdowns, and even the supply of coke to the hospitals had become inadequate.[1]

Things were literally moving rapidly toward the end. Signs of total anarchy loomed before us. Coal trains no longer reached their destinations but were stopped en route by Gauleiters who confiscated them for their own needs. The buildings in Berlin were unheated; gas and electricity were available only during restricted hours. A howl arose from the Chancellery: Our coal authority had refused to let it have its full consignment for the rest of the winter.

Faced with this situation we could no longer carry out our programs, but only try to produce parts. Once our remaining stocks were used up, armaments production would cease. In drawing this conclusion

* In October 1944 the necessary materials for poison-gas production were still being manufactured: methanol (21,500 tons per month in 1943) at the rate of 10,900 tons in October 1944; cyanide (1234 tons in 1943) at the rate of 336 tons in October 1944.

I underestimated—as no doubt the enemy air strategists did also—the large stocks of materials that had been accumulated in the factories.[2] An extensive search showed that high production of armaments could in fact be continued, but only for a few months more. Hitler accepted a last "emergency or supplementary program," as we called it, with a calm that seemed truly uncanny. He did not waste a word on the obvious implications, although there could be no doubt what these were.

Around this time Hitler, at a situation conference, commented in the presence of all the generals: "We have the good fortune to have a genius in our armaments industry. I mean Saur. All difficulties are being overcome by him."

General Thomale put in a tactful word: "*Mein Führer,* Minister Speer is here."

"Yes, I know," Hitler replied curtly, annoyed at the interruption. "But Saur is the genius who will master the situation."

Oddly enough, I swallowed this deliberate insult without any perturbation, almost indifferently. I was beginning to take my leave of Hitler.

On October 12, 1944, when the military situation in the West had settled down again and it became possible to speak of a front once more—not of a helplessly retreating horde of men—Hitler took me aside during a situation conference, told me I must not say a word to anyone, and then revealed that he was going to carry out a great offensive in the West by concentrating all available forces. "For that you must organize a special corps of German construction workers, one sufficiently motorized to be able to carry out all types of bridge building even if rail transportation should be halted. Stick to the organizational forms that proved their value in the western campaign of 1940."[3] I pointed out to Hitler that we scarcely had enough trucks left for such a task. "Everything else must be put aside for the sake of this," he declared emphatically. "No matter what the consequences. This will be the great blow which must succeed."

Around the end of November, Hitler said once again that he was staking everything on this offensive. Since he was sure of its success, he added nonchalantly that it was his last effort: "If it does not succeed, I no longer see any possibility for ending the war well. . . . But we will come through," he added, and promptly strayed off into more and more expansive and fantastic notions: "A single breakthrough on the western front! You'll see! It will lead to collapse and panic among the Americans. We'll drive right through their middle and take Antwerp. Then they'll have lost their supply port. And a tremendous pocket will encircle the entire English army, with hundreds of thousands of prisoners. As we used to do in Russia!"

About this time I met Albert Vögler to discuss the desperate situation the bombings had produced in the Ruhr. He asked me bluntly: "When are we going to call it quits?"

I indicated that Hitler was planning to stake everything on a last effort.

Obstinately, Vögler continued: "But does he fully realize that after that we have to call it quits? We're losing too much of our substance. How will we be able to reconstruct if industry goes on taking such a beating even for a few months more?"

"I think," I replied, "that Hitler is playing his last card and knows it, too."

Vögler gave me a skeptical look. "Of course, it's his last card, now that our production is collapsing all over the place. Is this operation going to be directed against the East, to take off the pressure there?"

I avoided an answer.

"Of course, it will be on the eastern front," Vögler said. "Nobody could be so crazy as to strip the East in order to try to hold back the enemy in the West."

From November on, General Guderian, the army chief of staff, repeatedly called Hitler's attention to the threat to Upper Silesia resulting from the Russian troop concentrations on the eastern front. Naturally, he wanted the divisions assembled for the offensive in the West shifted to the eastern theater of war, to avoid a total breakdown there. At the Nuremberg Trial a number of the defendants attempted to justify the continuance of the war beyond the winter of 1944–45 on the grounds that Hitler had only wanted to save the lives of the refugees from the East and to keep German soldiers from Russian imprisonment. But the decisions he made at that time are proof to the contrary.

I held the view that it was essential to play this "last card" as impressively as possible. I arranged with Field Marshal Model, the commander of Army Group B, to keep him supplied with improvised armaments aid during the offensive. On December 16, the day of the attack, I set out from Berlin, bound for a small headquarters in a hunting lodge near Bonn. Riding through the night in a Reichsbahn diesel car, I saw the switching yards east of the Rhine jammed with freight cars. The enemy bombers had prevented the movement of supplies for the offensive.

Model's headquarters was situated in a narrow wooded valley in the Eifel mountains; it was a large hunting lodge owned by a wealthy industrialist. Model had not built bunkers for fear of attracting the attention of enemy reconnaissance planes to the site months beforehand. He was in good humor, for the surprise assault had succeeded in breaking through the front; his troops were advancing rapidly. We were having the right sort of weather too, just what Hitler had wanted. He had said: "We must have bad weather, otherwise the operation cannot succeed."

As a camp follower I tried to get as close as possible to the front. The advancing troops were in good spirits, for low-lying clouds hampered all enemy air activity. But, by the second day of the offensive, transportation had already reached a chaotic state. Motor vehicles could move only a foot at a time along the three-lane highway. My car took an hour on the average to move two miles, wedged in as it was by ammunition trucks. I kept fearing that the weather might improve.

Model offered all sorts of reasons for this confusion—lack of discipline in newly formed units, for example, or the chaos in the hinterland. But whatever the reasons, the whole scene showed that the army had lost its erstwhile famous talent for organization—surely one of the effects of Hitler's three years of command.

The first destination of our laborious progress was a blown-up bridge on the northern wing of the Sixth SS Armored Army. In order to make myself useful I had promised Model to find out how the bridge could be repaired as quickly as possible. The soldiers took a skeptical view of my presence on the scene. My adjutant heard one of them explain: "The Fuehrer rapped him because the bridge isn't ready yet. Now he's got orders to clean up the mess himself." And in fact, the bridge building was going forward very sluggishly. For the construction crews from the Todt Organization, which we had carefully assembled, were stuck in the inextricable traffic jams east of the Rhine, along with the greater part of the engineering materials. Thus the imminent end of the offensive was obviously in the offing, if only because of the lack of essential bridge-building materials.

Inadequate supplies of fuel also hampered operations. The armored formations had started the attack with meager fuel reserves. Hitler, with his optimistic improvidence, had counted on their being able to supply themselves later on from captured American stocks. When the offensive threatened to grind to a halt, I helped Model by telephoning orders to the gasoline plants of the nearby Ruhr area to improvise tank car trains, which they then managed to get to the front.

But the flow of supplies ceased when the foggy weather changed in a few days and the cloudless sky filled with innumerable enemy fighter planes and bombers. A drive by day became a problem even for a fast passenger car; we were often glad to seek the shelter of a small patch of woods. Now the supply services could only operate during the night, groping their way forward, virtually without any visibility, almost from tree to tree.* On December 23, Model told me that the offensive had definitely failed—but that Hitler had ordered it to continue.

---

* In my travel report, December 31, 1944, I wrote to Hitler:

Vehicles must move at night without headlights. Since all daytime travel is unsafe and nighttime travel is slow, our troop movements amount to only one-half to

Up to the end of December, I stayed in the area of the offensive, visited various divisions, was under fire from low-flying planes and artillery, and saw the ghastly consequences of a German attack on a machine-gun position. Hundreds of our soldiers lay sprawled in a small area; they had simply been mowed down. Late that evening I visited Sepp Dietrich, a former sergeant in the old German army, now commander of an SS armored force. He had set up headquarters in the vicinity of the Belgian border town of Houffalize. One of the few Old Fighters of the early days of the party, in his own plain fashion he too had parted ways psychologically with Hitler. Our conversation soon turned to the latest batch of commands. Hitler had decreed with increasing insistence that encircled Bastogne be taken "at any cost." He refused to understand, Sepp Dietrich grumbled, that even the elite divisions of the SS could not effortlessly overrun the Americans. It was impossible to convince Hitler that these were tough opponents, soldiers as good as our own men. "Besides," he added, "we are receiving no ammunition. The supply routes have been cut by the air attacks."

As if to illustrate our helplessness, our nocturnal talk was interrupted by a low-level attack from huge four-motored bomber formations. Howling and exploding bombs, clouds illuminated in red and yellow hues, droning motors, and no defense anywhere—I was stunned by this scene of military impotence which Hitler's military miscalculations had given such a grotesque setting.

Protected by darkness, I left Dietrich's headquarters at four o'clock in the morning of December 31 and drove off with Manfred von Poser, my liaison officer to the General Staff. It took us until two o'clock the following morning to reach Hitler's headquarters. Again and again we had to seek cover from fighter planes. It had taken us twenty-two hours to cover a distance of little more than two hundred miles.

Hitler's western headquarters, from which he had directed the Ardennes offensive, was at one end of a solitary grassy valley near Bad Nauheim, a mile northwest of Ziegenberg. Hidden in woods, camouflaged as blockhouses, the bunkers had the same massive ceilings and walls as all the other places at which Hitler stayed.

Three times since my appointment as a minister I had tried to de-

---

one-third of the enemy movements, even when the roads on our side are as good as theirs. The enemy can maneuver in broad daylight and with lights on at night. An additional serious obstacle, especially to bringing up supplies, is the condition of the roads in the Eifel region and the Ardennes. . . . Most of the highways have rises and curves which make them as difficult to traverse as Alpine roads. . . . The combat strategy handed down from above, and the resultant orders, do not always take these severe supply difficulties into account. In all the planning the question of supplies seems to take second place. . . . But if supplying has not been properly calculated and provided for, the operation is doomed.

liver my New Year's wishes to Hitler personally, and each time something thwarted my intention. In 1943 it had been the icing of an airplane, in 1944 motor damage on the flight from the coast of the Arctic Ocean when I was returning from the front.

Two hours of this year of 1945 had passed when I at last, after passing through many barriers, arrived in Hitler's private bunker. I had not come too late: adjutants, doctors, secretaries, Bormann—the whole circle except for the generals attached to the Fuehrer's headquarters, were gathered around Hitler drinking champagne. The alcohol had relaxed everyone, but the atmosphere was still subdued. Hitler seemed to be the only one in the company who was drunk without having taken any stimulating beverage. He was in the grip of a permanent euphoria.

Although the beginning of a new year in no way dispelled the desperate situation of the year past, there seemed to be a general feeling of thankfulness that we could begin anew at least on the calendar. Hitler made optimistic forecasts for 1945. The present low point would soon be overcome, he said; in the end we would be victorious. The circle took these prophesies in silence. Only Bormann enthusiastically seconded Hitler. After more than two hours, during which Hitler spread around his credulous optimism, his followers, including myself, were transported in spite of all their skepticism into a more sanguine state. His magnetic gifts were still operative. For it was no longer possible to produce conviction by rational arguments. We ought to have come to our senses when Hitler drew the parallel between our situation and that of Frederick the Great at the end of the Seven Years' War, for the implication was that we faced utter military defeat.[4] But none of us drew this conclusion.

Three days later, in a grand conference with Keitel, Bormann, and Goebbels, we were given a further dose of unrealistic hopes. Now a *levée en masse* was to bring about the turnaround. Goebbels became insulting when I spoke up against this; I argued that total conscription would strike our remaining programs to such an extent that it would be equivalent to the total collapse of whole industries.[5] Dismayed and indignant, Goebbels stared at me. Then, turning to Hitler, he cried out solemnly: "Then, Herr Speer, you bear the historic guilt for the loss of the war for the lack of a few hundred thousand soldiers! Why don't you say yes for once! Consider it! Your fault!" For a moment we all stood there fretful, stony, indecisive—then Hitler decided in favor of Goebbels and winning the war.

This conversation was followed by an armaments discussion in which Goebbels and his state secretary, Naumann, sat in as Hitler's guests. As had been common lately, Hitler passed me over in the course of the discussion; he did not ask my opinion but turned only to Saur. I was cast in the role of a mute listener. After the conference Goebbels remarked to me that it had struck him as strange to see with what indifference I let Saur push me aside. But all that was involved by now was empty talk. The failure of the Ardennes offensive meant that the war was over. What followed was only the occupation of Germany, delayed somewhat by a confused and impotent resistance.

I was not the only one who avoided such tussles. An air of general indifference had overcome headquarters. It could not be explained solely as the result of lethargy, overwork, and Hitler's psychological influence. Instead of the violent clashes, the tensions of the preceding years and months among numerous hostile interests, groups, and cliques fighting for Hitler's favor and trying to shift the responsibility for the more and more frequent defeats, there now prevailed a disinterested silence which was in itself an anticipation of the end. When, for example, during this period Saur succeeded in having Himmler replaced by General Buhle as chief of armaments for the army,* it was hardly commented on, although it meant a loss of power for Himmler. There was no real atmosphere of work any longer. Whatever was happening made no impression, since everything was overshadowed by awareness of the inexorable end.

My trip to the front had kept me away from Berlin for more than three weeks—but in fact it was no longer possible to govern from the capital. The chaotic conditions everywhere made central guidance of the armaments organization more and more complicated—and also more and more meaningless.

On January 12, the great Soviet offensive in the East, which Guderian had predicted, finally began. Our defensive line collapsed along a broad front. Even the more than two thousand modern German tanks which were standing still in the West could no longer have countered the superiority of the Soviet troops at this point.

A few days afterward we were standing around in the so-called Ambassadors' Room at the Chancellery, a tapestried anteroom to Hitler's main office, waiting for the situation conference to begin. When Guderian arrived—he had been delayed by a call on Japanese Ambassador Oshima—an orderly in a plain black-and-white SS uniform opened the door to Hitler's office. We walked across the heavy, handwoven rug to the map table by the windows. The huge table top, a single slab of marble, had come from Austria; it was blood-red, striated with the beige and white cross sections of an ancient coral reef. We took our positions on the window side; Hitler sat facing us.

The German army in Courland was hopelessly cut off. Guderian

* *Führerprotokoll,* January 3–5, 1944, Point 24. Saur had repeatedly protested to Hitler that Himmler's deputy, SS Obergruppenführer Jüttner, kept interfering with the system of self-responsibility we had established for industry. When he heard the details, Hitler was so angry that he had Himmler replaced.

tried to convince Hitler that this position should be abandoned and the army transported across the Baltic Sea. Hitler disagreed, as he always did when asked to authorize a retreat. Guderian did not give in, Hitler insisted, the tone sharpened, and finally Guderian opposed Hitler with an openness unprecedented in this circle. Probably fired by the effects of the drinks he had had at Oshima's, he threw aside all inhibitions. With flashing eyes and the hairs of his mustache literally standing on end, he stood facing Hitler across the marble table. Hitler, too, had risen to his feet.

"It's simply our duty to save these people, and we still have time to remove them!" Guderian cried out in a challenging voice.

Infuriated, Hitler retorted: "You are going to fight on there. We cannot give up these areas!"

Guderian held firm: "But it's useless to sacrifice men in this senseless way," he shouted. "It's high time! We must evacuate those soldiers at once!"

What no one had thought possible now happened. Hitler appeared visibly intimidated by this assault. Strictly speaking, he really could not tolerate this insubordination, which was more a matter of Guderian's tone than his argument. But to my astonishment Hitler shifted to military arguments, maintaining that a withdrawal to the ports was bound to result in general disorganization and even higher losses than continuing the defense. Once again Guderian vigorously pointed out that every tactical detail of the retreat had already been worked out and that carrying out the operation was quite possible. But Hitler stuck to his decision.

Was this clash the symptom of disintegrating authority? Hitler had still had the last word. No one had stalked out of the room. No one had declared that he could no longer assume the responsibility for what was coming. This was why Hitler's authority remained fundamentally intact, after all—although for a few minutes we had literally been numbed by this violation of the court tone. Zeitzler had voiced his objections more moderately; in his voice, even while contradicting Hitler, traces of veneration and loyalty had remained. But for the first time matters had come to an open quarrel in the larger circle. The novelty was almost palpable. New worlds had opened out. To be sure, Hitler had still saved face. That was a great deal. But at the same time it was very little.

In the face of the rapid advance of the Soviet armies it seemed to me advisable to travel to the Silesian industrial area once more to make sure that my orders for the preservation of the industries were not being undermined by local authorities. On January 21, 1945, I went to Oppeln and met Field Marshal Schörner, newly appointed commander of the army group which, as he informed me, existed in name only. Their tanks and heavy weapons had been destroyed or captured in the course of a lost battle. No one knew how far the Russians were from Oppeln. In any case, the headquarters officers were leaving; in our hotel only a few overnight guests remained behind.

In my room hung an etching by Käthe Kollwitz: *La Carmagnole.* It showed a yowling mob dancing with hate-contorted faces around a guillotine. Off to one side a weeping woman cowered on the ground.

In the desperate situation of a war rolling rapidly to its end, I was gripped by increasing anxieties. The weird figures of the etching haunted my fitful sleep. Obsessive notions of my own terrible end, repressed by day or smothered in activity, came to the surface. Would the populace rise in fury and disappointment against its former leaders and kill them as in *La Carmagnole?* Friends and close acquaintances sometimes talked about our own dark futures. Milch usually declared firmly that the enemy would make short work of the leadership of the Third Reich. I shared his view.

A telephone call from Colonel von Below, my liaison man to Hitler, startled me out of the torments of that night. The previous week I had urgently pointed out to Hitler that since the Ruhr had now been cut off from the rest of the Reich, the loss of Upper Silesia would necessarily bring about rapid economic collapse. In a teletype message on January 21, I had again called Hitler's attention to the importance of Upper Silesia and asked permission to ship "at least 30 to 50 percent of the January production" to Schörner's army group.[6]

The purpose of this message was also to support Guderian, who was still trying to persuade Hitler to stop the offensive efforts in the West and throw the few still functioning armored forces into the breach in the East. At the same time I had pointed out that the Russian enemy was "carrying out his supply tasks in close formation, visible from a great distance in the present snowy landscape. Since the commitment of the German fighter planes in the West is yielding hardly any tangible results, it might be good to apply this weapon concentratedly here, where it is still highly esteemed." Below reported that Hitler, with a sarcastic smile, had declared my remark was to the point but had issued no orders. Did Hitler think that his real enemy lay in the West? Did he feel solidarity with, let alone sympathy for, Stalin's regime? I recalled a good many earlier remarks of his which could possibly be interpreted in that sense and which might be seen as the motivation for his conduct at this time.

The next day I tried to continue my journey to Kattowitz, the center of the Silesian industrial region, but I never got there. Rounding a curve on the sheet-ice road, I collided with a heavy truck. My chest had crushed the steering wheel and even twisted the steering column, and I sat, gasping for air, on the steps of a village tavern, pale and distraught. "You look like a cabinet minister after a lost war," Poser said wryly. The car was out of commission; an ambulance took me back. When I was on my feet again I was at least able to find out by telephone from my assistants in Kattowitz that all the arrangements we had made were being carried out.

On the ride back to Berlin, Hanke, the Breslau Gauleiter, showed me through the party headquarters, a building by the great architect Schinkel which had recently been renovated. "The Russians will never get their hands on this," he exclaimed emotionally. "I'd rather burn it down." I remonstrated, but Hanke insisted. He didn't give a damn about Breslau if it were about to fall into the enemy's hands, he said. But finally I succeeded in convincing him of the artistic importance of at least this building and in talking him out of his vandalism.*

Back in Berlin, I tried to show Hitler some of the innumerable photos I had taken during my trip of the miseries of the refugees. I had the vague hope that the pictures of these fugitives—women, children, and old men, trudging painfully toward a wretched fate in the bitter cold—might stir Hitler to pity. I thought I might be able to persuade him at least to stem the advance of the Russians by sending some troops from the West. But when I presented the pictures to Hitler, he roughly pushed them aside. It was impossible to tell whether they no longer interested him or affected him too deeply.

On January 24, 1945, Guderian sought out Foreign Minister Ribbentrop. He explained the military situation to him and declared bluntly that the war was lost. Ribbentrop hemmed and hawed, and tried to slide out of the affair by informing Hitler at once, with an expression of astonishment, that the chief of staff had formed his own opinion of the military situation. Two hours later at the situation conference Hitler spluttered that any defeatist statements of this sort would be punished with the greatest severity. Each of his assistants, he said, was at liberty to speak to him directly. "I most emphatically forbid generalizations and conclusions in regard to the whole situation. That remains my affair. In the future anyone who tells anyone else that the war is lost will be treated as a traitor, with all the consequences for him and his family. I will take action without regard to rank and prestige!"

No one dared say a word. We had listened silently; just as silently we left the room. From now on an additional guest frequently appeared at the situation conferences. He kept in the background, but his presence

---

* But not for long: A few months later he waged the battle of Breslau without regard for human lives or historic buildings and even had his old friend, the mayor, Dr. Spielhagen, publicly hanged. Then, as I heard from the designer Flettner, shortly before the surrender of Breslau he flew out of the besieged city in one of the few existing prototype helicopters.

alone was exceedingly effective. He was Ernst Kaltenbrunner, the Gestapo chief.

In view of Hitler's threats and his increasing unpredictability, on January 27, 1945, I sent the three hundred most important members of my Industry Organization a concluding report on our armaments work during the past three years. I also called together my former associates in my architectural work and asked them to collect photographs of our designs and store them in safe places. I had little time to spare, nor did I want to bare my feelings and my cares to them. But they understood: This was my farewell to the past.

On January 30, 1945, I had von Below, my liaison officer, hand Hitler a memorandum. By sheer chance, the date it bore was the twelfth anniversary of his taking power. Realistically, I declared that the war was over in the area of heavy industry and armaments and, given this situation, food, household heating, and electricity should have priority over tanks, airplane motors, and ammunition.

To finally dampen Hitler's wild dreams of future armaments achievements in 1945, I included a chart of the scanty production of tanks, ordnance, and ammunition to be expected in the next three months. The memorandum concluded: "After the loss of Upper Silesia, the German armaments industry will no longer be able even approximately to cover the requirements of the front for ammunition, ordnance, and tanks. . . . From now on the material preponderance of the enemy can no longer be compensated for by the bravery of our soldiers." Hitler had again and again asserted that our lacks would be balanced out by miracles of courage from the moment the German soldier was fighting on German soil for the possession of his native land. My memorandum was intended as a reply to this theory.

After receiving this memorandum, Hitler ignored me and even pretended not to notice my presence during the situation conference. But on February 1 he finally summoned me, ordering that Saur come along also. After everything that had passed I was prepared for an unpleasant clash. But the very fact that he received us in his private study in the Chancellery residence indicated that I was not a candidate for the punishment he had threatened for "defeatism." He did not make Saur and me stand, as was his habit when he wanted to show his anger, but very pleasantly offered us the upholstered easy chairs. Then, he turned to Saur, his voice sounding tense. He seemed constrained; I sensed an embarrassed attempt simply to overlook my opposition and to talk about the everyday problems of armaments manufacture. In a determinedly calm manner he discussed the possibilities of the next few months. Saur, by mentioning favorable factors, tried to offset the depressing tone of my memorandum. Hitler's optimism did not seem entirely unfounded.

After all, my forecasts had quite often proved mistaken during the past years, since the enemy rarely proceeded with the consistency on which my calculations were based.

I sat by sulkily, without participating in the dialogue. It was only toward the end that Hitler turned to me: "You are perfectly entitled to let me know your estimate of the armaments situation, but I forbid you to convey such information to anyone else. You are also not permitted to give anyone a copy of this memorandum. But as for your last paragraph"—at this point his voice became cool and cutting—"you cannot write that sort of thing to me. You might have spared yourself the trouble of such conclusions. You are to leave to me the conclusions I draw from the armaments situation." He said all this very softly, without any sign of excitement, whistling somewhat between his teeth. The effect was not only much more definite but far more dangerous than one of his furies, for whatever he said in a rage could easily be taken back next day. Here, I felt quite distinctly, I was hearing Hitler's last word on the subject. Then he dismissed us. He was curt to me, cordial to Saur.

On January 30, I had already had Poser send out six copies of the memorandum to six departments of the army General Staff. To comply formally with Hitler's order, I asked to have these returned. Hitler told Guderian and others that he had placed the memorandum in the safe unread.

I promptly began preparing still another report. Saur, I knew, basically shared my views of the armaments situation. I decided that this time Saur was to write and sign the report, that this was the only way to make him declare himself. It indicates my nervousness at the time that I had our conference take place secretly in Bernau where Dieter Stahl, who was in charge of our ammunition production, owned a factory. Each of the participants at this conference agreed that Saur must be made to send in a report which echoed my declaration of bankruptcy.

Saur writhed like an eel. He would not venture as far as a written statement, but he did finally agree to confirm my pessimistic forecast at our next conference with Hitler. But the next meeting with Hitler ran its usual course. As soon as I finished my report, Saur began trying to balance out the somber note I had struck. He spoke of a recent consultation with Messerschmitt and drew some first sketches of a new four-motored jet bomber from his briefcase. Although building a plane with a range sufficient to reach New York would have taken years even under normal conditions, Hitler and Saur went into raptures over the dire psychological effects of an air raid upon the skyscraper canyons of New York.

During February and March of 1945, Hitler occasionally hinted that he was contacting the enemy by various means, but he would never go into details. My impression was that he was trying to create an atmosphere of utter irreconcilability which left no roads open. At the time of the Yalta Conference, I heard him giving instructions to Lorenz, the press secretary. He was dissatisfied with the reaction of the German newspapers and demanded a sharper, more aggressive tone: "Those warmongers in Yalta must be denounced—so insulted and attacked that they will have no chance to make an offer to the German people. Under no circumstances must there be an offer. That gang only wants to separate the German people from their leadership. I've always said: Surrender is absolutely out of the question!" He hesitated: "History is not going to be repeated!" In his last radio address Hitler took up this idea and assured "these other statesmen once and for all that every attempt to influence National Socialist Germany by empty phrases of the Wilsonian type presumes a naiveté that is foreign to present-day Germany." The only one who could release him from his duty of uncompromisingly representing the interests of his people, he continued, was he who had appointed him. He meant the "Almighty," to whom he repeatedly alluded in this speech.[7]

During the years of military victory Hitler had associated largely with the circle of generals around him. With the approaching end of his rule he visibly withdrew into that intimate clique of old party members with whom he had launched out on his career. Night after night he sat with Goebbels, Ley, and Bormann for a few hours. No one was admitted to these gatherings; no one knew what they were talking about, whether they were reminiscing about their beginnings or talking about the end and what would come after it. I listened in vain for at least a single feeling remark about the future of the defeated nation. They grasped at every straw, made much of even the vaguest signs of a turning point; yet they were in no way prepared to regard the fate of the entire nation as nearly so important as their own. "We will leave nothing but a desert to the Americans, English, and Russians"—this was the standard close to any discussion of the matter. Hitler agreed, although he did not express himself in such radical terms as Goebbels, Bormann, and Ley. Actually, a few weeks later it turned out that Hitler was more radical than any of them. While the others were talking, he concealed his attitude behind a pose of statesmanship, but it was he who issued the orders for smashing the foundation of the nation's existence.

At a situation conference early in February the maps showed the catastrophic picture of innumerable breakthroughs and encirclements. I drew Doenitz aside: "Something must be done, you know."

Doenitz replied with unwonted curtness: "I am here only to represent the navy. The rest is none of my business. The Fuehrer must know what he is doing."

It is significant that the group who gathered day after day around the map table, facing a Hitler who sat there exhausted and obstinate, never considered taking any joint action. Undoubtedly Goering had long since become corrupt and increasingly unnerved. Nevertheless, from the day the war broke out he had been one of the few persons who saw, realistically and without illusions, the fundamental change which Hitler had wrought by bringing on the war. If Goering, as the second man in the state, had joined with Keitel, Jodl, Doenitz, Guderian, and me in presenting Hitler with an ultimatum, if we had demanded to know his plans for ending the war, Hitler would have been forced to declare himself. But Hitler had always shied away from confrontations of this sort. And now he could less than ever afford to give up this fiction of a unanimous leadership.

Around the middle of February, I called on Goering one evening in Karinhall. I had discovered from studying the military map that he had concentrated his parachute division around his hunting estate. For a long time he had been made the scapegoat for all the failures of the Luftwaffe. At the situation conferences Hitler habitually denounced him in the most violent and insulting language before the assembled officers. He must have been even nastier in the scenes he had with Goering privately. Often, waiting in the anteroom, I could hear Hitler shouting at him.

That evening in Karinhall, I established a certain intimacy with Goering for the first and only time. Goering had an excellent Rothschild-Lafite served at the fireplace and ordered the servant not to disturb us. Candidly, I described my disappointment with Hitler. Just as candidly, Goering replied that he well understood me and that he often felt much the same. However, he said, it was easier for me, since I had joined Hitler a great deal later and could free myself from him all the sooner. He, Goering, had much closer ties with Hitler; many years of common experiences and struggles had bound them together—and he could no longer break loose.

A few days later Hitler shifted the parachute division concentrated around Karinhall to the front south of Berlin.

At this time a high-ranking SS leader hinted to me that Himmler was preparing decisive steps. In February 1945, the Reichsführer-SS had assumed command of the Vistula Army Group, but he was no better than his predecessor at stopping the Russian advance. Hitler was now berating him also. Thus what personal prestige Himmler had retained was used up by a few weeks of commanding frontline troops.

Nevertheless, everyone still feared Himmler, and I felt distinctly shaky one day on learning that Himmler was coming to see me about something that evening. This, incidentally, was the only time he ever called on me. My nervousness grew when Theodor Hupfauer, the new chief of our Central Office—with whom I had several times spoken rather candidly—told me in some trepidation that Gestapo chief Kaltenbrunner would be calling on him at the same hour.

Before Himmler entered, my adjutant whispered to me: "He's alone."

My office was without window panes; we no longer bothered replacing them, since they were blasted out by bombs every few days. A wretched candle stood on the table; the electricity was out again. Wrapped in our coats, we sat facing one another. Himmler talked about minor matters, asked about pointless details, spoke of the situation at the front, and finally made the witless observation: "When the course is downhill there's always a floor to the valley, and once that is reached, Herr Speer, the ascent begins again."

Since I expressed neither agreement nor disagreement with this proverbial wisdom and remained virtually monosyllabic throughout the conversation, he soon took his leave. I never found out what he wanted of it, or why Kaltenbrunner had called on Hupfauer at the same time. Perhaps they had heard about my critical attitude and were seeking allies; perhaps they merely wanted to sound us out.

On February 14, I sent a letter to the Finance Minister offering to turn over "the entire sizable increase of my personal fortune since the year 1933 for the benefit of the Reich." This action was intended to help stabilize the mark, whose value had been maintained with difficulty only by coercive measures and which would inevitably collapse as soon as the coercion ended. When the Finance Minister, Count Schwerin-Krosigk, discussed my offer with Goebbels, he encountered eloquent opposition. The Propaganda Minister would have been particularly affected had he felt under pressure to imitate my example.

Another idea of mine had even smaller prospects of adoption. Recalling it today makes me aware of the romantic and fantastic state of mind I was in during that period. At the end of January, I discussed the hopelessness of the situation very cautiously, feeling my way, with Werner Naumann, state secretary in the Propaganda Ministry. The conversation arose by chance; we happened to find ourselves together in the Ministry air-raid shelter. Assuming that at least Goebbels was capable of lucidity and logic, I sketched the outlines of a grand final stroke. What I had in mind was a joint undertaking by the government, the party, and the commanding generals. Hitler would issue a proclamation that the entire leadership of the Reich was prepared to surrender voluntarily to the enemy if in return the German people would be granted bearable conditions for their continued existence. Reminiscences of history, memories of Napoleon who had surrendered to the British after the collapse at Waterloo, were mingled in this rather operatic notion with Wagnerianisms about self-sacrifice and redemption. It was good that nothing ever came of it.

Among my associates recruited from industry, Dr. Lüschen, head of the German electric industry, member of the board of directors and chief of research and development in the Siemens concern, was particularly close to me personally. He was a man of seventy on whose experience I gladly leaned. He foresaw difficult times for the German people but had no doubts about eventual recovery.

Early in February, Lüschen visited me in my small apartment in the rear building of my Ministry on Pariser Platz. He took a slip of paper from his pocket and handed it to me, saying: "Are you aware of the passage from Hitler's *Mein Kampf* that is most often quoted by the public nowadays?"

I read: "The task of diplomacy is to ensure that a nation does not heroically go to its destruction but is practically preserved. Every way that leads to this end is expedient, and a failure to follow it must be called criminal neglect of duty." He had found a second fitting quotation, Lüschen continued, and he handed me another slip: "State authority as an end in itself cannot exist, since in that case every tyranny on this earth would be sacred and unassailable. If a racial entity is being led toward its doom by means of governmental power, then the rebellion of every single member of such a *Volk* is not only a right, but a duty."[8]

Lüschen took his departure without a word, leaving these quotations behind. Uneasily, I paced back and forth in my room. Here was Hitler himself saying what I had been trying to get across during these past months. Only the conclusion remained to be drawn: Hitler himself— measured by the standards of his own political program—was deliberately committing high treason against his own people, which had made vast sacrifices for his cause and to which he owed everything. Certainly more than I owed to Hitler.

That night I came to the decision to eliminate Hitler. My preparations, to be sure, went no further than the initial stages and therefore have a touch of the ridiculous about them. But at the same time they are evidence of the nature of the regime and of the deformations in the character of its actors. To this day I shudder at the thought of what that regime had led me to—I who had once wanted nothing more than to be Hitler's master builder. Even at this late date I still occasionally sat opposite him at table, occasionally even leafed through old building plans with him—all the while I was thinking how to obtain poison gas to destroy the man who in spite of our many disagreements still felt some liking for me and treated me with more forbearance than he did anyone else. For years I had lived in his entourage, where a human life meant nothing; but all that seemed to be none of my affair. Now I realized that this atmosphere had not left me untouched. I was not just entangled in a thicket of deceptions, intrigues, baseness, and killing. I myself had become part of this perverted world. For twelve years, when you came right down to it, I had lived thoughtlessly among murderers. Now, at the moment of the regime's doom, I was on the point of receiving from Hitler himself, of all people, the moral impulse to attempt murder against him.

At the Nuremberg Trial, Goering ridiculed me and called me a second Brutus. Several of the defendants reproached me with: "You broke the oath you swore to the Fuehrer." But this appeal to the oath was empty; it was simply a way to escape the obligation to think independently. If nothing else, Hitler himself robbed this sham argument of its rationale, as he did for me in February 1945.

On my walks in the Chancellery gardens I had noticed the ventilation shaft for Hitler's bunker. Camouflaged by a small shrub, level with the ground and covered with a thin grating, was the opening of the air intake. The air that was drawn in passed through a filter. But no filter worked against our poison gas tabun.

Chance had brought me into closer personal relations with the head of our munitions production, Dieter Stahl. The Gestapo had questioned him about a defeatist remark on the impending end of the war. The penalties were all too serious. He had asked my help. Since I knew Gauleiter Stürtz of Brandenburg quite well, I was able to quash the affair.

About the middle of February, a few days after Lüschen's visit, I was sitting with Stahl in a small room in our Berlin air-raid shelter. Outside, a heavy air raid was in progress. The situation promoted candid conversation. In that dreary room with its concrete walls, steel door, and plain chairs, we talked about conditions in the Chancellery and the catastrophic policy being pursued there. At one point in our talk, Stahl gripped my arm and exclaimed: "It's going to be frightful, frightful!"

I began discreetly asking about the new poison gas and whether he could obtain it. Although the question was extremely unusual, Stahl answered readily enough. There was a pause in the conversation. I found myself saying: "It is the only way to bring the war to an end. I want to try to conduct the gas into the Chancellery bunker."

In spite of the confidential relationship that had arisen between us, I was myself shocked by my own frankness. But Stahl showed no signs of either consternation or excitement. Soberly, he promised that in the next few days he would look around for ways to obtain the gas.

A few days later Stahl told me that he had got in touch with the head of the munitions department in the Army Ordnance Office, Major Soyka. Perhaps, he had said, there were ways of rebuilding artillery shells, which were made in Stahl's factory, for poison-gas experiments. Actually, every medium-level employee in the poison-gas factories had easier access to tabun than the Minister of Armaments or the chief of the Directing Committee for Munitions. In the course of our discussions, it turned out that tabun became effective only after an explosion. This made it impracticable for my purpose, for an explosion would have shattered the thin-walled air ducts. By this time it was the beginning of March. But I continued to pursue my plan, for this seemed the only way to eliminate not only Hitler, but Bormann, Goebbels, and Ley at the same time, during one of their nocturnal chats.

Stahl thought that he would soon be able to obtain one of the traditional types of gas for me. Ever since the building of the Chancellery, I had been acquainted with Henschel, the chief engineer of the building. I suggested to him that the air filters had been in use too long and needed renewing; for Hitler had occasionally complained in my presence about the bad air in the bunker. Quickly, much more quickly than I could possibly act, Henschel removed the filtering system, so that the bunker was without protection.

But even if we could have obtained the gas immediately, those days would have passed fruitlessly. For when I invented some pretext at this time to inspect the ventilation shaft, I found a changed picture. Armed SS sentinels were now posted on the roofs of the entire complex, searchlights had been installed, and where the ventilation shaft had previously been at ground level there now rose a chimney more than ten feet high, which put the air intake out of reach. I was stunned. My first thought was that my plan had been discovered. But actually the whole thing was the operation of chance. Hitler, temporarily blinded by poison gas during the First World War, had ordered the building of this chimney because poison gas is heavier than air.

Basically I was relieved that my plan had been finally thwarted. For three or four weeks more I was beset by fears that our plot might still be uncovered. Sometimes I became obsessed with the notion that my intention could be read in my face. After all, since July 20, 1944, there was always the risk that a man's family would be called to account—my wife and above all our six children.

The building of the chimney had done more than ruin this particular plot. The whole idea of assassination vanished from my considerations as quickly as it had come. I no longer considered it my mission to eliminate Hitler but to frustrate his orders for destruction. That, too, relieved me, for all my feelings still existed side by side: attachment, rebellion, loyalty, outrage. Quite aside from all question of fear, I could never have confronted Hitler pistol in hand. Face to face, his magnetic power over me was too great up to the very last day.

The total confusion of my emotions can be seen in the fact that however aware I was of the amorality of his conduct, I could not suppress a pang at his inexorable decline and at the collapse of a life built so entirely on self-assurance. From this point on, I felt toward him a mixture of abhorrence, pity, and fascination.

In addition I felt fear. In the middle of March, when I again had to send in a report dealing with the taboo subject of the lost war, I decided to accompany it with a personal letter. In a nervous hand, using the green ink which was the prerogative of a government minister, I began drafting it. Not entirely by hazard I wrote it on the back of the sheet on which my secretary had copied the quotation from *Mein Kampf* in the special large type used for communications for Hitler. By this mechanism I was trying to remind Hitler of his own call to rebellion in a time of lost war.

"The enclosed memorandum," I began, "is something I have had to write. As Reich Minister of Armaments and War Production it is my duty to you and to the German people." Here I hesitated and recast the sentence, placing the German people before Hitler. Then I continued: "I know that this letter must necessarily have grave consequences for me personally."

At this point the draft, which has been preserved, breaks off. I had also put a line through this sentence. In its new form, my fate is cast entirely in Hitler's hands. The change was trivial: ". . . may possibly have grave consequences for me personally."

29

Doom

During this last stage of the war, I found distraction and relief in being active. I left it to Saur to worry about armaments production, which was winding down anyhow.[1] For my part I kept in as close touch as possible with my industrial associates so we could discuss urgent problems of provisioning and of transition to a postwar economy.

The Morgenthau Plan was made to order for Hitler and the party, insofar as they could point to it for proof that defeat would finally seal the fate of all Germans. Many people were actually influenced by this threat. We, on the other hand, had long since taken a different view of what lay in the future. For Hitler and his henchmen had pursued aims similar to the Morgenthau Plan, only far more drastically, in the occupied territories. But experience showed that in Czechoslovakia, Poland, Norway, and France industries had developed again, even contrary to German intentions, since the temptation to reactivate them for our own ends was greater than the manias of embittered ideologues. And once anyone began to revive industry, he found he had to maintain the economic fundamentals that underlay it, to feed and clothe people and to pay wages.

Such, at any rate, had been the course of things in the occupied territories. We thought the one prerequisite for a repetition in Germany was that the productive mechanism should remain relatively intact. My work toward the end of the war, and especially after abandoning my plan to assassinate Hitler, was directed almost exclusively toward saving the industrial substance, in defiance of all difficulties and without ideological or nationalistic bias. But since this was the very reverse of official policy, it led me further along the course of lies, deception, and schizophrenia on which I had already embarked.

At a situation conference in January 1945, Hitler handed me a foreign press report. "You know I ordered everything in France to be destroyed. How is it possible that French industry is already approaching its prewar production only a few months later?" He glared indignantly at me.

"Probably it's a propaganda report," I replied calmly. Hitler knew all about false propaganda reports, and the affair was dismissed.

In February 1945, I once again flew to the Hungarian petroleum region, to the remaining coal area of Upper Silesia which we still held, and to Czechoslovakia and Danzig. Everywhere I extracted pledges from the local representatives of my Ministry to follow our line. The generals, too, indicated their sympathy with my efforts.

In the course of this journey I made an interesting observation at Lake Balaton in Hungary. I witnessed the open deployment of a number of SS divisions which Hitler intended to commit to a large-scale offensive. But the plan for this operation was subject to strictest secrecy. It seemed all the more grotesque, therefore, that these forces wore badges on their uniforms identifying them as elite formations. But even more grotesque than this open deployment for a "surprise" offensive was Hitler's belief that with a few armored divisions he could overthrow the newly established, strong position of the Soviets in the Balkans. He thought the peoples of southeastern Europe were already tired of Soviet rule after only a few months. In the desperate mood of these weeks he persuaded himself that a few initial successes would change everything. There would surely be a popular uprising against the Soviet Union, and the populace would make common cause with us against the Bolshevik enemy, until victory was won. It was fantastic.

My subsequent visit in Danzig brought me to the headquarters of Himmler in his capacity of Commander in Chief of the Vistula Army Group. The headquarters was a comfortably equipped special train. By chance I was present at a telephone conversation between him and General Weiss, and heard Himmler cut off all arguments for abandoning a lost position with a stereotyped reply: "I have given you a command. You'll answer with your head for it. I'll call you to account personally if the position is lost."

But when I visited General Weiss the next day, the position had been abandoned in the course of the night. Weiss appeared unimpressed by Himmler's threats. "I am not committing my troops for insane demands that cost heavy casualties. I am doing only what is possible." Hitler's and Himmler's threats were beginning to lose their effectiveness. On this trip, too, I had my Ministry photographer take pictures of the endless lines of

refugees trekking in mute panic toward the West. Once again Hitler refused to look at the photos. With resignation rather than vexation he
pushed them far away from him on the large map table.

On my trip to Upper Silesia, I met General Heinrici, a sensible man
with whom I had to collaborate confidentially during the last weeks of
the war. At that time, in the middle of February, we decided that the railroad installations which would be needed in the future for distributing
coal to southeast Germany were not to be destroyed. Together, we visited
a mine near Ribnyk. Although the mine was in the immediate vicinity of
the front, the Soviet troops were allowing work to continue there. The
enemy, too, seemed to be respecting our policy of nondestruction. The
Polish workers had adjusted to the change in the situation. They were
working as efficiently as ever, in a sense repaying us for our pledge that
we would preserve their place of work if they refrained from sabotage.

Early in March, I went to the Ruhr for a survey of what would be
needed for the impending end and the new beginning. The industrialists
were most anxious about the transportation question. If the coal mines
and steel works were preserved but all the bridges destroyed, then the
circulation among coal, steel, and rolling mills would be broken. That
same day I went to see Field Marshal Model about it.* He was in a state
of fury. He told me that commands had just come from Hitler to attack
the enemy on his flank at Remagen, using certain specified divisions, and
recapture the bridge. "Those divisions have lost their weapons and have
no fighting strength at all. They would be less effective than a company!
It's the same thing all over again: At headquarters they have no idea what
is going on. . . . Of course, I'll be blamed for the failure." In his irritation
at Hitler's orders, Model was all the readier to listen to my proposals. He
promised that in the fighting in the Ruhr area he would spare the indispensable bridges and especially the railroad installations.

To forestall the blowing up of bridges, which boded so ill for the future, I arranged with General Guderian[2] to issue an edict on "measures of
destruction in our own country," whose purpose was to forbid any demolition which would "hinder the supplying of our own population." Certain
demolitions were absolutely essential, but these were to be kept to a minimum; as far as possible only minor stoppages of traffic were to be undertaken. Guderian meant to issue this order on his own responsibility for
the eastern theater of war. But when he tried to persuade General Jodl,
who was in charge of the western theater, to sign it, he was referred to
Keitel. Keitel took possession of the draft and said he would discuss it with
Hitler. The result could be predicted: At the next situation conference

* That same day Model decided not to use the largest pharmaceutical plant in
Germany, Bayer-Leverkusen, as an artillery base. He agreed to inform the enemy
and request him to spare the factory.

Hitler made a great scene over Guderian's proposal and reiterated the strict orders for destruction.

In the middle of March, I sent Hitler another memorandum in which I again frankly expressed my opinion on the measures that must be taken at this stage of the war. The memorandum violated all the taboos he had set up in recent months, as I well knew. But only a few days before I had convoked my industrial associates to a meeting in Bernau and told them that I would risk my head to keep the factories from being demolished, no matter how much the military situation deteriorated. At the same time I once again sent out a circular letter to all my branch offices ordering them to avoid destruction on principle.[3]

To coax Hitler into reading my memorandum at all, the first pages began in the usual tone with a report on coal production. But by the second page I was presenting a list in which the armaments factories were already ranked last. I gave civilian needs precedence: food, gas, electricity.* Abruptly, the text went on to say that "the final collapse of the German economy" could be expected "with certainty" within four to eight weeks, and that afterward the war "could not be continued on the military plane." Then, appealing directly to Hitler, I wrote: "No one has the right to take the viewpoint that the fate of the German people is tied to his personal fate." The primary obligation of leadership in these last weeks of the war must be "to help the people wherever possible." I concluded

---

* Weeks earlier we had already drawn up complete plans. On February 19, one day after Hitler ordered me by decree "to distribute all the transportation facilities of the armed forces, the armaments industry, agriculture, and industry among the prime users and to establish the order of priorities for shipments" I gave the following orders in my "Instructions Concerning the Transportation Situation": "Anything which is vital to preserving the strength of the German nation naturally takes precedence over everything else. As far as possible food and other necessities of life must be provided for the population." The transportation crisis forced me to make this decision, since freight-car loadings had dropped to a third of the former figure.

Thanks to the pressure exerted by Riecke, the state secretary in the Ministry of Food, I was able to obtain a decree from the Planning Bureau on March 2, 1945, allowing me to order the Bureau of Construction to provide the food-producing industries and the farm machinery plants with electricity and coal and to have the nitrogen plants repaired before the hydrogenation plants. These were the last of my many decrees on priorities. I did not even mention the armaments industry.

Pools of trucks which we kept in reserve for urgent armaments transports were provided with the necessary fuel and dispatched to deliver the seed for the next crops, for the state railroad had announced that it could no longer handle this task. During these weeks we carried out a special program to fill Berlin's warehouses with enough food to last for several months. A special offer I made to State Secretary Zintsch of the Ministry of Education was accepted, and our trucks began to move precious art objects from the Berlin museums to the salt caves along the Saale River. The objects thus saved today form the heart of the Dahlem museum's collection.

the memorandum: "At this stage of the war it makes no sense for us to undertake demolitions which may strike at the very life of the nation."

Until then I had opposed Hitler's policy by a pretense of optimism in conformity with the official line, arguing that factories should not be destroyed because we would want to put them back in operation quickly after the reconquest. Now, on the contrary, I declared for the first time that the material substance of the nation had to be preserved "even if a reconquest does not seem possible. . . . It cannot possibly be the purpose of warfare at home to destroy so many bridges that, given the straitened means of the postwar period, it will take years to rebuild this transportation network. . . . Their destruction means eliminating all further possibility for the German people to survive."*

I did not dare hand this memorandum to Hitler without preparation. He was too unpredictable, and an instant order to have me shot was quite conceivable. I therefore gave the twenty-two-page document to Colonel von Below, my liaison officer at the Fuehrer's headquarters, with instructions first to summarize it for him at a suitable moment. Then I requested Julius Schaub, Hitler's adjutant, to tell Hitler that I would like to have a photograph of him with a personal dedication for my impending fortieth birthday. I was the only close associate of Hitler's who had not asked him for such a photograph during the entire twelve years. Now, at the end of his rule and of our personal relationship, I wanted to let him know that although I was opposing him and had had to face up to the fact of defeat, I still revered him and valued the distinction of a dedicated photograph.

Still I was apprehensive and took steps to put myself out of his reach immediately after handing over the memorandum. That same night I planned to fly to Königsberg, already threatened by the Soviet armies. I was to have a conference with my assistants there, where I would again urge my plea against needless demolitions. At the same time, I thought, I would bid Hitler farewell.

And so on the evening of March 18, I went to the situation conference with my fateful document. For some time the conferences had no longer

---

* In this memorandum I used Berlin as an example of what would happen if bridges were blown up: "The planned demolition of the bridges in Berlin would cut off the city's food supply, and industrial production and human life in this city would be rendered impossible for years to come. Such demolitions would mean the death of Berlin." I also pointed out to Hitler the consequences for the Ruhr area: "If the numerous railroad bridges over the smaller canals and valleys, or the viaducts, are blown up, the Ruhr area will be unable to handle even the production needed for repairing the bridges." In my March 15 memorandum, I also demanded of Hitler that preparations be made so that when the enemy approached only a code word need be issued to assure that civilian and army stocks, including food stocks, would immediately be distributed among the people.

been taking place in Hitler's resplendent office, which I had designed seven years ago. Hitler had transferred them to his small study in the deep shelter. With melancholy bitterness he commented to me: "Ah, you know, Herr Speer, your beautiful architecture no longer provides the proper frame for the situation conferences."

The subject of the March 18 conference was the defense of the Saar, now hard pressed by Patton's army. As he had done once before in the case of the Russian manganese mines, Hitler suddenly turned to me for support: "Tell the gentlemen yourself what a loss of the Saar coal will mean to you!"

Completely off my guard, I blurted out: "That would only speed up the collapse." Stunned and embarrassed, we stared at each other. I was just as surprised as Hitler. After an awkward silence, Hitler changed the subject.

That same day Field Marshal Kesselring, the Commander in Chief in the West, reported that the populace was playing a negative role in the struggle against the advancing American forces. More and more often the people did not allow our own troops to enter the villages. Deputations would go to the officers to beg them not to cause the destruction of localities by defending them. In many cases the troops had yielded to these desperate pleas.

Without a moment's compunction, Hitler turned to Keitel and told him to compose an order to the Commander in Chief and the Gauleiters: The entire population of the threatened areas was to be forcibly evacuated. Dutifully, Keitel sat down at a table in the corner to draw up the order.

One of the generals present tried to persuade Hitler that it was impossible to carry out the evacuation of hundreds of thousands of persons. There were no longer any trains available. Transportation had long since broken down completely. Hitler remained obdurate. "Then let them walk!" he replied. That, too, could not be organized, the general said. Provisioning would be needed; the torrent of humanity would have to be led through less populated areas; and besides the people did not even have proper shoes. He was not given a chance to finish. Imperviously, Hitler turned away.

Keitel had drafted the order and read it to Hitler, who approved it. Its text ran:

> The presence of the population in the battle zone threatened by the enemy imposes difficulties upon the fighting troops, as it does on the population itself. The Fuehrer therefore issues the following command: West of the Rhine, or in the Saar Palatinate, as the case may be, all inhabitants are to be evacuated at once from the area, beginning directly behind the main battlefield. . . . Removal is to take place in a general southeasterly direction and

south of the line formed by St. Wendel, Kaiserslautern, and Ludwigshafen. Details to be settled by Army Group G in association with the Gauleiters. The Gauleiters will receive the same order from the Chief of the Party Secretariat. Chief OKW *(signed)*, Field Marshal Keitel.*

No one objected when Hitler concluded: "We can no longer afford to concern ourselves with the population." Together with Zander, Bormann's liaison man to Hitler, I left the room. Zander was in despair. "But that's impossible. It will be an utter disaster. No preparations have been made!"

Impulsively, I said that I would give up my flight to Königsberg and drive west that very night to see what I could do to help.

The situation conference was over, it was past midnight, and my fortieth birthday had begun. I asked Hitler whether I might see him for a moment. He called his orderly: "Bring that picture I've signed," and handed me, with cordial birthday wishes, the red leather case stamped with the Fuehrer's emblem: This was the usual container in which he presented his silver-framed photos. I expressed my thanks and set the case down on the table as I prepared to hand him my memorandum. But Hitler was saying: "Lately it's been hard for me to write even a few words in my own hand. You know how it shakes. Often I can hardly complete my signature. What I've written for you came out almost illegible."

At that I opened the case to read the inscription. It was in fact scarcely legible, but couched in unusually cordial terms, joining thanks for my work with the assurance of lasting friendship. It was hard for me at this point to respond to the gift by presenting him with the memorandum in which I dryly set forth the collapse of his whole mission.

Hitler received it without a word. To bridge the awkwardness of this moment, I informed him that I would be driving to the West instead of flying to Königsberg that night. While I was still in the bunker, telephoning for my car and driver, I was again summoned to Hitler. "I've thought it over. It will be better if you take my car and have my driver Kemptka drive you." I objected on various grounds. Finally, Hitler agreed that I could use my own car, but that Kemptka must drive me. I felt rather uneasy, for the warmth Hitler had shown when he handed me his photo-

---

* Here we have an example of the chaos created by Hitler's sudden reactions. Shortly before this, on the same day, March 18, Keitel had sent a teletype message saying: "The Fuehrer has unequivocally [!] decided to carry through the disengagement and evacuation measures wherever necessary in those western sectors directly threatened by the enemy." But those who did not obey this order were completely "covered": "During the disengagement and evacuation, military operations, food transport and coal transport must not be impeded."

The next day, March 19, 1945, Bormann issued implementation instructions for Hitler's latest order. These provided that "in case transportation is not available, evacuation should be undertaken in horse- or ox-drawn wagons. If necessary the male part of the population should proceed on foot."

graph, a warmth to which I had almost succumbed, was now gone without a trace. I could feel his ill humor as he dismissed me and was already at the door when he said, as if cutting off the possibility of any answer: "This time you will receive a written reply to your memorandum!" He made a brief pause, then in an icy tone continued: "If the war is lost, the people will be lost also. It is not necessary to worry about what the German people will need for elemental survival. On the contrary, it is best for us to destroy even these things. For the nation has proved to be the weaker, and the future belongs solely to the stronger eastern nation. In any case only those who are inferior will remain after this struggle, for the good have already been killed."[4]

I was relieved when I at last sat at the wheel of my car in the fresh night air, Hitler's chauffeur at my side and Lieutenant Colonel von Poser, my liaison officer to the General Staff, on the rear seat. Kemptka had agreed that we would take turns driving. By this time it was about half past one in the morning, and speed was of the essence if we were to cover the three hundred odd miles of autobahn to the headquarters of the Commander in Chief, West, near Nauheim, before daybreak—for then the enemy hedgehopping fighters appeared. We had the radio tuned to the broadcaster for the night fighters and kept the grid map on our knees: "Night fighters in grid Number—. . . . Several Mosquitoes in grid—. . . . Night fighters in grid—. . . ." This way we knew exactly where the enemy was. If a formation were approaching us, we would switch to our parking lights and feel our way slowly along the edge of the road. As soon as our square on the grid map was free of the enemy, we switched to high beam and foglights, turned on the big jacklight, and with our supercharger howling, roared down the autobahn. By morning we were still on the road, but low-lying clouds had brought air activity to a standstill. At headquarters,* I first of all lay down for a few hours sleep.

Toward noon I had a meeting with Kesselring, but our talk proved fruitless. He behaved as a soldier pure and simple and was not inclined to discuss Hitler's orders. On the other hand, the party representative on his staff proved surprisingly more amenable to reason. As we paced back and forth on the terrace of the castle, he assured me that he would do his best to suppress reports on the behavior of the population which might affect Hitler badly.

During a simple meal with his staff, Kesselring had just offered a brief toast to my fortieth birthday when a formation of enemy fighter planes suddenly descended on the castle with a high-pitched whining sound. At the same moment the first burst of machine-gun fire struck the

---

* This headquarters was located in a small castle atop a cliff, connected with bunkers by a stairway. It was the headquarters I had built for Hitler in 1940 which he had rejected at the time.

windows. Everyone threw himself to the floor. Only now did the alarm siren sound. The first heavy bombs crashed in the immediate vicinity. While the explosions boomed on either side of us, we rushed through the smoke and plaster dust into the bunkers.

This attack was obviously aimed at the western defense headquarters. The bombs continued to fall without a pause. The bunker swayed but was not hit directly. When the attack was over, we continued our conferences, at which we were now joined by Hermann Röchling, the Saar industrialist, a man in his seventies. In the course of the conversation Kesselring told Röchling that the Saar would be lost in the next few days. Röchling accepted the news almost indifferently. "We have lost the Saar once before and won it back. Old as I am, I shall see it return to our possession again."

The next stage in our journey was Heidelberg, where the Armaments Staff for southwest Germany had been transferred. This was a chance for me to pay a brief birthday visit to my parents. By day the autobahn could not be traversed because of the planes. Since I knew all the secondary roads from my boyhood, Röchling and I drove through the Odenwald. It was warm, sunny spring weather. For the first time we talked with complete frankness. Röchling, formerly an admirer of Hitler, made it quite clear that he thought it senseless fanaticism to continue the war.

It was late evening by the time we reached Heidelberg. The news from the Saar sounded good; scarcely any preparations for demolitions had been made. Since it was now only a matter of days before the area fell into Allied hands, even a command from Hitler could no longer do damage.

Then, during a toilsome drive over roads blocked by retreating troops, we were furiously sworn at by tired and battered soldiers. It took until midnight for us to reach the army headquarters, situated in a wine-growing village of the Palatinate. SS General Hausser was more sensible in the interpretation of insane orders than his Commander in Chief. Hausser thought that the ordered evacuation could not possibly be carried out and that blowing up the bridges would be irresponsible. Five months later, a prisoner of war being taken from Versailles, I rode in a truck through the Saar and the Palatinate. Both the railroad installations and the highway bridges were largely intact.

Stöhr, the Gauleiter of the Palatinate and the Saar, declared flatly that he would not implement the order for evacuation which he had received. A rather curious conversation developed between the Gauleiter and the Minister of Armaments and War Production.

"If you cannot carry out the evacuation and the Fuehrer calls you to account, you can say I told you the order had been canceled."

"No, very kind of you, but I'll take it on my own responsibility."

I insisted: "But I'll gladly put my head on the block for it."

Stöhr shook his head. "No, I'm doing it. I want to take this on my own shoulders." That was the only point on which we could not agree.

Our next destination was Field Marshal Model's headquarters, a hundred and twenty-five miles away in the Westerwald. In the morning hours the American low-level planes appeared. We abandoned the main roads and by way of secondary roads finally reached a small, peaceful village. Nothing indicated that this was the command headquarters of an army group. Not an officer or soldier, not a car or motorcycle courier was in sight. All automobile traffic was banned by day.

In the village inn I sat with Model and took up the discussion we had begun in Siegburg about preservation of the railroad installations in the Ruhr area. While we were talking, an officer came in with a teletype message. "This concerns you," Model said, both embarrassed and perplexed. I sensed that it was bad news.

It was Hitler's "answer in writing" to my memorandum. On every point it ordered the exact opposite of the things I had called for on March 18. "All military, transportation, communications, industrial, and supply facilities, as well as all resources within the Reich" were to be destroyed. The message was the death sentence for the German people; it called for application of the scorched earth principle in its most sweeping form. The decree further stripped me of all my powers; all my orders for the preservation of industry were explicitly revoked. Now the Gauleiters were put in charge of the program of destruction.[5]

The consequences would have been inconceivable: For an indefinite period there would have been no electricity, no gas, no pure water, no coal, no transportation. All railroad facilities, canals, locks, docks, ships, and locomotives destroyed. Even where industry had not been demolished, it could not have produced anything for lack of electricity, gas, and water. No storage facilities, no telephone communications—in short, a country thrown back into the Middle Ages.

It was obvious from Field Marshal Model's attitude that my situation had changed. He now talked to me with a distinct air of aloofness and avoided all further discussion of our actual subject, the safeguarding of the Ruhr industries.[6] Tired and distraught, I lay down to sleep in a farmhouse. After a few restless hours I walked across the fields and climbed a hill. The village lay peacefully below me in the sunlight under a thin veil of mist. I could see far out over the hills of Sauerland, the land lying between the Sieg and the Ruhr rivers. How was it possible, I thought, that one man wanted to transform this land into a desert. I lay down in the fern. Everything seemed unreal. But the soil gave off a spicy fragrance; the first green sprouts of plants were springing from the ground. As I walked back, the sun was setting. I had taken my resolve. The execution of that order must be prevented. I called off the conferences I had arranged for that evening in the Ruhr. It was better to explore the situation in Berlin first.

The car was fetched from its hiding place under trees. In spite of lively air activity, I set out that night, with dimmed lights, for the East. I leafed through my notes while Kemptka sat at the wheel. Many of these notes concerned the conferences I had held in the past two days. Indecisively, I went over the pages. Then I began to tear them up inconspicuously and to scatter the pieces out the window. During a stop, I happened to notice the running board. The strong wind of the car's movement had pressed those betraying scraps of paper in a small heap in the corner. Covertly, I kicked them into the roadside ditch.

30

Hitler's Ultimatum

EXHAUSTION PRODUCES A STATE OF INDIFFERENCE. THUS I WAS NOT AT ALL agitated when I met Hitler in the Chancellery on the afternoon of March 21, 1945. He asked me briefly about the trip, but he was terse and did not mention his "reply in writing." It seemed to me pointless to bring it up. Without asking me to join them, he listened to Kemptka's report for over an hour.

Ignoring my demotion, I handed Guderian a copy of my memorandum that same evening. I offered another copy to Keitel who, however, refused to take it; he wore an expression of horror, as if it were a dangerous high explosive. I tried in vain to find out the circumstances in which Hitler's command had been issued. There was an air of coolness all around me, as after the time my name had been discovered on the ministerial list of the July 20 conspiracy. Obviously, Hitler's entourage regarded my present state as a fall into ultimate disfavor. I had actually lost all influence over the area that concerned me most: the preservation of the industry I was supposed to be running.

At this time two decisions by Hitler proved to me that he was resolved on the utmost ruthlessness. In the W ∍hrmacht communiqué of March 18, 1945, I read of the execution of four officers charged with not having blown up the Rhine bridge at Remagen in time. Model had just told me that they were completely innocent. The "shock of Remagen," as it was called, kept many of the responsible men in a state of terror until the end of the war.

That same day I heard, or rather had it hinted to me, that Hitler had ordered the execution of General Fromm. A few weeks before Minister of Justice Thierack had remarked to me, offhandedly and completely unmoved, between two courses of a meal: "Fromm's going to lose his bonnet soon too!" My efforts to speak up for Fromm that evening remained fruitless; Thierack was not in the least impressed. Consequently, a few days later I sent him a five-page official letter in which I refuted most of the charges against Fromm, insofar as I knew what they were, and offered to appear before the People's Court as a witness for the defense.

That was probably an unprecedented request on the part of a Reich minister. Only three days later, on March 6, 1945, Thierack wrote me curtly that I would have to obtain permission from Hitler in order to testify. "The Fuehrer has just informed me," Thierack continued, "that he has no intention of issuing an exceptional permission to you in the case of Fromm. I therefore will not include your statement in the records of the court."[1] The executions also made me aware of the nature of the risk I was running.

I was stubborn. When, on March 22, Hitler invited me to one of his armaments conferences, I again had Saur represent me. From his notes, it was clear that he and Hitler had frivolously ignored the realities. Although armaments production had long since come to an end, they occupied themselves with projects as though the whole of 1945 were still at their disposal. For example, they discussed the totally nonexistent crude-steel production and also decided that the 8.8 centimeter antitank gun for the troops was to be produced in "maximum quantities" and the production of the 21 centimeter mortars was to be increased. They gloried over the development of entirely new weapons: a new special rifle for the parachute troops—with "maximum ejection speed," of course—or a new supercaliber 30.5 centimeter mortar. The minutes also recorded an order of Hitler's that five new variants of existing types of tanks were to be demonstrated to him within a few weeks. In addition, he wanted to investigate the effect of Greek fire, known since classical antiquity, and he wished to have our jet fighter-bomber, the Me-262, rearmed as quickly as possible as a fighter plane. In ordering this last action, he was tacitly conceding the error he had made a year and a half before, when he had persistently refused the advice of all the experts.[2]

I had returned to Berlin on March 21. Early in the morning three days later I received the news that British troops had crossed the Rhine on a broad front, north of the Ruhr, without meeting any resistance. Our troops were helpless, as I had already heard from Model. As late as September 1944 our strenuous production of armaments had made it possible to erect a new defensive front in a short time out of weaponless armies. This could no longer be done. Germany was being overrun.

I drove to the Ruhr area once more. Saving its industry was the crucial question for the postwar era. In Westphalia a flat tire forced us to stop. Unrecognized in the twilight, I stood in a farmyard talking to the farmers. To my surprise, the faith in Hitler which had been hammered into their minds all these last years was still strong. Hitler could never lose the war, they declared. "The Fuehrer is still holding something in reserve that he'll play at the last moment. Then the turning point will come. It's only a trap, his letting the enemy come so far into our country." Even among members of the government I still encountered this naive faith in deliberately withheld secret weapons that at the last moment would annihilate an enemy recklessly advancing into the country. Funk, for example, asked me: "We still have a special weapon, don't we? A weapon that will change everything?"

That very night, I began my conferences with Dr. Rohland, the chief of the Ruhr staff, and his most important assistants. Their report was terrifying. The three Gauleiters of the Ruhr region were determined to carry out Hitler's demolition order. Hörner, one of our technical assistants who was, unfortunately, at the same time chief of the party technical office, had drawn up a plan of destruction at the Gauleiters' command. Regretfully, but with the air of a man accustomed to obedience, he explained the details of his scheme that was to eliminate the industry of the Ruhr for the foreseeable future. The plan was a technical masterpiece: Even the coal mines were to be flooded, and their restoration prevented for years to come by destruction of the lift machinery. Barges loaded with cement were to be sunk to block the transshipment ports and the canals of the Ruhr. The Gauleiters wanted to begin their first demolitions next day, since the enemy troops were advancing rapidly in the northern part of the Ruhr. But the Gauleiters had so little transportation at their disposal that they were dependent on aid from my armaments organization. They hoped to find an ample supply of explosives, blasting caps, and fuses in the mines.

Rohland immediately summoned some twenty reliable coal-mining men to the former Thyssen castle of Landsberg, the seat of the Ruhr staff. After a brief conference it was jointly decided, as though this were one of the most natural acts in the world, that all dynamite, blasting caps, and fuses were to be thrown into the sumps of the mines. One of our men was instructed to use what meager fuel was available to drive all the trucks under our command out of the Ruhr area. If necessary, trucks and gasoline were to be placed at the disposal of the fighting troops, which would make them absolutely unavailable to the civilian sector. Finally, I promised Rohland and his associates fifty submachine guns—we were still producing thousands—to be used for guarding power plants and other important industrial installations against the Gauleiters' demolition squads. In the hands of determined men defending their own places of work, these

weapons represented considerable force, since the police and party functionaries had only recently been compelled to deliver their weapons to the
army. What this amounted to, really, was open revolt.

Gauleiters Florian, Hoffmann, and Schlessmann were at this time
meeting at the Hotel Bleibergquelle near Langenberg. Disobeying all of
Hitler's injunctions, on the next day I made another effort to win them
over to my view. I had a heated dispute with Gauleiter Florian of Düsseldorf. He took the line that if the war were lost, it was not the fault of Hitler or the party, but of the German people. Only miserable creatures would
survive such a catastrophe anyhow. But I was able to make Hoffmann and
Schlessmann see some reason. In spite of this, they were in a quandary:
The Fuehrer's orders must be obeyed, they said, and no one could relieve
them of their responsibility. They were altogether perplexed, all the more
so since Bormann had meanwhile passed on a new order from Hitler even
more radically calling for destruction of the basis of the nation's life.*
Hitler once again commanded that "areas which we cannot at present
hold, and whose occupation by the enemy is probable, must be evacuated." To forestall any objections, the edict continued: "From the many
descriptions he has received, the Fuehrer is aware of the great difficulties
involved in implementing this order. The Fuehrer's demands are based
on precise and cogent deliberations. The absolute necessity of evacuation
is not open to question."

Any such resettlement of millions of people from the territories west

---

* The decree read as follows:

Re: Reception of fellow Germans transferred from evacuated areas. I am delegated to report as follows:

On March 19, 1945, the Fuehrer issued an order on demolitions which you
have already received or which you will find enclosed. At the same time the
Fuehrer unequivocally ordered that areas which we cannot at present hold, and
whose occupation by the enemy is probable, must be evacuated.

The Fuehrer has imposed upon the Gauleiters of districts near the front the
solemn obligation to do all that is humanly possible to assure total evacuation,
that is the withdrawal from the threatened areas of every single fellow German
[*Volksgenosse;* a word with race-theory overtones]. From the many descriptions
he has received, the Fuehrer is aware of the great difficulties involved in implementing this order.

The Fuehrer's demands are based on precise and cogent deliberations. The
absolute necessity of evacuation is not open to discussion.

If the evacuation and transportation of so many fellow Germans is a difficult
problem, providing them with shelter in the interior districts of Germany will be
no less difficult. This seemingly impossible task of housing our fellow Germans
from the evacuated areas must be accomplished. The Fuehrer expects that the
districts of the interior will display the needful understanding for the inescapable
demands of the hour.

We must improvise in every possible way in order to master the present
situation in each region.

of the Rhine and the Ruhr, from the dense population centers of Mannheim and Frankfurt, could only be undertaken in rural areas, chiefly in Thuringia and the lowlands of the Elbe. The inadequately dressed and poorly fed urban population was supposed to flood into a countryside without sanitary provisions, shelter, or food. Famine, disease, and misery were inevitable.

The assembled Gauleiters agreed that the party no longer had any power to carry out these orders. But to our general astonishment, Florian read aloud the text of a ringing summons to the party functionaries of Düsseldorf, which he intended to have posted throughout the city. It called for: setting fire to all remaining buildings of the city upon the approach of the enemy, evacuation of all the inhabitants. Let the enemy march into a burned out, deserted city![3]

The two other Gauleiters had meanwhile become uncertain of themselves. They were ready to accept my interpretation of the Fuehrer's order—that the Ruhr's industry was still important for armaments production, all the more so since in the struggle for the Ruhr we could supply the troops with ammunition directly from the factories. Therefore the destruction of the power plants, which was to have begun next day, was postponed, and the order for demolition was transformed into an order to temporarily paralyze the factories.

Immediately after this conference I again called on Field Marshal Model in his headquarters. He proved to be willing to keep the fighting as far from the industrial area as possible and thus reduce demolitions to a minimum. He would also refrain from ordering the destruction of any factories.[4] For the rest, he promised to keep in close contact with Dr. Rohland and his associates during the next few weeks.

From Model, I learned that American troops were advancing upon Frankfurt. A precise front line could no longer be determined, and Kesselring's headquarters had just been shifted farther to the east. About three o'clock in the morning I arrived at Kesselring's old headquarters near Nauheim. After a talk with his chief of staff, General Westphal, I was satisfied that he too would interpret the demolition order in a merciful sense. Since even the chief of staff had no idea of how far the enemy had advanced in the course of the night, we detoured to the east, driving through the Spessart and the Odenwald to Heidelberg, and thus passed through the small town of Lohr. Our troops had already withdrawn; a curiously expectant mood hovered over the silent streets and squares. At one intersection stood a solitary soldier with a couple of bazookas. He looked at me in surprise.

"What in the world are you waiting for?" I asked him.

"For the Americans," he replied.

"And what will you do when the Americans come?"

He hesitated only a moment. "Get the hell out of here."

Here as well as everywhere else I had the impression that people thought the war was over.

At the Armaments Staff office for Baden and Württemberg in Heidelberg lay orders from Gauleiter Wagner of Baden commanding the destruction of the water and gas works in my native city, as in all other cities in Baden. We found a simple method of thwarting these orders. We went ahead and prepared the written copies but put the letters into the mailbox of a town that was on the point of being occupied by the enemy.

The Americans had already taken Mannheim, only twelve miles away, and were slowly advancing toward Heidelberg. After a nocturnal discussion with Mayor Neinhaus of Heidelberg, I offered a last service to my native city—by writing to SS General Hausser, whom I already knew from my work in the Saar, and asking him to declare Heidelberg a hospital city to be surrendered without a fight. At dawn I bade my parents good-by. During the last hours we spent together they, too, had displayed that uncanny calm and composure which had come over the suffering people. Both were standing at the front door of our house as I got into the car. My father came quickly up to the car once more, and while clasping my hand one last time looked silently into my eyes. We had a premonition that we would never see each other again.

Retreating troops without arms or equipment were blocking the road to Würzburg. A wild pig had ventured out of the woods in the half-light of morning and was being noisily chased by soldiers. In Würzburg I called on Gauleiter Hellmuth, who invited me to an ample breakfast. While we did justice to the excellent country sausages and eggs, the Gauleiter explained with the greatest matter-of-factness that to carry out Hitler's decree he had ordered destruction of the Schweinfurt ball-bearings industry. The factory heads and the party authorities were already waiting in another room for instructions. The plan was well conceived: The oil baths of the special machines were to be set afire. Experiences in the air raids had already shown that such fires would reduce the machinery to useless scrap iron. At first I could not convince him that such destruction was foolish. He asked me when the Fuehrer intended to apply the decisive secret weapon. He had heard, from Bormann and Goebbels, that commitment of this weapon was impending.

As I had done so often, I had to tell him that this secret weapon did not exist. I knew that this Gauleiter was one of the sensible ones and pleaded with him not to carry out Hitler's scorched earth order. Given the situation, I argued, it was madness to deprive the people of the foundations for a continued national life by demolishing industrial facilities and bridges. I also mentioned the German troops that were being concentrated east of Schweinfurt to counterattack in the center and recapture our armaments industries. In saying this I was not even lying, for the top leadership was actually planning a counterattack in the near future. The tired old argument that Hitler could not continue his war without ball bearings finally had its effect. Convinced or not, the Gauleiter was not eager to win immortal fame for having ruined all chance of victory by destroying the Schweinfurt factories.

After Würzburg the weather cleared. Only occasionally did we now encounter small units marching on foot, without heavy arms, to meet the enemy. These were training units which had been raised for the final offensive. The inhabitants of the villages were busy digging pits in their gardens; they were burying their family silver and other valuables. Everywhere we encountered the same friendly, obliging attitude on the part of the rural populace. However, nobody wanted us to take cover between houses from low-flying planes, since this might endanger the houses. "*Herr Minister,* would you mind moving on to the next house, down the road a piece?" someone called out of a window.

Precisely because the populace was so peaceable and resigned and because well-equipped troop units were nowhere to be seen, the large number of bridges prepared for dynamiting struck me as even more insane than it had at my Berlin desk.

In the towns and villages of Thuringia, party formations, chiefly SA units, were tramping aimlessly about the streets in their uniforms. Sauckel had called up the "great levy," mostly elderly men or children of sixteen. This was the *Volkssturm* that was supposed to confront the enemy, but nobody could supply them with weapons. A few days later Sauckel issued one more noble injunction to fight to the last, then took off in his car for southern Germany.

Late in the evening of March 27, I arrived in Berlin. I found a changed situation there.

In the meantime Hitler had issued orders that SS Gruppenführer Kammler, already responsible for the rocket weapons, was to be in charge of the development and production of all modern aircraft. Thus I had lost my jurisdiction over air armaments. What was more, since Kammler could employ my own assistants in the Ministry, an impossible organizational and bureaucratic snarl had been created. In addition, Hitler had explicitly commanded that Goering and I accept our subordination to Kammler by countersigning the decree.

I signed without objecting, furious and insulted though I felt at this latest humiliation. That day I stayed away from the situation conference. Almost at the same time Poser informed me that Hitler had sent Guderian on leave. Officially this was a furlough for health reasons, but everyone familiar with the inside story knew that Guderian would not return. Thus I was losing one of the few men in Hitler's military entourage who had not only supported me by action but constantly encouraged me to continue my present course.

On top of everything else my secretary brought me the orders issued by the chief of the Signal Corps in accordance with Hitler's edict of total destruction: the wires and installations of the post office, the railroad system, the waterways, the police, and electric-power transmission lines were all to be smashed and severed. By "explosion, fire, or dismantlement," all telephone, telegraph and relay offices, the switches of the long-distance cables, the masts, antennas, and broadcasting and receiving facilities of the radio stations were to be rendered "thoroughly useless." To prevent the enemy from making even temporary repairs in the communications network of the occupied areas, all stocks of spare parts, all cable and wire, even the switching diagrams, cable diagrams, and descriptions of equipment, were to be fully destroyed.[5] But General Albert Praun intimated to me that he would use judgment in carrying out this brutal order.

On top of all this I received confidential information that armaments were to be turned over to Saur, but under the direction of Himmler, who was to be appointed Inspector General for War Production.[6] This seemed to mean that Hitler intended to drop me. Shortly afterward Schaub telephoned and in an unusually acid tone let me know I was to see Hitler that evening.

I felt considerable apprehension when I was led into Hitler's office deep underground. He was alone, received me frostily, did not shake hands, scarcely replied to my greeting, and in a sharp, low voice immediately came to the point: "Bormann has given me a report on your conference with the Ruhr Gauleiters. You pressed them not to carry out my orders and declared that the war is lost. Are you aware of what must follow from that?"

As if he were reminded of something remote, his voice softened as he spoke, the tension lessened, and almost in the tone of a normal person he added: "If you were not my architect, I would take the measures that are called for in such a case."

Partly in a spirit of open rebellion, partly from sheer exhaustion, I answered impulsively rather than courageously: "Take the measures you think necessary and grant no consideration to me as an individual."

Apparently Hitler had lost the thread; there was a brief pause. He continued in a friendly manner, and I had the impression that he had already carefully considered and determined this course: "You are overworked and ill. I have therefore decided that you are to go on leave at once. Someone else will run your Ministry as your deputy."

"No, I feel perfectly well," I replied resolutely. "I am not going on leave. If you no longer want me as your minister, dismiss me from my post."

Even as I said this I remembered that Goering had already rejected this solution a year ago. Hitler now answered decisively, and in a tone of finality: "I do not want to dismiss you. But I insist that you begin your sick leave immediately."

I remained stubborn: "I cannot keep the responsibility of a minister

while another man is acting in my name." Then, with a shade of concilia-
tion, and almost as if I were taking an oath, I added: "I cannot, *mein
Führer*." That was the first time in the course of the conversation that I
had used this form of address.

Hitler appeared unmoved. "You have no choice. It is impossible for
me to dismiss you." And then, as if likewise wishing to make a gesture
hinting at his own weakness, he added: "For reasons of foreign and domestic policy, I cannot spare you."

Encouraged, I replied: "It's impossible for me to go on leave. As long
as I am in office I must conduct the affairs of the Ministry. I am *not* sick!"

There was a lengthy pause. Hitler sat down, and I did also, unasked.
In a relaxed tone, Hitler continued: "Speer, if you can convince yourself
that the war is not lost, you can continue to run your office."

From my memoranda, and no doubt from Bormann's report, he knew
quite well how I regarded the situation and what conclusions I had drawn.
Evidently all he wanted from me was lip service, a verbal statement that
would bar me from saying otherwise in the future.

"You know I cannot be convinced of that," I replied sincerely but
without defiance. "The war is lost."

Hitler launched into recollections. He spoke of the other difficult situations in his life, situations in which all had seemed lost but which he
had mastered by perseverance, energy, and fanaticism. He went on and
on, forever, it seemed to me, carried away by his memories of the early
days of struggle. He drew on such examples as the winter of 1941–42, the
threatening transportation crisis, even my own stupendous achievements
in armaments production. I had heard all that from him many times, knew
these monologues almost by heart, and could have continued them myself
almost word for word. He scarcely changed the tone of his voice, but perhaps the very drone of it made his sermon more compelling. I had had a
similar feeling years ago in the teahouse, when I had tried to resist his hypnotic eyes.

Now, since I remained silent and only looked steadily at him, he surprisingly lowered his demand: "If you would believe that the war can
still be won, if you could at least have faith in that, all would be well."
He had passed into an almost pleading tone, and for a moment I thought
that in his piteousness he was even more persuasive than in his masterful
poses. Under other circumstances I would probably have weakened and
given in. This time, what kept me from submitting to his spell was the
thought of his destructive plans.

Agitated, and therefore probably speaking a shade too loudly, I said:
"I cannot, with the best will in the world. And after all, I do not want to
be one of the swine in your entourage who tell you they believe in victory
without believing in it."

Hitler did not react. For a while he stared into space, then again
began talking about his experiences in the *Kampfzeit*, the days before the

party had come to power. He reverted once again, as he had often done during these weeks, to Frederick the Great's unexpected salvation. "One must believe that all will turn out well. . . . Do you still hope for a successful continuance of the war, or is your faith shattered?" Once again Hitler reduced his demand to a formal profession of faith that would be binding upon me: "If you could at least hope that we have not lost! You must certainly be able to hope . . . that would be enough to satisfy me."

I did not answer.

There was a long, awkward pause. At last Hitler stood up abruptly. Now he was very unfriendly again and declared with the sharpness he had shown at the beginning of the interview: "You have twenty-four hours to think over your answer! Tomorrow let me know whether you hope that the war can still be won." Without shaking hands, he dismissed me.[7]

As if to dramatize what lay in store for Germany after Hitler's command, immediately after this discussion a teletype message came from the Chief of Transportation. Dated March 29, 1945, it read: "Aim is creation of a transportation wasteland in abandoned territory. . . . Shortage of explosives demands resourceful utilization of all possibilities for producing lasting destruction." Included in the list of facilities slated for destruction were, once again, all types of bridges, tracks, roundhouses, all technical installations in the freight depots, workshop equipment, and sluices and locks in our canals. Along with this, simultaneously all locomotives, passenger cars, freight cars, cargo vessels, and barges were to be completely destroyed and the canals and rivers blocked by sinking ships in them. Every type of ammunition was to be employed for this task. If such explosives were not available, fires were to be set and important parts smashed. Only the technician can grasp the extent of the calamity that execution of this order would have brought upon Germany. The instructions were also prime evidence of how a general order of Hitler's was translated into terrifyingly thorough terms.

In my small emergency apartment in the rear wing of the Ministry, I went to bed, exhausted, and let my mind cast about for how I was to answer Hitler's twenty-four-hour ultimatum. Finally I got up and began writing a letter. At first the text moved inconsistently between a desire to make Hitler see reason and an attempt to meet him halfway. But then it continued bluntly: "When I read the demolition order (of March 19, 1945) and, shortly afterward, the stringent evacuation order, I saw these as the first steps toward carrying out these intentions." At this point I gave my answer to the question he had posed as an ultimatum: "But I can no longer believe in the success of our good cause if during these decisive months we simultaneously and systematically destroy the foundations of our national existence. That is so great an injustice to our people that should it be done, Fate can no longer wish us well. . . . I therefore beg you not to carry out this measure so harmful to the people. If you could revise your policy on this question, I would once more recover the faith and the courage to continue working with the greatest energy. It no longer lies in our hands," I continued my response to Hitler's ultimatum, "to decide how Fate will turn. Only a higher Providence can still change our future. We can only make our contribution by a strong posture and unshakable faith in the eternal future of our nation."

I closed not with the *Heil, mein Führer,* customary in such private letters, but used my last words to further my point and invoke the one hope that still remained to us: "May God protect Germany."*

As I reread this letter, I found it a weak performance. Perhaps Hitler decided that anything I wrote at this point would express a rebellious attitude which would force him to take stern measures against me. For when I asked one of his secretaries to type the letter—which since it was meant only for him I had written almost illegibly by hand—on Hitler's special typewriter with its oversized letters, she telephoned back: "The Fuehrer has forbidden me to receive any letters from you. He wants to

---

* Further excerpts from this letter:

My feeling is that if I should quit my post at this critical moment, even at your orders, I would be guilty of deserting the German people, not to speak of my loyal associates. Nevertheless I am duty-bound to tell you bluntly and without embellishment how the course of events looks to me, irrespective of the possible consequences for me. Unlike so many of your co-workers I have always spoken frankly to you, and I shall continue to do so. . . .

I believe in the future of the German people. I believe in a Providence that is just and inexorable, and thus I believe in God. It pained me deeply during the victorious days of 1940 to see how many among our leaders were losing their inner integrity. This was the moment when we should have commended ourselves to Providence by our decency and inner modesty. Then Fate would have been on our side. But during those months we were weighed in the balance and found too light for ultimate victory. We wasted a year of precious time luxuriating in our easily won success when we could have been girding ourselves for battle. This is why we were caught unprepared in the decisive years of 1944 and 1945. If all our new weapons had been ready a year earlier, we would be in a very different position now. As if we were being warned by Providence, from 1940 on all our military undertakings were dogged by unprecedented ill luck. Never before has an outside element such as the weather played such a decisive and devastating role as in this, the most technological of all wars: The cold in Moscow, the fog around Stalingrad, and the blue sky above the winter offensive in the West in 1944.

I can continue to carry out my duties with a sense of honor, with conviction, and with faith in the future, only if you, *mein Führer,* continue to uphold our life as a people. I shall not enter into a discussion of the way your orders of March 19, 1945, will inevitably crush our last remaining industrial potential and produce panic and horror among the population. These matters are of the highest importance, but they do not involve the principle that concerns me here. . . . You will understand my inner conflict. I cannot throw myself into my work or generate the necessary confidence if even while I am urging my workers to supreme efforts I know that we are planning to destroy the very foundations of their lives.

see you here and have your answer verbally." Shortly afterward I was told to come to Hitler at once.

Toward midnight I drove down Wilhelmstrasse, now shattered by bombs, the few hundred yards to the Chancellery, still without knowing what I was going to do, or answer. The twenty-four hours were up; I had not arrived at an answer. I left it to the moment of confrontation to decide what I would say.

Hitler stood before me, not at all sure of himself, seeming rather anxious. He asked tersely: "Well?"

For a moment I was confused. I had no answer ready. But then, simply to say something, without reflection and without completely committing myself, my lips spoke the words: *"Mein Führer,* I stand unreservedly behind you."

Hitler did not answer, but he was moved. After brief hesitation he shook hands with me, as he had not done when he received me. His eyes filled with tears, as they so often did nowadays. "Then all is well," he said. He showed plainly how relieved he was. I too was shaken for a moment by his unforeseen rush of feeling. Once again something of the old relationship could be felt between us.

I quickly saw a way to profit by the situation: "If I stand unreservedly behind you, then you must again entrust me instead of the Gauleiters with the implementation of your decree."

He authorized me to draw up a document which he would sign at once; but when we talked about it, he yielded not an iota on the destruction of industrial installations and bridges. And on this note I took my leave. By now it was one o'clock at night.

In one of the rooms of the Chancellery I drafted my instructions "to assure uniform implementation of [the] decree of March 19, 1945." In order to avoid any further discussion, I did not even try to undo its provisions. I merely made sure of two things: "Implementation will be undertaken solely by the agencies and organs of the Ministry of Armaments and War Production. . . . The Minister of Armaments and War Production may, with my authorization, issue instructions for implementation. He may pass detailed regulations on procedures to the Reich Defense Commissioners."*

Thus I was reappointed. And I smuggled in one sentence which gave

---

* The decree read as follows:

THE FUEHRER   *Fuehrer's Headquarters*
                                         March 30, 1945

To assure uniform implementation of my decree of March 19, 1945, I hereby order as follows:

1. The orders given for destroying industrial installations are aimed exclusively at preventing the enemy from using these installations and facilities to increase his fighting strength.

me significant leeway: "The same effect can be achieved with industrial installations by crippling them." But to placate Hitler, I added another provision that total destruction of particularly important plants would be ordered by me. I never gave any such orders.

Hitler signed this decree in pencil, almost without discussion, after he had made a few corrections in a trembling hand. He showed that he was still on top of the situation by one revision he made in the first sentence of the document. I had framed it as generally as possible, explaining that the purpose of the destructive measures was to prevent "the enemy from using these installations and facilities to increase his fighting strength." Seated wearily behind the map table in the situation room, Hitler limited it just to the industrial installations.

I think Hitler realized that he was making some important concessions. We talked a bit after he affixed his signature, and I found him willing to grant "that the scorched earth idea had no point in a country of such small area as Germany. It can only fulfill its purpose in vast spaces such as Russia." I made a note of this point and filed it away.

As usual, Hitler's actions were double-edged. That same evening he had ordered the commanders in chief "to intensify to the most fanatical level the struggle against the enemy who is now in movement. The na-

---

2. No measures may be taken which would impair our own fighting strength. Production must be continued up to the last possible moment, even at the risk that a factory may fall into the enemy's hands before it can be destroyed. Industrial installations of all sorts, including food-producing plants, may not be destroyed until they are immediately threatened by the enemy.

3. Although bridges and other transportation installations must be destroyed to deny the enemy their use for a prolonged period, the same effect can be achieved with industrial installations by crippling them lastingly.

Total destruction of particularly important plants will be ordered on my instructions by the Minister of Armaments and War Production (e.g., munitions plants, essential chemical plants, etc.).

4. The signal for crippling or destroying industrial complexes and other plants will be given by the Gauleiter and defense commissioner, who will supervise the process.

Implementation will be undertaken solely by the agencies and organs of the Ministry of Armaments and War Production. All the agencies of the party, the state and the armed forces are to assist when needed. The Minister of Armaments and War Production may, with my authorization, issue instructions for implementation. He may pass detailed regulations on procedures to the Reich Defense Commissioners.

6. These guidelines apply to plants and installations in the immediate war zone.

(Signed) Adolf Hitler

The decree pertained only to industry; the orders for destruction of shipping, railroad installations, communications, and bridges remained in effect.

ture of this struggle permits no consideration for the population to be taken."[8]

Within the hour I gathered together all available motorcycles, automobiles, and orderlies and descended on the printing plant and the teletype offices, determined to halt, by virtue of my restored authority, the destruction that was already in progress. By four o'clock in the morning I was having my implementation orders distributed—without, as was provided, bothering with Hitler's authorization. I boldly renewed all my previous instructions on the safeguarding of industrial installations, power plants, gasworks, and waterworks as well as food plants—the same instructions that Hitler had declared invalid on March 19. I promised that detailed instructions for the total destruction of industry would be forthcoming—and never issued them.

Again without authorization from Hitler, I ordered ten to twelve food trains to proceed to the immediate vicinity of the encircled Ruhr area. Together with General Winter of the Wehrmacht Operations Staff, I drew up an edict which was intended to stop the destruction of bridges; but Keitel frustrated this. I made an agreement with SS Obergruppenführer (Lieutenant General) Frank, who was responsible for the Wehrmacht's stockpiles of clothing and food, to distribute the supplies among the civilian population. Malzacher, my representative in Czechoslovakia and Poland, was to prevent the destruction of bridges in Upper Silesia.[9]

The next day at Oldenburg I met with Seyss-Inquart, the Commissioner General for the Netherlands. During a pause in the drive I practiced using a pistol, the first time in my life I had ever handled one. After carefully sounding him out, Seyss-Inquart, to my surprise, admitted that he had opened communications with the enemy. He did not want to inflict any more damage on Holland and especially wished to prevent large-scale flooding, which Hitler was planning. I came to a similar agreement with Gauleiter Kaufmann of Hamburg, whom I visited on the way back from Oldenburg.

On April 3, immediately after my return, I sent out orders forbidding the blowing up of sluices, locks, dams, and canal bridges.[10] More and more teletype messages, of increasing urgency, came pouring in requesting special orders for dealing with industrial plants. I answered each of these by ordering that the works be temporarily crippled.*

---

* For instance, a radio message from Gauleiter Uiberreither read as follows:

Radio message—PZR No. 5/6 0830   4/3/45
To Reich Minister Albert Speer
Berlin W 8

Concerning Fuehrer's orders of March 19, I request detailed instructions as to which armaments plants in my Gau are not to be destroyed under any circum-

Fortunately, in making such decisions I was able to count on support. Dr. Hupfauer, my political deputy, had formed an alliance with the state secretaries of the principal ministries in order to limit the effect of Hitler's policy. One member of his circle was Bormann's deputy, Gerhard Klopfer. We had pulled the rug out from under Bormann; his orders were issued into a vacuum, so to speak. During this last phase of the Third Reich he may have dominated Hitler; but outside the headquarters bunker other laws prevailed. Even Ohlendorf, the chief of the SD (Sicherheitsdienst, the dreaded Security Service), told me in prison that he had been regularly informed of my actions but had allowed the reports to stop at his desk.

Actually, in April 1945, I had the feeling that in collaboration with the state secretaries I was able to do more in my area than Hitler, Goebbels, and Bormann put together. On the military side I had good relations with General Krebs, the new chief of staff, since he had formerly been a member of Model's staff. But even Jodl, Buhle, and Praun, the chief of the Signal Corps, showed an increasing understanding of the real situation.

I was aware that if Hitler knew what I was doing, he would have seen it as high treason. I had to assume that this time I would have to pay the full penalty. During these months of playing a double game I followed a simple principle: I stayed as close to Hitler as possible. Every

---

stances. Since the military situation is completely fluid, a surprise enemy breakthrough can be expected at any moment. I call your attention to the aircraft factories in Marburg, Steyr, Daimler-Puch-Graz, and relocated factories. The fate of the armaments plants in upper Styria should be determined on the basis of the military situation in the Lower Danube region, but I have no information about that. Should the hydroelectric or steam power plants on the Drau and the Mur be destroyed before they can fall into the hands of the enemy undamaged? Your guidelines are only partly applicable here, since there is no definite front line.

(Signed) Gauleiter Uiberreither

My answer read:

Berlin, April 3, 1945

To Gauleiter Uiberreither, Graz

According to the Fuehrer's orders of March 30, 1945 there is to be no scorched earth. All installations and plants should be crippled so that the enemy will derive no additional military potential from them. In almost every case expert crippling by engineers will be sufficient and will fulfill the conditions stipulated by the Fuehrer. This applies to the plants mentioned in your cable. The Fuehrer's order of March 30, 1945, was intended to eliminate the varied interpretations that could be attached to the order of March 19, 1945, and to establish his unequivocal commitment to the method of crippling. Destruction is therefore permissible only if crippling would not achieve the desired effect. In addition the Fuehrer proclaims: Work until the last possible moment. Power plants are to be crippled only.

(Signed) Speer

absence furnished cause for suspicion, but an existing suspicion could be observed or eliminated only by someone who was constantly in his presence. I was not suicidally inclined; I had already set up an emergency hiding place in a primitive hunting lodge sixty miles from Berlin. In addition Rohland was keeping another hiding place ready for me in one of the numerous hunting lodges belonging to Prince Fürstenberg.

Even in the situation conferences at the beginning of April, Hitler was still talking about counteroperations, about attacks upon the Western enemy's exposed flanks—the Allied troops were now beyond Kassel and moving forward at a swift pace toward Eisenach. Hitler continued to send his divisions from one place to the other—a cruel, phantom war game. For when I would come back from a visit to the front and check the previous day's movements of our troops on the map, I could only note that I had seen nothing of them in the region I had driven through— and what troops I had passed consisted of soldiers without heavy weapons, armed solely with rifles.

I, too, was now daily holding a minor situation conference at which my liaison officer to the General Staff gave me the latest information— contrary to an order of Hitler's incidentally, for he had forbidden the military to brief nonmilitary government authorities on the military situation. Poser was able to tell me with fair exactness from day to day which area would be occupied by the enemy in the next twenty-four hours. These sober reports had nothing in common with the deliberately misty situation reporting that went on in the bunker underneath the Chancellery. There, nothing was said about evacuations and retreats. It seemed to me that the General Staff under General Krebs had finally abandoned giving Hitler accurate information and had settled for keeping him busy with war games. When, contrary to the situation report of the evening, cities and whole areas proved next day to have already fallen, Hitler remained perfectly calm. Now he no longer flew at the members of his entourage, as he had done only a few weeks before. He seemed resigned.

At the beginning of April, Hitler had summoned Field Marshal Kesselring, the western Commander in Chief, to him. By chance I happened to be present at this ridiculous conversation. Kesselring tried to explain the hopelessness of the situation to Hitler. But he had spoken no more than a few sentences when Hitler seized the floor and began lecturing the Field Marshal on how he intended to annihilate the American wedge advancing toward Eisenach by attacking it on the flank with a few hundred tanks. He would create a colossal panic and thus drive the Western enemy back out of Germany again. Hitler went off into long explications of the notorious inability of American soldiers to accept defeats, although the Battle of the Bulge had just proved the opposite. At the time I was angry with Kesselring for agreeing, after only briefly demurring, to these fantasies and entering into a discussion of Hitler's plans with seeming seriousness. But I realized later that there was no point getting excited about battles that would never be fought.

At one of the subsequent conferences Hitler again explained his idea of a flank attack. As dryly as possible I interjected: "If everything is destroyed, the recovery of these areas will do me no good at all." Hitler said nothing. I ventured a step further: "I cannot rebuild the bridges so quickly."

Hitler, obviously in a euphoric mood, replied: "Don't worry, Herr Speer, not as many bridges have been destroyed as I have ordered."

Just as good-humoredly, almost jokingly, I replied that I felt rather odd at being pleased with the disobedience of an order. To my surprise, Hitler was prepared to look at a new decree I had prepared.

When I showed Keitel the draft, he lost his temper for a moment. "Why still another change! We already have the demolition order. . . . No war can be waged without blowing up bridges!" Finally he agreed to my draft, though making minor emendations in the text, and Hitler signed the new instructions. It was now official policy to do no more than cripple transportation and communications facilities and to postpone destroying bridges until the last moment. Once again, three weeks before the end, I extracted Hitler's consent to this final statement: "With regard to all measures for demolition and evacuation, it must be borne in mind . . . that when lost territory is recovered these installations should be usable for German production."[11] Hitler did, however, strike out a clause that destruction should be postponed "even if the enemy's rapid movement creates the risk that a bridge . . . may fall into his hands before it can be destroyed."

That same day General Praun, the chief of the Signal Corps, revoked his order of March 27, 1945, canceled all demolition instructions, and even quietly ordered the safeguarding of the stockpiles, since they might be handy after the war for restoring the communications network. Hitler's reason for destroying communications was in any case senseless, he commented, since the enemy carried his own cable and radio stations with him. I do not know whether the Transportation Chief canceled his decree on laying waste to all transportation facilities. Keitel, in any case, refused to issue new instructions on the basis of Hitler's latest decree since this might be subject to further interpretation.[12]

Keitel quite rightly took me to task for having created unclear command relationships by eliciting from Hitler his order of April 7. In the nineteen days between March 18 and April 7, 1945, no less than twelve contradictory decrees had been issued on this question. But the chaotic command situation made it possible for men of good will to limit chaos in the future.

31

The Thirteenth Hour

—————

IN SEPTEMBER, WERNER NAUMANN, STATE SECRETARY IN THE PROPAGANDA Ministry, had invited me to stiffen the will to fight by speaking on the German radio network. Suspecting a trap by Goebbels, I begged off. But now that Hitler had seemingly swung over to my line, I saw a radio address as an opportunity to call upon the public in general to avoid senseless demolitions. As soon as Hitler's April 7 decree was published, I let Naumann know that I would be willing to make a speech and then drove off to Milch's hunting cottage by secluded Stechlin Lake.

In this last phase of the war we were trying to prepare for whatever might come. In order to be able to defend myself if necessary, I spent some time on the lake shore practicing shooting at a dummy. In between I worked on my radio speech. By evening I was satisfied; I was able to hit the dummy several times in rapid succession, and my speech seemed to convey my message without exactly exposing me. Over a glass of wine I read it aloud to Milch and one of his friends.

"It is a mistake to believe in the appearance of miraculous secret weapons which will take the place of the full commitment of the individual soldier!" I said, among other things. We had not destroyed the industries of the occupied territories, I continued, and now I regarded it as our duty to guard the foundations of civilized life in our own country also. "All those overzealous people who refuse to understand this need must be punished with the utmost severity. For," I went on, using the characteristically bombastic language of the time, "they are sinning against the most sacred possession of the German people: the source of our nation's vitality."

I paid lip service to the theory of recovering the lost territory, then dwelt a bit on the phrase "transportation wasteland," which our chief of transportation had used: "The people must do everything in their power to make sure such plans are thwarted. If we act prudently and with common sense in this emergency, supplies can be made to last until the next harvest."

I finished my reading. Equably and stoically, Milch commented: "The meaning comes out clearly, but the Gestapo will see it too."

On April 11 the radio recording truck was already at the door of the Ministry and workmen were laying cable in my office when a telephone call reached me: "Come to the Fuehrer and bring the text of the speech with you."

I had prepared a special version for the press which blurred the strongest statements,[1] although I fully intended to read the original text aloud. I took the less dangerous version with me. Hitler was sitting in his bunker office having tea with one of his secretaries. A third cup was brought for me. It was a long time since I had sat opposite him and seen him in so intimate and relaxed a mood. He ceremonially adjusted his thin metal-framed glasses, which gave him the look of a schoolteacher, took a pencil, and after the first few pages began cutting whole paragraphs. Refraining from any discussion, he occasionally remarked in a quite friendly tone: "Let's leave that out," or, "But this passage is superfluous." His secretary freely picked up the pages Hitler laid aside. She read them through and remarked regretfully: "A pity, such a nice speech." Hitler dismissed me amiably, with what sounded like a piece of very friendly advice: "Do make a new draft."*

In the cut version the speech had lost all point. And unless I had Hitler's approval I could not use the broadcasting facilities of the Reich network. Since Naumann, too, did not mention the matter again, I let it be forgotten.

In December 1944 the Berlin Philharmonic Orchestra gave its last concert of the year. Wilhelm Furtwängler had invited me to come to the conductor's room. With disarming unworldliness he asked me straight out whether we had any prospect of winning the war. When I replied that the end was imminent, Furtwängler nodded; he had come to the same conclusion. I felt he was in danger, since Bormann, Goebbels, and Himmler had not forgotten many of his frank remarks as well as his defense of the blacklisted composer Hindemith, and I advised him not to return from an

* Saur told me during our imprisonment in Nuremberg that Hitler had said at the time: "Speer is still the best of them all."

impending concert tour in Switzerland. "But what is going to become of my orchestra?" he exclaimed. "I'm responsible for it." I promised to look after the musicians during the coming months.

Early in April 1945, Gerhart von Westermann, the general manager of the Philharmonic, informed me that on Goebbels's orders the members of the orchestra were to be conscripted in the last call-up for the defense of Berlin. I telephoned Goebbels and gave all the reasons why the musicians should not be drafted into the People's Militia. The Propaganda Minister reproved me sharply: "I alone raised this orchestra to its special level. My initiative and my money made it what it has become, what it represents to the world today. Those who come after have no right to it. It can go under along with us."

Remembering the system Hitler had used at the beginning of the war to save favored artists from being drafted, I had Colonel von Poser go to the draft boards and destroy the papers of the Philharmonic musicians. In order to give the orchestra financial support as well, my Ministry arranged a few concerts.

"When Bruckner's *Romantic Symphony* is played, it will mean the end is upon us," I told my friends. That final concert took place on the afternoon of April 12, 1945. The Philharmonic Hall was unheated and everyone who wanted to hear this last concert in the imperiled city sat huddled in overcoats. Electricity was usually cut off at the hour of the concert, but for this one day I ordered the current to be kept on so that the hall could be lighted. The Berliners must have wondered. For the beginning I had ordered Brünnhilde's last aria and the finale from *Götterdämmerung*—a rather bathetic and also melancholy gesture pointing to the end of the Reich. After Beethoven's violin concerto came the Bruckner symphony, dear to me especially for its architectonic final movement. That was the last music I would hear for a long time to come.

When I returned to the Ministry, I found a message from the office of the Fuehrer's adjutant to telephone at once. "Where in the world have you been? The Fuehrer has been waiting for you."

When I arrived in the bunker, Hitler caught sight of me and rushed toward me with a degree of animation rare in him these days. He held a newspaper clipping in his hand. "Here, read it! Here! You never wanted to believe it. Here it is!" His words came in a great rush. "Here we have the miracle I always predicted. Who was right? The war isn't lost. Read it! Roosevelt is dead!"

He could not calm down. He thought this was proof of the infallible Providence watching over him. Goebbels and many others were bubbling over with delight as they exclaimed how right he had been in his reiterated conviction that the tide would turn. Now history was repeating itself, just as history had given a hopelessly beaten Frederick the Great victory at the last moment. The miracle of the House of Brandenburg!

Once again the Tsarina had died, the historic turning point had come, Goebbels repeated again and again and again. For a moment this scene stripped the veil from the deceitful optimism of the past several months. Later on, Hitler sat exhausted, looking both liberated and dazed as he slumped in his armchair. But I sensed that he was still without hope.

Innumerable fantasies burgeoned in the wake of the news of Roosevelt's death. A few days later Goebbels suggested to me that since I had so much credit in the bourgeois West, what would I think of using one of our long-range planes to fly to meet Truman, the new American President? But such ideas vanished as rapidly as they cropped up.

On yet another of these early days of April, I happened into Bismarck's former sitting room and found Dr. Ley surrounded by a sizable group, among them Schaub and Bormann, several adjutants and orderlies. Ley came rushing toward me with the news: "Death rays have been invented! A simple apparatus that we can produce in large quantities. I've studied the documentation; there's no doubt about it. This will be the decisive weapon!" With Bormann nodding confirmation, Ley went on, stuttering as always, to find fault with me: "But of course your Ministry rejected the inventor. Fortunately for us he wrote to me. But now you personally must get this project going. Immediately. At this moment there's nothing more important."

Ley went on to rail at the inadequacy of my organization, which he said was calcified and overbureaucratized. The whole thing was so absurd that I did not bother to contradict him. "You're absolutely right," I said. "Why don't you take it over personally? I'll be glad to give you all the powers you'll need as 'Commissioner for Death Rays.'"

Ley was delighted with this proposal. "Of course. I'll take charge of it. In this matter I'll even be glad to act as your subordinate. After all, I started as a chemist."

I suggested an experiment, recommending that he use his own rabbits; all too often results were faked by using doctored animals, I said. A few days later I actually received a telephone call from Ley's adjutant. He gave me a list of electrical equipment needed for the experiment.

We decided to carry on with this farce. My friend Lüschen, the head of our entire electrical industry, was told the story and asked to hunt up the devices the inventor wanted. He soon returned and informed me: "I was able to supply everything except one circuit breaker. We don't have any with the particular circuit-breaking speed requested. But the 'inventor' insists on this particular item. You know," Lüschen continued, laughing, "you won't guess what I've found out. This particular circuit breaker has not been made for about forty years. It's mentioned in an old edition of the *Graetz* [a physics textbook for secondary schools] from around 1900."

Such wild notions flourished as the enemy approached. In all seriousness Ley also advanced the following theory: "When the Russians overrun us from the east, the torrent of German refugees will be so heavy that it will press upon the West like a migration of the nations, break through, flood the West and then take possession." Even Hitler mocked such crackpot theories on the part of his labor leader, but during that last period he liked to have Ley close at hand.

In the first half of the month of April, Eva Braun unexpectedly and unbidden arrived in Berlin and declared that she would not leave Hitler's side again. Hitler urged her to return to Munich, and I too offered her a seat in our courier plane. But she obstinately refused, and everyone in the bunker knew why she had come. Figuratively and in reality, with her presence a messenger of death moved into the bunker.

Hitler's physician, Dr. Brandt, a permanent member of the Obersalzberg circle since 1934, had left his wife and child in Thuringia to be "rolled over"—as the phrase of the day had it—by the Americans. Hitler appointed a summary court-martial, the judges to consist of Goebbels, the youth leader Axmann, and SS General Berger. But Hitler dominated the case, acting both as prosecutor and supreme authority wrapped into one, as it were; he demanded the death penalty and formulated the charges against Brandt: that Brandt had known he could have brought his family safely to Obersalzberg. In addition there was suspicion that he had sent secret documents to the Americans, using his wife as courier. Hitler's chief secretary of many years burst into tears. "I no longer understand him," she said of Hitler. Himmler came to the bunker and reassured the troubled entourage. Before the court-martial could take place an important witness had to be interrogated, he told us, and added slyly: "This witness is not going to be found."

This incident had placed me in an embarrassing situation also, for on April 6 I had moved my family to an estate in the vicinity of Kappeln in Holstein, far from big cities on the Baltic.* Now that had suddenly become a crime. When Hitler had Eva Braun ask me where my family was, I lied, saying that they were on a friend's estate in the vicinity of Berlin. This satisfied Hitler, but he wanted me to promise that we too would go to Obersalzberg when he retreated there. At that time he still intended to lead the final struggle in the so-called Alpine Redoubt.

Even if Hitler left Berlin, Goebbels declared, he wanted to meet his end in Berlin. "My wife and my children are not to survive me. The Americans would only coach them to make propaganda against me." But when

---

* The plan for the division of Germany was known by now. Holstein had been assigned to the British. I was certain that the British would behave fairly to the families of prominent Nazis. Also, the estate was situated in the command sector assigned to Doenitz, whom I planned to join when the end was upon us.

I visited Frau Goebbels in Schwanenwerder in the middle of April, I learned that she could not face the thought that her children were to die. Nevertheless she apparently gave in to her husband's decision. A few days later I proposed to her that at the last moment a barge of our transport fleet be tied up at night at the landing stage of the Goebbels property in Schwanenwerder. She and the children could hide below deck until the barge had been moved to a tributary on the western side of the Elbe. We would supply food enough so that she could remain there for some time undiscovered.

After Hitler had stated that he would not survive a defeat, many of his closest associates vied with each other in protesting that there would be nothing left for them but suicide too. But I felt that they had a moral duty to face trial by the enemy. Two of the most successful air force officers, Baumbach and Galland, worked with me during the last days of the war developing a weird plan for laying hands on the most important members of Hitler's entourage and preventing them from committing suicide. Every evening, we had discovered, Bormann, Ley, and Himmler drove out of Berlin to various suburban villages that were spared air raids. Our plan was simple: When the enemy night bombers dropped white parachute flares, every car stopped and the passengers fled into the fields. Flares fired by signal pistols would undoubtedly produce similar reactions. Then a troop of soldiers armed with submachine guns would overpower the six-man escort squads.

Flares were actually brought to my home, the selection of soldiers discussed, details considered. In the general confusion it would have been possible to bring the arrested men to a secure place. To my surprise Dr. Hupfauer, Ley's former chief assistant, insisted that the coup against Bormann be carried out by party members seasoned by experience at the front. No one in the party was so hated as Bormann, Hupfauer said; Gauleiter Kaufmann was claiming the privilege of personally killing "the Fuehrer's Mephistopheles."

But after hearing about these fantastic schemes of ours, General Thomale, chief of staff of the Armored Forces, convinced me in a nocturnal conversation on the open road that it was not for us to intervene in the judgment of God.

Meanwhile, Bormann was pursuing his own schemes. After Brandt was arrested, I was warned by State Secretary Klopfer that the arrest had been engineered by Bormann and that it was also meant as a blow against me. Bormann evidently thought—quite wrongly, by the way—that Brandt was the chief mainstay of my influence with Hitler. Klopfer suggested that I be very careful about making any careless remarks.[2]

The enemy radio also broadcast several news items that worried me. One story was that I had helped a nephew of mine, who had been sentenced by a court-martial for reading some of Lenin's writings, to regain his freedom.[3] Another report said that my associate Karl Hettlage, who had always been in bad grace with the party, was on the verge of arrest. And a Swiss newspaper was supposed to have claimed that von Brauchitsch, the former Commander in Chief of the army, and I were the only people with whom the Allies could deal on the terms of a surrender. Perhaps the enemy was deliberately spreading such reports to produce dissension in the leadership; perhaps they were rumors.

During these days of disintegration the army quietly assigned me several reliable frontline officers armed with submachine guns who took up quarters in my home. For emergencies they had an eight-wheeled armored reconnaissance vehicle ready, with which we could presumably have escaped from Berlin. To this day I have never learned on whose orders or on the basis of what information this was done.

The assault on Berlin was imminent. Hitler had already appointed General Reymann to be commandant of the city for the battle. At first Reymann remained subordinate to General Heinrici, the Commander in Chief of the army group which extended from the Baltic Sea along the Oder River to about sixty miles south of Frankfurt an der Oder. Heinrici was a man I trusted, for I had known him a long time and only recently he had helped me to surrender the industry of the Rybnicker coal basin intact. So when Reymann insisted on preparing every bridge in Berlin for demolition, I drove to Heinrici's headquarters near Prenzlau. That was on April 15, one day before the beginning of the great Russian offensive against Berlin. For technical reinforcement I brought with me the Berlin municipal superintendent of roads, Langer, and the Berlin chief of the Reichsbahn, Beck. At my request Heinrici ordered Reymann to attend the conference.

The two technicians demonstrated that the planned demolitions would mean the death of Berlin.[4] The commandant of the city referred to Hitler's orders to defend Berlin by every possible expedient. "I must fight, and therefore I must be able to destroy bridges."

"But only in the direction of the main blow?" Heinrici interjected.

"No, wherever there is fighting," General Reymann said.

I asked whether all the bridges in the center of the city were also to be destroyed if the fighting came down to street battles. Reymann said yes. This was the moment for some platonic reasoning. I had it down to a pattern by now. "Are you going to fight because you believe in victory?" I asked.

The general was taken aback for a moment; then he had no choice but to answer this question affirmatively.

"If Berlin is thoroughly destroyed," I said, "then industry will be wiped out for the foreseeable future. And without industry the war is lost."

General Reymann was in a quandary. He did not know what to do Fortunately, General Heinrici came to the rescue with specific orders. The explosives were to be removed from the blasting charges on the vital arteries of the Berlin railroad and highway network. Bridges would be blown up only in the actual course of important military actions.*

After our associates had left, Heinrici turned to me again and said privately: "These instructions will assure that no bridges will be destroyed in Berlin. For there will not be any battle for Berlin. If the Russians break through to Berlin, one of our wings will pull out to the north and the other to the south. In the north, we'll base our defense line on the east-west canal systems. But I'm afraid that the bridges there will have to go."

I understood. "Then Berlin will be taken quickly?"

The general agreed. "At least without much resistance."

The next morning, April 16, I was awakened very early. Lieutenant Colonel von Poser and I wanted to post ourselves on a height above Oder-bruch near Wriezen to watch the last decisive offensive of this war, the Soviet assault on Berlin. But dense fog prevented us from seeing anything. After a few hours a forester brought us word that all the troops were re-treating and that the Russians would soon be here. So we retreated also.

We passed by the great ship elevator of Nieder-Finow, a technical marvel of the thirties and the key to shipping from the Oder to Berlin. Everywhere along the hundred and twenty foot high iron framework demolition charges had been skillfully placed. We could already hear ar-tillery fire some distance away. A lieutenant of the Engineers reported that all preparations for demolition had been completed. Here people were still acting on Hitler's demolition order of March 19, and there was considerable relief at von Poser's last-moment instructions to the contrary. But we felt rather discouraged, for obviously the order of April 3, 1945, to leave waterways intact had not reached all the troops.

With the communications network going to pieces, it seemed hope-less to send out new instructions via teletype. But General Heinrici's sym-pathy with my views prompted me to return to my plan of appealing directly to the public and trying to recall people to reason. Amid the con-fusion of the battles, I hoped, Heinrici would be able to place at my dis-posal one of the radio stations within the territory of his army group.

After driving on another twenty miles Poser and I found ourselves in Goering's animal paradise, the lonely woods of Schorfheide. I dismissed my escort, sat down on the stump of a tree, and drafted a rebel's speech which I wrote out at one swoop. Only five days ago Hitler had censored my official speech to such an extent that it was no longer worth giving.

---

* Of nine hundred and fifty bridges in Berlin, eighty-four were destroyed. Un-doubtedly this favorable result was due in part to Heinrici's attitude. In addition, two of my associates, Langer and Kumpf, undertook to disrupt the demolition of bridges even during battles.

This time I wanted to issue a call for resistance, to bluntly forbid any damage to factories, bridges, waterways, railroads, and communications, and to instruct the soldiers of the Wehrmacht and the militia to prevent demolitions "with all possible means, if necessary by the use of firearms." The speech also called for surrendering political prisoners, which included the Jews, unharmed to the occupying troops, and stipulated that prisoners of war and foreign workers not be prevented from making their way back to their native lands. It prohibited Werewolf* activity and appealed to cities and villages to surrender without a fight. Once again I concluded with rather excessive solemnity that we believe "unshakably in the future of our nation, which will remain forever and always."[5]

I had Poser carry a hasty note scribbled in pencil to Dr. Richard Fischer, general manager of the Berlin Electricity Works, to make sure that the supply of current to the most powerful of the German radio stations, in Königswusterhausen, would be continued until it was taken by the enemy.[6] That station, which was regularly broadcasting the Werewolf messages, was as its last act supposed to broadcast my speech issuing a ban against Werewolf activities.

Late that evening I met General Heinrici again; he had meanwhile moved his headquarters back to Dammsmühl. There would be a brief period in which the radio station belonged to the "battle zone" and thus would have passed from government authority to that of the army—this was the time for me to give my speech. Heinrici, however, thought that the station would be occupied by the Russians before I finished talking. He proposed that I record the speech on a phonograph record and leave it with him. He would have it broadcast just before the Soviet troops reached the station. But in spite of all Lüschen's efforts, no suitable recording apparatus could be located.

Two days later Gauleiter Kaufmann sent me an urgent message to come to Hamburg; the navy was preparing to demolish the port installations. At a conference in which the chief representatives of industry, the shipyards, the port authorities, and the navy participated, the Gauleiter made so good a case for preservation that the decision was taken to destroy nothing.[7] In a house along the Aussenalster, I continued my conference with Kaufmann alone. Well-armed students had assumed the task of guarding him. "It would be best for you to stay here in Hamburg with us," the Gauleiter urged me. "Here you're safe. We can depend on my men in any emergency."

Nevertheless I drove back to Berlin and reminded Hitler that he,

---

* "Werewolves" were supposed to be guerrilla fighters who would put up last-ditch resistance to the Allied forces in all parts of Germany. The Allies took this threat seriously, but after the war ended the Werewolves proved to be only another fictional creation of the Goebbels propaganda machine. No such resistance ever appeared. —*Translators' note.*

who had gone down in the party's history as the "conqueror of Berlin," would lose his reputation if he now ended his life as the destroyer of this city. Ludicrous though this remark may sound, it fitted into the framework of ideas that we all shared at the time, particularly Goebbels, for he believed that he would heighten his posthumous fame by committing suicide.

We had a situation conference on the evening of April 19. Hitler said that he was acceding to a proposal of Gauleiter Goebbels that all reserves would be committed to fighting the decisive battle outside the capital itself, though at the very gates of Berlin.

32

Annihilation

———

In the last weeks of his life, Hitler seemed to have broken out of the rigidity which had gradually overcome him during the preceding years. He became more accessible again and could even tolerate the expression of dissent. As late as the winter of 1944, it would have been inconceivable for him to enter into a discussion of the prospects of the war with me. Then, too, his flexibility on the question of the scorched earth policy would have been unthinkable, or the quiet way he went over my radio speech. He was once more open to arguments he would not have listened to a year ago. But this greater softness sprang not from a relaxation of tension. Rather, it was dissolution. He gave the impression of a man whose whole purpose had been destroyed, who was continuing along his established orbit only because of the kinetic energy stored within him. Actually, he had let go of the controls and was resigned to what might come.

There was actually something insubstantial about him. But this was perhaps a permanent quality he had. In retrospect I sometimes ask myself whether this intangibility, this insubstantiality, had not characterized him from early youth up to the moment of his suicide. It sometimes seems to me that his seizures of violence could come upon him all the more strongly because there were no human emotions in him to oppose them. He simply could not let anyone approach his inner being because that core was lifeless, empty.

Now, he was shriveling up like an old man. His limbs trembled; he walked stooped, with dragging footsteps. Even his voice became quavering and lost its old masterfulness. Its force had given way to a faltering, toneless manner of speaking. When he became excited, as he frequently did in a senile way, his voice would start breaking. He still had his fits of obstinacy, but they no longer reminded one of a child's temper tantrums, but of an old man's. His complexion was sallow, his face swollen; his uniform, which in the past he had kept scrupulously neat, was often neglected in this last period of life and stained by the food he had eaten with a shaking hand.

This condition undoubtedly touched his entourage, who had been at his side during the triumphs of his life. I too was constantly tempted to pity him, so reduced was he from the Hitler of the past. Perhaps that was the reason everyone would listen to him in silence when, in the long since hopeless situation, he continued to commit nonexistent divisions or to order units supplied by planes that could no longer fly for lack of fuel. Perhaps that was why no one said a word when he more and more frequently took flight from reality and entered his world of fantasy, when he spoke of the clash between East and West which must be on the point of erupting—when he bade us realize that it was inevitable. Although the entourage could scarcely have been blind to the phantasmal character of these ideas, his constant repetitions had some sort of hypnotic effect—as when, for example, he claimed he was now in a position to conquer Bolshevism by the strength of his own personality and in alliance with the West. It sounded believable when he assured us that he was continuing to live only for this turning point, that he personally wished his last hour had come. The very composure with which he looked forward to the end intensified sympathy and commanded respect.

In addition he had again become more amiable and more willing to drop into his private mood. In many ways he reminded me of the Hitler I had known at the beginning of our association twelve years before, except that he now seemed more shadowy. He centered his amiability on the few women who had been with him for years. For a long time he had shown special liking for Frau Junge, the widow of his servant who had been killed at the front; but he also favored his Viennese diet cook. His longtime secretaries, Frau Wolf and Frau Christian, also formed part of this private circle during the last weeks of his life. For months now he had shown a preference for taking his teas and meals with them. Scarcely any men still belonged among his intimates. I too had long since ceased to be invited to his table. The arrival of Eva Braun also introduced a number of changes in his habits, although it did not put a stop to his probably innocent relations with the other women about him. He must have been motivated by some simple belief that women were more loyal in misfortune than men could be. Indeed, he sometimes seemed to distrust the show of faith by the men of his staff. The exceptions were Bormann, Goebbels, and Ley, whom he seemed still to be sure of.

Around this shadowy Hitler the apparatus of command continued to run mechanically. Apparently there was still some momentum here which went on operating even when the motor was running down. This residual force seemed to keep the generals moving along the same track even at the very end, when the radiations of Hitler's will were beginning to weaken. Keitel, for example, continued to press for the destruction of bridges even when Hitler was now willing to spare them.

Hitler must have noticed that the discipline in his entourage was also slackening. Formerly, whenever he had entered a room everybody had risen until he sat down. Now conversations continued, people remained seated, servants took their orders from guests, associates who had drunk too much went to sleep in their chairs, and others talked loudly and uninhibitedly. Perhaps he deliberately overlooked such changes. These scenes affected me like a bad dream. They corresponded to the changes which had been taking place for several months in the Chancellor's residence: The tapestries had been removed, the paintings taken down from the walls, the carpets rolled up, and valuable pieces of furniture had been stowed away in an air-raid shelter. Stains on the wallpaper, gaps in the furnishings, scattered newspapers, empty glasses and plates, a hat that someone had tossed on a chair, added up to an impression of a place in the midst of moving day.

For some time Hitler had abandoned the upper rooms. He claimed that the constant air raids disturbed his sleep and interfered with his ability to work. In the bunker he could at least get some sleep, he said. And so he had converted to an underground life.

This withdrawal into his future tomb had, for me, a symbolic significance as well. The isolation of this bunker world, encased on all sides by concrete and earth, put the final seal on Hitler's separation from the tragedy which was going on outside under the open sky. He no longer had any relationship to it. When he talked about the end, he meant his own and not that of the nation. He had reached the last station in his flight from reality, a reality which he had refused to acknowledge since his youth. At the time I had a name for this unreal world of the bunker: I called it the Isle of the Departed.

Even during this last period of his life, in April 1945, I still occasionally sat with Hitler in the bunker bent over the building plans for Linz, mutely contemplating the dreams of yesteryear. His study roofed with more than sixteen feet of concrete, then topped with six feet of earth, was undoubtedly the safest place in Berlin. When heavy bombs exploded in the vicinity this massive bunker shook, as it fortunately passed the shock waves on to the sandy soil of Berlin. Hitler would give a start. What had become of the formerly fearless corporal of the First World War? He was now a wreck, a bundle of nerves who could no longer conceal his reactions.

Hitler's last birthday was not actually celebrated. Formerly on this day lines of cars had driven up, the honor guard had presented arms, dignitaries of the Reich and of foreign countries had offered their congratulations. Now all was quiet. For the occasion Hitler had, it is true, moved from the bunker to the upper rooms, which in their state of neglect provided a fitting framework to his own lamentable condition. A delegation of Hitler Youth who had fought well was presented to him in the garden. Hitler spoke a few words, patted one or another of the boys. His voice was low. He broke off rather abruptly. Probably he sensed that his only convincing role now was as an object of pity. Most of his entourage avoided the embarrassment of a celebration by coming to the military situation conference as usual. No one knew quite what to say. Hitler received the expressions of good wishes coolly and almost unwillingly, in keeping with the circumstances.

Shortly afterward we were standing, as we had done so often, in the confined space of the bunker, around the situation map. Hitler had taken his seat facing Goering. The latter, who always made such a point of his attire, had changed his uniform quite remarkably in the past few days. To our surprise the silver-gray cloth had been replaced by the olive-drab of the American uniform. Along with this his two-inch wide gold-braided epaulets had given way to simple cloth shoulder strips to which his badge of rank, the golden Reich Marshal's eagle, was simply pinned. "Like an American general," one of the participants in the conference whispered to me. But Hitler seemed not to notice even this change.

The impending attack on the center of Berlin was being discussed. The night before the idea had been bandied about of not defending the metropolis and, instead, transferring to the Alpine Redoubt. But overnight, Hitler had decided to fight for the city in the streets of Berlin. At once everyone began clamoring that it was essential to shift the headquarters to Obersalzberg, and that now was the last moment remaining.

Goering pointed out that only a single north-south route through the Bavarian Forest was still in our possession and that the last escape route to Berchtesgaden might be cut off at any time. Hitler became indignant. "How can I call on the troops to undertake the decisive battle for Berlin if at the same moment I myself withdraw to safety!" Goering in his new uniform sat pale and sweating opposite him, his eyes wide, as Hitler talked on, whipping himself up by his own rhetoric: "I shall leave it to fate whether I die in the capital or fly to Obersalzberg at the last moment!"

As soon as the situation conference was over and the generals dismissed, Goering turned to Hitler, utterly distraught. He had urgent tasks awaiting him in South Germany, he said; he would have to leave Berlin this very night. Hitler gazed absently at him. It seemed to me that he was deeply moved by his decision to remain in Berlin and stake his life on the outcome. With a few indifferent words, he shook hands with Goering, giving no sign that he saw through him. I was standing only a few feet away from the two and had a sense of being present at a historic moment: The leadership of the Reich was splitting asunder. With that, the birthday situation conference ended.

Along with the other participants in the conference I had left the room in the usual informal way, without bidding good-by to Hitler personally. Ignoring our original intention, Lieutenant Colonel von Poser urged me to leave that very night. The Soviet army had launched the final attack on Berlin and was obviously advancing swiftly. For days all the preparations for our flight had been made; important baggage had been sent on ahead to Hamburg and two mobile homes belonging to the construction section of the Reichsbahn had been set up at Eutin Lake, near Doenitz's headquarters in Plön.

In Hamburg, I once again visited Gauleiter Kaufmann. Like me, he found it beyond understanding that the struggle was being continued at all costs in this situation. Encouraged by these remarks, I gave him the draft of the speech I had written the week before, sitting on that tree stump. I was not sure how he would take it. "You ought to deliver this speech. Why haven't you done so yet?"

After I had explained the difficulties, he suggested: "Won't you give it on our Hamburg station? I can vouch for the technical head of our radio station. At least you can have the speech recorded at the station."[1]

That same night Kaufmann took me to the bunker in which the technical staff of the Hamburg station had set up their headquarters. After passing through deserted rooms to a small recording studio, he introduced me to two sound engineers who obviously already knew what I was up to. The thought shot through my head that within a few minutes I would be completely at the mercy of these total strangers. In order to cover myself and perhaps win their complicity, I told them before beginning the speech that afterward they could decide whether they agreed with what I said or whether they wanted to destroy the disks. Then I sat down in front of the microphone and read my speech from the manuscript. The engineers said nothing; perhaps they were frightened, perhaps convinced by my words, though not to the point of declaring themselves on the matter. At any rate they raised no objections.

Kaufmann took the records. I told him the conditions under which he could broadcast this speech without authorization from me. Those conditions throw light on my state of mind in those last days of the Third Reich: If I were murdered at the instigation of political enemies, among whom I chiefly counted Bormann; if Hitler heard of my actions and condemned me to death; if Hitler were dead and his successor continued his desperate policy of annihilation.

Since General Heinrici did not intend to defend Berlin, the capture of the city and the end of the regime seemed likely within a few days. In fact Hitler, as I was informed by SS General Berger[2] and also by Eva Braun, had wanted to take his own life on April 22. But Heinrici had meanwhile been replaced by General Student, commander of the parachute troops. Hitler regarded him as one of his most energetic officers and felt he could depend upon him all the more in this situation because he thought the man was rather stupid. This change in personnel alone revived his courage. Simultaneously, Keitel and Jodl were commanded to throw all available divisions into the fight for Berlin.

At this point I myself had no work; the armaments industry no longer existed. Nevertheless I was driven about by an intense inner restlessness. For no good reason at all I decided to spend the night on the estate near Wilsnack where I had spent so many weekends with my family. There I met one of Dr. Brandt's assistants. He told me that Hitler's doctor was now being held prisoner in a villa in a western suburb of Berlin. He described the place, gave me the telephone number, and mentioned that the SS guards were not so very forbidding. We discussed whether I might be able to liberate Brandt in the confusion that must now be gripping Berlin. But I also wanted to see Lüschen again. I wanted to persuade him to flee from the Russians, to the West.

These were the reasons that took me to Berlin for the last time. But the far more powerful magnet behind these reasons was Hitler. I wanted to see him one last time, to tell him good-by. Now I felt as if I had stolen away two days before. Was that to be the end of our many years of association? For many days, month after month, we had sat together over our joint plans, almost like co-workers and friends. For many years he had received my family and me at Obersalzberg and had shown himself a friendly, often solicitous host.

The overpowering desire to see him once more betrays the ambivalence of my feelings. For rationally I was convinced that it was urgently necessary, although already much too late, for Hitler's life to come to an end. Underlying everything I had done to oppose him in the past months had been the desire to prevent the annihilation that Hitler seemed bent on. What could be greater proof of our antithetical aims than the speech I had recorded the day before, and the fact that I was now awaiting his death impatiently? And yet that very expectation brought out once again my emotional bond to Hitler. My wish to have the speech broadcast only after his death sprang from the desire to spare him the knowledge that I too had turned against him. My feelings of pity for the fallen ruler were growing stronger and stronger. Perhaps many of Hitler's followers had similar emotions during these last days. On the one hand there was sense of duty, oath of allegiance, loyalty, gratitude—on the other hand the bitterness at personal tragedy and national disaster—both centered around one person: Hitler.

To this day I am glad that I succeeded in carrying out my intention to see Hitler one last time. It was right, after twelve years of association, to make this gesture in spite of all antagonisms. At the time, it is true, I acted under an almost mechanical compulsion when I set out from Wilsnack. Before my departure I wrote my wife a few lines both to encourage her and to let her know that I did not intend to join Hitler in death. About fifty-five miles from Berlin a stream of vehicles heading toward Hamburg blocked the entire road: jalopies and limousines, trucks and delivery vans, motorcycles, and even Berlin fire trucks. It was impossible to thrust on in the face of these tens of thousands of vehicles. It was a mystery to me where all the fuel had suddenly come from. Probably it had been hoarded for months for just this crisis.

There was a divisional staff in Kyritz. From there I telephoned the villa in Berlin where Dr. Brandt was being held prisoner, awaiting execution of the death sentence. But on special orders from Himmler, however, he had already been moved to northern Germany. I could not reach Lüschen either. Nevertheless, I did not change my decision, but briefly informed one of Hitler's adjutants of the possibility that I would be coming that same afternoon. At divisional staff headquarters I had learned that the Soviet forces were advancing rapidly, but that encirclement of Berlin was not expected for a while; the airport of Gatow on the bank of the Havel might remain in the possession of our troops for some time. Therefore Poser and I went to the large Rechlin Airport in Mecklenburg, which was used for testing planes. Here I was well known, for I had been present at many flight tests, and could count on having a plane placed at my disposal. From this airfield fighter planes were starting out for low-level attacks on the Soviet troops south of Potsdam. The commandant was willing to have me taken in a training plane to Gatow, where two Storks, single-motored reconnaissance planes with low landing speed, would be held in readiness for the second lap of our journey. While last-minute preparations were made, I studied the positions of the Russian forces on the maps at staff headquarters.

Escorted by a squadron of fighter planes, we flew southward at an altitude of somewhat over three thousand feet a few miles from the battle zone. Visibility was perfect. From above, the battle for the capital of the Reich looked innocuous. After an unmolested century and a half Berlin was once more being conquered by enemy troops—but it all seemed to be taking place in an uncannily peaceful landscape whose roads, villages, and small towns I knew so well from innumerable drives. All that could be seen were brief, inconspicuous flashes from artillery or exploding shells, looking no more impressive than the flare of a match, and burning farm buildings. But on the eastern boundary of Berlin, far off in mist, larger billows of smoke could be discerned. The roar of the motor drowned out the distant noises of battle.

The escort squadron flew on to attack ground targets south of Potsdam, while we landed in Gatow. The airfield was almost deserted. Only General Christian, who as Jodl's assistant belonged to Hitler's staff, was getting ready to leave by plane. We exchanged a few trivial phrases. Then I and my escort entered the two Storks—enjoying the sense of adventure, for we could also have driven by car—and skimmed over the same route which I had driven with Hitler on the eve of his fiftieth birthday. To the surprise of the few drivers on the broad avenue, we landed just in front of the Brandenburg Gate. We stopped an army vehicle and had it drive us to the Chancellery. By this time it was late afternoon; it had taken some ten hours to cover the hundred miles between Wilsnack and Berlin.

It was not at all clear to me if I was running a risk in meeting with Hitler. Moody as he was, I had no idea how he might feel toward me after these two days. But in a sense I no longer cared. Of course I hoped the encounter would turn out all right, but I had also to take a bad outcome into consideration.

The Chancellery which I had built seven years before was already under fire from heavy Soviet artillery, but as yet direct hits were relatively rare. The effect of these shells seemed insignificant compared to the rubble that a few American daylight air raids had made of my building during the past few weeks. I climbed over a hurdle of burned beams, walked under collapsing ceilings, and came to the sitting room in which, a few years ago, our evenings had dragged on, where Bismarck had held social gatherings and where Hitler's adjutant Schaub was now drinking brandy, in the company of a few people, few of whom I knew. In spite of my telephone call they had ceased expecting me and were astonished to see me turn up. Schaub's cordial welcome was reassuring and seemed to indicate that no one at headquarters knew anything about my Hamburg recording. Then Schaub left us to announce my arrival. Meanwhile, I asked Lieutenant Colonel von Poser to enlist the aid of the Chancellery telephone switchboard to locate Lüschen and ask him to come to the Chancellery.

Hitler's adjutant returned: "The Fuehrer is ready to see you." How often in the past twelve years had I been ushered into Hitler's presence with these words. But I was not thinking of that as I descended the fifty-odd steps into the bunker, but if I would be ascending them with a whole skin. The first person I met below was Bormann. He came forward to meet me with such unwonted politeness that I began feeling more secure. For Bormann's or Schaub's expressions had always been reliable guides to Hit-

ler's mood. Humbly, he said to me: "When you speak with the Fuehrer . . .
he'll certainly raise the question of whether we ought to stay in Berlin
or fly to Berchtesgaden. But it's high time he took over the command in
South Germany. . . . These are the last hours when it will be possible.
. . . You'll persuade him to fly out, won't you?"

If there were anyone in the bunker attached to his life, it was obviously Bormann, who only three weeks earlier had enjoined the functionaries of the party to overcome all weaknesses, to win the victory or die
at their posts.[3] I gave a noncommittal reply, feeling a belated sense of
triumph at his almost imploring manner.

Then I was led into Hitler's room in the bunker. In his welcome there
was no sign of the warmth with which he had responded a few weeks
before to my vow of loyalty. He showed no emotion at all. Once again
I had the feeling that he was empty, burned out, lifeless. He assumed
that businesslike expression which could be a mask for anything and asked
me what I thought about Doenitz's approach to his job. I had the distinct
feeling that he was not asking about Doenitz by chance, but that the question involved his successor. And to this day I think that Doenitz liquidated
the hopeless legacy that unexpectedly became his lot with more prudence,
dignity, and responsibility than Bormann or Himmler would have done.
I voiced my favorable impression of the admiral, now and then enriching
my account with anecdotes which I knew would please Hitler. But with
the wisdom of long experience I did not try to influence him in Doenitz's
favor, for fear that this would drive him in the opposite direction.

Abruptly, Hitler asked me: "What do you think? Should I stay here
or fly to Berchtesgaden? Jodl has told me that tomorrow is the last chance
for that."

Spontaneously, I advised him to stay in Berlin. What would he do
at Obersalzberg? With Berlin gone, the war would be over in any case,
I said. "It seems to me better, if it must be, that you end your life here in
the capital as the Fuehrer rather than in your weekend house."

Once more I was deeply moved. At the time I thought that was a
piece of good advice. Actually it was bad, for if he had flown to Obersalzberg the battle for Berlin would probably have been shortened by a
week.

That day he said nothing more of an imminent turning point or that
there was still hope. Rather apathetically, wearily and as if it were already a matter of course, he began speaking of his death: "I too have
resolved to stay here. I only wanted to hear your view once more." Without excitement, he continued: "I shall not fight personally. There is always the danger that I would only be wounded and fall into the hands
of the Russians alive. I don't want my enemies to disgrace my body
either. I've given orders that I be cremated. Fräulein Braun wants to depart this life with me, and I'll shoot Blondi beforehand. Believe me,

Speer, it is easy for me to end my life. A brief moment and I'm freed of everything, liberated from this painful existence."

I felt as if I had been talking with a man already departed. The atmosphere grew increasingly uncanny; the tragedy was approaching its end.

During the last months I had hated him at times, fought him, lied to him, and deceived him, but at this moment I was confused and emotionally shaken. In this state, I confessed to him in a low voice, to my own surprise, that I had not carried out any demolitions but had actually prevented them. For a moment his eyes filled with tears. But he did not react. Such questions, so important to him only a few weeks before, were now remote. Absently, he stared at me as I faltered out my offer to stay in Berlin. He did not answer. Perhaps he sensed that I did not mean it. I have often asked myself since whether he had not always known instinctively that I had been working against him during these past months and whether he had not deduced this from my memoranda; also whether by letting me act contrary to his orders he had not provided a fresh example of the multiple strata in his mysterious personality. I shall never know.

Just then General Krebs, the army chief of staff, was announced. He had come to give the situation report.* In that respect nothing had changed. The Commander in Chief of the armed forces was receiving the situation reports from the fronts as always. Only three days before the situation room in the bunker could hardly hold the crowd of high-ranking officers, commanders of various departments of the Wehrmacht and SS, but now almost all had left in the meantime. Along with Goering, Doenitz and Himmler, Keitel and Jodl, air force Chief of Staff Koller, and the most important officers of their staffs were now outside of Berlin. Only lower-ranking liaison officers had remained. And the nature of the report had changed. Nothing but vague scraps of news were coming from outside. The chief of staff could offer little more than conjectures. The map he spread out in front of Hitler covered only the area around Berlin and Potsdam. But even here the data on the status of the Soviet advance no longer corresponded with the observations I had made a few hours before. The Soviet troops had long since come closer than the map indicated.

To my astonishment, during the conference Hitler once again tried

---

* Krebs was acting for the "ill" Guderian. Hitler had officially assigned the supreme command of the armed forces to Keitel and limited himself to commanding the troops in Berlin. But I had the impression that he did not want to recognize this as a fact. Even as commander of Berlin, Hitler did not leave his bunker; he issued all his orders from his desk. Apparently this meeting on April 23 was what was called a "minor" situation conference, since neither the commandant of Berlin nor the other troop commanders attended.

to make a display of optimism, although he had only just finished talking with me about his impending death and the disposition of his body. On the other hand, he had lost much of his former persuasiveness. Krebs listened to him patiently and politely. Often in the past, when the situation was clearly desperate but Hitler continued undeterred to conjure up a favorable outcome, I had thought he was the captive of obsessional ideas. Now it became evident that he spoke two languages at once. How long had he been deceiving us? Since when had he realized that the struggle was lost: since the winter at the gates of Moscow, since Stalingrad, since the Allied invasion, since the Ardennes offensive of December 1944? How much was pretense, how much calculation? But perhaps it was merely that I had just witnessed another of his rapid changes of mood and that he was being as sincere with General Krebs as he had earlier been with me.

The situation conference, which ordinarily went on for hours, was quickly ended. Its very brevity revealed that this remnant of a headquarters was in its death throes. On this day Hitler even restrained from swooping us off into the dream world of providential miracles. We were dismissed with a few words and left the room in which so dreary a chapter of errors, omissions, and crimes had been played out. Hitler had treated me as an ordinary guest, as if I had not flown to Berlin especially for his sake. We parted without shaking hands, in the most casual manner, as if we would be seeing each other the next day.

Outside the room I met Goebbels. He announced: "Yesterday the Fuehrer took a decision of enormous importance. He has stopped the fighting in the West so that the Anglo-American troops can enter Berlin unhindered." Here again was one of those mirages which excited the minds of these men for a few hours and aroused new hopes which as quickly as they had come would be replaced by others.

Goebbels told me that his wife and six children were now living in the bunker as Hitler's guests, in order, as he put it, to end their lives at this historic site. In contrast to Hitler, he appeared to be in fullest control of his thoughts and emotions. He showed no sign of having settled his accounts with life.

By this time it was late afternoon. An SS doctor informed me that Frau Goebbels was in bed, very weak and suffering from heart attacks. I sent word to her asking her to receive me. I would have liked to talk to her alone, but Goebbels was already waiting in an anteroom and led me into the little chamber deep underground where she lay in a plain bed. She was pale and spoke only trivialities in a low voice, although I could sense that she was in deep agony over the irrevocably approaching hour when her children must die. Since Goebbels remained persistently at my side, our conversation was limited to the state of her health. Only as I was on the point of leaving did she hint at what she was really feeling: "How happy I am that at least Harald [her son by her first marriage] is alive." I too felt confined and could scarcely find words—but what could anyone say in this situation? We said good-by in awkward silence. Her husband had not allowed us even a few minutes alone for our farewell.

Meanwhile, there was a flurry of excitement in the vestibule. A telegram had arrived from Goering, which Bormann hastily brought to Hitler. I trailed informally along after him, chiefly out of curiosity. In the telegram Goering merely asked Hitler whether, in keeping with the decree on the succession, he should assume the leadership of the entire Reich if Hitler remained in Fortress Berlin. But Bormann claimed that Goering had launched a coup d'état; perhaps this was Bormann's last effort to induce Hitler to fly to Berchtesgaden and take control there. At first, Hitler responded to this news with the same apathy he had shown all day long. But Bormann's theory was given fresh support when another radio message from Goering arrived. I pocketed a copy which in the general confusion lay unnoticed in the bunker. It read:

> To Reich Minister von Ribbentrop:
>
> I have asked the Fuehrer to provide me with instructions by 10 P.M. April 23. If by this time it is apparent that the Fuehrer has been deprived of his freedom of action to conduct the affairs of the Reich, his decree of June 29, 1941, becomes effective, according to which I am heir to all his offices as his deputy. [If] by 12 midnight April 23, 1945, you receive no other word either from the Fuehrer directly or from me, you are to come to me at once by air.
>
> (Signed) Goering, Reich Marshal

Here was fresh material for Bormann. "Goering is engaged in treason!" he exclaimed excitedly. "He's already sending telegrams to members of the government and announcing that on the basis of his powers he will assume your office at twelve o'clock tonight, mein Führer."

Although Hitler had remained calm when the first telegram arrived, Bormann now won his game. Hitler immediately stripped Goering of his rights of succession—Bormann himself drafted the radio message—and accused him of treason to Hitler and betrayal of National Socialism. The message to Goering went on to say that Hitler would exempt him from further punishment if the Reich Marshal would promptly resign all his offices for reasons of health.

Bormann had at last managed to rouse Hitler from his lethargy. An outburst of wild fury followed in which feelings of bitterness, helplessness, self-pity, and despair mingled. With flushed face and staring eyes, Hitler ranted as if he had forgotten the presence of his entourage:

"I've known it all along. I know that Goering is lazy. He let the air force go to pot. He was corrupt. His example made corruption possible in our state. Besides he's been a drug addict for years. I've known it all along."

So Hitler had known all that but had done nothing about it.

And then, with startling abruptness, he lapsed back into his apathy: "Well, all right. Let Goering negotiate the surrender. If the war is lost anyhow, it doesn't matter who does it." That sentence expressed contempt for the German people: Goering was still good enough for the purposes of capitulation.

After this crisis, Hitler had reached the end of his strength. He dropped back into the weary tone that had been characteristic of him earlier that day. For years he had overtaxed himself; for years, mustering that immoderate will of his, he had thrust away from himself and others the growing certainty of this end. Now he no longer had the energy to conceal his condition. He was giving up.

About half an hour later Bormann brought in Goering's telegram of reply. Because of a severe heart attack Goering was resigning all his powers. How often before Hitler had removed an inconvenient associate not by dismissal, but by an allegation of illness, merely to preserve the German people's faith in the internal unity of the top leadership. Even now, when all was almost over, Hitler remained true to this habit of observing public decorum.

Only now, at the very last hour, had Bormann reached his goal. Goering was eliminated. Possibly Bormann also was aware of Goering's failings; but he had hated and now overthrown the Reich Marshal solely because he had held too much power. In a way I felt sympathy for Goering at this time. I recalled the conversation in which he had assured me of his loyalty to Hitler.

The brief thunderstorm staged by Bormann was over; a few bars of *Götterdämmerung* had sounded and faded. The supposed Hagen had left the stage. To my surprise, Hitler was amenable to a request of mine, though I made it with considerable trepidation. Several Czech managers of the Skoda Works were expecting an unpleasant fate from the Russians because of their collaboration with us. They were probably right about that. On the other hand, because of their former relations with American industry they were placing their hopes of safety on flying to American headquarters. A few days before Hitler would have strictly outlawed any such proposal. But now he was prepared to sign an order waiving all formalities so that the men could fly to safety.

While I was discussing this point with Hitler, Bormann reminded him that Ribbentrop was still waiting for an audience. Hitler reacted nervously: "I've already said several times that I don't want to see him." For some reason the idea of meeting Ribbentrop annoyed him.

Bormann insisted: "Ribbentrop has said he won't move from the threshold, that he'll wait there like a faithful dog until you call him."

This figure of speech softened Hitler; he had Ribbentrop summoned. They talked alone. Apparently Hitler told him about the escape plan of the Czech managers. But even in this desperate situation the Foreign Minister fought to defend his jurisdictional rights. In the corridor he grumbled to me: "That is a matter for the Foreign Office." In a somewhat milder tone he added: "In this particular case I have no objection if the document will say: 'At the suggestion of the Foreign Minister.'" I added these words, Ribbentrop was content, and Hitler signed the paper. This was, so far as I know, Hitler's last official dealing with his Foreign Minister.

In the meantime my paternal adviser of the past few months, Friedrich Lüschen, had arrived at the Chancellery. But all my efforts to persuade him to leave Berlin remained vain. We told each other good-by. Later, in Nuremberg, I learned that he had committed suicide after the fall of Berlin.

Toward midnight Eva Braun sent an SS orderly to invite me to the small room in the bunker that was both her bedroom and living room. It was pleasantly furnished; she had had some of the expensive furniture which I had designed for her years ago brought from her two rooms in the upper floors of the Chancellery. Neither the proportions nor the pieces selected fitted into the gloomy surroundings. To complete the irony, one of the inlays on the doors of the chest was a four-leaf clover incorporating her initials.

We were able to talk honestly, for Hitler had withdrawn. She was the only prominent candidate for death in this bunker who displayed an admirable and superior composure. While all the others were abnormal—exaltedly heroic like Goebbels, bent on saving his skin like Bormann, exhausted like Hitler, or in total collapse like Frau Goebbels—Eva Braun radiated an almost gay serenity. "How about a bottle of champagne for our farewell? And some sweets? I'm sure you haven't eaten in a long time."

I was touched by her concern; she was the first person to think that I might be hungry after my many hours in the bunker. The orderly brought a bottle of Moet et Chandon, cake, and sweets. We remained alone. "You know, it was good that you came back once more. The Fuehrer had assumed you would be working against him. But your visit has proved the opposite to him, hasn't it?" I did not answer that question. "Anyhow, he liked what you said to him today. He has made up his mind to stay here, and I am staying with him. And you know the rest, too, of course. . . . He wanted to send me back to Munich. But I refused; I've come to end it here."

She was also the only person in the bunker capable of humane considerations. "Why do so many more people have to be killed?" she asked. "And it's all for nothing. . . . Incidentally, you almost came too late. Yesterday the situation was so terrible it seemed the Russians would quickly occupy all of Berlin. The Fuehrer was on the point of giving up. But Goebbels talked to him and persuaded him, and so we're still here."

She went on talking easily and informally with me, occasionally bursting out against Bormann, who was pursuing his intrigues up to the last. But again and again she came back to the declaration that she was happy here in the bunker.

By now it was about three o'clock in the morning. Hitler was awake again. I sent word that I wanted to bid him good-by. The day had worn me out, and I was afraid that I would not be able to control myself at our parting. Trembling, the prematurely aged man stood before me for the last time; the man to whom I had dedicated my life twelve years before. I was both moved and confused. For his part, he showed no emotion when we confronted one another. His words were as cold as his hand: "So, you're leaving? Good. *Auf Wiedersehen.*" No regards to my family, no wishes, no thanks, no farewell. For a moment I lost my composure, said something about coming back. But he could easily see that it was a white lie, and turned his attention to something else. I was dismissed.

Ten minutes later, with hardly another word spoken to anyone, I left the Chancellor's residence. I wanted to walk once more through the neighboring Chancellery, which I had built. Since the lights were no longer functioning, I contented myself with a few farewell minutes in the Court of Honor, whose outlines could scarcely be seen against the night sky. I sensed rather than saw the architecture. There was an almost ghostly quiet about everything, like a night in the mountains. The noise of a great city, which in earlier years had penetrated to here even during the night, had totally ceased. At rather long intervals I heard the detonations of Russian shells. Such was my last visit to the Chancellery. Years ago I had built it—full of plans, prospects, and dreams for the future. Now I was leaving the ruins of my building, and of the most significant years of my life.

"How was it?" Poser asked.

"Thank God, I don't have to play the part of a Prince Max of Baden,"* I answered with relief. I had correctly interpreted Hitler's coolness at our parting, for six days later, in his political testament, he excluded me and appointed Saur, his favorite for some time, as my successor.

The road between the Brandenburg Gate and the Victory Column had been converted into a runway by the use of red lanterns. Labor squads had filled the holes from the latest shell hits. We started without incident;

* Prince Max of Baden was appointed Imperial Chancellor at the end of the First World War. In that capacity he declared the Kaiser's abdication, negotiated the Armistice, and turned the government of Germany over to the Socialists—for all of which acts he was much criticized.—*Translators' note.*

I saw a shadow rush by the right side of the plane: the Victory Column. Then we were in the air, and undisturbed. In and around Berlin we saw many large fires, the flashes of artillery, flares that looked like fireflies. Still, the scene could not be compared with that produced by a single heavy air raid on Berlin. We headed toward a gap in the ring of artillery fire, where the darkness was still tranquil. Toward five o'clock, with the first glimmers of dawn, we arrived back at the Rechlin airfield.

I had a fighter plane readied to deliver the Fuehrer's order concerning the Skoda managers to Karl Hermann Frank, Hitler's deputy in Prague—I never did find out if the messenger arrived. Since I wanted to avoid being chased along the roads by low-level English fighters, I postponed driving to Hamburg until evening. Himmler, I heard at the airfield, was staying only twenty-five miles away at the hospital that had sheltered me a year before under such curious circumstances. We decided to visit him, landing in our Stork on a nearby field. Himmler was quite surprised to see me. He received me in the very room where I had lain during my illness, and to make the situation even more grotesque, Dr. Gebhardt was also present.

As always, Himmler displayed that special brand of cordiality toward a fellow official which effectively cut off all intimacy. He was interested chiefly in my experiences in Berlin. Undoubtedly he had heard of Hitler's treatment of Goering by now, but he passed over it. And even when I somewhat hesitantly told the story of Goering's resignation, he maintained that it meant nothing. "Goering is going to be the successor now. We've long had an understanding that I would be his Premier. Even without Hitler, I can make him Chief of State. . . . You know what he's like," he added with a conniving smile and without the slightest embarrassment. "Naturally I'll be the one to make the decisions. I've already been in touch with various persons I mean to take into my cabinet. Keitel is coming to see me shortly. . . ." Perhaps Himmler assumed that I had come to see him to wheedle a post in his new government.

The world in which Himmler was still moving was fantastic. "Europe cannot manage without me in the future either," he commented. "It will go on needing me as Minister of Police. After I've spent an hour with Eisenhower he'll appreciate that fact. They'll soon realize that they're dependent on me—or they'll have a hopeless chaos on their hands." He spoke of his contacts with Count Bernadotte, which involved transfer of the concentration camps to the International Red Cross. Now I understood why I had seen so many parked Red Cross trucks in the Sachsenwald near Hamburg. Earlier, they had always talked about liquidating all political prisoners before the end. Now Himmler was trying to strike some private bargains with the victors. Hitler himself, as my last talk with him had made apparent, had put such ideas far behind him.

Finally, Himmler after all held out a faint prospect of my becoming a minister in his government. For my part, with some sarcasm I offered him my plane so that he could pay a farewell visit to Hitler. But Himmler waved that aside. He had no time for that now, he said. Unemotionally, he explained: "Now I must prepare my new government. And besides, my person is too important for the future of Germany for me to risk the flight."

The arrival of Keitel put an end to our conversation. On my way out I heard the Field Marshal, in the same firm voice with which he so frequently addressed high-flown sentimental declarations to Hitler, now assuring Himmler of his unconditional loyalty and announcing that he was entirely at his disposal.

That evening I returned to Hamburg. The Gauleiter offered to have my speech to the people broadcast by the Hamburg station at once, that is, even before Hitler's death. But as I thought of the drama that must be taking place during these days, these very hours, in the Berlin bunker, I realized that I had lost all urge to continue my opposition. Once more Hitler had succeeded in paralyzing me psychically. To myself, and perhaps to others, I justified my change of mind on the grounds that it would be wrong and pointless to try to intervene now in the course of the tragedy.

I said good-by to Kaufmann and set out for Schleswig-Holstein. We moved into our trailer on Eutin Lake. Occasionally I visited Doenitz or members of the General Staff, who like me were at a standstill, awaiting further developments. Thus, I happened to be present on May 1, 1945, when Doenitz was handed the radio message* significantly curtailing his rights as Hitler's successor. Hitler had appointed the cabinet for the new President of the Reich: Goebbels was Chancellor; Seyss-Inquart, Foreign Minister; and Bormann, Party Minister. Along with this message came one from Bormann announcing that he would be coming to see Doenitz shortly.

* The first radio message, dated April 30, 1945, 6:35 P.M. read:

Grand Admiral Doenitz:
In place of the former Reich Marshal Goering the Fuehrer has designated you as his successor. Written authorization on the way. Immediately take all measures required by the present situation.

Bormann

The radio message sent on May 1, 1945, at 3:18 P.M. read:

Grand Admiral Doenitz: (Top Secret! Only via officer.)
Fuehrer deceased yesterday at 3:30 P.M. Testament of April 29 appoints you Reich President, Minister Goebbels Chancellor, Reichsleiter Bormann Party Minister, Minister Seyss-Inquart Foreign Minister. On the Fuehrer's instructions the testament sent out of Berlin to you and to Field Marshal Schörner, to assure its preservation for the people. Reichsleiter Bormann will try to get to you today to orient you on the situation. The form and time of announcement to the troops and public are left to you.
Confirm receipt.

Goebbels   Bormann

"This is utterly impossible!" Doenitz exclaimed, for this made a farce of the powers of his office. "Has anyone else seen the radio message yet?"

Except for the radioman and the admiral's adjutant, Lüdde-Neurath, who had taken the message directly to his chief, no one had. Doenitz then ordered that the radioman be sworn to silence and the message locked up and kept confidential. "What will we do if Bormann and Goebbels actually arrive here?" Doenitz asked. Then he continued resolutely: "I absolutely will not cooperate with them in any case." That evening we both agreed that Bormann and Goebbels must somehow be placed under arrest.

Thus Hitler forced Doenitz, as his first official function, to commit an act of illegality: concealing an official document.* This was the last link in a chain of deceptions, betrayals, hypocrisies, and intrigues during those days and weeks. Himmler had betrayed his Fuehrer by negotiations; Bormann had carried off his last great intrigue against Goering by playing on Hitler's feelings; Goering was hoping to strike a bargain with the Allies; Kaufmann had made a deal with the British and was willing to provide me with radio facilities; Keitel was hiring out to a new master while Hitler was still alive—and I myself, finally, had in the past months deceived the man who had discovered me and furthered my career; I had even at times considered how to kill him. All of us felt forced to these acts by the system which we ourselves represented—and forced also by Hitler, who for his part had betrayed us all, himself and his people.

On this note the Third Reich ended.

On the evening of that May 1, when Hitler's death was announced, I slept in a small room in Doenitz's quarters. When I unpacked my bag I found the red leather case containing Hitler's portrait. My secretary had included it in my luggage. My nerves had reached their limit. When I stood the photograph up, a fit of weeping overcame me. That was the end of my relationship to Hitler. Only now was the spell broken, the

---

* Strictly speaking, Doenitz could not claim that his succession to Hitler was constitutionally legal, since the constitution of the German Reich would have required an election. Rather, his legitimacy as Hitler's successor was based on his predecessor's charisma, a fact which Doenitz confirmed in his public acts by constantly invoking Hitler's last will and testament. Thus, this first official act of Doenitz's was illegal only insofar as he was disregarding an important aspect of Hitler's testament after first assenting to it by accepting the functions of the office.

Hitler's idea of imposing his choices of cabinet ministers on his successor was, by the way, one of the most absurd inspirations of his career as a statesman. Again, he failed to make clear, as in other cases during the past years, who was to have the ultimate decision-making power: the Chancellor rather than his cabinet or the President. According to the letter of the testament, Doenitz could not dismiss the Chancellor or any of the ministers, even if they proved unfit for office. Thus, the most important power of any President had been denied him from the outset.

magic extinguished. What remained were images of graveyards, of shattered cities, of millions of mourners, of concentration camps. Not all these images came into my mind at this moment, but they were there, somehow present in me. I fell into a deep, exhausted sleep.

Two weeks later, staggered by the revelations of the crimes in the concentration camps, I wrote to the chairman of the ministerial cabinet, Schwerin-Krosigk: "The previous leadership of the German nation bears a collective guilt for the fate that now hangs over the German people. Each member of that leadership must personally assume his responsibility in such a way that the guilt which might otherwise descend upon the German people is expiated."

With that, there began a segment of my life which has not ended to this day.

EPILOGUE

33

Stations of Imprisonment

KARL DOENITZ, THE NEW CHIEF OF STATE, WAS STILL CAUGHT UP IN THE IDEAS of the National Socialist regime, just as I was, and more than either of us imagined. For twelve years we had served that regime; we thought it would be cheap opportunism now to make a sharp turnabout. But the death of Hitler broke that mental bind which had for so long warped our thinking. For Doenitz this meant that the objectivity of the trained military officer came to the fore. From the moment he took over, Doenitz held that we should end the war as quickly as possible, and that once this task was done, our work was over.

On that very May 1, 1945, one of the first military conferences took place between Doenitz as the new Commander in Chief of the armed forces and Field Marshal Ernst Busch. Busch wanted to attack the superior British forces advancing on Hamburg, while Doenitz was against any offensive measures. All that should be done, he said, was to keep the way to the West open as long as possible for the refugees from the East. Columns of them were blocked near Lübeck; a delaying action by the German troops in the West should be continued only to allow the flow to continue, Doenitz said. Busch made a great to-do about the Grand Admiral's no longer acting in Hitler's spirit. But Doenitz was no longer moved by such exhortations.

The day before, in a dispute with the new Chief of State, Himmler had been made to understand that there was no place for him in the new government. Nevertheless, the next day he turned up unannounced at Doenitz's headquarters. It was around noon, and Doenitz invited Himmler and me to dine with him—though not out of any special friendliness. However much he disliked Himmler, Doenitz would have regarded it as discourteous to treat a man who had so recently held so much power with contempt. Himmler brought the news that Gauleiter Kaufmann intended to surrender Hamburg without a fight. A leaflet addressed to the populace was now being printed, Himmler said, to prepare the way for the impending entrance of British troops into the city. Doenitz was angry. If everyone acted on his own, he said, his assignment no longer had any point. I offered to drive to Hamburg to talk with Kaufmann.

Kaufmann, well protected in his headquarters by his bodyguard of students, was no less agitated than Doenitz. The commandant of the city had received orders to fight for Hamburg, he told me. But the British had issued an ultimatum that if Hamburg were not surrendered, they would order the heaviest bombing the city had ever received. "Am I supposed to follow the example of the Gauleiter of Bremen?" Kaufmann continued. "He issued a proclamation calling on the people to defend themselves to the last, and then cleared out while the city was demolished by a frightful air raid." He was so determined to prevent a battle for Hamburg, Kaufmann told me, that if necessary he would mobilize the masses to active resistance against the defenders of the city.

I telephoned Doenitz and told him of the threat of open rebellion in Hamburg. Doenitz asked time to consider. About an hour later he issued the order to the commandant to surrender the city without a fight.

On April 21, at the time I was recording my speech at the Hamburg radio station, Kaufmann had proposed that the two of us let ourselves be taken prisoner together. Now he renewed this offer. But I rejected this idea, as I also did the plan for a temporary flight which our champion dive-bomber pilot, Werner Baumbach, had earlier suggested to me. Baumbach had the use of a long-range four-motored seaplane which throughout the war had plied between northern Norway and a German weather station in Greenland to supply the station with provisions. Baumbach proposed that we use it to take me and a few friends to one of the many quiet bays of Greenland for the first few months after the occupation of Germany. Boxes of books were already packed, as well as medicines, writing materials, and a great deal of paper (for I wanted to start on my memoirs without delay). We would also take along rifles, my faltboat, skis, tents, hand grenades for fishing, and food.* Ever since seeing the Udet film SOS Iceberg I had dreamed of a lengthy vacation in Greenland. But since

---

* In those days Greenland seemed so distant and isolated that even intensive air reconnaissance scarcely seemed a real threat. The supply planes for these weather stations could carry enough fuel to fly to England, where we planned to turn ourselves in late in the fall of 1945.

Doenitz was now head of the government, I canceled this plan, with its combination of panic and rank romanticism.

Burning oil trucks and automobiles shot up only minutes before lay by the side of the road, with English fighter planes flying overhead, as I drove back to Eutin Lake. In Schleswig the traffic was heavier, a jumble of military vehicles, civilian cars, columns of people on foot, some soldiers, some civilians. When I was occasionally recognized, no one said anything angry. There was an air of friendly, regretful constraint about the way people greeted me.

I arrived at the headquarters in Plön on the evening of May 2. Doenitz had already moved to Flensburg to evade the rapidly advancing British troops. But I met Keitel and Jodl, who were on the point of leaving to join their new master. Doenitz had taken up quarters on the passenger ship *Patria*. We had breakfast together in the captain's cabin, and there I presented him with an edict prohibiting the destruction of any facilities, including bridges. He promptly signed it. Thus I had achieved at last every point of the program I had demanded of Hitler on March 19—although it was now far too late.

Doenitz at once saw the merit of my making a speech urging the German people in the areas already captured by the enemy to hurl all their energies into reconstruction. The speech was intended to counteract the lethargy "which has come over the people as a result of the paralyzing horror and the immeasurable disillusionment of recent months." All Doenitz asked was that I show the speech to Schwerin-Krosigk, the new Foreign Minister, at the present headquarters of the government, the naval school at Mürwik near Flensburg. Schwerin-Krosigk also agreed to the broadcast if I would add a few sentences to explain the present policy of the government. He dictated these to me.* The only stations in our possession which could still broadcast, Copenhagen and Oslo, were hooked in when I read the speech in the Flensburg studio.

When I stepped out of the broadcasting studio, I found Himmler waiting for me. We still held valuable territories such as Norway and Denmark, he reminded me self-importantly, territories which we could regard as pledges for our security. These were of sufficient importance to the enemy so that we could negotiate concessions for ourselves in exchange for the assurance that we would surrender them intact. My speech

---

* It was an abridged version of the speech I had recorded at the Hamburg radio station on April 21, 1945. The addition requested by Schwerin-Krosigk read: "Only for this reason [to avoid casualties in the civilian population] does the Grand Admiral feel compelled to continue the fighting. The sole purpose of the struggle which is still being waged is to prevent the Germans fleeing from the Soviet armies, or threatened by them, from perishing. This last obligation in Germany's heroic struggle is what our people, who have borne all the sufferings of this war so gallantly, must now assume."

suggested that we would hand over these areas without a fight and without asking anything in return; it was consequently a harmful speech, Himmler argued. He then surprised Keitel by proposing that a censor be installed to pass on all public announcements of the government; he himself would be glad to assume this task. But that same day Doenitz had already rejected similar suggestions from Terboven, Hitler's governor in Norway. On May 6, Doenitz signed an order prohibiting demolitions of any kind in the still occupied territories, parts of Holland and Czechoslovakia, Denmark and Norway. This was the final rejection of any policy of pledges, as Himmler called it.

In the same spirit the Grand Admiral said no to any plan to transfer himself and the new government to Denmark or Prague, despite the fact that Flensburg might be occupied by the British any day. Himmler in particular felt drawn to Prague. An old imperial city, he urged, was more fitting as the headquarters of a government than historically insignificant Flensburg. He omitted to add that by moving to Prague we would be passing from the sphere where the navy held power into the sphere of the SS. Doenitz finally cut off the discussion by stating flatly that we would certainly not continue our activities beyond the German borders. "If the British want to capture us here, let them do it!"

Himmler then began pressing Baumbach, who had been placed in charge of the government air squadron, to provide him with a plane so that he could escape to Prague. Baumbach and I decided that we would land him on an airfield already held by the enemy. But Himmler's intelligence service was still functioning. "When people fly in your planes," he snarled at Baumbach, "they don't know where they're going to land."

A few days later, as soon as communications with Field Marshal Montgomery had been established, Himmler gave Jodl a letter asking him to have it passed on to Montgomery. As General Kinzl, the liaison officer to the British forces, told me, Himmler asked for an interview with the British Field Marshal under a safe-conduct. Should he be taken prisoner he wanted it established that by the laws of war he had a right to be treated as a high-ranking general—since he had been Commander in Chief of the Vistula Army Group. But this letter never arrived. Jodl destroyed it, as he told me in Nuremberg.

As happens in critical situations, those days revealed the characters of men. Gauleiter Koch of East Prussia, at one time Reich Commissioner for the Ukraine, arrived in Flensburg to demand a submarine so that he could escape to South America. Gauleiter Lohse made the same demand. Doenitz flatly refused. Rosenberg, now the oldest Reichsleiter of the National Socialist party, wanted to dissolve the party. He alone had the right to issue such an order, he declared. A few days later he was found almost lifeless in Mürwik. He spoke of having poisoned himself, and a suicide attempt was suspected, but it turned out that he was merely drunk.

On the other hand some manifested courageous attitudes. A good many of the leaders refrained from disappearing into the masses of refugees swarming into Holstein. Seyss-Inquart, the Reich Commissioner for the Occupied Netherlands, rode a PT boat through the enemy blockade at night to confer with Doenitz and me, but he refused the chance to remain at the seat of government and returned to Holland in his PT boat. "My place is there," he said mournfully. "I'll be arrested immediately after my return."

On May 4 came the armistice in northwest Germany, followed three days later, on May 7, 1945, by the unconditional surrender in all the theaters of war. A day later that capitulation was again solemnly sealed by the signatures of Keitel and three representatives of the branches of the Wehrmacht at the Soviet headquarters in Karlshorst, near Berlin. After the signing the Soviet generals, whom Goebbels's propaganda had always represented as barbarians without manners or knowledge of civilized conduct, served the German delegation a good meal, complete with champagne and caviar, as Keitel told us.* Keitel obviously had no feeling that after such a step, which meant the end of the Reich and imprisonment for millions of soldiers, it would have been in better taste to refuse the champagne on the victor's table and have taken only what was necessary to still the pangs of hunger. His gratification at this gesture on the part of the victors testified to a sad lack of dignity and sense of decorum. But after all, it had already been much the same at Stalingrad.

The British troops encircled Flensburg. There was now only a tiny enclave in which our government still had executive authority. The "Control Commission for the OKW," under Major General Rooks, installed itself on the *Patria* and soon began functioning as a liaison office to the Doenitz government. To my mind, the capitulation meant that the Doenitz government had done its job in bringing the lost war to an end. On May 7, 1945, I proposed that we issue a last proclamation to the effect that since we no longer had any freedom of action, all we could do was to wind up such matters that had arisen out of the surrender. "We expect that the enemy will nevertheless call us to account for our former activities exactly like all the other responsible members of the National Socialist regime." In making this remark I wanted to forestall any misinterpretation of our gesture.[1]

However, State Secretary Stuckardt, now heading the Ministry of the Interior, took a different view. He wrote a memorandum stating that Doenitz as Chief of State and legitimate successor to Hitler had no right

---

* On May 6, 1945, the *Berliner Zeitung* printed a report from Chuikov's headquarters: "After the signing Keitel and his companions were treated to caviar, vodka, and champagne in the villa placed at their disposal. The meal differed in no respect from the Allies' banquet."

to surrender his position; he must hold it so that the continuity of the German Reich would be preserved and the legitimacy of future governments would not be imperiled. Doenitz, though at first more disposed to follow my line, agreed with Stuckardt. Thus, the continuance of his government was assured for a whole fifteen days more.

The first British and American newspapermen arrived, and each of their stories aroused unrealistic hopes of the most varied kind. Simultaneously, SS uniforms vanished. Overnight Wegener, Stuckardt and Ohlendorf had become civilians. Gebhardt, Himmler's intimate, actually transformed himself into a Red Cross general. Moreover a government structure began to arise—a consequence of its members having nothing to do. Doenitz, in the old fashion of Imperial Germany, appointed a Chief of the Military Cabinet (Admiral Wagner) and a Chief of the Civilian Cabinet (Gauleiter Wegener). After some debate it was resolved that the Chief of State would continue to be addressed by the title of Grand Admiral. An information service was set up: An old radio set provided the latest news. Even one of Hitler's big Mercedes limousines had found its way to Flensburg and served to convey Doenitz to his home all of five hundred yards from the offices of the government. A photographer from Heinrich Hoffmann's studio appeared to take pictures of the new government at work. I remarked to Doenitz's adjutant that the tragedy was turning into a tragicomedy. Correctly as Doenitz had acted up to the capitulation and sensibly as he had worked to bring the war to a quick end, he was now complicating everything and our situation in a totally confusing manner. Two members of the new government, Ministers Backe and Dorpmüller, had vanished without a trace. Rumor said they had been taken to Eisenhower's headquarters to begin drafting measures for the reconstruction of Germany. Field Marshal Keitel, still chief of the High Command of the armed forces, was taken prisoner. Our government was not only impotent; the victors did not deign to notice it.

We composed memoranda in a vacuum, trying to offset our unimportance by sham activity. Every morning at ten a cabinet meeting took place in the so-called Cabinet Room, a former schoolroom. It looked as if Schwerin-Krosigk was trying to make up for all the cabinet meetings that had not been held during the past twelve years. We used a painted table and chairs collected from around the school. At one of these sessions the acting Minister of Food brought a few bottles of rye from his stores. We fetched glasses and cups from our rooms and discussed how to reshuffle the cabinet to bring it in line with the changing times. A hot debate arose over the question of adding a Minister for Churches to the cabinet. A well-known theologian was proposed for the post, while others regarded Pastor Niemöller as the best candidate. After all, the cabinet ought to be made "socially acceptable." My tart suggestion that a few leading Social Democrats and liberals be brought forth to take over our functions went unnoticed. The Food Minister's stocks helped to liven the mood of the meeting. We were, I thought, well on the way to making ourselves ridiculous; or rather, we already were ridiculous. The seriousness that had prevailed in this building during the surrender had vanished.

On May 15, I wrote Schwerin-Krosigk that the government of the Reich must consist of people who could enjoy the confidence of the Allies; the composition of the cabinet must be changed and the closer associates of Hitler replaced. Moreover, I said, it was "as foolish to entrust an artist with paying off debts as—in the past—to put a champagne salesman in charge of the Foreign Ministry." I asked to "be relieved of the affairs of the Minister of Economics and Production." I received no reply.

After the capitulation subordinate officers of the American and British forces turned up here and there and moved around unabashed in rooms where our "seat of government" was located. One day in the middle of May an American lieutenant appeared in my room. "Do you know where Speer is?" he asked. When I identified myself, he explained that American headquarters was accumulating data on the effects of the Allied bombings. Would I be willing to provide information? I said I would.

A few days earlier the Duke of Holstein had offered me the Castle of Glücksburg, several miles from Flensburg, as quarters for me and my family. That same day I sat in the sixteenth-century castle, built out into the water, with several civilians of my age belonging to the USSBS, the United States Strategic Bombing Survey, who were attached to Eisenhower's staff. We discussed the mistakes and peculiarities of the bombings on both sides. The next morning my adjutant reported that many American officers, including a high-ranking general, had arrived at the entrance to the castle. Our guard of soldiers from a German armored force presented arms,* and so—under the protection of German arms, as it were—General F. L. Anderson, commander of the bombers of the American Eighth Air Force, entered my apartment. He thanked me in the most courteous fashion for taking part in these discussions.

For three days more we went systematically through the various aspects of the war in the air. On May 19 Chairman Franklin d'Olier of the USSBS, along with his vice-chairman, Henry C. Alexander, and his assistants, Dr. Galbraith, Paul Nitze, George Ball, Colonel Gilkrest, and Williams, visited. From my own work I could appreciate the great importance of this division for the American military operations.

* Even after the cease-fire, the German troops around Doenitz's government seat were allowed to bear light arms. At this meeting I stated, according to the minutes for May 19, 1945, that "I have no need of collecting credits in order to avert misinterpretations of my actions. The political aspects will be examined by other quarters."

During the next several days an almost comradely tone prevailed in our "university of bombing." It came to a sudden end when Goering's champagne breakfast with General Patton produced banner headlines all over the world. But before that happened General Anderson paid me the most curious and flattering compliment of my career: "Had I known what this man was achieving, I would have sent out the entire American Eighth Air Force merely to put him underground." That air force had at its disposal more than two thousand heavy daylight bombers. It was lucky General Anderson found out too late.

The place where my family was staying was twenty-five miles from Glücksburg. Since the worst that could happen was that I would be arrested a few days earlier, I drove out of the enclave around Flensburg and thanks to the careless unconcern of the British reached the occupied zone without trouble. The British soldiers who were strolling in the streets paid no attention to my car. Heavy tanks stood in the villages, their cannon protected by canvas hoods. So I arrived safely at the door of the country house where my family was staying. We were all delighted at this prank, which I was able to repeat several times. But perhaps I strained British nonchalance too much after all. On May 21, I was taken back to Flensburg in my car and locked in a room at Secret Service headquarters, watched over by a soldier with an automatic rifle on his knees. After a few hours I was released. My car had vanished; the British took me back to Glücksburg in one of their cars.

Early in the morning two days later my adjutant came rushing into my bedroom. The British had surrounded Glücksburg. A sergeant entered my room and announced that I was a prisoner. He unbuckled his belt with its pistol, laid it casually on my table, and left the room to give me an opportunity to pack my things. Soon afterward a truck brought me back to Flensburg. As we rode off I could see that many antitank guns were trained on Glücksburg Castle. They still thought I might be capable of far more than I was. Shortly afterward the Reich war flag, which had been raised every day at the naval school, was taken down by the British. If anything proved that the Doenitz government, try though it might, was not a new beginning, it was the persistence of this flag. As a matter of fact, at the beginning of our days in Flensburg, Doenitz and I had agreed that the flag must remain. We could not pretend to represent anything new, I thought. Flensburg was only the last stage of the Third Reich, nothing more.

Under normal circumstances a fall from the heights of power might be attended by grave inner crises. But to my astonishment the fall took place without any perceptible turmoil. I also adapted quickly to the conditions of imprisonment. I ascribe that to my twelve years of training in subordination. For in my own mind I had already been a prisoner under Hitler's regime. Relieved at last of the responsibility for daily decisions, I was overpowered during the early months by a craving for sleep such as I had never felt before. A slackening of the mind took place, although I tried not to let it show.

In Flensburg all of us, the members of the Doenitz government, met again in a room that resembled a waiting room. There we sat on benches along the walls, each of us surrounded by suitcases with his personal possessions. We must have looked much like emigrants waiting for their ship. A melancholy mood prevailed. One by one we were summoned to an adjoining room to be registered as prisoners. Depending on their dispositions, the new prisoners returned angry, insulted, or depressed. When my turn came, I too was affronted by the embarrassing physical examination to which I was subjected. Probably it was a consequence of Himmler's suicide; he had kept a poison pill concealed in his gum.

Doenitz, Jodl, and I were led into a small courtyard in which a dramatically large number of machine guns were directed toward us from the windows of the upper floor. Newspaper photographers and movie cameramen had their turn, while I tried to give the impression that this spectacle, which was intended only for the newsreels, did not concern me at all. Then we were squeezed into several trucks along with the others from the waiting room. Ahead of us and behind us, as I could see at curves in the road, we had an escort of thirty to forty armored vehicles— a rare honor for me, accustomed as I was to driving around in my car alone and without protection. At an airport we were loaded into two two-motored cargo planes. Sitting on suitcases and crates, we already very much looked our part of "captives." We were not informed of our destination. It took some getting used to, the fact that we would never know where we were being moved to, after so many years in which we had taken it for granted that we were the ones who determined our destinations. On only two of these journeys was the end completely clear: the one to Nuremberg and the one to Spandau.

We flew over coastal landscapes and then for a long time over the North Sea. Were we bound for London? The plane veered to the south. To judge by the look of the land and the cities we were over France. A large city appeared. Reims, some insisted. But it was Luxembourg. The plane landed; outside a cordon of American soldiers was drawn up in two rows. Each of them had his automatic rifle trained on the narrow lane which we would walk between them. I had seen such a reception only in gangster films when the criminals are finally led off to justice. In open trucks, seated on crude wooden benches and guarded by soldiers again with their guns at the ready, we were taken through several villages where the people in the streets whistled and shouted at us, epithets we could not make out. The first stage of my imprisonment had begun.

We stopped at a large building, the Palace Hotel in Mondorf, and were led into the lobby. From outside we had been able to see Goering and other former members of the leadership of the Third Reich pacing back and forth. The whole hierarchy was there: ministers, Field Marshals, Reichsleiters, state secretaries, and generals. It was a ghostly experience to find all those who at the end had scattered like chaff in the wind reassembled here. I kept to one side, eager to absorb as much as possible of the quiet of the place. Just once I spoke to Kesselring, asking him why he had continued to blow up bridges instead of sparing them after the command communications to Hitler had been broken. With his inflexible military mentality he replied that bridges had to be destroyed as long as fighting was going on; as Commander in Chief nothing concerned him but the safety of his soldiers.

Soon quarrels over rank began. Goering was Hitler's proclaimed successor of earlier years, Doenitz the Chief of State whom Hitler had appointed at the last moment; but as Reich Marshal, Goering was also the highest-ranking military officer. There was a muffled battle between the new Chief of State and the deposed successor over the question of who should take precedence in the Palace Hotel of Mondorf (which had been emptied of all persons but ourselves and our guards) and who in general was top dog of us all. No agreement could be reached. Soon the two principals avoided meeting at the door, while each took the presiding seat at two different tables in the dining room. Goering especially never forgot his station. When Dr. Brandt once casually referred to all he had lost, Goering interrupted snappishly: "Oh, come, don't you talk! You haven't any reason to complain. After all, what did you have! But I! When I'd had so much. . . ."

Barely two weeks after we were taken to Mondorf I was told that I was going to be transferred. From then on the Americans treated me with just a shade of respect. Many of my fellow prisoners interpreted this transfer overoptimistically as a call to assist in the reconstruction of Germany, for they were not yet used to the idea that things really could be managed without us. I was delegated to bring regards to friends and relatives. A car waited outside the entrance to the Palace Hotel, not a truck this time but a limousine, and my guard was not an MP with a submachine gun but a lieutenant who saluted courteously. We drove westward past Reims toward Paris. In the center of the city the lieutenant got out at an administration building and soon returned equipped with a map and fresh orders. We headed upstream along the Seine. In my confusion I thought that we were making for the Bastille, quite forgetting that it had long ago been torn down. But the lieutenant became uneasy; he compared street names until I realized with relief that he had lost his way. Clumsily, in my school English, I offered to pilot us; but it was only with some hesitation that he told me our destination was the Trianon Palace Hotel in Versailles. I knew the way there well; it was where I had stayed in 1937 when I was designing the German pavilion for the Paris World's Fair.

Luxury cars and honor guards at the doors indicated that this hotel was no prison camp but had been taken over by the Allied staffs. It was actually Eisenhower's headquarters. The lieutenant vanished inside while I sat quietly watching the spectacle of high-ranking generals driving up. After a long wait a sergeant conducted us down an avenue. We drove past several meadows straight toward a small palace whose gates opened for us.

For several weeks I stayed at Chesnay. I ended up in a small room on the third floor of the rear wing. Its appointments were spartan: an army cot and a chair. The window was laced over with barbed wire. An armed guard was posted at the door.

The next day I had the opportunity to admire our little palace from the front. Surrounded by ancient trees, it was situated in a small park beyond whose high wall the adjacent gardens of the Palace of Versailles could be glimpsed. Fine eighteenth-century sculptures created an idyllic atmosphere. I was allowed a half-hour walk every day; an armed soldier followed me. We were forbidden to make contact with the other prisoners, but after a few days I learned a bit about them. They were almost exclusively leading technicians and scientists, agricultural and railroad specialists, among them former Minister Dorpmüller. I recognized Professor Heinkel, the aircraft designer, as well as one of his assistants. I also caught glimpses of many other people with whom I had worked. A week after my arrival my permanent guard was withdrawn, and I was allowed to walk about freely. With that, the monotonous period of solitude came to an end and my psychological state improved. New prisoners arrived: various members of my Ministry, among them Fränk and Saur. We were also joined by technical officers of the American and British forces, who wanted to expand their knowledge of German conditions. My assistants and I agreed that we ought to place our experience in the technology of armaments at their disposal.

I could not contribute very much; Saur had by far the better knowledge of details. I was extremely grateful to the commandant, a British parachute major, when he rescued me from this dreary interim by inviting me to take a drive with him.

We drove past small palace gardens and parks to Saint-Germain, the beautiful creation of Francis I, and from there along the Seine toward Paris. We passed the Coq Hardi, the famous restaurant in Bougival where I had spent pleasant evenings with Cortot, Vlaminck, Despiau, and other French artists, and reached the Champs Elysées. Here the major proposed a stroll, but I said no in his interest; there was always the chance I might be recognized. Crossing the Place de la Concorde we turned into the quais along the Seine. There fewer people were about; we ventured a walk and then returned by way of Saint-Cloud to our palatial prison camp.

A few days later a large bus drew up in the prison yard. A whole busload of "tourists" was quartered with us, among them Schacht and General Thomas, the former chief of the Armaments Office. Also among the bus passengers were prominent prisoners from German concentration camps who had been liberated by the Americans in South Tyrol, taken to Capri, and then transferred to our camp. Word went around that Pastor Niemöller was among them. We did not know him personally, but among the new arrivals was a frail old man, white-haired and wearing a black suit. The designer Flettner, Heinkel, and I agreed he must be Niemöller. We felt great sympathy for this man so visibly marked by many years of concentration camp. Flettner took it upon himself to go over to the broken man and express our sympathy. But he had no sooner addressed him than he was corrected: "Thyssen! My name is Thyssen. Niemöller is stand-ing over there." And there he stood, looking youthful and self-possessed, smoking a pipe—an extraordinary example of how the pressures of long imprisonment can be withstood. Later, I often thought about him. The bus drove into the palace courtyard again a few days later and whisked its former passengers off again. Only Thyssen and Schacht were left be-hind with us.

When Eisenhower's headquarters was shifted to Frankfurt, a column of some ten American military trucks appeared at our quarters. We pris-oners were assigned our places in two open trucks with wooden benches. The other trucks took the furnishings. As we passed through Paris, at every traffic stop a crowd assembled shouting insults and threats. East of Paris we paused in a meadow for a midday rest. Guards and prisoners mingled—a peaceful scene. Our first day's destination was supposed to be Heidelberg. I was glad when we did not make it that night, for it would have pained me to be in prison in my home town.

The next day we reached Mannheim. The city seemed lifeless; the streets were deserted, the buildings shattered. A German private in torn uniform, his face roughly bearded, a cardboard carton on his back, stood dully by the side of the road: the image of defeat. At Nauheim we turned off the autobahn. Soon afterward we began climbing a steep road and ended up in Kransberg Castle. In the winter of 1939, I had fitted out and rebuilt this large castle, three miles from Hitler's command center, as a headquarters for Goering. A two-story wing had been added for Goering's large staff of servants, and we prisoners were now quartered in this annex.

Here, in contrast to Versailles, there was no barbed wire. Even the windows on the top floor of our servants' wing provided a clear view of the landscape. The wrought-iron gate which I had designed was not locked. We were allowed to move about freely in the whole area of the castle. Five years before I had laid out an orchard above the castle, surrounded by a wall some three feet high. Here we could sprawl at ease, with a grand view of the Taunus woods and far below us the village of Kransberg with its gently smoking chimneys.

Compared with our fellow countrymen, who were going hungry in their freedom, we were inappropriately well off, for we received the same rations as American troops. But in the village, the prison camp had a bad reputation. Apparently the surrounding populace believed we were being beaten and starved; rumor had it that Leni Riefenstahl was pining away in the dungeon of the tower. Actually we had been brought to this castle to answer questions on the technical conduct of the war. It was the gathering point for all kinds of specialists: almost the entire leadership of my Ministry, most of my department heads, most of the leading men in munitions, tank, automobile, ship, aircraft, and textile production, the important figures in chemistry, and such designers as Professor Porsche. But interrogators seldom found their way to us. The prisoners grumbled, for most of them rightly hoped that once they had been pumped dry of information they would be released again. Wernher von Braun and his assistants joined us for a few days. He had received offers from the United States and England for himself and his staff, and we discussed these. The Russians, too, had contrived to use the kitchen staff at the heavily guarded Garmisch camp to smuggle an offer of a contract to him.

For the rest, we banished boredom by early-morning sports, a series of scientific lectures, and once Schacht recited poetry, giving astonishingly emotional renderings. A weekly cabaret was also conjured up. We watched the performances—the scenes repeatedly dealt with our own situation—and sometimes tears of laughter ran down our faces at the tumble we had taken.

One morning, shortly after six o'clock, one of my former assistants roused me from sleep: "I've just heard on the radio that you and Schacht are going to be tried at Nuremberg!" I tried to keep my composure, but the news hit me hard. Much as I believed in principle that as one of the leaders of the regime I must take responsibility for its crimes, it was hard for me at first to adjust to the reality. I had felt some trepidation at seeing photographs of the interior of Nuremberg prison in the newspaper. Weeks ago I had read that some of the chief members of the government had been put there. But while my fellow defendant Schacht soon had to exchange our pleasant prison camp for the jail at Nuremberg, weeks were to pass before I was taken there.

Although this meant that I was facing charges of the gravest sort, one would never have known it from the behavior of the guards toward me. The Americans said cheerily: "You'll soon be acquitted and the whole thing forgotten." Sergeant Williams increased my rations so that, as he said, I would have my strength for the trial, and the British commandant invited me for a drive the day we met. We drove alone, without guards, through the Taunus woods, lay down for a while under a huge fruit tree, tramped about the woods, and he told me about hunting bears in Kashmir.

It was beautiful September weather. Toward the end of the month an American jeep swung in through the gate: the squad that had come to get me. At first the British commandant refused to turn over his prisoner before he had received orders from Frankfurt. Sergeant Williams provided me with innumerable biscuits and asked repeatedly whether I needed anything from his stores. By the time I finally entered the jeep, almost the entire camp community had assembled in the castle yard. Everyone wished me well. I shall never forget the kindly and troubled expression in the eyes of the British colonel as he bade me good-by.

34

Nuremberg

THAT EVENING I WAS DELIVERED TO THE NOTORIOUS INTERROGATION CAMP
of Oberursel near Frankfurt, greeted with crude mocking jokes by the
sergeant in charge, and fed a thin, watery soup with which I nibbled my
British biscuits. I thought nostalgically of beautiful Kransberg. That night
I heard the rough shouts of the American guards, anxious replies and
screams. In the morning a German general was led past me under guard,
his face weary and desperate.

Finally, we were moved on in a canvas-covered truck. I sat squeezed
in tightly with others; among them I recognized the Mayor of Stuttgart,
Dr. Strölin, and Admiral Horthy, the Regent of Hungary. We were not
told our destination, but it was obvious: Nuremberg. We arrived there
after dark. A gate was opened; I stood for some minutes in the corridor of
a block of cells which I had seen in the newspaper a few weeks earlier.
Before I knew it, I was locked into one of them. Opposite me, Goering
peeped out the opening[1] in his cell door and shook his head. A straw pal-
let, tattered and filthy old blankets, impassive indifferent guards. Although
all four floors of the building were occupied, an eerie silence prevailed,
interrupted only by the occasional clang of a cell door when a prisoner
was led off for interrogation. Goering, across the corridor from me, walked
endlessly back and forth in his cell; at regular intervals I saw part of his
massive body passing the peephole. Soon, I too began pacing my cell, at
first back and forth and then, the better to utilize the space, around and
around.

After about a week during which I was ignored and remained in uncertainty, there came a change—a modest one for an ordinary person, for me an enormous one: I was transferred to the sunny side of the prison on the fourth floor, where there were better rooms with better beds. Here the American warden, Colonel Andrus, paid a first visit to me: "Very pleased to see you." As camp commandant in Mondorf he had insisted on the utmost strictness, and I thought I could detect some mockery in his words. On the other hand, it was a pleasure to see the German staff again. The cooks, mess attendants, and barbers had been carefully picked from among prisoners of war. But because they too had known the meaning of imprisonment, they behaved helpfully toward us whenever there were no supervisory personnel about. They managed to whisper to us a good many bits of news from the papers, as well as good wishes and encouragements.

If I opened the top pane of the high cell window the patch of sunlight that entered was just big enough for me to sunbathe the upper part of my body. Lying on blankets on the floor, I changed my position as the sun moved until its last slanting ray was gone. There was no light; there were no books or even newspapers. I was wholly cast on myself and had to fend off my growing depression without external aids.

Sauckel was frequently led past my cell. Whenever he saw me, he made a face, gloomy but at the same time rather embarrassed. Finally my door too was unlocked. An American soldier awaited me, a note in hand on which were written my name and the room of the interrogating officer. We passed through courtyards and down staircases into the halls of the Nuremberg Palace of Justice. On the way I passed Funk obviously coming from an interrogation; he looked extremely worn and downcast. At our last meeting we had both been free men in Berlin. "This is how we meet again!" he called out in passing. From the impression he made upon me, tieless and in an unpressed suit, with sallow, unhealthy complexion, I could only deduce that I must be making a similar wretched impression. For I had not seen myself in a mirror for weeks, and that was how it was going to be for years. I also saw Keitel standing in a room facing several American officers. He too looked shockingly run-down.

A young American officer awaited me. He pleasantly invited me to sit down and then began asking for explanations of various matters. Apparently Sauckel had tried to make a better case for himself by branding me as solely responsible for the importation of foreign workers. The officer proved to be well disposed and of his own accord composed an affidavit which straightened out this matter. This somewhat eased my mind, for I had the feeling that since my departure from Mondorf a good deal had been said about me on the principle of "Incriminate the absent."

Shortly afterward I was presented to the deputy prosecutor, Thomas Dodd. His questions were sharp and aggressive; we clashed frequently.

I did not want to be cowed and answered candidly and without evasions, giving no thought to my future defense. I deliberately omitted many details which might have sounded like extenuations. Back in my cell, I had the feeling: "Now you're in the trap." And in fact these statements later constituted an essential part of the charge against me.

At the same time, however, the interrogation gave me a certain feeling of buoyancy. I believed and still believe that I acted rightly in offering no excuses and not sparing my own person. Anxiously, but with the resolution to continue along the same path, I waited for the next interrogation, which had already been announced. I was not called again. Perhaps the prosecution had been impressed by my candor; I do not know the reason. All that followed were several politely formal question sessions with Soviet officers, who were accompanied by a heavily rouged stenographer. Seeing these men badly shook the stereotyped image I still held at that time. After every reply the officers would nod and say, *"Tak, tak,"* which sounded odd but merely meant, as I soon found out, "So, so." Once the Soviet colonel asked me: "But surely you have read Hitler's *Mein Kampf?*" Actually, I had only leafed through it, partly because Hitler had told me the book was outmoded, partly because it was hard reading. When I said no, he roared with laughter. Somewhat insulted, I withdrew the reply and declared that I had read the book. After all, that was the only believable answer. But in the course of the trial this lie returned to haunt me. In cross-questioning the Soviet prosecution brought up this time I had contradicted myself. Then, under oath, I had to tell the truth and admit that at the interrogation I had spoken a falsehood.

At the end of October all the defendants were assembled in the lower story. The whole wing of cells had been cleared of other prisoners. The silence was uncanny. Twenty-one persons were awaiting their trial.*

Rudolf Hess, flown in from England, had also appeared, wearing a blue-gray coat, walking handcuffed between two American soldiers. Hess wore an absent-minded but at the same time obstinate expression. For years I had been accustomed to seeing all these defendants in magnificent uniforms, either unapproachable or jovially expansive. The whole scene now seemed unreal; sometimes I imagined I was dreaming.

Nevertheless, we were already behaving like prisoners. Who, for example, in his days as a Reich Marshal or Field Marshal, as a Grand Admiral, minister, or Reichsleiter, would have thought that he would ever submit to intelligence testing by an American military psychologist? And yet this test was not only not resisted, everyone in fact strove to do the best he could on it and see his abilities confirmed.

The surprise victor in this test, which embraced memory span, reac-

---

* The twenty-second defendant, Bormann, was to be tried in absentia; Robert Ley had committed suicide before the trial began.—*Editor's note.*

tion speeds, and imagination, was Schacht. He came out on top because the test allowed additional points with increasing age. Seyss-Inquart, though no one would have foreseen it, achieved the highest actual point score. Goering, too, was among the top scorers; I received a good median rating.

A few days after we had been separated from the other prisoners, a commission consisting of several officers entered the deathly stillness of our cell block. They went from cell to cell. I heard them speaking a few words that I could not understand, until finally my door opened and a printed copy of the indictment was unceremoniously handed to me. The preliminary investigation had been concluded; the actual trial was beginning. In my naïveté I had imagined that each of us would receive an individual indictment. Now it turned out that we were one and all accused of the monstrous crimes that this document listed. After reading it I was overwhelmed by a sense of despair. But in that despair at what had happened and my role in it, I found the position I felt I should take in the trial: to regard my own fate as insignificant, not to struggle for my own life, but to assume the responsibility in a general sense. In spite of all the opposition of my lawyer and in spite of the strains of the trial, I held fast to this resolve.

Under the impact of the indictment I wrote to my wife:

> I must regard my life as concluded. Only then can I shape its finale in the way I consider necessary. . . . I must stand here as a minister of the Reich and not as a private individual. I have no right to consider all of you or myself. My sole wish is that I may be strong enough to stick to this position. Strange as it may sound, I am in good spirits when I have relinquished all hope and become uncertain and nervous as soon as I think I have a chance. . . . Perhaps, by my bearing, I can once more help the German people. Perhaps I shall accomplish it. There are not many here who will.*

At this time the prison psychologist, G. M. Gilbert, was going from cell to cell with a copy of the indictment, asking the defendants to write their comments on it. When I read the partially evasive, partially disdainful words of many of my fellow defendants, I wrote, to Gilbert's astonishment: "The trial is necessary. There is a shared responsibility for such horrible crimes even in an authoritarian state."

* Letter to my wife, October 17, 1945. Also, on this subject, I wrote to my wife on December 15, 1945: "I am duty-bound to face this tribunal. In view of the fate of the German people one may be too solicitous for one's own immediate family." In March 1946: "I cannot put up a cheap defense here. I believe you will understand, for in the end you and the children would feel shame if I forgot that many millions of Germans fell for a false ideal." Letter to my parents, April 25, 1946: "Don't solace yourselves with the idea that I am putting up a stiff fight for myself. One must bear one's responsibility here, not hope for favoring winds."

I still regard it as my greatest feat of psychic courage to have held to this view throughout the ten months of the trial.

Along with the indictment we were presented with a long list of German lawyers, from whose ranks each of us could choose his defender if we had no proposals of our own. Much as I strained my memory, I could not recall a single lawyer. The names on the list were completely unknown to me, so I asked the court to make a choice. A few days later I was taken to the ground floor of the Palace of Justice. At one of the tables a slight man with strong glasses and a low voice stood up. "I am supposed to be your lawyer, if you agree. My name is Dr. Hans Flächsner, from Berlin." He had friendly eyes and an unassuming manner. When we discussed various details of the indictment, he displayed a sensible, unhistrionic attitude. Finally he handed me a form. "Take this with you and consider whether you want me for your defense attorney." I signed it there and then and did not regret it. In the course of the trial Flächsner proved to be a circumspect, tactful lawyer. But what mattered more to me, he felt a sympathy toward me out of which, during the ten months of the trial, a real mutual affection developed that has lasted to this day.

During the preliminary investigation the prisoners were prevented from meeting. Now this regulation was relaxed, so that we crossed paths more often in the prison yard, where we could talk without surveillance. The trial, the indictment, the invalidity of the international tribunal, profound indignation at the disgrace—again and again as we walked our rounds of the yard I heard the same subjects and opinions. Among the twenty other defendants I found only one who shared my views. That was Fritzsche, with whom I could consider in detail the principle of responsibility. Later Seyss-Inquart also showed some understanding of this. With the others, all discussion was useless and wearing. We were speaking different languages.

On other questions also we naturally enough held divergent opinions. In what light we were going to describe Hitler's rule for purposes of this trial was acutely important. Goering, though he had had strong reservations about some practices of the regime, was all in favor of whitewashing Hitler. Our only hope, he held, was to use this trial to promote a positive legend. I felt that it was unethical to deceive the German people in this way; I also thought it dangerous because it would make the transition to the future more difficult for the whole nation. Only the truth could accelerate the process of cutting free from the past.

I had a certain insight into Goering's real motives when he observed that the victors would undoubtedly kill him but that within fifty years his remains would be laid in a marble sarcophagus and he would be celebrated by the German people as a national hero and martyr. Many of the prisoners had the same dream about themselves. On other subjects Goering's arguments were less effective. There were no differences among us, he said; we were all sentenced to death from the start and none of us had a chance. It was pointless to bother about a defense. I remarked: "Goering wants to ride into Valhalla with a large retinue." In actuality Goering later defended himself more stubbornly than the rest of us did.

At Mondorf and Nuremberg, Goering had undergone a systematic withdrawal cure which had ended his drug addiction. Ever since, he was in better form than I had ever seen him. He displayed remarkable energy and became the most formidable personality among the defendants. I thought it a great pity that he had not been up to this level in the months before the outbreak of the war and in critical situations during the war. He would have been the only person whose authority and popularity Hitler would have had to reckon with. Actually, he had been one of the few sensible enough to foresee the doom that awaited us. But having thrown away his chance to save the country while that was still possible, it was absurd and truly criminal for him to use his regained powers to hoodwink his own people. His whole policy was one of deception. Once, in the prison yard something was said about Jewish survivors in Hungary. Goering remarked coldly: "So, there are still some there? I thought we had knocked off all of them. Somebody slipped up again." I was stunned.

My vow to accept responsibility for the entire regime could not be kept without some severe psychological crises. The only way of getting out of it was to escape trial by suicide. Once I tried using a towel to stop the circulation in my sick leg, in order to produce phlebitis. Remembering from one of our lectures in Kransberg that the nicotine from even a cigar, crumbled and dissolved in water, could be fatal, I kept a crushed cigar in my pocket for a long time. But from the intention to the deed is a very long way.

The Sunday divine services became a great support for me. Even as recently as my stay in Kransberg I had refused to attend them. I did not want to seem soft. But in Nuremberg I threw aside such prideful feelings. The pressure of circumstances brought me—as, incidentally, it did almost all the defendants with the exception of Hess, Rosenberg, and Streicher—into our small chapel.

Our suits had been put in mothballs; the Americans had provided us, during our imprisonment, with cotton gabardine fatigues dyed black. Now clothing-room clerks came to our cells. We were allowed to choose which of our clothes should be cleaned for the trial. Every detail was discussed with the commandant, down to the matter of sleeve buttons.

After a last inspection by Colonel Andrus, on November 19, 1945, we were led into the still empty courtroom, each of us escorted by a soldier, but without handcuffs. Seats were formally assigned. At the head were Goering, Hess, and Ribbentrop. I was placed third from last on the second bench, in agreeable company: Seyss-Inquart on my right, von Neurath on my left. Streicher and Funk sat right in front of me.

I was glad that the trial was beginning, and almost all of the defendants expressed the same view: If only it were all over at last!

The trial began with the grand, devastating opening address by the chief American prosecutor, Justice Robert H. Jackson. But I took comfort from one sentence in it which accused the defendants of guilt for the regime's crimes, but not the German people. This thesis corresponded precisely with what I had hoped would be a subsidiary result of the trial: that the hatred directed against the German people which had been fanned by the propaganda of the war years and had reached an extreme after the revelation of those crimes, would now be focused upon us, the defendants. My theory was that the top leadership in a modern war could be expected to face the consequences at the end precisely because they had previously not been exposed to any danger.* In a letter to my defense attorney who was trying to define the line we would follow, I declared that viewed within the total framework everything that we would be discussing as points in my favor appeared to me unimportant and ludicrous.

For many months the documents and testimonies accumulated. These aimed to prove that the crimes had been committed, without regard to whether any one of the defendants had been personally connected with them. It was horrible, and could only be borne because our nerves became more blunted from session to session. To this day photographs, documents, and orders keep coming back to me. They were so monstrous that they seemed unbelievable, and yet none of the defendants doubted their genuineness.

Along with this, the daily routine continued: from morning to twelve noon the trial sessions; recess for eating in the upper rooms of the Palace of Justice; from two until five o'clock second session; then return to my cell where I changed clothes quickly, gave my suit out for pressing, had supper, and then usually was taken to the conference room for the defense where I discussed the course of the trial with my lawyer until nearly ten o'clock and made notes for the coming defense. Finally, I returned exhausted to my cell late in the evening and immediately fell asleep. On Saturdays and Sundays the court did not hold sessions, but we worked all

---

* Letter to my wife, December 15, 1945: "If I had not had my assignment, I would have been a soldier, and what then? Five years of war are a long time, and I would almost certainly have had more to endure and would perhaps have suffered a worse fate. I am glad to accept my situation if by so doing I can still do something for the German people." Letter of August 7, 1946: "In such situations one should not think only of one's own life. Every soldier on the battlefield is faced with danger of death and has no choice in the matter."

the longer with our lawyers. Generally there remained little more than half an hour daily for a walk in the prison yard.

In spite of our common situation no sense of solidarity arose among us, the defendants. We split up into groups. A significant instance was the establishment of a "generals' garden"—a small section, no larger than twenty by twenty feet separated from the rest of the prison garden by low hedges. Here our military men trudged steadily around in self-elected isolation, although the small walking area must have been very uncomfortable. We who were civilians respected this division. For the noon meals the prison command had put a number of separate rooms at our disposal. My table mates were Fritzsche, Funk, and Schirach.*

In the meantime we had regained some hope that we would come out of the trial with our lives, since the general indictment had been followed by a detailed indictment for each defendant. Clear distinctions were made in these. Consequently, Fritzsche and I at this point were counting on milder judgments, for the charges against us were comparatively less harsh.

In the courtroom, however, we encountered only hostile faces, icy dogmas. The only exception was the interpreters' booth. From there I might expect a friendly nod. Among the British and American prosecutors there were also some who occasionally manifested a trace of sympathy. I was taken aback when the journalists began laying bets on the extent of our penalties, and their list of those slated for hanging sometimes included us too.

After a pause of several days devoted to the final preparations of the defense, the "counterattack" began. A few of us expected a great deal of it. Before Goering mounted the witness stand, he had promised Funk, Sauckel, and others to take their responsibility upon himself and thus exonerate them. In his early statements, which had a considerable ring of courage, he kept this promise. But the closer he approached to details, the more disappointed grew the faces of those who were counting on him, for he then pared down his own responsibility point by point.

In his duel with Goering, Prosecutor Jackson had the advantage of surprise. There were always fresh documents he could pull out of his swollen briefcase. But Goering could take advantage of his adversary's basic ignorance of the material. In the end Goering merely fought for his life, using evasions, obfuscations, and denials.

Ribbentrop and Keitel, the next two defendants, behaved in the same

---

* The prison psychologist, G. M. Gilbert, has revealed in his *Nuremberg Diary* (New York: Farrar, Straus & Young, Inc., 1947), p. 158, that the different groups were established deliberately by the prison command to prevent Goering from "terrorizing the defendants."—*Translators' note.*

way. They too repudiated any responsibility: Whenever confronted with a document that bore their signatures, they justified it on grounds of an order from Hitler. Disgusted, I blurted out the remark about the "letter carriers on high salaries," which afterward was printed in newspapers throughout the world. When I consider the matter today, they were basically telling the truth: They were actually not much more than transmitters of Hitler's orders. Rosenberg, on the other hand, made an impression of honesty and consistency. All the efforts of his lawyer both before and behind the scenes to persuade him to recant his so-called ideology came to nothing. Hans Frank, Hitler's lawyer and later Governor General of Poland, also shouldered his responsibility. Funk reasoned skillfully and in a way that stirred my pity. Schacht's attorney drew on all his rhetorical resources to make his client out a rebel conspirator; his efforts ended only in his weakening rather than strengthening the actual exonerating evidence in Schacht's favor. Doenitz, for his part, fought obstinately for himself and his submarines; it gave him great satisfaction when his lawyer was able to present an affidavit from Admiral Nimitz, commander of the American Pacific fleet, stating that he had conducted his own submarine warfare on the basis of the same principles as the German naval leadership. Raeder gave the impression of objectivity; Sauckel's simplemindedness seemed rather pathetic; Jodl's precise and sober defense was rather imposing. He seemed to be one of the few men who stood above the situation.

The order of testimony followed the seating order. My nervousness increased, for now Seyss-Inquart, my neighbor, was already in the witness chair. A lawyer himself, he had no illusions about his situation; he had been a direct participant in deportations and the shooting of hostages. He seemed controlled and concluded his testimony with a statement that he must take responsibility for what had happened. By a lucky chance, a few days after the testimony which sealed his death sentence he received the first good news about his son, who up to this time had been missing in Russia.

When I went to the witness stand, I had stage fright. I hastily swallowed a tranquilizing pill the German doctor had prudently handed to me. Opposite me, about ten paces away, Flächsner stood at the defense attorney's desk; on my left, at a higher level, sat the judges.

Flächsner opened his thick manuscript. Questions and answers began. At the outset I stated: "If Hitler had had any friends, I would certainly have been one of his close friends"—by which I was trying to explain something that up to this point not even the prosecution had asserted. A vast number of details referring to the documents presented were discussed. I corrected misunderstandings but tried not to sound apologetic or evasive.* In a few sentences I assumed responsibility for all the orders from Hitler which I had carried out. I took the position that in every government orders must remain orders for the subordinate organs of the government; but that the leadership on all levels must examine and weigh the orders it receives and is consequently co-responsible for them, even if the orders have been carried out under duress.

What mattered more to me was to assert my collective responsibility for all the measures of Hitler, not excluding the crimes, which were undertaken or committed in the period from 1942 on wherever and by whomever. "In political life there is a responsibility for a man's own sector," I said to the court.

> For that he is of course fully responsible. But beyond that there is a collective responsibility when he has been one of the leaders. Who else is to be held responsible for the course of events, if not the closest associates around the Chief of State? But this collective responsibility can only apply to fundamental matters and not to details. . . . Even in an authoritarian system this collective responsibility of the leaders must exist; there can be no attempting to withdraw from the collective responsibility after the catastrophe. For if the war had been won, the leadership would probably have raised the claim that it was collectively responsible. . . . I have this obligation all the more since the chief of government has withdrawn from his responsibility to the German people and to the world.[2]

To Seyss-Inquart, I expressed these ideas in more vivid fashion:

> How would it be if the scene suddenly changed, and we all acted as if the war had been won? Can't you just see how each of us would rush to put his merits and his achievements in the forefront? Now the thing has been switched; instead of decorations, honors, and gifts, death sentences are being dispersed.

During the past several weeks Flächsner had tried in vain to reason me out of accepting responsibility for things that had happened outside my Ministry. To do so, he said, could have fatal consequences. But after

---

* In court I clearly acknowledged my share of the responsibility for the forced-labor program: "I was grateful to Sauckel for every worker he provided me with. Often when we failed to meet armaments quotas because of a shortage of workers, I would put the blame on Sauckel. . . . Of course I knew that foreign laborers were working in the armaments plants. I assented to this. . . . I have made it clear enough that I approved of Sauckel's labor policy [of bringing forced labor] from the occupied areas to Germany. . . . The laborers were for the most part brought to Germany against their will, and I raised no protest against this policy. On the contrary, at the beginning, until the autumn of 1942, I tried to have as many workers as possible brought to Germany."

my admission I felt my spirits lightened. I was glad I had not tried to dodge the issue. Having made this matter clear, I believed I could now launch into the second part of my testimony which dealt with the last phase of the war. I believed it important to present these data, chiefly for their effect on the German people. If they learned of Hitler's intentions to destroy the very basis of life for the German people after the loss of the war, it would help the nation turn its back on the past.* Here was strong evidence to counter the creation of a Hitler legend. But when I said these things, I encountered stiff disapproval from Goering and other defendants.[3]

In court I intended merely to mention my plan to assassinate Hitler, chiefly in order to show how dangerous Hitler's destructive intentions had seemed to me. "I prefer not to go into the details," I said. The judges put their heads together. The presiding judge then turned to me: "The court would like to hear the details. We will hold our recess now." I did not want to make any further statements on the matter, for fear of seeming to boast about it. I sketched the story with considerable reluctance and agreed with my defense attorney that he was not to use this part of my testimony in his final plea.[4]

Back in the safe track of our interrogation manuscript, the concluding part of my testimony ran rapidly through the last period of the war without interruption. In order to diminish any impression of special merits, I deliberately qualified my remarks: "All these measures were not even so dangerous. From January 1945 on, it was possible inside Germany to carry out any reasonable measure contrary to the official policy. Every sensible person welcomed such measures. Everyone involved knew what our [counter-] orders meant. Even longstanding party members came to the nation's aid in that period. Jointly we were able to do a great deal to undercut Hitler's insane orders."

Flächsner closed his manuscript with visible relief and went to his seat among the other lawyers. Justice Jackson, the chief U.S. prosecutor, took his place. For me that was no surprise, for the previous evening an American officer had come rushing to my cell to tell me that Jackson had decided to cross-examine me himself. In contrast to his usual manner, Jackson began quietly, in an almost benevolent voice. After he had again ascertained by documents and questions that I admitted co-responsibility for the employment of millions of forced laborers, he discussed the second part of my testimony in a favorable light. I had, he said, been the only man who had had the courage to tell Hitler to his face that the war was

---

* Letter to my wife, June 1946: "What matters most to me is that I manage to tell the truth about the end. That is what the German people must be told." Letter, mid-August: "The best way I can help my people is to speak the truth about the whole madness. There are no benefits for me in this course, nor do I want any benefits."

lost. I interposed, saying that Guderian, Jodl, and many of the commanders of army groups had also defied Hitler. When he asked the further question, "Then there were more plots than you have told us?" I replied rather evasively: "In that period it was remarkably easy to concoct a plot. You could accost almost anyone on the street. If you told him what the situation was, he would answer: 'It's sheer madness.' And if he had the courage, he would offer his aid. . . . It was not so dangerous as it looks from here, for there were perhaps a few dozen irrational people; the other eighty million were extremely rational as soon as they realized what was involved."[5]

After a further cross-examination by General Raginsky, the representative of the Soviet prosecution—an examination full of misunderstandings because of errors by the interpreters—Flächsner once more stepped forward. He handed the court a sheaf of written statements by my twelve witnesses. With that, the presentation of my case was over. For hours I had been gripped by severe stomach pains. Back in my cell, I threw myself on my cot, overwhelmed equally by physical pain and mental exhaustion.

35

Conclusions

FOR THE LAST TIME THE PROSECUTORS TOOK THE FLOOR. THEIR SUMMATIONS concluded the trial. For us only our final speeches remained. Since these were to be broadcast in full over the radio, they had a special significance. They were our last chance to address our own people, but also our last chance, by admitting our guilt, by facing squarely the crimes of the past, to show the nation that we had led astray a way out of its quandary.[1]

The nine months of trial had left their marks on us. Even Goering, who had entered the trial with an aggressive determination to justify himself, spoke in his final speech of the terrible crimes that had been brought to light, condemned the ghastly mass murders, and declared that he could not comprehend them. Keitel stated that he would rather choose death than be entangled again in such horrors. Frank spoke of the guilt that Hitler and the German people had laden upon themselves. He warned the incorrigibles against the "way of political folly which must lead to destruction and death." His speech sounded overwrought, but it expressed the essence of my own view also. Even Streicher in his final speech condemned Hitler's "mass killings of Jews." Funk spoke of frightful crimes that filled him with profound shame. Schacht declared that he stood "shaken to the depths of his soul by the unspeakable misery which he had tried to prevent." Sauckel was "shocked in his inmost soul by the crimes that had been revealed in the course of the trial." Papen declared that "the power of evil had proved stronger than that of good."

(519)

Seyss-Inquart spoke of "fearful excesses." To Fritzsche "the murder of five million people" was "a gruesome warning for the future." On the other hand they all denied their own share in these events.

In a sense my hopes had been realized. The judicial guilt had been concentrated to a large extent upon us, the defendants. But during that accursed era, a factor in addition to human depravity had entered history, the factor that distinguished our tyranny from all historical precedents, and a factor that would inevitably increase in importance in the future. As the top representative of a technocracy which had without compunction used all its know-how in an assault on humanity,* I tried not only to confess but also to understand what had happened. In my final speech I said:

> Hitler's dictatorship was the first dictatorship of an industrial state in this age of modern technology, a dictatorship which employed to perfection the instruments of technology to dominate its own people. . . . By means of such instruments of technology as the radio and public-address systems, eighty million persons could be made subject to the will of one individual. Telephone, teletype, and radio made it possible to transmit the commands of the highest levels directly to the lowest organs where because of their high authority they were executed uncritically. Thus many offices and squads received their evil commands in this direct manner. The instruments of technology made it possible to maintain a close watch over all citizens and to keep criminal operations shrouded in a high degree of secrecy. To the outsider this state apparatus may look like the seemingly wild tangle of cables in a telephone exchange; but like such an exchange it could be directed by a single will. Dictatorships of the past needed assistants of high quality in the lower ranks of the leadership also—men who could think and act in-

---

* The readiness of technicians to carry out any order is, of course, not limited to our country. A year later, Harry L. Stimson (U. S. Secretary of State from 1929–33, Secretary of War from 1911–13 and 1940–45) wrote an article, "The Nürnberg Trial: Landmark in Law," *Foreign Affairs* (1947) in which he said:

> We must never forget, that under modern conditions of life, science, and technology, all war has become greatly brutalized, and that no one who joins in it, even in self-defense, can escape becoming also in a measure brutalized. Modern war cannot be limited in its destructive method and the inevitable debasement of all participants. . . . A fair scrutiny of the last two World Wars makes clear the steady intensification in the inhumanity of the weapons and methods employed by both, the aggressors and the victors. In order to defeat Japanese aggression, we were forced, as Admiral Nimitz has stated, to employ a technique of unrestricted submarine warfare, not unlike that which 25 years ago was the proximate cause of our entry into World War I. In the use of strategic air power the Allies took the lives of hundreds of thousands of civilians in Germany and in Japan. . . . We as well as our enemies have contributed to the proof that the central moral problem is war and not its methods, and that a continuance of war will in all probability end with the destruction of our civilization.

dependently. The authoritarian system in the age of technology can do without such men. The means of communication alone enable it to mechanize the work of the lower leadership. Thus the type of uncritical receiver of orders is created.

The criminal events of those years were not only an outgrowth of Hitler's personality. The extent of the crimes was also due to the fact that Hitler was the first to be able to employ the implements of technology to multiply crime.

I thought of the consequences that unrestricted rule together with the power of technology—making use of it but also driven by it—might have in the future. This war, I continued, had ended with remote-controlled rockets, aircraft flying at the speed of sound, atom bombs, and a prospect of chemical warfare. In five to ten years it would be possible for an atomic rocket, perhaps serviced by ten men, to annihilate a million human beings in the center of New York within seconds. It would be possible to spread plagues and destroy harvests. "The more technological the world becomes, the greater is the danger. . . . As the former minister in charge of a highly developed armaments economy it is my last duty to state: A new great war will end with the destruction of human culture and civilization. There is nothing to stop unleashed technology and science from completing its work of destroying man which it has so terribly begun in this war. . . ."[2]

"The nightmare shared by many people," I said, "that some day the nations of the world may be dominated by technology—that nightmare was very nearly made a reality under Hitler's authoritarian system. Every country in the world today faces the danger of being terrorized by technology; but in a modern dictatorship this seems to me to be unavoidable. Therefore, the more technological the world becomes, the more essential will be the demand for individual freedom and the self-awareness of the individual human being as a counterpoise to technology. . . . Consequently this trial must contribute to laying down the ground rules for life in human society. What does my own fate signify, after all that has happened and in comparison with so important a goal?"

After the course the trial had run, my situation was, as I saw it, desperate. My last sentence was by no means intended as a theoretical profession of faith. I considered my life at its close.[3]

The court recessed for an indefinite period to consider the verdicts. We waited four long weeks. During this time of almost unbearable suspense, exhausted by the preceding eight months of mental torment, I read Dickens's novel of the French Revolution, *A Tale of Two Cities.* He describes how the prisoners in the Bastille looked forward with tranquillity and often with cheerful serenity toward their fate. But I was incapable of such inner freedom. The Soviet prosecution had urged the death sentence for me.

On September 30, 1946, in freshly pressed suits, we took our seats in the dock for the last time. The court wanted to spare us the movie cameras and photographers at this juncture. The spotlights which earlier had illuminated the large courtroom to allow the recording of each of our emotions were extinguished. The room assumed an unusually gloomy aspect as the judges entered and defendants, lawyers, prosecutors, spectators, and press representatives rose in their honor for the last time. As on every day of the trial, the presiding judge, Lord Lawrence, bowed to all sides, to us, the defendants, as well. Then he sat down.

The judges took turns. For several hours they monotonously read out the most dreadful chapter in German history. Still, the condemnation of the leadership seemed to me to exonerate the German people from judicial guilt. For if Baldur von Schirach, for many years leader of the German youth and one of Hitler's closest associates, and if Hjalmar Schacht, Hitler's Minister of Economics at the beginning of the rearmament, were acquitted of having prepared and carried out aggressive warfare—then how could any ordinary soldier, let alone women and children, be burdened with the guilt? If Grand Admiral Raeder and Hitler's deputy, Rudolf Hess, were acquitted of having participated in the crimes against humanity—how could a German engineer or worker be held answerable?

I also hoped that the trial would exert a direct influence upon the occupation policies of the victorious powers. They for their part could not very well mete out to our people the treatment they themselves had just defined as criminal. In this, I had mainly in mind the main charge against me: forced labor.[4]

There followed the justification of the verdict for each individual case, but as yet without announcement of the verdict itself.[5] My own activities were described in a cool and unbiased fashion, in total accord with what I myself had already declared during my interrogation. My responsibility for the deportation of foreign workers was stated; then that I had opposed Himmler's plans solely on the tactical grounds of their effect on production but had used his concentration camp inmates without protest and had requisitioned Soviet prisoners of war for work in the armaments industry. It added to my culpability that I had raised no humane and ethical considerations in these cases, thus helping to forge the policy of raising foreign laborers by force.

None of the defendants, including those who could certainly count on the death sentence, lost his composure as the judges read out these charges. In silence, without any outward sign of emotion, they listened. It still remains incredible to me that I was able to stick it out through the trial without breaking down and that I was able to listen to the reading of the judgment with anxiety, but still with a measure of strength and self-control. Flächsner was overoptimistic: "The judgment means you'll receive perhaps four or five years."

The next day we, the defendants, saw each other for the last time before the announcement of the individual sentences. We met in the basement of the Palace of Justice. One after the other we entered a small elevator and did not return. In the courtroom above the sentence was announced. Finally it was my turn. Accompanied by an American soldier, I rode up in the elevator. A door opened, and I stood alone on a small platform in the courtroom, facing the judges. Earphones were handed to me. In my ears the words reverberated: "Albert Speer, to twenty years imprisonment."

A few days later I accepted the sentence. I waived the right to an appeal to the Four Powers. Any penalty weighed little compared to the misery we had brought upon the world. "For there are things," I noted in my diary a few weeks later, "for which one is guilty even if one might offer excuses—simply because the scale of the crimes is so overwhelming that by comparison any human excuse pales to insignificance."

Today, a quarter of a century after these events, it is not only specific faults that burden my conscience, great as these may have been. My moral failure is not a matter of this item and that; it resides in my active association with the whole course of events. I had participated in a war which, as we of the intimate circle should never have doubted, was aimed at world dominion. What is more, by my abilities and my energies I had prolonged that war by many months. I had assented to having the globe of the world crown that domed hall which was to be the symbol of new Berlin. Nor was it only symbolically that Hitler dreamed of possessing the globe. It was part of his dream to subjugate the other nations. France, I had heard him say many times, was to be reduced to the status of a small nation. Belgium, Holland, even Burgundy, were to be incorporated into his Reich. The national life of the Poles and the Soviet Russians was to be extinguished; they were to be made into helot peoples. Nor, for one who wanted to listen, had Hitler ever concealed his intention to exterminate the Jewish people. In his speech of January 30, 1939,[6] he openly stated as much. Although I never actually agreed with Hitler on these questions, I had nevertheless designed the buildings and produced the weapons which served his ends.

During the next twenty years of my life I was guarded, in Spandau prison, by nationals of the four powers against whom I had organized Hitler's war. Along with my six fellow prisoners, they were the only people I had close contact with. Through them I learned directly what the effects of my work had been. Many of them mourned loved ones who had died in the war—in particular, every one of the Soviet guards had lost some close relative, brothers or a father. Yet not one of them bore a grudge toward me for my personal share in the tragedy; never did I hear words of recrimination. At the lowest ebb of my existence, in contact with these ordinary people, I encountered uncorrupted feelings of sympathy, helpfulness, human understanding, feelings that bypassed the prison rules. . . . On the day before my appointment as Minister of Armaments and War Production I had encountered peasants in the Ukraine who had saved me from frostbite. At the time I had been merely touched, without understanding. Now, after all was over, I once again was treated to examples of human kindness that transcended all enmity. And now, at last, I wanted to understand. This book, too, is an attempt at such understanding.

"The catastrophe of this war," I wrote in my cell in 1947, "has proved the sensitivity of the system of modern civilization evolved in the course of centuries. Now we know that we do not live in an earthquake-proof structure. The build-up of negative impulses, each reinforcing the other, can inexorably shake to pieces the complicated apparatus of the modern world. There is no halting this process by will alone. The danger is that the automatism of progress will depersonalize man further and withdraw more and more of his self-responsibility."

Dazzled by the possibilities of technology, I devoted crucial years of my life to serving it. But in the end my feelings about it are highly skeptical.

Afterword

IN WRITING THIS BOOK MY INTENTION HAS BEEN NOT ONLY TO DESCRIBE THE past, but to issue warnings for the future. During the first months of my imprisonment, while I was still in Nuremberg, I wrote a great deal, out of the need to relieve some of the burden that pressed so heavily upon me. That was also the motivation for further studies and notes undertaken during 1946 and 1947. Finally, in March 1953 I decided to set down my memoirs in coherent form. Was it a disadvantage or an advantage that they were written under conditions of depressing solitude? At the time I was often startled by the ruthlessness with which I judged others and myself. On December 26, 1954, I finished the first draft.

When I was released from Spandau prison on October 1, 1966, consequently, I found more than two thousand pages of my own writing at my disposal. Then, with the aid of the documents of my Ministry preserved in the Federal Archives in Koblenz, I reworked this material into the present autobiography.

I am indebted to the editors who discussed many problems with me over two years, Wolf Jobst Siedler, head of the Ullstein and Propyläen publishing houses, and Joachim C. Fest, member of the advisory board of these publishers. Their keen questions helped me frame many of the general observations in this book, as well as my treatment of the psychological and atmospheric aspects of events. My fundamental view of Hitler, his system, and my own part in it, as I had set it down fourteen years earlier in the first version of my memoirs, was confirmed and reinforced by our conversations.

I am also indebted to Dr. Alfred Wagner, UNESCO, Paris, to Archivist Dr. Thomas Trumpp and Frau Hedwig Singer of the Federal Archives, Koblenz, and to David Irving for permitting me to use several previously unpublished diary entries of Jodl and Goebbels.

Notes

Unless otherwise indicated and with the exception of family letters, all documents, letters, speeches, and such, as well as the *Office Journal*, are in the Federal Archives (Bundesarchiv) in Koblenz, catalogued under the inventory number R 3 (Reich Ministry of Armaments and War Production).

The *Office Journal* is a day-by-day record kept in my department from 1941 to 1944. It covered my activities first as Inspector General of Buildings and later as Armaments Minister. [References in text to "the Minister" indicate author.—*Translators' Note*]

The *Führerprotokoll* is the record of Hitler's activities.

CHAPTER 1: *Origins and Youth*

1. For six hundred consecutive years, starting in 1192, Reich Marshals from the von Pappenheim family became Quartermasters General of the German Army. In addition they were Chief Army Provosts and responsible for military roads, transportation, and health. (K. Bosl, *Die Reichsministerialität* [Darmstadt, 1967]).
2. These remarks on music and literature as well as those on the occupation of the Ruhr and the inflation are taken from letters I wrote at the time to my future wife.
3. The concluding lines from Heinrich Tessenow, *Handwerk und Kleinstadt* (1920).

CHAPTER 2: *Profession and Vocation*

1. This quotation and the one following are cited from the unpublished transcript of notes taken by Wolfgang Jungermann, a student of Tessenow, on his lectures from 1929 to 1932.
2. Quoted from memory.

CHAPTER 3: *Junction*

1. See *Die neue Reichskanzlei* (Munich: Zentralverlag der NSDAP, no year).

CHAPTER 5: *Architectural Megalomania*

1. Writing in 1787, Goethe suggested in *Iphigenie on Taurus* that even "the best man" finally "becomes accustomed to cruelty" and "in the end makes a law of that which he despises"; habit makes him "hard and almost unknowable."
2. To this end we planned to avoid, as far as possible, all such elements of modern construction as steel girders and reinforced concrete, which are subject to weathering. Despite their height, the walls were intended to withstand the impact of the wind even if the roofs and ceilings were so neglected that they no longer braced the walls. The static factors were calculated with this in mind.
3. Sir Neville Henderson, *Failure of a Mission* (New York, 1940), p. 72.
4. Both pictures were painted (from photographs) by Hitler's official painter, Professor Knirr, whom Hitler always rewarded handsomely for his work. A photograph from a later period shows that Knirr was also commissioned to do a portrait of Hitler's father.
5. According to Rolf Wagenführ, *Die deutsche Industrie im Kriege 1939–1945* (Berlin, 1954), p. 86, German expenditures for war production in 1944 amounted to seventy-one billion marks. *Die deutsche Bauzeitung*, Vol. 1898, Nos. 5, 9, 26, and 45, contain details about the future site for German national celebrations.
6. The Olympic Stadium built in Berlin in 1936 had a volume of only 9,886,800 cubic feet.
7. From an unpublished speech delivered by Hitler on January 9, 1939 to the workers constructing the new Chancellery building.

CHAPTER 6: *The Greatest Assignment*

1. See *Reichsgesetzblatt*, January 30, 1937, p. 103.
2. In this way the necessary switches and sidings and the repair shops could

be located far outside of Berlin and would no longer interfere with the future architectural development of the city.

3. The site covered an area of about 8150 acres. Given the present-day standard density of 48 inhabitants per acre, that would yield 400,000 inhabitants.

4. As long ago as 1910, the city plan by Professors Brix and Genzmer which won first prize in a contest on Berlin was based on the projection that Berlin would have ten million inhabitants by the year 2000 *(Die deutsche Bauzeitung*, No. 42 [1910]).

5. John Burchardt (Dean of Massachusetts Institute of Technology) and Bush-Brown have observed in *The Architecture of America* (1961), a volume published for the centennial of the American Institute of Architects, that there was little difference between Fascist, Communist, and democratic taste at least insofar as it was expressed through official channels. As examples of the neoclassic style in Washington, D.C., Burchardt mentions the Federal Reserve Building (designed by Crete, 1937), the Roman rotunda of the Jefferson Memorial (Pope, 1937), the National Gallery (Pope, 1939), the Supreme Court, and the National Archives.

CHAPTER 7: *Obersalzberg*

1. Built in neo-Gothic style between 1862 and 1924. The tower was restricted to a height three feet less than that of St. Stephan's Cathedral.

CHAPTER 8: *The New Chancellery*

1. In the Berlin Sportpalast on January 9, 1939, Hitler delivered an address to mark the completion of the new Chancellery. In this unpublished speech he once more referred to the speed with which the Chancellery had been built. As early as 1935, Hitler had commissioned me to work out a design for a sizable enlargement of the Chancellery.

2. Dr. Grawitz, an SS Major General (Gruppenführer) and chief of the SS medical corps, had given him this advice.

3. Ultraseptyl.

4. Ilya Mechnikov studied bacteria, toxins, and immunity; he was awarded the Nobel Prize in 1908.

5. From the unpublished speech delivered in Berlin's "German Hall" on August 2, 1938, to celebrate the raising of the ridgepole for the new Chancellery.

6. From Hitler's speech on January 9, 1939.

7. See Friedrich Hossbach, *Zwischen Wehrmacht und Hitler 1934–1938* (Göttingen, 1949), p. 207.

8. Today the Theodor-Heuss Platz.

9. From my memorandum to Hitler, September 20, 1944.

10. See *Die Reichskanzlei* (Munich: Eher-Verlag), p. 6of.

CHAPTER 9: *A Day in the Chancellery*

1. Every day Hitler did have innumerable meetings with Gauleiters, acquaintances and old party members who had achieved rank and prestige. But so far as I could observe, these discussions did not take care of any work. Hitler merely rambled on in the style of his table talk, touching informally on various problems which were occupying him. The conversation usually turned fairly quickly to unimportant matters. Hitler's appointment calendar undoubtedly would have given a very different impression of his capacity for work.

CHAPTER 10: *Our Empire Style*

1. These buildings are mentioned in the *Office Journal*, 1941.
2. The Tourism Building at the intersection of the grand avenue and Potsdamer Strasse.
3. *Office Journal*, 1941: "The Opera House stands opposite the Economics Ministry, the Philharmonic faces the Colonial Ministry." Around 1941 the architect Klaj reported to me that in the architecture section of the army High Command model houses suitable for Africa were being designed.
4. See also Goebbels's diary entry, May 12, 1943: "Either Frederick the Great should be provided with a magnificent mausoleum in the classic style, to be erected in the park at Sanssouci, or he should be interred in the great Soldiers' Hall of the projected ministry of war building."
5. The Berlin triumphal arch (including the arch aperture) would have had a volume of 83,543,460 cubic feet; the Arc de Triomphe in Paris would have fitted into it 49 times. The Soldiers' Hall was a cube 820 feet long, 295 feet deep, and 262 feet high. The field behind the hall, intended for the new High Command, measured 984 by 1476 feet. The entrance hall with the grand staircase in Goering's new building had a floor space of 158 by 158 feet and a height of 138 feet. The cost of this building was estimated at a minimum of 160 million Reichsmarks. The new Berlin Town Hall was planned to have a length of 1476 feet; its central structure would have been 197 feet high. The Navy High Command was to be 1050 feet long, and the new police headquarters 919 feet.
6. Field Marshal von Blomberg, until 1938 Minister of War, was married in January 1938. Hitler and Goering attended the wedding. Shortly afterward it was revealed that the Field Marshal's bride had been a prostitute, whereupon Hitler forced him to resign—thus strengthening Nazi party control over the army. There is considerable evidence that von Blomberg was the victim of an elaborate plot by Goering, Himmler, and possibly Hitler. See the detailed account of this episode in Hans Bernd Gisevius, *To the Bitter End* (Boston: Houghton Mifflin Company, 1947).
7. Hitler's speech at the raising of the ridgepole for the new Chancellery, August 2, 1938.
8. Albert Speer, "Neuplanung der Reichshauptstadt," in *Der Baumeister* (Munich, 1939), No. 1. Our building plans also became the target of the

typical Berlin wit, even though so little was known of what we really had in mind. Ulrich von Hassell notes in his diary that Furtwängler was supposed to have said to me: "It must be wonderful to be able to build on such a grand scale using your own ideas." To which I am supposed to have replied: "Imagine if someone told you: 'It is my unshakable will that the *Ninth* is to be performed from now on only on the harmonica.'"

9. *Office Journal,* March 28, 1941.
10. *Office Journal,* April 29, 1941.
11. *Office Journal,* March 31, 1941.

CHAPTER 11: *The Globe*

1. According to the preserved plan, the new assembly hall was to have an area of 22,596 square feet.
2. Working sketches for the project, drawn up at the time, are still in existence. On November 5, 1936, Hitler did the sketches based on the preliminary plans I had presented.
3. These ninety-eight-foot columns were made up of red granite sections about ten feet in diameter which were already being quarried in Sweden when the war broke out.
4. The 741,510,000 cubic feet was made up as follows: 331,914,000 cubic feet for the rotunda with its dome, 335,445,000 cubic feet for the square pedestal, 77,682,000 cubic feet for the four antechambers, and 282,480 for the turret.
5. According to K. Lankheit, *Der Tempel der Vernunft* (Basel, 1968), the dome of the building designed by Etienne L. Boullée to glorify *Raison* as the French Revolution interpreted it would have measured 853 feet in diameter.
6. In order to compensate for variations in the subsoil and to compact the foundation by its own dead weight, the construction engineers insisted on a solid slab 1050 by 1050 feet that would extend to a depth of 106 feet.
7. One axis of this square measured 1640 feet, the other 1476 feet.
8. Hitler drew sketches for this building on November 5, 1936, in December 1937, and in March 1940. Bismarck's official residence on Wilhelmstrasse had a volume of 459,000 cubic feet. The new Fuehrer's palace scheduled for completion in 1950 would have had a volume of 67,089,000 cubic feet, not counting the area set aside for offices and official business. Hitler's total volume of 42,372,000 cubic feet put Goering in his place, for the Reich Marshal envisioned only 19,479,800 cubic feet of construction. For this reason Hitler did not feel the need to return to the subject of Goering's building.

   The 919-foot garden façade of Hitler's palace could not compete with the 1890-foot façade of Louis XIV's Versailles, but this was only because the available space did not permit such a length, and I had to bend the two wings to form a U. Each of these wings measured 640 feet; the total length of the sides facing on the garden amounted to 2199 feet and exceeded Versailles by more than 300 feet.

The ground-floor layout sketch for this palace has been preserved; from it I can reconstruct how Hitler planned to utilize the space and the arrangement of the individual halls. From the great square one passed through a monumental gateway into a 361-foot-long court of honor which opened onto two more courts surrounded by columns. From the court of honor one entered reception halls, which opened into a suite of rooms. There would have been several such suites, each stretching 820 feet; one suite, on the north side of the palace, would even have been 1247 feet long. From there one passed through an antechamber into the great dining hall. Measuring 302 by 105 feet, it covered an area of 31,710 square feet. Bismarck's entire residence had an area of only 12,912 square feet, and would thus have fitted neatly into this hall. Under normal circumstances a dining hall requires 16 square feet per person; thus this hall would have had room for almost two thousand guests to dine simultaneously.

9. The reception room of the White House (the East Room) has a volume of 57,600 cubic feet; Hitler's had 741,510! The diplomats' route in the 1938 Chancellery was 722 feet long; the new one was to extend 1654 feet. The visitor crossed a reception room that measured 112 by 118 feet, a barrel-vaulted hall that was 591 by 220 feet, a square room measuring 92 feet on the side, a gallery 722 feet long, and a 92- by 92-foot antechamber. The thickness of the walls accounts for the discrepancy between the length of the rooms and the total length.

10. This includes the secretariat wing on the southwestern side of the square. Since these secretariats were also located in the new Chancellery, a total volume of 49,434,000 cubic feet would have been achieved, whereas Siedler's building amounted to only 706,200 cubic feet.

11. In the ridgepole raising speech on August 2, 1938, Hitler said:

> I am not only the Chancellor of the Reich; I am also a citizen. As a citizen I still live in the Munich apartment I had before coming to power. But as Chancellor of the Reich and Fuehrer of the German nation, I want Germany to have impressive public buildings like any other country; indeed, on the contrary, better than any other. And you will understand that I am too proud to move into former palaces. That I refuse to do. The new Reich will create new spaces for itself and its own buildings. I will not move into the old palaces. In the other nations—in Moscow they're squatting in the Kremlin, in Warsaw they're squatting in the Belvedere, in Budapest in the Königsburg, in Prague in the Hradschin. Everywhere they're squatting in some old building! My simple ambition is to present the new German Reich with buildings it need not be ashamed of in the presence of these princely edifices of the past. But above all, this new German republic is neither a boarder nor a lodger in the royal chambers of bygone days! While others are living in the Kremlin, in the Hradschin, or in a citadel, we will enshrine the prestige of the Reich in buildings born of our own times. . . . Who will move into these buildings I do not know. God

willing, the best sons of our *Volk*, no matter what their class background. But one thing I do know: No one in the whole world should
look down on these sons of our *Volk* for coming from the lowest classes.
The moment someone is called upon to be a representative of Germany,
he is the peer and equal of every foreign king or emperor.

And at the dedication on January 9, 1939:

> I have refused to move into the so-called Presidential Palace. Why,
> my fellow Germans? Because that is the house in which the Lord
> Chamberlain once lived. And you know that the Fuehrer of the Ger-
> man nation cannot live in the house once occupied by the Lord Cham-
> berlain! I would rather live on the fifth floor of a private dwelling than
> settle down in that palace. I never *could* understand the old Republic.
> Those gentlemen set up a republic for themselves, got rid of the old
> Reich, and then they moved into the residence of the former Lord
> Chamberlain. That is so undignified, German workers! They did not
> have the fortitude to give their own state a face of its own. I decided
> to do that, and it has remained my firm decision that the new state
> shall receive its own official buildings.

Considering the extent of Hitler's plans for the future, known only to
him and to me, it is hardly surprising that he should have been so concerned with working out a rationale for his personal craving for prestige.

12. I estimated that the hall would cost roughly two hundred marks per cubic
    meter (35.31 cubic feet) and the other buildings three hundred marks per
    cubic meter.
13. The SS barracks was south of the south station, about four miles from
    Hitler's government center; the barracks for the Grossdeutschland guards
    regiment was to be only 2825 feet north of the domed hall.

CHAPTER 12: *The Descent Begins*

1. The *Völkischer Beobachter* reported on August 23, 1939: "Tuesday morning [August 22], starting about 2:45 A.M., a very impressive display of
   northern lights could be seen in the northwestern and northern sky from
   Sternberg Observatory.
2. Remark reported by Hitler's adjutant, von Below.
3. Quoted from memory.
4. On November 23, 1937, at the dedication of the Sonthofen Ordensberg
   [Order Castle], tremendous cheers erupted when Hitler—after a speech that
   had been received quietly—unexpectedly shouted to the assembled party
   leaders: "Our Enemy Number One is England!" At the time I was astonished by the spontaneity of this cheering. I was also surprised at Hitler's
   suddenly turning against England, for I had assumed all along that England
   still held a special place in his wishful thinking.
5. As late as June 26, 1944, Hitler said in a speech delivered to a group of
   leading industrialists at Obersalzberg: "I did not want to repeat the mistake

of 1899, 1905, and 1912, namely the mistake of waiting, of hoping for a miracle that would enable us to get by without fighting it out."

6. See Hitler's statement to Hermann Rauschning that if the coming war could not be won, the Nazi leadership would opt for dragging the whole continent into the abyss. (Rauschning, *Hitler Speaks* [London, 1939].)

7. Neville Henderson, *Failure of a Mission* (New York, 1940), p. 202f.: "My impression was that the mass of the German people, that other Germany, were horror-struck at the whole idea of the war which was being thus thrust upon them. . . . But what I can say is that the whole general atmosphere in Berlin itself was one of utter gloom and depression."

CHAPTER 13: *Excess*

1. *Office Journal*, 1941: "On May 12, Herr Speer conferred with the Fuehrer at Obersalzberg concerning future parades on the grand avenue; Colonel Schmundt was present. The Fuehrer had already contemplated placing the reviewing stand in front of the ministries. The troops were to march by in the order of the campaigns in which they had participated, proceeding from south to north through the triumphal arch."

2. According to my letter dated February 19, 1941 to the National Socialist Party Treasurer, the cities were: Augsburg, Bayreuth, Bremen, Breslau, Cologne, Danzig, Dresden, Düsseldorf, Graz, Hanover, Heidelberg, Innsbruck, Königsberg, Memel, Münster, Oldenburg, Posen, Prague, Saarbrücken, Salzburg, Stettin, Waldbröl, Weimar, Wolfsburg, Wuppertal, and Würzburg.

3. From the transcript of my discussion with Hitler on January 17, 1941. In my memorandum to Bormann dated January 20, 1941, I returned the post of Commissioner of Construction to his staff. On January 30, 1941, I wrote to Dr. Ley resigning from Beauty of Labor and from supervision of all the building projects of the German Labor Front. According to the *Office Journal*, supervision over all construction of party centers was restored to the party treasurer, M. X. Schwarz. I also surrendered the right to pass on architectural writings and to appoint Gau architects entrusted with the National Socialist welfare projects. I informed Rosenberg that in the professional journal we put out together, *Baukunst im Dritten Reich*, my name would in the future appear without the title Commissioner of Construction for the National Socialist Party.

4. My suggestion to Dr. Todt about halting construction and his reply are recorded in the *Office Journal*.

5. These data are taken from the final report in the *Office Journal* for 1941. According to notations in late March and early September 1941, Norway was commissioned to provide 31,200,000 cubic yards of uncut granite and 12,050,000 cubic yards of cut granite, and Sweden was to provide 5,473,000 cubic yards of uncut and 6,890,000 cubic yards of cut granite. Sweden alone had a contract for granite deliveries with a total value of two million Reichsmarks per year, guaranteed for a period of ten years.

6. This statement of Hitler's is recorded in the *Office Journal,* November 29, 1941. The orders to Admiral Lorey are also quoted in the *Office Journal.*
7. Details from the *Office Journal* entries for May 1 and June 21, 1941, and from the *Führerprotokoll,* May 13, 1942, Point 7.
8. *Office Journal,* November 24, 1941, and January 27, 1942.
9. *Office Journal,* Autumn 1941 and January 1, 1942.
10. *Office Journal,* November 11, 1941.
11. *Office Journal,* May 5, 1941.

CHAPTER 14: *Start in My New Office*

1. Letter from Dr. Todt, January 24, 1941.
2. In the *Office Journal,* May 10, 1944, this passage is quoted from one of my speeches: "In 1940, when Dr. Todt was appointed Minister of Armaments and Munitions, the Fuehrer summoned me officially. Hitler told me that Todt's job of equipping the armed forces was so overwhelming that one person could not also handle the construction program at the same time. I asked the Fuehrer to reconsider his intention of putting me in charge of construction. For it was evident to me how much this job meant to Dr. Todt and what an inner struggle he would have before he could relinquish it. He would have been very unhappy with this solution. The Fuehrer reconsidered."
3. On May 8, 1942, only three months after my appointment, Hitler reassured Rosenberg: "The Fuehrer then repeated several times that Speer's Ministry would be dissolved the moment the peace treaty was signed, and his duties would be assigned to others." (Rosenberg's notation, Nuremberg Document 1520 PS.) In the same vein I wrote to Hitler on January 25, 1944 from Hohenlychen, where I lay ill: "I need hardly emphasize to you, *mein Führer,* that I have never aspired to enter the realm of politics, either in wartime or after the war. I regard my present activities simply as wartime service, and I am looking forward to the time when I will be able to devote myself to artistic matters which are more to my liking than any ministerial post or political work."
4. See also the *Office Journal,* February 12: "Attempts to trespass on the territory of the Minister (Funk, Ley, Milch) during the first days after he assumed the new posts were at once recognized and nipped in the bud." Ley is mentioned in this account because shortly after my appointment he wrote an attack in the Berlin party organ *Angriff* which earned him a rebuke from Hitler. See Goebbels's diary, February 13 and 25, 1942.

CHAPTER 15: *Organized Improvisation*

1. From my speech to the district economic advisers, delivered April 18, 1942.
2. In a memorandum to me on November 5, 1942, Goering confirmed this indirectly: "I then with great pleasure delegated these powers to you

from my general authority, so as to prevent any working at cross-purposes. Otherwise I would have had to ask the Fuehrer to let me resign as Commissioner of the Four-Year Plan."

3. From the decree concerning the Commissioner General for Armaments.
4. *Office Journal*, March 2, 1942.
5. See Walther Rathenau, *Die neue Wirtschaft* in *Gesammelte Schriften* (1917), Vol. 5.
6. There is an extensive literature on the organizational activities of the Armaments Ministry, including such works as Gregor Janssen's *Das Ministerium Speer* and Rolf Wagenführ's *Die deutsche Industrie im Kriege 1939–1945* (Berlin, 1954) which deal with the organization of arms production and present the production statistics far more thoroughly than I ever could. According to the decree on distribution of duties (October 29, 1943), the directive committees and pools were responsible for enforcing uniformity, for setting norms for multiple utilization of separately manufactured parts, for economics in raw materials, for substitutions in raw materials to save scarce metals, for production bans on certain items, for output comparisons, for exchange of information, for encouraging waste-free stamping, for development of new processes, for limiting production types, for setting company production schedules, for concentration of production, for converting and increasing capacities, for providing labor where needed, for reassignment of tasks, for ordering, for distribution and proper use of machinery, for economies in the use of electricity and gas, and other such duties.

   The chairmen of the development commissions had to decide if the amount of time and the technical risks involved in a development program bore a reasonable relation to its potential military or economic usefulness and, should the development be undertaken, if there would be adequate facilities for producing the item.

   The directors of the directive committees, the pools, and the development commissions were under my immediate supervision.

7. According to a memorandum form Personnel Chief Bohr, June 7, 1944.
8. *Office Journal*, 1942.
9. From the *Indexziffern der deutschen Rüstungsfertigung*, January 1945. The statistics were based on the prices of the individual items of military hardware; price increases were not taken into account to avoid inflating the statistics. The monetary value that munitions production represented within the total armaments outlay for the three branches of the armed forces amounted to 29 percent; therefore, when this monetary value was doubled, it had a strong impact on the total armaments index.

   The effectiveness of our work in the three most important areas of armaments can be seen from the following survey:

   1. The number of tanks was increased fivefold from 1940 to 1944, while their gross weight rose 7.7 times. This result was achieved with a 270 percent increase in the labor force and with a 212 percent increase in steel consumption. Thus, the tank committee had saved 79 percent in labor and 93 percent in steel in comparison with the production levels of 1941.

2. A 1941 price index of the total munitions production for the army, navy, and air force stood at 102; in 1944 the figure had risen to 306. This tripling of the total munitions capacity was achieved with a 67 percent increase in labor and a 182 percent increase in steel consumption. Thus, here too, despite the fact that mass-production methods had been applied before we took over, there was a reduction of 59 percent in the number of workers per unit of production, although we could achieve only a 9.4 percent reduction in steel consumption.

3. The price index for all artillery increased 3.3 times from 1941 to 1944. This increase represented an increase in the labor force of only 30 percent, of steel consumption of only 50 percent, and of copper consumption of only 38 percent. (The percentages in these three examples are taken from my speech delivered at the Wartburg, July 16, 1944.)

The organizations for agriculture and forestry were structured along similar lines of autonomy, with the same good results.

10. Speech delivered April 18, 1942. By employing the principle of trust, "something which may strike administrative bureaucrats as a sheer impossibility," I continued, "we may succeed in destroying a system which, if it were allowed to continue, would increasingly become a serious drag on the whole war economy." Doubtlessly I was exaggerating when, two years later, on August 24, 1944, I told my assistants in the armaments organization "our placing of so much trust in factory managers and technicians is absolutely unique."

Fourteen days previously, on August 10, 1944, I stated to the same group: "Our administrative system had been structured in such a way that each of us, down to the individual workman, was exposed to total suspicion; each was treated as if he might try at any moment to betray the state. In order to avoid such betrayal, double and triple safeguards had been instituted, so that, for instance, if a factory manager slipped through one barrier—perhaps the price controls—he would be caught by the surplus-profits tax, and then the regular taxes followed, so that in the end nothing was left over. This basic attitude toward the German people must be changed; this mistrust has to be replaced in the future by trust. Merely by substituting trust for mistrust within the administrative system six to eight hundred thousand employees can be made superfluous"—whom, of course, I wanted to employ in the armaments factories.

11. See letter to Hitler, September 20, 1944, quoted in Chapter 27.

12. Speech to fellow armaments workers, August 1, 1944.

13. Quoted in the *Office Journal*, February 19, 1943.

14. See letter of September 20, 1944.

15. "Decree by the Fuehrer for the Protection of the Armaments Industry," March 21, 1942.

16. On May 26, 1944, after an argument with SS Group Leader Kammler, who had had a director of the BMW motor works arrested for sabotage, I presented at our subsequent meeting for department heads a set of "Guidelines for Procedure in the Event of Human Error in the Armaments Industry." "A body of industrialists should rule on the misconduct before the courts or the SS take up the matter. The Minister will not tolerate

arrests or sentences unless the person in question has received a hearing."
(Office Journal.)

17. In connection with the subject of this chapter see the speech delivered in
Essen to a group of industrialists on June 6, 1944.

18. Nine months before I had made a vain attempt to stop the flood of in-
coming letters. Unimportant mail was to be stamped "Return to sender.
Not critical for the war effort!" with a facsimile of my signature. Office
Journal, February 11, 1943.

19. The artillery figures for 1941 include the antitank guns and antiaircraft
guns. In 1941 production of machine guns and aircraft reached one-half of
that of 1918; but the increased use of gunpowder and dynamite for bombs
and mines (land and underwater) caused production to rise by 250 percent. These statistics for weaponry and aircraft may be compared only in a
limited sense, for since 1918 the technical standards for military hardware
had risen considerably. (The production figures for 1918 are from Wagenführ, op. cit.) For a long time production of munitions lagged behind that
of the First World War. In a speech delivered August 11, 1944, I made
the comparison perfectly clear: "During the First World War better results
were achieved in many areas, and particularly in the area of munitions,
than in our own munitions production up to about 1943. Only in recent
months has the peak munitions production of that world war—in Germany,
the Protectorate, and Austria combined—been surpassed."

20. The difficulties which our highly elaborate and autocratic bureaucracy
created for itself and others in our war economy are illustrated by the
following strange case, which I described in detail in a speech of April
28, 1942:

On February 11, 1942, an armaments firm in Oldenburg ordered
a quart of alcohol from its supplier in Leipzig. First, a requisition slip
from the Reich Monopoly Bureau was needed. The Oldenburg firm
submitted its request for such a slip but was referred to the Economic
Group, from which it was to secure a certificate of urgent need. The
Economic Group in turn referred the matter to its Regional Office in
Hanover, which requested and received a declaration that the alcohol
was to be used for technical purposes only. On March 19, after more
than five weeks, the Hanover office announced that it had already
returned the order to the Economic Group in Berlin. On March 26 the
Oldenburg firm made inquiries and was told that its request had been
approved and sent on to the Reich Monopoly Bureau; at the same time
it was explained that further correspondence with the Economic Group
was pointless since the group had no contingency control over alcohol.
In the future, the company should apply to the Monopoly Bureau—
which, we should note, it had tried to do in the first place, but to no
avail. A new application to the Monopoly Bureau, submitted on March
30, was followed twelve days later by the reminder that the Monopoly
Bureau was supposed to be informed of the monthly consumption of
alcohol but that nevertheless the one quart of alcohol was as a generous
gesture being released from a firm in Oldenburg.

Now, eight weeks after its first request, the firm happily sent a messenger to the depot, only to have him told that before the alcohol could be picked up a certificate had to be obtained from the Food Rationing Board, a division of the Agriculture Department. When queried, the local Food Rationing Board stated that it could license alcohol for drinking purposes only and not for manufacturing or technical uses. Meanwhile, April 18 had arrived, and the one quart of alcohol ordered on February 11 was still not in the hands of the firm that had ordered it, despite the fact that the alcohol was urgently needed for a specific purpose.

CHAPTER 16: *Sins of Omission*

1. In my final summary on January 27, 1945, almost three years later, I stated: "Given a similar concentration of all our energies and ruthless removal of all impediments, we could have achieved in 1940 and 1941 the armaments production of 1944."

2. *The Times* (London), September 7, 1942, "The Speer Plan in Action." *The Times* was not the only paper to be well informed on what was going on in my Ministry. About that time another English paper carried details which were news even to me.

3. From speech delivered April 18, 1942.

4. The memorandum of March 20, 1944, sent by my Commissioner for Factory Conversions to Martin Bormann reads: "In accordance with your memo of March 1, 1944, I have seen to it that the important tapestry factories and similar production centers for art goods are not to be closed down." On June 23, 1944, Bormann wrote: "Dear Herr Speer: The Commission on Crafts has reminded the Pfefferle Company (with which you are acquainted) of the ban on the production of picture frame moldings, picture frames, and the like; the company's special authorization from the House of German Art was not accepted. I am requested to inform you that the Fuehrer wishes no further obstacles placed in the way of the Pfefferle Company's work, much of which has been specially ordered by the Fuehrer. I would be grateful if you would issue the appropriate instructions to the Production Department. *Heil Hitler!* Yours, Bormann."

5. According to Point 18 of the *Führerprotokoll,* June 20, 1944, I reported to the Fuehrer that "at the moment a good 28,000 workers are building additions to the Fuehrer's headquarters." According to my memorandum of September 22, 1944, some 36,000,000 marks were spent for bunkers in Rastenburg, 13,000,000 for bunkers in Pullach near Munich to provide for Hitler's safety when he visited Munich, and 150,000,000 for the bunker complex called the "Giant" near Bad Charlottenbrunn. These projects required 328,000 cubic yards of reinforced concrete (including small quantities of masonry), 277,000 cubic yards of underground passages, 36 miles of roads with six bridges, and 62 miles of pipes. The "Giant" complex alone consumed more concrete than the entire population had at its disposal for air-raid shelters in 1944.

6. On my initiative, my deputy in Franconia, Chief Architect Wallraff, put

difficulties in the way of Goering, for the Veldenstein project had not been authorized. In revenge, Goering had Wallraff shipped to a concentration camp. He was freed at our request after we had invoked the Fuehrer's decree of March 21, 1942.

7. Speech to Central Planning.

8. About this time my associates gave me reports on the achievements of Ernest Bevin, the socialist Minister of Labor in England, who had organized the entire labor force into battalions which he could move to wherever they were needed. Later, in prison, I read more about this extraordinary feat of organization: "England's industrial war production was the most intensive of any country at war. The entire civilian population of England, including women, was really one enormous, mobile labor army which was sent around the country as ruthlessly as any army in the field and committed wherever it was needed at the moment. This total mobilization of the English labor force was the work of Bevin." (From an article in the *Mercator* [1946].) Goebbels's diary entry for March 28, 1942, shows that we too at first considered mobilizing all the German labor reserves: Sauckel: "From a press dispatch I note that the employment of women It should not be too difficult to mobilize at least another million German workers; we need only to work energetically and not be frightened by the recurrent difficulties."

9. November 9, 1941. See *Proceedings of the International Military Tribunal,* (English edition), Vol. XXIII, p. 553.

10. Two years later, on January 28, 1944, I voiced the following reproach to Sauckel: "From a press dispatch I note that the employment of women has progressed much further in England than here. Of a total population of 33 million between the ages of 14 and 65, 22.3 million are active in the armed forces or in the economy. Of 17.2 million women, 7.1 million are employed full-time and another 3.3 million, part-time. Thus, out of 17.2 million women, 10.4 million are employed, or 61 percent. By comparison, in Germany, out of about 31 million women between the ages of 14 and 65, 14.3 million are employed full or part-time. That makes 45 percent. Thus the percentage of working women is appreciably lower than in England." We therefore possessed a reserve labor force of 16 percent or 4.9 million women. (Nuremberg Document 006 Speer.) At the time I was not aware that even before the war, in June 1939, State Secretary Syrup of the Ministry of Labor had presented a plan for mobilizing 5.5 million unemployed women for war production; these would have been added to the 13.8 million women already employed. He also considered it a possibility that 2 million women could be transferred from peacetime jobs to the metal and chemical industries and to agriculture. (Minutes of the meeting of the Reich Defense Council, June 23, 1939, Nuremberg Document 3787 PS.)

11. From Sauckel's proclamation, April 20, 1942. (Nuremberg Document 016 PS.)

12. According to Charles Webster and Noble Frankland, *The Strategic Air Offensive against Germany* (London, 1961), Vol. IV, p. 473, in June 1939 England had 1,200,000 domestic servants, but only 400,000 by June 1943.

In Germany the number declined from 1,582,000 on May 31, 1939, to 1,442,000 on May 31, 1943.

13. These statistics are taken from the speech I delivered on April 18, 1942, to the district economic advisers. Of a total crude steel production of 31.2 million metric tons per year in 1942, 2.8 million were still not going into armaments.

14. Up to this time General Hannecken had handled these matters for the Economics Ministry; he was in a weak position vis-à-vis both Hitler and Goering.

15. At the Nuremberg Trial this right to reserve decision incriminated Goering in the eyes of the prosecution. When I was interrogated I was able to declare with a clear conscience: "Goering would have been no help to me; we had practical work to do." The prosecution accepted this explanation.

16. At the first meeting of Central Planning on April 27, 1942, out of a monthly crude steel production of 2 million metric tons 980,000 tons were allocated to the army, navy, and air force for armaments. This meant that the previous quota of 37.5 percent had been increased to 49 percent, exceeding the allotment of 46.5 percent during the First World War (Minutes of Central Planning, April 27, 1942). By May 1943 we had raised the allocation for the armaments producers to 52 percent (Minutes of Central Planning, May 4, 1943). In 1943 the armaments industry thus received 5,900,000 more metric tons of crude steel than before I had taken office. The percentage share of the increased steel production amounted to 1,300,000 metric tons.

17. Wagenführ, *Die deutsche Industrie im Kriege 1939–1945* (Berlin, 1954) compares the cutbacks in consumer goods production in Britain and Germany. Using the 1938 figure as a base of 100, production in 1940 was still 100 in Germany and was 87 in England. In 1941 it was 97 in Germany, 81 in England; in 1942 it was 88 in Germany and 79 in England. But it should be taken into account that even before the war England had had unemployment, probably resulting in a lower standard of living than Germany's.

18. *Führerprotokoll,* June 28–29, 1942, Point 11.

19. *Führerprotokoll,* March 5–6, 1942, Point 12; March 19, 1942, Point 36; May 13, 1942, Point 20; and May 18, 1942, Point 9. The *Office Journal,* May 21, 1942, reports Dorpmüller's declaration of bankruptcy and his offer to have me made "traffic dictator."

20. Hitler's remarks are included in a rather lengthy transcript in the *Führerprotokoll,* May 24, 1942.

21. In 1942 we managed to produce 2637 locomotives, whereas in 1941 the large number of models in production kept the industry down to 1918 locomotives. In 1943, using one standard model, we produced 5243 locomotives, 2.7 times as many as 1941 and twice as many as in the previous year.

22. *Führerprotokoll,* May 30, 1942.

23. *Office Journal,* May 6, 1942.

24. *Office Journal,* 1942: "On June 4 the Minister flew back to Berlin. . . .

That evening there was a lecture in Harnack House on atom-smashing and the development of the uranium machine [*sic*] and the cyclotron."

25. As late as December 19, 1944, I wrote to Professor Gerlach, who had been placed in charge of the uranium project: "You can always count on me to help you overcome any obstacles that may interfere with your work. Despite the very heavy drain on the labor force by the armaments industry, the relatively small [!] needs of your project can still be met."

26. *Führerprotokoll*, June 23, 1942, Point 15, states only: "Reported briefly to the Fuehrer on the conference on splitting the atom and on the backing we have given the project."

27. *Office Journal*, August 31, 1942, and March 1944. In 1940 twelve hundred metric tons of uranium ore had been seized in Belgium. Mining of domestic ore in Joachimstal was not pushed with any real urgency.

CHAPTER 17: *Commander in Chief Hitler*

1. The ninety-four sections of the *Führerprotokoll* with their 2222 points of discussion have been preserved in their entirety and provide a clear picture of the range of these conferences. After the meetings I dictated the general items while Saur and other colleagues dictated points dealing with their areas. But these records do not accurately convey the nature of the discussions. For in order to bolster the authoritativeness of our decisions we would preface them with the words, "The Fuehrer has decided," or, "In the Fuehrer's opinion," even if we had fought these items through over his objections, or had ourselves proposed something that merely did not elicit any protest from Hitler. In this respect my strategy resembled Bormann's. In 1942, as the minutes indicate, I had twenty-five conferences on armaments with Hitler, in 1943 twenty-four. In 1944 these discussions were reduced to thirteen, a sign of my dwindling influence. In 1945, I had only two opportunities to discuss armaments questions with Hitler, since from February 1945 on I let Saur represent me at the conferences. See also W. A. Boelcke, ed., *Deutschlands Rüstung im Zweiten Weltkrieg: Hitlers Konferenzen mit Albert Speer 1942–1945* (Frankfurt am Main, 1969).

2. Based on the Czech 38 T tank. In October 1944, I tried once more to win Hitler over to the idea of light tanks: "On the southwestern front (Italy) reports on the cross-country mobility of the Sherman have been very favorable. The Sherman climbs mountains which our tank experts consider inaccessible to tanks. One great advantage is that the Sherman has a very powerful motor in proportion to its weight. Its cross-country mobility on level ground (in the Po Valley) is, as the Twenty-Sixth Armored Division reports, definitely superior to that of our tanks. Everyone involved in tank warfare is impatiently waiting for lighter and therefore more maneuverable tanks which, simply by having superior guns, will assure the necessary fighting power."

3. Quotation from Hitler's speech at Obersalzberg, June 26, 1944, to a large group of industrialists.

4. If I recall rightly, the cadets' training academy was committed to the area around Astrakhan.
5. From November 20 to November 24, I was at Obersalzberg. Hitler left there on November 22 for his headquarters at Rastenburg.
6. The State Opera House on Unter den Linden, destroyed by bombing, was rebuilt on orders from Goering issued April 18, 1941.

CHAPTER 18: *Intrigues*

1. Three weeks after Hitler's January 8, 1943, draft call he issued a proclamation urging fulfillment of an increased production quota for tanks.
2. Meeting of Central Planning, January 26, 1943. The agenda was concerned with "the transfer of one million Germans to the armaments factories. My demands were not met. The number of persons employed were:

	May, 1943	May, 1944
Trade, banking, insurance	3,100,000	2,900,000
Administration	2,800,000	2,800,000
Transportation	2,300,000	2,300,000
Crafts, manual arts	3,400,000	3,300,000
Social services	1,000,000	900,000
Domestic services	1,400,000	1,400,000
	14,000,000	13,600,000

(These statistics are taken from the United States Strategic Bombing Survey, *Effects of Strategic Bombing,* which in turn bases its information on the *Kriegswirtschaftliche Kräftebilanz des Statistischen Reichsamtes.)* The decrease of 400,000 employed can probably be explained by the retirement of older persons, since the young were being drafted into the armed forces. On July 12, 1944, I repeated the old argument to Hitler: "The bombing phase of the war has shown that a life in ruins—without restaurants, without amusement spots, without the domestic amenities, without fulfillment of many everyday human needs—is perfectly possible. It has shown that business and banking can survive on only a fraction of their previous activity . . . [or] that, for example, passengers on public conveyances continue to pay their fares even if all tickets have been lost in fires, or that the taxation agencies still receive their payments even when the Finance Bureau's records have all been destroyed."
3. In opposition to everyone else, Sauckel argued at a meeting held January 8, 1943, in the Cabinet Room that it was not necessary to call up women. The labor force was still adequate, he held. *(Office Journal.)*
4. This view of Hitler stands in contrast to the impression given by Goebbels's diary for the same period. Goebbels undoubtedly planned to publish parts of his diary once the war had been won. Perhaps it was for this reason that he suppressed any criticism of Hitler; but perhaps he was also afraid that his personal papers might some day come under scrutiny without prior warning.

5. See also the detailed account Goebbels gives in his diary of the meetings at Obersalzberg, at Hitler's headquarters, and in Goering's residence in Berlin.

CHAPTER 19: *Second Man in the State*

1. Keitel directed that "all prisoners of war captured in the East after July 5, 1943 are to be sent to the camps of the High Command of the Armed Forces. From there they are to be put to work immediately or transferred to the Commissioner for Labor Assignment or to the mines." (Document USA 455.)

   Hitler's reactions were unpredictable. When Canadian soldiers landed at Dieppe on August 19, 1942 they killed some workers from the Todt Organization who were building bunkers there. The Canadians probably mistook them for political army functionaries, since they had brownish uniforms and swastika armbands. At the Fuehrer's headquarters, Jodl took me aside and said: "I think it would be best not to mention this to the Fuehrer. Otherwise he will order reprisals." I said nothing myself, but since I forgot to pass the warning on to my representative in the Todt Organization, Dorsch, he reported the incident to Hitler. Far from threatening revenge, Hitler proved amenable to Jodl's argument that the High Command of the Armed Forces had made a regrettable oversight in failing to inform the enemy via Switzerland that the Todt Organization workers wore uniforms resembling those of combatants. Jodl said he would rectify this at once. At the time I suggested that the swastika armbands be dropped, but Hitler rejected this proposal.

2. The preparations had taken so long that it was now too late to build any major fortifications before winter. Hitler therefore ordered (*Führerprotokoll*, July 8, 1943, Point 14) that in the East about 260,000 cubic yards of cement should be used per month, starting in the spring and continuing for six to seven months. According to the *Führerprotokoll*, May 13–15, 1943, Point 14, some 780,000 cubic yards were used on the Atlantic Wall. Hitler even assented to "a correspondingly smaller amount of construction on the Atlantic Wall."

3. As late as the beginning of October 1943, Hitler "did not agree that a stationary rear line should be built behind the Dnieper front," even though a few days earlier this river had already been crossed by Soviet troops. (*Führerprotokoll*, September 30–October 1, 1943, Point 27.)

4. Our efforts to simplify submarine construction were successful. The old type of submarine had taken eleven and a half months to build in drydock. Thanks to prefabrication, construction time for the new type was reduced to only two months in the shipyards, which were prime bombing targets. (Data furnished by Otto Merker, March 1, 1969.)

5. During the winter of 1944, disorganization began to take its toll in the armaments industry, but since the naval program was now going full swing eighty-three U-boats were delivered between January and March 1945. According to the report of the British Bombing Survey Unit, *The Effects of Strategic Bombing on the Production of German U-Boats*, in the same period forty-four submarines were destroyed in the shipyards. The total, including

U-boats lost in the yards, thus amounted during the first quarter of 1945 to forty-two per month. To be sure, the stepped-up naval program had a depressing effect on shipbuilding as a whole, for the index of seagoing vessel construction showed a reduction from bombings, from 181 in 1943 to 166 in 1944, a drop of 9 percent.

CHAPTER 20: *Bombs*

1. The USSBS (United States Strategic Bombing Survey) puts the losses for 1943 at 9 percent ("Area Studies Division Report," Tables P and QS 18). With a production of 11,900 medium-weight tanks in 1943, that percentage represented a loss of about 1100 tanks.

2. In Russia our 8.8 centimeter antiaircraft gun with its precision sight had proved to be one of the most effective and feared antitank weapons. From 1941 to 1943, we produced 11,957 heavy antiaircraft guns (8.8 to 12.8 centimeter), but most of them had to be deployed for antiaircraft purposes within Germany or in rear positions. During the same period, 12,006 of the heavy caliber weapons (7.5 centimeters and up) were delivered, but only 1155 of these were 8.8's. Fourteen million rounds of 8.8 or higher caliber flak ammunition were used for purposes other than antitank ammunition, for which only 12,900,000 rounds were provided.

3. *Führerprotokoll,* June 4, 1942, Point 41: "Discussed with the Fuehrer the telephone call between the Reich Marshal and Grohé, supporting the Reich Marshal."

4. The Möhne Valley reservoir had a volume of 4,731,540,000 cubic feet, the Sorpe Valley reservoir 2,507,010,000. When the Sorpe Valley reservoir was out of action, the two remaining Ruhr reservoirs contained only 1,176,230,000 cubic feet or 16 percent of the necessary amount of water. According to a statement made February 27, 1969 by Dr. Walter Rohland (the engineer who during the last years of the war headed the Ruhr staff), if the Ruhr reservoirs had all been destroyed, the shortage of water for cooling the coke works and blast furnaces would have reduced production in the Ruhr district by 65 percent. And in fact the temporary failure of the pumping stations had led to a noticeable decrease in gas production by the coke works. The major consumers could be supplied with only 50 to 60 percent of their needs. (*Office Journal,* May 19, 1943.)

5. See *Führerprotokoll,* September 30–October 1, 1943, Point 28, and *Office Journal,* October 2, 1943.

6. *Office Journal,* June 23, 1943: "The partially successful choice of bombing targets by the British has prompted the Minister to intervene in the choice of targets for the German air force. Previously, according to the testimony of the responsible air force officers, the Air Force General Staff has paid little attention to armaments facilities. The Minister appointed a committee consisting of, among others, Dr. Rohland (steel expert), General Manager Pleiger (representative of the coal industry), and General Waeger (head of the Ordnance Bureau); he gave the chairmanship to Dr. Carl (of the power industry), who was recalled from the army for this purpose." On

June 28, I informed Hitler of the formation of this committee. (Führer-protokoll, Point 6.)

7. For example, the entire industry of the Dnieper region depended on one major power plant. According to a memorandum dated February 12, 1969 by Dr. Richard Fischer, Commissioner for Power Supply, a 70 percent loss of power suffices to bring industry to a near halt, since the remainder is essential for supplying the needs of daily life. The distance from Smolensk, at that time still in German hands, to the power stations outside Moscow was 370–430 miles, to the Urals 1115 miles.

8. See Hermann Plocher, The German Air Force versus Russia, 1943 (Air University, 1967), p. 223ff.

9. Führerprotokoll, December 6–7, 1943, Point 22: "Reported to the Fuehrer on the suggestion submitted by Dr. Carl for the proposed Russian operation and gave him exhaustive background studies for examination. The Fuehrer once again stresses that I am right to suggest that only a surprise attack would have any effect; in his opinion a division into three separate operations, as suggested by the air force, would not be suitable."

10. See Office Journal, mid-June 1944: "The systematic way in which the enemy is attacking specific branches of the armaments industry is something new. Knowledge of the weak links in our own armaments establishment has induced the Minister to undertake a survey of the Russian economy. There, too, certain targets could be pinpointed which, if destroyed, would cripple large parts of the armaments industry. The Minister has been trying for a year to persuade the air force to do something, even if a one-way mission proves necessary." And in Führerprotokoll, June 19, 1944, Point 37: "The Fuehrer considers the destruction of the power plants in the Urals and in the upper Volga region decisive for the outcome of the war. He does not, however, feel that the present range and supply of bombers would be sufficient." On June 24, 1944, I asked Himmler, who had shown interest in my plan as early as March, to invite my technical assistant, Dr. Carl, to come and present the plan, in my presence if possible. The problem was to find volunteers for a one-way flight. After the attack the pilots would abandon their planes over remote areas, parachute to earth, and try to make their way back to the German front.

11. On July 25, shortly after midnight, 791 British planes attacked Hamburg, and on July 25 and 26 came daylight raids by 235 American bombers, followed on July 27 by the second night raid, staged by 787 British planes, and a third by 777 British planes on July 29. This succession of heavy attacks ended August 2 with a mission flown by 750 British bombers.

12. After the August 17 air raid the total number of ball bearings produced decreased, according to the Statistischer Schnellbericht zur Kriegsproduktion (January 1945), from 9,116,000 to 8,325,000. Since there was full production during the first half of August, it must have dropped in the second half to 3,750,000 or by 17 percent. With 52.2 percent of the production concentrated in Schweinfurt, this one attack knocked out 34 percent of our production. In July, 1,940,000 ball bearings measuring 6.3 to 24 centimeters in diameter were produced.

13. Answer to an RAF questionnaire, "The Effects of the Bombings," p. 20.

Webster and Frankland, *op. cit.*, Vol. II, p. 62ff., indicate that the Director of Bomber Operations, Air Commodore Bufton, was fully aware of the importance of Schweinfurt. Two days before the first attack he wrote to Marshal Bottomley stressing that the American daylight attack had to be followed up by a more powerful night attack and that the crews of the attacking planes should be read a declaration before setting out:

"History may prove that tonight's operation, in conjunction with the day attack which is taking place at this moment, will be one of the major battles of this war. If both operations are successful, German resistance may be broken and the war ended sooner than would be possible in any other way." He wanted the crews to know that "every vital piece of mechanism is dependent upon ball bearings" and that owing to extreme vulnerability to fire and water "literally millions" of bearings could be converted into "so much scrap metal." Finally he suggested that the crews should be told that they had "the opportunity to do more in one night to end the war than any other body of men."

But Air Marshal Harris was determined to stage a series of attacks on Berlin. His list of targets of the same priority as Schweinfurt included cities with aircraft plants: Leipzig, Gotha, Augsburg, Brunswick, Wiener-Neustadt, and others.

14. In fact 60 of the 291 attacking bombers were shot down. After the second attack was staged on October 14, 1943, 32 percent of the total production capacity, including 60 percent of Schweinfurt's, had been destroyed; percentages based on comparison with the undisrupted production for July. The German capacity for ball bearings 6.3 to 24 centimeters in diameter had been reduced by 67 percent.

15. On certain machines we managed to conserve 50 percent of the ball bearings.

16. Air Marshal Harris successfully opposed further attacks on Schweinfurt. He pointed out that similar strategic bombing raids on economic targets such as the Ruhr dams, a molybdenum mine and on hydrogenation plants had proved unsuccessful. He did not realize that they had failed only because of an inadequate follow-up. On January 12, 1944, Air Marshal Bottomley urged Air Marshal Charles Portal to order Sir Arthur Harris "to destroy Schweinfurt at the earliest possible date." On January 14, Harris was informed that the British and American air force staffs were in full agreement with the strategy of "attacking selected key industries known to be vulnerable and vital to the enemy's war effort." Sir Arthur protested again and had to be commanded on January 27 to attack Schweinfurt. (See Webster and Frankland, *op. cit.*) It was not until February 22, 1944 that the American and British air forces began to carry out this order in coordinated day and night attacks.

17. The production of ball bearings 8.3 centimeters in diameter and larger dropped from 1,940,000 in July 1943 to 558,000 in April 1944. The total number available decreased from 9,114,000 in July 1943 to 3,834,000 in April 1944 or to 42 percent. In considering the production figures for April 1944 we must take into account that the enemy allowed us to rebuild freely throughout that month, so that the degree of destruction just after

the series of attacks was significantly higher. After these attacks the ball-bearing industry was spared. Thus in May we were able to increase production to 25 percent more than April's figure, to 700,000 bearings 6.3 centimeters in diameter. In June we reached 1,003,000 bearings, and in September 1944 we had again reached 1,519,000 or 78 percent of our original production. In September 1944 we manufactured 8,601,000 bearings of all sizes or 94 percent of the production before the bombings.

18. According to *Indexziffern der deutschen Rüstungsproduktion*, January 1945.

19. *Office Journal*, January 7–11, 1944.

20. *Office Journal*, August 2, 1944. On the same day I issued the following decree: "Transfer of bearing production to underground facilities is of the greatest urgency. The necessary labor force has hitherto not been provided because the agencies responsible have not obeyed their orders [!]." A few months earlier, on May 10, 1944, I explained to the committee (only key phrases were recorded): "Bearings, etc., extraordinarily difficult to popularize. Means not yet found for making people see that this is as urgent and important as tanks and artillery. In my opinion have to hammer away at that harder. Not the fault of the Jägerstab [Fighter Staff; a special committee set up to speed and coordinate fighter production]; rather my old worry which keeps recurring: I have no grasp of propaganda techniques." Just issuing an order proved insufficient—even in the Third Reich, even in wartime. We, too, were at the mercy of the willingness of the people involved.

21. German News Agency (DNB) report, August 21 and 22, 1943.

CHAPTER 21: *Hitler in the Autumn of 1943*

1. See R. Brun, *Allgemeine Neurosenlehre* (Basel, 1954): "The patient no longer regulated his need for physical and mental rest automatically and disregarded excessive strain. . . . The conscious will is thwarted by an unconscious negation, which the patient attempts to overcome by frantic, tense overexertion. The excessive fatigue which gradually builds up would vanish if the patient allowed himself a rest period, but instead this fatigue is used by the unconscious 'devil's advocate' to disguise deeply rooted inferiority feelings."

2. *Führerprotokoll*, November 13–15, 1943, Point 10: "The restoration of the National Theater and the Prince Regent Theater in Munich is to be subsidized by the Ministry." These projects were never completed.

3. The explosives industry had difficulty in keeping pace with the rising production of munitions for the army and for antiaircraft operations. The index for the production of explosives rose from 103 in 1941 to 131 in 1942 to 191 in 1943 to 226 in 1944. But the index for munitions production, including bombs, rose from 102 in 1941 to 106 in 1942 to 247 in 1943 to 306 in 1944. Although these two indexes do not provide directly comparable figures, they do indicate that if more bombs had been produced, there would not have been enough explosives to fill them.

4. *Führerprotokoll,* June 18, 1943: "Pointed out to the Fuehrer that personal inspection of the Ruhr by him is urgently necessary. As soon as he can find time the Fuehrer will make the trip." He never did find the time. Goebbels, too, wrote a month later in his diary (July 25, 1943): "Above all these letters repeatedly ask why the Fuehrer does not visit the areas that have come under heavy bombing."

5. In his diary Goebbels often recorded remarks by Hitler, as for instance on September 10, 1943: "What today we cannot help seeing as a great misfortune may later seem a piece of great good fortune. Time and again crises and calamities in the struggle waged by our movement and our state have proved to have been for the best from a historical point of view."

6. *Office Journal,* 1943: "By acting quickly the Minister obtained a decree from the Fuehrer assuring him total control of Italian armaments production. This decree, already signed by the Fuehrer on September 12, was re-signed on the thirteenth in order to indicate that the rights it granted remained intact despite the Duce's liberation. The Minister feared that the formation of a new Fascist regime in Italy would interfere with his preempting Italian industry to serve the needs of the German armaments industry."

CHAPTER 22: *Downhill*

1. Thus coal mining in the Ukraine was supposed to resume in April 1942, and at the same time munitions production facilities were to be established near the front. By the end of August 1943, Soviet military successes had brought this program to a standstill. The so-called Protectorate of Bohemia and Moravia was controlled de facto by the SS, whose hold no one dared to challenge. There all sorts of articles were manufactured for the use of the SS troops. In the summer of 1943 the Ministry proposed a plan for producing an additional one thousand light tanks per month by making use of available machinery and skilled labor in Bohemia and Moravia. In October 1943, Hitler finally directed Himmler to stop SS production and grant the armaments organizations the same powers we already held in Germany. (*Office Journal,* October 8, 1943.) But since we were unable to operate in that industrial region until the end of 1943, the first sixty-six of the "Czech tanks" were not ready until May 1944. In November 1944, the production was 387 tanks.

2. *Führerprotokoll,* September 11–12, 1943, Point 14.

3. *Office Journal,* September 17, 1943: "Before a late supper at the official guest house there was a final discussion, after the Minister had again conferred alone with Bichelonne, who had requested a private meeting to talk over the Sauckel operation. His government had forbidden him to discuss these matters officially." At the Central Planning meeting, March 1, 1944, Kehrl reported: "Out of this discussion [between Speer and Bichelonne] arose the idea of restricted industries which would be protected from Sauckel. The plan is backed by Germany's solemn commitment, as confirmed by my minister's signature."

4. See *Office Journal,* September 21, 1943.

5. *Führerprotokoll,* September 30–October 1, 1943, Point 22.

6. A grotesque example demonstrates the extent to which the Gauleiters, as Hitler's immediate subordinates, disregarded decisions by the official agencies: Leipzig was the headquarters of the Reich's Central Agency for the Fur Trade. One day the local Gauleiter, Mutschmann, informed the director of the agency that he had appointed one of his friends as the director's successor. The Minister of Economics protested vigorously, since the director of a central agency could be appointed only by Berlin. The Gauleiter summarily ordered the director to vacate his post within a few days. In the face of this power clash, the Minister of Economics resorted to an absurd solution: The night before the post was to be handed over to the Gauleiter's friend, trucks from Berlin drove up to the doors and transferred the entire fur trade agency, including its files and its director, to Berlin.

7. In my speech of November 30, 1943, I laid down certain principles for any future planning: "The centers of cities should not be rebuilt in conformity with pretentious artistic notions; rather, reconstruction should save the cities from the kind of traffic congestion we had before the war and which certainly threatens to be even worse after the war. . . . It is clear that we must be as economy-minded as possible in our planning."

   In my December 18, 1943, memorandum to the Gauleiters I expanded on this theme: "Demobilization will necessitate large projects to absorb the huge labor force which will suddenly become available. . . . If we make our plans for urban reconstruction well in advance, we will avoid wasting valuable time after the war for city planning and will not have to resort to stopgap measures which in the long run would obstruct the planned development of our cities. . . . If we start building with the same determination and innovative energy that we see at present in our armaments industry, an extraordinarily large number of housing units will be constructed each year. Therefore, it is essential that we think in terms of areas big enough for the purpose. . . . If we do not prepare adequately, we will be forced in the immediate postwar era to resort to measures that will seem totally incomprehensible a few years later."

8. See also Manstein, *Aus einem Soldatenleben* (Bonn, 1965).

9. From my memorandum, "The Importance of Nikopol and Krivoi Rog for German Steel Production," November 11, 1943.

10. From my memorandum, "Alloys in Armaments Production and the Importance of Chromium Imports from the Balkans and Turkey," November 12, 1943.

11. See also the record of Hitler's telephone conversation with Saur on December 20, 1943, printed in *Hitlers Lagebesprechungen.*

12. See *Office Journal,* October 13, 1943: "By far the most upsetting item for the department heads was the Minister's plan of assigning one or more representatives from industry to each department. . . . Since this new arrangement involved personal qualities rather than factual issues, strong feelings were aroused."

13. Dr. Gerhard Fränk and Erwin Bohr.

14. Aside from Doenitz, who was assigned exactly the same type of plane, I was the only leader who was regularly in a position to travel in his own

plane. My ministerial colleagues no longer had private planes. Nowadays, Hitler himself seldom flew, while Goering, as an "old" flier, felt somewhat nervous about using "newfangled machines."

15. *Führerprotokoll*, June 28–29, 1944, Point 55: "The Fuehrer stated very firmly that he would never agree to production of the submachine gun unless it were designed for ordinary rifle ammunition. Besides, he is almost completely convinced that the rifle suits the purpose better." On January 14, 1944, two weeks after the trip to Lapland, the infantry program was initiated. The increases it brought about can be seen from the following table:

Average Monthly Production

	1941	1943	Nov. 1944
Rifles	133,000	209,000	307,000
Submachine guns	——	2,600	55,100
New rifles 41 and 43	——	7,900	32,500
Machine guns 42 and 43	7,100	14,100	28,700
Rifle ammunition	76,000,000	203,000,000	486,000,000
Submachine gun ammunition	——	1,900,000	104,000,000
Rifle grenades	——	1,850,000	2,987,000
Mines	79,000	1,560,000	3,820,000
Hand grenades	1,210,000	4,920,000	3,050,000
Bazooka shells	——	29,000	1,084,000

16. *Office Journal*, January 4, 1944: "Hoping that with Himmler's and Keitel's aid he could stem the threatening reactivation of the Sauckel operations, the Minister has taken a rail motorcar to a conference presided over by the Reichsführer-SS and attended by Waeger (chief of the Armaments Bureau), Schmelter (Department of Labor Mobilization), Jehle, and Kehrl (director of the Planning Department). The question on the agenda was: Who was to have the final word on transporting laborers from France to Germany?"

17. Notation by Lammers, January 1944 (US Exhibit 225): "Minister Speer explained that he needed an additional one and half million workers; to be sure, that would depend on whether it proves possible to increase the production of iron ore. If this proves impossible, he will not need any additional workers. Sauckel stated that in 1944 he would have to import at least two and a half and probably three million new workers; otherwise production would decline. . . . Hitler's decision: The Commissioner for Labor Assignment is to furnish at least four million new workers from the occupied areas."

18. By teletype, January 4, 1944, to my deputy in Paris (Nuremberg Document 04 Speer) and by letter to Sauckel, January 6, 1944 (05 Speer). The International Military Tribunal at Nuremberg declared in its judgment that "employees of these [restricted] factories were immune to deportation to Germany, and any worker who received orders to go to Germany could avoid deportation by going to work in one of the restricted factories.

. . . [As a mitigating circumstance] it must be acknowledged that Speer's arrangement kept many workers at home. . . ."

19. *Office Journal,* January 1944.

CHAPTER 23: *Illness*

1. See "Report to the Fuehrer," No. 1, January 25, 1944.
2. "Report to the Fuehrer," No. 5, January 29, 1944, includes twelve pages on the difficulties in my Ministry.
3. From the case history: "On admission, January 18, 1944, the patient appeared exhausted. . . . Extremely heavy drainage from the left knee joint." February 8, 1944: "After standing sudden onset of extreme pain in the extensor muscles of the back, left side, and the iliopsoatic muscle. Anteriorly radiating pain as in lumbago. Suggests acute muscular rheumatism. . . ." Yet Gebhardt's internist, Dr. Heissmeyer, had noted symptoms of pleurisy. Gebhardt ignored his findings in the treatment and clung to his wrong diagnosis.
4. From Dr. Koch's testimony, March 12, 1947 (Nuremberg Document 2602):

> In the course of the treatment differences arose between Gebhardt and me. I thought that the damp climate of Hohenlychen was affecting Speer's recovery adversely, and after I had examined the patient and concluded that he was strong enough to be moved, I suggested that he be taken south [to Meran]. Gebhardt opposed this suggestion violently. He took cover behind Himmler, with whom he discussed the matter over the telephone several times. All this struck me as very odd. I had the impression that Gebhardt was using his position as a doctor to play some political game. But I do not know what it was and I did not bother myself over it then; I wanted to be a doctor and nothing else. I then tried several times to persuade Gebhardt to change his mind. Finally, the whole business became too much for me, and I asked to speak with Himmler myself. In a telephone conversation that lasted a good seven or eight minutes I managed to persuade him to let Speer be moved to Meran. Even at the time it seemed very peculiar that Himmler should have the power of decision in a medical matter, but I did not let it disturb me, since I intentionally kept out of things which did not fall within the sphere of medicine. I should also like to mention that I had the impression Speer was greatly reassured when I was present and holding a protective hand over him.

> In February 1945, when I had a minor collision with a truck in Upper Silesia and was slightly injured, Gebhardt immediately boarded a special plane to bring me back to his hospital. My assistant, Karl Cliever, thwarted this plan without giving me any reasons, although, as he indicated at the time, he had some. Toward the end of the war French Minister Bichelonne had Gebhardt operate on his knee at Hohenlychen. He died a few weeks later of a pulmonary embolism.

5. *Office Journal,* March 23, 1944: "In the meantime, Dr. Gebhardt, in his capacity as SS Gruppenführer, has been entrusted by the Reichsführer-SS [Himmler] with the safety of the Minister."
6. I heard this from Gauleiter Eigruber himself at the Armaments Conference in Linz, June 23–26, 1944.
7. This account, including the quotations, follows Dorsch's memorandum of April 17, 1944, and my own of August 28, 1944. At the same time Goering put Dorsch in charge of constructing many underground hangars to protect fighter planes at their home bases in the Reich. When I sent Fränk to represent me at the April 18 meeting on these new construction projects, Goering refused to let Fränk join him and Dorsch.
8. Burgmann, an official of the old school, had become something of an intimate of Hitler's while working on the building projects for Berlin and Nuremberg.
9. Message from Bormann, March 1, 1944.
10. That same day Hitler signed my draft, which read as follows: "I commission the director of the Todt Organization headquarters, Ministerial Director Dorsch, to supervise the construction of the six underground hangars I have ordered, while retaining his other functions in your Ministry. You must provide the necessary prerequisites for a rapid execution of this project. In particular you must try to achieve a meaningful balance between this and other projects essential to the war effort; if necessary obtain my ruling on questions of priority."
11. This and the following quotations are taken from the *Office Journal* and from my speech to the department heads on May 10, 1944, in which I gave a summary of the discussion.
12. See my speech of May 10, 1944.
13. Letter from Goering, May 2, 1944, in reply to my letter of April 29, 1944.

CHAPTER 24: *The War Thrice Lost*

1. See *Führerprotokoll,* May 22–23, 1944, Point 14.
2. The first attack, on May 12, destroyed 14 percent of our capacity. This figure and the ones given in the text are taken from my memoranda to Hitler dated June 30 and July 28, 1944, as well as from my study, "The Effects of the Air War," September 6, 1944.
3. The number of day and night fighter planes produced had increased from 1017 in January 1944 (before the wave of attacks) to 2034 in June. The monthly average was only 849 in 1943. I defended myself against Goering's accusations as follows (*Führerprotokoll,* June 3–5, 1944, Point 20): "I take this occasion to explain to the Fuehrer that the Reich Marshal is in error when he accuses me of equipping the army at the expense of the air force during the past two years. In spite of the bombings, airplane production was doubled in three months—and not by diverting production capacity from army equipment, as the Reich Marshal thinks, but by calling upon reserves already existing within the air armaments industry itself.
4. See *Führerprotokoll,* June 3–5, 1944, Point 19.

5. Decree, June 20, 1944. Goering tried to save face by directing that "arming the German air force shall be carried out responsibly by the Minister of Armaments and Munitions in accordance with the tactical requirements and technical specifications established by the Commander in Chief of the air force.

6. On April 19, 1944, four weeks before the attacks on the fuel industry, I wrote to Hitler: "Whereas in 1939 our hydrogenation plants were producing 2 million metric tons equivalent of petroleum (including automobile fuel), the construction of new facilities up to 1943 provided an increase to 5.7 million metric tons, and the facilities scheduled for completion this year will raise the yearly output to 7.1 million metric tons." The machinery and components of these additional installations, with their extra capacity of 1.4 million metric tons per year or 3800 tons daily, could now be used for repairing the damaged plants. Thus Hitler's stubborn refusal in 1942 to relinquish this extra capacity turned out to have had its good side after all.

7. See memorandum, June 30, 1944. Although some production continued, by December 1944 the air raids had deprived us of 1,149,000 metric tons of airplane fuel, twice the amount of Keitel's reserves. Theoretically these reserves were supposed to last only until August, since there had been a production loss of 492,000 metric tons. They were stretched past September 1, 1944, but only by restricting airplane use to a dangerous degree.

    It was more difficult for the enemy to knock out ordinary gasoline and diesel fuel production becauses the refineries were widely dispersed. In July 1944 gasoline production decreased to 37 percent, diesel fuel production to 44 percent. In May 1944 the gasoline and diesel fuel reserves together amounted to 760,000 metric tons. Production before the attacks was 230,000 metric tons.

    A monthly average of 111,000 tons of bombs was dropped over Germany during the second quarter of 1944. Only one-twentieth of that amount (5160 metric tons) was dropped on the fuel industry in May, only one-fifth (20,000 tons) in June. In October 1944 the RAF dropped one-seventeenth of its bombs on fuel facilities, the American air force one-eighth. In November 1944, however, the RAF dropped one-quarter and the Americans one-third of their bomb loads on fuel plants. (See W. F. Craven and J. L. Cate, *The Army Air Forces in World War II* [Chicago, 1949] Vol. II, and Wagenführ, *Die deutsche Industrie im Kriege 1939–1945, Op. cit.*). Since the RAF's night attacks using a mix of incendiary and explosive bombs proved particularly effective against fuel plants and refineries, before November the RAF missed a great opportunity for striking the closer, more easily spotted targets in the Ruhr area and along the coast.

8. From memorandum dated July 28, 1944.

9. Craven and Cate, *op. cit.*, Vol. II.

10. Hitler established these guidelines on August 13, 1942 in the presence of Keitel, Schmundt, Admiral Kranke, General of the Engineers Jakob, Dorsch, and me. (*Führerprotokoll*, August 13, 1942, Point 48.)

11. As recorded on June 5, 1944; in addition nearly 6,000,000 cubic yards were used for submarine pens and other projects in France.
12. See *Führerprotokoll*, June 3–5, 1944, Point 16. Development of the V-1 had moved rapidly thanks to the energetic intervention of Milch, who had gone to the rocket test site in Peenemünde and realized that the complicated procedure was producing only meager results. In the face of the tacit resistance even of my Ministry, he was able to earn the credit for having developed and, produced, at only a fraction of the cost and effort, a different weapon which did everything that had been expected of the Peenemünde rocket.
13. In his June 26, 1944 speech to the industrialists, after the three military catastrophes, Hitler stated: "I often feel that we will have to undergo all the trials the devil and hell can devise before we achieve Final Victory. . . . I may be no pious churchgoer, but deep within me I am nevertheless a devout man. That is to say, I believe that he who fights valiantly obeying the laws which a god has established and who never capitulates but instead gathers his forces time after time and always pushes forward—such a man will not be abandoned by the Lawgiver. Rather, he will ultimately receive the blessing of Providence. And that blessing has been imparted to all great spirits [!] in history."
14. Three weeks previously, in my Essen speech of June 6, 1944, I had denounced these leanings and promised that in peacetime our machinery for controlling industry would be dissolved.
15. See *Führerprotokoll*, June 19–22, 1944, Point 20: "Gave the Fuehrer background documents for his speech; he was satisfied with the material."
16. Bormann refused (letter of June 30, 1944) to publish the speech, which has since appeared in *Es spricht der Führer*, ed. Hildegard von Kotze and Helmut Krausnick (Gütersloh, 1966).

CHAPTER 25: *Blunders, Secret Weapons, and the SS*

1. At the end of the war, I learned from Galland that insufficient interest on the part of the top leadership had caused a delay of about a year and a half.
2. The figures are taken from Program 225, which was in effect from March 1, 1944 on but which could only be implemented in part. According to this program, Me-262's were to be produced at the following rate: 40 in April 1944, increasing to 60 in July, remaining at 50 from July through October, rising to 210 in January 1945, to 440 in April 1945, to 670 in July 1945, and to 800 in October 1945.
3. See *Führerprotokoll*, June 7, 1944, Point 6. Despite my doubts, Hitler stood by his order "that the Me-262's in production must be used exclusively as bombers."
4. See *Führerprotokoll*, June 10–22, 1944, Point 35.
5. See travel report, September 10–14, 1944.
6. According to the *U. S. Air University Review*, Vol. XVII, No. 5 (July–August 1966), a four-engine B-17 (Flying Fortress) cost $204,370. A V-2,

on the other hand, according to David Irving's precise documentation, cost only 144,000 Reichsmarks, or one sixth that of the bomber. Six rockets delivered four and a half metric tons of explosives (1650 pounds per rocket). Each one was destroyed by use. A B-17 bomber, on the other hand, could be sent on any number of missions, had a range of 1000 to 2000 miles, and could deliver two tons of explosives on the target. On Berlin alone 49,400 metric tons of explosives and bomb shrapnel were dropped, damaging or totally destroying 20.9 percent of the dwelling units (Webster and Frankland, *The Strategic Air Offensive against Germany* [London, 1961], Vol. IV). To deliver the same load over London we would have had to use 66,000 large rockets, or the production of six years.

At a conference on propaganda directed by Goebbels, I had to admit (August 29, 1944): "It is doubtful whether the V-2 can prove psychologically decisive in any way. In a purely technical sense it cannot. . . . Psychological effects do not enter into what I have to say. I can only assure you that it always takes time for a new weapon . . . to reach real effectiveness and demonstrate what it can achieve."

7. See *Führerprotokoll*, June 23, 1944, Point 21.
8. This December 12, 1942 order empowered the planners to finish the designs for the project and to order the machine tools, which required a lead time of many months. The designers could also initiate negotiations with the suppliers and rush the necessary allotments into the production process.
9. See *Führerprotokoll*, July 8, 1943, Points 18, 19, and 20.
10. Further details may be found in David Irving, *Die Geheimwaffen des dritten Reiches* (Gütersloh, 1965).
11. See *Führerprotokoll*, August 19–22, 1943, Point 24.
12. My predecessor, Dr. Todt, had received the honorary rank of brigadier general in the air force, which placed him at a definite disadvantage during clashes with his opponents, who held much higher ranks. This was sufficient reason for me to renounce this practice, which I also disapproved of on more general grounds.
13. See *Führerprotokoll*, September 20–22, 1942, Point 36.
14. The head of the Armaments Delivery Office, Dr. Walter Schieber, asserted in a letter dated May 7, 1944 (Nuremberg Document 104 PS) that establishment of the concentration camp annexes called "labor camps" was justified, despite much friction with the SS, because "the technical and the human success would outweigh the drawbacks."
15. See *Office Journal*, January 13, 1944.
16. See Ley's letter dated May 26, 1944 and my reply written the following day.
17. See *Führerprotokoll*, June 3–5, 1944, Point 21.
18. See E. Georg, *Die wirtschaftlichen Unternehmungen des SS* (Stuttgart, 1963).
19. See *Führerprotokoll*, June 3–5, 1944, Point 21.
20. Eugene Davidson, "Albert Speer and the Nazi War Plans," *Modern Age*, No. 4 (1966).

CHAPTER 26: *Operation Valkyrie*

1. These measures were approved at the Central Planning meeting of May 19, 1944. Seven days later, on May 26, 1944, the enemy air forces began the raids that succeeded in destroying twenty-six Seine bridges within a short period of time.
2. See Jodl's diary for June 5, 1944; also *Führerprotokoll,* June 8, 1944, Point 4: "The Fuehrer agrees to my instructions in case of an invasion, as set forth in my May 29 letter to Jodl."
3. The detailed decree, "Re: Valkyrie," issued on July 31, 1943 by General Fromm as chief of army ordnance and commander of the Reserve Army, refers to a previous decree dated May 26, 1942.
4. See my letter to Thierack, March 3, 1945, exonerating Fromm.
5. See Hitler's decree of July 13, 1944.
6. See *Office Journal,* July 9, 1944.
7. See *Office Journal,* July 20, 1944.
8. This schedule is printed in *Der 20. Juli* (Berlin: Berto-Verlag, 1961).
9. This is clear from Remer's report, submitted two days later.
10. See my letter to Thierack dated March 3, 1945.
11. *Führerprotokoll,* July 6–8, 1944, Point 2.
12. See Kaltenbrunner's report to Bormann, dated October 12, 1944, in Karl Heinrich Peter, *Spiegelbild einer Verschwörung. Die Kaltenbrunner-Berichte an Bormann und Hitler über das Attentat am 20. Juli 1944. Geheime Dokumente aus dem Ehemaligen Reichssicherheitsamt* (Stuttgart, 1961).
13. I heard about this remark from Walter Funk.
14. As Hauptamtleiter (Department Chief) in the party, I ranked lower than the Reichsleiters who were normally entitled to be present at such party meetings.
15. Parts of this speech of Hitler's were published; see Domarus, *Hitlers Reden* (Munich, 1965).
16. From my testimony at Nuremberg on June 20, 1946. I was able to cite Schacht as another witness.
17. See *Office Journal,* end of August and September 20, 1944.

CHAPTER 27: *The Wave from the West*

1. From a speech delivered to my assistants on August 31, 1944.
2. See *Office Journal,* August 10 and 31, 1944.
3. See letter dated September 20, 1944.
4. This demand was aimed directly against Bormann's ambitions. I asked Hitler to let me "give the Gauleiters the necessary orders in all armaments and production matters without having to involve the chief of the Party Secretariat [Bormann]." The Gauleiters were to be instructed "to report directly to me and to put themselves directly in contact with me even when principles of armaments and war production are at issue." But

Bormann's primitive power system depended precisely on his constantly giving the Gauleiters new tasks to perform for the state, while insisting that "all information go through him as a matter of principle" and that "for the sake of consistency all orders to the Gauleiters be issued only through him." In this way he insinuated himself between the ministries and the men responsible for executing ministerial orders and thus made both dependent on him.

5. The *Office Journal* records that a week later, at the beginning of October, "Dr. Goebbels and Reichsleiter Bormann as well as the Gauleiters and their party agencies are constantly criticizing the armaments plants. . . . The Minister is now trying to settle who will have the say in armaments questions in the future. In spite of all arrangements with Dr. Goebbels, the Minister is repeatedly overruled. Admonitions to the Gauleiters never get past Dr. Goebbels; telephone messages are not answered until the damage is done. Tension and irritation are rising on both sides." About a week later, infuriated with the treatment I was receiving, I ordered the director of the Central Division for Culture and Propaganda to see to it "that my name no longer appears in the press."

6. See the report on my travels from September 26 to October 1, 1944. A month later, in my report on a visit to the Southwest Army Group (October 19–25, 1944), I pointed out to Hitler—citing Chief of Staff Guderian in support of my contention—that in September the fighting troops had received only a fraction of the weapons sent to them.

Inquiries to the Quartermaster General revealed that in September the following amounts had been assigned for direct supply to the fighting troops on all fronts :

	Supplies for front divisions	Supplies for newly formed divisions
Pistols	10,000	78,000
Submachine guns	2,934	57,660
Machine guns	1,527	24,475
2 cm. flak	54	4,442
3.5 cm. flak	6	948
7.5 cm. flak	180	748
8 cm. mortars	303	1,947
12 cm. mortars	14	336
Light field howitzers	275	458
Heavy field howitzers	35	273
Trucks	543	4,736
Caterpillar tractors	80	654
Tanks	317	373
Self-propelled guns	287	762

7. According to the report on my trip of September 1944, the First Army deployed around Metz was defending an 87-mile front, for which it still had 112 field pieces, 52 tanks, 116 heavy antitank guns, and 1320 machine guns. For the defense of Aachen with its important industries the Eighty-First Army Corps had only 33 field pieces, 21 tanks, and 20 heavy anti-

tank guns. In the same report I told Hitler: "The supply of heavy weapons is so inadequate that the lines may be broken through at any point. One hundred tanks, each with a five-man crew, can easily crush the resistance of ten thousand soldiers who lack heavy weapons."

8. See *Führerprotokoll,* June 19–22, 1944, Point 9.

9. See Nuremberg Document RF.71 which quotes Sauckel as suggesting as early as April 26, 1944 that Hitler issue the following order: "To the Commander in Chief West and to the military commanders of France, Belgium, and Holland: In case of an invasion able-bodied labor must at all costs be kept out of the hands of the enemy. The armaments situation in the Reich requires that such labor be immediately placed at the disposal of the German armaments plants in as large numbers as possible." On May 8, 1944 the official minutes of a negotiating session between Sauckel and the French government included the following: "Gauleiter Sauckel states that in the event of an invasion he has given his staff a mobilization plan providing that any workers who become available will be transported to Germany with the utmost efficiency." Following the cabinet meeting presided over by Lammers on July 11, 1944, Keitel informed the military commanders of France "that drastic measures must be taken for capturing French workers." I decided on the contrary that "despite the invasion, production in France must be continued, and deportation of labor to the Reich should be considered only for factories producing high-priority machinery which is in short supply." (*Office Journal.*)

10. Telegram sent September 13, 1944 to the Gauleiters of the Ruhr area: "On principle, plants are only to be crippled temporarily by removing various elements to safety, particularly the electrical ones." For mining and the steel industry such measures were planned only as a last resort; these facilities, therefore, were almost certain to be exempted.

11. Quotation from an editorial by Helmut Sündermann, the acting press chief, written September 7, 1944. A few weeks later Sündermann explained regretfully to me that Hitler had dictated this text to him, down to the very details.

12. From my travel report, September 10–14, 1944.

13. On September 16, 1944, Bormann agreed to extend these instructions of Hitler's to the occupied areas in the West—Holland, France, and Belgium—and to all the eastern, southern, and northern Gaus of the Reich. In a letter written September 19, 1944, to the chairman of the Armaments Commission and to the armaments inspectors I assumed responsibility for all cases in which a factory had to be surrendered intact to the enemy. "In the future I will consider it worse to cripple a factory too hastily than to leave it intact if the order to cripple comes too late." On September 17 it was established that if the anthracite and soft-coal mines on the left bank of the Rhine were occupied, the technical directors would remain with a skeleton staff in order "to prevent flooding of the shafts or other harm to the mining facilities." On October 5, 1944, instructions were also issued to the power plants by the Central Electricity Agency, which was directly under my Ministry.

14. See my memorandum of September 5, 1944, and the *Führerprotokoll,*

August 16–20, Point 5: "The Fuehrer has established a 'minimal economic area'; the idea is to determine in detail how long this area can achieve an increased degree of armaments production using only the available supplies and facilities in the area."

15. Memorandum, September 5, 1944. Our nickel and manganese supplies lasted five months longer than our chromium reserves. And, since we had replaced thousands of miles of copper cable in the high-tension lines with aluminum cable, we had a seventeen-month supply of copper on hand, although copper had once been one of our most critically scarce metals.

16. These quotations are taken from the travel reports for September 26–October 1, October 19–25, and December 7–10, 1944.

17. Diary entry by Jodl, November 10, 1944.

18. The quotation about stretching explosives by adding mineral salts is taken from my memorandum of December 6, 1944 on nitrogen supplies. Nitrogen was essential for explosives production. Before the attacks Germany and the occupied areas were producing a total of 99,000 metric tons per month. In December 1944, that figure had dropped to 20,500. In September 1944, 4100 tons of additives were used with 32,300 tons of explosives; in October, 8600 tons with 35,900 tons; and in November, 9200 tons with 35,000 tons. (Interim report issued by the Planning Bureau in January 1945.)

19. According to "Output Survey" issued by the Technical Bureau on February 6, 1945, deliveries of day and night fighter planes before the attacks on the aircraft factories were 1017 in January 1944. In February, during the attacks, they amounted to 990, in March to 1240, in April to 1475, in May to 1755, in June to 2034, in July to 2305, in August to 2273, and in September to 2878. These increases were largely achieved by cutting back other production, particularly production of multiengined models. Accordcording to the *Indexziffern der deutschen Rüstungsendfertigung* (January 1945), the total weight of all the planes delivered rose from an index figure of 232 in January 1944 to only 310 in September, or by 34 percent. During this period the percentage of total plane production represented by fighter planes rose (by weight) from 47.7 to 75.5 percent.

20. See *Führerprotokoll*, August 18–20, Point 10.

CHAPTER 28: *The Plunge*

1. See memorandum, November 11, 1944.

2. There is no doubt that the enemy's hopes for an end to the war in the winter of 1944–45 would have been fulfilled if the chemical industry had been knocked out. For, in general, transportation recovered much faster than we expected. Thus, for instance, daily freight-car loadings (averaging 139,000 in 1943) were still 70,000 in January 1945, 39,000 in February, and 15,100 in March—still a ninth of the original loadings. Thanks to its large reserve stocks the armaments industry was able to meet a quota which called for more raw materials than were being transported at the time. The index of total armaments production was 277 in

1944 (223 in 1943). In January 1945 it had dropped by 18 percent to 227, in February by 36 percent to 175, in March 1945 by about 50 percent to 145—and this with a ninth of the original transportation. In 1943 there were 225,800 metric tons (so-called Quartermaster-General tons) of munitions produced. In January 1945 this type of production still amounted to 175,000 tons, or 75 percent of the 1943 figure—although the nitrogen supply was only one eighth as large. In 1943 the average monthly delivery of tanks, tank destroyers, heavy artillery, and self-propelling guns was 1009; in January 1945 it was 1766. In 1943 there were 10,453 trucks and light tractors produced; in January 1945 there were 5089. In 1943 there were 1416 half-track tractors produced; in January 1945 there were 916—but only one fourth of the previous amount of fuel was available for running these vehicles. The disastrous developments in the chemical industry were thus the decisive factor in diminishing our combat readiness.

3. *Führerprotokoll*, October 12, 1944, Point 27.
4. In Hitler's opinion, only the death of Tsarina Elizabeth saved Frederick from tasting to the dregs a defeat that had already been decided.
5. *Führerprotokoll*, January 3–5, 1945, Point 23.
6. From the teletype message to Hitler, January 21, 1945, and the memorandum, January 16, 1945.
7. See Hitler's radio address, January 30, 1945.
8. The first quotation is from page 693, the second from page 104 of the 1935 edition of *Mein Kampf*. In my cell at Nuremberg I found the following quotation on page 780; it completes the two previous ones: "But then all those will be called before the judgment seat who today, in possession of power, trample on laws and rights, who have led our people into destitution and ruin, and who, when their Fatherland was suffering, valued themselves above the life of the community."

CHAPTER 29: *Doom*

1. I also left it to Saur to brief Hitler on the armaments situation. On January 20, according to the records, I had my last such conference with Hitler; after that he held the regular sessions on February 14 and 26 and on March 8 and 22 with Saur.
2. The draft of March 15, 1945, was prepared with the technical assistance of Colonel Gundelach, chief of staff to the Commanding General of the Army Engineers.
3. Instructions dispatched by circular letter, March 12, 1945.
4. I quoted this remark of Hitler's in the letter I wrote to him on March 29, 1945. At that time I softened it with, "If I did not misunderstand you. . . ." But this phrase was merely intended to give Hitler a chance to pretend he had not made the statement. In the same letter I summarized the impact Hitler's words had on me as follows: "These words shook me to the core."
5. The Fuehrer's order for the destruction that was to be purposefully carried out in the Reich read in full:

The struggle for the very existence of our people forces us to seize any means which can weaken the combat readiness of our enemy and prevent him from advancing. Every opportunity, direct or indirect, to inflict the most lasting possible damage on the enemy's striking power must be used to the utmost. It is a mistake to believe that when we win back the lost territories we will be able to retrieve and use these transportation, communications, production, and supply facilities that have not been destroyed or have been temporarily crippled; when the enemy withdraws he will leave us only scorched earth and will show no consideration for the welfare of the population.

Therefore, I order:

1. All military, transportation, communications, industrial, and food-supply facilities, as well as all resources within the Reich which the enemy might use either immediately or in the foreseeable future for continuing the war, are to be destroyed.

2. Those responsible for these measures are: the military commands for all military objects, including the transportation and communications installations; the Gauleiters and defense commissioners for all industrial and supply facilities, as well as other resources. When necessary, the troops are to assist the Gauleiters and the defense commissioners in carrying out their task.

3. These orders are to be communicated at once to all troop commanders; contrary instructions are invalid.

This decree was directly contrary to the requests I had made in my March 18 memorandum: "If the war advances farther into Reich territory, measures should be taken to assure that no one has the right to destroy industrial installations, coal mines, electric plants, and other facilities, nor transportation installations and inland waterways. Demolition of bridges as planned would do more lasting damage to the transportation network than all the bombing of the past few years."

6. Kesselring had added the notation: "To be implemented by the Commander in Chief of the army group," thus placing all responsibility for disregarding the orders on the shoulders of his subordinate, Field Marshal Model.

CHAPTER 30: *Hitler's Ultimatum*

1. See my letter, March 3, 1945, to Minister of Justice Thierack and his reply, March 6.

2. See the "Minutes of the Conference with the Fuehrer, March 22, 1945," signed by Saur.

3. So far as I know, Florian decided not to publish the proclamation after all. It is possible that he made his remarks about the worthlessness of the German people during some earlier discussion.

4. Hitler had ordered that the army command was to be responsible for demolitions within a five- to nine-mile-wide "war zone."

5. The "implementation instructions for the Fuehrer's order of March 19, 1945 (re: communications facilities)," issued at 4 P.M. March 27, read:

> Communications facilities are to be destroyed by dynamiting, fire or demolition. Items to be rendered totally unusable are: telephone, telegraph and amplification stations and centrals (wire lead-in points, switchboards, junction boxes, pylons and, if sufficient time is available, above-ground lines and long-distance cables), stocks of telegraph equipment of all types, cables and wiring, factory records (cable layout plans, wiring diagrams, descriptions of devices, etc.), the major radio facilities (broadcasting and receiving stations, towers, antennas. Efforts should be made to remove beforehand especially valuable parts. . . . Special orders follow for the national capital and its immediate environs, in particular for the radio stations in Nauen, Königswusterhausen, Zeesen, Rehmate, and Beelitz.

6. After my release from imprisonment Seebauer, who at the time had been one of my department heads, informed me that during my illness in the spring of 1944 Hitler had already picked Saur to be my successor.

7. In his last situation conference on April 27, 1945, Hitler reacted more sharply: "Failure to obey one of my orders would mean immediate annihilation, a leap into the void for any party leader. . . . I can scarcely believe that a party leader to whom I gave an order would dare not to carry it out." (Stenographic record, printed in *Der Spiegel*, No. 3 [1966].)

8. The order, transmitted through Jodl, was issued on March 29 and forwarded on March 30 to the Reichsleiters and Gauleiters by Bormann.

9. These instructions and measures are enumerated in the *Geheime Reichssache* (a "classified" information sheet), March 30, 1945.

10. My teletype message to all the waterways directors under my jurisdiction read: "On the basis of the Fuehrer's decree of March 30, 1945, destruction of locks, sluices, dams, drawbridges, and harbor installations is strictly forbidden unless I have given instructions to the contrary.—Copy, for information, to: Wehrmacht Operations Staff; request transmission to subordinate military agencies."

11. Hitler's decree of April 7, 1945, read as follows (with the passage Hitler crossed out in italics):

> To assure uniform execution of my decree of March 19, 1945 I decree the following for transportation and communications:
>
> 1. Operatively important bridges must be destroyed in such a way that they cannot be used by the enemy. Areas or sectors (rivers, parts of the autobahn, etc.) where such bridges are to be destroyed will be determined from case to case by the High Command of the armed forces. The harshest penalties must be inflicted if these bridges are not destroyed.
>
> 2. All other bridges must not be destroyed until the defense commissioners along with the competent agencies of the Ministry of Transportation and the Ministry of Armaments and War Production determine that the approach of the enemy makes it essential to halt production or transportation to those areas.

To assure that production continues until the last possible moment, I ordered in my decree of March 30, 1945, that transportation must be maintained up to the last possible moment [*even if the enemy's rapid movement creates the risk that a bridge (with the exception of those designated in point 1) may fall into his hands before it can be destroyed*].

3. All other objects and installations important for vehicular movement (other manufactured objects of every sort, rails, ballast, and repair shops), as well as the communications facilities of the postal system, the railroad system, and of private companies are to be effectively incapacitated. With regard to all measures for demolition and evacuation it must be borne in mind that, with the exception of the instances treated separately under point 1, when lost territory is recovered these installations should be usable for German production.

Headquarters, April 7, 1945   Adolf Hitler

This decree had the following advantages: It could hardly be expected that the agencies involved would ever make the necessary evaluations in time. The orders to destroy railroad and communications facilities, locomotives and freight cars, and to sink ships, were now canceled. The threat of harsh penalties was restricted to the most important bridges, since the penalties did not apply to points 2 and 3.

12. On April 7, 1945, Keitel dispatched an "urgent" teletype message merely giving instructions for the total destruction of bridges important to military operations. He avoided any positive interpretation of the positive elements of Hitler's decree, thus sabotaging their effectiveness.

CHAPTER 31: *The Thirteenth Hour*

1. The first draft of this speech was written April 8, 1945; the draft softened for the benefit of the press is dated April 10, 1945.
2. Dr. Gerhard Klopfer declared in his affidavit of July 1947:

A short time later Speer requested Dr. Hupfauer to ask me how I felt about his intention to publicly defend Dr. Brandt during the proceedings against him. I thereupon informed him that I had the distinct impression that the proceedings against Brandt were also aimed against Speer himself. I asked him therefore not to appear in public, giving the originator of the proceedings [Bormann] the desired pretext for launching a possibly planned attack against Speer.

3. Hitler's air force adjutant, von Below, had taken care of this matter.
4. I had outlined these consequences to Hitler in my memorandum of March 15, 1945. See footnote on p. 437 in Chapter 29.
5. The complete text of this speech, written April 16, 1945, follows:

Never before in history has a civilized people been struck so hard; never have the destruction and war damage been so great as in our country, and never has a people borne the hardships of war with greater endurance, hardiness, and loyalty than you. Now all of you are depressed, shaken to the core. Your love is turning to hate, your endurance and hardiness to fatigue and indifference.

This must not be. In this war the German people has displayed a determination which in days to come will, if history is just, be accorded the highest honor. Especially at this moment we must not weep and mourn for what is past. Only desperately hard work will enable us to bear our fate. But we can help ourselves by realistically and soberly deciding what the essential demands of the hour are.

And here we find there is only one main task: to avoid everything that could rob the German people of its basis for life, a basis already so diminished. Preservation of our places of work, of the transportation network, and of all other installations necessary to the feeding, clothing, and sheltering of our people is the first prerequisite for preserving our strength as a nation. In this phase of the war, therefore, we must avoid anything which could inflict further damage on our economy.

As the Minister responsible for all production, for the preservation of roads, waterways, and power plants and for the restoration of transportation, I therefore order, in agreement with the highest authorities of the various branches of the armed forces:

1. Destruction or crippling of any bridge, plant, waterway, railroad, or communications facility is henceforth prohibited.

2. All explosive charges on bridges are to be spiked and all other preparations for demolition or incapacitating are to be eliminated. If a plant has already been crippled, the parts removed are to be returned.

3. Local measures to protect the plants and the railroad and communications networks should be instituted at once.

4. These instructions apply not only to the Reich but also to occupied Norway, Denmark, Bohemia, Moravia, and Italy.

5. Anyone who acts counter to these instructions is consciously and intentionally inflicting harm on the German people and thus becomes an enemy. The soldiers of the armed forces and the militia are hereby instructed to proceed against these enemies of the people with all possible means, if necessary by the use of firearms.

In not destroying bridges that were intended to be blown up, we are giving our enemies an advantage in their operations. For this reason, but more for the sake of humane warfare, we urge our enemies to cease air raids on German cities and villages even if these contain installations important to the war effort. For our part we must make arrangements for the orderly surrender of cities and towns which are completely encircled. Cities which lack effective means of defense should be declared open cities.

To avoid injustices and serious blunders during this last phase of the war, the following instructions are issued in the interests of the German people:

1. Prisoners of war and foreign workers are to remain in their places of work. Those who are already on the move should be directed toward their home countries.

2. In the concentration camps the political prisoners, including the Jews, should be separated from asocial elements. The former are to be handed over unharmed to the occupying forces.

3. Punishment of all political prisoners, including the Jews, is to cease until further notice.

4. Service of the Volkssturm [People's Militia] against the enemy is voluntary. In addition it is the militia's duty to assure law and order within the country. Until the enemy occupation begins, members of the National Socialist Party are obligated to work with the militia in order to demonstrate that they wish to serve the people to the end.

5. The activities of the Werewolf and similar organizations must cease at once. They give the enemy a just pretext for reprisals and also threaten the foundations of our strength as a nation. Order and meeting our obligations are essential prerequisites to the survival of the German people.

The destruction which this war has brought upon Germany can be compared only with that of the Thirty Years' War. But losses in human lives from hunger and epidemics must never be allowed to take on the proportions they did then. The enemy alone can decide whether he will try to win his place in history as a decent and generous victor by conferring on the German people the honor and conditions deserved by an opponent who, although vanquished, can be said to have fought bravely and well.

But each one of you can do his part to protect our people from the worst. During the next few months you must summon up even more of the determination to rebuild that you, German workers and factory directors, and you, German railroad men, have shown time and again during the devastating air raids. The last few months of paralyzing horror and boundless disappointment have produced an understandable lethargy. But that must go now! God will only help a nation that does not give up, even in so desperate a situation.

For the immediate future I give you the following guidelines to be followed in areas already occupied by the enemy:

1. The most important task is repair of the damaged railroads. Therefore, if the enemy gives permission or orders, every possible means must be employed, no matter how primitive, to carry out this work of reconstruction. For transportation makes it possible to provide food to large areas in which the population would otherwise face grave shortages. And only if you manage to patch up a transportation network will you ever be reunited with your families. Therefore, it is in the personal interest of each one of you to do everything possible to restore transportation.

2. Industrial and manual workers, who have performed incomparable feats during this war, are under obligation to carry out as quickly as possible all assignments connected with rebuilding the railroads; other tasks should be put aside for the time being.

3. During six years of war the German farmer has been highly self-disciplined; he has been an example to the nation in delivering his

products according to his own instructions. In the days to come every German farmer must raise his production to the highest possible level. It can be taken for granted that the German farmer will cultivate this year's crop in fullest awareness of his duty. He knows how large a responsibility he bears to the German people.

4. Food must receive transportation priority over everything else. Food-producing plants must receive electricity, gas, coal, or wood before any other factories are supplied.

5. Government bureaus must not be dissolved. Bureau chiefs bear full responsibility for keeping them in operation. Anyone who leaves his place of work without his supervisor's permission is committing a crime against the nation. Administration is necessary if we are to preserve the German people from chaos.

If we work with the same determination that we have demonstrated during the past few years, the German people will survive without more great losses. Transportation can be fairly adequately restored within two or three months. According to our calculations, modest but sufficient food supplies can be maintained in the area west of the Oder River until the next harvest. Whether our enemies will permit this remains to be seen. But I pledge to devote all my strength, up to the very end, to the survival of the German people.

The military blows which Germany has received during the last few months have been shattering. Our fate is no longer in our own hands. Only a more merciful Providence can change our prospects for the future. We ourselves, however, can help save ourselves not only by going about our work industriously, facing the enemy with dignity and self-confidence, but also by becoming more modest in our hearts, by practicing self-criticism, and by believing unshakably in the future of our nation, which will remain forever and always.

May God protect Germany!

6. The note read:

April 16, 1945

Dear Herr Fischer:

Since the communications lines will soon be severed, I may need to resort to the radio transmitters for issuing basic instructions, for instance concerning crippling rather than destroying, etc. You are personally responsible for providing electricity to the stations up to the last moment, including the Werewolf station in Königswusterhausen. Power may be shut off only after enemy broadcasts prove that the transmitting facilities have been seized.

Cordially, Speer

7. Next I went to the Commander in Chief of the army group, Field Marshal Busch, who agreed that even if there was fighting the Elbe bridges in Hamburg would not be destroyed. At the same time he agreed not to use the Wiesmoor Power Station in the Ems region (15,000 kilowatts) as a military base. This power plant was important as a source of emergency electricity to Hamburg, since in the near future coal shipments or overland deliveries could not be counted on.

CHAPTER 32: *Annihilation*

1. Kaufmann had tried to contact the British in order to surrender Hamburg, although Hitler had declared the city a fortress. On April 22, the Königswusterhausen station was no longer available.
2. SS General Berger told me this at Nuremberg.
3. It had already been decided that in the event of a military partitioning of Germany a northern area would be under Doenitz's command, while Hitler reserved control of the southern area for himself. However, on April 2, 1945, Bormann uttered the following challenge to the party functionaries: "Anyone who leaves his Gau under enemy attack without specific orders from the Fuehrer, anyone who does not fight to the last breath, is a groveling coward. He will be considered a deserter and treated as such. Pluck up your courage and overcome your weaknesses. The word of the hour is: Victory or death!"

CHAPTER 33: *Stations of Imprisonment*

1. See the letter to Doenitz, May 7, 1945. On May 5, I had already reported to Doenitz via his "Chief of the Civilian Cabinet," Wegener: "As soon as the problem of handing over the areas now occupied and the last unoccupied parts of the Reich has been settled, I shall resign from directing the activities of the two ministries and shall no longer be available as a member of the government now being formed." Doenitz asked me to stay on. On May 15, I again directed the following request to Schwerin-Krosigk: "When the list of ministers is presented, the following must be noted: (1) Herr Speer considers it essential that he be replaced by a suitable successor as Minister of Economics and Production, so that he may place himself at the disposal of the Allies. His experience may be called on temporarily during the transition for reconstruction of manufacturing and the building industry. . . ."

CHAPTER 34: *Nuremberg*

1. In each of the heavy oak cell doors was an opening about ten inches square through which the prisoners could be observed.
2. These quotations are from the examination by Flächsner and the cross-examination by Jackson.
3. In a letter to my wife in August 1946, I described the reaction of my co-defendants: "Most of the defendants have taken a very sour view of my activities during the last phase of the war. I can imagine pretty well what steps they would have taken had they found out at the time. There would not have been much left of the family."
4. After a pause I replied to the tribunal: "I hesitate to describe details, because such things are unpleasant. I am doing so only because the court has

requested it. . . . I do not intend to cite my role during this phase as part of my defense."

5. From the cross-examination by Jackson.

CHAPTER 35: *Conclusions*

1. In general the authenticity of the documents presented was questioned neither by the defense attorneys nor by the defendants. Whenever a document was challenged, the prosecution withdrew it from evidence, with one exception: the Hossbach transcript of the meeting at which Hitler announced his war aims. In his memoirs Hossbach has since confirmed the authenticity of that document.

2. Almost two decades later President Kennedy said at his press conference of August 20, 1963: "What we now have . . . will kill three hundred million people in one hour." (*The New York Times*, August 21, 1963.)

3. In mid-August, I wrote to my family about my final speech and my prospects in the trial: "I must be prepared for anything. It is hard to say who will be more deserving of pity after the sentencing. . . . Flächsner has become a pessimist. For my part, I must not place my personal fate in the foreground. My concluding words will therefore not even deal with my case." Early September 1946: "Yesterday I had my final say. I tried once more to do my duty. But I doubt that it will be acknowledged. I must travel a straight and narrow path even if no one understands that today.

4. These hopes were deceived. As Eugene Davidson points out in *The Trial of the Germans* (New York: Macmillan, 1966), as early as February 17, 1946, under Allied Control Law Number 3, General Clay introduced a compulsory labor policy into the American Zone. On March 28, 1947, I wrote in my Nuremberg diary:

> Deportation of labor is unquestionably an international crime. I do not reject my sentence, even though other nations are now doing the same thing we did. I am convinced that behind the scenes during the discussions about German prisoners of war someone will point to the laws on forced labor and to their interpretation and prosecution by the Nuremberg Tribunal. Could the discussion of this matter in our press be so open and critical if for months on end forced labor had not been publicly denounced as a crime? . . . The conviction that my sentence is "unjust" because "the others" are making the same mistake would make me more unhappy than the sentence itself. For then there would be no hope for a civilized world. Despite all the mistakes, the Nuremberg Trial was a step in the direction of recivilization. And if my twenty years of imprisonment could help the German prisoners of war to get home only one month earlier, it would be justified.

5. It became obvious that the victors were sitting in judgment over their vanquished enemies. This was most apparent from a passage in the Doenitz judgment: "These orders [to sink ships without warning] prove that Doenitz is guilty of violating the Protocols [of London]. . . . In consideration

of Admiral Nimitz's answer to the questionnaire that in the Pacific Ocean from the first day of its entry into the war the United States practiced unrestricted submarine warfare, the penalty imposed on Doenitz is not based on his infractions of the international regulations for submarine warfare." In this case technical developments (use of aircraft, better navigational procedures) had taken precedence over legal conventions, overwhelmed them and pushed them aside. Here was one example of how modern technology is capable of creating new legal concepts, to the detriment of humanity—concepts which can result in legalized death for countless human beings.

6. Hitler repeated the announcement of his intentions on January 30, 1942: This war will not end "as the Jews imagine, by the extermination of the European-Aryan peoples, but the outcome of this war will be the annihilation of Jewry."

Index

Aachen, 290, 403–404
Abel, Adolf (architect), 51
Abyssinia, Italian invasion of, 71
Adolf Hitler Endowment Fund of German Industry, 87, 265
Adolf Hitler Schools, 25n., 122–123
Africa Corps, 246; surrender of, 215, 292
Air Ministry, 289, 322, 332; building plans for, 136–137
Air-raid shelters, 182, 217
Air raids:
—German: on Warsaw, 227; on England, 281–282, 283; misdirection in Russia, 282–283; on London, 283, 284; V-weapons, 355–356, 364–365, 369
—Western Allied: on Berlin, 182, 286, 287–289, 478; on German cities, 213, 215, 255, 262, 263, 278, 283–289, 314, 363; 1944, effect on transportation, 224; on dockyards, 274; effects on armaments production, 278, 284–286, 336, 346–348, 349–350, 406, 407; armaments emergency caused by, 229, 346; on Cologne, 279–280; on Ruhr reservoirs, 280–281, 347n.; selective bombing, 280–281, 282, 285–287, 347n., 352; on Hamburg, 283–284; on ball-bearing plants, 284–286, 347n.;

Hitler's disinterest in their effects on citizenry and civilian casualties, 299–300; on aircraft industry, 332, 347n.; on fuel industry, 346, 348, 349–350, 406; on Ploesti oil fields, 348; Rommel on, 353; in support of Normandy invasion, 354, 355; average daily bomb tonnage (1944), 365; precision of, 377; prevent supply movement for Ardennes offensive, 416, 417, 418; on Bremen, 494; Speer's evaluations of, for RAF and USSBS, 285, 499–500
Air warfare, 278–291; Hitler's plan for subjugation of England by, 183, 229; Hitler's disinterest, 242, 281, 299–300; area bombing vs. nerve center pinpoint attacks, 280, 281–283, 352; technological vs. military use, 283; Hitler's mistaken emphasis on offensive vs. defensive use and weapons in, 363–366; Speer's discussions with USSBS, 499–500. See also Antiaircraft defense
Aircraft carriers, 166
Aircraft industry: Allied bombing of, 332, 347n.; put under Speer's Ministry, 348–349; Hitler's order to stop production, 407–409. See also Bomber planes; Fighter planes; Jet planes

(573)

A portion of the
original manuscript
of Albert Speer's
notes. They were
written during his
first years in Spandau
prison and are the
basis for these
memoirs.